VOICE & DATA COMMUNICATION HANDBOOK

Fifth Edition

About the Author

Regis J. (Bud) Bates Jr.
President
TC International Consulting, Inc.
PO Box 51108
Phoenix, AZ 85076
Tel. (480) 706-0912, Fax (480) 759-7502
http://www.tcic.com

Mr. Bates has more than 39 years of experience in telecommunications and information systems. TC International Consulting (TCIC) is a full service management consulting organization that specializes in planning, designing, and integrating information technologies. TCIC leads the pack in strategic development and implementation of new technologies for carriers and corporations alike.

Mr. Bates is a systems expert who specializes in network operations and planning for telecommunications and management information systems. As president of TCIC, he performs strategic planning, business continuity planning, and technology innovation for his client companies. Mr. Bates has helped Fortune 100–500 companies design, setup, and manage wireless LANs, LANs, and WANs using SONET, ATM, MPLS, VoIP, and VPN architectures.

Mr. Bates is also a sought after professional instructor and he teaches using instructor-led learning formats. He spends some of his time working with the major telecommunications manufacturers in training their staff members on the innovations of technology and the convergence of voice and data networks for the future both in a wired and a wireless environment. Many of his materials are used throughout the higher education institutions around the world in certification and graduate level classes in telecommunications management.

Mr. Bates authored over 16 technology-oriented books, many of which were best sellers for McGraw-Hill. Bud received his degree in Business Management from Stonehill College (BS) in Easton, Massachusett. He holds various wireless and wired certifications.

Much of his time lately has been devoted to VoIP, IP telephony, wireless LANs, securing WLANs, and WiMAX. Bud continues to develop courseware and write about the topics that fascinate him.

Donald W. Gregory is a partner with Computer Sciences Corporation's Consulting Group (CSC). Prior to joining CSC, he spent several years at Arthur Andersen, International Harvester/Navistar, and Digital Equipment Corp. During most of that time he has specialized in the design and implementation of data and voice communications networks.

VOICE & DATA COMMUNICATION HANDBOOK

Fifth Edition

Regis (Bud) Bates
Donald Gregory

New York   Chicago   San Francisco
Lisbon   London   Madrid   Mexico City
Milan   New Delhi   San Juan   Seoul
Singapore   Sydney   Toronto

The **McGraw·Hill** Companies

Cataloging-in-Publication data is on file with the Library of Congress.

McGraw-Hill books are available at special quantity discounts to use as premiums and sales promotions, or for use in corporate training programs. For more information, please write to the Director of Special Sales, Professional Publishing, McGraw-Hill, Two Penn Plaza, New York, NY 10121-2298. Or contact your local bookstore.

Voice & Data Communication Handbook, Fifth Edition

1234567890 FGR FGR 019876

ISBN-13:   978-0-07-226335-0
ISBN-10:   0-07-226335-0

Sponsoring Editor
Jane Brownlow

Editorial Supervisor
Jody McKenzie

Project Manager
Gita Raman

Acquisitions Coordinator
Jennifer Housh

Copy Editor
Surender Nath Shivam

Proofreader
Yomnam Ojen Singh

Indexer
Robert Swanson

Production Supervisor
Jean Bodeaux

Composition
International Typesetting
and Composition

Illustration
International Typesetting
and Composition

Art Director, Cover
Brian Boucher

Cover Designer
Brian Boucher

Contents at a Glance

Contents

Chapter 16   Routers and Switches in the Networking Role   517

Chapter 17   Voice over Internet Protocols (VoIP)   543

Acknowledgments

Well, here I am again, finalizing the latest update for McGraw-Hill. This one is extra special because it is the fifth edition of the *Voice and Data Communications Handbook!* Things have really changed so we decided to change the structure and the content considerably. We certainly hope that this one meets your needs as we think it will!

This update deals with the issues surrounding the convergence of voice and data. As always, I chose to write the way I think, that is, in a nontechnical fashion. I hope that this is consistent with you the reader, because there is little published geared for the novice and business professional. Besides restructuring the flow of the chapters, we eliminated much of the "old stuff" and added something new this time. We have added more on the "how to do it" with screen shots and some detail lists.

To be fair about this production we owe a lot of credit to many people. Some of the people interacted with us regularly, others only occasionally. First, we must thank Jane Brownlow, McGraw-Hill's executive editor on this book. Jane had a real task of trying to keep after us to get this book completed, even though every deadline was missed. In addition to Jane, is Jennifer Housh who e-mailed weekly looking for the week's submission of new chapters to keep the project on schedule. I know that I frustrated Jennifer many times when delays kept slipping into the production. Numerous other people aided in the editing and production of the book—far too many to name. They know who they are and can give themselves a pat on the back for their efforts. Then there are the vendors and manufacturers we talk to daily regarding products, services, and opportunities. All add to the knowledge in this book.

This team of people all pulled together to make this fifth edition of the *Voice and Data Communications Handbook* a reality. They deserve the credit.

Finally, as always, I want to thank you the reader for giving up your time to read this book. I receive many calls and e-mails from readers who just want to let me know that they enjoyed my opinion or the way I present an idea. I hope I can continue to win your support. My best wishes to you all!

Thank you all
Regis J. (Bud) Bates Jr.

Introduction

Welcome to the world of converged telecommunications! We are about to embark on a descriptive and narrative overview of the telecommunications industry. This book is designed to help "clear the air" for you.

Because this is the fifth edition, it is possible that you have ventured down this trail before. Have no fear; we have changed this book considerably, with every attempt to give you more current information. You will still get something out of this book.

No magic exists here, merely an understanding of what converged telecommunications is all about: the principles of voice and data as they converge into a VoIP and IP telephony architecture. Moreover, we use discussions on standards and protocols only as needed to get you up to speed on the technologies. We intend to make things as simple as possible as we cover the various techniques and terminology used throughout this book. Be aware, however, that no matter how simple we attempted to make this information and no matter how smoothly we attempt to steer you through the guides outlined, this is a technical subject.

Therefore, from time to time, we may start sounding a little "techie." This is not done to impress or confuse you—we just cannot think of a way to make our explanation any more basic without destroying the flow. At any rate, this book is designed to give you a fundamental understanding of the overall concepts used in the telecommunications arena, using voice, data, LAN technologies, and now wireless technologies too. Changes have been occurring at an escalating pace, so we must continue to look back at the history in order to see the future.

Format

The format of this book is arranged to walk you right through the evolution of the industry. We have changed some of the older format by putting a bit more of a "how to" and installation screens shots of the various techniques. We certainly hope you like these changes, as we attempt to satisfy the needs of many customers who have asked for these changes.

We approach the historical deployment of a network throughout the country on the basis of the original Bell System, and we look at the regulatory scene and the various legal issues that arose. Early on, we discuss the impact of the Telecommunications Act of 1996 and what has changed since the initial decisions. This one act opened the door to competition in the areas of telephony, long distance, cable services, and many other technologies. Many skeletons still lie on the side of the road to competition. Many organizations have been bankrupted; still others are barely surviving.

Next, we touch on the fundamentals of the voice evolution from the telephone company and end-user perspective. We look at the basic characteristics of the human voice and how the telephone network was developed. The discussion of network evolution encompasses the distinct dialing plans and how things have changed to accommodate phenomenal growth. We look at how the telephones have changed over the years. The discussion also shows how the telephone set converts a sound wave into an electrical wave and prepares the electricity for transmission across the network.

We enjoyed coming up with the best way to present certain models. The open system interconnection (OSI) section gets a little comical in the discussion of the standards that we use in just about all aspects of the industry. We think you'll really enjoy the way we present this very complex model, and how we can try to make all things simple if we take them one step at a time. So, draw your own conclusions and see whether this doesn't make more sense after you get through this chapter.

We discuss the explosion of the Internet around the world and how it works. This should be rewarding to read and will help you understand why things happen so slowly when you dial into the World Wide Wait!

We next consider the changes following the introduction of digital standards. The old network was built as an analog system. It served us well. We hope that you will understand the differences between digital and analog after reading this.

We explore the use of a digital network instead of an analog network, attempting to make this discussion simple, but again, there are some parts that get a bit complicated. Read this one in earnest; it is your future.

Many of our chapters look to moving data across a communications system called a local area network (LAN). The LAN evolves into a campus area network (CAN), a metropolitan area network (MAN), a wide area network (WAN), and a foreign area network (FAN). Is your head still spinning? An area that will probably be of deep concern is the LAN and now the wireless LAN (WLAN) technologies. These have become so commonplace that most of us take them for granted. We also show you how you might use some of the TCP/IP tools to determine if you are connected. Read this one with the knowledge that when it breaks, we can help!

ATM (not the automated teller machines) and frame relay are fast packet systems. They mimic packet switching on steroids. But if you read this section and don't scream, "I want it now," you missed something. You'll see!

Following the discussions of these networking concepts, we discuss the newer competitive way to access the high-speed communications services through xDSL and CATV company services. Using this springboard, we will look at the speeds and capacities of these wired services.

Our discussion leads to some of the finer points of networks, such as the SS7 evolution for call setup and teardown. However, this is only one part of what SS7 brings to the networking strategies, because we can use SS7 for all the features and functions that bring new capabilities.

The speed of fiber brings us closer to the terabit throughput. With all the emphasis on SONET and dense wave-division multiplexing (DWDM), we get the higher multiplexed rates and the benefits of different colors of light (so to speak).

We discuss a subject that normally causes even the strong of heart to shudder: the use of an analog telephone line to transmit critical data. How can we make digital data look like a voice call? What are the tools that will enable us to get the information in a usable and understandable form? This section gets quite lengthy and, from time to time, a bit technical; however, you need to understand this concept.

We also look at the demand rising for Voice over IP protocols and Voice over the Internet. Our intent is to get you talking and thinking about the services; then do more individualized research on your own.

Also the convergence of voice and data paves the way for the VoIP PBX and Voice over the LAN. See how we have attempted to simplify this form of connection. If all else fails, there is always a VoIP provider who promises the world of savings and instant connectivity. All you have to do is install their box.

Sounds lake a new form of monopoly, doesn't it? But wait for the sixth edition of this book, we are sure that the telephone companies (remember the old monopolies) still have a few tricks up their sleeves to attract you back to their services. The words are triple and quadruple play (voice, data, video, and IM) as the carriers offer you the old network in a new way!

After all this discussion of the wired network solutions, we then take a different approach. This is a discussion of connectivity without wires. We look at cellular communications and personal communications. The world is heading for an unconnected mode. Wireless voice and data are the rave of the industry (well almost!). Enjoy learning how the wired and wireless future will share the same trail. Discussions will also look at the third generation (3G) of wireless communications.

We hope that you are intrigued and will read on.

CAUTION This is not a novel; it is not intended to be read from cover to cover. So, allot some time each day and take a chapter or a group of chapters together to gain an appreciation for the overall world of telecommunications. There is no reason this book cannot give you the tools necessary to deal with the novice or pro alike. Take some time to familiarize yourself with the ideas of the book; use the examples and analogies. Enjoy the stories and heed their message.

ONE CLOSING THOUGHT Many of our readers have sent us messages (e-mail, voice mail, letters) stating that we were technically incorrect with some of our concepts. Upon discussing this with them, we find that we are not incorrect, but we did not provide sufficient technical or engineering specific detail for their needs or their liking. Wonderful! That is exactly what we were trying to do. Our philosophy with this book is the KISS method (keep it silly and simple). If you are looking for techno-babble as designed by propeller heads, there are many other books on the market.

If you want to learn the basics without having a degree in engineering or in tech-speak, you came to the right place. Let's have some fun!

Voice Communications

After reading this chapter and completing the questions, you will be able to:

- Discuss the characteristics of a voice
- Understand the concept of bandwidth
- Converse about the variations of a conversation (amplitude and frequency)
- Discuss the capacities of the various media used to carry information
- Listen for the changes and differences in a conversation
- Explain how the telephone networks are laid out
- Discuss how the telephone set works

The telephone set transmits sound to the receiving party. If the telephone network and the telephone set were designed to carry voice signals from one point to another, then the characteristics of the voice signal had to be known. A great amount of time and effort went into studying the actual variables associated with sound created by our vocal chords. From these studies, you can derive the fundamental concepts of a telecommunications network. This implies the telephone set is designed to carry only voice. In reality, this is correct because all the effort was directed toward carrying the voice in its truest possible form from the sender to receiver. The word "telecommunications" involves this very basic concept. A definition is in order here because we cover the characteristics of the telephone network and its capability to carry the human voice.

Telecommunications is the transmission of information—in the form of voice, data, video, or images, across a distance, over a medium, from a sender to a receiver—in a usable and understandable manner.

The Medium

A medium is any form of transmission capacity used to carry signals. In the telecommunications world, this can be in the form of copper wires, coaxial cables, optical fiber (glass or plastic), or air (radio signals). Other forms of media also exist, for example, this book uses paper as the medium to get the information to the reader. But we're dealing with a telephony concept, so we'll stick to these types of analogies. Depending on the medium used, the distances over which information is transmitted can vary greatly. However, strides have been made since the late 1870s, when the telephone set was first invented. Now we can transmit any information over thousands of miles as simply as we do over inches. The information takes on the form of electrical energy to re-create the sound waves generated by our voices in a representative form, so listeners at the distant end can understand the message.

Sound

Sound is the banging of air molecules together at a rapid rate. As we generate sound with our vocal chords, we're banging these air molecules together to produce intelligible information that can be used and understood by others. This is in the form of air pressure changes. Hold your hand in front of your mouth as you speak. Feel the air pressure hitting your hand? This is the effect of sound as we generate the changes in air pressure. Our vocal chords, therefore, are moving back and forth and banging the molecules of air together.

An old question asks, "If a tree falls in the forest and no one is there to hear it, does it create sound?" The answer must be an obvious "yes." Although no one is there to hear it, the air pressure changes caused by the tree falling to the ground—regardless of where it falls—must still be producing sound. If we put a tape recorder in the forest and the tree falls, the sound will, most likely, be captured by the recorder. Even though no one is there, the recorder still captures the noises created by the air changes.

The telephone set converts sound waves to their analog equivalent in the form of electrical pulses, which are then carried across the telephone network. *Analog* is the analogous form of the voice wave being created in a "look-alike" electrical wave. We can, therefore, assume that to communicate across the medium (wires) we must have some form of sound. The sound will be converted into electricity. The electricity is then sent across the telephone wires.

The banging together of air molecules at a rapid pace creates human speech. This is called *compression* and *rarefaction*. The human voice produces sound at a constantly changing set of frequencies (pitch) and amplitudes (loudness). To re-create the sound faithfully, the sound waves (or air pressure changes) are converted from sound into electricity. This is what the telephone set does.

As the electrical equivalent of sound is created, compare the sound wave to an electrical wave. Electricity is typically generated in an analog form by rotating the electromagnetic energy around a center point. As the energy is on the rise, it increases the amplitude to a peak level in decibels, and then reverses direction and begins to fall. Because the wave is concurrent, its electrical field has both a positive and a negative side. As the signal

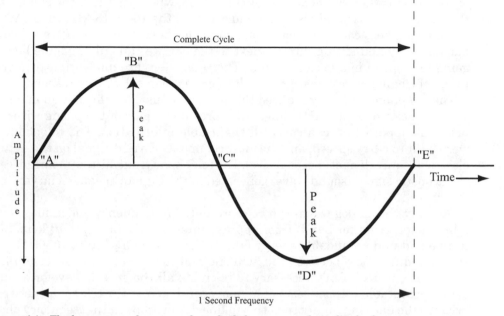

Figure 1.1 The human sound wave produces both frequency and amplitude changes.

decreases from the peak of the positive energy, therefore, it moves back toward the zero line. As with a magnet, two poles exist: positive and negative. So, as the wave gets to the zero line, it continues to fall to the negative side of the voltage line until it hits some peak at the bottom of the energy field. From there, it, in turn, rises back up to the zero line (value) again. This, in effect, constitutes a 360 degree cycle around the baseline or one complete rotation. This rotation is called a *sinusoidal wave*. This sinusoidal wave shown in Fig. 1.1 is the analogous re-creation of the human sound wave in its electrical form. This single wave cycle over a specified period of time, usually one second, is called *one hertz*, named after the man who discovered this concept. Hertz is normally abbreviated *Hz*.

The sound wave produced by a human voice has a constantly changing variable energy in both signal strength (the amplitude) and the number of rotations around the baseline over a period of time (the frequency). Voice characteristically creates 5000 cycles of information per second. This is abbreviated into 5 kilohertz. *Kilo* means thousands and is represented by the *k* in kHz.

The human ear is responsive to variations in frequency and amplitude at rates from 25 to 22,000 Hz. This means the ear can receive and discern all the information contained in the human voice. This is important in telephony.

Differences exist in human responsiveness to sound. For example, older humans can discern sounds ranging only up to 7 to 8 kHz because of abuses and deterioration of the eardrums. People who have fired a weapon (rifle or handgun) without proper ear protection can have damaged the upper and lower frequency responses, limiting the range of frequencies they can hear. A younger person, who hasn't had the chance to damage the ears, can receive and discern sound waves in the 16- to 18-kHz range. When we see these youngsters carrying those boom boxes on their shoulders; however, with the box blaring away and sitting directly next to the ear, we can only imagine how the ear is going to respond in a matter of time. The youngsters are inadvertently narrowing the range of frequency responses to which their ears can selectively respond.

The telephone company realized the majority of usable information in a human conversation can fit in a 3-kHz range, so it provides a pair of telephone wires—typically made of copper—that can carry all the usable information. The telephone networks were built to carry speech, and the most commonly carried signal on the network is the electrical equivalent of speech (voice). The telephone transmitter (mouthpiece) converts the acoustic signal (sound wave) generated in the human speaker's larynx into electrical waves.

Actually, the analog waves can be represented in frequency and analog changes over a broad spectrum (or band) from approximately 30 Hz to about 10 kHz. Most of the usable and understandable energy falls in the spectrum of 200 to 3500 Hz. If we subtract the differences between the high end and the low end, the spectrum is 3300 Hz, or 3.3 kHz, wide. It isn't necessary to re-create all the speech waveforms precisely to get an acceptable transmission of human speech across the telephone network. This is because the ear isn't highly sensitive to fine distinctions in the frequency changes, and the human brain can make up for any variations in the speech form by interpretation. Of course, if something doesn't come across the wire clearly enough, the human brain intervenes and causes the mouth to say, "What?" This, in turn, can cause the speaker at the transmitting end to generate the signal over again by repeating the words.

Because the cost of transmitting the signal across a telephone network is directly proportional to the range of frequencies carried, the telephone company uses a bandpass filter on the circuit. A bandpass filter allows portion of the frequency band to pass through the channel. Everything else is filtered off. Commercially acceptable and usable information is transmitted in what is called a *band-limited channel*. This means all the usable information is allowed to pass onto the circuit, but the extraneous information that doesn't add significantly to the conversation is filtered off. If the extra energy is put onto the wire and carried from end to end, the costs go up at an equal rate; this is wasteful. So the telephone company limits the amount of information you can pass on the wire.

What Is Bandwidth?

One of the toughest concepts for anyone to understand is bandwidth. To the novice, bandwidth becomes even more perplexing when it's bandied about by telephone company personnel, engineers, and others. But bandwidth is the basis of most of what we do in the telecommunications and telephony world.

Think of bandwidth as a water pipe (or a garden hose). The larger the pipe, the more water that can flow through the pipe. The smaller the pipe, the smaller the flow of water. Be careful not to confuse flow with pressure! We can constrain the pipe and cause

Figure 1.2   Bandwidth can be compared to a pipe or a hose. The larger the pipe, the more water flows.

the flow to gush out of the pipe, but did more water flow? Now, in telecommunications terms, think of bandwidth as a communications pipe. The bigger the pipe, the more information that flows through it. The smaller the pipe, the less information that can be carried through the pipe.

Bandwidth is similar to this garden hose analogy, as shown in Fig. 1.2. *Bandwidth* is the range of frequencies that can be carried across a given transmission channel. If more information is sent, more bandwidth is necessary. Therefore, a 3-kHz channel has 3 kHz of bandwidth. This is fine because all the usable information of a voice-grade conversation is contained in this amount of bandwidth. In actuality, the telephone companies break the available electromagnetic spectrum into slices, each about 4 kHz wide. Then, these 4-kHz slices (called *channels*) are limited with bandpass filters, as shown in Fig. 1.3. Consider the spigot analogy, turning the water on faster or slower via the spigot valve. The result is we receive 3 kHz of the available 4-kHz slices.

Other forms of bandwidth requirements exist. For comparative purposes, we can see the differences in capacities used in various forms of bandwidth allocations, as shown in Table 1.1.

MHz (megahertz) is a new term here, which represents millions of frequency changes per second. You can imagine the amount of information carried in a TV signal, where sound, motion, and voice are all on the same channel. Think of how a video signal on a TV station would look if the channel were restricted to carrying only 3 kHz of information. By the time some moving picture was created on the set, the viewer would have lost interest.

TABLE 1.1   **Summary of Channel Capacities to Carry Different Forms of Information**

Service	Bandwidth Allotted
Voice channel	3 kHz
High-fidelity music	15 kHz
CD stereo player	22 kHz
FM radio station	200 kHz
TV channel on CATV	6 MHz
TV channel actually used	4.5 MHz

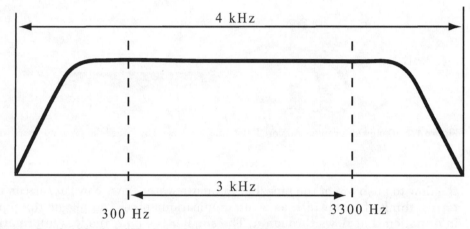

Figure 1.3   Bandwidth of a 4-kHz channel shows the usable amount of 3 kHz.

The frequency spectrum of a TV channel, as shown in Table 1.1, shows a community antenna television (CATV) channel is actually allocated 6 MHz of capacity. Yet, the amount actually used approximates 4.5 MHz. The difference is the band limitation on the channel, much the same as with the voice channel. In this case, the amount of flow is in the millions of cycles per second (a big pipe is needed here). The band-limited channel uses bandpass filters, so a guard band is between the TV channels. In other words, as you watch Channel 3 on your TV set, the filters are placed on the line to prevent frequencies and information from Channels 2 and 4 from overflowing onto Channel 3. These guard bands are placed on every channel, thereby restricting the 6-MHz channel to only 4.5 MHz of usable information. The same holds true on a telephone channel as shown in Fig. 1.4. Here the 4-kHz channel has the guard bands created through the use of the bandpass filters.

The same concept holds true for nearly all the channel capacities used in the telecommunications industry. The available bandwidth is a function of need and cost. You get what you need, but any more is too expensive.

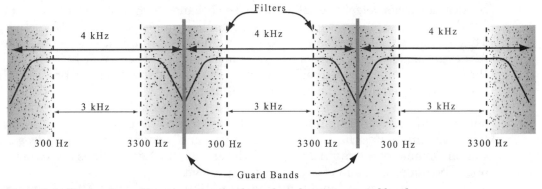

Figure 1.4   The bandpass filter separates the channels and creates a guard band.

Voices

The human voice is a consolidation of the waves of electrical energy carried across the given channel capacity. Humans generate a combination of amplitude and frequency changes in a continuing flow. If the changes are held constant, then the conversation becomes monotone, highly unacceptable for the average conversation. Indeed, if everything were held constant, the recipient of the information would be lulled to sleep. We use the variations in our voices to reflect deviations in emotion, accentuation, or articulation and emphasis on certain points. Every voice generates a different pattern of amplitude and frequency changes. This is what gives every individual a unique and recognizable speech tone.

Interesting to note is the female voice pattern typically generates more changes in amplitude than in frequency. This accounts for the squeaky sound in the female voice. Conversely, the male vocal pattern generates more frequency changes than amplitude shifts. This accounts for the low-pitched, grainier tones of the male. These are averages; every human is different and the norm can be deviated from at any time. When someone is highly emotional, there are definite shifts from that person's normal voice patterns. The pitch might go up by varying degrees, showing the results of stress or anger.

The telephone links are designed to handle this widely varying pattern of shifts. From time to time, though, the voice pattern might exceed the differences in the allotted bandwidth. Then the frequencies in the voice go above or below the normal range. At this point, the bandpass filters start to remove the excesses. What can result is a pattern of tinny or flattened speech conversations. This can be also heard if someone uses the letters F and S where the frequency ranges on these two sounds might exceed the bandpass ranges; they get flattened.

Other Services

Because the telephone network was built to carry voice, the other services that we want to communicate, such as data, facsimile, images, and video must be transmitted within the same constraints as voice calls. The network allows any telephone set to contact any other telephone set across a 3-kHz bandwidth. If you want to communicate anything else, such as data, it must be accommodated on this same 3-kHz bandwidth. This invokes a limitation on the speed of our data communications channel capacities. Although modems can transmit signals more quickly, they must be constrained into the size of the pipe. A video conference transmission also reflects non-real-time motion because of the channel capacities on a dial-up basis.

If you need to move more information across the channels, you have two choices. One option is to dedicate a high-speed line between the two or more ends. However, this approach eliminates the possibility of "any-to-any" connection and requires planning well in advance of communicating with the end points. Leased lines between the points might be underused and could be more expensive.

Another option is to have the bandpass filters moved out to (for example) 8 kHz between the end points. Unfortunately, similar limitations are here. If the switching networks in the middle and the receiving end aren't equipped to handle the 8 kHz capacity, our call is then funneled down into the lowest common denominator. We would have to know every location we would be communicating with, losing the benefits of the any-to-any connection. Also, no guarantee exists that the switching systems will route the call over the same path on a switched dial-up connection every time. This would force us back into a 3-kHz channel along the route selected if it's different every time, eliminating the benefits of the wider channel capacity.

The Telephone Network

A *network* is a series of interconnections that form a cohesive and ubiquitous connectivity arrangement when tied together. Whew! This sounds ominous but, to make this a little simpler, let's look at the components of what constitutes the telephone network.

Generally, a network is a series of interconnection points. Over the years, the telephone companies developed the connections throughout the United States and the world so that a level of cost-effective service can be provided to their customers. To build out this connectivity, the telephone companies installed wires to the customer's door, whether the customer is business or residential. The spot where these wires terminate is called the demarcation point (demarc) or the minimum point of penetration (MPOP). The position of the demarcation point depends on the legal issues involved. In the early days of the telephone network, the telephone companies owned everything, so they ran the wires to an interface point, and then connected their telephone sets to the wires at the customer's end.

New regulations in North America changed this connection to a point at the entrance to the customer's building. From there, the customers hook up their own equipment, items they purchase from a myriad of other sources. Throughout many parts of the world, where full divestiture hasn't yet taken place, the telephone companies (or PTTs) still own the equipment. Other areas of the world have a hybrid system under which customers might or might not own their equipment. The combinations of this arrangement are almost limitless, depending on the degree of privatization and deregulation.

However, the one characteristic common in most of the world to date is the local provider owns the wires from the outside world to the entrance of the customer's building. This is called the local loop.

A Topology of Connections Is Used

In the *local loop*, the topological layout of the wires has traditionally been a single wire pair or multiple pairs of wires strung to the customer's location. This has always been an issue of money. Just how many pairs of wires are needed for the connection of a single line set to the network? The answer (one pair) is obvious. But, for some other types of service, such as digital circuits and connections, the answer is one or more (typically two) pairs. Depending on the customer, the number of wires run to the location has been contingent on the need versus the cost. As a result, the use of a single or dual pair of wires has been the norm. More recently, the local providers have been installing a four-pair (eight-wire) connection to the customer location. This is because the customer (both business and residential) has begun to use voice lines, separate fax lines, and separate data communications hookups. Each of these requires a two-wire interface, so the need for multiple pairs has grown. Installing multiple pairs the first time is far less expensive than installing a single pair of wires every time the customer asks for a new service. Many of the telephone companies are now adding sophistication to the local loop, however, by using a single pair of wires to the consumer's door (business or residential) and providing a xDSL service. For example, a customer can now use Voice over DSL, Data over DSL and Fax over DSL. The xDSL service only requires a single pair of telephone wires.

So, the topology is a dedicated local connection of one or more pairs from the telephone provider to the customer location, which is called a *star configuration*. The telephone company connection to the customer originates from a centralized point called a central office (CO). In a star configuration, all wires home back to a centralized point, the CO.

Once the hundreds or thousands of wire pairs get to the CO, things change. The provider at that point might be using a different topology. At the local telephone company's office, the wires are terminated in what is called a *wire center*. The *wire center* is nothing more than a large extension of the customer's hookup. Thousands of hookups come together in this centralized point. From the wire center, a series of spokes is run out to the customer, to other central offices, to higher-level offices in the hierarchy, or to any location desired. The wire center is also called a *frame*; all the wires are connected to the frame.

At this frame, a series of cross-connections is made. These are either to other wires that go to other locations or to a switching center where the telephone company's central computer (in older offices around the world, this can be an electromechanical system) resides. This is called the *switch*. Most of the equipment today is a stored-program, common-controlled computer system that just happens to process cross-connections for telephone calls. Remember one fundamental fact: the telephone network was designed to carry analog electrical signals across a pair of wires to re-create a voice conversation at both ends. This network was built to carry voice. Only in the past 30 years have we been transmitting other forms of communication, such as facsimile, data, and video.

The switch makes routing decisions based on some parameter, such as the digits dialed by the customer. As these decisions are being made quickly, a cross-connection is made in logic. This means the switch sets up a logical and physical connection to another set of wires. The connection can be back to the frame, where the wires serve a neighboring pair of wires connected to our next-door neighbor or to another connection that links another central office. The possibilities are only limited by the physical arrangements in the office itself.

Between and among the offices built by the carriers (the local and the long-distance providers) is a set of connections usually laid out in a ring, but also possibly in a star configuration. These are the facilities that carry traffic and they're called *interoffice trunks*. In some COs, these are copper wires; in others, they are fiber optic wires; and, in still others, they may be on radio systems.

Throughout this network, more or fewer connections are installed, depending on the anticipated calling patterns of the user population. Sometimes there are many connections among many offices. At other times, it can be simple and single connection.

Tied all together, then, is a series of local links to the customer locations, through a central office where switching and routing decisions are made, then on out to a myriad of other connections from telephone companies, long-distance suppliers, and other providers. This is the basis of the telephone network.

The Local Loop

The basic model for our interface to the telephone company network is the single-line telephone set. It stands to reason that we need to connect this set to the telephone company CO. The pair of twisted wires running from the telephone company's CO is called the *local loop*. Each subscriber, or customer, is delivered at least one pair of wires per telephone line. As a wireless world is rapidly approaching us, the equivalent of a single pair of wires will exist, even though only air is in between the CO and the customer. More telephone providers are looking at the use of wireless local loop configurations to satisfy growing demand and reduce the cost of provisioning the service. Installing a wireless connection to the consumer is less expensive than digging up the ground and laying wires and cables to the door.

Exceptions to this rule occur in rural areas where the telephone company might share multiple users on a single pair of wires. This is called a *party line* and, again, this is a financial decision. If the number of users demanding telephone service exceeds the number of pairs available, a Telco might well offer the service on a party or shared set of wires. Rural parts of America still have some of these party lines. In other parts of the world, these may still be the more common way of conducting business.

The phone company distributes its outside plant, or distribution, to the customer by running large bundles of twisted pairs toward the customer location. Figure 1.5 shows how this is done using feeders, which are composed of 50 to over 3000 pairs of wires.

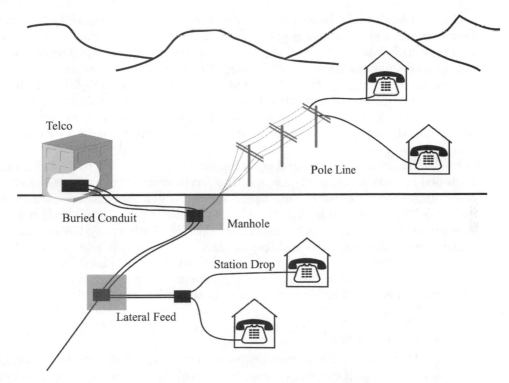

Figure 1.5 The local loop is made up of a series of wires that fan out laterally.

600 Pairs of Wire

Figure 1.6 A 600-pair cable is used in the feeder and distribution network.

Figure 1.6 is the bundle of wires consisting of 600 pairs. The wires are color-coded to allow access to specific pairs in these bundles.

The feeders are run to splice points or breakout points called *manholes* or *handholes*. At this point, the splicing of two reels of cable takes place, assuming the cable on a single reel wasn't sufficient. A lateral distribution can also take place here. *Lateral distribution* is the breakout of a number of pairs to run in a different direction. The lateral distribution or branch feeder is then strung to various customer locations. The end of the pair to the final customer location is called the *customer pair* or *station drop*.

In this outside plant—from the CO to the customer location—90 percent of all problems occur. This isn't to imply the Telco is doing a lousy job of delivering service to the customer. These cables are exposed more to cable cuts because of construction (commonly called *backhoe fade*), flooding at the splice locations, rodent damage, and many other risks.

In the traditional analog dial-up telephone network, each pair of the local loop is designed to carry a single telephone call to service voice conversations. This is a proven technology that works for the most part and continues to get better as the technologies advance. The cables can be delivered via a telephone pole (aerial distribution), buried conduit (underground feed), or direct buried cables. Either way, the service is one with which we are familiar with and feel comfortable. What was just described is the connection at the local portion of the network. From there, the local connectivity must be extended out to other locations in and around a metropolitan area or across the country. The connections to other types of offices are then required.

The Network Hierarchy (Pre-1984)

Prior to 1984, most of the network was owned by AT&T and its local Bell Operating Companies (BOCs). It evolved through a series of interconnections based on volumes of calls and growth. A layered hierarchy of office connections was designed around a five-level architecture. Each of these layers was designed around the concept of call completion. The offices are connected together with wires of various types, called *trunks*. These trunks can be twisted pairs of wire, coaxial cables (like the CATV wire), radio (such as microwave), or fiber optics. The trunks vary in their capacities, but generally high-usage trunks are used to connect between offices. Figure 1.7 shows the hierarchy prior to the divestiture of AT&T, with the five levels evident.

The class 5 office is the local exchange or end office. It delivers dial tone to the customer. The end office, also called a *branch exchange*, is the closest connection to the end user. Think of a tree: all the activity takes place at the ends of the branches and the customers are the leaves hanging off the branches. Calls between exchanges in a geographical area are connected by direct trunks between two end offices, which are called interoffice trunks. Over 19,000 end offices in the United States alone provide basic dial tone services.

The class 4 office is the toll center. A call going between two end offices not connected together is routed to the class 4 office. The toll center is also used as the connection to the long-distance network for calls where added costs are incurred when a connection is made. This toll center may also be called a *tandem office*, meaning calls have to pass through (or tandem through) this location to get somewhere else on the network. A basic arrangement of a tandem switching system is shown in Fig. 1.8. The tandem office usually doesn't provide dial tone services to the end user. However, this is a variable where a single office might provide various functions. The tandem office can also be just

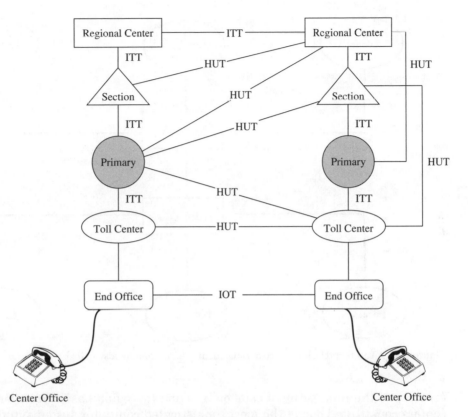

Figure 1.7   Network hierarchy pre-1984 used five different levels within the architecture.

a *toll*—a connecting arrangement that's a pass-through from various class 5 offices to the toll centers. Again, this varies depending on the arrangements made by the telephone providers. The ratio of toll centers that serve local long distance is approximately 9 to 1. Prior to divestiture, approximately 940 toll centers existed.

The class 3 office is the primary center. Calls destined within the same state area are passed from the local toll office to the primary center for completion. These locations are served with high-usage trunks used strictly for passing calls from one toll center to another. The primary centers never serve dial tones to an end user. The number of primary centers prior to divestiture was approximately 170, spread across the country among the various operating telephone companies (both Bell and independent operating companies).

The class 2 office is the sectional center. A sectional center is typically the main state switching system used for interstate toll connections designated for the processing of long-distance calls from section to section. Approximately 50+ sectional centers existed before the divestiture of the Bell System. These offices didn't serve any end users, but would serve between primary centers around the country. The class 1 office is the regional center and ten regional centers existed across the country. The task of each

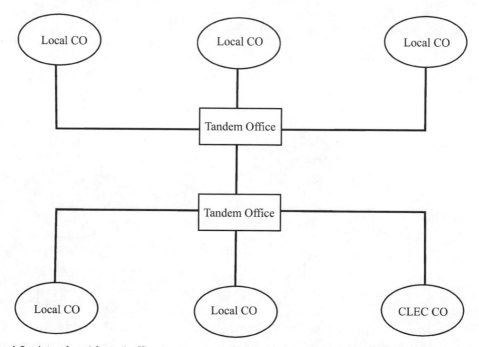

Figure 1.8 A tandem (class 4) office arrangement. The tandem is also called a Bell Access Tandem.

center was the final setup of calls on a region-by-region basis. However, the regional centers constituted one of the most sophisticated computer systems in the world. The regional centers continually updated each other regarding the status of every circuit in the network. These centers were required to reroute traffic around trouble spots (for example, failed equipment or circuits) and to keep each other informed at all times. As mentioned, this was all prior to the divestiture of the local BOC by AT&T.

The Network Hierarchy (Post-1984)

After 1984 the network took a dramatic turn, with the separation of the BOCs from AT&T. Many users screamed that things would fall apart and service would be affected, but none of this came true. This doesn't mean a lot of confusion didn't occur because it did. Things kept humming along for the most part, though, and calls were completed through this series of interconnecting points called the network.

The hierarchy of the network shown in Fig. 1.9 introduced a new set of terms and connections. The BOCs were classified the same way as independent telephone companies. They are all called local exchange carriers (LECs) and now Incumbent Local Exchange Carriers (ILECs). The seven spin-off companies formed because of the divestiture became Regional Bell Holding Companies (RBHCs), which had regulated arms called the Regional Bell Operating Companies (RBOCs). Each RBOC had the Bell Operating Companies in its geographical area. Additionally, the RBHCs also had

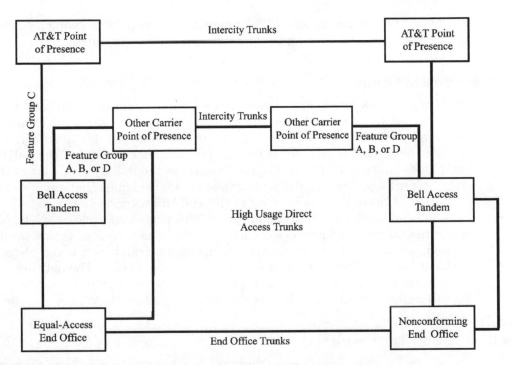

Figure 1.9 The network after divestiture shows some very distinct changes.

an unregulated side of the business, where they could enter into new ventures (such as equipment sales, finance, and real estate).

Equal access, or the capability of every interexchange carrier (IEC or IXC) to connect to the BOC for long-distance service, became a reality. Equal access was designed to allow the same access to other long-distance competitors that AT&T had always enjoyed prior to divestiture. Prior to divestiture, a customer attempting to use an alternative long-distance supplier would have to dial a seven- or ten-digit telephone number to get to this supplier's switch. Then, when this connection was completed, a computer would answer the call and place a tone on the line. From there, the caller would have to enter a seven- to eleven-digit authorization code. This code identified the caller by telephone number, caller name and address, and billing arrangements. Only after the computer (switch) verified this information, would it then send dial tone to the caller's ear. The caller would then have to dial the ten-digit telephone number of the requested party. This could involve lengthy and frustrating call set-up times—especially when the number called was busy.

Users chose not to use these alternative carriers because of the time and the number of digits required and the frustration of attempts to call busy numbers. That is, unless the organization forced the user to dial across the carriers' networks. The reason for all the digits was simple. The telephone company didn't pass on the caller information to the alternate carrier (MCI, Sprint, ITT, and so forth) that it passed to AT&T. Thus, the choice of many callers was AT&T because the process was simpler. Now the caller information is passed on in an equal basis, so the access is equal.

The Public-Switched Network

The U.S. public-switched network has always been the largest and the best in the world. Over the years, the network has penetrated to even the most remote locations around the country. Primary call-carrying capacity in the United States is through the public-switched network. Because this is the environment that AT&T and the Bell Operating Companies built, we still hear people refer to it as the Bell System. However, as we've already seen, significant changes have taken place to change that environment.

The public network allows access to the end office, connects through the long-distance network, and delivers to the end point. This makes the cycle complete. Many companies use the switched network exclusively; others have created variations depending on need, finances, and size. The goal of the network hierarchies is to complete the call in the least amount of time and over the shortest route possible. The network is dynamic enough, however, to pass the call along longer routes through the hierarchy to complete the call in the first attempt wherever possible.

The North American Numbering Plan

The network numbering plan was designed to allow for the quick and discreet connection to any phone in the country. The North American numbering plan (NANP), as it is called, works on a series of ten numbers as shown in Table 1.2.

The Area Code   Note some changes have occurred in this numbering plan. When this plan was originally formulated, the telephone numbers were divided into three sets of digits. The first was a three-digit area code or numbering plan assignment (NPA). This started with a digit from 2 to 9 in the first slot of the sequence. In the second slot, the number was set as 0 or 1. In the third slot, it could be any digit from 1 to 0 (with 0 representing 10). The reasons behind this sequence were clever. For example, the first digit didn't use a 0 or 1 because these digits were used for access to operators (0) or operator services such as credit card calling. The 1 was used to send a significant digit to the local switching office indicating the call was long distance; this enabled the switch to immediately start setting up a toll connection immediately to the toll center or tandem office. Thus, the exclusion of 0 and 1 in the first digit of the area code facilitated the

TABLE 1.2   The North American Numbering Plan As It Evolved

Timing	Area Code	Central Office Code	Station Subscriber Number
Original	N 0/1 X	N N X	X X X X
Pre-1995	N 0/1 X	N X X	X X X X
Post-1995	N X X	N X X	X X X X

quicker call setup. In the second slot, the digit was only a 1 or 0. This was used by the switching office equipment in a screening mode. As soon as the system sampled the second digit and saw a 0 or 1, it knew this three-digit sequence was an area code. The third slot was any digit; having no special significance, it was processed normally. Back in the early 1960s, we recognized we were running out of area codes, given that only 160 were available ($8 \times 2 \times 10 = 160$). In reality, only 152 were allowed for use by the various states because certain ones were allotted for special services (the N11 area codes, for example, 211, 311, 411, and so forth, were always reserved). Close administration of the area code assignments kept this scheme working until 1995, when the inevitable occurred. From the outset, the use of the entire numbering plan was limited, so it had to grow. In 1995, the area codes were expanded by allowing any digit in the center slot of the three-digit sequence. This expansion created 640 new area codes for the NANP. Our current rate of consumption of telephone numbers is alarming. When we think back to the beginning days of the networks, customers had a single number that sufficed. Now, the average household has three or more numbers (a second line for fax, a third line for modem, a fourth line for teens, separate number for cell phones, and so forth).

The Exchange Code   Following the area code is another three-digit sequence called the *exchange code*, which is a central office designator that lists the possible number of central office codes that can be used in each area code. The exchange code originally was set up in the sequence NNX, meaning the first and second numbers used the digits 2 through 9, for the same reasons as in the area code. The digits 1 and 0 were reserved for operator and long-distance access and the 0/1 exclusion in the exchange code prevented this three-digit number from being confused with an area code. In the third number slot of the exchange code, any digit could be used. The greatest limitation in the exchange codes was that we would run out. With NNX, we have 640 possible exchange numbers to use ($8 \times 8 \times 10 = 640$), but these were used quickly.

In the late 1960s, we began planning the use of an exchange code-numbering plan that changed the sequence to NXX, expanding the number of exchange codes in each of the area codes to 800. This added some relief to the numbering plan. When using the NXX sequence, though, the need arose for a forced 1 in advance of the 10-digit telephone number, so the call screening and number interpretation in a switch wouldn't get confused. This met with some resistance but, ultimately, customers got used to the idea. The first two locations to use this revised numbering plan were Los Angeles and New York City early in 1971.

The Subscriber Extension   The last sequence in the numbering plan is the subscriber extension number. This is a four-digit sequence that can use any digit in all of the slots, allotting 10,000 customer telephone numbers in each of the exchange codes. Because the four-digit sequence can be composed of any numbers, the intent is to give every subscriber his or her own unique telephone number. This hasn't changed yet, although the possibility that we can still run out of numbers always exists. Therefore, two ideas have been bandied around: add two, three, or four more digits to the end of the telephone number or add one or two more digits to the area code or exchange code.

In either method, users will be asked to dial more digits, an idea that's never popular, but might become a necessity. However, this is far more complicated than just adding a few more digits here and there. The whole world will be impacted by any such decision and the length of time required to implement such a global change will be extraordinary.

Currently in North America, several new area and exchange codes have been installed where only one existed. This forces users in the area to dial 11 digits (1 plus the 10-digit telephone number) for local, as well as long-distance calls.

Wiring Connections: Hooking Things Up

The Telco uses a variety of connections to bring the service to the customer locations. The typical connection is the two-wire service we keep discussing. This two-wire interface to the network is terminated in a demarcation point, as required by law. Normally, Telco terminates in what is described as a block; this can be the standard modular block for a single-line telephone. If the customer has multiple lines, Telco terminates in a 66 block or an RJ-21X or other form of multiline connector shown in Fig. 1.10. These are fancy names for their termination points. The typical modular connector uses an RJ-11C for telephones connected to a two-pair interface (not to be confused with the two wires) or an RJ-45X as a four-pair interface for both voice and data. Another version of connector for digital service is an eight-conductor (four-pair) called the RJ-48X.

When a Telco brings in a digital circuit, it terminates the four-wire circuit into a newer RJ-68 or a smart jack. There's no major mystique in any of these connectors.

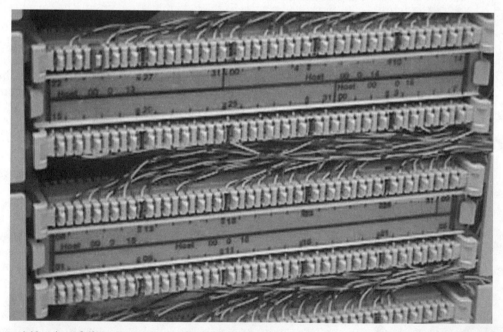

Figure 1.10 A multiline connector is used to terminate a bundle of wires, shown here in the Telephone company block.

Figure 1.11   The block used for an RJ-11 has four pins.

The number is strictly a uniform service code, so the Telco can keep it all straight. When ordering a circuit, however, the Telco asks how you want it terminated. The rule of thumb in a multiline environment is to use the RJ-21X (which is a 66 block with an amphenol connector on it). Sounds complex, doesn't it? A single line terminates in an RJ-11C or RJ-12. These various single line connectors are shown in Fig. 1.11, which is the RJ-11C or the RJ-12.

The Telephone Set

Most people take the telephone set for granted. How can this device that we have known and used since we were old enough to stand up be worth mentioning? Why should we even care? This attitude is not uncommon. Since the early days of the telephone network installation, users have accepted the device as the norm with no real concern. We had the device, and all we had to do use it. It always worked!

For the most part, this is true. However, from time to time telephones do break, and when they do, we feel lost. We do not have the foggiest idea of what went wrong or what to do to fix it.

When AT&T and its BOCs installed and controlled the original telephone network under its monopoly, we were left with the fear that if we tinkered with the telephone set and broke it, we would lose our phone privileges. Can you imagine that? Of course, since the breakup of the Bell System, things have changed considerably. The set now belongs to the end user. We can do anything we want with it or to it. If we break it, we buy a new one. Simple?

The Function of the Telephone Set

Earlier we stated that the voice can create sound wave changes at a rate ranging from 100 to 5000 times per second, and amplitudes and frequencies are constantly changing. From this understanding of how the human voice works, we then must understand that the network was built to carry voice. How then does the voice get put onto a telephone company network and carried to the other end of the line? The sound waves must travel down the one pair of wires that the telephone company has provided. The challenge is to convert sound into something that the telephone network deals with: electricity. Yes, electricity is what runs across copper wires. The telephone company delivers a pair of copper wires to our door and then attaches a telephone set to those wires. So, the function of the telephone set is to convert sound into electricity. It will therefore act as a change agent as shown in Fig. 1.12.

Conversely, when a voice is sent through the wires as electricity, the process must be reversed at the receiving end. Therefore, the telephone set must also function to convert this electricity back into sound. The change process must work in two ways. The "from" and "to" functions are what the set must accomplish. Figure1.13 is a representation of the reverse process.

Figure 1.12   The telephone converts sound into electricity.

Figure 1.13   The set also converts electricity back into sound.

But wait, there's more. On the top of the telephone set, two little buttons are spring-loaded. They must have a function too. The switch hook, as these buttons are called, is a mechanism that originates and finalizes calls. When you press the springy-dingies on the top of the set, the dial tone goes away. If you lift the handset off the base of the telephone, you hear the dial tone (this is called *going off hook*). So, these buttons request and relinquish the dial tone from the telephone company.

By now, you will notice that the telephone is a complex piece of equipment. The invention of Alexander Graham Bell has come a long way from its founding. Nevertheless, functionally it still does the same thing. The first telephone sets had no dial pads; all calls were handled by a telephone company operator. In order to make a call, you would have to "flash" the operator and request the called party.

So, let's back up a little and look at the pieces of a telephone set, at least generically. The telephone set consists of multiple pieces, each of which serves at least one function. Without one or more of the pieces, communication might not take place. They are all intertwined to work together so that we have constant service at any time. Figure 1.14 is the telephone in all its glory.

The Pieces

The telephone set is made up of the following major components.

The Base All of the components are either housed inside or attached to the base. It is typically a plastic or space-age healed plastic case that will withstand many impacts, such as being dropped from a table or desk. This case protects the inner workings and other components from exposure to the most dangerous part of a telephone network: humans.

Figure 1.14 The telephone set shown here is one of the more common ones people used.

We tend to spill things on the set. We also drop it or knock it over. When we are frustrated on the phone, we slam it down or beat it on the desk, taking out our anger and irritation on this device that is always supposed to work. Without the casing to protect the telephone, we would never have service. This casing also protects the inside of the phone from dust and other elements floating around in the air.

The Handset   The handset shown in Fig. 1.15 houses two separate components, the transmitter and the receiver. The handset is ergonomically designed to fit the distance from the mouth to the ear. The transmitter is located at the bottom portion of the handset, so that it is positioned in front of the mouth when we hold the handset to our face. The receiver is located at the top of the handset so that it rests against our outer ear when we hold the handset to our face. The first handsets consisted only of an ear mechanism; the transmitter was a stationary mount on the front of the base.

Now we move to the inner pieces of the handset. Figure 1.16 shows the handset with the transmitter and receiver indicated. Note that the wires also connect the pieces. Two wires run from the earpiece and two wires run from the mouthpiece. Remember that the telephone is going to convert sound into electricity. The wires carry the electricity created at the mouthpiece to the telephone set. The second set of wires carries electricity from the telephone set to the earpiece. So, the handset contains a four-wire circuit: two wires for the transmitter and two wires for the receiver. Each side of the function has its own two-wire electrical circuit at this point. Modern-day functions of the following parts are still the same. Although newer solid-state components have replaced the pieces, they perform the same functions as the pieces described in the following paragraphs.

The Transmitter   As mentioned in the discussion about the farmer wanting to see the inside of the telephone set, the transmitter houses some very sophisticated components. The first portion of the transmitter houses a diaphragm just under the outer casing of the mouthpiece. The diaphragm is a very sensitive membrane that will vibrate with air pressure changes. When we speak into the mouthpiece of the telephone set, we are really creating air pressure changes with our vocal cords. The sound pressure we create causes air pressure changes that move at the same frequency as the changes we

Figure 1.15   The handset houses the transmitter and receiver.

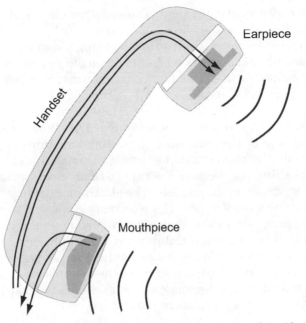

Figure 1.16 The transmitter and receiver are connected with two wires each inside the handset.

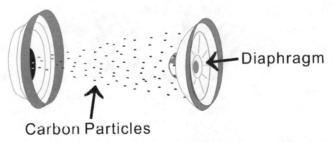

Figure 1.17 The transmitter has a diaphragm and loosely packed carbon particles that create the electricity.

produce by vibrating our vocal chords. The pressure changes cause the membrane on the diaphragm to move back and forth at the same frequency (see Fig.1.17).

Behind the diaphragm are loosely packed carbon particles. When the diaphragm moves back and forth, it causes the carbon particles to move back and forth. This produces an electrical resistance to the charge that occurs at the same frequency and amplitude as the sound pressure changes created by the voice. The result is an analog sine wave that is directly (mostly) proportional to the frequency and amplitude of the voice, or the electrical equivalent of sound. This electrical energy is carried away from the transmitter across the wires behind the mouthpiece.

The resistance also protects us from creating a signal that is too strong for the rest of the components and network elements. If we did not restrict the flow of the energy, we could cause damage to equipment, not to mention what we could do to your eardrums. What?«el»What?«el»What?

The Receiver   The receiver is shown in Fig. 1.18. When voice or other telecommunication in the form of electrical energy is being transmitted to us from the far end (the other party on the phone call), the network carries this electricity to the telephone set. The wires behind the receiver are run up to an electromagnet that is mounted inside the receiver portion of the handset. The electromagnet is attached to a diaphragm similar to that in the mouthpiece. The electricity comes through the wires to the magnet, and the magnet vibrates at the same frequency as the received energy. As the magnet vibrates, it causes the membrane on the diaphragm to move back and forth. This back-and-forth motion causes air pressure changes (vibrations) that are at the same frequency as the transmitted energy. As the air pressure changes occur, they cause the air waves to bounce off the inner eardrum, which is what produces sound to our ears. See Fig. 1.19 for the eardrum comparison.

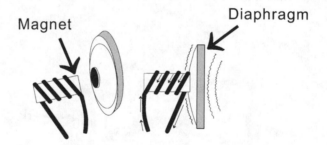

Figure 1.18   The receiver uses an electromagnet to change the electricity back into air pressure.

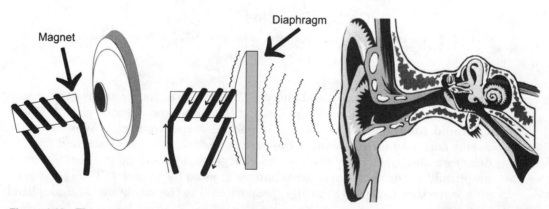

Figure 1.19   The eardrum receives air pressure and converts it into sound.

The transmitter and receiver complete the conversion of sound to electricity and electricity back to sound. We often refer to the handset functions as E&M, or the ear-and-mouth communications process. The E represents the direction of flow to the ear or to the receiver, and the M represents the direction of energy from the mouth or the transmitter.

The Connector or the Handset Cord   Coming from the handset and proceeding to the base of the telset is a coiled wire. It doesn't have to be coiled; that just makes it easier to manage. Inside the curly wire are four wires: two from the transmitter and the receiver, respectively. The modern sets use a connector that is called an RJ-11C. This is the four-wire connector that has a little spring-loaded clip on it to plug and unplug the connector into the female receptacle. The cord is double-ended with male RJ-11C connectors. This is also a matter of convenience. Because the cords and the connectors are the most likely pieces to wear out, it makes sense to use a plug-and-play module. Older versions of this cord used a screw-down version (called a spade lug), but this required that the telephone set be opened up to get at the screw mounts. Remember, this was an area that we were not allowed into.

A funny thing happens along this connector cord, however. When it gets to the base of the telephone set, it is plugged into the female version of the RJ-11. But inside this jack, a hybrid arrangement takes place. One of the transmitters and one of the receiver wires are connected to each other as shown in Fig. 1.20. The other two wires that continue into the set are covered in the next section. The important thing here is to understand why the transmitter wire gets connected to the receiver wire. This creates a loopback

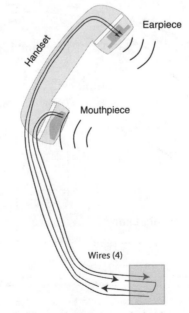

Earpiece

Handset

Mouthpiece

Wires (4)

Figure 1.20   As the four wires enter the set, they go into a hybrid arrangement.

arrangement of sorts. The transmitted sound is looped right back to the ear. We can hear everything we say in the conversation because the energy is transmitted back to the earpiece. You are probably asking yourself why this is done. The process produces what is called *side tone*. This side tone is a means of letting us know that an electrical connection across the network still exists. When you speak into a telephone during a conversation and you hear yourself, you recognize that there is still a connection to the distant end. You can also regulate your volume when you hear yourself speak. When you speak into the set and you hear nothing or the sound is dead, you recognize that there is no one out there—in other words, that you have been cut off. This is part of your basic training in telephone usage. Although no one ever explained this to you, it has been learned through experience.

The Inside of the Telephone   Once the wires are run from the handset to the base of the telephone, two wires go into the set. Actually, these wires meet up with a whole network of cross-connects (connections from place to place) inside the set, but we are concerned with the two wires. As shown in Fig. 1.21, one of the wires, the transmitter wire, is connected inside the set to the dial pad (whether rotary or tone dial). This is used as an addressing mechanism. The telephone network uses a decimal numbering system in the form of a sequence of digits that we dial to the called party. The dial pad is used to send these digits out to the telephone company for delivery to the called party. This wire connected to the dial pad is also cross-connected to the switchhook (the spring-loaded buttons). The same wire is used to connect to another jack (RJ-11, RJ-12, or other), which is connected in turn to the outside world.

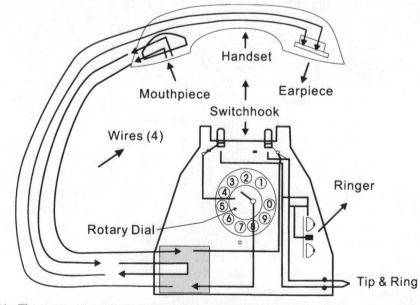

Figure 1.21   The transmitter wire is connected to the dial pad and the switchhook. The receiver wire connects to the ringer.

The second wire from the handset cord is connected through the network of wires to a ringer. The ringer can be in the form of a bell or a turkey warbler (electronic ringer), but the function is what is important here. The ringer is a receiver wire function. It is used to alert you that someone wants to speak to you. If you do not have a ringer, you'd have to pick up the handset every now and then and listen to see whether someone is on the line. This would be inconvenient for you, not to mention for the caller, who would never know whether you would pick up the handset. Callers would be in limbo forever. So the ringer is a crucial component of the set and the process.

The Switchhook Already mentioned and equally important is the switchhook function. This is the portion of the set that actually gets the dial tone from the telephone company or, when we are through with the call, gives the dial tone back. In reality, what happens is that an electrical wiring circuit is physically connected from the telephone company office to our telephone set. This circuit gives us access to the services offered by the telephone company, mainly the dial tone and the ability to make and receive calls. Under normal conditions, we do not have a dial tone at our set. This is a service that we must request.

To request the service, we lift the handset off the switchhook. When we do this, the little buttons pop up. At the same time, they "make" the circuit by adding a resistance across the wires. The telephone company equipment constantly monitors all of its connections to end users. When the central office computer (now they are computers) sees a change in the resistance across the wires, it recognizes this as a request for a dial tone. Actually, the Telco installs a battery on the local loop. The battery current flows down the receive wire and gets stopped at the handset where the circuit is in the "break" mode. When we go off hook and "make," we have actually connected the transmit and receive wires together. This creates a continual loop as the battery current flows from the Telco to the handset and then gets looped right back to the central office (CO). This is how the CO recognizes the change in the state of the telephone set. We call this a loop start circuit.

After we create the loop, the Telco starts the process by returning the dial tone. If the dial tone is available, it will be provided immediately. In the time it takes us to go off hook and bring the handset up to our ear, the dial tone is there. Actually, it gets there much faster than that if everything is functioning properly.

As we use the line and make calls, we will use the other components in the telephone set, but the central office computer will monitor the line (wires) for the time when we are finished with our calls. When we disconnect, we place the handset back into the cradle. This pushes the spring-loaded buttons back down and breaks the circuit. The central office computer sees this change on the wires and recognizes that we are done. Therefore, the central office computer takes the dial tone away from us and provides it to other users who require it. Then the process starts all over again. The phone company uses a 10:1 ratio of users to dial tone. For every ten users, the company knows that statistically only one user requires service.

The Dial Pad It really does not matter whether you have a newer set or an older one. The dial pad uses the set to address the network. When we have our dial tone, we then start a sequence of dialed digits indicating to the central office with whom we want to speak. As mentioned, the first telephone sets did not have a dial pad. Everything was manually performed through the telephone company operators. If you needed to speak to someone, you got the operator by going off hook. The off-hook process created the "make" on the circuit (looped the battery back to the operator) that lit a light or created a visual indication to the telephone company operator. The operator would answer and converse with you. At this point, you would pass on the name or number of the requested party and the operator would provide the connection. It was quite simple, but as things got busier, the human involvement became an issue. You could be on the line waiting for an operator forever if things were busy at the central office.

The rotary telephone set shown Fig. 1.22 was the first attempt to automate the process. Initially, it was well received; however, over time it became a nuisance. The rotary set is an electromechanical device. As you dialed the number, you would rotate the dial in a clockwise direction. When the dial was released, the counterclockwise return to the normal position created a series of electrical interrupts or pulses across the line to the telephone company office. The CO would interpret these pulses and make the necessary routing decisions. The main problem that led to frustrations was that statistically four attempts were necessary to make a call and speak to the intended party. Either the network was busy, the called party was busy, the phone at the receiving end went unanswered, or some other event got in the way. Thus, users felt frustration with this set, especially because it took so long to dial a number.

The pulses are generated at 10 per second (10 PPS), which also created long call setup times because of the slowness of the dial pad. Additionally, because it was electromechanical, the system was prone to failures. The rotary set might stick or misdial the digits, or otherwise thwart the user. Users began to complain, and the manufacturers had to respond. The primary manufacturer at the time was Western Electric, a division of AT&T.

The Touch-Tone phone was the second edition of the dial pad. This changed the look and feel of the dialing process. Instead of using the rotary dial to electromechanically produce the digits, this phone created by AT&T's Western Electric Division employed

Figure 1.22   The rotary dial pad was inconvenient to use but got the job done.

a tone dialing sequence. Using a group of tones that fall into the spectrum of voice frequency, the tone dialer has a set of buttons that send out frequency-based tones instead of electrical impulses.

The Touch-Tone telephone set was created to speed up dialing and call processing, reduce user frustration, increase productivity, and enable additional services through the dial pad. The touch tones are actually a dual-tone multifrequency (DTMF) system. Each of the numbers represented on the dial pad has both an X and Y matrix or cross-point. This was a decision that Western Electric made to create a number of tone generators that could be used at the set and tone receivers to be used at the central office. Western Electric did not want to have too many of these tone generators/receivers, because they are expensive. Therefore, under a dual-tone arrangement, they could get away with using only half of the generators needed to represent the same number of digits. See Fig. 1.23 for the tone dial pad and note the frequencies as they appear on the chart.

When you press a number, two separate tones are generated and sent to the CO simultaneously. Each number on the dial pad has its own distinct set of dual tones, so the system recognizes each as a discrete number. The reasoning behind the dual tones is that the human voice could not generate a harmonic shift in frequency quickly enough to recreate these tones. Therefore, the telecommunications systems can recognize the tone shifts as dialed digits instead of conversational path information (voice). For the most part, this works; however, from time to time humans can generate these quick harmonics. It is rare, but it can be done.

Tone dialing is faster than rotary because the tones are generated at 23 pps, much quicker than the rotary set. As the tone dial was introduced, a 12-button pad was created,

Figure 1.23 The Touch-Tone phone.

adding two extra numbers to the telephone. The older rotary set only had ten numbers (decimal). The two new buttons enabled new features and capabilities to be introduced in the telephone world, using the pound (#) and star (*) keys as delimiters when dialing into computers, and so on.

Tone dialing also helps to get the call through the network more quickly because the tones are sent at a much faster rate than that of rotary pulsing. This improves network performance because the network processes the call setup and teardown faster, it creates happier users because they can dial their numbers much more quickly than with the tedious rotary dial sequence, and it promotes overall satisfaction.

The Ringer   As already discussed, the ringer serves the purpose of alerting the called party that someone wants to converse. The ringer has no mystique other than it must be "told" via an electrical current to ring. The current from the central equipment out at the telephone company office is sent to a ringing generator that produces the current across the line. A 48V direct current from a battery in the office produces an 80V alternating current at 20 Hz output across the telephone line to the customer location. This is as simple as can be. Occasionally, differences appear in the way these things are laid out or the voltages that are applied to the line, but we are using norms in our examples.

Tip and Ring   Tip and ring is a phrase that Telco installers or repairers use all of the time. They love to talk about tip and ring. This is a description of the two wires that are connected to the telephone set from the outside world. You will recall that the four wires that left the handset went through a hybrid arrangement as they came into the telephone set. At this entrance point, only two wires were carried into the set to connect to the signaling systems inside the phone. The two wires, one from the transmitter and one from the receiver, now exit the set and proceed toward the telephone company connection. They call the transmit wire the "tip" and the receive wire the "ring."

Tip and ring are better described as the transmitter and receiver wires, but telephone company personnel held the words over from a bygone era. Tip and ring come from the use of the old operator cord boards. When the operator tested the line, the tip of an RCA jack was used. If a call was already in motion on a particular line, the operator would hear static on the line when tipping. If the line was not in use, the operator would not get any static from the tipping; the operator would then insert the jack on a cord board into the designated extension port on the board. This insertion would then cause a ringing voltage to be generated across the wires and your phone to ring. This system has all but disappeared here in the United States, but in several other parts of the world, cord boards still exist. That's the main reason for the mention of where this all came from.

Newer Sets

The telephone evolved over time. Conceptually, nothing has really changed, but the pieces continue to advance. Today's digital telephone sets provide far more than just a plain old analog telephone call. The older set functionally achieved interface to the network provided by the various carriers. This interface, with all of its electrical and mechanical components, got us to where we are today.

However, progress continues. Users wanted more features and functions from the devices placed on the desk or wall in offices and residences. Consequently, the migration to solid-state, microprocessor-controlled telephone sets became the wave of the future. The newer sets are digital. That means that they perform the same functions with less voltage, very discrete events are preprogrammed into them, and other characteristics of digital transmission will add to the quality of conversation.

The telephone set was a clear target for digital technology. Anyone can now manufacture a telephone set, or system for that matter, as long as they abide by certain registration techniques and parameters. On this set, several added features that enhance the call placement process are incorporated into the telephone set rather than being served by an external device. For example, some of the features that are now becoming the norm are as follows.

Questions

1. How many wires are used in the telephone handset?
   a. Two
   b. Four
   c. Six
   d. One

2. How does the telephone company CO know when you want to make a phone call?
   a. It can sense it
   b. The operator knows that a call is coming in
   c. The circuit gets closed in a loop
   d. There is no way the CO can tell

3. What is the purpose of the telephone set?
   a. To crack walnuts
   b. To give you something to do with your hands while you are talking
   c. To convert speech into airwaves
   d. To convert airwaves into electrical waves and electrical waves into airwaves

4. What is the purpose of the ringer?
   a. To notify you that someone wants to make a call
   b. To alert you that someone has just arrived
   c. To signal you that the phone company is charging for this call
   d. To alert you that someone wishes to speak with you

5. What two forms can the dial pad take on? (choose the two best answers)
   a. Round
   b. Square
   c. Rotary
   d. Touch pad
   e. Multi frequency

6. Into what format does the set convert human sound?
   a. Air
   b. Sound
   c. Electricity
   d. Pulses
   e. Tones

7. How many pulses per second does the rotary dial create?
   a. 5
   b. 7
   c. 9
   d. 10
   e. 12

8. How many tones does the Touch-Tone set create?
   a. 5
   b. 7
   c. 10
   d. 12

9. How long did it take to set up a phone call in the old days when we used a rotary phone?
   a. 10 seconds
   b. 43 seconds
   c. 37 seconds
   d. 1 second

10. What two variables are constantly changing in a voice conversation?
    a. Amplitude and frequency
    b. Analog and frequency
    c. Analog and Digital
    d. Amplitude and phase

11. What is the bandwidth of the actual channel?

    a. 3Khz

    b. 3.3Khz

    c. 4Khz

    d. 64Khz

12. What type of shifts is produced more by female voice?

    a. Amplitude

    b. Frequency

    c. Phase

    d. Harmonics

13. How many pairs of wire does the local loop use?

    a. 1

    b. 2

    c. 3

    d. 4

14. For what type of information is the most common use of the network built?

    a. Data

    b. Internet

    c. Video

    d. Voice

15. What is the bandwidth of the voice channel?

    a. 64Kbps

    b. 4KHz

    c. 3Khz

    d. 3.3Khz

16. Why is a modem limited to its speeds and throughput?

    a. The manufacturer made it that way

    b. The Public Utilities Commission allows it

    c. The FCC restricts it

    d. The telephone line can only carry that much speed and throughput

2

The Open Systems Interconnect Model (OSI)

After reading this chapter and completing the questions, you will be able to:

- Describe the OSI model
- Converse openly about the seven-layer architecture
- Compare the differences between the OSI and other models, such as TCP/IP, IBM SNA, and DEC DNA
- Understand the reasoning for using a model like this for transparent communications
- Describe the importance of reliable communications processes for moving data

The three-letter acronym OSI (*open systems interconnect*) appears in several places in this book. No one concept in this industry has been more misunderstood, but that is what happens when several different operations are merged into one.

Introduction to the OSI Model

We first had a telephone industry. Later, we started to call it a telecommunications network—especially as newer services were being supported on this one infrastructure. The merger started when we introduced data processing into the telecommunications industry. Now, we have the convergence network. The data processing industry had already become entrenched in its own jargon and concepts. As long as the data processing function was localized to the mainframe and all transactions were performed in the computer room, no problem existed. However, like all things, this industry evolved. Soon the movement was from the computer room to the desktop, where users wanted connectivity to the mainframe. This was accomplished through the use of specialized wiring systems. Nothing is new here, other than that these special wires were very expensive. The wires had to carry the data from the terminal to the computer and also do the reverse. This was accomplished with the use of traditional communications techniques—by converting the data into electrical energy and carrying it down the wire—and the data was represented in digital form without notice.

Then it happened: Not only did we need connectivity from the desktop to the computer room, we also needed it from a desktop across town or across the country. Now the process was going to change the way we conducted business. The data communications industry became the next battleground. The data processing people all thought that data processing and data communications should be similar enough so that they would control the deployment. The telephony people felt that this computer stuff was a pain anyway, so they were content to let it reside in the data processing arena.

However, some problems existed with this whole situation. To send the data across town or across the entire country, it would be necessary to use a device called a modem. Recall that we talked about this in an earlier chapter, but there the modem was used to make the data look like voice. As long as the data looked like voice, the data folks wanted to send it back to the telephony department, especially when they didn't understand or care to understand how this analog network functioned.

Thus, the marriage of the three techniques began back in the late 1950s and into the 1960s. The evolution was slow because the telephone monopoly controlled the delivery of the transport system. The data processors were looking for a way to make the network digital to avoid the digital-to-analog and the analog-to-digital conversions. This seemed like too many steps, and as each step was taken, there was a risk of introducing errors into the data stream.

Things rolled along nicely, but the data processing evolution kept going from the mainframe environment to one leaning toward distributed computing. Organizations were cropping up that would offer smaller-scale computers (midi[*] and mini) that could handle very specific functions and off-load this process from the mainframe. Once again, this started the ball rolling. Many of the computers in use at the time were not compatible with each other. This led to a new set of predicaments. As the smaller computer companies were competing with the mainframe world, two major players were doing battle—IBM and DEC. Each had its own hardware and software platforms. Now organizations began to move computers from different manufacturers into their buildings. No problem; these were very specific application processors, so there need be no conflict. That was true, but a user who needed access to the mainframe and the specialty machine now required two separate sets of wires run to the desk and two different terminals on top of the desk. This is reminiscent of the situation portrayed the historical section of this book, where the interconnection of various telephone companies would not work and users needed two or three phones on their desks to intercommunicate. The battle was being fought over compatibility rather than technology. The problems were just starting.

First, let's take another look at this from the perspective of the managers of the computing systems. In Fig. 2.1, the organization had a mainframe that was based on

---

*A mid-range computer, such as a departmental or branch office system, made by the computer manufacturers like DEC and Data General.

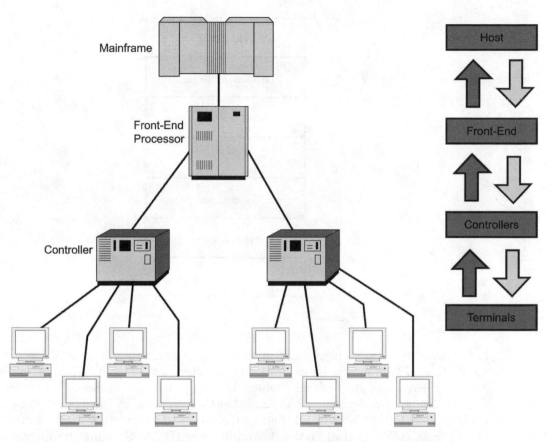

Figure 2.1 The hierarchy in a mainframe environment.

architecture created by the manufacturer—in this case, IBM. The hierarchy of this architecture allowed various connection arrangements based on the device's level on the planes of the architecture. Figure 2.1 shows how the transfer of information among and between users would take place. Things worked pretty well because IBM had everything in place; they delivered the hardware, the software, the connections, and the talent to make everything work together. This was all based on a proprietary and closed architecture called systems network architecture (SNA). Figure 2.2 shows the architecture in its stack. This is a seven-layered architecture that IBM created to make everything work in harmony. Using this structure, IBM would fix something that did not work—for a fee, of course.

The SNA architecture

Later, as the specialty machines appeared, the provider used a separate approach. This provider was created as a result of spin-offs from IBM. The founders of this particular company (DEC) were upset with the strategy and direction that IBM used. Therefore, they created their own offshoot company to offer lower-end machines to the customer,

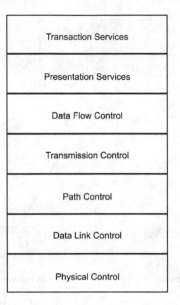

Transaction Services
Presentation Services
Data Flow Control
Transmission Control
Path Control
Data Link Control
Physical Control

Figure 2.2   The SNA architecture.

but at more reasonable prices and in a more open environment. DEC, of course, being an offshoot of IBM used a lot of similar approaches. Let's face it. When an engineer or manager leaves one place of employment, it's tough to leave behind all learned information, so the cross-pollination of ideas and goals took root. In the design and rollout of their products, DEC introduced their own closed and proprietary architecture (shown in Fig. 2.3), called Digital Network Architecture (DNA) that just happened to have seven layers. These seven layers were based on DEC hardware, software, connections, and talent to make everything work in harmony. Sounds familiar, doesn't it?

Progressive end users who had embarked on a multivendor approach in meeting their computing needs would be faced with two separate architectures to work with. The third aspect of this is that many users wanted to be connected to both systems. Ultimately the end user wanted to be able to access these two platforms, hardware, software, applications shared data sets, or whatever from a single device. Moreover, many of the specialty applications that the users wanted required the data that was stored in the mainframe. This meant that the users were re-keying the data from printed reports that came from the mainframe. This left a new set of problems:

- The timeliness of the data was suspect. Because it had to be re-keyed, it could be obsolete before it was ever entered.

- The accuracy of the information was questionable because data entry errors are not uncommon.

- The cost of the information was now more expensive because the input was done at least twice.

DNA

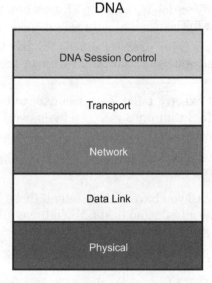

Figure 2.3 DEC's DNA architecture.

- The frequency of the input was becoming exponential because as soon as the data was printed out from the mainframe, it could be obsolete as a result of changes made by other users. Unfortunately, this was changed in the mainframe, but the update in the specialty machine was not automatic.

Therefore, the scenario became almost comical. Here's an illustration to make this concept easier to understand. This is a hypothetical situation—all names of people and companies are used only for the purposes of this example. Do not try this yourself, as it was tested by professionals who are skilled at ducking the issues.

Let's use an example of an organization that has two suppliers of computing platforms. One is an ABC mainframe; the other is a DEF BAX. The company has users attached to both machines, and has received complaints about the connections. Users are getting confused when they try to log on for sessions on both machines. The IT manager decides to go to the vendors and ask whether a way to provide transparent connectivity exists. The dialogue goes something like this:

IT Mgr: Hello, ABC? I've got this ABC mainframe where the users are attached using a 333X terminal. I also have a DEF BAX system and my users are using a VL2000/3000 type terminal to connect to the BAX.

ABC: Yes, what can we do for you?

IT Mgr: Well, what I'm trying to do is let my BAX users log onto the mainframe and view or manipulate the data on the ABC host. When the need dictates, I'd also like for my users to pull the data from the host and move it over to the BAX where the user can modify or delete the data. Then, when they are done, they should be able to save it back to the original data set on the host.

ABC: So, you want your users to access the data on the host, use it, modify it, or whatever. Then you want that data saved on the host so that others can see it and use it. Is that correct?

IT Mgr: That's it exactly. I also want the user to be able to use the same keystrokes on their terminal that my 333X terminals use.

ABC: OK! There's no problem, we have the perfect solution for you.

IT Mgr: You do! That's great! This is exactly what I was hoping to hear. What do I have to do?

ABC: It's simple. All you have to do is sell all those DEF terminals and the BAX, then buy all ABC terminals and hosts. You'll have full transparency and everyone will enter the exact same keystrokes.

That's not exactly what the IT manager was hoping to hear. So off to DEF. The dialogue will be somewhat the same.

IT Mgr: Hello, DEF? I have these two systems, one a BAX using VL2000/3000 terminals serving a special application. I also have this ABC mainframe that is serving some of my back office functions like accounting, billing, inventory control, and so on. What I'd like to do is provide seamless and transparent connectivity between the two computers and let any user access any data from the terminals at their desk. This can be a VL2000/3000 or a 333X. Do you have a way of handling this for me?

DEF: You have a BAX and an AB who?

IT Mgr: An ABC host.

DEF: Oh, this is easy. We have these requests all the time and we help our customers through this arrangement very easily. As a matter of fact, we can do it all for you.

IT Mgr: You can? This is great. I knew you folks would come through for me. What do I have to do?

DEF: It's really quite simple. Sell all those other devices, buy more BAXs and VL2000/3000s. It will work transparently and everyone will love it!

Once again the dilemma—what was the IT manager to do? Fortunately others had already gone through this problem and a new supplier had emerged: the third-party manufacturers of "black boxes."* The box was not black; the name referred to the fact that no one really knew what it did. It was a protocol converter. All the user knew was that if somebody on one system typed the normal way at a terminal, the commands and data typed went into the black box as DEF and came out the other side as ABC, and vice versa.

---

*Black box was the name given to any device when we did not really know what was going on inside, it just did what it was supposed to do. The reference to black box is not to the Black Box Company in Pittsburgh, PA, who offers several excellent products and services.

These protocol converters were not inexpensive; but they were certainly a more attractive option than the other choices that the IS manager got. So, the IS manager bought a third-party converter and attached it to both machines. With a connection to each machine, the converter sat in the middle. This is shown in Fig. 2.4, where the two hosts are connected to the converter. All is solved. Or is it?

After the installation, things appear to be working fairly well. Then one day they start to go awry. The IS manager calls ABC and asks if anything different has been done with the system or code. The converter worked fine yesterday, but today nothing seems to be functioning. ABC, of course, responds that it has done nothing. It would, therefore, suggest it must be those other folks. Now, the IS manager goes to DEF and gets the exact same response. So, it must be those others. Finally, off to the third-party supplier, who of course suggests that it has done nothing different so it must be those others. The result of all this is shown in Fig. 2.5. This is called the finger-pointing routine. Point and hide is really what happened.

Even if nothing went wrong, things might not be exactly the same as what the end user accesses at the various machines through protocol converters. The follow-up to

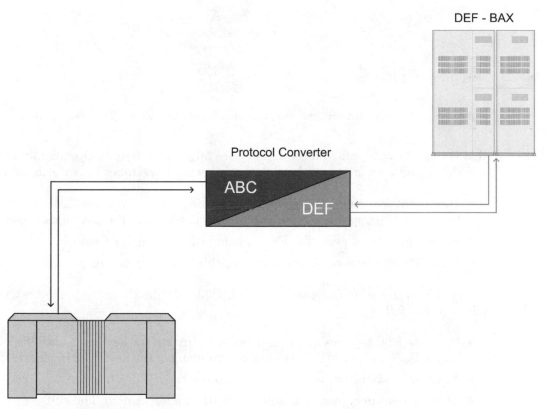

Figure 2.4 A black box was used to create transparency.

Black Box Vendor

ABC

DEF

IS-Manager

Figure 2.5   When a problem occurred, the finger-pointing started, leaving the IS manager at a loss.

this is that the code sets and command lines might be different. Specifically, in a 333X world, the end user might go through the following keystrokes to perform a function:

- To repaint a screen with a blank accounting form, press the CMD key, which is located at the upper left corner of the keyboard, using the left index finger.
- At the same time, press the F9 key using the right index finger.
- Voilà! The new screen appears with the blank form ready to go.

To perform the same function from a VL2000/3000 device in the same host, the user might do the following:

- Press the ESC key, located in the upper left corner of the keyboard, with the left index finger. Because no CMD key exists, a remapping of the keyboard must take place.
- At the same time, press the F9 key with the right index finger.
- At the same time, press the shift key with the left thumb. The shift key is on the lower left side of the keyboard.
- At the same time, press the ALT key with the right thumb. The ALT is located at the lower right side of the keyboard.

- At the same time, press the space bar with your left big toe. The space bar is located at the bottom center of the keyboard.

- Voilà! You now have the screen repainted with the blank form ready to be filled in! Figure 2.6 shows what this might look like.

Obviously, by now you have recognized that this is strictly in jest. There are past ills in the industry; but they have not been this bad. The issue was that transparency in connectivity, communications, and use of the data was not to be had easily. The result was that the users put pressure on their coordinating committees in the industry to come up with a resolution. In 1978, the International Organization for Standards (ISO) was asked to come up with a solution that would allow the transparent communications and data transfer between and among systems regardless of manufacturer. This was originally thought of as the task of the data communications devices. Thus, a new committee was formed to evaluate how this might happen. Everyone in the industry held their breath. What form of solution would be achieved? Because this was a committee made up of users, vendors, and manufacturers of the systems as well as standards members, what could be expected? The result was to come several years later, with what we now have come to know as the ISO OSI reference model. No, they did not just reverse the letters of the organization; this stands for the open systems interconnect reference model. It is a seven-layer architecture, just like the other two architectures that already existed (SNA and DNA)—two of the member companies of the committee were IBM and DEC. This seven-layered architecture is shown in Fig. 2.7. The seven layers will be covered in more detail later, but are listed here:

- The application layer sits at the very top of the model. This is the direct interface with the application used when requesting a service. This layer provides

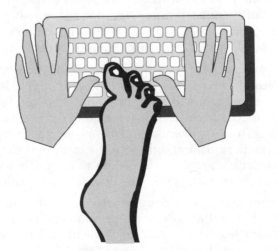

Figure 2.6   Using protocol converters was not that transparent.

OSI

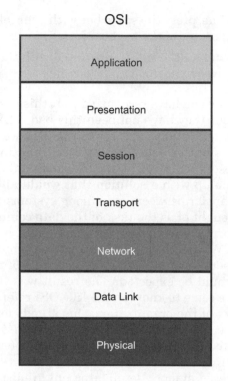

Figure 2.7   The OSI reference model.

communications services to the end user. This layer supports application and end-user processes. Communication partners are identified, quality of service (QoS) is identified, user authentication and privacy are considered, and any constraints on data syntax are identified. Everything at this layer is application-specific. This layer provides application services for file transfers, e-mail, and other network software services. Telnet and FTP are applications that exist entirely in the application level. Tiered application architectures are part of this layer.

- The presentation layer sits below the application layer and provides a service to the application layer. This is where formatting, code conversions, data representation, compression, and encryption are handled for the application. This layer provides independence from differences in data representation (e.g., encryption) by translating from application to network format, and vice versa. The presentation layer works to transform data into the form that the application layer can accept. This layer formats and encrypts data to be sent across a network, providing freedom from compatibility problems. It can also be called the syntax layer.

- The session layer, located under the presentation layer, is responsible for the establishment and maintenance of connections to a process between two different users or systems. The control of the direction of data transfer is handled here. This layer establishes, manages and terminates connections between applications.

The session layer sets up, coordinates, and terminates conversations, exchanges, and dialogues between the applications at each end. It deals with session and connection coordination.

- The transport layer is right below the session layer. The transport layer controls the connection for error recovery and flow control. It is responsible for assuring error-free data delivery end to end in a cost-efficient manner. This layer provides transparent transfer of data between end systems, or hosts. It ensures complete data transfer.

The next three layers deal with the network-specific issues of the communications process. Whereas the upper four layers deal with the end-to-end communications and data transfer, the bottom three layers are concerned with the node-to-node connection. This portion of the network may be provided by a single entity (such as a carrier, PTT, or third-party communications company).

- The network layer sits just under the transport layer and is responsible for the switching and routing of the connection, creating logical paths, known as virtual circuits. Also, this layer is responsible for taking the data that is to be shipped from node to node, not end user to end user, and breaking it into smaller pieces to accommodate the transmission system. Congestion control, alternate routing, and other such connectivity services are handled here. The network layer provides establishment of the connection, transfer of the data, releasing the connection, and in some cases, the transfer of data in a connectionless service. Addressing, internetworking, error handling, congestion control and packet sequencing are functions of this layer.

- The data link layer is responsible for the delivery of the information to the medium. It will create frames of information, if required, and send the frames along to the wires. Additionally, this layer is responsible for the reliability of the information and error checking on a node-to-node basis. At this layer, data packets are encoded and decoded into bits. It furnishes transmission protocol knowledge and management and handles errors in the physical layer, flow control and frame synchronization. The data link layer is divided into two sublayers: the media access control (MAC) layer and the logical link control (LLC) layer. The MAC sublayer controls how a computer on the network gains access to the data and permission to transmit it. The LLC layer controls frame synchronization, flow control and error checking.

- The physical layer that sits below the data link layer is the actual electrical or mechanical interface to the physical medium. In this layer, we have the physical pieces and the necessary components based on the dependency of the medium. This layer is responsible for transmitting the bits onto the guided medium (wires)—electrical impulse, light, or radio signal—through the network at the electrical and mechanical level. It specifies various physical portions such as the voltage levels, the pins to use in placing the voltage onto the link, and whether the signal will be electrical or photonic (fiber) or modulated onto a nonguided (radio)-based service. Fast Ethernet, RS232, and ATM are protocols with physical layer components. We will see how all of these pieces tie together in later text.

Even with all of the effort that was placed on creating this set of protocols and the entire architecture, many industry and end user groups were somewhat frustrated. They wanted a single solution to provide the transparent communications between systems of different manufacturers; and what they got was still another seven-layer architecture. They were amazed that the standards committees would do such a thing. In reality, this was the best way to provide the solutions, but it took a while to sink in. The seven layers are independent of each other; even though they provide services to the upper layer and rely on the lower layer, some freedom still exists. This is important because in the event that any protocol suite in one of the seven layers needs to be changed, the rest of the architecture will remain intact. A single solution would not have done that.

Figure 2.8 compares the three seven-layer architectures—the OSI as a base, the SNA, and the DNA—to see how they line up against each other. In fairness to both DEC and IBM, their architectures were in place before the OSI model was created; therefore,

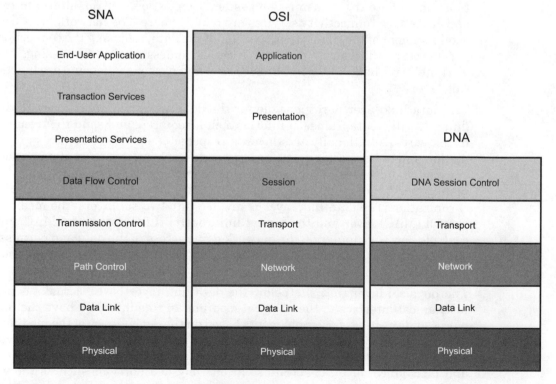

Figure 2.8 Comparing OSI, DECNet, and SNA.

they cannot be expected to be the same. DEC, over the years, has changed the architecture of its DECnet protocols to be more consistent with the OSI. However, IBM has basically done nothing over the past 27 years to change. IBM felt that it already had the single largest and most widely accepted architecture installed at all of the Fortune 1000 companies, so therefore there was no need to change what already worked. So, even though the OSI architecture was developed around 1978, it was not totally accepted until 1984, and there have been very few implementations of it. In 1988, it was finally ratified as a true standard. More implementations were seen overseas than in North America.

Part of the reason was the cost of moving over to a new architecture. The U.S. government wanted a standard applied to all of their purchases in the past. In an effort to initiate OSI acceptance and implementation, the GSA specified a modified version of the OSI reference model. If you wanted to sell something of a computing or data communications nature to the government, you had to comply with their modified version. It was called the Government Open Systems Interconnect Profile (GOSIP). Yes, you guessed it; the US government was responsible for creating gossip. (Author's comment: Wait a minute, that was GOSIP, not gossip! Let's try to keep these things straight.)

This model has been the reference on which many of the changes of the past 25+ years have been based. Although very few manufacturers have attained fully open systems, they have attempted to use the OSI as a model for their future compliance. It must be remembered that there was little incentive for any manufacturer to comply fully with the OSI model because the openness could potentially jeopardize future revenue streams. Not to pick on any vendor, but when you bought a computer system using SNA from a large computer manufacturer, it was also an unwritten rule that most, if not all future software and hardware purchases would be from that same vendor. If you bought from that vendor, you were assured that your purchases would fit seamlessly into your existing hardware and software platforms. If you went the third-party route and something did not work, you could expect little support from IBM. Thus, IBM's future revenue streams flowed from the proprietary nature of their architecture. If a completely open attitude and platform were introduced, it would work with any hardware you acquired.

Now back to this complex model. The seven layers always confused even those with a rigorous background in the data processing or data communications industry. Furthermore, these folks took 5- and 10-day workshops, only to leave even more confused than when they went in. How can we show you in one chapter of text how this works and keep it simple? We assume that you are likely a novice or getting into some new portion of the industry, and that this is your reference manual. So, let's try it with our usual method: a story. We can hope that by the time this works through, you will have a basic understanding of the function of the model and each of the layers as they play into the industry. Here goes!

Figure 2.9 shows a situation where two people (Don and Bud) are thinking about moving to a new area in a suburb of a major city. There is no subdivision yet; but there is a lot of property that can easily be broken down into perfectly sized lots, all with a great view.

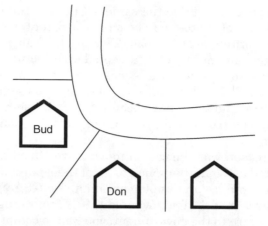

Figure 2.9 Building on new subdevelopment areas.

These two players meet with a builder who owns the land and ask for their respective lots, which just happen to be right next to each other. The builder agrees to build both Bud's and Don's houses at a certain price.

Now that the agreements have been reached, both parties decide that they'd like their houses rather quickly. So, they both go back to the builder and ask that the process be accelerated. The builder, of course, will balk at the idea of doing the job too quickly. However, perseverance wins out and the two potential homeowners get the builder to cave in and speed up the construction.

The result is that in two weeks, the houses are ready to go. Now Bud and Don can move in. Immediately, a couple of things become apparent. Because the houses were built so quickly, the builder did not have time to notify the local incumbent local exchange carrier (ILEC) or competitive local exchange carrier (CLEC) that the owners were moving in. So, the two owners take possession, but they have no form of telephony service. Here are Don and Bud, living next door to each other without a means of communicating. What options do they have?

Immediately, they both call the local telephone company (ILEC or CLEC) and are told that the installation of facilities in their new area will take 6 to 12 months. This is too long for next-door neighbors to be without a communications method. So, they consider their options and come up with the choices shown in Table 2.1. The option is shown in the first column, and the pros and cons are in the other two columns. These are not all-inclusive; we have limited our list to a few options.

In the figures illustrating the table results, benefits and losses are associated with the communications options. Therefore, Don and Bud decide to model their communications device after the service that they really wanted—the telephone. The two neighbors aren't going to go out and build a central office. After all, they really just want the convenience of speaking with each other. So, they decide to build on a model. Let's use the OSI model and make sure that this all ties in while we provide transparent communications.

Bud comes up with the idea that he and Don need to send their information across a medium. The earlier options used the airwaves as the medium; but weather conditions

TABLE 2.1   **Summary of Communications Options**

Option	Benefits	Deterrents
Use a megaphone and yell out the window from one house to the other (see Figure 2.10).	• Easy to install • Relatively short distances • Can be implemented immediately	• What if one person isn't home? • What if Bud wants to talk to Don at 2:00 a.m.? • -Loss of transmission due to distances. • -Noisy for other neighbors in the area. • Total lack of privacy.
Throw pebbles at the window, when the receiver hears the pebbles on the window, open the window and yell out (see Figure 2.11).	• Pebbles are readily available • The method of signaling each other is straightforward	• Given the distances, the throw will take some effort. This can cause damage. • -In inclement weather, this can be inconvenient and awkward.
Use a flashlight and send the signals in Morse code.	• Easy to use • Quick communications	• Don doesn't know Morse Code. • -During daylight hours, the sun may diminish the light. • Batteries can fail.
Go next door and visit.	• Easy to accommodate	• Weather may make this difficult.
Have our conversations during the visit.	• Doesn't cost anything	• What about those 2:00 a.m. conversations? • The inconvenience will outweigh the benefits.

Figure 2.10   A megaphone isn't a good choice, but it could work.

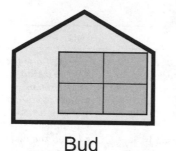

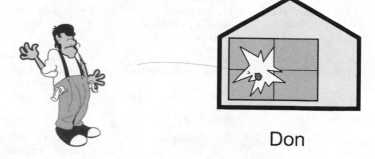

Figure 2.11   Throwing pebbles (or rocks) may not be a good alternative.

and other factors limited this. Therefore, both neighbors agree to use a physical medium. They decide to install a piece of everyday common household string between both of their houses. This is shown in Fig. 2.12, where the string is run in a direct line of sight between both parties. The string is laid out and the two parties are connected with the medium.

Given that the physical string is now attached, can the two parties communicate? It is somewhat obvious that something is still missing. Therefore, the neighbors decide that they have to use the model to handle their next step. Don comes up with the idea that they need to address the physical medium with some electrical or mechanical interface (layer 1 of the OSI). They decide that an electrical interface is not applicable because they do not have an electrical conductor in the string. So all they need is a mechanical interface. Don suggests that each neighbor attach a tin can on his end of the link to build this interface. Using everyday household tin cans on both ends of the string, Don and Bud have now addressed the bottom layer of the OSI model (see Fig. 2.13).

A problem has arisen with this arrangement. To make this all work properly and transparently, everyone must build the connection in the same way. Bud has attached the string through the side of the can, whereas Don has attached the string to the bottom of the can. Although this might work, when you pull the string tight, the can at Bud's end is in an awkward position. This means that the two have to agree how they will connect the two cans to the string to make this work more efficiently. The agreement is that they will both take an empty can, punch a hole through the bottom, and then attach the string from the outside of the can, through the hole in the bottom, and knot it off inside the can. Then, they will pull the string tight to get a good connection. Now, the bottom layer of the OSI is handled.

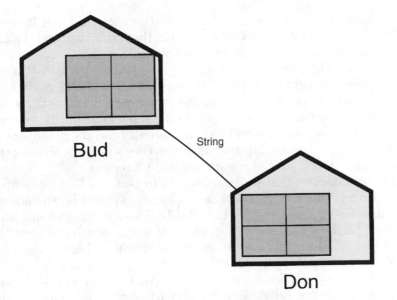

Figure 2.12 A piece of ordinary string produces a physical connection (medium).

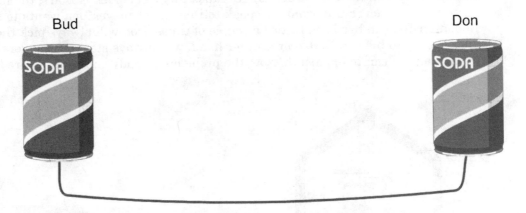

Figure 2.13 Two tin cans are used to satisfy the mechanical interface (layer 1 OSI).

The strings are now attached the same way; so can the parties now communicate? Well, maybe! Bud decides to test it out; so he picks up the tin can on his end and starts to talk to Don. Don is preoccupied with the television set and does not hear that the communications system is being used. The whole conversation is wasted thus far. So, the parties need a means of using the link. They build a protocol that will solve this problem. First, the two parties agree that they should have an alerting mechanism to let the other party know that a conversation is requested. They decide that when one party wants to talk to the other, the originating party will grab the can on his end and yank on it three times. This will cause the can on the other end to rattle around. When the called party sees the can bouncing around, he will know that the party on the other end wants to talk. To use the data link (layer 2), Bud and Don establish a protocol called the yank and rattle. One end yanks the string, causing the can on the other end to rattle. Now they have overcome this obstacle.

We can skip by layer 3 of the model for now. Is it obvious why? Look at Fig. 2.14; and it should become fairly clear. The strings are attached to both parties directly. The connection is a point-to-point private line. No switching or routing decisions need to be made, because the connection always goes to the same location. Therefore the network layer doesn't apply per se, so it will be transparent. Now, the neighbors have the necessary connection and the alerting mechanism; so they should be able to communicate without much ado, correct? Maybe not, but see what happens.

Bud now decides that he wants to talk to Don. So, Bud picks up the can and yanks three times. This causes Don's can to bounce around on the other end, which alerts Don that Bud wants to talk to him. Kind of like a ringing phone, isn't it? So Don jumps up and grabs the can, picks it up, places it to his mouth and says, "Hello." At the same time, Bud is yelling into the can on the other end of this connection for Don to pick up: "Don. Hello, Don, are you there?"

Are these two parties communicating? No, they are not. Both have the can to their mouths; and no one is listening. If both parties are talking and no one is listening, then the information transfer is nil. So, a new set of protocols is required. Let's introduce the transport layer in the OSI model now. Because this whole idea is Bud's, the neighbors agree that whenever Bud wants to speak to Don, or whenever Don wants to speak to Bud, after the can has been rattled a couple of times, Don will always pick the can up and place it to his ear. Bud, on the other hand, will always start the conversation off by placing the can to his mouth. Now, the problems already encountered are handled.

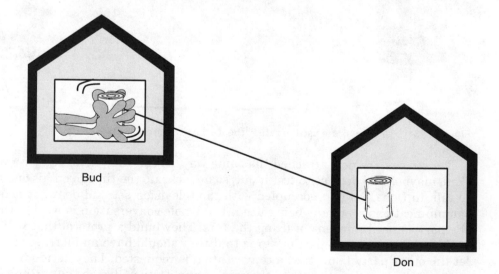

Bud

Don

Figure 2.14 The point-to-point connection doesn't need a network layer. No switching decisions need to be made.

So, we should be able to communicate without any further complications, right? Here is the transmission process as it has been defined.

Bud: (Yanks the string).

Don: (Picks up the can on his end and places it to his ear because that's the rule).

Bud: "Hi, Don! Can I borrow your lawn mower today?"

Don: (Takes the can from his ear and places it to his mouth and begins responding) "No way, you told me last week that you were going to finally buy your own."

Bud: (At the same time Don is responding) "I know I told you last week that I was going to buy my own, but I haven't had a chance to get to the store yet."

Now, both parties are talking at the same time. After a given amount of time, they will probably both be listening at the same time. The communications flow is not working properly. So, they have to add a new set of protocols to allow the orderly transfer of the information. The problem stems from the half duplex nature of the link. Only one transmitter/receiver is on each end. Two possible solutions exist. These are as follows:

First, a new string could be run between both parties. On this new string, Don and Bud will attach two new cans, just as they did for the first connection. Each can will be labeled T or R. The T can on Don's end will be connected to the R can at Bud's end, and vice versa. Now, when an alert comes in, each party will pick up the two cans at his end. The T can will be placed in front of each party's mouth, and the R can will be placed in front of each party's ear (see Fig. 2.15). Now, there are two separate transmission paths, one for transmitting and one for receiving. This is probably the best option; but Bud and Don are reluctant to do this because it adds the complexity of maintaining two strings between their houses and requires twice as many cans on each end. This will take up too much space in their homes.

The alternative to this communications dilemma is the use of a set of rules (protocol) that will define the session layer (the control of the data transfer between the two ends). The session layer will work like this. Because this is Bud's idea, whenever Bud or Don yanks on the string, Don always listens first and Bud always talks first. The problem occurs when the transmitting end is done sending and wants to await the reply: The two parties need to know how to time this out properly. So, Bud will talk first (Have you noticed that Bud talks a lot?). When Bud finishes his statement, he will use an "over" protocol. When Don hears the word over, he will take the can from his ear and place it to his mouth. At the same time, Bud will take the can from his mouth and place it to his ear. Then, Don finally gets a chance to talk. When Don finishes, he will say "over," and the process will reverse back to the beginning; and so on.

Now the two parties have the ability to communicate with each other. Essentially, they can send their information back and forth as they had planned. Now that this whole scenario is established, you have probably noticed that a couple of layers were missed in the OSI model. These would be handled transparently by Don and Bud because they are working with the same communications protocols. However, let's go back and look at these layers to see how they will play out under our scenario. The three we

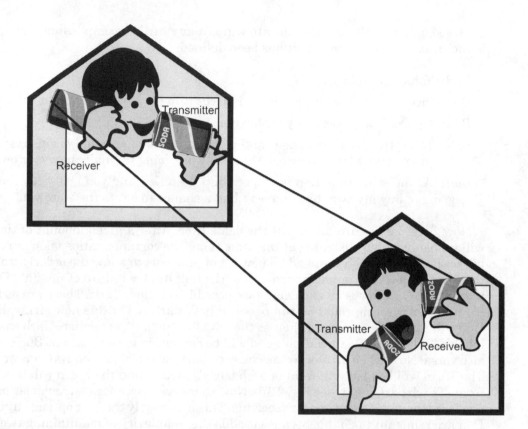

Figure 2.15 Two separate cans allow simultaneous transmission or reception, not the converse.

have yet to address are the network, presentation, and application layers. So, we shall complicate the issue by introducing the following add-on needs.

Just as Don and Bud get the communications working by the rules established, a new neighbor, Helen, moves in next door to Don. This is going to happen all around the neighborhood; and we should be prepared. Helen is neighborly and decides that she might have a need to speak to Don and Bud from time to time. The rules already in place can be used to provide the connectivity between all three parties: Fig. 2.16 shows this. To set up communications between Helen and Don, a string can be run between the two houses and cans attached to the string. The rule will be as follows: because Don was here first, Don will always speak first and Helen will listen, regardless of whom rattles the can. The "over" protocol can also be used to provide the session layer, and so on. Now, Helen also needs to talk to Bud, but, as the figure shows, in order for this to happen, they need to run the string from Helen to Bud. This is not a problem for Helen or Bud. As a matter of fact, we can even color-code the cans (red for Don, blue for Bud).

This scenario is a problem for Don. In order for Bud and Helen to connect the string to each location, the string must go in one side of Don's house, pass through and exit the other side to connect to Bud. Don will therefore have to leave his windows open on both

Figure 2.16 Adding a third party may complicate the process (for Don).

Figure 2.17 By using the relay point, we satisfy the bottom three layers of the model.

sides of his house at all times for this to work. Don doesn't like this idea; so he offers to become a network layer relay point. The process, as shown in Fig. 2.17, will work this way. When Bud wants to speak to Helen, he will pick up the one can that is associated with this communications system. He will then yank the can, causing Don to pick up and immediately listen. Bud will then say, "Don, this is a call for Helen." On hearing this, Don, who has two cans and strings, will grab the other can that is connected to the string to Helen's. Don will yank the can, causing Helen to pick up the can and listen. Don speaks first on this connection, so this is fine; he has a can to his ear from Bud and the other can to his mouth leading out to Helen. When Don knows that Helen is on the link, he will say, "Stand by for a message from Bud." At this point, Bud will speak to Don, who in turn will automatically relay everything he hears to Helen. Now the routing of the information is accommodated. The network layer is met, of sorts.

A problem exists with this whole scenario that isn't as obvious. Helen only speaks German. Bud only speaks English. Now the problem is: if Bud speaks English into the can connected to Don, how do we make the format or language conversion into something that is usable and understandable to Helen? Luckily, when Don was in school, he took German 101. He didn't excel; but he has a working knowledge of the language. Now, when Don hears Bud say, "Good morning, Helen," in English, Don will relay the information out through the other can in German as: "Guten Tag!" When Bud finishes and says, "over," the process switches. Bud takes the can from his mouth and moves it to his ear. Don takes the can connected to Bud and moves it from his ear to his mouth; at the same time, he takes the can connected to Helen and moves that one from his mouth to his ear.

Helen in turn moves the can from her ear to her mouth and begins to speak or respond. When Helen responds with "Morgen, wie gehts?" Don hears it and converts it to Bud as "Morning. How are you?" So it goes. The presentation layer has just been addressed to accommodate the format or protocol (language) conversion so that transparent communications can take place. The only layer in this case is the applications layer that has not been addressed. What is the application in this regard? Chit-chat: "I just called to say hello!"

By now, you should have an understanding from this simplistic comparison of how the process works through the OSI model. Furthermore, the importance of this all taking place transparently should be obvious. If we had to go through the trials and tribulations of information transfer every time we placed a call, this would be far too cumbersome. The next time a connection to another neighbor is needed, the same rules can be applied.

We already have a simplistic network here, so let's draw it to a conclusion by introducing a couple of other players. Mary moves in behind Bud. There will be a need for Mary to communicate with Bud, Don, and Helen. Rather than trying to run strings all around the neighborhood, we'll just use our relays and rules already in place. So, Mary connects a string to Bud. Communication to Bud is simple. To reach Don, the call will go through Bud to Don; to reach Helen, the call will go through Bud and Don to ultimately get to Helen. One added complication is that Mary only speaks French. Therefore, when Mary says "Bonjour." to Bud, he repeats the information to Don as "Good morning." Don then finally sends it to Helen as "Guten Morgen." Now, Roy moves in behind Don. The neighbors run a connection between Don and Roy—no problem. Roy only speaks pig Latin; but that's okay because Don can deal with it. Now, when Mary wants to speak to Roy, she calls through Bud in French, which Bud converts to English and sends on to Don. Don receives the message in English and converts it to pig Latin for Roy. The connection is sent through and routed/switched depending on the intended target location. Helen, as you recognize, is left out of this conversation; but she has no need to be connected. The result is shown in Fig. 2.18. The connection is routed and switched transparently between and among the neighbors. Don has also become very similar to a central switching system and service provider. Now for voice or data, the telecommunications network is built to handle communication from any user to any other, regardless of the language (format and protocol) or origin of creation (manufacturer). This is what the OSI model was designed to do for us.

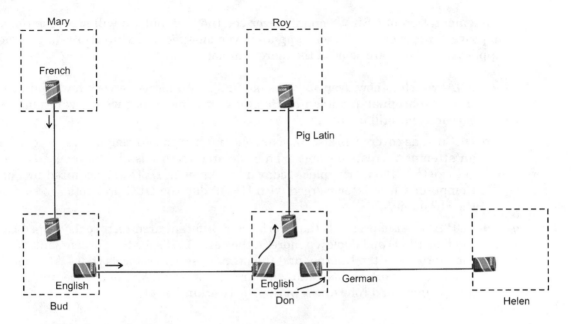

Figure 2.18   The layers can all be met through this network.

Is it here? Partially. Most manufacturers are implementing OSI compatibility in different ways. That's okay, but it might lead to some kludges. The issue is not how the arrangement is created, but the opportunity to have a universal set of rules and protocols that everyone can build to. That is what the OSI reference provides.

That description is probably more than most of us need to know about this. However, we should at least be aware of just what the reference was meant to do for the industry as a whole. If we substitute our players in the previous example, then we can have an organization using a computer platform manufactured by Company Bud. This is connected to or through a computer manufactured by Company Don and ultimately sharing and swapping information with a computer manufactured by Company Helen, and so on.... The communications network might well be used as a point-to-point, point-to-multipoint, or switched dial-up service. Protocols and services such as ISDN, X.25, switched 64 Kbits/s, and leased-line T1 have been applied, so that the connectivity arrangements adhere to those of the tin cans and string. Yes, some of the cans might be larger or rounder than others. As long as the same rules apply for electrically and mechanically attaching to the string (wires, light beams, and radio waves), then this should all work.

Other Network Architectures

Using the OSI as the reference is fine. It will be the basis of all future development. Other architectures were in existence or sprung up during the wait for the ubiquitous implementation of OSI. We might never see the end; but we will see variations and improvements over the OSI as it applies to vendor-specific architectures or proprietary applications. Here are some of the more common models:

- SNA, which is now over 32 years old and has undergone very few modifications from the original architecture. Some say it is dead, but we know of many large corporations still using it.

- DECnet, as covered, is also 32 years old, but has gone through several revisions in an attempt to create openness. This one architecture is all but gone. DEC no longer exists in the marketplace today as we knew it. DEC was acquired by Compaq Computer which later merged with HP. Today the DEC products are sold under the HP name.

- TCP/IP, a set of protocols that works on a different architecture developed back in the late 1960s and deployed more in the early 1970s for the government. Now it is the protocol for the Internet and the primary set of protocols that LAN, metropolitan area network (MAN), and wide area network (WAN) users are implementing for openness and robustness in their networking needs.

Internet Protocols (TCP/IP)

While the industry and standards bodies wrestled with openness in the communications and computing arenas, another evolving set of protocols emerged. This is also a layered architecture composed essentially of four layers. A result of a government contract to look at the internetworking of computers in the event of a national disaster, the protocols emerged from the original Advanced Research Projects Agency Network (ARPANET). Developed by Bolt, Beraneck, and Newman of Cambridge, this simple but robust set of protocols was geared toward linking systems in an open architecture. The transmission control protocol with Internet protocol (TCP/IP) continued its evolution from the original ARPANET to what we know as the Internet. The TCP/IP architecture is shown in Fig. 2.19. This is a four-layer stack that deals with the equivalent seven-layer architecture of OSI, SNA, and DNA.

Actually, the TCP/IP is now the most widely accepted set of protocols in the industry. Included in all forms of the UNIX operating systems and now the protocol of choice in many LAN-to-WAN environments, it is the "middleware" for interconnectivity. The two most prevalent features of this protocol stack are its ability to work with just about any environment because of it can use application program interfaces to emulate most services on other architectures and its ability to "packetize" the data and send it out.

IP

Internet Protocol, abbreviated IP, performs a packetization (called *datagrams*) of the user data to be sent between and among the various systems on a network. When a large file is sent down the protocol stack, the IP function is responsible for the

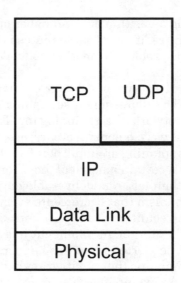

Figure 2.19 The TCP/IP protocol stack (architecture).

segmentation and packetization of this data. Then a header is placed on the datagram for delivery to the data link. The routing and switching of this data is handled at the IP (network) layer. To be somewhat simple in our analogy, IP is also a dumb protocol. When a datagram is prepared for transmission across the medium, IP does not specifically route the call across a specific channel. Rather, it just puts the header on the datagram and lets the network deal with it. Therefore, the outward-bound datagrams can take various routes to get from point A to point B. This means that the datagrams are not sequentially numbered as they are in other protocols. IP makes its best attempt to deliver the datagrams to the destination network interface; however, it makes no assurances that:

- The data will arrive.
- The data will be error free.
- The nodes along the way will concern themselves with the accuracy of the data and sequencing, or come back and alert the originator that something is wrong in the delivery mechanism.

This might sound strange in a networking environment, but it allows robustness to be achieved. The nodes along the network merely read the header information and route the datagram to the next logical downstream neighbor. This means that if anything gets corrupted on the network, the node will not know where to send the datagram, so it will throw it away. The network will not send a message back to the originator and let it know that the datagram did not get delivered. Another possibility is that the nodes along the network can send the datagram out on the basis of the best route (based on some costing algorithm or the number of points to pass through). Yet, in the transfer of the datagrams, if one of these routes is busy or broken, the datagrams will be rerouted around the problem to another node. This has great possibilities; but it can lead to a problem.

It is possible, in the IP routing of a datagram that it can be sent along the network in a loop (see Fig. 2.20). The routes might set up in a loop fashion, and the datagram will be circulating on the network like a spinning top. This doesn't cause concern if it is only one datagram; but if it were a general occurrence, the network could get quite bogged down with datagrams spinning around. Therefore, IP has a mechanism in its header information that allows a certain amount of "hops" or what is called time to live (TTL) on the network. Rather than let an undeliverable datagram spin around on the network, IP has a counter mechanism that decrements every time the datagram passes through a network node. If the counter (usually 16 hops or less) expires or gets set to 0, the node will discard the datagram. As you might imagine, if the network can throw away datagrams, we should be alerted when this happens. This is not part of the IP protocol; it does not tell the originator that a datagram has been discarded. Additionally, datagram number 4 (just an example) was spinning around the network for several hops and was finally discarded. Yet numbers 5, 6, and 7 go through the network without ado.

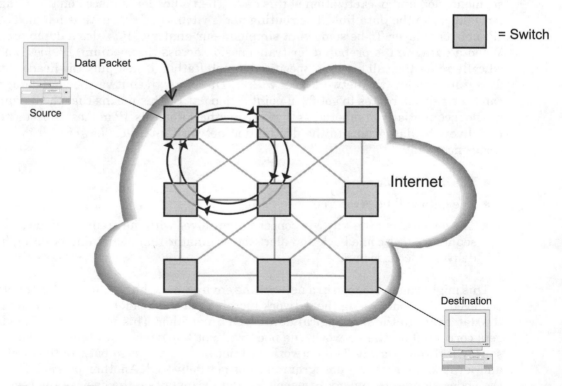

Figure 2.20 IP can send data into a loop, meaning it will not reach the destination computer. The switches could send the data around and around.

Thus, the later datagrams arrive at the destination, but datagram 4 is gone. IP does not have a mechanism to know that this has happened, and no numbering sequence to put everything back in order. Why would anyone favor such a dumb protocol? It is this robustness to deliver the datagrams across the network and throw away bad or undeliverable datagrams that helps to improve the efficiency of network utilization.

TCP

No network manager or administrator would easily accept not knowing whether data gets delivered across the network. Therefore, working together with IP is the transmission control protocol (TCP). TCP provides the smarts to overcome the limitations of IP. Here, the controls will be put in place to ensure that the reliable data stream is sent and delivered. At the sending end, TCP puts a byte count header on the information that will be delivered to the IP protocol layer. This is encapsulated as part of the data in the IP datagram. The receiving end, when it gets the datagrams, is responsible for putting the data back into its proper sequence and ensuring its accuracy. If things are not correct, the byte count acknowledgment (ACK) or nonacknowledged (NAK) message is sent back to the sending end. The sending end receiving a NAK will resend the bytes necessary to fill in the blanks. Furthermore, TCP holds all of the later received bytes (datagrams 5, 6, and 7 from the previous example) until it gets datagram four resent. Thus it buffers the data at the receiving end. This makes data reception and accuracy the responsibility of the end user (node), not the network responsibility. This is to prevent the network from getting bogged down if errors or loops are occurring. The network is, after all, a transport system, not a computer processing function.

Using TCP/IP, the network operates efficiently; and improvements are being seen every day as the quality of the circuits is improved with all of the fiber-optic backbones being installed. Therefore, the movement in the past 10 years has been heavily toward TCP/IP and the Internet.

We will go into much more detail on TCP and IP later in this book when we discuss many of the data protocols and the newer Voice over IP protocols.

Questions

1. What does OSI mean?
    a. Open Systems Interface
    b. Only System Interface
    c. Open Systems Interference
    d. Open Systems Interconnect
2. What organization is responsible for creating the OSI?
    a. ITU
    b. ISO

  c. IBM

  d. IEEE

3. In which year was the model ratified?

  a. 1978

  b. 1988

  c. 1974

  d. 1983

4. When the OSI model was being developed, it was to solve some of the problems we experience between:

  a. IBM and DEC

  b. Sun and HP

  c. IBM and Data General

  d. DEC and Data General

5. What organization created the Government Open Systems Interconnect Profile?

  a. International Telecomm Union

  b. CCITT

  c. US government

  d. IBM

6. How many layers does the OSI model have?

  a. 11

  b. 6

  c. 7

  d. 4

7. How many layers does the IBM's SNA have?

  a. 5

  b. 7

  c. 6

  d. 4

8. When DEC created their architecture, what did they call it?

  a. DECnet

  b. DNI

  c. DNA

  d. Digital networking standards

9. What layer did we eliminate when we used a point-to-point leased line?

   a. Application

   b. Transport

   c. Network

   d. Data link

10. What layer is responsible for the electrical and mechanical interface?

    a. 4

    b. 1

    c. 3

    d. 2

11. What layer performs the transparent transmission of information between the two ends?

    a. 7

    b. 6

    c. 4

    d. 5

12. What layer is responsible for translation and protocol conversion?

    a. Application

    b. Presentation

    c. Network

    d. Transport

13. The best way to handle data transmission is to let the data processing people handle it.   T/F.

14. When the world began to evolve to OSI what happened?

    a. It was widely accepted.

    b. Few people implemented it.

    c. The US government made everyone abide by it.

    d. The North Americans began to replace their IBM systems.

15. Why do we need the model anyway?

    a. It adds more cost to the price of a system.

    b. It provides for transparency in our networks.

    c. It guarantees nothing.

    d. It seemed like a nice thing to do.

16. What is the replacement protocol suite that the US government and the rest of the world is now implementing?

    a. DNA

    b. TCP/IP

    c. SNA

    d. GOSIP

17. How many layers does the TCP/IP protocol model have?

    a. 7

    b. 5

    c. 4

    d. 6

18. IP guarantees delivery and reliability of the data.   T/F.

3

Regulation in the Industry

After reading this chapter and completing the questions, you will be able to:

- List the major legal battles and regulations, and their effects on the industry
- Define RBOCs and their formulation
- List the main points of the Telecomm Act of 1996
- Describe the regulatory bodies
- Discuss the major standards committees

Because the telecommunications industry has been regulated extensively, the roles of the carriers, as well as their structure, have changed. We discuss these legal battles in depth and their effect on the industry to present day. Understanding their past is important because it explains certain constraints and limitations on some carriers today. This chapter explains how the service providers have changed from the initial rollout of telephone service to become the robust providers they now are. Regulation of the industry continues to be an area of rapid change and further reform. If you pay special attention to the headlines in today's newspapers, you will see additional changes being suggested and implemented. These changes are being discussed and studied on at least a monthly basis. Events in this arena are critical to future trends and to opportunities available in the telecommunications field.

The Importance of the Telephone

It is important to realize how communications took place prior to the inventions of this industry. Try to imagine how people stayed informed before the advent of telephones.

Within a community, people physically went to gathering places, or residences, to speak in person to others. Contact with other people outside your city was extremely limited, and other states must have seemed a world apart.

Information was disseminated primarily through newspapers, the U.S. Postal Service, and then the telegraph. Radio and newscasts did not exist. They became popular in the 1930s.

Imagine how people felt as the entire world began to open up for them with the availability of the telephone in the late 1870s. Distance no longer mattered, as you could have a two-way conversation with someone miles away from your home. It is easy to see why the telephone was so well received; it opened the door to almost unlimited opportunities.

Almost immediately, everyone wanted to have this device. It wasn't long before companies began to spring up all over the place to provide service and get in on the market of this revolutionary invention.

The Initial Formulation of the Carrier Network

Alexander Graham Bell was awarded the patent for the telephone in 1876. Bell had sought financial backing to make this invention profitable and to capitalize on its opportunity. At first, Bell approached Western Union, the largest telegraph company with his patent. He offered it to them for the sum of $100,000. Western Union officials were unimpressed. They thought the telephone was a toy or a fad for the rich, and they quickly turned down this offer.

Bell remained determined in the potential of his device and he acquired financial backing from two private investors: Gardiner Hubbard and Thomas Sanders. With this investment, they drew up the plans to create a company to provide the first telephone service. On July 1, 1877, the Bell Telephone Company was formed. For the next six months, the Bell Telephone Company began producing phones and provisioned wires in New Haven, Connecticut. In 1878, the first services were provided in Connecticut. The Bell Telephone Company continued expanding and opening offices in the major cities in the Northeast.

Shortly after rejecting Alexander Graham Bell's offer for the telephone, Western Union realized it had made a terrible mistake in dismissing Bell and his telephone. The company realized it was losing out on this invention and all the future revenue associated with it. Western Union approached two other inventors to create their own version of the telephone.

Western Union used Dr. Elisha Gray's patent for the receiver, and then went to Thomas Edison for the transmitter. After Bell patented the telephone, Edison had developed a transmitter that was superior and improved the quality of the set. In addition, Edison's experience with the distribution of electricity was used to assist in the wiring of residential and corporate sites. Edison had designed a series of electrical distribution grids, and he now began applying these ideas to the telephone system.

At this point, Western Union created the American Speaking Telephone Company (ASTC) and used the Gray/Edison device to provide service.

The Bell Company was furious that Western Union entered the telephone business, and they challenged ASTC's legitimacy based on the Bell patents. In 1878, Bell filed suit against ASTC for patent right infringement and, eventually, Bell prevailed in the courts. The settlement of this case came a year later when Western Union gave up all rights of telephone service and products, and even their network. In short, Western Union left the telephone industry. For giving up their place and the Edison/Gray patent, Western Union would receive a percentage of all the telephone rentals the American Bell Telephone Company made (until the Bell patent expired). In return, the American Bell Telephone Company agreed not to infringe into the telegraph manufacturing business. However, this didn't prohibit the American Bell Telephone Company from infringing on the telegraph industry. Over the next 25 years, they would buy controlling interest in Western Union and would also absorb Western Electric, the former manufacturing arm of Western Union.

The American Bell Telephone Company decided to create a sibling company in 1885—called American Telephone and Telegraph (AT&T)—to address this void in long-distance communications. AT&T was responsible for creating and maintaining a long-distance voice and telegraph network.

Shortly thereafter, the American Bell Telephone Company decided to buy controlling interest in the Western Union Company for the purpose of making Western Union the provider of AT&T hardware (telephones).

Also, around the same time as ASTC, the New England Telephone Company was formed. It assisted in the development of the two previously mentioned companies by both building telephones and providing additional network services. This means that the New England Telephone Company was in direct competition with the American Bell Telephone Company.

With several providers now in the mix, customers were now in a dilemma. Which carrier should they use? Were they all the same?

Each company was not the same. In fact, if you subscribed to one of these three individual companies, you couldn't communicate with a neighbor or business connected to another company's network. The interconnection between and among the companies didn't exist. For example, if a businessman needed to speak to three different businesses that used the services of the three different operating companies, three separate telephone lines and three different telephone sets would be required. This may be difficult to imagine, but it accurately represents the situation at that time.

Each of these small companies provided only local service. Without a connection from one city to another, long-distance communication was impossible. Still, there continued to be a demand to communicate with others who were some distance away.

Things were good for the American Bell Telephone Company up until 1894, when the patent on Bell's invention expired. The patent had allowed the American Bell Telephone Company, its subsidiaries, and its licensees to be the only legal provider of services in the United States. That meant every device and network was the property of the American Bell Telephone Company.

In 1899, AT&T had sustained such profitability and growth that it bought the assets of American Bell Telephone Company and incorporated it into its operations. What resulted was the creation of one of the largest, most influential companies ever. The sheer power of this organization became a force that took almost a century of rules and regulation to break up. This is not to say that AT&T wasn't necessary at the time but, in the long run, its sheer size and power became a hindrance.

With the expiration of the Bell patent, new providers began to spring up everywhere. By 1920, over 9000 local providers existed. AT&T did not welcome this competition; it saw its market share being taken by these small upstarts. AT&T decided it would not allow competitors to connect with their long-distance network, in an effort to ensure its position in the marketplace.

As with any new service, government regulatory control was lacking and true economics prevailed. Because there was such a tremendous upstart cost to become a long-distance provider, AT&T began to strangle out the competition.

Eventually, when these smaller companies began to lose subscribers (after all, who wants service where you can't talk with friends, businesses, and relatives outside your locality?) and became financially stressed, AT&T swooped in and bought them, increasing its overall network. From 1920 to 1943, AT&T practiced this procedure until the total number of competitors was down to around 1500. This wasn't totally a bad thing, as people using AT&T got what they always wanted: the ability to talk to people anywhere (as long as they were hooked up to AT&T).

However, AT&T still wasn't satisfied and pushed the envelope even further. AT&T enjoyed the position of being the largest provider with the largest network, and it began to put the pressure on the marketplace. They undercut competitors' prices and literally forced out all the competition, leaving customers in many areas with no local service at all.

As public outrage over AT&T grew, lawmakers began investigating the practices employed by AT&T.

Legal Battles and Regulation

When a new industry emerges, it is a new phenomenon and not widely understood by the masses. When dealing with technology, it is imperative that these businesses flourish and allow their products to benefit the public. In any business-free market, without checks and balances, however, one company will eventually rise to the top and dominate the marketplace. This process has been repeated time and time again in various industries (oil, manufacturing, software, and so forth). We will now focus on the major regulations, acts, and legal battles that have shaped and changed this industry. Some of these laws were interim solutions, whereas others changed the landscape in telecommunications forever.

Sherman Antitrust Act of 1890

The federal government passed the Sherman Antitrust Act in 1890 to deal with monopolies and price fixing. This act made every contract, combination (in the form of trust or otherwise), or conspiracy in restraint of interstate and foreign trade illegal. The Sherman Antitrust Act authorized the federal government to start proceedings against trusts (or companies) to dissolve them in the name of public interest.

Although the Sherman Laws originally dealt with Standard Oil, its significance cannot be understated.*

Kingsbury Commitment

AT&T had become a tremendously powerful entity that had dictated the marketplace in communications. Its practices were investigated by the government under the Sherman Antitrust Laws. Fearing that Congress would dissolve AT&T (which would have hurt tens of thousands of customers), AT&T decided to change its stance, settle the suit, and make changes. This was known as the *Kingsbury Commitment*.

In 1913, AT&T's Vice President Kenneth R. Kingsbury made a statement that AT&T would immediately make the following changes:

- Relinquish its holdings in Western Union (over a period of years, AT&T had purchased a controlling interest in its former competitor).

- Stop the practice of acquiring the independent telephone companies, unless authorized by the Interstate Commerce Commission (ICC).

- Allow the independent telephone companies to interconnect to the AT&T long-distance network.

1914 Clayton Antitrust Act

Although the Sherman Antitrust Laws created some change in the direction of AT&T and the communication industry, officials felt that the laws needed further reform to provide better monitoring of the industry. Knowing further regulations were needed, they supplemented the Sherman Laws further and created an overseeing agency for trust regulation. In 1914, the Sherman Act was supplemented by the *Clayton Antitrust Act*.

The main outcome of the Clayton Antitrust Act was the creation of the Federal Trade Commission (FTC), an independent presiding body of the federal government chartered to oversee competition of American businesses as part of a free and fair market. The Clayton Antitrust Act was part of the reforms to prevent the growth of monopolies and to preserve competition in the marketplace.

Despite the best efforts of this legislation, the issues of the communications industry were unique. The resources needed to provide free and fair competition to long-distance service were prohibitive. (After all, it took almost 20 years to get the AT&T network to its current state and its network was underutilized.) Trying to provide another option would cost tens of millions of dollars, decades of time, and a talent pool that was employed by AT&T. The leaders at AT&T, therefore, began petitioning lawmakers about the idea of only having one long-distance carrier. Their logic was that creating such

---

* Standard Oil was a company owned by John D. Rockefeller. Standard Oil, the largest oil company in the United States in the 1800s, engaged in price fixing. It laid the foundation of government regulation in the telecomm arena.

an expansive network was so costly and difficult, that they should be given exclusive rights because they were allowing others to interconnect with it. Congress looked into these claims, agreed with them, and passed legislation in 1921 to address the issue.

Graham-Willis Act

The *Graham-Willis Act* of 1921 established the telephone system as a natural monopoly. The Graham-Willis Act allowed AT&T to be a monopoly under the condition that it promised to cable up the entire country. AT&T's exclusive place as a long-distance carrier was protected if the company kept the commitment to connect all parts of the country to its network. Although this seemed acceptable at the time, what it did was to make AT&T temporarily exempt from the Sherman Antitrust Laws.

The Radio Act of 1927

Another communications invention—the radio—became available to the public in the 1920s. The first radio stations formed to provide content shows for the airwaves. These radio stations were regulated with the passing of the *1927 Radio Act,* which gave the Department of Commerce and the Interstate Commerce Commission the responsibility of regulating this new form of communication. See Fig. 3.1 for the breakdown of government agencies. The consumer side, presided over by the Federal Communications Commission (FCC), has four bureaus. The National Telecommunications and Information Administration (NTIA) presides over the government and the military.

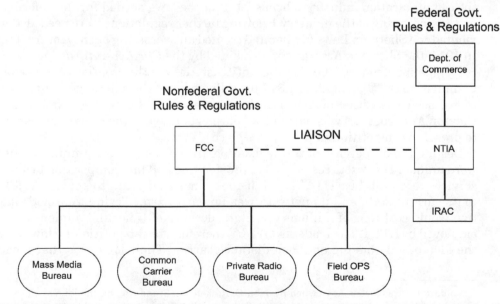

Figure 3.1 The organization of regulating agencies in the communications arena. The consumer side is presided over by the FCC; the NTIA presides over the government and military.

NOTE   These agencies receive their authority from Congress, under the Department of Commerce.

Communications Act of 1934

By 1934, there was pressure for one organization to regulate all telecommunications services, both wireless and wired. The *1934 Communications Act* enabled the creation (under the Department of Commerce) of the FCC. The function of the FCC is to be an independent government agency responsible with regulating both interstate and international communications over radio, television, wire lines, satellite, and cable media. Today, the FCC is the agency responsible for regulating all commercial communication services. It serves as the liaison between the consumer and the government.

NOTE   The government has its own agency to regulate governmental functions in its communications needs.

For years, AT&T had dominated the industry through its long-distance service monopoly and its Western Electric manufacturing subsidiary. It provided all telephone equipment and service through its normal distribution channels, the telephone companies.

The network was untouchable, with only AT&T products and services allowed for interconnection to the networks. This was an appeasement to AT&T, which stated the connection of a foreign piece of equipment on the network would disrupt the network and decrease its efficiency, as well as jeopardize national security. The government agreed and continued allowing only AT&T devices to be used for communication.

This stance was modified somewhat after World War II when the FCC permitted the connection of certain customer-owned and provided recorders to the telephone lines, so long as a protection device was used. This *protection device* was a piece of hardware that electrically isolated the non-AT&T equipment from the telephone network. (The isolation equipment, of course, had to be leased from AT&T).

Hush-a-Phone

In the 1950s, an innovation known as the Hush-a-Phone, an acoustically coupled device designed to eliminate noise and increase privacy, was tested before the FCC. Although this sounds impressive, the Hush-a-Phone was nothing more than a rectangular metal box-like cone that could be placed over a mouthpiece. Users spoke into the cone and their conversation would be kept private from others in public places. Prior to this invention, users would have to "cup" their hands over the mouthpiece to accomplish the same thing. Everyone wanted their own Hush-a-Phone! Well over a hundred thousand units sold before AT&T found out about it. Immediately, AT&T sued Hush-a-Phone because it had not approved this device for the public network. They had been granted exclusive rights for the public network and, clearly, this device was attached to the AT&T phone, causing a violation with regulations. The FCC agreed with AT&T's position and moved to prevent "foreign" devices from being connected to the telephone network, even though this device was only a mechanical privacy cone and was not electrically connected to the network in any way.

An appeals court later overturned this decision because the acoustic coupler was a nonelectrical device. Therefore, the court ruled it would pose no threat to the integrity of the network. However, the legal battle and costs associated with it forced the Hush-a-Phone company out of business, leaving AT&T to lose the battle but win the war, creating a chilling effect for others who would consider challenging its dominance.

The U.S. Naval Department was one of the users who fought for the use of the Hush-a-Phone. The Navy wanted to have the privacy of the Hush-a-Phone and the ability to record a conversation for documentation purposes. After losing the battle in court, AT&T suggested if a recording device were to be allowed on the network, then a beep should be sounded on the line periodically (every 15 seconds). This beep would alert the user at the far end that the conversation was being recorded. The Bell System suggested if a beep were introduced to the line, then an electrical input was required. You can probably see where this is headed. AT&T was fighting tooth-and-nail for its place as the sole provider of telecommunications services. Bell fought for the right to install the equipment on the line that provided the beep. This was made possible because the Hush-a-Phone decision was made based on a nonelectrical input. Therefore, the Bell System was then able to charge the U.S. Naval Department for the equipment that introduced the beep and all was settled. AT&T still kept market share by providing all the equipment to access the network or the equipment that allowed other manufacturers' products to interface with its network.

Even though the courts allowed third-party devices to be connected to the network, any device of electrical nature was still prohibited if it wasn't from AT&T (manufactured in its Western Electric Division).

The 1956 Consent Decree

In 1956, the Department of Justice (DOJ) filed an antitrust suit against the Bell System, which had previously been postponed because of World War II. In general, the suit was aimed at getting AT&T to divest itself of Western Electric. This was finally settled in what was known as the *1956 Consent Decree*. The result was this: AT&T could retain ownership of Western Electric if it only produced products for the Bell-operated companies. Regulators wanted to provide free and fair trade practices, as well as competition, so this decree went on to prevent the Bell System from offering commercial data-processing services, limiting Bell to providing telecommunications services under regulation. This still left the Bell System a regulated monopoly with no competition for equipment and services in its operating areas.

The Carterfone Decision

In 1968, however, the first true case was tested by a company called Carter Electronics of Texas. Carter made a device used to interconnect mobile radios to the telephone network via acoustic couplers (again avoiding an electrical connection as in the Hush-a-Phone).

But, despite the lack of direct electrical connection, AT&T vigorously contested the Carter product as dangerous to its network. Eventually, the FCC ruled against AT&T and for Carter. It permitted devices to be connected as long as adequate protective steps were taken. The FCC ruling was paramount in that the direct electrical connection of devices to the network was allowed so long as a protective coupler arrangement was still used. The decision had monumental impact because, prior to the Carterfone Decision, manufacturers had a limited outlet for their products. They typically sold their products to the independent operating telephone companies. Now, the floodgates were opened and these manufacturers had a whole new world of opportunity to market their products. Even the foreign manufacturers sped into the equipment market, offering end-user products that had previously been totally controlled by the Bell System. The European and Japanese marketers were quick to enter the PBX and terminal equipment business.

However, the use of a protective device was still an area of frustration with these equipment vendors. Rent for the Bell protective arrangements was a recurring cost that made the purchase of other equipment less attractive. The manufacturers continued to complain about this, and they made a case that AT&T was still protecting its marketplace, leaving no room for competition in the equipment industry.

1975 FCC Registration Program

The competitive complaints resulted in the 1975 FCC registration program for all products that could be attached to the telephone network. As long as a manufacturer could pass the requirements of the FCC registration (Part 68),* then its products could be attached to the network without the use of the protective devices. This began what was called the *interconnect business*.

The Execunet Decision

Still, additional activity took place. In the 1960s, a small microwave carrier company called Microwave Communications Incorporated (MCI) began constructing a microwave network between Chicago and St. Louis. MCI's initial intent was to provide alternate private-line services called *Execunet*, in a high-volume corridor. Private-line(s) service is a service for businesses that require a large number of connections to their other office locations. Rather than paying the normal rate to traverse the public network, high-volume users can directly dial branch offices for a fixed monthly fee. These lines, at the time, were part of the public network, but were terminated to preassigned locations (due to programming at the CO switch).

MCI sold its microwave service as an alternative to the AT&T private line service. Initially, MCI only offered the private, site-to-site, private office connectivity (with the permission of the FCC), but then it directly challenged AT&T by letting users in one

---

*Remember this part when we progress through this book, as many of the rules applied by the FCC will adhere to the Part 15 and Part 68.

town use its microwave link to access local dial tone in the other city and to make local phone calls in the far-end city. MCI took its interconnection request to the courts and won the right to interconnect its network with the telephone company network. At that point, MCI leased lines (in both locations) and allowed customers in St. Louis to dial MCI, and then have the call get local dial tone in Chicago. This new service directly violated FCC regulations. This was illegal and it was immediately reported to the FCC. The lengthy legal actions that followed nearly put MCI into bankruptcy (much like the Hush-a-Phone battle), but the little MCI company prevailed and became the "other common carrier" industry—one more step toward ending AT&T's monopoly. This was the *Execunet* service decision and created the birth of the Other Common Carrier industry. In addition, this decision now allowed the creation of another common carrier, Sprint. Now, three players were in the long-distance market and, slowly, the legislation was chipping away from the stranglehold AT&T had on the communications market.

The Bell Network Hierarchy (Pre-1984)

Prior to 1984, most of the network was owned by AT&T and its local Bell Operating Companies (BOCs). It was a creation based on growth to provide scalability as newer areas were provided with service. A layered hierarchy of office connections was designed around a five-level architecture (with the offices designated from class 5 through class 1). The offices are connected together with wires of various types, called *trunks*. These trunks can be twisted pairs of wire, coaxial cables (like the CATV wire), radio (such as microwave), or fiber optics. The trunks vary in their capacities, but generally high-usage trunks are used to connect between offices. Figure 3.2 shows the hierarchy prior to the divestiture of AT&T, with the five levels evident.

The End Office

The class 5 office is the local exchange or *end office*. It delivers dial tone to the customer. The end office, also called a *branch exchange,* is the closest connection to the end user. Think of a tree: all the activity takes place at the ends of the branches and the customers are the leaves hanging off the branches. Calls between exchanges in a geographical area are connected by direct trunks between two end offices, which are called *interoffice trunks*. Over 19,000 end offices in the United States alone provide basic dial-tone services.*

The Toll Center

The class 4 office is the *toll center*. A call going between two end offices that aren't connected together is routed to the class 4 office. The toll center is also used as the

---

*Prior to the 1984 divestiture, almost 66,000 end offices were in the United States. The equipment is smaller now and it can handle more connections, so the providers consolidated into fewer locations, saving space and money.

connection to the long-distance network for calls where added costs are incurred when a connection is made. This toll center may also be called a *tandem office*, meaning calls have to pass through (or tandem through) this location to get somewhere else on the network. A basic arrangement of a tandem-switching system is shown in Fig. 3.2. The tandem office usually doesn't provide dial-tone services to the end user.

However, this is a variable where a single office might provide various functions. The tandem office can also be just a *toll*—a connecting arrangement that's a pass-through from various class 5 offices to the toll centers. Again, this varies depending on the arrangements made by the telephone providers. The ratio of toll centers that serve local long distance is approximately 9 to 1. Prior to divestiture, approximately 940 toll centers existed.

The Primary Center

The class 3 office is the *primary center*. Calls destined within the same state area are passed from the local toll office to the primary center for completion. These locations are served with high-usage trunks used strictly for passing calls from one toll center to another.

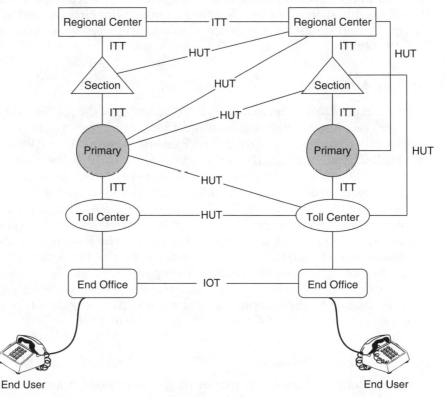

Figure 3.2 The pre-1984 hierarchy as it existed in North America under the Bell System.

The primary centers never serve dial tones to an end user. The number of primary centers prior to divestiture was approximately 170, spread across the country among the various operating telephone companies (both Bell and independent operating companies).

The Sectional Center

The class 2 office is the sectional center. A *sectional center* is typically the main-state switching system used for interstate toll connections designated for the processing of long-distance calls from section to section. Approximately 50 sectional centers existed before the divestiture of the Bell System. These offices didn't serve any end users, but they served among primary centers around the country.

The Regional Center

The class 1 office is the *regional center* and 10 regional centers existed across the country. The task of each center was the final setup of calls on a region-by-region basis. However, the regional centers constituted one of the most sophisticated computer systems in the world. The regional centers continually updated each other regarding the status of every circuit in the network. These centers were required to reroute traffic around trouble spots (for example, failed equipment or circuits) and to keep each other informed at all times. As mentioned, this was all prior to the divestiture of the local BOC by AT&T.

The Divestiture Agreement

The landscape of telecommunications has changed over the past century, mostly through court actions. Despite the many acts, and regulatory bodies, the players in the industry have largely remained unchanged. AT&T and its other ventures (Western Electric, Bell Labs) still controlled almost the entire marketplace. In 1982, the most monumental decision to be made since the inception of the monopoly in the telecommunications business was reached. In light of all the computer inquiries and consent decrees taking place, the DOJ was still investigating AT&T, Western Electric, and Bell Labs. This recent action started in early 1974, essentially reopening the actions that had been started after World War II, and was aimed at the complete breakup of the Bell System. In early 1981, the suit finally made it into the courts but, surprisingly, was brought to a halt on January 8, 1982, when an agreement was reached to drop the suit and submit a modification of the 1956 Consent Decree to the courts. Judge Harold Greene of the Federal District Court was presiding when this compromise was reached. This was called the 1982 Divestiture Agreement or the Modified Final Judgment (MFJ) of 1984.

Incumbent Local Exchange Carriers

The incumbent local exchange carrier (ILEC) is the telephone company serving your area and providing you with all the necessary services of installing and maintaining dial-tone. The term local exchange carriers (LEC) came into existence after the separation of the Bell System from AT&T. The modified final judgment decree specified that the local telephone company, or dial-tone provider, would be kept separate after divestiture. Prior to 1984, the carriers were called the BOCs, and they still are referred to this way. See Fig. 3.3 for example of the BOCs that existed before the divestiture agreement.

All these telephone companies were considered ILECs because the term fit better with the service they provided. This service was:

- The dial tone
- The local loop of wire connecting to their equipment and the customer location
- The telephone set to interface to the network
- The interface to the local and long-distance portions of the networks and the access to the long-distance network
- The billing and collection functions for all services
- The installation of all related pieces and components to give the end user access to the network
- The maintenance and repair functions

Figure 3.3 Out of AT&T, 23 Bell Operating Companies were formed. These BOCs presided over individual states in some instances but, in others, they presided over several states that were more rural.

This all changed in the 1984 divestiture of the network and telephone company interfaces. Consequently, the customer now must decide whom to talk to regarding services and equipment needs. However, with the telecommunications deregulation and privatization occurring throughout North America and other parts of the world, the way we (the consumers) used to do this process is becoming the way we will do it again. What goes around comes around. Soon, the ILECs will be able to compete and offer all the services (and more) that they offered prior to 1984!

Provisions of Divestiture

Recall that the 1956 Consent Decree was aimed at providing free and fair trade practices in the industry. Despite the small gains made in allowing other providers in the market place, further reform was needed to level the playing field. The courts were called on again to break up the monopoly of AT&T and the Bell System. This divestiture, or break up of the Bell system, was called the Modified Final Judgment (MFJ). The main idea was that local dial-tone service would remain a monopoly, but all other services would operate in a fair and competitive operating environment. Therefore, the local dial-tone business that would be provided by the LECs would remain regulated. The trade-off was this: AT&T would be allowed to enter other unregulated markets and services (previously off limits because of the 1956 Consent Decree). AT&T was now allowed to operate in long distance, equipment manufacturing, computer equipment, and sales markets.

Out of AT&T, the 23 Bell Operating Companies (BOCs) would be split up into several individual entities, each totally independent of the other. AT&T would keep Western Electric manufacturing, Bell Labs, and the Long Lines (Long Distance) division. The 23 Bell Operating Companies were to be consolidated into seven RBOCs. The decision to make seven RBOCs was an effort to provide services to the public without having so many redundant assets. Each company prior to this consolidation had to have duplicate divisions in almost every job function to maintain the network. Note, over time, these were consolidated back into four RBOCs: SBC, Verizon, BellSouth, and Qwest Communications. The coverage areas for these four RBOCs is shown in Fig. 3.4.

Some other important points of the MFJ include the following:

- AT&T had to transfer sufficient personnel, assets, and access to technical information to the new RBOCs, (or whatever new organization was owned by the RBOCs), to enable local exchange services or access to exchange services to be provided without any ties to AT&T.

- All long-distance services, links, personnel, and other facilities had to be relinquished by the BOCs and turned over to AT&T.

- All existing licensing agreements and contracts between AT&T or its subsidiaries and the BOCs had to be terminated.

- Equal access for all interexchange carriers into the RBOCs' switching systems had to be provided. (This broke down the special privilege AT&T enjoyed over

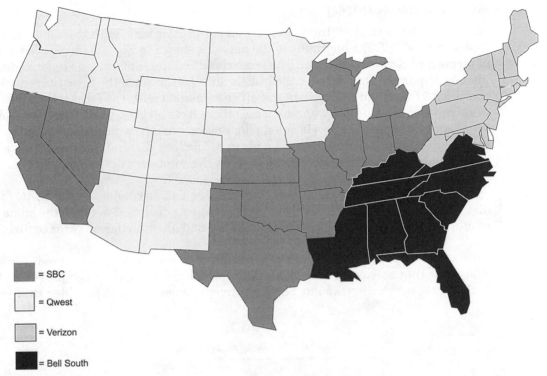

= SBC

= Qwest

= Verizon

= Bell South

Figure 3.4 Four RBOCs exist today: Qwest, SBC, Verizon, and Bell South. This diagram shows the states where the respective RBOCs provide services. The consolidation of regions was to eliminate inefficiencies and redundant positions.

its competition.) The equal access for all carriers was to be provided within two years. The only exceptions were electromechanical systems, where it was cost-prohibitive to make changes or for smaller companies serving fewer than 10,000 users.

- After the breakup, the RBOCs could provide, but couldn't manufacture, equipment.

- After the divestiture, the RBOCs could produce and distribute directories to subscribers.

- Carrying calls between and among offices would be defined as either local-exchange services or interexchange services. The LECs would hand off any interexchange call to an interexchange carrier (IEC/IXC). To define the boundaries of who carried the call and who shared in the revenue, a number of local access and transport areas (LATAs) were created. The calls inside a LATA were the responsibility of the LEC, and connections between LATAs were the responsibility of the IEC.

- Joint ownership or participation in the network between AT&T and the BOCs was prohibited. Although this was a common practice before the breakup, it wasn't supported after the breakup.

The Network Hierarchy (Post-1984)

After divestiture in 1984, the network took a dramatic turn, with the separation of the BOCs from AT&T. The hierarchy of the network shown in Fig. 3.5 introduced a new set of terms and connections. The BOCs were classified the same way as independent telephone companies. They are all called LECs and ILECs. Since the divestiture took place, the class 5 office and the tandem toll office remained with the local telephone companies. The sectional, primary, and regional offices have all been pretty much consolidated into a single device that provides long distance connectivity across the country. So the hierarchy has been shrunk from 5 levels to 3. The long distance portion of the network now belongs to many providers depending on their network development. This is truly a competitive marketplace.

Equal access, or the capability of every IEC or IXC to connect to the ILEC for long-distance service, became a reality. Equal access was designed to allow the same access to other long-distance competitors that AT&T had always enjoyed prior to divestiture.

Tariffs   Simply put, a *tariff* is a description of a service that is offered, the rate of charge for that service, and the rules under which the service is to be provided. A tariff is the basic service agreement between the customer and the provider that must be

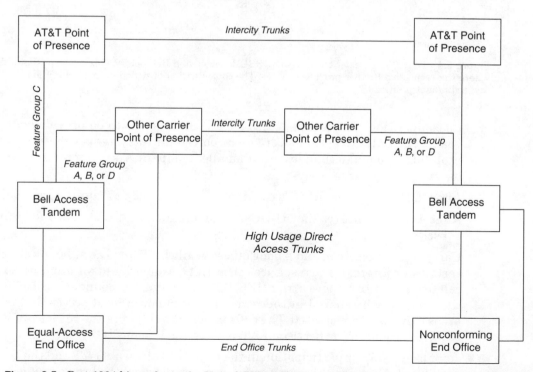

Figure 3.5 Post-1984 hierarchy in the United States. This is much different than the previous hierarchy, but this model now allows individual entities to handle routing within their own organization.

submitted to the regulators for approval. Before any changes in service can be offered, they must be approved by the regulators. This is a check and balance from the MFJ that ensures fair and free competition in the marketplace. In the United States, 50 different regulators are ruling on the tariffs—one for each state.

But who writes the tariff? The RBOCs and AT&T (as well as any other operator of long distance networks) write the tariffs. Although more and more services are being made available quicker than ever before, the universal escape clause is "the tariffs don't allow this service," which is a clear misrepresentation. The organizations write tariffs and submit them to their respective arbitrator, whether it's the FCC for interstate traffic (for AT&T) or the respective Public Utilities Commissions for the RBOCs. An easy way to avoid offering a service or to delay a customer request is to suggest the tariff doesn't allow something.

In the United States, the overseer function has been relegated to the Public Utilities Commission(s) of each state and the FCC. Local communications services are seen as the dominion of the PUC, whereas interstate tariffs are the dominion of the FCC.

In the rest of the world, rate settings and guidelines differ, depending on the country. Many of the telephone companies are under direct control or ownership of the local government. The telephone service is relegated to the post-office agencies, called Post, Telephone, Telegraph organizations (PTTs). The name stands for the services provided: postal, telephony, and telegraphy. Privatization continues to occur in several parts of the world. Telephone services are being removed from government control and passed on to private organizations. It stands to reason that these organizations may face stiff competition for the services, much the same as what has happened in the United States.

The Telecom Act of 1996

In February 1996, the Clinton Administration signed into law the Telecom Act of 1996. This act was the culmination of several years of trying to deregulate and provide a competitive marketplace in the telecommunications arena. This law, when enacted, opened the door to an open communications infrastructure. Essentially, what the administration implemented was the concept of an information superhighway.

The Telecom Act of 1996 opened the way for myriad new players to compete for the local dial-tone service. The days of monopolistic control in telecommunications had supposedly ended, allowing competition and choice in all areas of telecommunications. Why did a need exist for competition in local services?

In the United States, dial tone amounted to a $115 billion per year industry and all the emerging players want a piece of that action. What this means, however, is a group of new players called competitive local exchange carriers (CLECs) would emerge to provide dial-tone services, while the local telephone companies are unshackled and allowed to penetrate the long-distance arena and data service sectors. In addition, the Telecom Act of 1996 allows the long-distance companies (IECs/ IXC) to enter into new business opportunities. These include dial tone, cable TV services, high-speed Internet access, and two-way video communications capabilities after the infrastructure is in place.

Cable TV Companies as CLECs

We have been discussing voice companies so far, but technology over the past century has changed dramatically, especially since the 1970s. Cable TV companies emerged during that time (as well as satellite companies) and put their own connections to the customers' door. Having an access media to millions of consumers, cable TV companies began to enter into telephony and other forms of the communications business. As the cable companies look at their infrastructure, they already have a high-speed communications channel running either to or by everyone's door. They must recognize, however, that in the past, their primary service was to deliver one-way cable services (TV). To provide high-speed Internet access, enhanced capabilities, and voice communications, these companies were forced to create a two-way communications cable system. This means they either had to add new cables or provide high-speed fiber in the backbone network (to the curb), and then coax to the door. Although this sounds straightforward and easy, it does require significant investments on the part of the cable companies.

Emerging Areas of Business for the RBOCs   As a result of the Telecommunications Act, the original telephone companies (the BOCs) broke out into new markets, offering long distance for less and providing cable TV services, Internet access, and videoconferencing capabilities as part of their local infrastructure. Because the local two-wire cable facility (called the *local loop*) was not designed to sustain the high-speed communications, the Telcos must continue to update their cable infrastructures. These companies are enamored with technologies that use high-speed, digital subscriber links. Using various techniques, such as asymmetrical digital subscriber link (ADSL) or very high-speed digital subscriber link (VDSL), the telephone companies can provide high-speed communications to the customer's door. In the ADSL marketplace, they envision delivering up to 9 Mbps to a customer's door, whereas outbound from the customer to the network, the service will offer Plain Old Telephone Service (POTS) and up to 384 Kbps data transmission.

Regardless of the technique used, the telephone companies are in a position to find technologies to support and sustain these speeds on their local, single twisted pair of wires to the customer's door. This is their challenge. Beyond the high-speed communications, the telephone companies can also enter into manufacturing, long distance, and cable TV service.

Creation of the Internet Service Providers (ISPs)

With the passage of the 1996 Telecom Act, we mentioned that the Clinton Administration imagined an information superhighway. What President Clinton (or possibly Vice President Gore and others in the Clinton Administration) was referring to was an increase in competition to provide high-speed links to customers' doors and allow data services, along with voice, to be provided. As already mentioned, the telephone networks (local loops only) were not designed to carry data traffic, so data centric companies or networks needed to be created. These were the first Internet service providers (ISPs). The ISPs main function was to provide public user access to the Internet. Originally, access to the Internet was provided over telephone lines through modem communications. Users connected a modem to their computer, plugged in the phone line, and dialed the ISP for access. This is still a primary way for mobile commuters and citizens in rural areas to connect to the Internet today. ISPs also began offering access to DSL service and T1 service. ISPs serve as the interface between the user and the high-speed Internet backbone. They provide you with an account, e-mail, and sometimes a browser to access the vast information on the Internet in a useable fashion.

The Canadian Marketplace

In 1994, the Canadian Regulatory Telecommunications Committee (CRTC) endeavored to do something similar to what happened in the United States.

The goal was to deregulate or demonopolize the local dial-tone provisioning service. On May 1, 1997, the CRTC provided its interpretation of how it would deregulate and open the market to dial tone to a competitive environment.

One year after the Telecom Act of 1996 in the United States, the CRTC modeled many services and provisions of the law after those accomplished by the FCC. The reason was to provide consistent policies throughout all North America. While the CRTC endeavored to break up the dial-tone monopoly, the cable companies, the long-distance providers, and a rash of emerging facilities-based or nonfacilities-based players already filed and petitioned for the right to offer services. Once again, in the Canadian marketplace, the influx of new providers and new opportunities overwhelmed the consumers, even though the implementation is ongoing.

In both the U.S. and Canadian marketplaces, all the dial-tone and long-distance access services have traditionally been available via the local loop. Now, with the cable TV companies trying to get into this business, the dial tone could be provided on either a cable or a local loop. More and more opportunities exist for a wireless connection to the consumer, however, whether residential or business. The wireless dial-tone providers are constantly springing up around the country as they entertain the thought of the Personal Communications Service (PCS). Through a combination of dial tone, the TV services, the high-speed Internet access, and the multimedia communications capabilities to the local door all these activities will come to culmination. No one service alone may warrant all the new emerging players but, as a whole, this marketplace is enormous.

Therefore, as the Telecommunications Act and the CRTC deregulation rolled out in the Canadian marketplace, consumers experienced dramatic changes in the way they do business. Through the convergence of wired and wireless communications, dial tone, and long distance, a variety of other services emerged to create a competitive potential for consumers. One-stop shopping is the wave of the future.

Most surveys indicate this is a direct contrast to how people feel toward their cable TV and telephone companies. These two providers are all too often looked on with scorn or distaste. If an electric company does offer dial-tone service, you may also expect a significant hit rate in terms of customers signing up to use that utility as the provider for communications services. If the electric companies can provide dial tone and cable TV for less, they will do so across an infrastructure used for their own internal process control systems. This means their cost for providing dial tone across this high-speed fiber backbone, which was put in place over the years, will be marginal.

As we can see, the FCC regulates the use of radio frequencies (such as microwave, cellular, WLAN, and satellite), antennas, allowable power output and interference prevention and enforcement such as Part 15 mentioned above. Moreover, the FCC regulates all of the connection, carriers, bandwidth, and equipment used within the telecommunications networks across the United States. This was the Part 68 mentioned above. The FCC is the single entity that regulates all the domestic carriers, CATV companies and Cellular companies as needed on a domestic basis. The FCC also serves as liaison with international regulators.

International Organizations

Internationally we mentioned that the PTTs regulate and govern the telecommunications within their respective countries. Most of the PTTs that are still monopolistic, report to the postal organization (at one time AT&T was under the domain of the US Postal Service, but only for a short period).

However, there are standards committees that have a good amount of hands on development that pertain to the rules associated with international communications. These organizations include the following:

International Telecommunications Union (ITU)—an international standards setting body—comprises members around the world. The ITU has two significant subcommittees that set the standards involving this area:

ITU–Telecommunications Standardization Sector (ITU-TSS)

ITU–Radio Systems Sector (ITU-RSS)

These two organizations accept the standards that become law around many parts of the world.

Others

Other organizations that work on the committees are the following for U.S.-based telecommunications:

IEEE is a standards committee that sets the standards (but does not enforce them) for our LAN, MAN, WAN, and WLAN specifications. The IEEE comprises member companies that produce, manage, or operate telecommunications networks, and have a vested interest in the decision-making process for standards.

Many of the WLAN specifications today are regulated by the FCC but standards are set by the IEEE.

Internet Engineering Task Force (IETF) is a member group of concerned manufacturers, operators, users, and others that set the standards for the Internet. This includes many of the specifications that deal with TCP/IP, UDP, and now VoIP. ITU and IETF work together on the standards for VoIP whereby the ITU set the H.323 standards, the IETF set the standards for SIP and now jointly they are working on a standard for carriers called H.248 or MEGACO. More on these organizations and techniques will be covered in their respective chapters.

Questions

1. How many levels were originally used in the network hierarchy?

    a. Two

    b. Three

    c. Four

    d. Five

2. What portions of the network remained with the Bell Operating Companies after the breakup of the telephone network?

    a. Long lines

    b. Long distance

    c. Local dial tone

    d. All of the above

3. How many regional offices were used across North America in the beginning?

    a. One

    b. Ten

    c. One hundred

    d. None of the above

4. What was the name given to the parent companies of the Bell Telephone Companies after the divestiture agreement?

    a. BOC

    b. RBHC

    c. RBOC

    d. CLEC

5. What is the name of the wiring that the Telco brings to the consumer's door?

    a. Local loop

    b. Wire

    c. DSL

    d. Single mode fiber optics

6. The name given to the local telephone companies after the breakup of 1984 is _____.

7. What do we call the telephone companies that used to be part of AT&T?
   a. ILEC
   b. ISP
   c. DLEC
   d. CLEC

8. How many independent LECs are there?
   a. 140,000
   b. 122,000
   c. 50,000
   d. 1400

9. What is the term used for the new providers of dial tone?
   a. ILEC
   b. LEC
   c. DLEC
   d. CLEC

10. What is the responsibility of the IEC/IXC?
    a. Dial tone
    b. Long distance
    c. Equipment
    d. None of the above

11. What are the newer data suppliers called? _____.

12. When the independent telephone companies provide a service to their local community, they are called a(n) _____.
    a. CLEC
    b. DLEC
    c. ILEC
    d. ITP

13. What one organization overseers the bulk of the efforts of the ILECs, IXCs, CATV and others?
    a. PUC
    b. ICCC
    c. FCC
    d. FDA

Signaling System 7 (SS7)

After reading this chapter and completing the questions, you will be able to:

- Describe the signaling systems
- Understand what role signaling plays in a network
- Discuss the benefits of out of band signaling
- Compare the different types of circuits used in SS7

The ability of a caller to go off-hook anywhere in the world today, dial some digits, and then miraculously talk to someone continues to be a point of amazement. The ability for a network made up of millions of connections to perform a call setup almost instantly, and then tear it down just as fast is what really carries the mystique. How can the network figure out where to send the call so quickly, get the connection, and ring the telephone on the other end? All of this happens in less than a second and the user is oblivious as to the intricacies of what occurs. What happens behind the scenes constitutes the backbone of the signaling systems. The networks are now dependent on the ability to handle sub-second call setup and teardown.

Evolution of Signaling Systems

Several signaling systems have been introduced into the telecommunications networks. The current one in use is called *Signaling System Number 7* (SS7) in North America. In the rest of the world this is referred to as *Common Channel Interoffice Signaling System Number 7* (CCS7). Although the names are different, the functions and the purposes of the two systems are the same. As always, the North Americans do things one way, and the rest of the world does things a different way. This is an age-old problem, but one that we have learned to deal with and adjust to. The essence of the signaling system boils down to many different factors, but one of the most significant reasons the carriers employ these systems is to save time and money on the network. Following that fact, the carriers are also interested in introducing new features and functions of an intelligent network, as previously discussed. The best signaling systems are designed to facilitate this intelligence in the network nodes designated as signaling devices, separate and distinct from the switching systems that carry the conversations.

Pre-SS7

Prior to the implementation of common channel SS7, per-trunk signaling (PTS) was used exclusively in the networks. The PTS method was used for setting up calls between the telephone companies' exchanges. This method continues to be used in some parts of the world where SS7 may not yet be implemented. Admittedly, the number of exchanges using the PTS method is declining. SS7 is gaining in its deployment worldwide. However, the network is always in a state of change and this is no exception. PTS sends tones or multiple frequencies (MF) to identify the digits of the called party. The trunk also provides all of the intelligence for monitoring and supervision (call seizure, hang up, answer back) of the call. Telephone systems at the customer's location (PBXs) that are not Integrated Services Digital Network Primary Rate Interface (ISDN PRI) compatible use the PTS method. To route telephone traffic through the Public Switched Telephone Network (PSTN), it is necessary to communicate with the switches that make up the PSTN. Signaling is a means for transferring network-related information between switching nodes, and also between the end office switches and their subscribers.

Signaling is therefore used to do the following:

- Request service from the central office switch. This means that the customer goes off-hook and signals the network that service is required.
- Send information to the central office switch to route the call, via in-band DTMF addressing digits (1-480-706-0912).
- Alert the destination address a call is arriving via ringing voltage.
- Provide status information such as time call is connected and call supervision such as call termination (ended) for billing purposes.
- Handle the setup and teardown of all calls.

On a long-distance call, when a call setup is necessary, each leg of the call repeats the multifrequency (MF) call setup procedure until the last exchange in the loop is reached. In essence, the call is being built by the signaling as progress is occurring on a link-by-link basis. As each link is added to the connection, the network is building the entire circuit across town or across the country. Each leg of the call setup takes approximately 2 to 4 seconds, using the configuration shown in Fig. 4.1, with a total call setup taking approximately 6 to 12 seconds (at a minimum) from end to end.

This method is inefficient use of the circuitry. Although the call gets to its end destination, several complications could arise such as ring-no-answer or the line is busy.

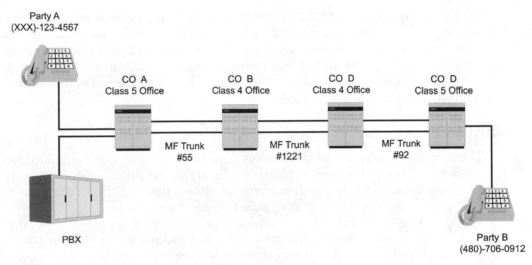

Figure 4.1   Per-trunk signaling preceded SS7 but was slow.

Regardless of the complications, the outcome is the same; the carrier ties up the network and never completes the call. Hence, there is no revenue generated. This inefficiency was costing the carriers a significant amount of money. Therefore, something had to be done to improve this method of call establishment. The call-establishment part of the connection could take as much as 24 seconds, then time out and never get to its destination. However, the carrier tied up parts of the network without getting a completion. This is no big deal when discussing one call. However, when a network carries hundreds of millions of calls per day, this accumulated lost time is extensive and expensive.

Channel-Associated Signaling (CAS)

When used for in-band signaling, channel-associated signaling provides all the information on the individual channel. No other signaling information is necessary as the line carries the call setup (signaling) and the call (talk). The following pieces are included in channel associated signaling:

- Call setup information (off-hook, dial tone, dialed digits, ring back, or busy tones) is transmitted in the same band of frequencies as used by the voice signal. Hence the word in-band signaling. All information concerning a call is carried on the same line.

- The talk path is switched over after the call setup is complete, using the same path that the call setup signals used.

- MF signaling is used for switch-to-switch call setup.

The primary benefit of CAS is that it is inexpensive to implement and can be used on any transmission medium. The fact that many networks were implemented using CAS bears this out. Moreover, several customer systems used in-band signaling (CAS) because it was easy to install and maintain. An equal amount of potential disadvantages were possible using CAS, so a new system had to be created to finesse the network connectivity and speed the process.

Introduction to SS7

The international standards bodies developed a digital signaling standard in the mid-1960s called *Signaling System Number 6* (SS6) that revolutionized the industry. Based on a proprietary, high-speed data communications network, SS6 later evolved to SS7. SS7 has now become the signaling standard for the world.

The success of the signaling standards lies in the message structure of the protocol and the network topologies. The protocol uses messages, much like the X.25 and other message-based protocols, to request services from other entities on the network. The messages travel from one network element to another, independent of the actual voice and data that they pertain to, in an envelope called a *packet*.

The first development of the SS6 in North America was used in the United States on a 2400-bps data link. Later these links were upgraded to 4800 bps. Messages in the form of data packets were used to request connections on voice trunks between central offices. Placing 12 signal units (of 28 bits each) assembled packets into a data block. This is similar to the methods used today in SS7 architectures.

SS6 used a fixed-length signal unit but SS7 uses variable-length signal units. The most recent version of SS7 uses a 56-Kbps data link throughout North America, whereas in the rest of the world CCS7 runs at 64 Kbps. The differences in the speeds between 56 and 64 Kbps result in the fact that many local exchange carriers and end-user systems have not fully deployed the use of enhanced call handling on the digital circuits. Consequently, the 56 Kbps is an anomaly in the SS7 networks. Further, the North American carriers were still installing SS6 through the mid-1980s (even though it was invented in the 1960s), while SS7 deployment began in 1983, leaving two separate signaling systems in use throughout North America.

SS6 networks are very slow, whereas SS7 is much faster. The use of a full DS-1 (1.544 Mbps) data link is still being considered in the North American marketplace.

Purpose of the SS7 Network

The primary purpose of SS7 was to access remote databases to look up and translate information from 800* and 900 calls. There were several benefits to using this lookup process so that the carriers do not have to maintain a full database at each switching node, but know how to get to the remote database and find the information quickly. The second purpose of the SS7 network and protocols was to marry the various stored program controlled systems throughout the network. This allows the quick and efficient

---

*The reference to 800 service includes 800, 866, 877 and 888 calls.

call setup and teardown across the network in 1 second. Moreover, this integration provides for better supervision, monitoring, and billing systems integration. Additional benefits of the SS7 network were geared to replacing the SS6 network, which as of today is well over 40 years old. Like anything else, the networks have served us well, but need upgrading on a regular basis due to technology changes and demands for faster, more reliable services. Most of the SS6 equipment has been removed.

SS7 networks allow the introduction of additional features and capabilities into the network making it attractive to the carriers so they can generate new revenues from the added features. SS7 also allows the full use of the channel for the talk path because the signaling is done out of band on its own separate channel. This is more efficient in the call setup and teardown process.

What Is Out-of-Band Signaling?

Out-of-band signaling is signaling that does not take place in the same path as the conversation. We are used to thinking of signaling as being in band. We hear dial tone, dial digits, and hear ringing over the same channel on the same pair of wires. When the call connects, we talk over the same path that was used for the signaling. Traditional telephony used to work this way as well. The signals to set up a call between one switch and another always took place over the same trunk that would eventually carry the call. This is what was referred to as CAS above.

In early days, out-of-band signaling was used in the 4-kHz voice-grade channel. In Fig. 4.2 we see the 4-kHz channel. The telephone companies used band-pass filters on their wiring to contain the voice conversation within the 4-kHz channel. The band-pass filters were placed at 300 Hz (the low pass) and at 3300 Hz (the high pass). The range of frequencies above the actual filter is 700 Hz (4000 − 3300 = 700). In this additional spectrum, in-band signaling was sent down the wires outside the frequencies used for conversation. Actually, the signals were sent across the 3500- and 3700-Hz frequencies. Although these worked, and were not in the talk path (out of the band), they were limited to the number of tones that could be sent. The result was also a limit to the states that could be represented by the tones.

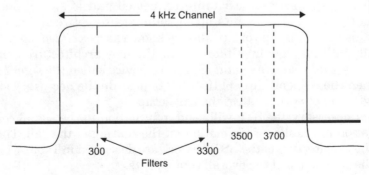

Figure 4.2 Out-of-band signaling shown on the 4-kHz channel.

Out-of-band signaling evolved to a separate digital channel for the exchange of signaling information. This channel is called a *signaling link*. Signaling links are used to carry all the necessary signaling messages between nodes. Thus, when a call is placed, the dialed digits, trunk selected, and other pertinent information are sent between switches using signaling links, rather than the trunks, which will ultimately carry the conversation.

It is interesting to note that while SS7 is only used for signaling between network elements, the ISDN D channel extends the concept of out-of-band signaling to the interface between the subscriber and the switch. With ISDN service, signaling that must be conveyed between the user station and the local switch is carried on a separate digital channel, called the *D channel*. The voice or data that comprises the call is carried on the B channel. In reality, the out-of-band signaling is *virtual* because the signaling information is actually running on the same path as the B channels. Time slots on the same physical paths separate the signaling and the conversational data flows. Therefore, the signaling is virtually out of band, while it is physically in the same bandwidth.

Why Out-of-Band Signaling?

Out-of-band signaling has several advantages that make it more desirable than traditional in-band signaling:

- It allows for the transport of more data at higher speeds (56 Kbps can carry data much faster than MF out pulsing).
- It allows for signaling at any time in the entire duration of the call, not only at the beginning.
- It enables signaling to network elements to which there is no direct trunk connection.

The SS7 Network Architecture

If signaling is to be carried on a different path than the voice and data traffic it supports, then what should that path look like? The simplest design would be to allocate one of the paths between each interconnected pair of switches as the signaling link. Subject to capacity constraints, all signaling traffic between the two switches could traverse this link. This type of signaling is known as *associated signaling*. Instead of using the talk path for signaling information, the new architecture includes the connection from the *signal switching point* (SSP) to a device called the *signal transfer point* (STP). It is then the responsibility of the STP to provide the necessary signaling information through the network to effect the call setup

When necessary, the STP will send information to the signal control point (SCP) for translation or database information on the routing of the call. The pieces combined to form the architecture of the SS7 network are described in Table 4.1 and shown in Fig. 4.3 with the connection of the overall components.

TABLE 4.1   Components of SS7 Networks

Component	Function
Signal switching point (SSP)	SSPs are the telephone switches (end offices and tandems) equipped with SS7-capable software and terminating signaling links. They generally originate, terminate, or switch calls.
Signal transfer point (STP)	STPs are the packet switches of the SS7 network. They receive and route incoming signaling messages toward the proper destination. They also perform specialized routing functions.
Signal control point (SCP)	SCPs are the databases that provide information necessary for advanced call processing capabilities.

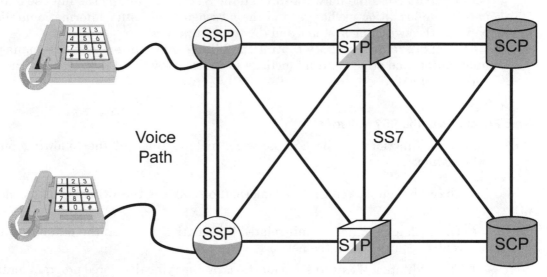

Figure 4.3   SS7 Architectural beginnings.

Figure 4.3 shows a typical interconnection of an SS7 network. Several points should be noted:

- Paired STPs perform identical functions. They are redundant. Together, they are referred to as a *mated pair* of STPs.

- Each SSP has two links (or sets of links), one to each STP of a mated pair. All SS7 signaling to the rest of the world is sent out over these links. Because the STPs are redundant, messages sent over either link (to either STP) will be treated equivalently.

- A link (or set of links) joins the STPs of a mated pair.

- Four links (or sets of links) interconnect two mated pairs of STPs. These links are referred to as a *quad*.

- SCPs are usually (though not always) deployed in pairs. As with STPs, the SCPs of a pair are intended to function identically. Pairs of SCPs are also referred to as mated pairs of SCPs. Note that a pair of links does not directly join them.

- Signaling architectures such as this, which provide indirect signaling paths between network elements, are referred to as providing *quasi-associated signaling*.

SS7 Interconnection

The actual linkage allows the local exchange offices to send the necessary information out of band across the signaling links. SS7 therefore uses messages in the form of packets to signal across the network through the STPs. This allows the full use of the talk path for information exchange, and the messaging paths for informational dialogue between the switching systems and the transfer points.

The links are used to pass control and billing information, network management information, and other control functions as necessary without interfering with the conversational path.

Basic Functions of the SS7 Network

The basic functions of the SS7 network include some of the following pieces of information:

- The exchange of circuit-related information between the switching points along the network.

- The exchange of non-circuit-related information between the databases and the control points within the network.

- The facilitation of features and functions by marrying the stored program control systems together throughout the network into a homogeneous network environment.

Further, the SS7 network allows these features to be put into place without unduly burdening the actual network call path arrangements.

- It handles the rerouting of network traffic in the event of circuit failures by using automatic protection switching services, such as found in SONET or alternate routing information.

- Because it is a packet-switching concept, the SS7 network prevents misrouted calls, duplication of call requests, and lost packets (requests for service).

- It allows the full use of out-of-band signaling using the ITU Q.931 signaling arrangements for call setup and teardown.

- It allows growth so that new features and functions can be introduced to the network without major disruptions.

Signaling Links

SS7 signaling links are characterized according to their use in the signaling network. Virtually all links are identical in that they are 56-Kbps (or 64-Kbps) bidirectional data links that support the same lower layers of the protocol; what is different is their use within a signaling network. The bidirectional nature of these links allows traffic to pass in both directions between signaling points. Three basic forms of signaling links exist, although they are physically the same. They all use the 56-Kbps in North America and 64-Kbps data facilities in nearly every other portion of the world. The three forms of signaling links are:

- *Associated signaling links.* The simplest form of signaling link is referred to as the *associated signaling link*, as shown in Fig. 4.4. In associated signaling, the link is directly parallel from the end office with the voice path for which it is providing the signaling information. This is not an ideal situation, because it would require a signaling link from the end office to every other end office in the network. There are some associated modes of signaling in use, but they are rare.

  Where one will most often find associated signaling deployed is at an end-user location using a single T1 and common channel signaling. Channel 24 on a T1 is the associated out-of-band signaling channel for the preceding 23 talk channels.

  In some cases, it may be better to directly connect two SSPs together via a single link. All related SS7 messages to circuits connecting the two exchanges are sent through this link. A connection is still provided to the home STP using other links to support all other SS7 traffic.

- *Nonassociated signaling links.* In the nonassociated signaling link arrangement there is a separate logical path from the actual voice path, as shown in Fig. 4.5. There are usually multiple nodes involved to reach the end destination, while the voice may have a direct path to reach the final destination. Nonassociated signaling is a common occurrence in many SS7 networks.

  The primary problem with this form of signaling is the number of signaling nodes that the call must use to progress through the network. The more nodes used, the more processing and delay that can occur. Nonassociated signaling involves the use of STPs to reach the remote exchange. To establish a trunk connection between the two exchanges, a signaling message will be sent via SS7 and STPs to the adjacent exchange.

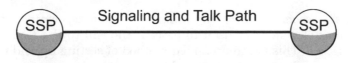

Figure 4.4 Associated signaling.

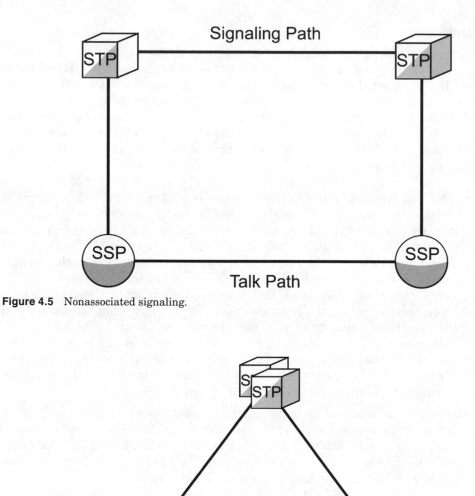

Figure 4.5   Nonassociated signaling.

Figure 4.6   Quasi-associated signaling.

■ *Quasi-associated signaling links.* In quasi-associated signaling, a minimum number of nodes are used to process the call to the final destination, as shown in Fig. 4.6. This is the preferred method of setting up and using an SS7 backbone because each node introduces additional delay in signaling delivery. By eliminating some of the processors on the setup, the delay can be minimized.

SS7 networks favor the use of quasi-associated signaling. In quasi-associated signaling, both nodes are connected to the same STP. The signaling path is still through the STP to the adjacent SSP.

The Link Architecture

Signaling links are logically organized by link type (A through F) according to their use in the SS7 signaling network. These are shown in Fig. 4.7 with the full linkage in place.

- *A link*. An access (A) link connects a signaling end point (SCP or SSP) to a STP. Only messages originating from or destined to the signaling end point are transmitted on an A link.

- *B link*. A bridge (B) link connects one STP to another STP. Typically, a quad of B links interconnect peer (or primary) STPs (the STPs from one network to the STPs of another network). The distinction between a B link and a D link is rather arbitrary. For this reason, such links may be referred to as *B/D links*.

- *C link*. A cross (C) link connects STPs performing identical functions into a mated pair. A C link is used only when an STP has no other route available to a destination signaling point due to link failure. Note that SCPs may also be deployed in pairs to improve reliability, unlike STPs; however, signaling links do not interconnect mated SCPs.

- *D link*. A diagonal (D) link connects a secondary (local or regional) STP pair to a primary (internetwork gateway) STP pair in a quad-link configuration. Secondary STPs within the same network are connected via a quad of D links. The distinction

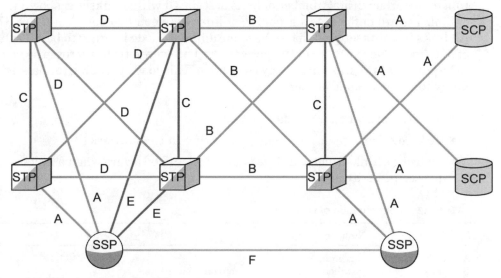

Figure 4.7   The signaling link architecture.

between a B link and a D link is rather arbitrary. For this reason, such links may be referred to as *B/D links*.

■ *E link*. An extended (E) link connects an SSP to an alternate STP. E links provide an alternate signaling path if a SSP's home STP cannot be reached via an A link. E links are not usually provisioned unless the benefit of a marginally higher degree of reliability justifies the added expense.

■ *F link*. A fully associated (F) link connects two signaling end points (SSPs and SCPs). F links are not usually used in networks with STPs. In networks without STPs, F links directly connect signaling points.

Links and Linksets

A linkset is a grouping of links joining the same two nodes. A minimum of one link to a maximum of 16 links can make up the linkset. Normally SSPs have one or two links connecting to their STPs, based on normal capacity and traffic requirements. This constitutes a one- or two-link linkset(s). SCPs have many more links in their linksets to handle the large amount of messaging for 800 and 900 numbers, calling cards, and AIN services.

Combined Linksets

Combined linkset is a term used to define routing from a SSP or SCP toward the related STP, where two linksets are used to share the traffic outward to the STP and beyond. The requirement is not that all linksets be the same size, but the normal practice is to have equally sized groupings of linksets connecting the same end node. Using a linkset arrangement, the normal number of links associated with a linkset is shown in Table 4.2.

Linksets are defined as a grouping of links between two points on the SS7 network. All links in a linkset must have the same adjacent node in order to be classified as part of a linkset. The switches in the network will alternate traffic across the various links, to be sure that the links are always available. This load spreading (or balancing) serves many functions. Some of them are:

■ To be aware when a link fails

■ To recognize when congestion is occurring in the network

■ To use the links when traffic is not critical and be aware when a link is down before it becomes critical

TABLE 4.2   Configuration of Linksets

Link Type	Number of Links
A links	Maximum of 16 links
B/D links	Installed in quads up to a maximum of 8 links
C links	Installed individually up to a maximum of 8 links

Routes and Routesets

The term *routeset* refers to the routing capability of addressing a node within the SS7 network. Every node within the network has a unique address. This address is referred to as a *point code*. The addressing scheme or point code is the major routing characteristic of the CCS7 (SS7) network. The terms *routeset* and *point code* are synonymous.

The point code is made up of nine digits broken down into three 3-digit sequences. An example of this is 245-100-000. Reading the point code from left to right, we find that:

- The first three digits refer to the *network identifier* (245)
- The next three digits refer to the *cluster number* (100)
- The final three digits refer to the *member number* (000)

In any given network, there can be 256 clusters and each can have 256 members. The network number in this case is for Stentor Communications in Canada.

The routing of SS7 messages to a destination point code can take different paths, or routes. From the SSP perspective, there are only two ways out from the node, one toward each of its mated STPs. From that point on the STPs decide what routes are appropriate, based on time, resources, and status of the network. From the SSP, various originating and terminating (destination) addressing scenarios are defined as follows:

- If the route chosen is a direct path using a directly connected link (SSP1-STPA), then the route is classified as an *associated route*.
- If the route is not directly connected via links (SSP1-SSP2), the route is classified as a *quasi-route*.
- All routing is controlled by nodal translations, providing flexible and network-specific routing arrangements. This is shown in Fig. 4.8.

SS7 Protocol Stack

The SS7 uses a four-layer protocol stack that equates to the seven-layer OSI model. These protocols provide different services depending on the use of the signaling network. The layers constitute two-part functionality: the bottom three layers are considered the communications transmission of the messages, whereas the upper portion of the stack performs the data processing function. Refer to Fig. 4.9 for the protocols.

The stack shows that the bottom three layers make up the *message transfer part* (MTP), similar to the X.25 network function. At one time SS7 messages were all carried on X.25. Now newer implementations use SS7 protocols, whereas in older networks or third-world countries X.25 may still be the transmission system in use.

The SCCP is used as part of the MTP when necessary to support access into a database, and occasionally for the ISDN user part. This extra link is the equivalent of the transport layer of the OSI model supporting the TCAP.

The SS7 network is an interconnected set of network elements that is used to exchange messages in support of telecommunications functions. The SS7 protocol is designed both

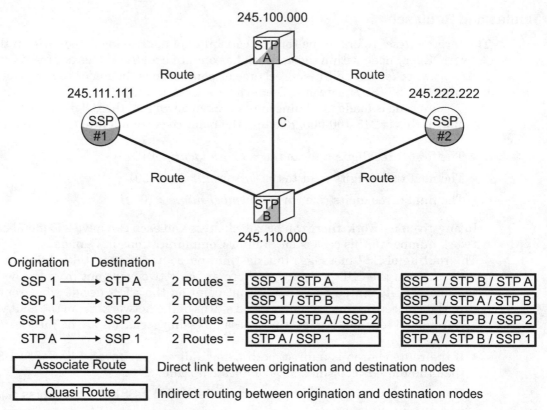

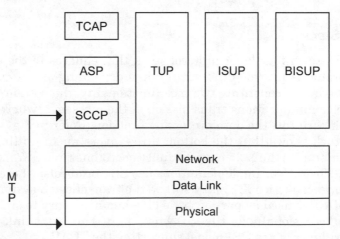

Figure 4.8 Routes and routesets.

Figure 4.9 SS7 protocols.

to facilitate these functions and to maintain the network over which they are provided. Like most modern protocols, the SS7 protocol is layered. Functionally, the SS7 protocol stack can be compared to the Open Systems Interconnection (OSI) reference model. Although OSI is a seven-layer stack designed to perform several communications and transparent functions, the SS7 protocol stack is similar but different.

Like any other stack, the SS7 protocol stack is specifically designed for reliable data transfer between different signaling elements on the network. Guaranteed delivery and the prevention of duplication or lost packets are crucial to network operations. To satisfy differing functions, the stack uses various upper-layer protocols, but consistently uses the same lower layers.

Basic Call Setup with ISUP

The important part of the protocols is the call setup and teardown. This next example is shown in Fig. 4.10. When a call is placed to an out-of-switch number, the originating SSP transmits an ISUP *initial address message* (IAM) to reserve an idle trunk circuit from the originating switch to the destination switch (1a). The IAM includes the originating point code, destination point code, circuit identification code dialed digits, and, optionally, the calling party numbers and name. In this example, the IAM is routed via the home STP of the originating switch to the destination switch (1b). Note that the same signaling links are used for the duration of the call unless a link failure condition forces a switch to use an alternate signaling link.

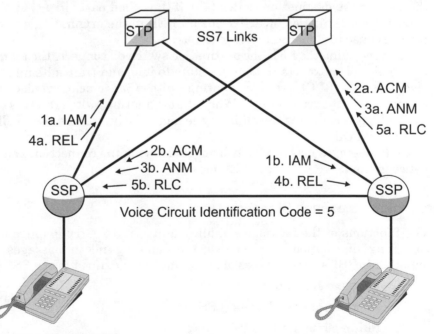

Figure 4.10   Call setup with ISUP.

The destination switch examines the dialed number and determines that it serves the called party, and that the line is available for ringing. The destination switch transmits an ISUP *address complete message* (ACM) to the originating switch (2a) via its home STP to indicate that the remote end of the trunk circuit has been reserved. The destination switch rings the called party's line and sends a ringing tone over the trunk to the originating switch. The STP routes the ACM to the originating switch (2b), which connects the calling party's line to the trunk to complete the voice circuit from the calling party to the called party. The calling party hears the ringing tone on the voice trunk.

In this example, the originating and destination switches are directly connected with trunks. If the originating and destination switches are not directly connected with trunks, the originating switch transmits an IAM to reserve a trunk circuit to an intermediate switch. The intermediate switch sends an ACM to acknowledge the circuit reservation request and then transmits an IAM to reserve a trunk circuit to another switch. This process continues until all trunks required to complete the connection from the originating switch to the destination switch are reserved.

When the called party picks up the phone, the destination switch terminates the ringing tone and transmits an ISUP *answer message* (ANM) to the originating switch via its home STP (3a). The STP routes the ANM to the originating switch (3b), which verifies that the calling party's line is connected to the reserved trunk and, if so, initiates billing.

If the calling party hangs up first, the originating switch sends an ISUP *release message* (REL) to release the trunk circuit between the switches (4a). The STP routes the REL to the destination switch (4b). If the called party hangs up first, or if the line is busy, the destination switch sends an REL to the originating switch indicating the release cause (e.g., normal release or busy).

Upon receiving the REL, the destination switch disconnects the trunk from the called party's line. It next sets the trunk's state to idle, and transmits an ISUP *release complete message* (RLC) to the originating switch (5a) to acknowledge the release of the remote end of the trunk circuit. When the originating switch receives (or generates) the RLC (5b), it terminates the billing cycle and sets the trunk state to idle in preparation for the next call.

ISUP messages may also be transmitted during the connection phase of the call (i.e., between the ISUP ANM and REL messages.

Functions of the Message Signaling Units

The functions of the message signaling units are to carry management information. Signaling information is passed over the signaling link in messages, which are called signal units (SUs). Three types of signal units are defined in the SS7 protocol:

1. Message signal units (MSUs)
2. Link status signal units (LSSUs)
3. Fill-in signal units (FISUs)

The signaling units handle basic error detection and correction. However, without the message transfer part (MTP) the signaling units are useless. They will not have a delivery mechanism without a MTP.

The Fill-In Signal Unit (FISU)

Signal units are transmitted continuously in both directions on any link that is in service. A signaling point that does not have MSUs or LSSUs to send will send FISUs over the link. The FISUs perform the function suggested by their name; they "fill up" the signaling link until there is a need to send real signaling information, as shown in Fig. 4.11. They also facilitate link transmission monitoring and the acknowledgment of other SUs. All three SU types have a set of common fields that are used by MTP Level 2. They are as follows:

- *Flag*. Flags delimit SUs. A flag marks the end of one SU and the start of the next. All transmission on the signaling link is broken up into 8-bit bytes referred to as octets. Signal units on a link are delimited by standard High-level Data Link Control (HDLC) pattern used in most ITU definitions. The flag is defined as the 8-bit pattern "01111110". While in theory, two flags are normally placed between SUs (one to mark the end of the current message and one to mark the start of the next message), in practice a single flag is used for both purposes. This is a slight variation from the HDLC frame format defined by the ITU.

- *Checksum*. The checksum is an 8-bit sum intended to verify that the SU has passed across the link error-free. The checksum is calculated from the transmitted message by the transmitting signaling point and inserted in the message. On receipt, the receiving signaling point recalculates it. If the calculated result differs from the received checksum, the received SU has been corrupted. A retransmission is requested.

- *Length indicator*. The length indicator indicates the number of octets between itself and the checksum. It serves both as a check on the integrity of the SU and as a means of discriminating between different types of SUs at level 2. FISUs have a length indicator of 0; LSSUs have a length indicator of 1 or 2 (currently all LSSUs have a length indicator of 1), and MSUs have a length indicator of greater than 2. According to the protocol, only 6 of the 8 bits in the length indicator field are actually used to store this length; thus the largest value that can be accommodated in the length indicator is 63. For MSUs with more than 63 octets following the length indicator, the value of 63 is used.

FCS		LI	FIB	FSN	BIB	BSN	FLAG
8	2	6	1	7	1	7	8

Figure 4.11   The FISU is used as a keep alive signal.

■ *BSN/BIB FSN/FIB.* These octets hold the backward sequence number (BSN), the backward indicator bit (BIB), the forward sequence numbers (FSN), and the forward indicator bit (FIB). These fields are used to confirm receipt of SUs and to ensure that they are received in the order in which they were transmitted. They are also used to provide flow control. MSUs and LSSUs are assigned a sequence number that is placed in the forward sequence number field of the outgoing SU. This SU is stored by the transmitting signaling point until the receiving signaling point acknowledges it. Because the 7 bits allocated to the forward sequence number can store 128 distinct values, a signaling point is restricted to sending 128 unacknowledged SUs before it must wait for an acknowledgment.

Link Status Signal Units (LSSU)

LSSUs are used to communicate information about the signaling link between the nodes on either end of the link. This information is contained in the status field of the SU as shown in Fig. 4.12. Because independent processors control the two ends of a link, there is a need to provide a means for them to communicate. LSSUs provide the means for performing this function. LSSUs are used primarily to signal the initiation of link alignment, the quality of received signaling traffic, and the status of the processors at either end of the link. Because they are sent only between the signaling points at either end of the link, LSSUs do not require any addressing information.

Message Signaling Units (MSU)

MSUs are the real functions of the SS7 network as seen in Fig. 4.13. All signaling associated with call setup and teardown, database query and response, and SS7 network management takes place, using MSUs. There are several different types of MSUs shown in Table 4.3. The functionality of the message signal unit lies in the actual content of the service information octet and the signaling information field. The service information octet is an 8-bit field that contains three types of information as follows:

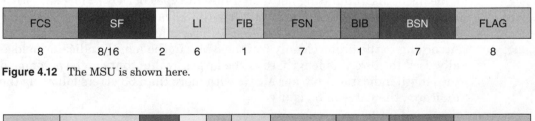

FCS	SF		LI	FIB	FSN	BIB	BSN	FLAG
8	8/16	2	6	1	7	1	7	8

Figure 4.12 The MSU is shown here.

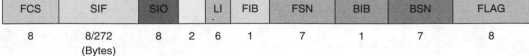

FCS	SIF	SIO		LI	FIB	FSN	BIB	BSN	FLAG
8	8/272 (Bytes)	8	2	6	1	7	1	7	8

Figure 4.13 The link status service unit.

TABLE 4.3   The Different Parts of the MSU

Service Indicator	MTP User
0	Signaling network management message (SNM)
1	Maintenance regular message (MTN)
2	Maintenance special message (MTNS)
3	Signaling connection control part (SCCP)
4	Telephone user part (TUP)
5	ISDN user part (ISUP)
6	Data user part (call and circuit related messages)
7	Data user part (facility regisration/cancellation message)

TABLE 4.4   The Routing Indicator Consists of Seven Octets

Octet Group	Function	Octets
Destination point code (DPC)	Contains the address of the node to which the message is being sent	3
Originating point code (OPC)	Contains the address of message originator	3
Signaling link selection	Distributes load among redundant routes	1

Four bits are used to indicate the type of information contained in the signaling information field. They are referred to as the service indicator.

Two bits are used to indicate whether the message is intended for use in a national or international network. They are generally coded with a value of 2, national network.

The remaining 2 bits are used to identify a message priority, from 0 to 3, with 3 being the highest priority. Message priorities do not control the order in which messages are transmitted; they are only used in cases of signaling network congestion.

The service indicator determines the format of the contents of the signaling information field. The first portion of the signaling information field is identical for all MSUs currently in use. It is referred to as the routing label. Simply stated, the routing label identifies the message originator, the intended destination of the message, and a field referred to as the signaling-link selection field, which is used to distribute message traffic over the set of possible links and routes. The routing label consists of seven octets as shown in Table 4.4.

ANSI versus ITU Standards for the SIO/SIF

ANSI and the International Telecommunications Union (ITU) differ somewhat in the way the fields are used for national and international interpretation. In the use of the SIF the first difference appears. Refer to Fig. 4.14 for the comparison.

The SIF in an MSU contains the routing label and signaling information (e.g., SCCP, TCAP, and ISUP messages). The routing label is comprised of the destination point code (DPC), originating point code (OPC), and signaling link selection (SLS) field. Each signaling point in the SS7 network is uniquely identified by a numeric point code address. An ANSI routing label uses seven octets; an ITU-T routing label uses four octets.

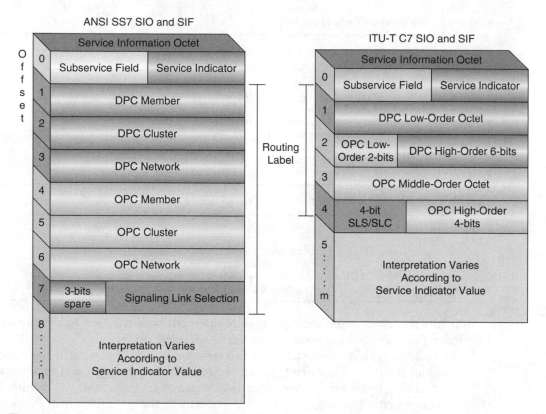

Figure 4.14   Comparing ANSI and ITU standard formats.

ANSI point codes use 24 bits (three octets); ITU-T point codes typically use 14 bits. For this reason, signaling information exchanged between ANSI and ITU-T networks must be routed through a gateway STP, protocol converter, or other signaling point which has both an ANSI and an ITU-T point code. (Note: China uses 24-bit ITU-T point codes that are incompatible with both ANSI and other ITU-T networks). Different implementations of higher level protocols and procedures further complicate interaction between ANSI and ITU-T networks.

An ANSI point code consists of network, cluster, and member octets (e.g., 245-16-0). An octet is an 8-bit byte, which can contain any value between 0 and 255. Telcos with large networks have unique network identifiers while smaller operators are assigned a unique cluster number within networks 1 through 4 (e.g., 1-123-9). Network number 0 is not used; network number 255 is reserved for future use.

ITU-T point codes are pure binary numbers. However, like ANSI point codes, ITU-T point codes may also be given network, cluster, and member designations. For example, the point code 5557 may be stated as 2-182-5 (binary 010 10110110 101). In ITU-T implementations, the SLS is interpreted as the signaling link code in ISUP messages.

Cyclic redundancy check (CRC): The CRC value is used to detect and data transmission errors. This uses a simple algorithm defined by the ITU, standardly accepted worldwide.

SS7 Applications

At this point we switch gears and look at some of the applications that are possible because of SS7 implementations. The use of advanced intelligent network (AIN) features, ISDN features, and wireless capabilities all became a reality because of the functions of SS7 integration. Some of the features are listed here; remember they are formulated and possible because of SS7, although they may be part of other systems or concepts. These include:

- 800/900 services
- Enhancements in 800 services within call centers
- 911 enhancements
- Class features
- Calling card toll fraud prevention
- Credit card approval and authentication
- Software/virtual defined private networks
- Call tracing
- Call blocking

It is with the SS7 protocols and signaling systems that all these features and functions are possible. Many of the features are possible through the stored-program CO switches. However, when we activate features that work across the network (or world), SS7 facilitates the delivery mechanism. Other systems will be introduced in the future to implement more intelligence in the networks, such as the advanced intelligent networks (AINs) but they will require the infrastructure of the signaling systems to enact and carry their messages.

Local Number Portability (LNP)

Prior to SS7, 800 numbers were not portable. If a company moved, they had to get a new number. The Telecom Act of 1996 mandated that personal phone numbers should also be portable. Telcos are required to support the porting of telephone numbers within a geographic area, increasing the demands on the SS7 network.

Seamless Roaming

Seamless roaming in cellular networks uses SS7 to share subscriber information from Home Location Registers (HLRs) so users do not have to register their cell phones with other providers when they travel. All cellular providers can access each other's databases via SS7, enabling their subscribers to roam seamlessly from one network to another, while still allowing the home network to track and bill for all calls.

SS7 over IP (S7IP)

The sigtran protocols specify the means by which SS7 messages can be reliably transported over IP networks. This is architecturally based on two components:

- A common transport protocol for the SS7 protocol layer being carried, and
- An adaptation module to emulate lower layers of the protocol.

Suppose the MTP Level 3 is being used. The sigtran protocols provide the equivalent functionality of MTP Level 2. On the other hand, if ISUP or SCCP are being used, sigtran provide both MTP Level 2 and 3 functionality. If using TCAP, sigtran provides the functionality of SCCP (connectionless classes) and MTP Levels 2 and 3.

The sigtran protocols provide all functionality needed to support SS7 signaling over IP networks, including:

- In-sequence delivery of signaling messages within a single control stream
- Identification of the originating and terminating signaling points
- Flow control
- Identification of voice circuits
- Error detection, retransmission and other error correcting procedures
- Recovery from outages
- Congestion avoidance on the Internet
- Security capabilities and future needs

The limitations required by narrowband SS7 networks, such segmenting and reassembling messages greater than 272 bytes do not apply to IP networks and therefore not supported by the sigtran protocols.

Performance Considerations for SS7 over IP

SS7 messages transported over IP networks must meet the rigid performance requirements imposed by both ITU SS7/C7 standards and, of course, user expectations. The ITU standard specifies that the end-to-end call setup delay cannot exceed 20 to 30 seconds after the ISUP *initial address message* (IAM) is transmitted. However, the user community demands faster response times. For this reason, VoIP networks must be engineered to satisfy user expectations and ITU standards for performance.

Stream Control Transmission Protocol

To reliably transport SS7 messages over IP networks, the IETF sigtran working group devised the Stream Control Transmission Protocol (SCTP). SCTP allows the reliable transfer of signaling messages between signaling endpoints in an IP network.

To establish an association between SCTP endpoints, one endpoint provides the other endpoint with a list of its transport addresses (multiple IP addresses in combination with an SCTP port). These transport addresses identify the addresses which will send and receive SCTP packets.

IP signaling traffic is usually composed of many independent message sequences between many different signaling endpoints. SCTP allows signaling messages to be independently ordered within multiple streams to ensure in-sequence delivery between associated endpoints. By transferring independent message sequences in separate SCTP streams, it is less likely that the retransmission of a lost message will affect the timely delivery of other messages in unrelated sequences (called head-of-line blocking). TCP/IP does enforce head-of-line blocking, therefore the sigtran Working Group recommends SCTP rather than TCP/IP for the transmission of signaling messages over IP networks.

SCTP provides:

- Acknowledged error-free non-duplicated transfer of signaling information
- In-sequence delivery of messages within multiple streams, with an option for order-of-arrival delivery of individual messages
- Bundling of multiple messages into a single SCTP packet (optional)
- Data fragmentation as required
- Congestion avoidance behavior and resistance to flooding (denial-of-service) and masquerade attacks

To meet stringent SS7 signaling reliability and performance requirements for carrier-grade networks, VoIP network operators ensure that there is no single point of failure in the end-to-end network architecture between an SS7 node and a media gateway controller. To achieve carrier-grade reliability in IP networks, links in a linkset are typically distributed amongst multiple signaling gateways, media gateway controllers are distributed over multiple CPU hosts, and redundant IP network paths are provisioned to ensure survivability of SCTP associations between SCTP endpoints.

Transporting MTP over IP

For MTP messages transported over SS7 or IP networks, the following requirements are specified by the International Telecommunication Union:

- MTP Level 3 peer-to-peer procedures require a response time within 0.5 to 1.2 seconds.
- No more than 1 in 2^7 messages will be lost due to transport failure.

- No more than 1 in 2^7 messages will be delivered out of sequence (including duplicated messages) due to transport failure.

- No more than 1 in 2^7 messages will contain an error that is undetected by the transport protocol or 1 in 2^7 for ANSI (American National Standard Institute) specifications.

- Availability of any signaling route set is 99.9998% or better.

- Message length (payload accepted) is 272 bytes for narrowband SS7 and 4091 bytes for broadband SS7.

To achieve the functional and performance requirements for MTP, the IETF sigtran Working Group has recommended three new protocols: M2UA, M2PA, and M3UA.

MTP2 User Adaptation Layer (M2UA)

M2UA transports SS7 MTP Level 2 user signaling messages over IP using the Stream Control Transmission Protocol (SCTP). The M2UA protocol layer provides the equivalent set of services to its users as MTP Level 2 provides to MTP Level 3. M2UA is used between the Signaling Gateway and Media Gateway Controller in VoIP networks. The signaling gateway receives SS7 messages over an MTP Level 1 and Level 2 interface from a signaling end point (SCP or SSP) or signal transfer point (STP) in the public switched telephone networks. The signaling gateway terminates the SS7 link at MTP Level 2 and transports MTP Level 3 and above to a Media Gateway Controller or other IP endpoint using M2UA over SCTP/IP.

MTP2 User Peer-to-Peer Adaptation Layer (M2PA)

Like M2UA, M2PA transports SS7 MTP Level 2 user part signaling messages over IP using the Stream Control Transmission Protocol (SCTP). Unlike M2UA, M2PA supports full MTP Level 3 message handling and network management between any two SS7 nodes communicating over an IP network. IP signaling points function as traditional SS7 nodes using the IP network instead of the SS7 network. Each switched circuit or IP signaling point has an SS7 point code. The M2PA protocol layer provides the same set of services as MTP Level 2 provides to MTP Level 3.

Signaling points may use M2PA over IP or MTP Level 2 over standard SS7 links to send and receive MTP Level 3 messages. M2PA facilitates the integration of SS7 and IP networks by enabling nodes in switched circuit networks to access IP telephony databases and other nodes in IP networks using SS7 signaling. Conversely, M2PA allows IP telephony applications to access SS7 databases, such as local number portability, calling card, freephone, and mobile subscriber databases. In addition, using M2UA over IP may result in cost advantages if traditional SS7 links are replaced by IP connections. M2PA and M2UA differ in the following ways as shown in Table 4.5.

TABLE 4.5   Comparing M2PA and M2UA Differences

M2PA	M2UA
The signaling gateway is an SS7 node with a point code.	The signaling gateway is not an SS7 node and has no point code.
SS7 links connect between the signaling gateway and IP signaling points.	Signaling gateway and media gateway controller connections are not SS7 links.
Signaling gateways can have upper SS7 layers, such as SCCP.	Signaling gateway has no upper SS7 layers as it has no MTP Level 3.
MTP Level 3 used for management procedures.	Uses M2UA management procedures.
IP signaling points processes MTP Level 3 MTP Level 2 primitives.	The media gateway controller transports MTP Level 3 and MTP Level 2 primitives to the signaling gateway's MTP Level 2 for processing.

MTP Level 3 User Adaptation Layer (M3UA)

M3UA transports MTP Level 3 user part signaling messages (e.g., ISUP, TUP, and SCCP) over IP using the Stream Control Transmission Protocol (SCTP). TCAP or RANAP messages, as SCCP user protocols, may be carried by SCCP using M3UA or by a different sigtran protocol called SUA.

M3UA is used between a signaling gateway and a media gateway controller or IP telephony database. The signaling gateway receives SS7 signaling using MTP over a standard SS7 link. The signaling gateway terminates MTP-2 and MTP-3 and delivers ISUP, TUP, SCCP and/or any other MTP-3 user messages, as well as certain MTP network management events, over SCTP associations to media gateway controllers or IP telephony databases.

If an IP endpoint is connected to more than one signaling gateway, the M3UA layer at the IP endpoint maintains the status of configured SS7 destinations and route messages according to the availability and congestion status of the routes to these destinations via each signaling gateway.

M3UA does not impose a 272-octet signaling information field (SIF) length limit as specified by SS7 MTP Level 2. Larger information blocks can be accommodated directly by M3UA/SCTP without the need for segmentation/reassembly as specified by the SCCP and ISUP standards. A signaling gateway will enforce the maximum 272-octet limit when connected to a SS7 network that does not support the transfer of larger information blocks to the destination.

Transporting SCCP over IP

SUA (SCCP User Adaptation Layer) is transports SS7 SCCP user part signaling messages (e.g., TCAP and RANAP) over IP using SCTP. SUA is used between a signaling gateway and an IP signaling endpoint and between IP signaling endpoints. SUA supports both SCCP unordered and in-sequence connectionless services and bidirectional connection-oriented services with or without flow control and detection of message loss and out-of-sequence errors.

For connectionless transport, SCCP and SUA interface at the signaling gateway. The SCCP user appears to be located at the signaling gateway. SS7 messages are routed to the signaling gateway based on point code and SCCP subsystem number.

The signaling gateway then routes SCCP messages to the remote IP endpoint. If redundant IP endpoints exist, the signaling gateway(s) can load share amongst active IP endpoints using a round-robin approach. The signaling gateway may also perform Global Title Translation (GTT) to determine the destination of an SCCP message. The signaling gateway routes on global title, i.e., digits present in the incoming message, such as called party number or mobile subscriber identification number.

For connection-oriented transport, SCCP and SUA interface at the signaling gateway to associate the two connection sections needed for connection-oriented data transfer between an SS7 signaling endpoint and an IP endpoint. Messages are routed by the signaling gateway to SS7 signaling points based on the destination point code (in the MTP-3 address field) and to IP endpoints based on IP address (in the SCTP header).

SUA can also be used to transport SCCP user information between IP endpoints directly rather than via the signaling gateway. The signaling gateway is needed only to enable interoperability with SS7 signaling in the switched circuit network.

Questions

1. The older signaling system (SS6) was created in 1960s.   T/F
2. SS7 was first deployed in the industry in what year?
   a. 1980
   b. 1982
   c. 1983
   d. 1989
3. The preferred form of associated signaling is_____.
   a. Nonassociated
   b. Associated
   c. Fully associated
   d. Quasi associated
4. The telephone carriers were still installing SS6 through_____.
   a. 1983
   b. 1985
   c. 1980
   d. 1973

5. The Central Office is now called the_____.

   a. STP

   b. SSP

   c. SCP

   d. TCAP

6. SS7 uses a _____ layer protocol stack.

   a. 7

   b. 4

   c. 3

   d. 5

   e. 6

7. Out of band signaling means that the signals are carried inside the voice channel. T/F

8. Originally, the carriers used frequencies that carried signaling information using_____.

   a. 300–3300

   b. 100–400

   c. 3600–3900

   d. 3500–3700

9. TCAP is the application support for the SS7 networks. T/F

10. The location where the databases are kept is called:

    a. STP

    b. Database engines

    c. SCP

    d. SSP

11. The ISUP has all the components necessary to handle call setup and teardown. T/F

12. The protocols used to carry the message are called:

    a. X.25

    b. IP

    c. TCP

    d. MTP

13. The original SS6 used _____ different signaling units.

14. The signaling units used in the SS6 networks were made up of _____ bits.

15. SS7 circuits run on links that operate at:

    a. 1.544 Mbps

    b. 56 Kbps

    c. 66 Kbps

    d. 4.8 Kbps

16. The B and D links are the same functionally.   T/F

17. The routeset and the _____ are synonymous.

    a. Route

    b. Linkset

    c. Point code

    d. Database

18. STPs are usually installed in _____.

    a. The middle of the network

    b. Mated pairs

    c. Stand alone mode

    d. Half duplex

19. The _____ is used with the MTP when a translation is needed from a database.

    a. STP

    b. SCP

    c. SNMP

    d. SCCP

20. Point codes are made up of _____ digits.

    a. 12

    b. 32

    c. 16

    d. 9

Switching Systems

After reading this chapter and completing the questions, you will be able to:

- Describe the switching components
- Articulate the hierarchy of the network
- Explain the function of a PBX
- Discuss the differences between the market providers
- Describe the basic features and functions of a PBX
- Describe a key telephone system (KTS)
- Compare the differences of a PBX and KTS

Recall in Chapter 1, we discussed a hierarchy of dial tone services. Also discussed was the network both pre- and post-1984 network hierarchies based on the legal breakup of the AT&T from its subsidiary telephone companies.

The discussions brought an idea of always on communications through the use of the telephone company services of dial tone. The dial tone is provided by a switching system known as the central office. This central office is central to the community, normally placed in the center of an area to be served. While applying this central concept, the providers built very expensive buildings and placed the telephone systems here. These systems are called *switches*. Switches define the way a call arrives at the Bell Central Office and gets processed through to a distant end. A switching system is the equipment that receives the initial call, makes a decision on forwarding the call to a next location (this is a very fast process of connecting line in to a line out) whether it is next door or across the country. To do this, the systems use the North American numbering plan discussed in Chapter 1. The 10 digits represent the means of looking up the best routing to get to the dialed number. Because there are no real routing decisions except call in to call out, the switching occurs very fast. Switching occurs at layer two

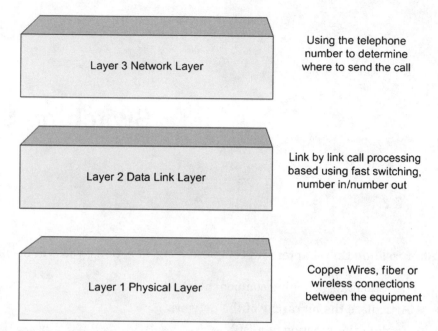

Figure 5.1 Comparing the various levels of OSI to the dial process.

of the OSI model, but the dialing plan uses layer three of OSI. Refer to Fig. 5.1 for an approximation of what occurs at the various layers of the model when dealing with the telephone call. This is the example we used in Chapter 2, the OSI model.

Most of the process revolves around the network put in place over the past 130+ years. The telecommunications providers were quick to build a robust and recoverable network to support life-line services. To switch a call across the network, a series of interconnections are used as shown in Fig. 5.2. Regardless of where the call is destined to go, it will traverse one of many possible routes. But these are network calls being switched on telephone company backbones. Moreover, the handsets connected to the network are using a central office switching system to handle all call processing. This is the norm when dealing with basic dial tone services. But what if an organization has hundreds or thousands of employees in a location (or spread across the country)? That is where a PBX comes into play. An organization can replace the single line telephones with an equivalent of the central office.

Let's start off with a quick definition of a private branch exchange.

Private: It belongs to an organization or individual; not a public service.

Branch exchange: The telephone company hierarchy listed the class 5 office as the central office or the branch exchange. This is where the dial tone is provided. So the branch (think of it as the limbs of the network hierarchy tree) exchange offers dial tone to the end user.

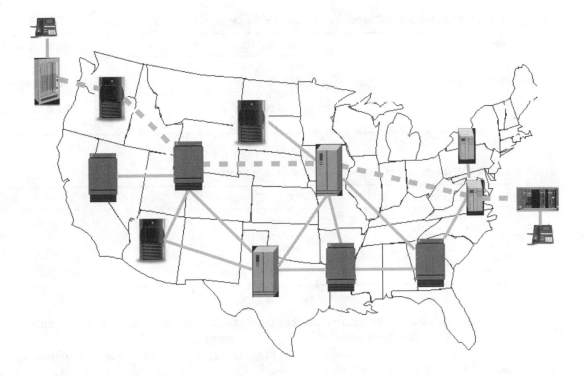

Figure 5.2 The call procedure across a network.

A traditional private branch exchange (PBX) is the typical telephone system for large organizations. It provides internal dial tone for a private organization to make and receive a large volume of calls. In this environment, an organization that is served by a central office dial tone from the local exchange company might need the capacity of high-volume calling and handling services. Clearly, a traditional single-line telephone set with a dial-tone line for each user will work. But, it will only just work. It will not satisfy the needs of the organization.

Moreover, it will be expensive. Assume that a dial-tone line costs $30 per month. If the organization has a multitude of users, the cost per month will be significant. Table 5.1 highlights some of the typical costs associated with basic dial-tone service for various numbers of employees. These numbers are only representative, but they should get our point across. The table reflects the basic monthly cost and the annualized cost of renting a dial-tone line from the local carrier.

You can clearly see from these numbers that the use of a basic dial-tone service can get quite expensive. As a matter of fact, many organizations say that telecommunication is the most expensive item in their corporate expense registers, second only to personnel costs. This is both good and bad. It is good that organizations are depending on telecommunications more, as opposed to more expensive alternatives (such as travel,

TABLE 5.1   Summary of Dial-tone Line Costs for the Organization

Number of Users	Monthly Cost at $30.00	Annualized Cost
100	$3,000	$36,000
500	$15,000	$180,000
1,000	$30,000	$360,000
2,500	$75,000	$900,000
10,000	$300,000	$3,600,000

TABLE 5.2   Summary of Single-line Set Equipment Costs

Number of Users	Cost of Equipment
100	$6,000
500	$30,000
1,000	$60,000
2,500	$150,000
10,000	$600,000

personnel, and other sales and marketing costs). Pound for pound, telecommunications still produce a greater return on every dollar spent.

Back to the point; the costs can be staggering to a financial or senior managerial person in an organization. The dial-tone line costs listed in Table 5.1 give the user only dial-tone access. This is a full-time dedicated access line for two-way service for every single user. If you add just a single-line telephone set for each of these users, then some capital costs are associated with the ownership of these lines. Table 5.2 shows the costs of a single-line set for every user, at a base price of $60 per single-line telephone set. These are, again, basic assumptions on the purchase of these sets; one could do better.

Again, you can see that the equipment costs can mount quickly. But what is wrong with this picture? Well for starters, the single-line set limits what the user can do with the basic dial-tone service. Also, the single-line set does not allow for intercommunication between the users within the organization, unless they tie up their dial-tone lines as follows:

- Grab the dial tone by going off-hook.

- When dial tone is received, dial the digits (seven or ten) of the desired internal party.

- When the ring is generated and the party answers, conduct a conversation.

But this completely ties up two outside lines for the two parties to converse. If a customer tries to call either of these two parties, the customer will get a busy tone. That is, unless the call hunts to some other number. If the call does hunt, then a third outside

---

*Many parts of North America now must dial 10 digits for local calls because of the addition of new area codes in their operating area. This overlay of area codes may cause some concern for many of the PBX owners because they have to program the new area code without the use of 1+ dialing, whereas other area codes require the 1+.

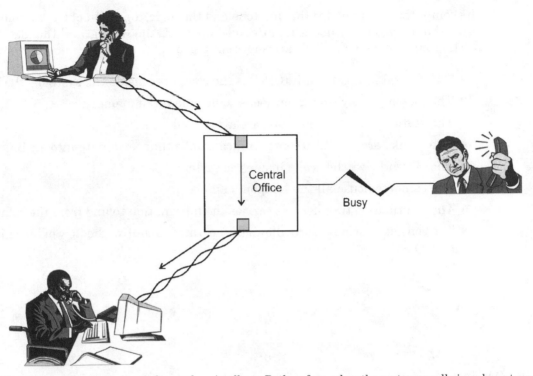

Figure 5.3 The single line is busy when A talks to B; therefore, when the customer calls in, a busy tone is received.

line is occupied, while a message is taken at the rollover line. Customers can be denied access, and can get frustrated. All of this occurs while the two parties could be talking to each other in the next office as shown in Fig. 5.3. Note that however long the wires are running back to the central office where the dial tone is provided; the call uses twice the resources to get the two conversationalists together. Clearly, this is not an optimal use of telecommunications services.

It should be obvious from the preceding discussion that larger organizations require the larger capacity and capability of a PBX. These systems have names that come in many flavors, such as private automated branch exchange (PABX).

The generic term PBX is a private (customer owned and operated) branch exchange (like a central office, it switches and routes calls internally or externally and provides a dial tone to the internal users). The PBX marketplace is inundated with acronyms and features. However, they all do similar things; they primarily process voice calls for the organization. These devices are computer systems that just happen to do voice. Now they also do other things, such as providing data communications and data access.

On average, the all-digital PBX will cost approximately $750 to $1000 per station. A station is the end-user device, and the figure includes the cost of all the associated hardware to support that telephone set. Included in this generic price is the card inside the computer that provides the dial tone and the logic, a portion of the common equipment that serves many users, and the telephone set, the wiring, and the installation. The components of the PBX are shown in Fig. 5.4.

- The central processor unit (CPU) is the computer inside the system—the brains.
- The memory—any computer needs some amount of memory.
- The stations, or telephone sets, are also called lines.
- The trunks are the Telco central office trunks that terminate into a PBX.
- The network switches calls inside the system.
- The cabinets house all the components.
- The information transfer bus carries the information to and from the computer.
- The console or switchboard allows the operator to control the flow of incoming calls, and so on.

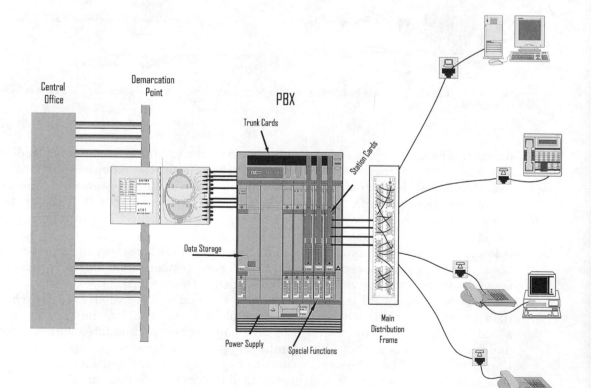

Figure 5.4   The components of a PBX.

Figure 5.5 A PBX.

- The common logic and power cards facilitate the system's operation.
- The battery backup insures against power failures.
- The wiring infrastructure connects it all.

The PBX is a stored-program, common-controlled device. As a telephone system, it is a resource-sharing system that provides the ability to access a local dial tone and outside trunks to the end user. This stored-program controlled system today is all-digital architecture. An actual picture of a PBX is shown in Fig. 5.5.

Further, all of the wires come to a central point at the main distribution frame (MDF) where blocks are used to terminate the wires in a centralized location. The MDF is shown in Fig. 5.6.

Additionally, the use of the main distribution frames internally may be in a telephone closet where patch panels are used to orchestrate the moves, adds, and changes to the telephone wires running out to the desktop user. The patch panel can be used for voice, data, or LAN connections, but it is best to keep them separate. Figure 5.7 is a sample of a patch panel in a closet.

Analog Systems

The analog system used analog components to handle the call setup and tear-down for the entire system. A voice call is introduced into the system in much the same way that

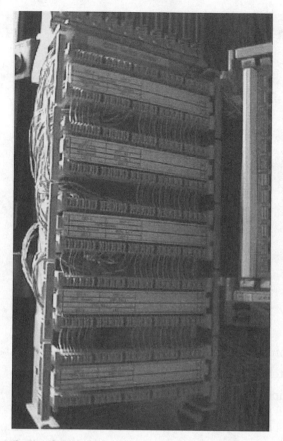

Figure 5.6 The main distribution frame.

a business or residential user's input is introduced to the telephone company network. As the user generates a call, the telephone handset is picked up from the cradle. At this point, an input/output (I/O) request signal is sent to the main architecture of the PBX, which is usually a computer. Once the signal is sent to the common control, the system then returns a dial tone. The user then dials the digits for the party desired. This dialing sequence is done in-band on the wires in the talk path of the caller. The digits, either rotary (pulse) or tone (DTMF), are sent down the wires to the telephone system.

From there, the telephone system kicks in and generates a request through the architecture to a trunk card. The trunk card serves as the interface to the central office (CO) to request an outside dial tone. The PBX, upon receiving dial tone at the trunk card interface, then regenerates the pulses or the tones across the line to the central office. The CO processes these digits in the same manner that it processes individual line requests from a residential user. From the telephone company's perspective, this is the easiest way to process the information.

Figure 5.7   A patch panel in a closet.

Digital PBX

All newer systems are digital. As computer architecture, the system processes the information in its digital format. A digital coder/decoder (codec) in the telephone set converts the analog voice conversation into a digital format. The digital signals are then carried down the wires to the PBX heart (the CPU) for processing. If a call must go outside to the world, the PBX has to determine the best route to process the call onto. In the case where the call will be traversing the telephone company's central office links on an analog circuit, the PBX must format the information for the outside link. In this case, a digital-to-analog conversion will take place. Even if the call is to traverse a digital link to the world, the PBX might have to go through a digital-to-digital conversion. This is because the digital signal at the PBX interface is a unipolar signal, whereas the signal to the telephone company is a bipolar signal as shown in Fig. 5.8.

The PBX market has been plagued by soft sales. This is a function of the recession, the rightsizing and downsizing of corporate America, and the overall unsettled market from a technological standpoint. End users are uncertain of what to buy and when on the market curve they should buy. Therefore, the vendors resort to major markdowns, and they often throw in several other goodies. The buyer's market prevails in the PBX industry. As a result, significant discounts can be obtained if you work with the vendor and understand the product being offered. Many vendors will also compete severely with their distributors. Remember, this is a buyer's market. Table 5.3 is a summary of how the costs would look for the acquisition of a digital PBX, the basic telephone system for an organization. This table reflects three important pieces of the billing

TABLE 5.3   Summary of Costs for a 1000-Line Digital PBX

Item	Price
Cost of hardware, software, training, all telephone sets, and interfaces with installation of the hardware	$350,000
Cost of wiring and installation for the building infrastructure	$350,000
Markup and profit	$300,000
Total	$1,000,000

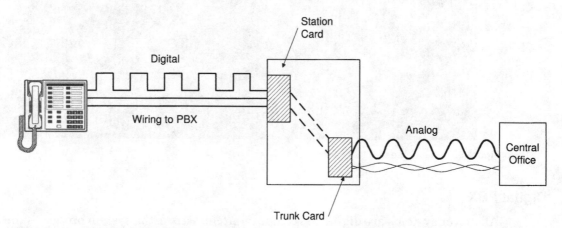

Figure 5.8   The digital signal from the PBX is converted to analog to the Telco.

arrangements. It would not be unethical to see how the vendors price out their systems against this model. In Table 5.3, we use an average price per port of $1000. The costs associated with a 1000-user system would, therefore, be as they appear in Table 5.3.

Another item of note is the third line item, that being profit. We always want our vendors to survive for another day, no two ways about that. However, we do not want to pay a 30 percent total markup on a system for profit. In actuality, the margin is 37 percent, and we will see why later. This is unheard of. So, the discounts that might be passed along from the vendor might well be from the profit picture. Suppose that the vendor offers a discount of 20 percent off the top of the price. The total price is $1,000,000 and the discount is 20 percent, so you can expect to pay $800,000. That should make you feel pretty good, to get a $200,000 discount off the top of your system. But, wait! What if the vendor came back and said that the total discount is only $70,000? Where did we go wrong? Well, the issue is where the numbers are being calculated. The vendor discounted the 20 percent from the top of the system cost ($350,000 × 0.2 = $70,000). Now, you are paying around $930,000 total for the system, installed. That is not exactly what you thought you were getting a discount on. The vendor will explain that the cost of the wiring cannot be discounted because they use a subcontractor and have to pay this third party for the installation. True, but the vendor also marks up the cost of the wiring and installation. That $350,000 fee to install and wire the system is probably only a $280,000 to $300,000 charge from the subcontractor. So, the manufacturer or distributor is getting a piece of the pie for the installation too.

Yes, this is true. Regardless of how we slice and dice the numbers, this is still a very lucrative sale for the vendor. With a $50,000 to $70,000 markup on the wiring (which is conservative), a $300,000 profit margin, and the remaining cost of the system ($280,000), you can imagine just how much the vendor is making on this system, can't you? Well, now look at the margins based on this new evidence (see Table 5.4).

Can you see anything wrong with this picture? Even though the vendor has given a 20 percent discount to you, and you feel so special for negotiating such a difficult deal for the vendor, and a great one for the organization, the overall margin of profit that the vendor has achieved is still 37 percent. This still leaves a lot of room for negotiation before the deal is done. If you consider that there is still room to cut the cost in the profit margin, the profits on the subcontracted piece of the wiring, and the overall system cost, then the dealing has only begun. In many cases, the ability to subcontract the wiring (for example) might produce more productive and competitive results. In this case, many organizations will act as the general contractor for the overall telephone system and then contract for the wiring separately from the telephones. An example of the wiring costs might look like the numbers shown in Table 5.5, where a separate contract is issued for the installation of a four-pair cable installed at 1000 user locations, the horizontal wiring between the telephone closets and the main distribution frame, and any ancillary cabling needed to implement the system.

Keep in mind that these figures are generic, and will require separate bids from various installation companies. If, however, you now consider this figure, and recognize that the wiring contractor has already built in the necessary profit margins to make money on the installation, then the PBX price now has a different perspective. The margin for

TABLE 5.4   Summary of New Profit Margins with a 20 Percent Discount on the System Cost

Item	Original Cost	New Cost	Profit	Margin
PBX system	$350,000	$280,000		
Wiring and installation	$350,000	$350,000	$70,000.00*	20
Margin and profit	$300,000	$300,000	$300,000.00	30
Total	$1,000,000	$930,000	$370,000.00	37

*Excludes the wiring contractor's profit margin for the installation and wiring

TABLE 5.5   Summary of Wiring Costs

Cost per User Location	Extended Price
Cost of wiring a 1000-user system at $250–280	$250,000–280,000
Cost for PBX manufacturer at $350	$350,000
Difference	$70,000–100,000

the hardware, installation, and warrantee on the PBX is now subject to serious negotiation (see Table 5.6).

As you can now imagine, the cost for the telephone system is $280,000 with a profit margin of $300,000 (over 100 percent markup). No vendor will ever approach this structure; these are comparative pricing scenarios. However, if you consider that a 30 percent markup is what the vendor is entitled to, the following summary gives us a whole new structure to deal from. The intent is not to jeopardize the stability and profitability of the supplier, but to maximize the comfort between the two parties. This case will obviously consume a lot of time and effort. But, the overall results are significant (see Table 5.7).

Clearly the price has changed significantly. The system is now being considered at approximately $644 per user instead of $1000. This accounts for a $356,000 discount overall. This is the way you can look at using the system pricing, rather than just accepting standard pricing. The pricing can vary quite a bit from the original proposal.

Central Office Centrex

An alternative to the purchase of a telephone system is called Centrex. Centrex is a service offered by the incumbent local exchange carrier (ILEC), the CATV companies, and CLECs. They bundle their services at a price that is very competitive with buying the pieces individually. In many cases, the CLECs have service offerings that add features not typically available from the ILEC. The consumer benefits from this one. Centrex stands for central exchange, or PBX services provided from the central office (exchange). The LECs, either the Bell Telephone Companies or the independent telephone companies, all

TABLE 5.6   Summary of New Cost Structure and Margins

Item	Cost	Percent Margin
PBX	$280,000	
Markup	$300,000	
Subtotal	$580,000	115
Wiring (as a separate contract and separate margins)	$280,000	15
Total	$860,000	

TABLE 5.7   Final Configuration of System Pricing

Item	Original Pricing	Revised Pricing	Difference
PBX	$350,000	$280,000	$70,000
PBX (markup at 30 percent of contract)	$300,000	$84,000	$216,000
Wiring	$350,000	$280,000	$70,000
Totals	$1,000,000	$644,000	$356,000
Percentage			35.6 percent

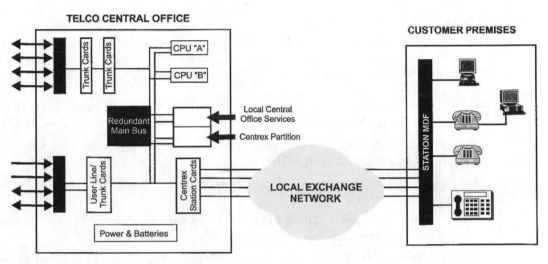

Figure 5.9 Central office Centrex components.

have a service offering. The Centrex service is a partition inside the CO, which provides telephone service on a private basis to businesses (see Fig. 5.9).

Centrex is usually rented on a line-by-line basis, month to month. Some companies have long-term agreements to hold down costs, but charging a monthly rate is more prevalent. Costs per line can range from $20 to $25 a month, depending on the company and the serving Telco. However, with very large organizations, a long-term contract can be negotiated with the provider. This will result in costs that are in the range of $10 to $12 per month for a Centrex line. The overall result is a monthly savings of $10 to $15 per month per line. With a 1000-line system, this can be a significant savings. An example is the 1000-line system that we were using in the PBX comparison. Here, a system can cost approximately $12,000 per month on a long-term agreement. The $12,000 is for the dial tone and features; anything else is an extra. The user must still buy the station equipment (telephone sets).

The components of a Centrex are as follows:

- Central office, which is the serving office
- CPU or computer
- Station cards
- Switching network
- Line cards
- Memory
- Common logic and power cards
- Bus to carry information to and from the CPU

Centrex Service

The primary suppliers, as already stated, are the LECs. They provide the service as part of the central office function. Centrex service is available in 34 countries. The list of Centrex providers includes:

- *Bell Operating Companies:* The four regional Bell Operating Companies (SBC/AT&T, Qwest, Bell South, and Verizon/MCI) are the largest sellers of Centrex (ILECs).
- *Independent operating companies:* These are such companies as Contel GTE, Centel, and Commonwealth (ILECs).
- *Resellers of Centrex service:* Many arrangements have been made with resellers around the country.
- *Bell authorized agents:* These are authorized agents of the ILEC, but are not employees of the company.
- *CATV companies:* These companies represent as much as 15 percent of the dial tone in the industry now.
- *CLECs:* The few that still remain.
- *Electric companies:* A few provide dial tone and thus, Centrex.

Peripheral Devices

The list of peripheral devices for the key systems, PBX, and Centrex markets is virtually unlimited. The devices range from items as simple as an external bell to very sophisticated management systems. The pieces are too numerous to list here (and change too frequently), but a lot of negotiating room still exists for any component you might need.

Some of the devices that might appear in the picture are as follows:

- Automatic call distribution
- Voice mail/answering machines
- Automated attendant
- Call detail recording
- Modem pools
- Multiplexers
- Head sets (wired and wireless)
- Display sets (telephones)
- Paging systems
- Least cost call routing
- Network management systems
- Design tools

Key Telephone Systems

Another form of equipment is used in a smaller environment. If the user office is small or if a branch office is involved, a key telephone system is used. A key telephone system is another form of a resource-sharing device that is used to reduce the number of outside telephone lines and provide access to many end users.

The equipment selection depends on the size of the organization and the need for communications connectivity. Many small branch offices, small businesses, home businesses, and other such organizations require only a limited amount of telephone sets and can get by with a key telephone system. Figure 5.10 illustrates a key telephone system. This type of system usually consists of a predetermined number of telephone sets to outside lines. Note the reference to lines in this example; the telephone company sees the system as an end-user connection in much the same way as a single-line telephone set. Therefore, the customer gets by with the use of lines instead of trunks. The nomenclature for a key system is normally outlined in the number of lines and the number of sets; for example, 1648 equates to 16 outside telephone lines and 48 telephone sets that comprise the system. These are maximums on the systems; smaller amounts can be used where appropriate.

A key telephone system is composed of the following pieces:

- The key service unit (KSU) is the heart and brain of the telephone system.
- Line cards are the interfaces to the telephone company lines. They effectively provide the off-hook and on-hook signals to the central office in lieu of the individual telephone sets.

25 Pair Amphenol Connector

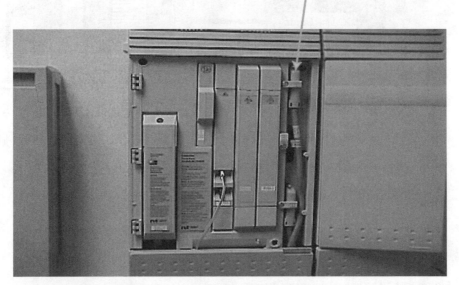

Figure 5.10   A key telephone system.

- Station cards are the cards that control the intelligence and interface to the end user's key system. The station card interfaces with the end user and the line cards for the access control of the system.

- Intercom cards are not always required. Some systems use an intercommunication card for internal connectivity, whereas others have this feature built into their functionality on the backplane of the system.

- Telephone sets are variable-user interfaces, whether they are single-line or digital multiline sets. The telephone set controls the intelligence that a user is allowed to access within the system.

- Power supplies and logic cards.

- The wiring infrastructure that is used to connect the sets to the KSU central processor unit (CPU), the brains of the system.

Figure 5.11 represents several of these different pieces that might be included. For example, we see that the telephone company has brought in central office lines and terminated them in either an RJ-21X or an RJ-11. From there, the graph shows a 66 block, sitting side by side with the RJ-21X, where a straight cross-connect arrangement

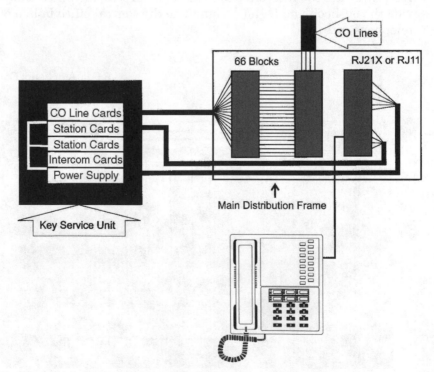

Figure 5.11 The key telephone system components.

is taking place. A fanned-out, 25-pair cable is punched down on the left side of the 66 block. We can refer to this 66 block as the vendor block, whereas the RJ-21X is the Telco block. The cable is run from the vendor block with the fanned-out, 25-pair cable into the key service unit, or the intelligence of the key telephone system. Here we might use an amphenol connector, a 25-pair pre-wired connector, for termination in the key service unit. The amphenol is also shown in Fig. 5.10 inside the key systems on the right side of the picture. This merely simplifies the process of providing the connectivity.

Looking at the other pieces, the system has central office line cards as opposed to the trunk cards that would appear on a PBX. Station cards are then installed, which provide the intelligence to the individual telephones that are installed within the system. Intercom cards enable intercommunication to prevent the problem that was mentioned earlier in the PBX section. One does not want to tie up all of the outside lines for two parties to be able to talk to each other internally. Therefore, the intercommunications device, or intercom, provides for the station-to-station talk path. Many key systems have an unlimited number of intercoms, whereas others have a very specific number of intercom paths available. This depends on the manufacturer.

From the key service unit, we see two lines drawn over to another 66 block that would run in a separate telephone closet. We would call these lines horizontal runs. The horizontal run connects the key service unit to the telephone closet, where the 66 block is a termination point. The purpose of this horizontal run is to bundle cable pairs together using 25, 50, or 100 pairs of wire to the telephone closet.

On termination on the 66 block, a separate station drop is run to the individual desktop device. At this particular point, the station drop is used on the basis of a two-, three-, or four-pair wiring system. Each key system requires a different number of wires to the telephone set. For the key telephone systems available on the market today, a single-pair cable system can be used. However, it would be imprudent for the telecommunications personnel to install only one pair of wires to every desktop. The reason is probably obvious; it would leave the possibility of being short of cables for the future. *(Authors' Note*: Even in today's environment with a single cable serving up voice, data and video, the need for added cables will always be there.)

Once a telephone set is installed on that station drop using a single pair of wires, the inevitable would happen. The next day, users would complain that they needed additional wires for fax or modem connectivity. The telecommunications manager who has not installed enough wires to meet such needs is caught in a bind. Therefore, it is recommended that a four-pair cabling system is always installed regardless of the number of pairs a contractor requests.

The four-pair cabling system allows flexibility for additional wires for fax, modem, or any other type of external communications connection. Moreover, the authors typically recommend the use of 2 four-pair cables to every desktop. This allows enough future flexibility so that the expensive cost of labor to rewire the building can be avoided. Each of the four-pair cables should be terminated in what is known as an RJ-45 jack. The RJ-45 jack, an eight-pin interface, is the standard plug for the future. All four-cable pairs should be terminated into the eight-pin interface. All too often telecommunications personnel use jacks with less capacity than the RJ-45 and do not terminate all the wires. This means that extra wires are in the wall, but are unusable. It would require a lot of labor to reinforce the wires.

Most key telephone systems today are computer-stored, programmed-controlled systems that are similar to the PBX discussed earlier in this chapter. As a matter of fact, it is becoming far more difficult to differentiate the PBX and the key system. Key systems can be as large as 200+ ports, whereas PBXs now come with as few as 50+ ports. Functionally, these two types of systems provide the same services and features. The differences are so subtle that it is becoming almost a moot point to call them by different names. These systems are used extensively throughout the industry, so they are fairly perfected in terms of having simple connections, being rich in features, and having significant penetration in the business community.

The key systems are used by larger organizations too. In departments where groups of people require connectivity to each other or where a consolidation of features is required behind a Centrex or PBX, the key system offers some solutions. Although many organizations try to emulate the key system in a PBX with multiline sets, it is often more prudent to install the key service unit. Many dual systems provide the access to features of the PBX and the clustering of workers of a key system.

Why Key Systems?

It is not uncommon to hear business users question the need for a key system. The obvious choice is to go to the telephone company and rent a single line for each user in the organization, branch office, sales office, or home-based business. However, the same arguments that were discussed at the beginning of this chapter hold equally true for the key system. It would be frivolous to rent a single line for every user in a sales or service office. The intent of the sales office is to provide a location where the sales force can schedule work and visit from time to time for meetings and report writing. However, the sales force might be road-based, with a primary emphasis on visiting the customer and meeting the customer's needs. According to this analysis, employees and outside lines should not have a one-to-one relationship. Of course, this assumes that the sales force is out of the office when calling on customers.

If the organizational charter is to telemarket, the entire scenario changes dramatically. When the office force drops in at varying intervals, it is unlikely that everyone will be around at one time. Therefore, a 3:1 ratio can usually be achieved, with three telephone sets being used for each outside line. This can save a significant amount of money in a small office and even more in the larger office environment. Table 5.8 shows a comparison of the use of outside lines on a 3:1 ratio. This does not include the costs for

TABLE 5.8   Comparison of Line Rentals with and without a Key System

Number of Users	Without Key System	With Key System	Difference
10 @$20	$200	$ 80	$120 monthly
20 @$20	$400	$140	$260 monthly
30 @$20	$600	$200	$400 monthly

TABLE 5.9   Summary of Key Telephone System Costs for Various Numbers of Users

Number of Users	Key Equipment Costs
10	$ 5000
20	$10,000
30	$15,000

the key system; the costs will be shown in a later comparison. Suffice it to say that the comparison here is based on the recurring monthly telephone company costs.

The obvious reason an organization would choose a key system is the recurring monthly savings of $120 to $400, as shown in Table 5.8. However, the cost of the key system is not shown. The primary savings shown in this table are the cost of renting a telephone line for each user as opposed to sharing the number of lines with the resulting savings. Now we can add the cost of the capital equipment for the key telephone system. A typical key system with installation, hardware, software, and warrantee will cost an average of $500 per user. A comparative analysis of the costs associated with the acquisition of the system is shown in Table 5.9.

You can see from this table that the costs have been applied in a linear fashion. Better discounts might be available as the system gets larger. Further, the system costs are associated with a basic telephone system. Other features that increase cost include:

- Voice mail
- Station message detail recording
- Automated attendant
- Least-cost routing
- Data and voice simultaneously
- Automatic call distribution

Each of these features raises the cost of a telephone system. The wiring is typically sold to a user on the basis of the vendor's approach to installation. For example, many of these key systems use a two-wire (one-pair) connection to the desktop; others might use a four-wire (two-pair) connection and so on. In general, a good rule of thumb is to install a four-pair connection to every desk, whether you believe you need it or not. This will only minimally increase the cost of the wiring, but it is a good deal. The cost of the wire ranges approximately from $0.03 to $0.05 per foot for the added pairs. All things considered, the little add-on for the wires makes for an insignificant increase to the overall system. However, over the life of the system, the extra pairs of wires pay for themselves in no time. If a user needs a modem or fax machine, for example, then the extra wires are necessary. To have an installer come back and pull an entire new pair of wires will cost from $250 to $350 (In New York City as much as $600), mostly the expense is for labor. This can also be disruptive in the workplace. Table 5.10 compares the equipment costs and the monthly rental costs for the telephone lines to show the overall impact. Taking the comparative numbers from the original tables (Tables 5.8 and 5.9); we see the following cost structure.

Although this table might look like it is a break-even outcome whether or not one uses a telephone system in lieu of the monthly rental of a line per user, some basic assumptions are being made here. The equipment cost for the non-key system is for the purchase of basic analog single-line sets. No multiline sets are involved in this scenario.

The monthly equipment costs are associated with a 3-year depreciation cost on a straight-line basis. In reality, the finance department would likely write the capital off over 5 years. The finance department would also write the equipment off at an accelerated rate based on the IRS and financial policies accepted.

The 1-year differences must be spread over the number of years the system is in place. After the payback period is achieved, the numbers change significantly.

Table 5.11 covers the same system costs over a 5-year depreciation cycle, in which the system life is a 10-year period. In this case, after the fifth year, the equipment costs disappear and only the recurring monthly costs remain. These are simple calculations—any increases in the line costs are not included and factoring for maintenance is not built in. The assumption here is to look at the overall differences between having a system or not. The same assumptions from Table 5.10 are used: the number of users, the cost of equipment at $60 per single-line set (written off, in this case, over 5 years), the line costs held constant over the 5- and 10-year life cycle, and so on.

TABLE 5.10   Summary of Costs for Key System versus Non-key System

Number of Users	Total 1-Year Cost without Key System			Total 1-Year Cost with Key System		
	Line Cost	Equipment Cost	Depreciation@ 3 Years	Line Cost	Equipment Cost	Depreciation@ 3 Years
10	$200	$ 600	$2600	$80	$5000	$2660
20	$400	$1200	$5200	$140	$10,000	$4980
30	$600	$1800	$7800	$200	$15,000	$7400

TABLE 5.11   5- and 10-Year Comparative Costs

Users	Non-Key Costs	Line Costs Monthly	Total			
			5 Years	10 Years		
10	$600	$200	$12,600	$24,600		
20	$1200	$400	$25,200	$49,200		
30	$1800	$600	$37,800	$73,800		
	Key Costs	Line Costs	Total		Difference	
			5 Years	10 Years	5 Years	10 Years
10	$5000	$80	$9800	$14,600	$2800	$10,000
20	$10,000	$140	$18,400	$26,800	$6800	$22,400
30	$15,000	$200	$27,000	$39,000	$10,800	$34,800

This table provides a much different picture of the financial impact of using the key telephone system. On the basis of an example of 30 users, the difference in raw costs over the 5-year period is $10,800; over 10 years, the key equipment will save $34,800. These are significant savings over the life of the equipment when you consider that the entire organization might only be 30 people. The equipment will obviously pay for itself over both the 5- and 10-year period. Remember also that the key system includes the features and functions of a telephone system and includes multiline sets. The non-key system comparison includes only single-line sets and no added features. Each of these will change the equation and show a better payout for the key telephone system. Having drawn this to a conclusion, you can now see why an organization might consider the installation of a resource-sharing arrangement such as a key telephone system. However, a financial calculation is not the only factor involved in this choice.

The system's approach has other advantages. For example, one advantage is the use of the intercommunications channel, called the *intercom*. The intercom frees the outside lines for incoming customer calls when two workers in the same office need to communicate. Using the intercom, party A calls party B on the internal communications paths in the system. Some systems have a fixed number of intercom paths, whereas others have an unlimited number. This is a function of the manufacturer equipment. When using the alternate system (the non-key telephones), the choices are far more restrictive. If party A wants to talk to party B, the two outside telephone lines associated with these two individuals are busy. The customer calls coming into the building for either party are blocked until they terminate their conversation. The customer might become frustrated and take his or her business elsewhere if this is a constant occurrence.

Moreover, it is far easier to add features and services in the key telephone system than in the single-line telephone set. Users will like the features that can be achieved in the key system, such as:

- Call transfer to another party
- Call hold by pressing a feature button
- Three-way or conference calling
- Consultation hold, where a call can be placed on hold while the user confers with another user in the system
- Speed dialing on an individual or system basis
- Speakerphones
- Hands-free dialing

Some of these features are displayed in Fig. 5.12, where the buttons are allocated for the use of the specific features. No one telephone set or system offers everything the user wants exactly the way he or she wants it.

Newer key telephone systems will use a soft key approach, where a visual display panel such as a light-emitting diode (LED) or liquid crystal display (LCD) is used on

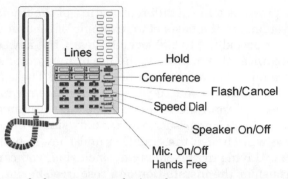

Figure 5.12   Features on sets for key system vendor interfaces.

Figure 5.13   The features are soft keys as you move through the menus.

the telephone set. As features and functions are activated, instead of fixed keys on the telephone set, the display will have a series of buttons whose functions change as you move through the menus on the system, as shown in Fig. 5.13. Although these are a little more expensive, they may add flexibility over time.

When a user activates a feature, a new set of menu options appears for each of the soft keys. This provides a very flexible arrangement, but we must be aware that the end user's ability to grasp and use these features will make the sole decision of their effectiveness. Merely throwing features and functions at an end user does not assure ease of use or connectivity establishment. Users may feel intimidated by soft keys with LCD-driven menus and not use the capabilities of the system. We must be concerned with this risk. Therefore, it is highly recommended that the telecommunications manager select a few users to be pilots (guinea pigs) for testing this system before going to a state-of-the-art telephone system. This checks the ease of use and the users' ability to absorb the information and use the features. One should not select the super or power users, but take a mix of power users and novices alike to guarantee a good cross-representation of internal users. This will help ensure a win/win situation when installing a key telephone system. Without it, one may install a system that is not fully utilized and is expensive due to these limited features. We do not want to waste corporate monies on features and functions that people will not be able to use merely for the sake of having glitzy equipment.

The telephone interfaces in Fig. 5.14 show different ways that a key system can be connected to the outside lines. Often the telephone company brings in individual two-wire analog circuits (lines) and terminates these in an RJ-11C jack. This is the case for smaller systems of less than 10 lines. However, if the system is larger and more connections are required, the telephone company might be asked to terminate the lines in an RJ-21X. This is a call that can be made by the vendor who is requesting the service for its customers. Frankly, the connections have no major difference other than some not-so-obvious benefits.

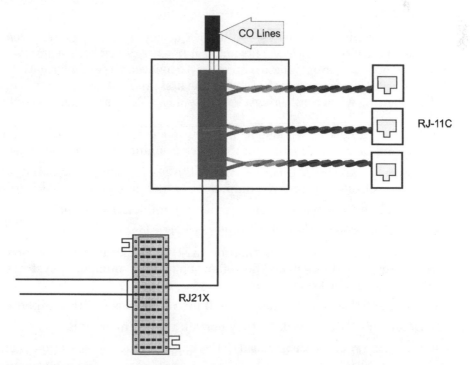

Figure 5.14   Telco interfaces to a key system vary.

For example, using the RJ-21X consolidates the RJ-11s into a single block that supports 25 two-wire connections. This is a little cleaner than having 25 individual RJ-11s installed on a wall. The convenience of testing and troubleshooting at one spot on the wall has some benefit.

However, the individual RJ-11s can be used in lieu of the larger block. Although these might take up more wall space, if the telephone system ever fails, a user can go into the telephone equipment room and unplug one of the circuit connections to the key system, plug in a single-line telephone set (2500 set), and make calls to obtain repairs from the telephone company or equipment vendors. Furthermore, if critical calls must be made, many users can take advantage of this special access method into the lines.

These systems have been around for a long time, so dealing with this connectivity has no mystique. For the most part, vendors have these systems down to a science. Users also have them under control. No major management issues appear in dealing with a key system, except when the system fails. The vendor can usually rectify this situation quickly when problems arise. The interface is a two-wire analog connection that is similar to the residential connection. The main problems a user will have concern the power. We always recommend that a backup battery be provided with the installation so that a critical component of the system's performance can be preserved with the supplemental power. The backup battery adds some minor costs, possibly a few hundred dollars at the most, but it buys a lot of comfort and protection for the end user.

The Vendor Proposal

When dealing with the purchase of the PBX or key telephone system, you will be better equipped if all of the known benefits and features are discussed. The growth capacity of the system before a major upgrade is required is a beneficial piece of information. Never assume that the best deal is placed on the table on the first proposal. As a matter of fact, we prefer to do the following when considering a key system, a PBX, or any other piece of equipment:

- Conduct a needs assessment. Determine the needs of the organization—to meet the core business functions of the office or plant, or other objectives.

- Determine the buying motivations. Is the system being considered to allow growth, replace obsolete or broken equipment, or just deliver a needed feature?

- Conduct user surveys to see whether any hidden needs exist.

- Document the needs and the buying motivation.

- Send out a request for information (RFI) to gather information about the players in your area, the systems they offer, the average number of systems they have installed, and the typical sizes.

- Prequalify the bidders that you will use on the basis of the responses to the RFI.

- Determine future needs as they pertain to system growth.

- Develop a request for proposal (RFP) based on the consolidation of all the information gathered.

- Obtain budgetary approval in advance for some value of the system intended for purchase. Allow some discretionary funding for added features or growth that you didn't anticipate. Never buy a system that only satisfies today's needs; make sure that you have plenty of room to grow.

- Release the RFP and formulate a target due date for responses.

- Analyze the information and begin to select a short list of possible suppliers that you feel comfortable with. This includes checking references of other customers who are using a system similar to the one you are considering.

- Negotiate the contract. Be firm. Make sure all costs are shown and documented.

- Allow plenty of time for the whole process.

These steps are generic enough that the process can be used straightforwardly for any system or service that is being considered. You can never do too much homework to evaluate a system or a supplier. However, you can get caught into a "paralysis by analysis" syndrome, where the process takes too long. This whole process for a key system can be completed in a matter of weeks before getting to final negotiation. Nowhere is it written that such a study should take months to years. Technological advances and the product life cycles are such that you can only decide on the technology on the basis of the information that is available today. Things will change at a very fast rate.

Questions

1. What does PBX stand for?
    a. Private Branch Telephone
    b. Public Branch Exchange
    c. Private Branch Exchange
    d. Private Bell Exchange

2. What is the name for the Bell Branch Exchange or Central Office?
    a. Root and Branches
    b. End User System
    c. Central Exchange
    d. Class 5 Office

3. Who are the primary users of a PBX?
    a. Bell Systems
    b. CLECs
    c. End user
    d. Corporate users

4. What is the motivation to use a PBX?

   a. Technical only

   b. Financial only

   c. Financial and technical

   d. It is a nice thing to do

5. The least cost method of installing a PBX is to use a _____ at every user's desk?

   a. Multiline set

   b. Single line set

   c. Dial tone

   d. Hybrid set

6. When a user wants to acquire a PBX, the costs are fixed and non-negotiable. T/F

7. At the entrance to the building, all the wires are terminated on the _____.

   a. SDF

   b. BDF

   c. MDF

   d. IDF

8. Another name for the MDF is the demarc.   T/F

9. A PBX is usually installed with redundant critical components.   T/F

10. Centrex is an alternative to buying a PBX.   T/F

11. Centrex can be rented on a month-to-month basis.   T/F

12. Key telephone systems are used for smaller locations.   T/F

13. The following is not a prime candidate for using a key telephone system.

   a. Corporate headquarters

   b. One person shop

   c. Small office

   d. Home office

14. A KTS is used as a _____.

   a. Telephone company offering

   b. Regional telecommunications service

   c. Resource-sharing device

   d. Dedicated system for a user

15. A 1648 telephone system means that the system supports
    a. 16 telephones and 48 lines
    b. 48 telephones and 16 sets
    c. 48 lines and 48 sets
    d. 48 telephones and 16 lines
16. The brain of the key systems is called
    a. Brain
    b. KTS
    c. KSU
    d. Memory
17. All key systems use an unlimited number of intercom cards.   T/F
18. A pre-wired, 25-pair connector used on a key system is called
    a. Multipair connector
    b. RJ-66
    c. RJ-45
    d. Amphenol
19. The connector used at the main distribution frame and throughout the building is called
    a. 66 block
    b. RJ-45
    c. RJ-21X
    d. RJ-11
20. One advantage of a key telephone system is that all users have a single line set.   T/F
21. The ratio used to provide lines to telephones in a key system is:
    a. 10:1
    b. 5:1
    c. 2:1
    d. None of the above
22. The average cost of a key system per user is $1000.   T/F

23. How many telephone lines does the RJ-21x support?

    a. 25 four-wire connections

    b. 24 four-wire connections

    c. 25 two-wire connections

    d. 24 two-wire connections

24. How many wires are in an RJ-11?

    a. Four

    b. 25

    c. Two

    d. Eight

25. How many wires are in an RJ-45

    a. Four

    b. Six

    c. 25

    d. Eight

26. The single line set is called a 2500 set.   T/F

6

Modulation and Multiplexing

After reading this chapter and completing the questions, you will be able to:

- Describe modulation techniques used in the network
- Discuss the difference between modulation and multiplexing
- Explain the implementation of the T Carrier system
- Discuss the differences between the analog and digital systems to carry the voice and data
- Discuss the T1 modulation process
- Describe the framing and formatting of a T1 as a multiplexing system
- Explain why there are differences in the digital transmission protocols
- Converse about the use of ESF and SF protocols

Modulation plays a key role in any communication system. The type of modulation used depends on the type of the communication channel. Modulation refers to the process of typically encoding digital data into analog signals for transmission. When transferring data over phone lines, for example, a modem modulates the data into audible tones "carried" on the range of frequencies between 0 Hz and 4 KHz. Once the data reaches its intended destination, another modem demodulates the signal (converts it back to its original form) into digital data. Cable TV networks also use modulation techniques to transfer data. Instead of audible tones, however, cable has sophisticated digital modulation schemes to greatly increase the amount of data that can be sent.

Modulation consists in superimposing the user or subscriber signal on a carrier signal (a constant tone), which is more adequate to the transmission medium. Modulation is the process of impressing information (voice, image, data, etc.) onto the carrier wave for transmission. A band-limited range of frequencies that comprise the message (called the baseband) is translated to a higher range of frequencies. The band-limited message is preserved (i.e., every frequency in that message is scaled by a constant value). To make this a bit simpler, if we change the constant carrier on a channel by adding the message information (the baseband) then the result is a new wave that has the combined baseband and carrier. To show this in a picture usually helps, refer to Fig. 6.1 for the beginning process using an unmodulated signal. This figure is actually showing the signal in a time domain, that being the signal is passed across a period of time.

The unmodulated signal can also be represented in a frequency domain. The graphic shown in Fig. 6.2 is the same carrier tone, this time shown in a frequency domain (for a voice channel use 4 kHz). This shows the constant frequency in the graphic.

In the process of modulation one at least of the three basic parameters of the carrier (amplitude, frequency, or phase) is changed according to the user modulating signal. Modulation can be applied to direct current (mainly by turning it on and off), to alternating current, and to optical signals. Think of blanket waving shown in Fig. 6.3 as

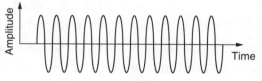

Figure 6.1   The unmodulated signal is a constant carrier tone shown in a time domain.

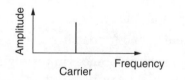

Figure 6.2   The unmodulated signal in a frequency domain.

Figure 6-3   The signal is modulated into the air by the movement of the blanket.

a form of modulation used in smoke signal transmission (the carrier being a steady stream of smoke). Morse code uses a binary (two-state) digital code similar to the code used by today's computers. For most of radio and telecommunication today, the carrier is alternating current (ac) in a given range of frequencies. Common modulation methods include:

- Amplitude modulation (AM), in which the voltage applied to the carrier is varied over time
- Frequency modulation (FM), in which the frequency of the carrier waveform is varied in small but meaningful amounts
- Phase modulation (PM), in which the natural flow of the alternating current waveform is delayed temporarily

These variants are sometimes known as continuous wave modulation methods to distinguish them from pulse code modulation (PCM), which is used to encode both digital and analog information in a binary way. Radio and television broadcast stations typically use AM or FM. Most two-way radios use FM, although some employ a mode known as single sideband (SSB). More complex forms of modulation are phase shift keying (PSK) and quadrature amplitude modulation (QAM).

Modem Modulation and Demodulation

A computer with an online or Internet connection that connects over a regular analog phone line includes a modem. This term is derived by combining beginning letters from the words modulator and demodulator. In a modem, the modulation process involves the conversion of the digital computer signals (high and low, or logical 1 and 0 states) to analog audio-frequency tones.

Digital highs are converted to a tone having a certain constant pitch; digital lows are converted to a tone having a different constant pitch. These states alternate so rapidly that, if you listen to the output of a computer modem, it sounds like a hiss or roar. The demodulation process converts the audio tones back into digital signals that a computer can understand.

In communications, the process in which some characteristic of a wave (the carrier wave) is made to vary in accordance with an information-bearing signal wave (the modulating wave); demodulation is the process by which the original signal is recovered from the wave produced by modulation. The original, unmodulated wave may be of any kind, such as sound or, most often, electromagnetic radiation, including optical waves. The carrier wave can be a direct current, an alternating current, or a pulse chain. In modulation, it is processed in such a way that its amplitude, frequency, or some other property varies. The wave is then modulated within a modulated envelope as seen in Fig. 6.4.

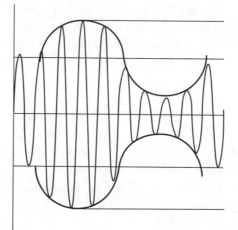

Figure 6.4   The modulated envelope.

Amplitude Modulation

Amplitude modulation is the modulation method used in the AM radio broadcast band. In this system the intensity, or amplitude, of the carrier wave varies in accordance with the modulating signal as seen in Fig. 6.5. When the carrier is thus modulated, a fraction of the power is converted to sidebands extending above and below the carrier frequency by an amount equal to the highest modulating frequency. The sidebands are shown in Fig. 6.6. If the modulated carrier is rectified and the carrier frequency filtered out, the modulating signal can be recovered. This form of modulation is not a very efficient way to send information; the power required is relatively large because the carrier, which contains no information, is sent along with the information.

In a variant of amplitude modulation, called SSB modulation, the modulated signal contains only one sideband and no carrier. The information can be demodulated only if the carrier is used as a reference. This is normally accomplished by generating a wave in the receiver at the carrier frequency. SSB modulation is used for long-distance telephony, such as in the amateur radio bands, and telegraphy over land and submarine cables.

Frequency Modulation

In FM, the frequency of the carrier wave is varied in such a way that the change in frequency at any instant is proportional to another signal that varies with time. The frequency modulation shown in Fig. 6.7 is shown in a time domain, whereas Fig. 6.8 shows the frequency modulation in a frequency domain. Its principal application is also in radio, where it offers increased noise immunity and decreased distortion over the AM transmissions at the expense of greatly increased bandwidth. The FM band has become the choice of music listeners because of its low-noise, wide-bandwidth qualities; it is also used for the audio portion of a television broadcast.

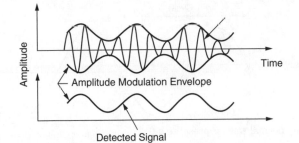

Figure 6.5 Amplitude modulation shown in a time domain.

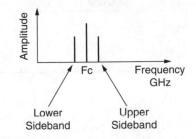

Figure 6.6 The sidebands shown in an AM technique.

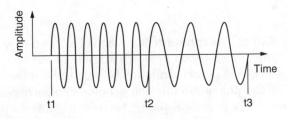

Figure 6.7 Frequency modulation shown in a time domain.

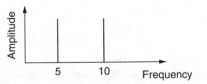

Figure 6.8 FM in a frequency domain.

Phase Modulation

Phase modulation, like frequency modulation, is a form of angle modulation. The modulation occurs when the sine wave angle is changed. As a start of the phase modulation, Fig. 6.9 looks at the normal sine wave using the full 360° cycle. This shows a continuous wave all set up at the same angle. In Fig. 6.10 the angle of the wave is shifted 180° out

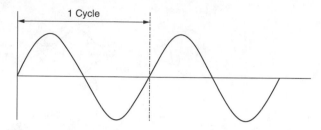

Figure 6.9   The normal wave represents a 0.

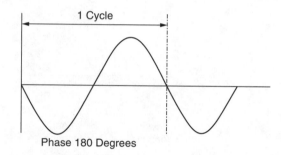

Figure 6.10   The wave using phase modulation is shown 180° out of phase represents a 1.

of phase. The shift allows the representation of a 1 or a 0 by reflecting a different phase of the signal. The two methods are very similar in the sense that any attempt to shift the frequency or phase is accomplished by a change in the other.

Variations of the phase modulation scheme can incorporate combinations of phase plus amplitude. This is called quadrature (four phases) plus amplitude or QAM. In Fig. 6.11 the use of the QAM technique is shown in a table format. The table shows that for each value a 4-bit combination is used.

Pulse Modulation

Pulse modulation involves modulating a carrier that is a train of regularly recurrent pulses. The modulation might vary the amplitude (PAM or pulse amplitude modulation), the duration (PDM or pulse duration modulation), or the presence of the pulses (PCM or pulse code modulation). PCM can be used to send digital data; audio signals on a compact disc use pulse code modulation.

Pulse code modulation is the most important form of pulse modulation because it can be used to transmit information over long distances with hardly any interference or distortion; for this reason it has become increasingly important in the transmission of data in the space program and between computers. Although PCM transmits digital instead of analog signals, the modulating wave is continuous. Digital modulation begins with a digital modulating signal.

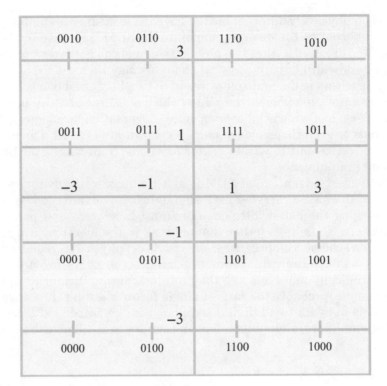

Figure 6.11 QAM values of amplitude and phase shown.

Multiplexing

The paths available for moving electronic information vary considerably in their respective capacities or bandwidths. If a company requires many paths over the same route (for example, many terminals each requiring a connection to one distant computer), it often makes sense to configure one large-capacity circuit and bundle all the smaller requirements into that one big path. The process of combining two or more communications paths into one path is referred to as multiplexing. There are three fundamental types of multiplexing, all of which have significant variations. These main types are:

- Space-division multiplexing (SDM)
- Frequency-division multiplexing (FDM)
- Time-division multiplexing (TDM)

SDM

SDM is the easiest multiplexing technology to understand. In fact, it is so simple it would hardly rate its own special term, except that it is the primary method by which literally millions of telephone signals reach private homes. With SDM, signals are placed on physically different media. Then those media are combined into larger groups and connected to the desired endpoints. In SDM, separate wave guides (e.g., wires, fiber, etc.) are used so that two physical channels do not interfere with one another. The entire bandwidth of both physical channels may be used simultaneously. A standard example of this is the multiple wires used in a bus, or ribbon cable, or telephones, etc.

For example, telephone wire pairs (which of course are also used for data communications), each of which can carry a voice conversation, are aggregated into cables with hundreds or even thousands of pairs, as shown in Fig. 6.12. The latter are run as units from Telco COs out to wiring center locations, from there splitting out to individual customer buildings.

The biggest advantage of SDM is also its biggest disadvantage: the physical separation of the media carrying each signal. It is an advantage because of the simplicity of managing the bandwidth; one only must label each end point of the medium appropriately. No failures (other than a break in the medium) can affect the bandwidth allocation scheme. But because there is a direct physical correlation between the physical link and the individual communications channel, a provider has some difficulty in electronically manipulating the path to achieve efficiencies of technology or scale. For example, probably the largest single factor blocking the conversion of the overall telephone network to all-digital technology is the embedded base of copper wire (and analog amplifiers) supplying telephone service to millions of homes and businesses.

FDM

FDM is inherently an analog technology. It achieves the combining of several digital signals onto (or into) one medium using a system in which signals are each allocated a unique portion of a shared frequency range. Each individual signal is modulated and translated in frequency so that it occupies the correct frequency segment of the composite signal spectrum and does not interfere with the other signals sharing the same band of frequencies. Individual signals are recovered from the composite signal by filtering.

One of FDM's most common applications is cable television. Only one cable reaches a customer's home, but the service provider can nevertheless send multiple television

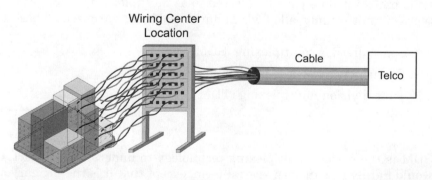

Figure 6.12 Space-division multiplexing (SDM) is a common system in the telephone company network.

channels or signals simultaneously over that cable to all subscribers. Receivers must tune to the appropriate frequency in order to access the desired signal. Figure 6.13 demonstrates the combining of signals on a cable television coaxial cable.

Certain modems have built-in FDM capabilities. Users can modify, with controls on the modem, how much bandwidth each connected digital device will be provided. An added concept is the use of FDM in microwave or CATV systems where the channels are up multiplexed into larger channels as shown in Fig. 6.14.

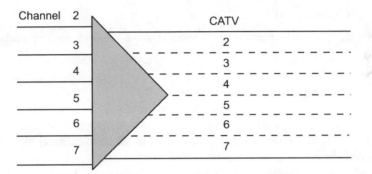

Figure 6.13   A CATV system is the most common form of FDM we use today.

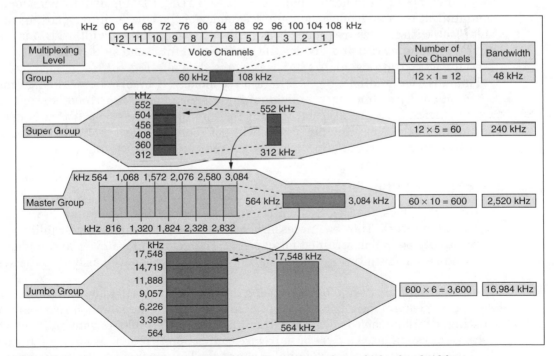

Figure 6.14   An up multiplexer creates larger groups of channels into higher bandwidth.

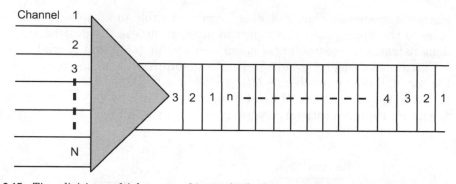

Figure 6.15 Time-division multiplexers combine multiple slower speed channels in the time domain.

TDM

More information can be conveyed in a given amount of time by dividing the bandwidth of a signal carrier so that more than one modulated signal is sent on the same carrier. Called multiplexing, the carrier is sometimes referred to as a channel and each separate signal carried on it is called a subchannel. The device that puts the separate signals on the carrier and takes them off of received transmissions is a multiplexer. Common types of multiplexing include FDM and TDM. FDM is usually used for analog communication and divides the main frequency of the carrier into separate subchannels, each with its own frequency band within the overall bandwidth. TDM is used for digital communication and divides the main signal into time slots, with each time slot carrying a separate signal. A TDM example is shown in Fig. 6.15.

Time-division multiplexing is a digital technology. It involves sequencing groups of a few bits or bytes from each individual input stream one after the other and in such a way that they can be associated with the appropriate receiver. If this is done sufficiently quickly, the receiving devices will not realize or care that some of the circuit time was used to serve another logical communication path.

Evolution of the T-Carrier System

In the early 1960s, the Bell System began to introduce and use a new digital technology in the network. This was necessary because the older carrier and cabling systems were rapidly becoming strained for capacity. The demand for newer and higher-speed communications facilities was building among customers as well as within the systems themselves.

When this digital technology was being introduced, it was deployed in the public network as a means of increasing the traffic capacity within the telephone company on the existing wire-pair cable facilities as interoffice trunks. The older systems, including the N-carrier system, used a two- or four-wire connection through an analog multiplexing device to deliver either 12 or 24 analog channels. This was still an inefficient use of the line capacity, and the analog service was noisy and required expensive line-treatment equipment. Therefore, the telephone company introduced its newer technology to overcome the limitations of the existing plant and transmission services.

Some of the problems with the analog systems were also related to the circuit quality. The older analog network meant that a call placed across the country from East to West Coast was significantly different from such a call made today. The static and noise on the line made the call sound more like it went to the moon and back. Because that's all that was available, that's what the user became accustomed to.

The use of older analog systems was ending within the telephone company networks. The telephone companies had to find a way of improving the utilization of the cable plant on an interoffice basis to overcome problems with underutilized pairs of wires; and the continued installation of inefficient systems was expensive and bulky. The average length of the wires between the telephone companies' offices was approximately 6.5 miles. As calling requirements continued to grow, the telephone companies needed to increase the traffic-handling capacity on these interoffice routes. They were in a quandary, however. First, they didn't want to continue running bulky cables between offices because there simply wasn't enough space. Second, costs for maintaining the cable plant were escalating. Something had to be done quickly. Figure 6.16 shows the use of wires between the telephone company offices. These wires provide the interoffice communications from telephone company to telephone company. The end user or customer was kept on the old analog twisted pairs of wire. From a user's perspective the changes were invisible, except that some improvement in call quality was evident.

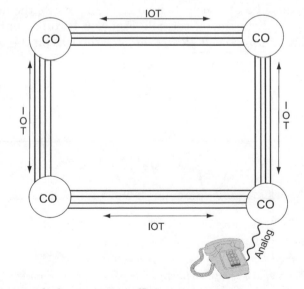

Figure 6.16 Links between telephone company offices.

Analog Transmission Basics

Before going much further, it would be prudent to furnish a brief description of the dial-up telephone network to aid in understanding the need for the digital architecture that was introduced through the use of the T-carrier system. The telephone system was designed around providing analog dial-up voice telephony. Everything was based on voice communications services on a switched (nondedicated) basis. A user could connect his or her telephone to that of another user on the network through either an operator-connected or dial-up (a later evolution) addressing scheme.

Because voice is the primary service provided, the telephone set has evolved into a device that takes the sound wave from the human vocal cords and converts that sound into an electrical current, represented by its analog equivalent. The human voice produces constantly changing variables of both amplitude (the height of the wave) and frequency (the number of cycle changes per second). As these constantly changing variables of amplitude and frequency are produced, the telephone set converts the sound pressure into an equivalent electrical wave. This electrical energy will be carried down a pair of wires. As the electrical energy is introduced into the wires (using twisted pairs of copper for this reference) certain characteristics begin to work on it. First, resistance occurs on the wire, impeding the flow of electricity and reducing the strength of the created signal. Second, the wires act as an antenna, drawing in noise (such as static, cross talk, or electricity from other conversations on wire pairs adjacent to yours). This loss of signal strength coupled with the introduced noise continues to distort the signal.

To overcome these problems, analog amplifiers are used to boost the signal strength back up to its original value. The amplifiers are normally placed on circuits greater than 18,000 to 20,000 feet in length. Figure 6.17 shows how the electrical signal on the wires is attenuated or weakened.

As the signal is boosted back to its original strength, the noise begins to accumulate, causing further distortion of the call. Figure 6.18 represents the analog amplifier on the line boosting up the signal. To overcome the loss on the line and to ensure that the

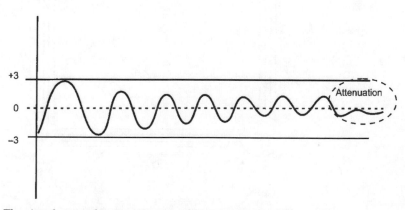

Figure 6.17 The signal strength attenuates over distance rather quickly.

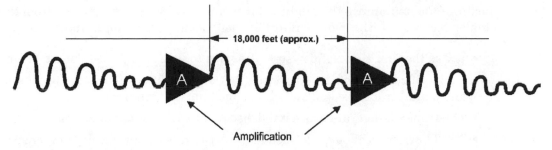

Figure 6.18 Amplifiers boost the signal back to its original strength.

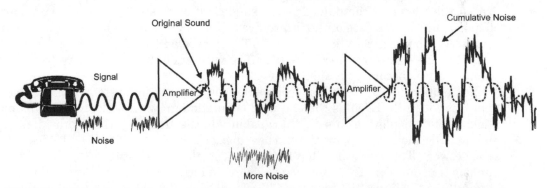

Figure 6.19 The signal and the noise become accumulative on the circuit because of the amplification.

signal gets to the other end, the telephone companies used analog amplifiers. These amplifiers were used on circuits to increase the strength of the analog transmission. However, they were prone to failures and had other qualities that were undesirable. Figure 6.19 is a representation of the problem encountered with the amplification process. As the signal is amplified, the signal and all the noise on the wires are amplified together. This does allow the signal to travel further, but after each amplification process, noise also accumulates. A good deal of the problem stems from the fact that the amplifier can't distinguish the analog signal from the noise. Therefore it amplifies everything.

The Evolution to Digital

The T-carrier system was developed to cope with these amplification problems. The telephone companies were looking to enhance the quality of calls and better utilize the cable facilities. The T-carrier system allowed them to increase the call-carrying capacity while taking advantage of the unused transmission capacity of their existing wire pair facilities and to improve the quality of transmission by migrating away from the older analog techniques. The evolution to T-carrier was important for a number of reasons:

- It was the first successful system designed to utilize digitized voice transmission.
- It identified many of the standards that are employed today for digital switching and digital transmission, including a modulation technique.
- The transmission rate was established at 1,544,000 bits per second.
- The T-carrier technology defined many of the rules, or protocols, and constraints in use today for other types of communications.

As mentioned earlier, the analog transmission capabilities were inefficient. In many cases, the telephone companies used a single pair of twisted wires to carry a phone call. This meant that as uses of the interoffice facilities grew, the cable plant grew exponentially. As more central offices (or end offices) were added, the need for meshing these together grew. Interconnecting each office with enough pairs of wire to service user demands was becoming a nightmare.

Remember that the telephone companies saw this carrier system as a telephone company service only. Even as the end user population grew, the telephone companies still held back on deploying this digital capability to the end user. These providers used the higher efficiencies to support the end user digitally, from end office to end office or through the network. The user was still relegated to a single conversation on a twisted pair using analog transmission. Thus this system operated in an analog format on the local loop, but digitally on the interoffice trunks (IOTs). In metropolitan areas, the telephone companies were reaping the benefits of the T-carrier system. Figure 6.20 is a representation of the telephone company deployment of analog/digital transmission capacities.

Some immediate benefits were achieved: the quality of transmission improved dramatically, and the utilization of existing wire facilities increased. A single four-wire facility on twisted wires could now carry 24 simultaneous conversations digitally at an aggregated rate of 1.544 Mbps.

As digital switching systems were introduced into the dial telephone network, they were designed around the same techniques employed in the T-carrier system. The digital switching matrices of the #4 and #5 electronic switching systems (ESSs) developed by Western Electric (now called Avaya) and the DMS systems developed by Northern Telecom, Inc. (now called Nortel Networks) utilize PCM internally, so that digital carrier systems and channels can be interfaced directly into the digital switching systems. By adhering to the standards set forth, the operating telephone companies and the long-haul carriers could build integrated digital switching and digital transmission systems that:

- Eliminated the need to terminate the digital channels or equipment to provide analog interfaces to digital switching architectures.
- Avoided the addition of quantizing noise that would be introduced by another digital-to-analog conversion process. Whenever a conversion of the signal from analog to digital or from digital to analog is necessary, the risk of errors and noise increases.

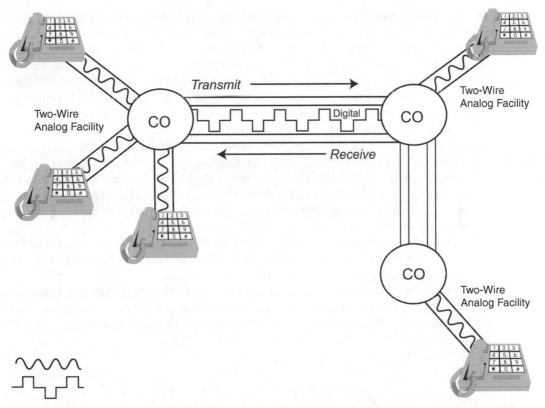

Figure 6.20 The telephone companies deployed analog-to-digital conversions in their networks.

These techniques were used to provide lower-cost, better-quality dial-up telephone services. However, this same technology underlies the idea of full end-to-end digital networking services that is the basis of integrated services digital networks (ISDN), the future and the higher-end broadband services that are emerging.

Analog-to-Digital Conversion

Prior to covering the T-carrier fundamentals, it would be appropriate to discuss the analog-to-digital conversion process. Digital architecture dictates the use of a digital bit stream; therefore the analog wave must be converted into a useable format. Digital pulses are represented by a 0 or a 1. As the analog signal is being transmitted to the network, it must be converted from a wave of varying amplitudes and frequencies to a digital format of 1s and 0s (or presence and absence of voltage).

The analog wave must be sampled often enough and converted to create a stream of 1s and 0s that is precise enough to be re-created at the distant end, producing a signal that sounds like the original conversation. According to the Nyquist rule, a digital signal is created by sampling the analog wave at twice the highest frequency on the line.

For an analog circuit, delivered by the local telephone company, the frequency range on a twisted pair of wires is represented in hertz (Hz). To maximize the utilization of the older carrier systems, the Telcos delivered a usable bandwidth of 3000 Hz (3 kHz), as compared to the 4000 Hz (4 kHz) capable of being carried on the line. The difference between the 3-kHz and 4-kHz services is in how the line is filtered. The human voice produces understandable information in the range of 300 to 3300 frequency changes per second. Therefore, the Telcos knew that all they had to provide to the user was 3 kHz of usable bandwidth. But for separation between conversations and to minimize cross talk and other interference, they allocated 4 kHz per analog line. Using Nyquist's rule, the sampling of an analog wave at twice the maximum frequency of the line meant that a minimum of 6600 samples per second should be sufficient to re-create the wave for the digital-to-analog and analog-to-digital conversion. However, to produce the quality of the higher range of frequencies of the human voice, the number of samples is rounded up to 8000 per second.

The sample now had to be created into a bit stream of 1s and 0s, as already stated. To represent the true tone and inflection of the human voice, enough bits need to be used to create a digital word. Using an 8-bit word creates enough different points on a wave to do just that. The wave is divided into 256 possible amplitude combinations at the moment of the sample itself. Figure 6.21 shows how the sampling is accomplished using two states and 8 bits to create 2^8 or 256 points on the analog wave. As each sample is taken, the amplitude of the wave is sampled.

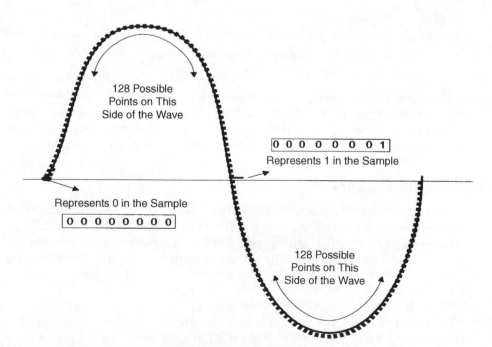

Figure 6.21   The analog wave is sampled to produce the digital values along the curve.

Once the sample has been taken and the digital equivalent created into an 8-bit word, the digital (or square) wave can be transmitted. The 1 represents the presence of voltage and the 0 represents the absence of voltage.

This conversion uses PCM to create the sample. Using PCM and the rules established, the transmission of the digital equivalent of the analog wave results in 8000 samples per second ∞ 8 bits per sample = 64,000 bits per second as the basis for a voice transmission in PCM mode. Whether the end user transmitted voice, data, or facsimile, the copper wires were used to carry the analog wave to the central office, where the wave was converted to a digital signal for transport across the telephone company network. At the far end, the receiving telephone company converted the digital signal back to its original analog equivalent for delivery to the customer. All this served to improve transmission quality for the telephone companies, but left the customer, who still received analog transmission to his or her premises, out in the cold.

As the telephone companies were reaping the benefits of their new transmission capability, the users began to request this service. More user demands created some upheaval within the Bell System. This technology was perceived to be a telephone company-only service. But users also wanted (demanded) end-to-end digital transmission to improve their throughput and quality. Because analog transmission was noisy, there was a limit to the types of signals users could exchange across the network. Specifically, the constant growth in computer technology and the deployment of terminals and printers around the country left the end user with limitations and restrictions that were becoming intolerable.

The Movement to End Users

Ultimately, the telephone companies had to install digital transmission to the customer premises. Originally this took the form of lower-speed digital data services (DDSs) at speeds of 2.4, 4.8, 9.6, and 56 Kbps digital. Newer introductions added 19.2–64 Kbps and high-capacity (HICAP) T1 services at 1.544 Mbps.

In order to deliver this digital capability to the customer, a special assembly or individual-case-basis (ICB) tariff arrangement was initially used. This emergence didn't occur until the mid-1970s. At first, this was done with some reluctance, but as the movement caught on the deployment was both quick and dynamic. The telephone companies had to modify the outside plant to accommodate the end-user needs. To do this, they first had to engineer the circuit. Next they had to remove all of the analog transmission equipment from the line. Then the circuit (now a four-wire circuit) had to be checked for splices, taps, bridges, and other problems that would introduce loss and noise and thereby impair transmission. These had to be removed or cleaned up. The next step was to provide digital equipment, called regenerators or repeaters, on the line.

With analog transmission, amplifiers are used on circuits over 18,000 feet in length. However, with digital transmission, repeaters are used at whatever intervals are necessary to ensure quality (typically 2000–6000 feet). In digital transmission—the presence or absence of a voltage—the signal can deteriorate very quickly. Therefore the telephone company needed four times as many repeaters as it had analog amplifiers.

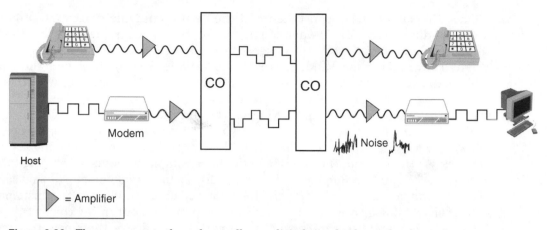

Figure 6.22   The movement to the end user allows a digital signal to be used end to end.

These repeaters or regenerators ensure that the proper signal is moved across the line. The signal is repeated to prevent it from falling below a threshold where it can't be distinguished from noise. Figure 6.22 is a representation of how the signal is actually recreated rather than amplified to produce the quality we have come to expect. As the signal moves across the wires, the same problems are inherent; resistance on the line depletes the signal strength, and noise is prevalent. The digital regenerator is placed close enough to get around this problem. Therefore the end user could move to an effective use of a four-wire circuit at 64 Kbps. The first deployment of this service was for voice, but data quickly became the dominant rider of the new digital transmission. It should also be noted that as T1 became more readily available, the primary use (75 percent) was to consolidate WATS lines onto a single digital trunk. This digital transmission capability was designed around the voice dial-up network; therefore, the service was a natural fit.

T1 Basics

T1 is characterized by the following operating characteristics:

A four-wire circuit: Because this technology evolved from the old twisted-pair environment, four wires were used. Two wires are used to transmit and two are used to receive. Other facilities can be used, but for now, think of it this way.

Full duplex: Transmission and reception can take place simultaneously. Many customers derive other uses, such as one way only for remote printing, file transfer, and so on, or two way for alternate service such as voice communications.

Digital: This is an all-digital service. Data, analog facsimile, analog voice, and the like are all converted to digital pulses (1s and 0s) for transmission on the line.

Time-division multiplexing: The digital stream is capable of carrying a standard 64-Kbps channel; 24 channels are multiplexed to create an aggregate of 1.536 Mbps. Time division allows a channel to use a slot 1/24 of the time. These can be fixed time slots made available to the channel.

Pulse code modulation: Using the example, the analog voice or other signal is sampled 8000 times per second; an 8-bit word is used to represent each sample, thus yielding the 64-Kbps channel capacity.

Framed format: T1 uses some very specific conventions to transmit information between both ends. One of these is a framing sequence that formats the samples of voice or data transmission. It's easy to think of a frame in terms of the 8-bit samples of the 24 channels being strung together in a logical sequence. After the 192 bits of information are compiled, a framing bit is added, creating a frame of 193 bits of information. A frame is shown in Fig. 6.23.

The framing bit can be equated to a pointer or address. Because the line is moving bits of information at 1,544,000 per second, it would be very easy to skew left or right and get information out of sequence. Therefore the extra 8000 bits of information (1 bit per frame, 8000 frames per second) create a locator for the equipment to lock in on. This pointer allows the devices to read a pattern of bits in order to know which frame is being received or transmitted and the location of each channel thereafter.

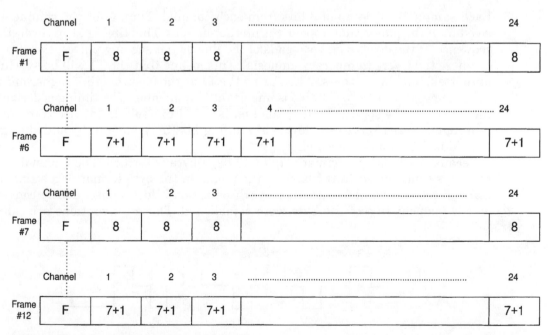

Figure 6.23 A framed format is used for the T1.

Framing has undergone several evolutions over the years. The first use of T1 service was for voice, so the information was easier to use.

The D4 superframe uses a framing pattern for voice and data. The framing pattern in the D4 superframe is a repeating 12-bit sequence (1000 1101 1100) that allows signaling bits to be "robbed" in the 6th and 12th frames of the superframe. The 8th bit from each sample in frames 6 and 12 is used to provide signaling.

Bipolar Format

T1 uses electrical voltage across the line to represent the pulses (1s). The bipolar format serves two purposes. It reduces the required bandwidth from 1.5 MHz to 772 kHz, which increases repeater spacing. And the signal voltage averages out to zero, allowing direct current (dc) power to be simplexed on the line to power intermediate regenerators. Think of it as an alternating current (ac) version of a dc line. Every other pulse will be represented by the negative equivalent of the pulse. For example, the first pulse will be represented by a positive 3 V (+3 V), the next pulse will be represented by a negative 3 V (–3 V), and so on. This effectively yields a 0 voltage on the line, because the + – + – equalizes the current. This bipolar format is also called alternate mark inversion (AMI). The mark is a digital 1. Alternate marks are inverted in polarity (+,–). The bipolar format is shown in Fig. 6.24.

Byte-Synchronous Transmission

Each sample is made up of 8 bits from each channel. Timing for the channels is derived from the pulses that appear within the samples. This timing keeps everything in sequence. If the devices on both ends of the line do not see any pulses, they lose track of where they were (temporary amnesia). This means that the T1 will be synchronous unto itself, but not to others. When using the T1 as the basis of other higher multiplexing schemes (like T2 and T3) this is important to remember. The timing is derived from the pulses on the specific link, so the link is timed to itself. If one needs to multiplex into higher-speed services, additional stuffing bits may have to be added to get the individual T1s timed to each other.

Because each sample is made up of 8 bits, a byte is formed. The transmitters and receivers synchronize on the basis of the pulses in the byte format. If a string of 0s is transmitted in several frames, then synchronization is lost. Consequently, conventions on the transmission of the byte were established. These conventions are called the

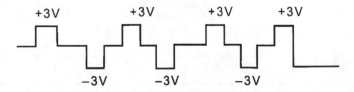

Figure 6.24 Alternating pulses vary in their polarity (bipolar).

1s density rule. What this means is that in order to maintain synchronization, a certain amount of 1s must be present.

For voice communication this doesn't pose a problem, because the voice generates a continuous change in amplitude voltages which, when encoded into an 8-bit word (byte), displays the presence of voltage (1s). However, in data transmission, strings of 0s are possible (even probable) when refreshing or painting screens of information. Hence the 1s density rule comes into play.

Simply put, the 1s density rule states that in every 24 bits of information to be transmitted, there must be at least three pulses (1s), and that no more than 15 0s can be transmitted consecutively. A more stringent requirement set by AT&T in the implementation of their digital transmission was that in every 8 bits of information, at least one pulse (1) must be present.

Think of how this affects data transmission. If your data must have at least one pulse per byte, you have to change the way you deliver data to the line. A technique known as pulse stuffing is used to meet these conventions. The 8th bit in every byte was stuffed with a 1. This limited the data transmission rate to 56 Kbps, because 7 usable bits plus a stuff bit had to be transmitted. The end-receiving equipment will receive 00000001 and not be able to tell if we sent 00000001 or if we sent 00000000 and the last bit was forced to a 1 for timing purposes. Because of this rule, we cannot trust the 8th bit, so we relegate ourselves to using 7 bits for data and the 8th bit for timing, all the time.

To overcome this bit stuffing, yet meet the one's density requirement, a technique was developed. This is known as bipolar eight 0 substitution (B8ZS—pronounced *bates*). This is shown in Fig. 6.25. At the customer location, B8ZS is implemented in

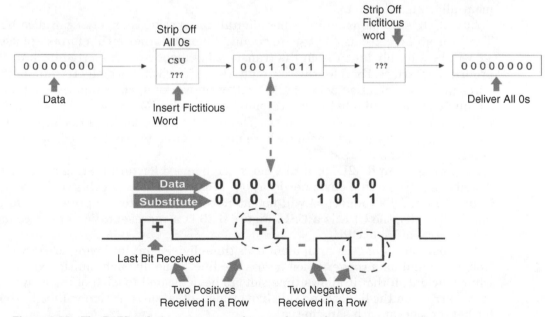

Figure 6.25 The B8ZS technique overcomes the ones density demands.

the channel service unit (CSU). As data bits are delivered to the CSU for transmission across the line, the CSU (a microprocessor-controlled device) reads the 8-bit format. Immediately recognizing that a string of 8/16/24 zeros will cause problems, it strips off the 8-bit byte and substitutes a fictitious byte.

- Eight 0s are stripped off the data stream and discarded.
- The CSU then inserts a substitute word (byte) of 00011011.

However, to let the receiving end know this is a substitute word and not real data, two violations to the bipolar or AMI convention are created. Remember that the bipolar convention states that alternating voltages will be used for the pulses. In the fourth and seventh positions, violations will be created that act as flags to the receiver that something is wrong.

Channelized or Nonchannelized

Generically, T1 is 24 channels of 64 Kbps each, plus 8 Kbps of overhead. This is considered channelized service. However, the newer multiplexing equipment can be configured in a number of ways. For example, the T1 can be used as a single channel of 1.536 Mbps (such as for a router connection to the WAN); or two high-speed data channels at 384 Kbps each and a video channel at 768 Kbps. These examples can be mixed into a variety of offerings. The point is that the service does not have to be configured in 24 channels, but can be nonchannelized into any usable data stream needed (equipment allowing, of course).

Any other suitable medium (fiber, digital microwave, coax, etc.) can also be used. The T1 is still treated as a four-wire circuit. When the other media forms are used, the T1 will be suitably taken from the transmission mode and converted back to the appropriate interface. For a four-wire circuit, the carrier will normally terminate the four wires into a demarcation point (DEMARC) or network interface unit (NIU). Individual circuits can be terminated into a recommended jack—RJ-48 (sometimes called dumb jacks) or RJ-68, (called smart jacks). These jacks serve as the interface to the four wires. In a larger environment or where multiple circuits are involved, other methods of termination can be used.

For example, an RJ-2IX or a BIX block can be used for terminating a T1 on a main distribution frame in a customer location. From the RJ-48, a cable (using a subminiature 15-pin DIN connector) will be extended to the customer premises equipment (CPE). Usually, the CPE is a CSU. Figure 6.26 is a representation of the connection from central office to CPE.

The customer premises equipment uses time-division multiplexing to carry the multiple voice and data conversation across the line. Time-division multiplexing is somewhat efficient in that it allows time slots to be dedicated to each of the conversations to be carried on the line. Using this fixed time slot, a conversation will be in the same bucket (or slot) at each sample time.

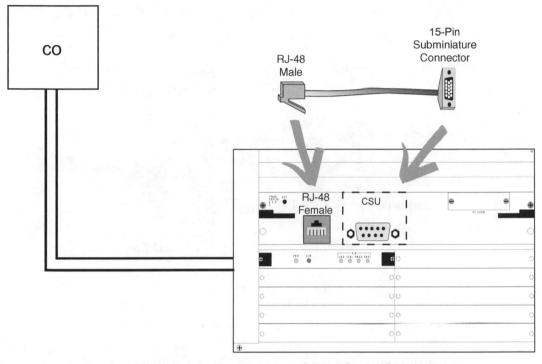

Figure 6.26 A typical connection from a CO to customer premises.

Remember that the equipment using the Nyquist rule operates at twice the highest frequency of the line. Therefore each individual conversation is sampled 8000 times per second. There are 24 (typical) paths being simultaneously multiplexed onto the T1. Each of these paths therefore carries one sample (1/8000 of a second) of voice, data, fax, video, etc.

The time slot is always present, and if no traffic is being generated between points across the line the time slot goes unused. The slot is empty. For this reason, time-division multiplexing is inefficient. Attempts to get the most amount of service from a T1 would be thwarted because of the fixed time slot problem. The TDM mux is shown in Fig. 6.27 with a number of connections for various services.

Digital Capacities

One of the by-products of the T-carrier system was that the transmission rate employed became the standard building block for a multiplexing hierarchy. In high-speed digital transmission systems, a carrier combines many lower-speed signals into an aggregate signal for transport. To simplify this process and to hold the line on the costs of equipment, standard rates were defined.

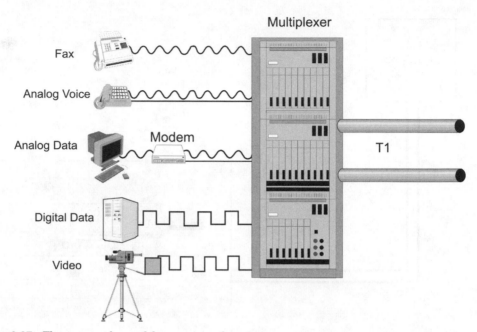

Figure 6.27   The mux can be used for a variety of services.

Each of the transmission rates was assigned a number that identified the rate and configuration for the signal. Each time a higher speed is created, the lower speeds are combined and extra bits (bit stuffing) are added to come up to the signaling rate. These extra bits allow the equipment (multiplexers) to compensate for distances, clocking, and so forth, which cause transmission delay cycles.

The designations for the digital transmission are called digital signal X. Many times people will transpose or intersperse these designators. For example, a T1 is often referred to as a DS1 in the industry. To clarify this point, T1 is the first level of the T-carrier system. It is physical components such as the wires, plugs and jacks, repeaters, and so forth. These physical devices combine to create the T1. DS1 is the multiplexed digital signal, first level, carried inside the T-carrier. The DS1 is the electrical signal (the pulses) running on the T1.

The digital hierarchy for North America includes the following:

DS0: Although originally not a formally defined rate, the DS0 is a 64-Kbps signal that makes up the basis for the DS1. 24 DS0s combined produce the DS1. The standard 64-Kbps pulse code modulation (PCM) signal is the basis for all of the future networks employing digital signaling. Included in this is the integrated service digital network (ISDN).

DS1: The digital signal level 1 is a TDM pulse code modulation aggregate of 1.544 Mbps, regardless of the medium used to carry the signal. The physical side of this capacity is called the T1.

DS1C: This is a digital signal equivalent to 2 DS1s, with extra (stuff) bits to conform to a signaling standard of 3.152 Mbps. Few (if any) of these circuit capacities are still in use today. In the early days of digital and data transmission, the 3 Mbps data rate was used to link mainframes together. The physical side of this circuit is called T1C.

DS2: This is a composite of four DS1s multiplexed together yielding an aggregate rate of 6.312 Mbps. The Bell System used a DS2 capability to deliver subscriber loop carrier (SLC-96) to customers. A total of 96 DS0s could be carried across the DS2. This service was used more by the LECs in their outside plant world. However, the 6 Mbps data rate is now becoming repopularized with the promise of ADSL technologies in the local loop. If we can get 6 to 8 Mbps downloads from the Internet on our local wires, the carriers stand to gain from not having to replace their infrastructure. This is also called a T2.

DS3: This 44.736-Mbps aggregate-multiplexed signal is equivalent to 28 DS1s or 672 DS0s. The T3 service is typically used by high-end data and voice customers who can afford the cost of this channel capacity.

DS4/NA: This 139.264-Mbps aggregate-multiplexed signal is equivalent to 3 DS3s or 2016 DS0s. The high-end and long-haul telecommunications carriers use this size of channel capacity. It is unlikely that a DS4 would ever be installed at a customer location.

DS4: This 274.176-Mbps aggregate-multiplexed signal is equivalent to 6 DS3s or 4032 DS0s.

These rates are based on the ANSI T1.107 guidelines. From an international perspective, the ITU has set a hierarchy of rates that differs from the North American standard. However, other rates are evolving for transmission capacities. The standard 64 Kbps is derived from using pulse-code modulation. In several vendor products, 64 Kbps for the transmission of voice and/or analog data is considered too much bandwidth to carry traditional voice or analog data. Therefore, lower speed capacities are derived at 32 Kbps.

Signaling

Signaling comes into play when dealing with voice and dial-up data services. Traditionally signaling is provided on a dial-up telephone line, across the talk path. This is referred to as in-band signaling. You might recall that the need to find bits to send between transmitter and receiver was accomplished in the 6th and 12th frames. Bit robbing, or stealing the 8th bit in each of the channels (1–24) in these two frames, allows for enough bits to signal between the transmit and receive ends. These ends can be customer premises equipment to the central office for switched services, or CPE to CPE for PBX-PBX connections, and so on.

The most common form of signaling on a T1 line is four-wire E&M signaling of type I, II, or III. It would be safe to say that the easiest implementation, acceptable to all vendors and carriers alike, is four-wire E&M type I.

Signaling is used to tell the receiver where the call or route is destined. The signal is sent through switches along the route to a distant end.

The common types of signals are:

- On-hook
- Off-hook
- Dial tone
- Dialed digits
- Ringing cycle
- Busy tone

Four-wire E&M is used for tie lines between switches. Occasionally, other services are bundled onto a T1 circuit. These could include:

- Direct inward dialing (DID)
- Direct outward dialing (DOD)
- Two-way circuit
- Off-premises extension (OPX)
- Foreign exchange service (FX)

With these other services, the type of signaling might differ. DID/DOD on a PBX might use ground-start trunks, which requires a ground to be placed on the individual circuit to alert the central office that service is requested or there is some other change on the line. Regardless of the type signaling or the services used, signaling requires bits of information. There is a way to overcome the robbed-bit signaling that limits data to 56 Kbps. *Common-channel signaling,* or CCS, is a method to get the clear channel capability back.

Remember that there are constant demands on the use of T1 for clear channel capacity. The use of bit stuffing to conform to the 1s density rule for timing was overcome by using B8ZS. Now, to overcome bit robbing for signaling, CCS can apply.

If the 24th channel in the digital signal is dedicated, 23 clear channels can pass 64,000 bits of information. The choice is how much to give up.

This common-channel signaling technique is also called the transparent mode for signaling. A single 64-Kbps channel (#24) is given up rather than 8 Kbps per channel [[×]] 24 (192 Kbps) for robbed bit. Carriers now use CCS7 (or SS7 as it is called in the United States) in their newer digital dial-up services under the auspices of Intelligent Networks and ISDN. In the T1 world, this means the primary rate interface (PRI) at 23B+D—simply stated, 23 bearer (B) channels at 64 Kbps clear channel, plus a data channel for signaling at 64 Kbps (D). The choices are not always obvious, but understanding the requirements helps to steer the decision better.

Clocking (Network Synchronization)

Any digital network synchronization between sender and receiver must be maintained. As the DS1 (the digital signal level 1 of 1.544 Mbps) is delivered to the network, it is likely that it will be multiplexed with other digital streams from many other users. All of these signals will then be transported as a single signal over high capacity digital links (DS3 and above). Further, if the line is directly interfaced to a digital switching device, then synchronization must be maintained between the customer's transmitter and the switch.

Synchronization is imperative in a digital transmission system. If the timing of arrival or transmission is off, then the information will be distorted. Regardless of whether voice, data, video, or image traffic is present, the presentation of a digital stream of 1s and 0s is contingent on a timed arrival between the two ends.

There are a number of ways to synchronize a digital network, but the issue must definitely be addressed. Some of the ways to address the synchronization deal with levels of synchronization.

The levels are:

- Bit
- Time slots for time-division multiplexing
- Frame

Bit Synchronization

As a digital stream of 1s and 0s is delivered to the line, the timing (or clocking) of the bit is important. The transmitter should be sending bits at the same rate the receiver can take them in. Any difference—faster or slower—could result in lost bits. Therefore, the bits must occur at a fixed time interval. This is a bit technical, but the timing for the bits is set up in a window of 648 nanoseconds (that is, 648 billionths of a second) and the pulse must occur in 1/2 of that window. Therefore, the pulse is 324 nanoseconds in duration. When we only have a 3-volt pulse, and it occurs for only 324 ns, one can see why the timing is crucial. A slight delay and the timing is off by a lot. If the timing is off enough, the pulse can wind up in the wrong time slot. This is called "jitter."

Time Slot

Whenever several links are connected or routed through a network processor, switching system, or end mode, the potential for lost bits, or degradation of the link increases exponentially. Using the pulse code modulation technique, 8 bits are encoded from each sample of information. These 8 bits are then assembled and placed into a time slot. As signals and links are processed through a network, it is the 8-bit pattern that is routed from time slot to time slot. Should a slippage or mismatch occur, multiple streams of information will be lost.

Frame Synchronization

After the data stream of 192 bits of information is assembled (8 bits × 24 channels), an extra overhead bit is added to let both transmitter and receiver know the boundaries of the frame (think of it as a start/stop bit sequence). When dealing with a T1, the bit sequencing is easier to derive. However, at multiplexing schemes above the T1 rate, additional bits are inserted in the data stream to maintain a constant clocking reference. The use of these overhead (or stuff) bits brings both transmitter and receiver up to a common signaling speed to maintain frame synchronization.

Potential Synchronization Problems

When a digital system is scheduled to receive a bit, it expects to do just that. However, clocking or timing differences between the transmitter and receiver can exist. Therefore, while the receiver is expecting a bit that the transmitter hasn't sent, a slip occurs. There will most likely be slips present because of multiple factors in any network. These can result from the two clocks at the ends being off or from problems that can occur along the link.

Along the link, problems can be accommodated. The use of pulse stuffing helps, but other methods also can help. Each device along the link has a buffer capability. This buffer creates a simple means of maintaining synchronization. Pulse stuffing is done independently for each multiplexer along the way, enhancing overall reliability of the network. However, pulse stuffing has its negatives too. The overhead at each multiplexer is basically a penalty. Further, at both ends the location and timing of each stuff bit must be determined, then signaled to the receiver to enable it to locate and remove the stuff bits. When de-stuffing occurs, a timing problem known as *jitter* can cause degradation of the signal. When passing through multiple switching sites, the signal must be de-stuffed from a received signal, and then re-stuffed to a newly transmitted signal. This is expensive in both equipment and overhead.

Obviously, when slippage occurs or if a problem exists in the network buffers, the retransmission of a frame or frames of information will be required. For voice, this isn't too bad, but for data transmission it can result in errors that can render the data unusable. The result will be retransmission requests (NAKS) that will affect the throughput of the link and potentially increase the burden on other systems to detect and correct the errors.

Performance Issues

Once a decision is made to use digital transmission capabilities and to consolidate 24 or more voice, data, or video circuits on a single T1, the performance of the T1 becomes an issue. The placing of all the eggs in a single basket is an issue to be dealt with.

The first users of this technology were risk takers. If 24 analog voice and data lines are being used and 1 fails, 23 are still working. However, when 24 lines are digitally encoded on a single circuit and 1 fails, they all fail. This is a concern to many users.

Further, it should be noted that failures do occur. A T1 is based on the four-wire circuit in an error-prone network. Equipment failures, cable cuts, flooded cable vaults, and the like, all contribute to circuit failures. If total circuit failures were the only problem, the risks would be minimized. But cases can occur that cause distortion, high bit-error rates, timing slips, and loss of framing sequence (to name a few), which can impair or disrupt transmission. The thought of all these situations can leave the potential user's knees weak.

A further statistic that causes concern is that 90 percent of all errors/failures will likely occur at the local loop (the last mile from central office to customer premises). This is not to imply that the local exchange carriers (LECs) are doing a poor job of provisioning these circuits. It is merely a statement of fact, because the local loop is exposed to more of the external problems mentioned above.

Considering average performances, the use of T1 technology is based on 7 days per week × 24 hours per day.

To ensure availability of the circuit and the call-carrying capacity of the channels, carriers, equipment vendors, and the like have all adopted to a new standard. This new standard is known as *extended superframe format* or ESF. Before delving into ESF, however, an understanding of the older format is appropriate.

D3/D4 Framing

First, the D3 and D4 framed formats were designed to format the channelized information of a T1. Because D3 was a voice-only (analog data input) and fixed format for input, the use of T1 was designed around tie lines, WATS lines, and dial-up analog data. The evolution to the D4 frame was to accommodate voice, data, and image. Both of these formats had their limitations. The superframe (SF) format used provisions to allow for signaling (robbed bit) and 1s density for timing (stuff bits). These two capabilities, combined with the framing bits, were constantly taking channel capacity from the T1. All of the user information was designed around a 56-Kbps data stream. The robbed or stuffed bits were designed around control. Yet, when looking at the potential for maintenance and diagnostic capabilities, no spare capacity exists for the data channels to do this, short of giving up additional overhead.

Maintenance Issues

Whenever a user of T1 with D3/D4 framing experienced problems on the line, the sequence of events became elongated and disruptive. Things would occur in the following order:

- The user would experience some hits on the line (or downtime) that affected data throughput. These hits would be in the form of loss of framing, loss of synchronization, bipolar violations, and such. Regardless of the problem, disruptions on the circuit for seconds or longer occurred. The user could see lights flashing on the channel service unit (CSU).

- The user would notify the appropriate carrier (either local exchange or interexchange carrier) of the problem. Further discussions would evolve regarding the errors and so on.

- To test the line, the carrier would ask the customer to get all users off the circuit and give the line to the carrier for testing. In many cases, this might be an immediate situation; in other cases, it was a scheduled event. Whether or not this was scheduled for a later time, the issue at hand was the need to give up 24 channels of voice, data, or image for a couple of hours for testing.

- The carrier would then test the line. A loopback arrangement would be used in some cases. The carrier would loop the circuit from the exchange office to the CSU or demarcation point. A pattern of 1s and 0s was transmitted to the customer premises and immediately shipped back around to the originating office. As the data was shipped out, a comparison was made with what was received back. If any errors were evident, the necessary fixes could be either done on the spot or scheduled.

- However, often the carrier conducted the tests and detected no problems. A technician might then be dispatched to the customer's premises to provide further testing. Equipment using test patterns (*quasi-random signal source* or QRSS) was used. Again, the possibility existed that no errors would be detected.

- The carrier would then give the circuit back to the customer. When challenged as to the nature of the problem, the carrier's response was *no trouble found* (NTF). Obviously, the customer had problems accepting this answer. The feeling that the carrier was either hiding something or just didn't know what was going on prevailed.

- Once the circuit was placed back in service (two hours later), the customer might see errors again. At this point the cycle would start all over again, usually with the same end result—NTF. Consequently, the working relationships and confidence levels between the customer and provider would become very strained.

Error Detection

The easiest way to describe errors on a T1 is as the process by which any logical 1 is changed to a 0 or a logical 0 is changed to a 1. These logic errors are the source of the corrupted data on the line. The errors can be caused by noise from a spike of electrical energy on the line (i.e., lightning) or induced by electromechanical interference (i.e., a large motor in a building). Further types of errors can be caused by cable losses, flooded cables, rodent damage, or cross talk on the line, to name a few. Equipment can introduce errors from the digital repeaters, multiplexers, or DACS on the line. Unfortunately, the process of detecting these errors can be tenuous. Any pulse (a 1) or absence of a pulse (a 0) transmitted along the line is subject to noise that can change the actual data. When traveling through equipment such as multiplexers, repeaters, DACS, CSU, DSU, and the like, the pulses are accepted as valid. The equipment therefore cleans up the valid pulses, but because the electronic systems can't differentiate between valid and erroneous pulses, it cleans up the entire data stream. Consequently, the receiver at the distant end accepts the clean, well-timed input as correct information. Hence errors are introduced and undetected.

You might think that an error on the line could be easily detected by the equipment because certain format problems might also be evident. For example, an error (an extra pulse on the line) might violate the bipolar format convention, or a dropped pulse might violate the 1s density rule. Clearly these would be easy to detect. However, if the signal must pass through equipment along the way, that equipment might clean up the errors. The equipment does have the ability to log an error on the inbound side, then reformat the signal on the outbound side and make it appear to be valid.

ESF—A Step to Correct the Problem

In the early 1980s, AT&T suggested the implementation of the extended superframe format as a means to provide nondisruptive error detection and perform nonservice affecting diagnostics on T1 circuits. This represented a step toward correcting the problem of lost customer confidence and the disruptive performance testing. As service providers, the interexchange carriers write tariffs to provide service within certain guidelines of availability. ESF helps to address this problem.

Essentially, because overhead on the circuit is at issue, customers are unwilling to give up more channel capacity for maintenance and diagnostics. ESF uses the 8 Kbps of overhead normally assigned for the framing format and therefore does not affect the data bandwidth.

What Does ESF Do?

Extended superframe format, as its name implies, extends the superframe from 12 consecutive frames of information to 24 frames of information. ESF takes advantage of newer technologies to use the 8 Kbps of framing overhead and uses only 6 bits (2 Kbps) for framing synchronization. Six additional bits are used for error detection by means of a cyclic redundancy check 6 (CRC-6). This leaves 12 of the framing bits for a facility data link communications channel (4 Kbps).

Using this shared facility, the carrier has the option of performing the three functions necessary to support the customer needs:

- Framing synchronization
- Error detection
- In-service monitoring and diagnostics

Framing

As already stated, the fundamental purpose of the bit pattern is framing synchronization. Framing is important because its loss can impact performance through incorrect synchronization. (Channel 1 could wind up connected to Channel X [2–24] if the framing is incorrect.) Errors might cause a loss of frame and disrupt the circuit, and far-end and/or intermediate equipment could be thrown into a loss-of-frame condition and thereby a loss of data. While the devices along the circuit are reframing data, throughput is disrupted for a period of time. Depending on the equipment in use, this loss could be quite substantial (approximately 200 ms). Newer equipment performs a reframing operation in less time (approximately 10–20 ms). This helps to improve performance. With ESF using only 1 of 4 bits, the delay could increase significantly unless the proper equipment is purchased.

CRC-6

Cyclic redundancy checking is designed to detect errors that occur on the line. Because the network is error prone, it is a foregone conclusion that errors will occur. Using CRC-6, an entire ESF (24 frames of information or 4632 bits) is checked for accuracy. This check is a fictitious number created by the CSU as it performs a mathematical computation on the 4632 data bits. When the math is calculated using a prime number polynomial, a 6-bit pattern is the end result. In the next ESF (24 frames), the result of this mathematics is transmitted to the distant end.

At the distant end, the receiving CSU calculates exactly the same mathematical operations on the ESF data and then computes an answer. When the next ESF is received, the result of the first calculation is contained in the CRC bits (6 bits) of the overhead. When the two results are compared, the answers should be the same. If, however, they differ, an error has occurred. The use of CRC-6 allows for an error detection efficiency of 98.4 percent, or, simply stated, detection of 63 of 64 errors and 99.9995 percent of bursts of errors less than 16.

The Facility Data Link

The 4 Kbps of overhead set aside for facility data link control is a synchronous communication channel. This channel can serve multiple purposes, one of which is the exchange of information between equipment devices along the circuit. AT&T publication 54016 specifies a set of standard message formats for communicating across the data link to the storage devices. The standard conforms to a basic X.25 (BX.25) link procedure and uses an AT&T standard known as telemetry asynchronous block serial protocol (TABS). The carrier or end user can communicate with the remote equipment (CSU) using a maintenance message format. Some of the maintenance messages allowed under the AT&T technical reference (54016) include:

- *Send 1-hour performance data reports:* This includes the existing status of the link; time since the last check (up to 24 hours); errored seconds; and failed seconds in the present 15-minute cycle, the overall 24-hour cycle, and the past four 15-minute cycle performances.

- *Send 24-hour errored seconds (ES) performance data:* The CSU will send specific error events logged within the past 24 hours in 15-minute increments.

- *Send 24-hour failed seconds (FS) performance data:* The CSU sends the 24-hour historical information of errored events logged in 15-minute increments.

- *Reset registers:* Empty the buffers and start counting errors all over again.

- *Send errored ESF:* The CSU will send the current count of errors accumulated (up to a maximum of 65,535).

- *Reset ESF register :* Empty the buffer and start at zero

Benefits of ESF

The reasons to use ESF are to increase circuit availability and improve performance. Once again, putting 24 channels (circuits) on one T1 puts the user at risk if performance is poor. Just about all of the major carriers (interexchange) have implemented ESF. Because all of the interexchange carriers internetwork—that is, they connect to each other—the use of the AT&T standard (54016) is the norm.

Vendors and carriers can see the improvements brought about by ESF. When a burst of errors occurs, the carrier need only access the CSU from the facility data link and query for status. The problem of old, the "no trouble found" situation, tends to fade into the background because the CSU has buffers to collect the errors for later retrieval. Further, with the facility of data link, the carrier can monitor real customer data traveling across the line nondisruptively. Errors occurring on the line can be seen and diagnosed in real time. This all leads to a better track record. In fact, many of the carriers will contractually guarantee circuit availability between 98.4 and 99.5 percent because of the proactive capability gathered in ESF.

This seemed to solve the problem for users and carriers alike. Despite the passive collection capability and the on-line diagnostics, the parties all began to create a working rather than an adversarial role.

Problems with ESF

Unfortunately, one player that is not mentioned in this scenario and yet is an essential ingredient in the total circuit is the local exchange carrier (LEC). An integral piece of the circuit is the "last mile," or the circuit running from the LEC to the customer premises. ESF was designed to function as a part of the customer premises equipment (CPE). However, the LEC by mandate cannot poll the CSU that stores the error information. Under the guidelines of the modified final judgment (MFJ), or what we know as divestiture, the LEC cannot go beyond a clearly defined demarcation point. This demarcation is the line termination in the RJ-48, RJ-68, or smart jack—where the LEC stops and customer takes over. Some of these limitations are falling aside with the deregulation of the telecommunications industry and the Telecommunications Act of 1996. Yet the local utilities commissions across North America have still held some of the barriers intact. Over time, the change will be finalized, but it is a phased project.

This point, therefore, excludes the LEC from benefits derived from ESF as defined by the AT&T technical reference (54016). To overcome this problem, the American National Standards Institute (ANSI) came up with a proactive approach to ESF: ANSI's standard T1.403 uses the CSU to monitor performance on the T1 line, then puts together an activity report every second and transmits this ESF report back out across the network. This solves the problem but leaves the door open to two sets of standards.

Questions

1. When did the Bell System begin to install T1 in the US?
   a. 1955
   b. 1934
   c. 1982
   d. 1960

2. What was the name of the inventor of the PCM technique?
   a. Alexander Bell
   b. Heinrich Hertz
   c. Harry Nyquist
   d. Dr. Watson

3. A T1 only carries 18 channels of voice or data.   T/F

4. To create the 64 Kbps trransmission we apply the following steps:
   a. Sample the channel at 2x the highest frequency
   b. Quantize the information
   c. Digitally encode the signal
   d. None of the above
   e. All of the above

5. The two framing formats currently in use are _____ and _____.

6. T1s are synchronized in three ways
   a. Bit
   b. Byte
   c. Frame
   d. CSU
   e. DSU
   f. All of the above
   g. a, b, and c only

7. AMI stands for
   a. Alternating Marked Information
   b. Available Mark Inverted
   c. Alternate Mark Inversion
   d. Any Mark Incident

8. The AMI format creates a bipolar signal.   T/F

9. Bipolar is shown by _____ and _____ 3 volt pulses.

10. The ones density rule means that the signal is densely populated with ones.   T/F

11. Ones density requires that_____% of the pulses transmitted will be ones.

12. The AT&T rule states that in every 8 bits there will be at least _____ pulse and there may be no more than _____ consecutive zeros.
    a. 1 and 24
    b. 3 and 24
    c. 3 and 8
    d. 1 and 8
    e. 1 and 15

13. The D4 framing format required that the link is tested disruptively.   T/F

14. To solve the problem by allowing non-disruptive testing, the _____ format was created.
    a. DS3
    b. D3
    c. D4
    d. ESK
    e. ESF

15. The T1 can be channelized or nonchannelized.   T/F

16. The newer framing format (ESF) uses a CRC-32 to do its error checking.   T/F

17. How many T1s are used to create a T3?
    a. 3
    b. 4
    c. 24
    d. 28
    e. None of the above

Wireless Communications

After reading this chapter and completing the questions, you will be able to:

- Discuss the evolution of cellular networks
- Explain the components of a radio system
- Describe laser communications
- Explain the distances and impairments of a radio communications
- Discuss the various options to modulate information onto a wireless channel

Wireless forms of communications are nothing new. Since the early days of civilization, various forms of communication took place without the advantage of physical connectivity. In tribal jungle environments, drums were a primary means of communicating. As message senders beat on either drums or hollowed out logs, the reverberating sounds were interpreted at the other end as shown in Fig. 7.1. In many situations, the drumbeat would travel only a limited distance, so various relay points were needed. The first receiver would acknowledge the sender's message through a series of return drumbeats, and then relay the same message to the next receiver. This limited form of transmission met the need but was subject to a lot of noisy interference and misunderstanding. Therefore, the message was sent repeatedly to minimize potential errors in interpretation. Crude, but it worked. Moreover, the use-limited distance didn't prevent others from "listening in" on the conversation undetected.

In early American times, Native American tribes used smoke signals as a limited distance form of communication. Drawbacks to smoke signals included distance limitations based on line-of-sight, a limited alphabet, and errors caused by the wind. If the smoke puff was blown away or dissipated too soon, the communication was lost.

The introduction of the semaphore flag deepened the scope of communication through an enhanced alphabet that could address the language needs, but was also limited to

Figure 7.1   Drums were an early means of communications.

line-of-sight daytime operation. Hardly a reliable or widely available capability, it was effective in certain circumstances. Because semaphore signaling allowed a full alphabet to be used, messages could be more extensive and detailed. Drawbacks were the limited distance (requiring constant relay of the information), the added time needed to send detailed messages, and the risk of undetected interception of the message.

In the nineteenth century, light beams were used for short haul communications, particularly in military contexts. Very detailed messages could be transmitted by a coded sequence (Morse code) of blinking lights from sender to receiver. Again, this was effective over limited distances and provided a quiet, yet visible means of communication. Drawbacks included limited distance, unauthorized reception of information due to visibility at various angles, and risk of interception. Security was always suspect, so a form of alphabetic encryption was introduced as a safeguard. This required an ever-changing code set, along with special handling and extra time to manually decipher the transmitted message. Further, the cipher code had to be kept current at all locations so that correctness could be achieved.

In radio transmission, human speech must first be converted to an electrical signal. This signal is analogous to the composition of the sound pressure changes produced by the human voice, hence the term analog communications. The analysis of sound waves is a key part of radio communications theory. Knowledge of radio principles is critical to understanding how the various wireless communications techniques function. In early telecommunications systems (particularly the telephony world), radio was an integral part of network development. As newer systems emerged, modifications and enhancements enabled networks to carry all forms of communication, including voice, data, telegraph, image, fax, and video.

Radio-Based Systems

As radio-based systems emerged, wireless communications became more readily avail able and easier to use. An electric transmitter was used to reproduce sound waves and modulate human speech onto a baseband radio frequency. If you need to go back and review the information on the modulation of the wave, refer back to Chapter 6. The radio wave carrying the transmitted signal could travel greater distances, allowing far more reliability and minimizing the relay process. Several portions of the radio frequency spectrum were allocated (assigned) to these transmission systems. Each carried its own particular capacities and had distance limitations associated with the band (range of frequencies) used for transmission.

Certain characteristics play an important role in the use of radio frequency. These should be understood in order to gain an appreciation of the use of radio frequency in our everyday life.

Free Space Communication

Radio systems propagate information in free space. This free space communication obviates some of the problems faced by other transmission systems. For example, wired systems require a physical medium and are difficult to install in certain geographic areas. Advantages of the radio system include the ability to:

- Span bodies of water, such as lakes or rivers as shown in Fig. 7.2, where a cable facility would require special treatment to prevent seepage onto the copper conductors.
- Overcome transmission obstacles posed by mountains and deep valleys as shown in Fig. 7.3, where cable costs would be prohibitive to install and difficult to maintain.
- Bypass the basic interconnection to the local telephone provider (Telco) or post telephone and telegraph (PTT) company.

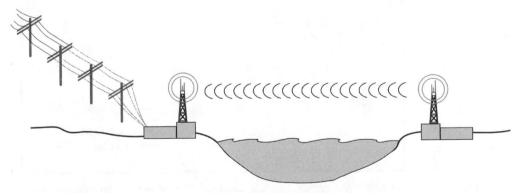

Figure 7.2 Radio systems overcome natural obstacles such as bodies of water.

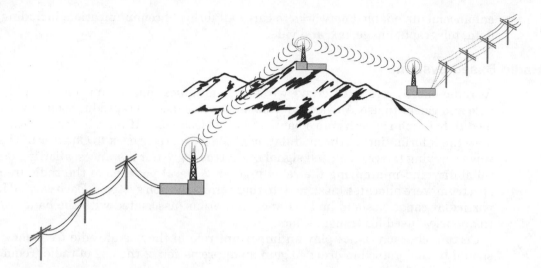

Figure 7.3 In some case, a radio system overcomes mountains and valleys.

Radio Frequency (RF)

Radio frequency has certain behavioral patterns that are important. The RF is divided into various parts of the spectrum each of the parts is allocated for use by the responsible agencies (such as the FCC in the United States). RF uses the signal propagation and creates several different behaviors.

■ *Free space loss*: Occurs as the RF travels through the air as shown in Fig. 7.4, also called attenuation.

Figure 7.4 Free space loss occurs over the distance. The higher the frequency used the quicker the attenuation.

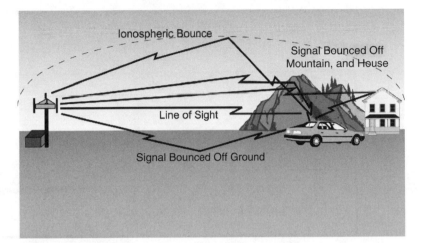

Figure 7.5   Reflection and multipath interference occurs as the signals bounce off various objects.

- *Reflection*: Occurs when a RF signal bounces off a smooth surface and changes directions as shown in Fig. 7.5. This is also called multipath fade or bounce.

- *Refraction*: Occurs when an RF signal is bent when passing through and being reflected by a medium with different density (can be the air).

- *Diffraction:* Occurs when a change in direction or intensity of a group of radio waves passes by an obstacle. This is also referred to as bending the wave.

- *Scattering*: Occurs when an RF signal strikes an uneven surface and causes the signal to be scattered in such a way that the resultant signals are insignificant.

- *Absorption*: Occurs when the RF signal is absorbed into the material of an object (it does not bounce off, pass through or bend around an object). RF is also prone to water absorption as shown in Fig. 7.6. This is true in higher frequency ranges.

- *Shadowing*: Terrain plays an important role in the use and design of networks. If the area is hilly, the signal strength behind the hills is attenuated even further as seen in Fig. 7.7. This phenomenon can also be observed when receiving normal FM radio in a car, when being far from the radio station. In one place the signal may be good, but after moving a meter or two (toward a red light!) the signal may be completely gone. The shadow is an area that no coverage is available based on the site design.

The Radio Frequency Spectrum

Because the waveform represents the electrical equivalent for analog transmission, it will also have a certain velocity with respect to distance and time. In free space radio transmission, the electromagnetic wave moves through the air at the speed of light (186,000 miles per second). Radio waves can be produced and transmitted across a wide

Figure 7.6 Absorption is a natural phenomenon where the RF signal is absorbed by the water in the air (such as heavy rain or humidity) or if a human body is nearby.

Figure 7.7 Shadowing is a common problem. Even if the initial deployment of RF systems works fine, changes can disrupt the overall performance.

range of frequencies, starting at about 10 kHz up through the millions of hertz (megahertz, or MHz) and even billions of hertz (gigahertz, or GHz). The spectrum ranges from radio frequencies through light frequencies and finally to x-rays and cosmic rays. Light frequencies operate in the THz (terahertz) range. A summary of the frequencies and wavelength is shown in Fig. 7.8.

Antennas

Antennas are used to collect the signal or to send the signal into the airwave. The Fresnel zone is the area that surrounds the transmitted signal (RF) from the antenna where the radio waves spread out after leaving the antenna, as shown in Fig. 7.9. Fresnel zone size is a function of the distance between antennas and the frequency used to transmit.

Line-of-sight (LOS) occurs when one antenna can "see" the other antenna. If a person stands next to one antenna and the other end is visible, then LOS exists. RF LOS is achieved when visual LOS exists, and there are no objects (trees, buildings) in the Fresnel zone (FZ) (no greater than 40 percent of the FZ can have obstacles in it).

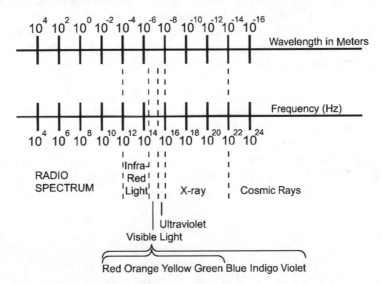

Figure 7.8 The RF spectrum shown in both frequencies and wavelength is a good comparison to use.

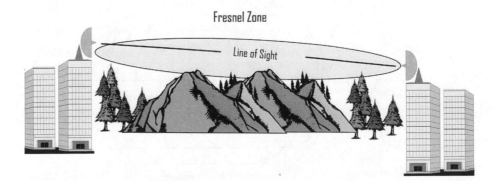

Figure 7.9 The Fresnel zone is the LOS required to communicate between antennas.

Radio Propagation

Depending on the band selected, the characteristics of propagation will vary. In general, when the signal is transmitted through an antenna device, the signal will travel along the earth's curvature. As the signal emanates in all directions (or in a point-to-point direction), the energy follows the earth's curvature. In some cases, reflected power off the earth's surface helps achieve the desired result. At lower frequencies (very low, low, and medium bands), the signal follows the curve of the earth's surface in what is typically called a ground wave. The distance that the wave travels is a function of the amount of power generated by the transmitting device. Power output is selected to cover specific distances and areas. This ground wave is shown in Fig. 7.10.

At the *high frequency* (HF) band, the ground wave is absorbed and attenuated very quickly. However, the radiated energy also has an upward movement in which the signal reaches approximately 40–300 miles above the earth shown in Fig. 7.11, entering the ionosphere. In the ionosphere, the radio waves get refracted at various angles and bounced back down to the earth. This type of transmission enables radio signals to be directionalized and transmitted at much lower power output.

At the very high frequency (VHF) band, the signal is transmitted in straight lines. A directional antenna can be used to direct the signal in an LOS path. A certain portion of the signal can be reflected off the ground along this same path and get to the same point. The design of this type of transmission requires great care, because the reflected wave can cause interference. Because the signal is being reflected off the earth's surface (or other surface), the path is longer. Therefore, the reflected signal can arrive later than the direct LOS signal. This delay, or out-of-phase signal, can distort the transmission.

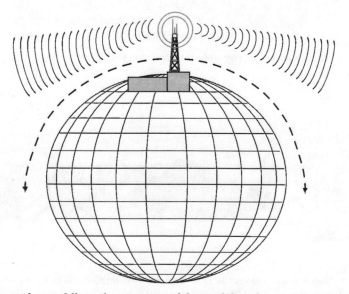

Figure 7.10 The ground wave follows the curvature of the earth based on gravitational pull.

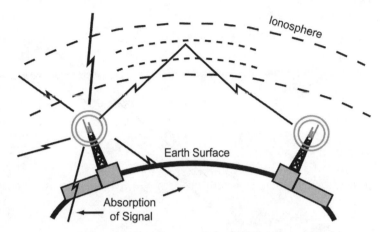

Figure 7.11   As high frequency communications is used, the ionosphere is used for bounce (refraction).

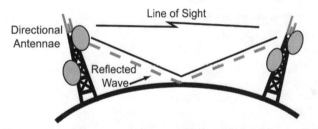

Figure 7.12   Very high frequency starts to demand line of sight communications, but a reflected path is also incorporated.

VHF transmission uses an LOS signal. The reflected wave is also shown in Fig. 7.12. In order to achieve LOS transmission, antenna height is critical. The greater the distance, the higher the antenna required.

At the ultra high frequency (UHF) band, the use of microwave signals is more prominent. In the microwave systems of today, high range frequencies are used for point-to-point communications. Several channels of communication can be multiplexed together and transmitted across the carrier. These microwave systems are used extensively by telephone companies and private organizations to carry telephone calls. Two sets of frequencies are required in microwave systems: a transmit frequency and a receive frequency. The lower bands of the frequency spectrum (LF and HF) are used as a one-way alternating transmission on a single frequency requiring one party to listen while the other speaks. A push to talk transmission is used. If both parties try to send at the same time, a jamming effect will render the transmission useless. Very specific transmission protocols are required so that the radio can be used effectively.

A microwave transmission uses two separate systems (a transmitter and a receiver). Each of the systems has its own frequency. Frequency 1 is used to transmit from west

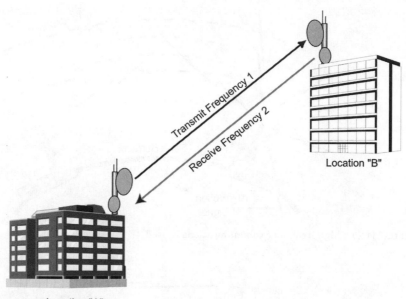

Figure 7.13   Microwave radio uses two separate frequencies to allow full-duplex operation.

to east, whereas frequency 2 is used to transmit from east to west, shown in Fig. 7.13. Newer microwave systems use a single transceiver. This simplifies the process and makes the communication easier.

Microwave Radio

As radio-based systems evolved, it was discovered that a microwave transmission could cover greater distance using repeaters. Basically, a repeater receives the radio signal on one antenna, converts the signal back into its electrical properties, then retransmits the signal out across a new transmitter. In some cases, the repeater changes the signal from one frequency to another. Line-of-sight transmission is used, and the height of the antenna is important to maintain this capability. An antenna array and tower is shown in Fig. 7.14.

However, limitations from power, path, and other sources still restrict the distances covered. The distance limitations vary for microwave transmissions in various frequency ranges. The typical distance for a 2 GHz microwave transmission is 30 miles between repeaters based on the curvature of the earth and the power output allowed by the regulatory bodies. The repeaters are shown in Fig. 7.15.

Each system will vary depending on external factors. For example, a 2–6 GHz radio installed atop Mt. Killington in Vermont could successfully achieve a 50–70 mile distance between systems without repeaters. The antenna's height in relation to the

Figure 7.14 Antennas are mounted on towers to get the height and distance necessary for the LOS.

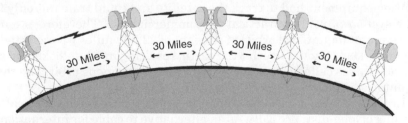

Figure 7.15 Repeaters are spaced approximately 30 miles apart.

earth's curvature allows greater transmission distance and minimizes interference from other sources. Also, the power output can be greater (although not required) at this height, because there's nothing else around.

The Path

The propagation path of a radio signal includes the direct wave, a reflected wave, and a surface wave. These combine to form the ground wave. Another portion of the wave, the refracted wave, is a function of atmospheric conditions. Each of these components affects the transmission of the radio signal in terms of loss (attenuation) and distortion. In microwave systems, the direct or free space wave is the controlling influence. However, the refracted wave must be considered as a deterrent to high-quality transmission, since it can cause multipath fading.

Other considerations must be looked at in path selection. For example, with LOS systems, it is the operator's responsibility to be aware of any construction plans along the path. A new building erected in the middle of the path can render transmission totally useless. Performance issues such as rain absorption must also be considered. Any system over the 8 GHz frequency range is prone to rain attenuation; that is, raindrops scatter or absorb the energy, impeding the reception of a high-quality signal.

Satellite Radio Communications

In 1960, microwave radio signals were transmitted up into the atmosphere to a repeater floating in space. The system was originally designed to bounce radio waves off an artificial object orbiting the earth. Earlier attempts to bounce radio waves off the moon were not as successful as had been hoped. The system worked, but the returning signal was so weak it couldn't be used. A similar attempt to bounce radio waves off an inflated weather balloon met with equally unrewarding results. Therefore, an active rather than a passive system became the next logical step.

An orbiting satellite offers several distinct advantages. A stronger signal can be obtained, and over very long distances the transmission signal requires only a single repeater. The connection is represented in Fig. 7.16. The satellite can be located in a polar, inclined, or equatorial orbit. The orbit can be either circular (equidistant) or elliptical (nonconcurrent) at different heights above the earth's surface. Early satellites were launched into elliptical orbits at lower heights than today's satellites. The orbit around the earth took from 1 to 2 hours, depending on the height and path. The earth station equipment had to track the satellite and could transmit only for limited periods. The system proved impractical for commercial use. Therefore, a circular orbit around the equator (equatorial orbit) at a height of 22,300 miles was selected. A satellite at this height takes 24 hours to orbit the earth, resulting in what looks like a stationary object. In fact, this is called a geostationary or geosynchronous orbit. The three satellites in an equatorial orbit are shown in Fig. 7.17

In the early days, satellite communications represented a radical change in the processing of long-distance calls. As an alternative to cable for international communication,

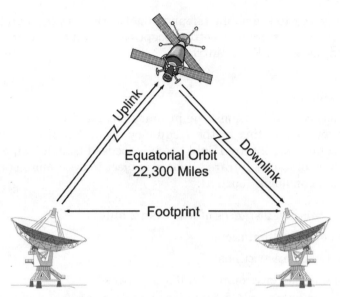

Figure 7.16   The satellite is located 22,300 miles above the earth when in equatorial orbit.

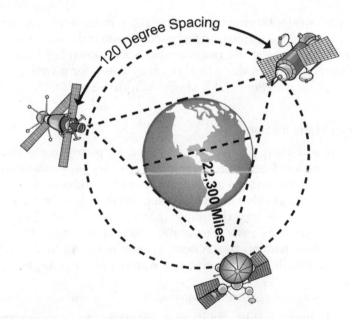

Figure 7.17   Three satellites is all it takes to cover the entire earth.

satellite transmission was very competitive. Further, in rural and underdeveloped areas, it provided quick connectivity solutions for users with a limited number of HF radio channels and allowed large amounts of bandwidth in areas that did not have a cable infrastructure in place. Maritime (ship-to-shore) communications improved through satellite access to the public telephone networks. Finally, satellite broadcasts of high-quality TV signals brought better reception as well as new information access to local communities and entire countries.

Laser Communications

In wireless communications, the primary means of transmitting light is through free space lasers. Operating in the frequency spectrum of laser beams in the terahertz range, an invisible infrared light beam is focused from a transmitter to a receiver over a very short distance. Infrared light is subject to even more specific curtailments than the radio technologies, such as:

- Transmission distances of less than 2 miles
- Line-of-sight limitations
- Bandwidth restrictions
- Proneness to environmental disturbances
- Disruption from fog, dust, heavy rain, and objects in its path

No single wireless technology can be 100 percent effective; each has its own limitations and strengths. Despite the technical bandwidth limitations, there are certain cost advantages and ease of use considerations that keep light-based systems high on the scale of acceptability in the minds of many users for a variety of applications such as voice, data, video, and now LAN traffic at native speeds.

Dynamics of Laser Transmission

An atmospheric laser transmission system helps overcome the stringent limitations and obstacles associated with other types of short haul communications. Transmission through the air, without the use of infrastructure, reduces the need for a right of way, as is necessary with a cable system. Further, infrared laser systems fall under the domain of nonlicensed technology, thereby removing many of the licensing requirements and associated delays and costs. For under the 2-mile range, this technique holds a wide range of exciting possibilities. A laser system is shown in Fig. 7.18.

The FSO technology approach has a number of advantages:

- Requires no RF spectrum licensing.
- Is easily upgradeable, and its open interfaces support equipment from a variety of vendors, which helps enterprises and service providers protect their investment in embedded telecommunications infrastructures.
- Requires no security software upgrades.
- Is immune to radio frequency interference or saturation.
- Can be deployed behind windows, eliminating the need for costly rooftop rights.

Figure 7.18 Laser communications (free space optics) systems are effective at under 2 miles. (*Source: LightPointe Communications*)

Vehicular Communications

In 1946, Illinois Bell Telephone Company (now a part of AT&T) introduced a mobile telephone service that would allow users driving in and around the Chicago area to communicate directly to and from vehicles. Using a radio-to-telephone interface, the telephone companies had a monopoly on this service. Users lined up by the hundreds if not the thousands to request mobile telephone service.

There was a 2-year wait in many areas of the country as the service rolled out. The reason was simple: the telephone companies mounted high-gain antennas on top of high-rise office buildings in the major downtown areas. From there, they would boom out a signal at approximately 200–250 watts. This is a very strong signal in any transmission. The antenna was on top of the highest building, and the power output was so great to get the best coverage possible. The FCC had only issued a limited number of frequencies for use in the mobile phone services.

All calls within the city had to be routed through the centralized tower because of the limited amount of channels. In this particular network, 12 channels were available. Each channel was used on a high-powered radio transmitter. Further, the system operated on a one-way (simplex) basis. Only one side of the call could speak at a time. This was analogous to the older two-way "push-to-talk" radio systems. The telephone companies were trying to provide coverage in approximately a 25-mile radius from the downtown area. Back in the late 1940s that was sufficient, because the work force was less mobile.

Problems with the Mobile Telephone Service

This arrangement worked for short periods, but, as newer demands were placed on the system, very limited channel capacity was strained. The limited number of channels led to the frequency reuse planning in the telephone companies.

Radio-based communications will travel greater distances as a function of the frequency used, antenna height, and output power. Even though the signal pattern was designed to provide coverage only in a 25-mile radius, it would cause interference to adjacent operators. As clearly shown in Fig. 7.19, another 50–75 miles bound the overlap areas. This means that the radio-based system could only use the assigned channels every 100 miles apart. The areas around the circle in this figure—the buffer zones—exist to prevent interference. You might recall from the bandwidth discussion earlier in this book that sidebands and frequency bandpass filters are used in the wired telephone world. Essentially the same holds true in the wireless world, where the telephone company allocated the buffer zones so that two conversations would not occur on the same channel. The figure shows that the signal was used in the center (thicker) core, but the overlap areas are shown in the lighter core.

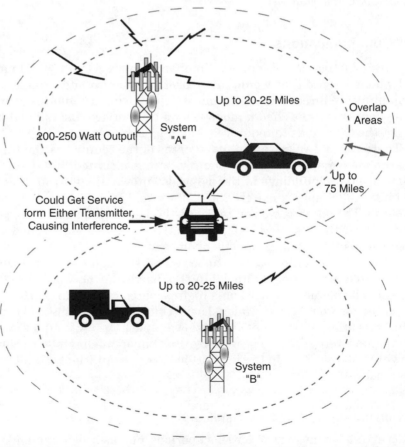

Figure 7.19 The interference and coverage patterns of the original MTS were greater than 25 miles and could be as much as 100 miles.

Cellular Communications

The carriers wanted to meet the demand for more services, but they just did not have the frequencies available. Therefore the engineers went back to the drawing board and created a new technique called cellular communications. The concept allows a honeycomb pattern of overlapping "cells" of communication. Because these cells can be minimal in size, it is possible to reuse the frequencies repeatedly. The goal of cellular was to make more service available to vehicular users.

In 1981, the FCC finally set aside 20 MHz of spectrum for cellular use. The spectrum was set aside for two separate carriers. The lower frequencies were reserved for wireline companies. Wireline companies are the regulated providers (the local telephone companies). The higher frequencies were assigned or reserved for nonwireline carriers, which are the competitors to the telephone carriers. Both operating carriers (the wireline and nonwireline) are licensed to operate in a specific geographic area. The areas are classified as the metropolitan service areas (MSA) and rural service areas (RSA). Each carrier had approximately 312 frequencies for voice/data communication and 21 frequencies for control channels.

The signal on conventional mobile radiotelephones degrades as the vehicle moved farther away from the base station. This degradation frustrated both the caller and the called party. As the user went beyond an area of coverage, the call would be cut off, further frustrating both calling and called parties.

With cellular communications, when a call is in progress and the caller moves away from the cell site toward a new cell, the call gets "handed off" from one cell to another. In Fig. 7.20, this process begins to take place. Here's how it works. Once a call is in progress and the handoff from cell to cell becomes necessary to keep it that way, the system initiates a change. As the cellular telephone approaches the imaginary line, the signal strength transmitted back to the cell site will start to fall. The cell site equipment will send a form of distress message to the mobile telephone switching office (MTSO), indicating that the signal is getting weaker. The MTSO then orchestrates the passing of the call from one cell site to another.

Immediately after receiving the message from the cell site, the MTSO sends out a broadcast to the other cell sites in the area. It issues a request to determine which site is receiving the cellular user's signal the most strongly; this is called a quality of service measurement. Each site responds accordingly.

As the responses come back to the MTSO, the particular cell receiving the signal the most strongly is then selected to accept the call. The MTSO directs the targeted cell site to set up a voice path in parallel to the site losing the signal. When this is ready, the MTSO sends a command to the cellular set to resynthesize, or go to the new frequency. The cellular set then retunes itself to the new frequency assigned to the receiving cell site, and the handoff takes place. This takes approximately 100–200 milliseconds to enact. Figure 7.21 shows the handoff.

This might sound a little more complicated than it really is. The designers recognized that the original radio systems put out way too much power. Using a lower-power output device, the radius of the radio transmission system is smaller. In fact, the

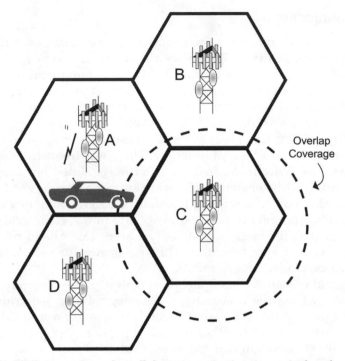

Figure 7.20 The handoff process in analog cellular communications is required as the vehicle roams from one cell to another.

cellular system was designed to operate in a range of approximately 3–5 miles. If the power output is reduced to 10 watts, the radio transmission will travel less distance. Therefore, the user must be closer to the equipment to receive the call. To accommodate this, the cellular "cells" include equipment placed (typically) in the center of each of these overlapping cells. The distance from the radio equipment to the user will be approximately 1–2 miles. Therefore, the system should work more efficiently. With only a 10-watt output, the frequencies used in each of the cells can be reused repeatedly. A separation of at least two cells must exist, but that was taken into account. Figure 7.22 is a representation of a cell network showing the honeycomb pattern.

The carriers have been getting better at providing this coverage as the years have gone by. Many of the cellular suppliers now have provided for a seamless transition from cell to cell anywhere in the country. To do this, they have developed an interface into another telephone- or landline-based technique called signaling system 7 (SS7). Using SS7, the carriers can now hand a call off across the country without user involvement. It just happens transparently. The SS7 linkage is shown in Fig. 7.23, where the MTSO equipment is tied into a computer system called a signal transfer point (STP). Recall the SS7 discussion from Chapter 4. In this figure, the MTSOs are tied to duplicate STPs as a means of providing redundancy in the network. With this interconnection, additional features were also provided in the cellular networks similar to the telephone networks.

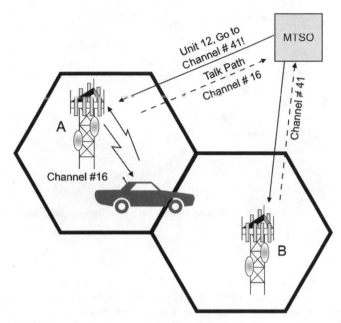

Figure 7.21 The handoff takes place under control of the mobile telephone switching office.

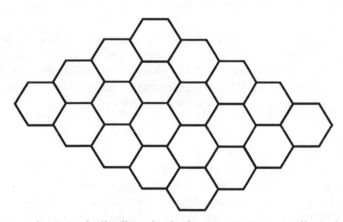

Figure 7.22 A honeycomb patter of cells allows for the frequency reuse more effectively.

Using either amplitude modulation or frequency modulation techniques, which were discussed in Chapter 6, to transmit voice on the radio signal uses all of the available bandwidth (or most of it). Distance, noise, and other interference demand power, amplification, and bandwidth to deliver a quality service. This means that the analog cellular carriers can support a single call on a single frequency (specific frequency). As such, the limitations of the systems are in channel availability on a given set of technologies.

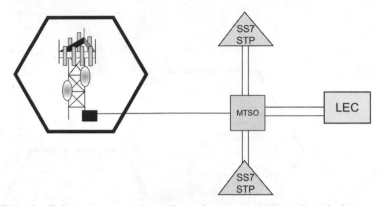

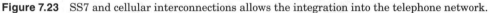

Figure 7.23   SS7 and cellular interconnections allows the integration into the telephone network.

If you consider the noisy nature of analog signals, you can also determine that quality is a matter of multiple factors, not the least of which will be congestion and atmospheric conditions, as covered in other sections of this book.

The analog system was designed to provide the benefit of quick communications while on the road. Because this is considered a service that would meet the telephone needs of users on the go, the thought of heavy penetration was only minimally addressed.

These evolutions in the analog arena were all driving forces in the use and acceptance of cellular communications. However, as congestion continued to go unchecked, the carriers entered a new era. The whole world has been evolving to digital transmission systems on the local and long-distance scene. This evolution to digital has many benefits for the standard wire-based carriers.

Digital Transmission

The cellular carriers continue to step into the digital world. This stems from the perspectives of compatibility and frequency utilization. If users can share a frequency or range of frequencies, then more users can be accommodated on less bandwidth. This has a definite financial impact on the carrier investment strategies. They could support more users on fewer frequencies and require less equipment. Many carriers still offer analog services as their primary service.

Digital

Digital transmission delivers better multiplexing schemes so that the carriers can get more users on an already strained radio frequency spectrum. Additional possibilities for enhancing security and reducing fraud are also addressed with digital cellular. Again, this appears to be a win-win situation for the carriers.

Once the decision was made to consider digital transmission, the major problem was how to achieve the switch, what flavor to use, and how to transfer the existing customer base seamlessly to digital. The options available to the carriers are:

- Time-division multiple access (TDMA) using global system for mobile (GSM)
- Code-division multiple access (CDMA)

Carriers and manufacturers are using both these system types. This creates a split in the industry, depending on the technique chosen and the carrier support. Whenever a user changes carriers, the likelihood of having to get a new set is very high.

GSM

GSM uses TDMA, a time-division multiplexing scheme where time slices are allocated to multiple conversations. Although TDMA usually deals with an analog-to-digital conversion using a typical pulse code modulation technique, it performs differently in a radio transmission. PCM is translated into a quadrature phase-shift keying technique, thereby producing a four-phased shift, doubling the data rate for data transmission (actually driving a voice call at 8 Kbps).

GSM Architecture

A GSM network is composed of several functional entities, whose functions and interfaces are shown in Fig. 7.24. The layout of a generic GSM network is shown. The GSM network can be divided into three broad parts. The subscriber carries the mobile

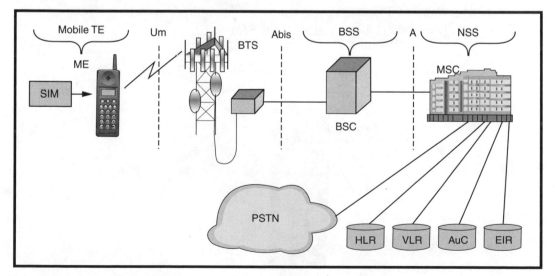

Fig 7.24 The GSM architecture.

station; the base station subsystem controls the radio link with the mobile station and the network subsystem, the main part of which is the mobile services switching center, performs the switching of calls between the mobile and other fixed or mobile network users, as well as management of mobile services, such as authentication.

Not shown is the operations and maintenance center, which oversees the proper operation and setup of the network. The mobile station and the base station subsystem communicate across the U_m (User interface modified for mobile) interface also known as the air interface or radio link. The base station subsystem communicates with the network service switching center across the A interface.

Subscriber Identity Module

The SIM shown in Fig. 7.25 provides personal mobility, so that the user can have access to all subscribed services irrespective of both the location of the terminal and the use of a specific terminal. By inserting the SIM card into another GSM cellular phone, the user is able to receive calls at that phone, make calls from that phone, or receive other subscribed services.

The mobile equipment is uniquely identified by the International Mobile Equipment Identity (IMEI). The SIM card contains the International Mobile Subscriber Identity (IMSI), identifying the subscriber, a secret key for authentication, and other user information. The IMEI and the IMSI are independent, thereby providing personal mobility. The SIM card may be protected against unauthorized use by a password or personal identity number.

The mobile phone actually consists of two separate components, each having its own specific role. The two components include the:

1. Mobile equipment
2. Subscriber identity module (or SIM card)

Figure 7.25   The SIM card inserts into the set.

Frequencies Allocated

In principle the GSM system can be implemented in any frequency band. However, there are several bands where GSM terminals are available. Furthermore, GSM terminals may incorporate one or more of the GSM frequency bands listed below to facilitate roaming on a global basis.

- *GSM 400*: 450.4–457.6 MHz paired with 460.4–467.6 MHz or 478.8–486 MHz paired with 488.8–496 MHz.
- *GSM 900*: Initially the 890–915 MHz frequencies paired with the 935–960 MHz were used in GSM Primary. Later additional channel capacity was added to be 880–915 MHz paired with 925–960 MHz bands. This added 10 MHz to the overall spectrum.
- *GSM 1800* (also called DCS 1800): 1710–1785 MHz paired with 1805–1880 MHz.
- *GSM 1900* (also called PCS in the United States): 1850–1910 MHz paired with 1930–1990 MHz.

In the above bands mobile stations transmit in the lower frequency sub-band and base stations transmit in the higher frequency sub-band.

TDMA Frames

In GSM, a 25-MHz frequency band is divided, using a FDMA scheme, into 124 carrier frequencies spaced one from each other by a 200-kHz frequency band. Normally, a 25-MHz frequency band can provide 125 carrier frequencies, but the first carrier frequency is used as a guard band between GSM and other services working on lower frequencies. Each carrier frequency is then divided in time using a TDMA scheme. This scheme splits the radio channel, with a width of 200 kHz, into eight bursts. The frame is shown in Fig. 7.26.

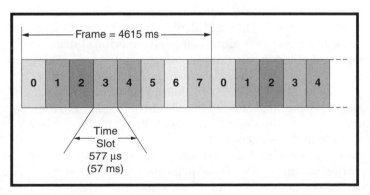

Figure 7.26   GSM TDMA frame.

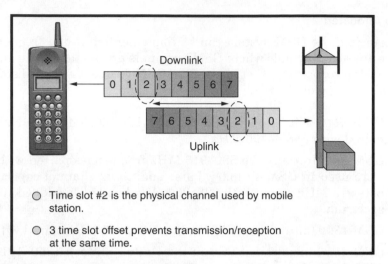

Figure 7.27 The three-time slot offset allows the phone to switch from send to receive.

A burst is the unit of time in a TDMA system, and it lasts approximately 0.577 ms. A TDMA frame is formed with eight bursts and lasts, consequently, 4.615 ms. Each of the eight bursts, that form a TDMA frame, is then assigned to an end user. One time slot is used for transmission by the mobile and one for reception. They are separated in time so that the mobile unit does not receive and transmit at the same time, a fact that simplifies the electronics.

A separation is used with a three-time slot offset so that the mobile will not have to send and receive at the same time. This is shown in Fig. 7.27 with the directional signals in each side of the channel.

GSM FDMA/TDMA Combination

To enable multiple access, GSM utilizes a blending of frequency division multiple access (FDMA) and Time-Division Multiple Access (TDMA). This combination is used to overcome the problems introduced in each individual scheme. In the case of FDMA, frequencies are divided up into smaller ranges of frequency slots and each of these slots is assigned to a user during a call. Although this method will result in an increase of the number of users, it is not efficient in the case of high user demand. On the other hand, TDMA assigns a time slot for each user for utilizing the entire frequency. Similarly, this will become easily overloaded when encountering high user demand. Hence, GSM uses a two-dimensional access scheme.

GSM uses the combined FDMA and TDMA architecture to provide the most efficient operation within the scope of price and reasonable data. The physical channels are TDMA times lots and the radio channels are frequencies. This scheme divides the entire frequency bandwidth into several smaller pieces as in FDMA and each of this

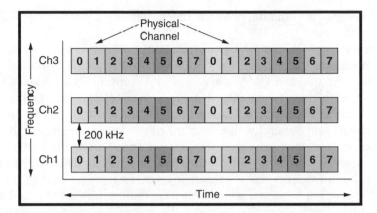

Figure 7.28   The 200-kHz channels are divided by frequency (FDMA) and the slotted by time (TDMA).

frequency slots is to be divided into eight time slots in a full-rate configuration. The FDMA/TDMA combination is shown in Fig. 7.28.

The cell sizes tend to be limited to a maximum radius of 35 km. The maximum timing advance is 63 bits (0–63). The duration of a single bit is 3.69 microseconds. Because the path has to be equalized is a two-way service, the maximum physical distance between the BTS and a mobile is half the maximum delay, or 70 km/2 = 35 km. The random access burst can accommodate a maximum delay over a distance of 75.5 km, that way the bursts can appear at the BTS receiver with a high possibility that they will not be covered by another mobile's normal burst. With larger cells, this cannot be assured.

CDMA

CDMA is a radical shift from the original FDMA and TDMA wireless techniques. This system has been gaining widespread acceptance across the world in the cellular industry. The cellular providers see CDMA as an upgrade opportunity for their capacity and quality. CDMA is a form of spread spectrum, a family of digital communications techniques. The core principle behind CDMA is the use of the noise-floor to carry radio signals.

As its name implies, bandwidth greater and wider than normal constrained FDMA and TDMA channels is used. Point-to-point communications is effective on the bandwidth that uses the noise waves to carry the signal spread across a significantly wider radio carrier. Spread spectrum, which was employed back in the 1920s, has evolved from military security applications. It uses a technique of organizing the radio frequency energy over a range of frequencies, rather than a modulation technique. The system uses frequency hopping with time-division multiplexing. At one minute the transmitter is operating at one frequency, at the next instant it is on another. The receiver is synchronized to switch frequencies in the same pattern. This is effective in preventing detection (interception) and jamming; thus, additional security is derived.

These techniques should produce increased capacities of 10 to 20 fold over existing analog systems.

Originally, conceived for commercial application in the 1940s, it was an additional 40 years before this technique became commercially feasible. The main factors holding back the use of CDMA were cost and complexity of operation. Today, the use of low-cost, high-density digital *integrated circuits* (ICs) that reduce the size and weight of the radio equipment makes the use of CDMA far more feasible. Another area is an educational one, whereby the carriers needed to understand that the use of optimal communications requires that the station equipment must regulate the power to the lowest possible levels to achieve the maximum performance. This, of course, flies in the face of the normal operations that the carriers learned during their training.

In 1989, spread spectrum CDMA was commercially introduced as the solution to the bandwidth demands of the industry. By using a spread spectrum frequency-hopping technique, developers announced that they could achieve the desired frequency reuse patterns everyone was looking for.

Spread spectrum can use one of two different techniques: *frequency hopping* (FH) or *direct sequence* (DS). In both cases, the synchronization between the transmitter and receiver is crucial. Both forms use a pseudorandom carrier; they just do it in different ways. Frequency hopping is not usually implemented in the commercial versions of CDMA. Direct sequence is used by commercially available CDMA. It is accomplished as a multiple of the more conventional waveform by using a pseudonoise binary sequence at the transmitter. Noise and interference across the waveform are uncorrelated with the pseudonoise sequence, and thus become like noise. This increases the bandwidth when they reach the detectors. The *signal-to-noise ratio* (SNR) can be enhanced by using filters that reject the interference.

Spread Spectrum and CDMA   The concepts of spread spectrum and of CDMA seem to contradict normal intuition. In most communications systems we try to maximize the amount of useful signals we can fit into a minimal bandwidth. In spread spectrum we try to artificially spread a signal over a bandwidth much wider than necessary. In CDMA we transmit multiple signals over the same frequency band, using the same modulation techniques at the same time. There are very good reasons for doing this. In a spread spectrum system we use some artificial technique to broaden the amount of bandwidth used.

Capacity Gain   When you use the Shannon-Hartly law for the capacity of a bandwidth-limited channel, it is easy to see that for a given signal power the wider the bandwidth used, the greater the channel capacity. So if we broaden the spectrum of a given signal we get an increase in channel capacity and/or an improvement in the signal-to-noise ratio. This is true and easy to demonstrate for some systems but not for others. "Ordinary" frequency modulation (FM) systems spread the signal above the minimum theoretically needed and they get a demonstrable increase in capacity. Some techniques for spreading the spectrum achieve a significant capacity gain but others do not.

The CDMA Cellular Standard With CDMA, unique digital codes, rather than separate radio frequencies are used to differentiate subscribers. The codes are shared by both the mobile station and the base station, and are called *pseudorandom code sequences*. All users share the same range of radio spectrum. For cellular telephony, CDMA is a digital multiple access technique specified by the TIA as IS-95. In 1993, the TIA gave its approval of the CDMA IS-95 standard. IS-95 systems divide the radio spectrum into carriers that are 1.25 MHz wide. One of the unique aspects of CDMA is that although the number of phone calls that a carrier can handle is certainly limited, it is not a fixed number. Rather, the capacity of the system will be dependent on a number of different factors.

CDMA changes the nature of the subscriber equipment from a predominantly analog device to a digital device. CDMA receivers do not eliminate analog processing in its entirety, but they separate the communications channels by a pseudorandom modulation technique that is applied to the digital domain, not based on frequencies. In fact, multiple users will occupy the same frequency band simultaneously.

Spread Spectrum Goals

Much of the action in the wireless arena includes the use of the frequency spectrum to its fullest while preserving its efficiency. The primary goal of spread spectrum systems is the substantial increase in bandwidth of an information-bearing signal, greater than required for basic communications.

This increased bandwidth, though not used for carrying the signal, can mitigate possible problems in the airwaves, such as interference or inadvertent sharing of the same channels. The cooperative use of the spectrum is an innovation that was not commercially available in the past.

Regulators around the world have set aside limited amounts of bandwidth to satisfy these services, so that the efficiency is kept high. The limited frequency spectrum allocated preserves upon the goal of using spectral efficiency, which is usually measured with one of the traffic engineering calculations (Erlang or Poisson) per unit in operation in a specified geography and in terms of per MHz. For example, cellular operators use a 25-MHz split between the two directions of communications: 12.5 MHz of transmit and 12.5 MHz of receive spectrum. As technology enhancements occur, practical ways of expanding the amount of coverage become a reality.

Principles of Spread Spectrum

Claude Shannon published the fundamental limits on communication over noisy channels in 1948 in the classic paper, "A Mathematical Theory of Communication" (Bell System Technical Journal, July 1948). Shannon showed that error-free communication is possible on a noisy channel provided that the data rate is less than the channel capacity.

Shannon's capacity (data rate) equation is the basis for spread spectrum systems, which typically operate at a very low SNR, but use a very large bandwidth in order to provide an acceptable data rate per user. Applying spread spectrum principles to the multiple access environments is a development occurring over the last decade.

Shannon's Equation

The equation essential states that the channel capacity "C" (error-free bps) is directly proportional to the bandwidth "W" and is proportional to the log of the signal-to-noise ratio "Log_2 (1 + S/N)." Shannon's equation *applies only* to the additive white gaussian noise (AWGN) channel. Fading, interference, distortion, etc. are not considered. The *channel capacity is a theoretical limit only*; it describes the best that can possibly be done with any code and modulation method.

$$C = W \times Log_2 \, (1 + S/N)$$

Orthogonal Sequences

Orthogonal signals or sequences have zero cross-correlation. Zero correlation is obtained if the product of two signals, summed over a period of time, is 0. For the special case of binary sequences, the values 0 and 1 may be viewed as having opposite polarity. Thus when the product (XORing in this case) of two binary sequences results in an equal number of 1s and 0s, the cross-correlation is 0.

Starting with a seed of 0, repeating the 0 horizontally and vertically, and then inverting the 0 diagonally generate orthogonal sequences. This process is to be continued with the newly generated block until the desired code length is generated. Sequences created in this way are referred to as "Walsh codes." See Fig. 7.29 for the seed sequence.

Walsh Codes

The orthogonal sequences used in cdmaOne systems are Walsh codes of length 64, as shown in Fig. 7.30. These Walsh codes are used on the forward link to identify each user's data. In any given sector, each forward channel is assigned a distinct Walsh code and they are reused in each sector. This is possible because a PN code with a unique time shift is used for spectral spreading.

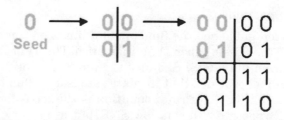

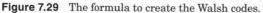

Figure 7.29   The formula to create the Walsh codes.

Walsh Chip within Symbol

Modulation Symbol Index	0123	4567	11 8901	1111 2345	1111 6789	2222 0123	2222 4567	2233 8901	3333 2345	3333 6789	4444 0123	4444 4567	4455 8901	5555 2345	5555 6789	6666 0123
0	0000	0000	0000	0000	0000	0000	0000	0000	0000	0000	0000	0000	0000	0000	0000	0000
1	0101	0101	0101	0101	0101	0101	0101	0101	0101	0101	0101	0101	0101	0101	0101	0101
2	0011	0011	0011	0011	0011	0011	0011	0011	0011	0011	0011	0011	0011	0011	0011	0011
3	0110	0110	0110	0110	0110	0110	0110	0110	0110	0110	0110	0110	0110	0110	0110	0110
4	0000	1111	0000	1111	0000	1111	0000	1111	0000	1111	0000	1111	0000	1111	0000	1111
5	0101	1010	0101	1010	0101	1010	0101	1010	0101	1010	0101	1010	0101	1010	0101	1010
6	0011	1100	0011	1100	0011	1100	0011	1100	0011	1100	0011	1100	0011	1100	0011	1100
7	0110	1001	0110	1001	0110	1001	0110	1001	0110	1001	0110	1001	0110	1001	0110	1001
8	0000	0000	1111	1111	0000	0000	1111	1111	0000	0000	1111	1111	0000	0000	1111	1111
9	0101	0101	1010	1010	0101	0101	1010	1010	0101	0101	1010	1010	0101	0101	1010	1010
10	0011	0011	1100	1100	0011	0011	1100	1100	0011	0011	1100	1100	0011	0011	1100	1100
11	0110	0110	1001	1001	0110	0110	1001	1001	0110	0110	1001	1001	0110	0110	1001	1001
12	0000	1111	1111	0000	0000	1111	1111	0000	0000	1111	1111	0000	0000	1111	1111	0000
13	0101	1010	1010	0101	0101	1010	1010	0101	0101	1010	1010	0101	0101	1010	1010	0101
14	0011	1100	1100	0011	0011	1100	1100	0011	0011	1100	1100	0011	0011	1100	1100	0011
15	0110	1001	1001	0110	0110	1001	1001	0110	0110	1001	1001	0110	0110	1001	1001	0110
16	0000	0000	0000	0000	1111	1111	1111	1111	0000	0000	0000	0000	1111	1111	1111	1111
17	0101	0101	0101	0101	1010	1010	1010	1010	0101	0101	0101	0101	1010	1010	1010	1010
18	0011	0011	0011	0011	1100	1100	1100	1100	0011	0011	0011	0011	1100	1100	1100	1100
19	0110	0110	0110	0110	1001	1001	1001	1001	0110	0110	0110	0110	1001	1001	1001	1001
20	0000	1111	0000	1111	1111	0000	1111	0000	0000	1111	0000	1111	1111	0000	1111	0000
21	0101	1010	0101	1010	1010	0101	1010	0101	0101	1010	0101	1010	1010	0101	1010	0101
22	0011	1100	0011	1100	1100	0011	1100	0011	0011	1100	0011	1100	1100	0011	1100	0011
23	0110	1001	0110	1001	1001	0110	1001	0110	0110	1001	0110	1001	1001	0110	1001	0110
24	0000	0000	1111	1111	1111	1111	0000	0000	0000	0000	1111	1111	1111	1111	0000	0000
25	0101	0101	1010	1010	1010	1010	0101	0101	0101	0101	1010	1010	1010	1010	0101	0101
26	0011	0011	1100	1100	1100	1100	0011	0011	0011	0011	1100	1100	1100	1100	0011	0011
27	0110	0110	1001	1001	1001	1001	0110	0110	0110	0110	1001	1001	1001	1001	0110	0110
28	0000	1111	1111	0000	1111	0000	0000	1111	0000	1111	1111	0000	1111	0000	0000	1111
29	0101	1010	1010	0101	1010	0101	0101	1010	0101	1010	1010	0101	1010	0101	0101	1010
30	0011	1100	1100	0011	1100	0011	0011	1100	0011	1100	1100	0011	1100	0011	0011	1100
31	0110	1001	1001	0110	1001	0110	0110	1001	0110	1001	1001	0110	1001	0110	0110	1001
32	0000	0000	0000	0000	0000	0000	0000	0000	1111	1111	1111	1111	1111	1111	1111	1111
33	0101	0101	0101	0101	0101	0101	0101	0101	1010	1010	1010	1010	1010	1010	1010	1010
34	0011	0011	0011	0011	0011	0011	0011	0011	1100	1100	1100	1100	1100	1100	1100	1100
35	0110	0110	0110	0110	0110	0110	0110	0110	1001	1001	1001	1001	1001	1001	1001	1001
36	0000	1111	0000	1111	0000	1111	0000	1111	1111	0000	1111	0000	1111	0000	1111	0000
37	0101	1010	0101	1010	0101	1010	0101	1010	1010	0101	1010	0101	1010	0101	1010	0101
38	0011	1100	0011	1100	0011	1100	0011	1100	1100	0011	1100	0011	1100	0011	1100	0011
39	0110	1001	0110	1001	0110	1001	0110	1001	1001	0110	1001	0110	1001	0110	1001	0110
40	0000	0000	1111	1111	0000	0000	1111	1111	1111	1111	0000	0000	1111	1111	0000	0000
41	0101	0101	1010	1010	0101	0101	1010	1010	1010	1010	0101	0101	1010	1010	0101	0101
42	0011	0011	1100	1100	0011	0011	1100	1100	1100	1100	0011	0011	1100	1100	0011	0011
43	0110	0110	1001	1001	0110	0110	1001	1001	1001	1001	0110	0110	1001	1001	0110	0110
44	0000	1111	1111	0000	0000	1111	1111	0000	1111	0000	0000	1111	1111	0000	0000	1111
45	0101	1010	1010	0101	0101	1010	1010	0101	1010	0101	0101	1010	1010	0101	0101	1010
46	0011	1100	1100	0011	0011	1100	1100	0011	1100	0011	0011	1100	1100	0011	0011	1100
47	0110	1001	1001	0110	0110	1001	1001	0110	1001	0110	0110	1001	1001	0110	0110	1001
48	0000	0000	0000	0000	1111	1111	1111	1111	1111	1111	1111	1111	0000	0000	0000	0000
49	0101	0101	0101	0101	1010	1010	1010	1010	1010	1010	1010	1010	0101	0101	0101	0101
50	0011	0011	0011	0011	1100	1100	1100	1100	1100	1100	1100	1100	0011	0011	0011	0011
51	0110	0110	0110	0110	1001	1001	1001	1001	1001	1001	1001	1001	0110	0110	0110	0110
52	0000	1111	0000	1111	1111	0000	1111	0000	1111	0000	1111	0000	0000	1111	0000	1111
53	0101	1010	0101	1010	1010	0101	1010	0101	1010	0101	1010	0101	0101	1010	0101	1010
54	0011	1100	0011	1100	1100	0011	1100	0011	1100	0011	1100	0011	0011	1100	0011	1100
55	0110	1001	0110	1001	1001	0110	1001	0110	1001	0110	1001	0110	0110	1001	0110	1001
56	0000	0000	1111	1111	1111	1111	0000	0000	1111	1111	0000	0000	0000	0000	1111	1111
57	0101	0101	1010	1010	1010	1010	0101	0101	1010	1010	0101	0101	0101	0101	1010	1010
58	0011	0011	1100	1100	1100	1100	0011	0011	1100	1100	0011	0011	0011	0011	1100	1100
59	0110	0110	1001	1001	1001	1001	0110	0110	1001	1001	0110	0110	0110	0110	1001	1001
60	0000	1111	1111	0000	1111	0000	0000	1111	1111	0000	0000	1111	0000	1111	1111	0000
61	0101	1010	1010	0101	1010	0101	0101	1010	1010	0101	0101	1010	0101	1010	1010	0101
62	0011	1100	1100	0011	1100	0011	0011	1100	1100	0011	0011	1100	0011	1100	1100	0011
63	0110	1001	1001	0110	1001	0110	0110	1001	1001	0110	0110	1001	0110	1001	1001	0110

Figure 7.30 Walsh 64 codes.

To provide a standard procedure between carriers specific Walsh codes are reserved for overhead channels. These are:

- *W0*: Pilot channel
- *W1-7*: Paging channels (W2-7 are optional and may be used for traffic)
- *W32*: Sync channel.

On the reverse link, the 64 Walsh codes are used as an orthogonal signaling set where every group of six symbols is represented by a Walsh code. This aids in signal recovery at the receiver in the base station.

The Move to 3G

Cell phones are everywhere you look. So are two-way pagers. Wireless handheld computers like the Treo, Black Berry, and Windows CE-based PDAs will be everywhere. With this wireless craze comes the desire for greater data access. It's no longer about using a phone to call your stockbroker—now it's about using your wireless device to check your portfolio, receive alerts, and make trades. The Internet and wireless personal devices are coming together. Emerging standards like 3G on the wireless carrier side, and the wireless application protocol (WAP) and wireless markup language (WML) on the data side, are leading toward a wireless Internet.

In the past, there has been much emphasis on the use of a wireless telephone set to conduct our day-to-day business. In 1992, global system for mobile (GSM) communications was rolling out fast in the European marketplace, whereas in North America the networks were divided into digital rollout using TDMA or CDMA technologies. North American TDMA has since given way to the rapid acceptance of a global standard of GSM. This meant that three different standards were being developed and used heavily throughout the world. Moreover, the analog networks were still fairly prominent using differing standards and frequencies. This meant that as an organization began to deploy a wireless strategy in the industry, compatibility issues continued to play a very dominant role in the decision process.

Competition to be the leader in the industry revolved around the technology selected. Many organizations were getting tied up in knots trying to decide which technology to use. Rather than worrying about the choice of GSM or CDMA, a user needs to select on the basis of:

- Coverage areas
- Pricing plans
- Cost of implementing
- Roaming charges (if any)
- Ease of use
- Long-term usage
- Battery life

Enter the Data

Just as the industry was wrestling with the choices between the use of analog or digital networks, and the use of the type of digital (CDMA, GSM) another phenomenon started to occur. The use of data transmission began to grow in use and in demand.

Users wanted to move away from the circuit switched data transmission to support packet switched data because of all the hype of the Internet and the use of packet switching technologies. Why not have the same efficiencies available on wireless networks? Therefore the movement was toward more data transmission at various speeds and the demand for:

- Better
- Faster
- Cheaper

To solve this problem, the evolution to third generation (3G) wireless standards set the stage to move from circuit data (dial up) to packet data (IP or X.25). The trend is toward packet switched data evolved the industry even more. The packets of data are destined to move us beyond just basic voice calls and slow speed data transfers. In fact, multimedia applications are actually where the industry is heading as shown in this figure. Packet data can handle a variety of data streams and formats, thus it is determined to be the best solution on the road to 3G wireless solutions.

What to Call the Data Systems of the Future

It was not long ago, when we had just gotten everyone on a single set of terms and definitions. The telecommunications industry was rife with different three letter acronyms (TLAs) that no one understood. Just when we thought it was safe to come out of the telephone closets and use some terms, the industry began creating all new ones for the wireless industry. The data speeds for the late 1990s operated at somewhere between 9.6 and 14.4 Kbps (if you were lucky). Later the industry wanted to raise the bar for data transmission so they created the means of transmitting high-speed circuit switched data (HSCSD) to operate at speeds of up to 64 Kbps.

In 2000, the industry began to test and deploy commercial data speeds as overlays to GSM and TDMA networks using a technique called general packet radio services (GPRS). GPRS is still evolving and being tested to support speeds initially at 20 Kbps, but ultimately should support speeds of 170 Kbps. No sooner was GPRS installed when the movement took us to a newer form of data transmission called enhanced data for GSM evolution (EDGE). Edge is going to ultimately take the speeds up to 384 Kbps packet switched IP or X.25 data.

The next step in the third generation of wireless communications is to use what is called universal mobile telecommunications services (UMTS). This is true third generation. UMTS is a set of standards designed to carry data at speeds of up to 2 Mbps. The bulk of these standards are designed around the GSM and CDMA architectures because of the proliferation of the technologies. In 2006, there were almost 2 billion GSM users worldwide. UMTS is one of the major new third generation mobile communications systems being developed within the framework which has been defined by the ITU and known as IMT-2000.

The subject of intense worldwide efforts on research and development throughout the present decade, UMTS has the support of many major telecommunications operators and manufacturers because it represents a unique opportunity to create a mass market for highly personalized and user-friendly mobile access to tomorrow's "Information Society."

UMTS will deliver pictures, graphics, video communications, and other wide-band information as well as voice and data, direct to people who can be on the move. UMTS will build on and extend the capability of today's mobile technologies (like digital cellular and cordless) by providing increased capacity, data capability, and a far greater range of services using an innovative radio access scheme and an enhanced, evolving core network. The launch of UMTS services from the year 2001 will see the evolution of a new, "open" communications universe, with players from many sectors (including providers of information and entertainment services) coming together harmoniously to deliver new communications services, characterized by mobility and advanced multimedia capabilities. The successful deployment of UMTS will require new technologies, new partnerships, and the addressing of many commercial and regulatory issues.

What About the CDMA Folks?

The whole while that the industry is rolling out the GSM/TDMA side of the business, the other part of the wireless industry has been moving also. In the CDMA architecture, we found that many of the high-speed circuit switched data services were good for 19.6–64 Kbps already. The first commercial launch of a cdmaOne network was in Hong Kong, in September 1995.

In June 2006, 155 operators have launched 151 CDMA2000 1X and 37 1xEV-DO commercial networks across Asia, the Americas and Europe. 31 1X and 40 1xEV-DO networks are scheduled to be deployed in the next year.

Some key benefits of the IS-95 air interface are soft handoffs (a make-before-break concept that reduces dropped calls) and increased capacity compared to AMPS networks. Currently the cdmaOne product portfolio was designed from the ground up

- Maximizes the advantages of CDMA digital wireless technology.
- Incorporates the efficiencies of IP—supports packet data at rates of up to 14.4 Kbps and packet-based transport on the backhaul.

The original IS-95-A air-interface standard was supplemented with the IS-95-B standard, which includes several improvements for hard-handoff algorithms in multicarrier environments and in parameters that affect the control of soft handoffs. Nonetheless, the primary change in the standard had to do with higher data rates for packet- and circuit-switched CDMA data: data rates of up to 115 Kbps can now be supported by bundling up to eight 14.4 or 9.6 Kbps data channels (14.4 Kbps × 8 = 115.2 Kbps). Today, some operators in Asia are implementing IS-95-B data with service rates of up to 64 Kbps.

CDMA2000 was designed with the Internet in mind, making it the platform on which to build innovative applications. CDMA2000 users receive myriad advanced services, including web browsing, m-commerce, MMS (multimedia messaging services), streaming video, games, enterprise solutions, and e-mail.

Demand for wireless data services and applications is taking off around the world and CDMA2000 operators are leading the industry in the range of services they offer, number of users they serve and revenue they generate from data. Capitalizing on the high-speed data capabilities and flexibility of CDMA2000 technologies, operators have introduced a variety of applications which enable their consumer and enterprise customers to access information, surf the Web, download music and video, send pictures, and play games.

CDMA2000 is an ideal platform for building advanced applications. It will deliver high data speeds of up to 3.1 Mbps—faster than fixed-line broadband solutions and it supports multiple application platforms. A wide range of devices with advanced data functionality for consumers and enterprise are available to choose from.

The term 1X, derived from 1XRTT (radio transmission technology), is used to signify that the standard carrier on the air interface is 1.25 MHz—the same as for IS-95-A and IS-95-B. This standard can be implemented in existing spectrum or in new spectrum allocations. The standard also paves the way for the next phase of third-generation networks cdma2000 3X (IS-2000-A).

In brief, cdma2000 1X, which is implemented in existing spectrum allocations:

- Delivers approximately twice the voice capacity of cdmaOne
- Provides data rates of 144 Kbps
- Backward compatible with cdmaOne networks and terminals
- Enhances performance

CDMA2000 1X can nearly triple the voice capacity of cdmaOne networks and delivers peak packet data speeds of 153 kbps (Release 0) or 307 kbps (Release 1) in mobile environments in a single 1.25 MHz channel.

CDMA2000 1xEV-DO (Evolution-Data Optimized) is a data centric technology that allows operators to offer advanced data services:

- CDMA2000 1xEV-DO Release 0 delivers up to 2.4 Mbps data speed; in commercial networks it delivers 300–600 Kbps in a single 1.25 MHz channel, the highest data rates of any wireless technology deployed today. It supports the most advanced data applications, such as MP3 transfers and video conferencing, TV broadcasts, video and audio downloads. It has been commercially available since 2002.

- CDMA2000 1xEV-DO Revision A (Rev A) delivers peak data speeds of 3.1 Mbps on the downlink and 1.8 Mbps on the uplink and incorporates quality of service (QoS) controls to manage latency on the network. With Rev A, operators will be able to introduce advanced multimedia services, including voice, data and broadcast over all-IP networks.

■ CDMA2000 Revision B (Rev B) standard was published in the first half of 2006. Rev B introduces a 64-QAM modulation scheme, and will deliver peak rates of 73.5 Mbps in the forward link and 27 Mbps in the reverse link through the aggregation of 15 1.25 MHz carriers within 20 MHz of bandwidth. A single 1.25 MHz carrier and an aggregated 5 MHz carrier in the forward link will deliver a peak rate of up to 4.9 Mbps and 14.7 Mbps, respectively. In addition to supporting mobile broadband data and OFDM-based multicasting, the lower latency characteristics of Rev B will improve the performance of delay-sensitive applications such as voice over Internet protocol (VoIP), push-to-talk over cellular, video telephony, concurrent voice and multimedia, and massive multiplayer online gaming. Rev B will be commercial in 2008.

IS-2000-A/cdma2000 3X

The cdma2000 3X standard was scheduled for completion in 2000. The term 3X, derived from 3XRTT, is used to signify three times 1.25 MHz or approximately 3.75 MHz. The cdma2000 3X multicarrier approach, or wideband cdmaOne, is an important part of the evolution of IS-95-based standards. In all likelihood, IS-2000-A will be followed by supplemental standards that offer additional functionality as the industry evolves. In short, cdma2000 3X:

■ Offers greater capacity than 1X

■ Supports data rates of up to 2 Mbps

■ Backward-compatible with 1X and cdmaOne deployments

■ Enhances performance even more

Third Generation (3G) Wireless

Third generation systems will provide access, by means of one or more radio links, to a wide range of telecommunication services supported by the fixed telecommunication networks and to other services that are specific to mobile users. A range of mobile terminal types will be encompassed, linking to terrestrial and/or satellite-based networks, and the terminals may be designed for mobile or fixed use.

Key features of 3G systems are a high degree of commonality of design worldwide, compatibility of services, use of small pocket terminals with worldwide roaming capability, Internet and other multimedia applications, and a wide range of services and terminals. According to the International Telecommunication Union (ITU) International Mobile Telecommunications 2000 initiative ("IMT-2000") 3G mobile system services are beginning to appear, subject to market considerations. Table 7.1 describes some of the key service attributes and capabilities expected of 3G systems:

Third-generation wireless technology combines two powerful innovations: wireless communications and the Internet. Today's wireless devices are designed to transmit voice and brief text messages and cannot handle digital multimedia and other high-bandwidth

TABLE 7.1 Summary of 3G Capabilities

3G System Capabilities	
Support of circuit and packet data	■ 144 Kbps or higher in high mobility (vehicular) traffic
	■ 384 Kbps for pedestrian traffic
	■ 2 Mbps or higher for indoor traffic
Interoperability and roaming	■ Ability to interoperate among carriers
	■ Roaming services available and transparent device determination
Common billing/user profiles	■ Sharing of usage/rate information between service providers
	■ Standardized call detail recording
	■ Standardized user profiles
Location and positioning services	■ Capability to determine geographic position of mobiles
	■ Report it to both the network and the mobile terminal
Support of multimedia services/ capabilities	■ Fixed and variable rate bit traffic
	■ Bandwidth on demand
	■ Asymmetric data rates in the forward and reverse links
	■ Multimedia mail store and forward
	■ Broadband access up to 2 megabits/second

Internet content. 3G devices, by contrast, provide high-speed mobile connections to the Internet and other communications networks, giving users full access to the rich content and commercial possibilities of the "information superhighway."

Mobile phones and other wireless devices such as personal digital assistants (PDAs) equipped with 3G technologies allow users to surf the Internet at high speeds, shown in Fig. 7.31. The immediate goal is to raise transmission speeds from approximately 9.6 Kbps to 2 Mbps. Many feel that 3G is overhyped comparing the rollout of 3G to the difficulties involved with creating standards for high-definition TV. Currently, the Internet is not friendly to mobile devices. But over time, the Internet will become more adaptable to mobility.

One of the biggest challenges facing 3G, and one that slowed work on the proposed standard was negotiation between hardware makers and carriers who had vested interests in wideband CDMA and TDMA/FDMA technologies. This appears to have been overcome with the introduction in late 1999 of a new radio access technology called universal terrestrial radio access (UTRA), which was proposed by the 3G Partnership Project and combines elements of all three techniques. The problem with the UTRA specification is that it appears to give service providers choices for how to implement multiplexing on their systems. And that could mean incompatibility. Currently there are five different standards that can be selected from to implement a 3G solution from the carriers' perspective.

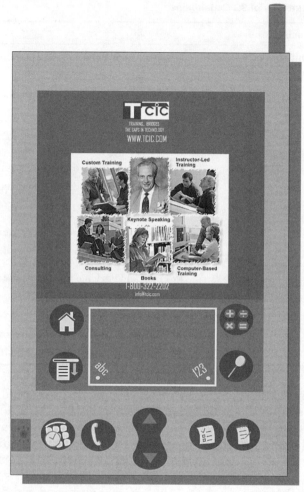

Figure 7.31 PDAs ready to surf the web with 3G.

Applications for 3G

Possible 3G applications are even more impressive. According to the International Telecommunication Union (ITU), 3G devices will be compact enough to fit into a pocket or handbag and will integrate the functions of a range of existing devices. The ITU suggests that the 3G device will function as a:

- Phone
- Computer
- Television
- Pager

- Videoconferencing center
- Newspaper
- Diary
- Credit card

It will support not only voice communications, but also real-time video and full-scale multimedia via a screen that can be pulled-out and flexible. It will also function as a portable address book and agenda, containing all the information about meetings and contacts, and able to remind you automatically before an important appointment, or automatically connect to an audio or videoconference at a specified time. It will automatically search the Internet for relevant news and information on preselected subjects, book your next holiday for you online, and download a bedtime story for your child, complete with moving pictures. It will even be able to pay for goods when you shop via wireless electronic funds transfer. In short, the new mobile handset will become the single, indispensable "life tool," carried everywhere by everyone, just like a wallet or purse is today.

Some applications are already on the market others are still developing. An example of this is the use of the 3G phones for TV reception. The TV included in the telephone is shown in Fig. 7.32. Think of a person driving down the road today. Everyone is out to deny us access to cell phones because it distracts the driver from their duties as a driver (causes accidents)! Now, instead of being distracted by a phone call, the risk is

Figure 7.32   Television reception at the handset. (*Source: Samsung*)

Figure 7.33   The video conferencing capability. (*Source: Nokia*)

that we will be watching our favorite talk show host or soap opera on the TV (oops, I mean phone) while attempting to drive to and from work. This is a possibility.

What of the road warrior who is on the go all week long and needs to conduct business. Here again the 3G phones can be used as a videoconferencing device. Now not only will we call our office, we can actually host a meeting while we drive down the road. We can see the party (parties) we are having a meeting with. The videoconferencing capability is shown in Fig. 7.33.

This just adds a new dimension to the overall risk of using the cellular phones. First we were told that they cause cancer (a claim that has never been truly proven). Then we could use the phone to download our e-mail. The WAP enabled phone allowed us to access our e-mail and web sites. What can we do besides making a phone call? These are the pieces 3G architectures were built for. To handle high-speed data access and all of the personalized communications needs prepares the network and the provider to be a one-stop shopping environment.

What Does It All Mean?

The sum of all the pieces is that much work still remains to be done before we see a true 3G architecture, handset and application working together. Like all other services, the piece parts are forming and being introduced as fast as the vendors can develop them. Many proprietary solutions are creeping into the business (even though 3G is supposed to be an open standard). The applications and the speed are what everyone seems to be concentrating upon. However, 3G was supposed to be a universal standard for all vendors to build to, so that compatibility and interoperability were assured. This is yet to happen, but there may be hope in the future.

Questions

1. In which year was cellular first introduced?
   a. 1978
   b. 1984
   c. 1990
   d. 1994

2. Cell sites operated at approximately _____ miles across.
   a. 10
   b. 7
   c. 12
   d. 3

3. The first cellular phones were made to operate in _____.
   a. Vehicles
   b. Shirt pockets
   c. Briefcases
   d. Wrist watches

4. What technology was used by the AMPS?
   a. Digital
   b. TDMA
   c. CDMA
   d. Analog

5. Cellular handoff occurs when the user is on the periphery of the cell.   T/F

6. As congestion occurred one of the first steps to get more utilization was to_____.
   a. Allow fewer users
   b. Build more networks
   c. Cell splitting
   d. Use less bandwidth

7. When the industry decided to move to digital, the selection was easy and straightforward.   T/F

8. The choices of digital were actually selected between two competing technologies:
   a. TDMA and FDMA
   b. ETDMA and N-AMPS

    c. IMTS and AMPS

    d. TDMA and CDMA

9. The PCS architecture allows more users and less cost.   T/F

10. Future networks will all be drive on TDMA.   T/F

11. Digital transmission will offer the ability to achieve data at much higher rates.   T/F

12. What does 3G stand for?

    a. Third Goal

    b. TDMA Generation

    c. TDMA Global

    d. Third Generation

13. What are the choices (technologies) that the vendors had?

    a. TMDA, CMDA, GSM

    b. FDMA, TMDA, GSM

    c. CDMA, TDMA, GSM

    d. TDMA/TDD, TDMA/FDMA, CDMA

14. How many users are on board with GSM?

    a. 100,000

    b. 2,000,000

    c. 1,500,000,000

    d. 2,000,000,000

15. In the future, the handset can be used for: (select only one)

    a. Video conferences

    b. Data terminal

    c. Watch

    d. ATM card

16. In future applications, which application will allow us to see the other end of a call?

    a. TV set

    b. Videoconferencing set

    c. Telephone set

    d. Global positioning system

17. The movement was toward more data transmission at various speeds and the demand for: (select only one)

    a. Better data

    b. Faster handset availability

    c. Cheaper quality of services

    d. Higher data error rates

18. What does GPRS mean?

    a. General Packet Data Services

    b. General Packet Radio System

    c. Generic Pocket Radio System

    d. General Packet Radio Service

Optical Communications

After reading this chapter and completing the questions, you will be able to:

- Discuss the benefits of the fiber standards
- Understand the speeds of SONET and SDH
- Determine what the differences are in WDM and DWDM
- Understand the SONET link architecture
- Explain the basic components of the model

In Chapter 7, we discussed the frequency spectrum of wireless networks. The RF spectrum is a finite resource. We also talked about invisible light in the form of infrared- and laser-based wireless systems. Visible and invisible light occupies a small portion of the overall electromagnetic spectrum. Visible light, which is represented as a rainbow of colors, is only part of the portion of the spectrum, which is commonly called light.

Radio occupies the spectrum up to about 1 GHz. Microwaves reside at 1 GHz through 150 THz frequency range. Terahertz (THz) is in trillions of cycles per second. Light is in the regime of 150–1500 THz. x-rays start at 1500 THz through 500,000 THz. Above that are the gamma rays.

Visible light is part of the spectrum that we can actually see. In Fig. 8.1 notice that the higher the frequency, the shorter the wavelength. The graphic shows much of the spectrum we know as visible light (in color it looks great, but in this book it appears in black and white). We differentiate the colors of the rainbow based on the light we can actually see. Our sight allows us to differentiate the color of the sunset from the color of a blue sky strictly on the frequency of the colors of light. Normally, the wavelength of light is measured in billionths of a meter. We call the wavelength of light nanometers (nm), which equal 10^{-9} meters. Visible light is in the range of 400–700 nm whereas the

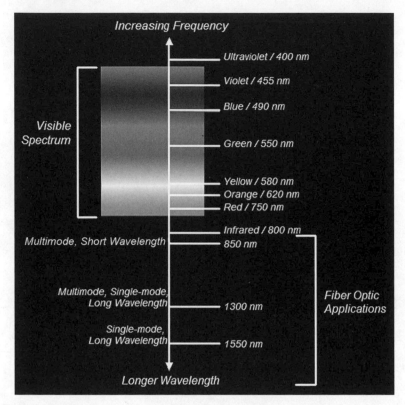

Figure 8.1 The light spectrum covers a range of frequencies and wavelengths.

light used for optical networks operates on 850–1550 nm. Note these are the wavelengths in the infrared ranges.

In optical communications the wavelengths are longer than visible light. Visible light has wavelengths that completes at around 700 nm. Light used in fiber optic communications has wavelengths at 850, 1310, and 1550 nm.

Light can be thought of in a couple different ways. As we described in Chapter 1, the sinusoidal wave (sine) is normally used to characterize the flow of light. After all, light is an analog wave moving down the optical glass in a fiber network. The wave has amplitude and it has a wavelength for one cycle.

A second course of action is to describe light by using ray diagrams. It represents the direction that the light is traveling. It is a good way to visualize where the light will go. One example of that is to describe the path that light follows in an optical fiber. Think of holding a flashlight shown in Fig. 8.2 and pointing the beam toward a distant wall. The representation here is the light shining on the wall through the lens of the flashlight. The signal in this free space (in the air) disperses, as opposed to the light carried down a fiber is contained inside the glass carrier.

Figure 8.2   The flashlight analogy describes the light in the form of a ray that passes through the lens.

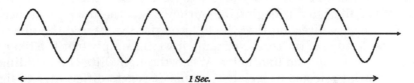

Figure 8.3   The frequency is shown as a sinusoidal wave.

Still a third way to describe light is to describe photons. These are the *particles* of light that carry a very small amount of energy. The photonic characteristics are used when getting into the physics of light.

Recall that the frequency is described as the number of cycles that occur in one second. This is measured in cycles per second—or hertz. The frequency is shown in Fig. 8.3. The frequency is also compared with the length of the wave, how great a distance it takes to complete one cycle. The wavelength is a more common means of describing the use of optical networks. Wavelength is usually represented as a lambda sign (λ). To calculate the wavelength of the light, we use the following formula:

$$f = c/\lambda$$

The formula solves for the frequency as a product of c (speed of light in a vacuum is 300,000,000 m/s) divided by the wavelength of the light. If we choose to rearrange the formula then we get:

$$\lambda = c/f$$

This formula shows that, as frequency goes up, wavelength goes down, and vice versa. This concept is true only for energy with a fixed speed, like electromagnetic energy. Using optical communications with a frequency of 193.4 THz we can apply the formula to get:

$$\lambda = 300,000,000 \, / 193.4 \times 10^{12}$$
$$\lambda = 300,000,000/193,400,000,000$$
$$\lambda = 1551.9 \text{ nm}$$

We'll be using the wavelength as a discussion point throughout this chapter. For now understand that wavelength will talk to the individual light beam used on a fiber based network.

Fiber Optics

A fiber optic cable has two parts the core (center or inside) and a cladding (outside covering). These two parts of the fiber work together to cause something called "total internal reflection" which is the key to fiber optics. The light beam is focused on the core of the fiber and it begins its journey down the fiber. Soon, because of a turn in the fiber or the direction that the light originally entered the fiber, the light reaches the outside edge of the core. Normally it would simply exit the fiber at this point, but this is where the cladding helps. When the light hits the cladding (which is made of a material selected especially because it reacts differently to light then the core material) instead of going on straight it reflects. This creates a tunnel effect in which the light bounces it way down the fiber until it exits at the other end of the fiber. An example of the construction of the fiber is shown in Fig. 8.4.

A third element includes a buffer/coating. The buffer has nothing to do with the confinement of the light in the core; its purpose is to protect the glass from scratches and moisture. Any glass material can be scratched or easily broken; fiber optic cable is the same. If the fiber is scratched, the scratch could propagate and leave the fiber in two pieces. Another important aspect of fiber is the need to keep them dry.

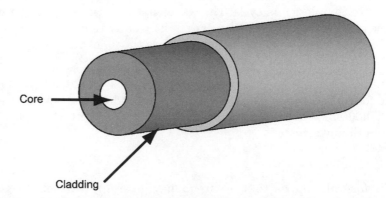

Figure 8.4 The fiber construction consists of a core, cladding, and buffer.

The core and the cladding are solid glass. The only differences between the two are the ways in which the glass was made. The core and the cladding have different impurities or dopants intentionally added to change the speed of light in the glass. These speed differences are what confine the light to the core. The buffer needs to be tough. Many people think that fiber can be handled like wire. The buffer is not insulation around the glass; it has nothing to do with the confinement of the light in the fiber. The buffer's purpose is to protect the glass from scratches and the effects of the environment. The buffer/coating is usually plastic or Kevlar to protect the fiber.

Figure 8.5 is an example of packaging options for fiber. The intent of this packaging is to include six fibers in a loose tube. The loose tube prevents the fibers from being stressed during installation. Stress in the fiber can induce problems in keeping the light confined. Inside this tube is a filling compound that will serve to prevent water and other liquid contaminants from destroying the fiber's light confinement capability. If water permeates inside the cable, the reflective and refractive components of the glass will change, thereby impairing the fiber.

Refraction and reflection are the two phenomena responsible for making optical fiber work. Reflection is familiar to everyone. Light from an object is returned (reflected), such as your image in a mirror. Refraction is probably less familiar, but we have all seen it in action. A drinking straw, in a glass of clear liquid, looks as if it is bent. We know it is not bent but that refraction is causing the straw to appear bent.

Both of these effects are described mathematically by relating the angle at which they intercept the material surface and the angle of the outgoing ray. In the case of reflection, the angles are equal. In glass, the speed of light is about two-thirds the speed of light in a vacuum. The relationship defines a quantity known as the *index of refraction*. The index of refraction is used to relate the speed of light in a material. Glass has an index of refraction of about 1.5. The reason that it is only a rough number is that glass has many different types, and all vary slightly in index of refraction among other parameters. Air has an index of refraction of about 1, while water has an index of refraction of 1.33.

Figure 8.6 is a view of the core of the fiber at the top and the cladding at the bottom. What must happen for the light to be confined within the core is reflection. Light in the

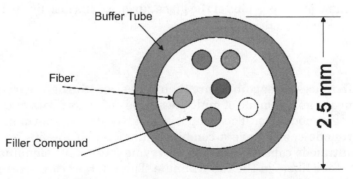

Figure 8.5   A six-fiber tube is packed with a filler compound to protect the fibers.

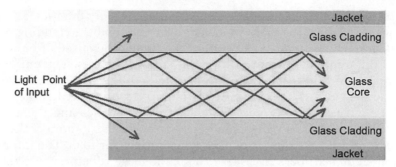

Figure 8.6   Light is both reflected and refracted inside the fiber.

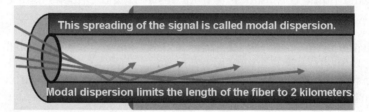

Figure 8.7   Modal dispersion occurs as the light spreads across the glass, thereby limiting the overall length as seen.

core will remain in the core by being reflected as it travels left to right in the picture. On the other hand, light that strikes the cladding at a different angle will undergo refraction in which the light exits the core and proceeds into the cladding. This is a detriment to optical communications. Light lost into the cladding cannot be used for intelligent communications with the far end. This graphic shows the condition under which light is mostly reflected and not refracted is that the index of refraction for the core is *greater* than the index of refraction for the cladding.

When the light is modulated from one end of the fiber to the other, the spreading of the light is called modal dispersion as seen in Fig. 8.7. The mode (or path) is dispersed across the various portions of the glass surface. This also limits the distance to approximately 2 km for multimode fiber.

Types of Fiber

The differences among fibers are their core sizes (the light-carrying region of the fiber). Multimode cable is made of multiple strands of glass fibers and has a much larger core than single mode fiber. The comparison of the sizes is shown in Fig. 8.8.

Multimode cables have a combined diameter in the 50–100 μm range. Each fiber in a multimode cable is capable of carrying a different signal independent from those on the other fibers in the cable bundle. These larger core sizes generally have greater bandwidth and are easier to couple and interconnect. It allows hundreds of rays of light

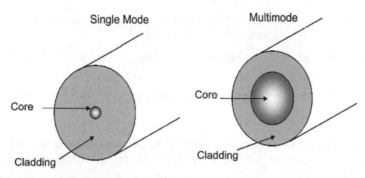

Figure 8.8   Single and multimode fiber compared.

to propagate through the fiber simultaneously. Multimode fiber today is used primarily in premise applications, where transmission distances are less than two kilometers.

Single mode fiber is a single strand of glass that has a much smaller core that allows only one mode of light to propagate through the core. Single mode fiber has a higher bandwidth than multimode and for this reason it is the ideal transmission medium for many applications. The standard single mode fiber core is approximately 8–10 μm in diameter. Because of its greater information-carrying capacity, single mode fiber is typically used for longer distances and higher-bandwidth applications.

While it might appear that multimode fibers have higher information carrying capacity, this is not the case. Single mode fibers retain the integrity of each light pulse over a longer distance, which allows more information to be transmitted. This is why multimode fibers are used for shorter distances and more often in premises at the corporate locations (i.e., high-rise offices, campus environments, and so forth).

Fiber-Based Networks

All digital transmission speeds discussed earlier were initially designed to be carried on the existing wired systems in place at the telephone company and interexchange carrier levels. These systems included microwave, coaxial, and twisted-pair copper wires. As newer fiber-optic systems were introduced, a new synchronous digital hierarchy (SDH) evolved. Throughout the world, SDH was accepted, yet in the United States the term *synchronous optical network* (SONET) was adopted. Although the international and United States versions of SDH/SONET are very close, they are not identical.

SONET defines a means to increase throughput and bandwidth through a set of multiplexing parameters. These roles provide certain advantages to the industry, such as:

- Reduced equipment requirements in the carriers' network
- Enhanced network reliability and availability
- Conditions to define the overhead necessary to facilitate managing the network better

- Definitions of the multiplexing functions and formats to carry the lower level digital signals (such as DS-1, DS-2, and DS-3)

- Generic standards encouraging interoperability between different vendors' products

- A flexible means of addressing current as well as future applications and bandwidth usage

SONET defines the optical carrier (OC) levels and the electrical equivalent rates in the synchronous transport signals (STS) for the fiber-based transmission hierarchy.

Background Leading to SONET Development

Prior to the development of SONET, the initial fiber-based systems used in the PSTN were all highly proprietary. The proprietary nature of the products included the following:

1. Equipment

2. Line coding

3. Maintenance

4. Provisioning

5. Multiplexing

6. Administration

The carriers (local and long-distance providers) were frustrated with the proprietary products because on interoperability problems, sole-source vendor solutions (which held the carriers hostage to one vendor) and cost issues. These carriers approached the standards committees and demanded that a set of operational standards be developed that would allow them to mix and match products from various vendors. In 1984, a task force was established to develop such a standard. The resultant standard became SONET.

The SONET Line Rates

SONET defines a technique to carry many signals from different sources and at different capacities through a synchronous, optical hierarchy. The flexibility and robustness of SONET are some of its strongest selling points. Additionally, in the past many of the high-speed multiplexing arrangements (DS-2 and DS-3) used bit interleaving to multiplex the data streams through the multiplexers. SONET uses a byte-interleaved multiplexing format. This is a strong point because it keeps the basic DS-0 intact throughout the network making it easier to perform diagnostics and troubleshooting. Byte interleaving simplifies the process and provides better end-to-end management.

The base level of a SONET signal is called the synchronous transport signal level-1 (STS-1) operating at 51.84 Mbps. The first step in using the SONET architecture

TABLE 8.1   SONET Rates

The SONET Hierarchy			
Electrical Signal	Optical Value	Speed	Capacity
STS-1	OC-1	51.84 Mbps	28 DS-1 or 1 DS-3
STS-3	OC-3	155.520 Mbps	84 DS-1 or 3 DS-3
STS-12	OC-12	622.08 Mbps	336 DS-1 or 12 DS-3
STS-24	OC-24	1.244 Gbps	672 DS-1 or 24 DS-3
STS-48	OC-48	2.488 Gbps	1344 DS-1 or 48 DS-3
STS-192	OC-192	9.953Gbps	5376 DS-1 or 192 DS-3
STS-768	OC-768	40 Gbps	21,504 DS-1 or 768 DS-3

Other rates exist, but these are the most popularly implemented.

is to create the STS-1. SONET specifies a synchronous transport signal (level 1) of 51.84 Mbps, which is a DS-3 with extra overhead. The overhead allows for diagnostic and maintenance capabilities on each STS. The optical equivalent of the STS-1 is an optical carrier level 1 (OC-1). This is the basic building block for chunks of bandwidth as they are multiplexed together to form much higher capacities. Increments of SONET include the capacities shown in Table 8.1. These transport systems and carrier levels work from the base of a T3 plus overhead creating an STS-1.

SONET goes further than just defining the multiplexed values of speed. It breaks the architecture of the link into three separate steps for purposes of defining the interfaces and defining responsibility. These layers include (a fourth is added here to describe the layer-by-layer responsibilities):

- *The photonic layer:* Deals with the transport of bits and the conversion from an STS electrical pulse into an OC signal in light pulses.

- *The section layer:* Deals with the transport of the STS-N frame across a physical link. The functions of the section layer include scrambling, framing, and error monitoring.

- *The line layer:* Deals with the reliable transport path of overhead and payload information across a physical system.

- *The path layer:* Deals with the transport of network services such as DS-1 and DS-3 between path terminating equipment.

SONET incorporates each of these into architecture such that overhead and responsibilities are clearly defined. This layered architecture is shown in Fig. 8.9. Note that the four layers are shown in this graphic. Actually, the photonic and section layers are one, but have been subdivided for clarity in showing the structure. The photonic and section layers deal with the physical medium or the OSI layer 1 protocols.

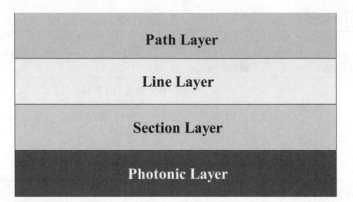

Figure 8.9   The SONET protocol stack.

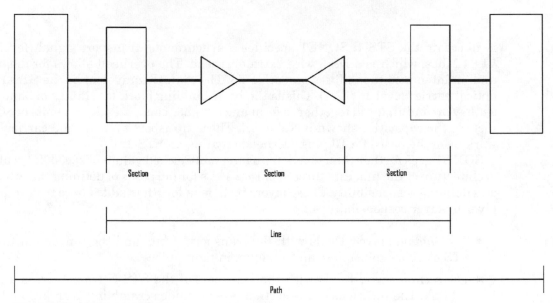

Figure 8.10   The link architecture.

The SONET architecture actually consists of three parts:

- The *section* is defined as the transport between two repeating functions or between line-terminating equipment and a repeater.
- The *line* is defined as the transport of the payload between two pieces of line-terminating equipment.
- The *path* is defined as the transport of the payload between two pieces of path-terminating equipment (such as multiplexers) or the end-to-end circuit.

This is shown in Fig. 8.10, where the pieces are laid out on a plane. The graphic shows how all the pieces work together in a fiber link. The fiber specification is what was originally used in SONET (and SDH internationally); however, newer microwave and satellite termination equipment is being introduced to provide the same capacities and formats. SONET defines the responsibility of the carriers in multiplexing the signal onto the physical medium, as well as the points of demarcation for the various carriers involved with the circuit.

SONET Frame Format

In each of the layers listed, overhead is added to the data being transported to assure that everything is kept in order and that errors can be detected. This overhead allows for testing and diagnostics along the entire route between the functions specified in the SONET layers. A new frame size is also used in the SONET architecture. The older M13 asynchronous format just couldn't cut the mustard. In order to get the network back to a synchronous timing element, a frame is created that consists of 90 octets (8-bit bytes) across and 9 rows (810 bytes) down. This is the OC-1 frame, or the equivalent of the DS-3 frame plus the extra overhead. However, with the change in size, the frequency of frames generated across the network is now brought back to 8000 per second. The 125-second clocking and timing for the digital network can be reestablished. The frame shown in Fig. 8.11 is 90 bytes (columns) wide and 9 rows high, yielding the 810-byte frame format.

Of the 90 columns, the first 3 ($3 \times 9 = 27$ bytes) are allocated for transport overhead. The transport overhead is divided into two pieces: 9 bytes (3 columns, 3 rows) for section overhead and the remaining 18 bytes (3 columns by 6 rows) for line overhead. This is for maintenance and diagnostics on the circuit.

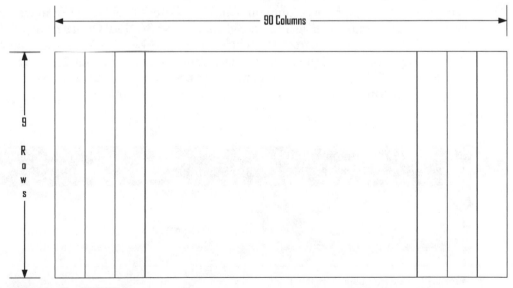

Figure 8.11   The SONET frame.

The 783 remaining octets (87 columns, 9 rows) are called the *synchronous payload envelope* (SPE). From the SPE, an additional 9 bytes (1 column, 9 rows) are set aside for path overhead. The path overhead accommodates the maintenance and diagnostics at each end of the circuit—typically, the customer equipment. Thus the leftover 774 bytes are reserved for the actual data transport.

$$774 \times 8 \text{ bits} = 6192 \text{ bits} \times 8000 \text{ frames per second } 49.536 \text{ Mbps}$$

ATM uses the STS payload as the transport of information by inserting 53 cells into the STS payload. This allows for the fluid and dynamic allocation of the bandwidth available. As it is advertised, ATM starts at 50 and 155 Mbps. To achieve the 155-Mbps rate three OC-1s are concatenated (kept together as a single data stream) to produce an OC-3C. This works out rather nicely.

While using the SONET specification for carrying the data, cells are mapped horizontally into the SONET frame shown in Fig. 8.12. However, newer things have occurred since the initial SONET standards were developed. Now SONET operates at speeds of up to the OC-192, which is the equivalent of 192 T3s. OC-192 is 9.958 Gbps of throughput. However, using a dense wave-division multiplexing (DWDM) concept (sending different colors of light onto the fiber) we can achieve approximately 32 OC-192s on a single piece of fiber (that is 320 Gbps). Moreover, the manufacturers are rapidly pursuing data rates at 1.6 Tbps on a single fiber. With these data rates being generated on the fiber, we shall see nearly unlimited bandwidth in the future. We continue to push the envelope in getting better, faster and cheaper.

One can only imagine where this will all lead. If we can get to 1.6 Tbps, then what about taking the next step to 10 Tbps? If we get to 10 Tbps, then what about stepping up to 100 Tbps? This is the way we have been pushing the carriers and manufacturers alike. They, of course, have been responding in kind.

The use of the higher-speed communications methods also leads to a newer transmission rate. Many vendors have announced that using SONET OC-192, they will deliver 10 Gbps Ethernet speeds across the wide area networks. This becomes a battleground for the various suppliers; the telephone companies want to deliver 1–10 gigabit speeds over their backbone, whereas the newer carriers want to deliver across SONET and Ethernet backbones and they do not care what form is provided here.

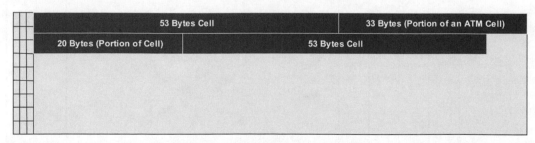

Figure 8.12 Cell mapping on SONET.

SONET Topologies

Several different topologies can be used in a SONET network using the various multiplexers. These include the normal topologies most networks have been accustomed to over the years. They include the following:

- Point to point
- Point to multipoint
- Hub and spoke
- Ring

The variations allow the flexibility of SONET in the wide area networks built by the carriers, but now becoming the method of choice at many large organizations. In each of the topologies, larger organizations are finding the benefits of installing highly reliable interoperable equipment at the private network interfaces and access to the public networks.

Point to Point

The simplest SONET/SDH topology is called point to point. It involves a direct fiber link between terminal multiplexers as path terminating equipment (PTE). The fiber span may include regenerators, depending on distance, but there will be no other intermediate network elements. This configuration might be used between two customer locations over dark fiber, or it could be used to connect two nodes within a carrier network.

The PTE performs a multiplex function so that, for example, multiple DS-1 signals can be transported between the two locations over the point-to-point link. If protection were required for this link, a linear protection scheme such as 1 + 1 or 1:1 would be used.

The SONET multiplexer, the entry level PTE for an organization (or the equipment installed by the LEC at the customer's premises to access the network) acts as a concentrator device for the multiple lower speed communications channels such as DS-1 and DS-3. In its simplest form, two devices are connected with an optical fiber (with any repeaters as necessary) as a point-to-point circuit. As the entry-level point into SONET architecture, the inputs and outputs are identical. In this environment, the network can act as a stand-alone environment and not have to interface with the public switched networks. See Fig. 8.13 for the point-to-point multiplexing arrangement.

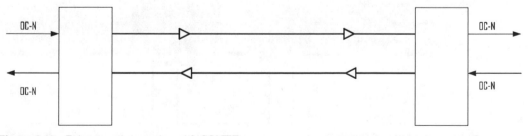

Figure 8.13   Point-to-point service with SONET.

Point to Multipoint

The linear bus topology has one or more intermediate points for dropping or adding traffic along the path. The intermediate nodes are add/drop multiplexers (ADMs). This topology is sometimes called *point-to-multipoint*. The benefit to this topology is that there are now multiple nodes that can communicate over the same fiber link. The ADMs would be administered to drop the appropriate traffic at each of the intermediate nodes. The paths could be at the VT level or at the STS level.

The operation at the ADMs could be drop and insert or drop and continue. Drop and insert implies that the dropped traffic channel is terminated at that location, and a new traffic channel can be inserted into the vacated time slot to communicate with a down stream node. Drop and continue means that the signal is dropped, but it is also transported to the down stream nodes. In the drop and continue case, a multicast function is performed.

In a large corporate network spanning the country (or any subset), a single high-speed link may be employed. The SONET add/drop multiplexer is used for the task, dropping circuits out without demultiplexing the entire high-speed signal. In Fig. 8.14, the ADM is installed between two far-end locations so that signals can be added or dropped off as necessary. This is a better solution than renting three different circuits between points A-B, A-C, and B-C, which adds to the complexity and cost. By using a circuit from A-B-C with ADMs, the service can usually be more efficiently accommodated.

Hub and Spoke

The hub and spoke method (sometimes referred to the star network) allows some added flexibility in the event of unpredicted growth or constant changes in the architecture of the network. SONET multiplexers can be hubbed into a digital cross-connect where it is concentrated and then forwarded on to the next node. This is used in many larger organizations where regional offices are located and district or branch offices are tied into the network through the hub. Once again the flexibility is there if a major change occurs in the network architecture or in the event of major campaigns in the organization. Hubs will act as the cross-connect points to link the various echelons in the

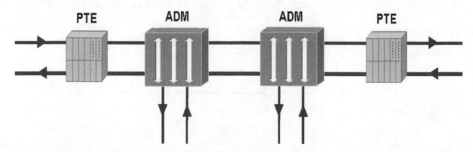

Figure 8.14 ADMs installed along the way create the point to multipoint connection.

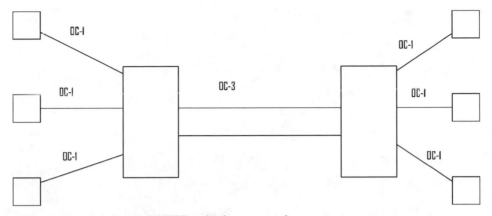

Figure 8.15 Hub and spoke in a SONET multiplexer network.

network together. These may be developed in a blocking or nonblocking manner. Typically, some blocking may be allowed. The hub and spoke arrangement is shown in Fig. 8.15.

Ring

The ring topology is the most common in today's service provider networks because it is the most resilient. Rings are based on two or four fibers. Transmission will be in one direction on one half of the fibers and in the opposite direction on the other half. Half the bandwidth can be reserved for protection. Quick recovery from a fiber cut anywhere on the ring can be accomplished by switching to the signal being transmitted in the opposite direction. Ring topologies have been so successful at providing reliable transport that even long-haul carriers often use multiple very large circumference rings in their nationwide networks.

ADMs are used at nodes on the ring for traffic origination or termination. It's not unusual for rings to be connected to other rings. In those cases, the cross-connects provide the interconnection function.

There are two dominant types of rings used in SONET networks, unidirectional path switched rings (UPSR) and bidirectional line switched rings (BLSR). Figure 8.16 shows a UPSR ring topology, whereas Fig. 8.17 shows the ring topology with dual fibers run (bidirectional service) between the ADMs.

In a ring architecture, where SONET automatic protection switching is employed, the best of all worlds comes to fruition. In this topology, ADMs are used throughout the network and a series of point-to-point links are installed between adjoining neighbors. The bidirectional capability places the most robustness into the network, however unidirectional services can also be installed. The primary advantage of the ring architecture is survivability in the event of a cable cut, or a failure in a network node. The multiplexers have sufficient intelligence to reroute or reverse direction in the event of a failure. If more than one fiber link is installed the systems could use alternate paths, but they must recover in milliseconds (which APS on SONET is designed to do).

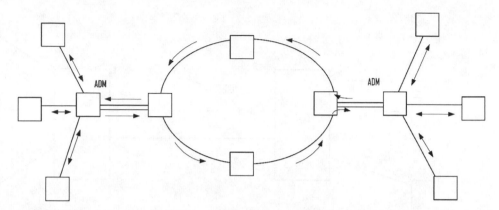

Figure 8.16   Ring architecture of SONET multiplexers using a unidirectional ring.

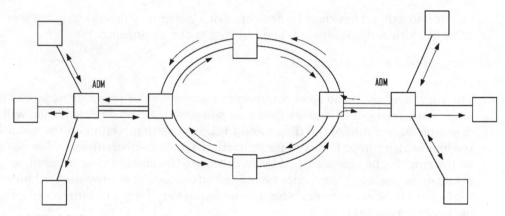

Figure 8.17   A bidirectional ring using SONET multiplexers.

While the ANSI committees were working on SONET though, another movement was underfoot. In Europe the standards committees were also wrestling with the logical replacement to the plesiochronous digital hierarchy (PDH), which is an asynchronous multiplexing plan to create high-speed communications channels. The Europeans came up with a separate multiplexing hierarchy called synchronous digital hierarchy (SDH) in support of the SONET standards.

Synchronous Digital Hierarchy (SDH)

Ever since the standards bodies approved the recommendations for the SDH (and SONET), the services have been effectively used to improve and revolutionize the industry. Significant cost efficiencies and performance improvements have been shown.

SDH provides a means for the rest of the world to use the capabilities of fiber based transport systems and multiplexing architectures to improve upon the older PDH, which was inefficient and expensive. The PDH evolved in response to the demand for plain old telephone services (POTS), and was not ideally suited to deliver the efficient use of bandwidth and high-speed services.

Digital networks continue to expand in complexity and penetration within the carriers' networks, now moving closer to the consumers' door. High-speed communications prior to the formulation of SDH in 1990, operated at speeds of up to 139.364 Mbps. However, the carriers implemented coaxial and radio-based systems operating at 140–565 Mbps. The networks were severely constrained due to the high cost of the transmission medium (coaxial cable especially). The multiplexing rates used plesiochronous rates, which led to the European PDH. After the development of fiber and the enhancements of integrated circuitry, the newer transmission speeds and complex networking architectures became realistic. In Europe, the evolution and deployment of ISDN also led to the proliferation of the B-ISDN standards, which allows a simple multiplexing technique.

Synchronous Communications

What does synchronous mean anyway? Why is it so important to the telecommunications industry? The easiest way to describe the need for synchronization is that the "bits" from one telephone call are always in the same location inside a digital transmission frame such as a DS-1. In the United States, telephone calls using digital transmission systems create a DS-0. The DS-0s are multiplexed 24 per DS-1 channel. DS-1 lines are synchronously timed and mapped, therefore, it is easy to remove or insert a call. Finding the location creates an easy add/drop multiplexing arrangement.

Plesiochronous

Plesiochronous means "almost synchronous." Variations occur on the timing of the line so bits are stuffed into the frames as padding. The digital bits (1s and 0s) vary slightly in their specific location within the frame creating "jitter." This occurs on a frame to frame basis creating ill timing and requiring some other actions to make everything bear some semblance of timing.

SDH Frame

The SDH forms a multiplexing rate based on the STM-N frame format. The STM stands for "Synchronous Transmission Module." The STM-N general frame format works as follows. Similar to the SONET OC-1 (albeit larger) the basic STM-1 frame consists of:

$$270 \text{ columns} \times 9 \text{ rows} = 2430 \text{ octets}$$
$$9 \text{ columns} \times 9 \text{ rows} = 81 \text{ octets section overhead}$$

The remaining 2349 octets create the payload. Higher rate frames are derived from multiples of STM-1 according to value of N. The standard STM-1 frame is shown in Fig. 8.18. This is similar but different from the frame in an OC-3.

The typical rates of speed and the appropriate STS and STM rates are shown in Table 8.2. Only three of the hierarchical levels are actually defined in the standard and are commercially available. These are the STM-1, STM-4, and STM-16.

As the data is prepared to place in the frame, several different modes of transport are available. At the input, the data flows into a container with a size designation. For example, the C11 is the equivalent of a T1 transport mechanism at 1.544 Mbps. The C12 will carry the E1 transport mechanism at 2.048 Mbps. Another transport is the C2, which is the equivalent of a DS-2 operating at 6.312 Mbps. Each of these levels

TABLE 8.2   Comparison of STS and STM Rates

Electrical Rate	Optical Rate	Speed
STS-1	STM-0	51.84 Mbps
STS-3	STM-1	155.52 Mbps
STS-9	STM-3	466.56 Mbps
STS-12	STM-4	622.08 Mbps
STS-18	STM-6	933.12 Mbps
STS-24	STM-8	1.244 Gbps
STS-36	STM-12	1.866 Gbps
STS-48	STM-16	2.488 Gbps

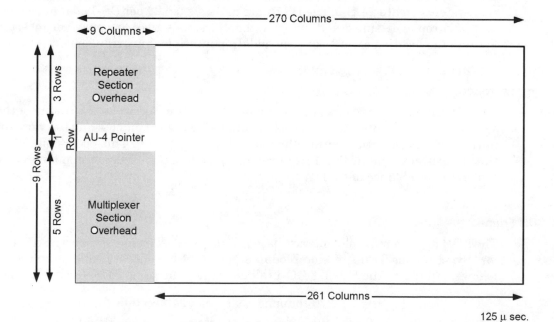

Figure 8.18   The STM-1 frame formats.

TABLE 8.3   Levels of Input as They Map into the Tributary Units

Equivalent	Rate	Input	Mapping	Aligning
DS-1	1.544 Mbps	C11	VC-11	TU-11
E-1	2.048 Mbps	C12	VC-12	TU-12
DS-2	6.312 Mbps	C2	VC-2	TU-2
E-3/T-3	34.368/44.736 Mbps	C3	VC-3	TU-3
E-3/T3	34.368/44.736 Mbps	C3	VC-3	AU-3
E-4	139.264 Mbps	C4	VC-4	AU-4

of container is then input into a virtual container (VC level N). This may sound very similar to the SONET virtual tributary (VT). SDH defines a number of *containers*, each corresponding to an existing plesiochronous rate. The information from a PDH signal is mapped into the relevant container. This is done similarly to the bit-stuffing procedure used in conventional PDH multiplexers.

Next, the virtual containers are mapped and multiplexed within the frame into a tributary unit level N. This completes the input from a container to a virtual container to a tributary unit. The levels are pretty much the same designation as shown in Table 8.3 below. The T1, E1, and T2 lines can be mapped and multiplexed into the virtual containers that convert the format needed within SDH. The containers are then aligned with the timing of the system to create a Tributary Unit (TU).

SDH brings the harmony to the overall multiplexing of the various signals and transport rates. It also acts as the gateway between SONET and SDH structure. It has been over a decade since the actual ratification of the standards, and now more than ever, the benefits are visible. Transcontinental links are now in heavy use across the world on fiber-based architectures.

Different Waves of Light on the Fiber

Over the past 15 years, several major improvements have been made in the use of optical fiber communications. In earlier discussions regarding the use of SONET and SDH the issue of bandwidth surfaced. Not only does the issue of bandwidth keep coming up, but the problem of just how quickly we consume all the bandwidth that is made available. No matter how much or how fast we improve our spectrum availability, newer applications crop up that literally "eat up" all the capacity available to us. The carriers have installed fiber optic cables as the backbone to links their interoffice networks. This creates a mainstay in their communications infrastructure. Using standard time-division multiplexing (TDM), their standard is to carry between 2.488 and 9.953 Gbps on a single fiber. The revolution to high bandwidth, applications and explosive use of the Internet has created capacity demands that exceeded the traditional TDM limits. TDM can only operate within the spectrum of the silicon that drives current technologies. What was once considered an inexhaustible amount of capacity when fiber optics was first introduced has literally vaporized. The depletion of the excess capacity we once had drove a new demand for more bandwidth. To meet these demands the use of wave-division multiplexing (WDM) surfaced.

To solve this problem, the use of frequency-division multiplexing with our light-based systems became a topic of research. What ensued was the ability to introduce various wavelengths (frequencies) of light on the same fiber cable, and the resultant increase in possible throughput. We have seen increases approximate between 16 and 30 times the original capacities of a single fiber. These capacities are now being pushed to the limit with variations being promised of up to 128 times the capacity of the existing fiber technologies. What this means is that the old days of having to replace the in-place fibers with new technology have been replaced with newer technology that uses the in-place fiber, necessitating only the change in electronics on the line. We can expect to see these advances provide virtually unlimited bandwidth without en masse changes in the infrastructure. The future holds the promise of reduced costs, increased bandwidth utilization, and ease of implementation that meets the demands of our higher speed communications.

Growing Demands

Clearly as we approached the turn of the century, the revolution from a voice centric network to a data and video centric network has permeated throughout our industries. Communications, once a narrowband service dominated by narrowband voice services, now demands the bandwidth capable of supporting broadband communications, video and multimedia. Just about every aspect of our lives has changed. Business, government, medicine, academia, and entertainment activities all depend on high-speed communications networking. Indeed, since the commercialization of the Internet, hundreds of millions of users are now engaged in surfing activities, music downloads, and videoconferencing and Voice over IP protocol.

Wave-Division Multiplexing

Ten years ago, the implementation of the OC-48 SONET specification had the industry believing that limitless bandwidth was available. One can just imagine that a mere decade ago the 2.5 ± Gbps capacities of the optical fiber networks was innovative and exceeded our wildest imaginations about how we would ever fill these communications channels. Yet, the industry began to recognize the changes in consumption patterns. The demand for multimedia communications, video WAN started to erode even the highest capacities available. To solve this problem, researchers began to experiment with the use of more than one light beam on the same cable. Light operates in the frequency spectrum similar to the older cable TV systems employing frequency-division multiplexing (FDM).

By using different radio frequencies on a cable TV system, the carriers were able to expand the number of TV channels available to them on the same coaxial systems. Why not do the same things with the various frequencies of light?

WDM, in contrast, can carry multiple data bit rates, allowing multiple channels to be carried on a single fiber. The technique quite literally uses different colors of light down the same fiber to carry different channels of information, which are then separated out at the distant end by a diffraction grating that identifies each color. All optical networks employing WDM with add/drop multiplexers and cross-connects permit this. Dense WDM (DWDM) systems multiplex up to 8, 16, 32 or more wavelengths in the 1550 nanometer (nm) window, increase capacity on existing fiber, and are data rate transparent.

WDM was first developed to increase the distance. Signals could be transported in long-distance networks, from 35–50 km to as much as 970 km or more with optical amplifiers. Subsequently, companies discovered that DWDM would work in metropolitan networks just as well. These DWDM ring systems can be connected with asynchronous transfer mode (ATM) switches and Internet protocol (IP) routers. ATM networks are expected to use SONET/SDH physical layer interfaces with OC-12 add/drop multiplexers. ATM can carry voice, video, and data communications in the same transport and switching equipment.

WDM systems require nonzero dispersion fiber. This type of fiber introduces a small amount of dispersion that decreases nonlinear component effects. Originally, SONET equipment makers expected to be forced to make reliable OC-192 (10 Gbps) systems or face stiff competition from DWDM manufacturers.

Thus, a new era was born in the use of wavelength-division multiplexing. By adding a tightly separated wavelength of light on the same cable, more capacity can be obtained. In normal fiber transmission, the use of two standard wavelengths was originally deployed, as shown in Fig, 8.19. First, a red band of light was used to transmit the signal from the originating end. A blue band is used at the opposite end. Therefore, the same cable can carry both send and receive traffic using different color bands. The original OC-48 transmission (operating at 2.5± Gbps) was exciting using a single wavelength of light and driving the signal over 20–30 miles of fiber. However, the carriers soon recognized that skyrocketing demand for the bandwidth would outpace the throughput of this single wavelength transmission.

Depending on the usage of various types, the life cycle of the OC-48 was anticipated to be approximately 2 years. Clearly the rapid increase in Internet access, cellular

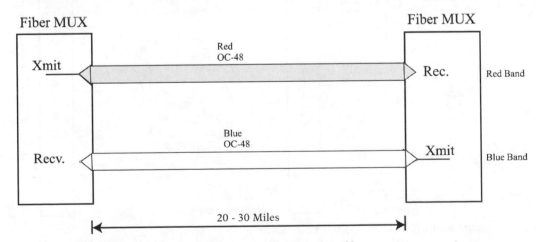

Figure 8.19   The colors of light separate the bands carried on the cable.

communications, high-speed data and the multimedia improvements were on a collision course with the capacity of this OC-48 architecture. Choosing to move to a higher-capacity multiplexing technique in TDM was a definite consideration. This led to the higher rate multiplexing at the OC-192 level (9.953 Gbps ±), a fourfold increase in the speed and throughput of the SONET networks. Yet, even though the increases were achieved to the OC-192 level, the initial implementation was with one wavelength of light.

At the same time, OC-48, using two wavelengths produced a 5-Gbps throughput on the same fibers, proving that the technology could work. Shortly after the introduction of the OC-192, strides were taken to introduce OC-48 running four wavelengths (10 Gbps) or a single OC-192 using one wavelength.

Shortly after 10 Gbps were demonstrated, the designers began to experiment with a 20-Gbps capacity using eight wavelengths of OC-48 and/or two wavelengths at the OC-192 rate. Now the stage was set to push the envelope as far as possible! It was only a matter of a few years before the developers began introducing quantum leaps in their multiplexing ability. Now with multiples of OC-48 and OC-192, the capabilities of fiber- based transmission exceed the wildest imagination. Capacities for the DWDM service are now ranging from 160 Gbps to as much as 400 Gbps. This is the first of many steps we can expect to see in the near future. Some rumors indicate 128 wavelengths of OC-192 being possible shortly after the turn of the century. That is 1.2 Tbps!

In Fig. 8.20, a variable number of wavelengths are selected in a WDM system that can carry many different wavelengths, exponentially increasing the throughput.

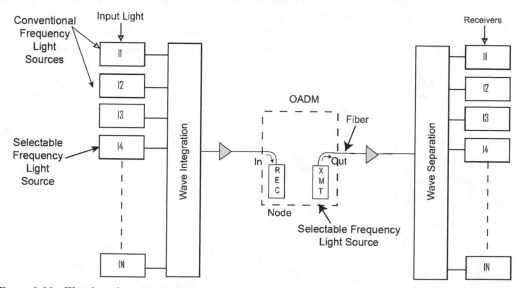

Figure 8.20   Wavelength-multiplexing systems.

TABLE 8.4   Summary of Fiber Compared to Other Forms of Media

Fiber-Based Advantages over Other Media	
Lower errors	BER approximates 10^{-15} for fiber whereas copper will be in the 10^{-4} to 10^{-8} range
Attractive cost per foot	Cost per foot on fiber is now approximately \$.15 compared to \$.13 for copper
Performance	Immune from RFI and EMI without extra cost of shielding on copper
Ease of installation	Ease of installation due to lower weight and thickness
Distances	Greater distance with fewer repeaters. Now can achieve 30–200 miles without repeaters. Copper and radio limited to less than 30 miles
Bandwidth improvements	Fiber nearing 1 Tbps, copper 100 Mbps and coax 1 Gbps
Capable of carrying analog and digital	Using TDM and WDM the fiber is both digital and frequency multiplexed increasing capacity

Benefits of Fiber Compared to Other Forms of Media

The benefits of fiber over other forms of media are shown in Table 8.4. However, it is important to note that the fiber has been used extensively in the long distance telecommunications networks and the local telephone company networks. It is more recent that a single mode fiber has worked its way into the end-user networks (LANs and CANs). With single mode fiber, the speeds are constantly being upped, while the error performances are continually being improved. This table concentrates on the bit-error rates and the speed of the cabling systems.

Wave-Division Multiplexing

Now back to the WDM concept. The combination of voice, data, and multimedia applications that are constantly putting pressure on the infrastructure add to the growing problem. Where normal digital transmission systems use TDM and cable TV analog technologies use FDM. WDM is a combination of the two schemes combined. The use of a TDM multiplexer breaks the bandwidth down to specific timeslots such as found in SONET based networks. However, by using the combination of frequency (different wavelengths) and time (time slots) the fiber can be used to carry orders of magnitude more than traditional fiber-based systems. Figure 8.21 shows the combination of the two multiplexing arrangements in a single format. Furthermore, several different wavelengths and colors of light can be used to produce far more capacity.

DWDM was developed to produce even better results on a single fiber pair than the original techniques deployed on the backbone networks. Expanding capacity with

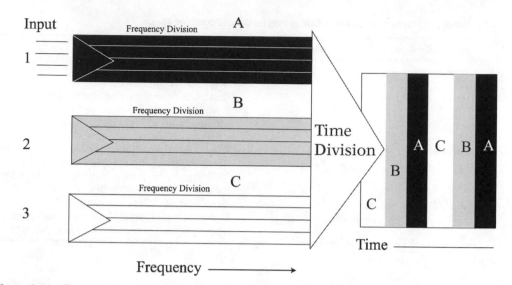

Figure 8.21   Combinations of frequency and time multiplexing produce the results in WDM.

DWDM can produce some significant improvements for today's technology. An example of this is the fact that some DWDM multiplexers can produce up to 240 Gbps on each pair of fibers. This equates to a call-carrying capacity of up to 3.1 million simultaneous calls on a single pair of fiber. Now many of the carriers have installed at least 12 pairs of fiber in their backbone networks. Performing the math yields 37.2 million calls simultaneously on the fiber using current technology before more fibers are required. This is obviously very attractive to the carriers who would prefer to get more service on their existing infrastructure rather than installing more glass in the ground. WDM is particularly useful when congestion begins to build up on the existing carrier based networks. Surely, the equipment is expensive but the cost of adding multiplexing equipment or changing it out, is far less expensive than digging up the ground to lay more fibers. The electronics for the DWDM multiplexers are rapidly becoming very cost efficient.

Using different light wavelengths, DWDM simultaneously transmits densely-packed data streams on a single fiber. By combining DWDM with special amplifiers and filtering equipment on the links, the carriers can achieve unprecedented throughput on their existing single mode fiber. Current technology supports approximately 16 different lengths on a single fiber (OC-192 is 10 Gbps, using 16 wavelength produces up to 160 Gbps in each direction). As stated earlier in the beginning of this chapter, 128 wavelengths are targeted for early in the new millennium. Table 8.5 is a summary of some of the benefits of the DWDM usage.

TABLE 8.5   Summary of Demand to Justify the Use of DWDM

Industry Demand	What Causes the Demand
Need for bandwidth	Internet access, cellular and personal communications (PCS) and data/voice integration and VoIP
Need for reliable communications	In order to guarantee the reliability customers are demanding, the carriers have been committing alternate routes and spare fiber capacity to back up existing infrastructure
More capacity	In order to get the service level agreements (SLA) and maintain the network in a fashion expected by the consumer, the carriers have to install backup circuits and fibers in their highest density routes
Higher performance on the network	Network dependency has become the norm. All forms of traffic must run on the existing infrastructure, and the carriers must provision capacity to meet the ever-changing demands of the network

Why DWDM though?

The more information that can be generated over a single fiber, the better the carriers like it. To be specific, before digging up the ground to lay more fibers, it is far less expensive to use the multiple wavelengths of light on a single fiber. Thus as the carriers sought to gain more utilization on the existing fiber, the incentive is for the manufacturers to continue to proliferate this technology.

The major manufacturers have obviously put all their resources into the development of the DWDM techniques to meet the rising demand from the carriers and the end users alike. Using 16 wavelengths (16λ) operating at the OC-192 rate yields 160 Gbps in each direction as shown in Figure 8.22 or 320 Gbps in one direction.

The use of fiber-based multiplexing also adds some other enhancements that were not traditionally available in the past. Because the signal never terminates in the optical layer, the interfaces can be bit-rate and format independent, allowing the service providers the opportunity to integrate DWDM easily with their existing equipment and infrastructure while gaining the access to the untapped resources and capacities in the existing fiber.

DWDM requires that the transmission lasers have a very tight wavelength tolerance so that the signals do not interfere with each other. After all, the systems carry 16 or 32 different wavelengths on a single fiber. It is imperative that the tolerances be held tightly to prevent mass destruction of the data signals being generated on the fibers. The International Telecommunications Union (ITU) has divided up the infrared spectrum into designated channels (wavelengths) that all optical equipment manufacturers adhere to as shown in Fig. 8.23. Note that the ITU wavelength grid is not very specific about the frequency separations, but the fixed frequency is precise.

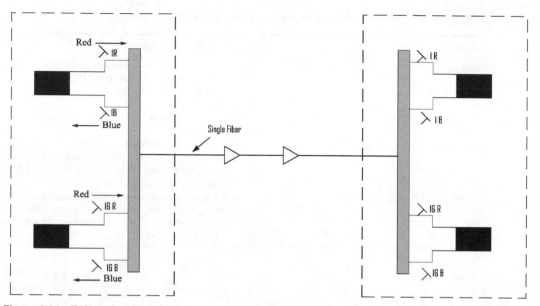

Figure 8.22 Bidirectional transmissions on a single piece of fiber.

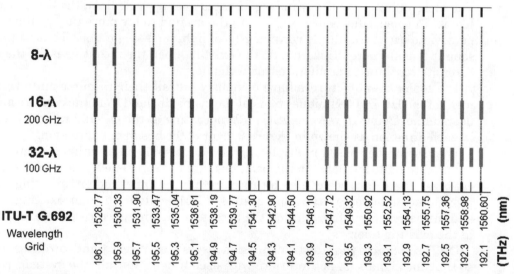

Figure 8.23 The recommended grid based on the ITU specifications.

The grid was originally done at 100 GHz (0.8 nm) spacing. For 200-GHz spaced products, manufacturers simply skip one channel every time they use a channel. Using much the same method, the 50- and 25-GHz channels can be calculated.

Table 8.6 is a summary of some of the other things that we are expecting to occur over the next 5 years in the area of fiber transport systems. This table takes advantage of

TABLE 8.6   A look at What DWDM and Fiber Rates Will Bring over the Next 5 Years

Technology and Capacities	Current vs. Future Technology
DWDM at OC-192 and 40λ	Current technology capable of carrying 40 different wavelengths (using ITU 100 GHz spacing) at 10 Gbps each or 400 Gbps. Currently the industry has achieved 320 Gbps with the 400 Gbps rate in the very near future.
DWDM at OC-192 and 80λ	The current spacing of 100 GHz as specified by the ITU is under attack. The near future holds the promise of doubling the number of wavelengths by using a 50-GHz spacing allowing up to twice as many wavelengths on the same fiber (80) each operating at 10 Gbps.
DWDM at OC-768 and 40λ	This is a turn of the century technology with up to 40 Gbps per wavelength and 40 wavelengths or a total of approximately 1.6 Tbps.
DWDM at OC-768 and 80λ	By the year 2002, we can probably expect to see the OC-768 plus the use of 80 wavelengths or a 3.2 Tbps throughput on the fiber.
DWDM at OC-192 and 160λ	By the year 2005 we can expect to see that the wavelengths decreased spacing and tighter tolerances on the fiber lasers yielding a total of 160 different wavelengths at 10 Gbps each or back to the 1.6 Tbps rate.
DWDM at OC-768 and 160λ	These 2008–2009 technologies will again double the capacity and yield 160 different wavelengths at the OC-768 rate (40 Gbps) or netting 6.4 Tbps on a single fiber.

the work being done in many of the labs and research facilities around the world. The ability to push the envelope is what the communications industry is driven.

WDM was first developed to increase the distance signals could be transported in long-distance networks, from 35–50 km to as much as 970 km or more with optical amplifiers. Subsequently companies discovered that DWDM would work in metropolitan networks just as well providing Metro-Ethernet at 1–10 Gbps. These DWDM ring systems can be connected with ATM switches and IP routers.

Protocol stacks for service transport over SONET/SDH and DWDM are emerging. Increasingly the dominant services are voice and IP. Today most voice service is circuit switched and is mapped into SONET via virtual tributaries. There are also some implementations that map voice into ATM for transport over SONET, for example voice over DSL. Not shown is Voice over IP (VoIP), which is also becoming increasingly common. In the VoIP case, we only really need the right half of the diagram. Voice becomes one of many services carried over IP as can be seen in Fig. 8.24. There are many ways that

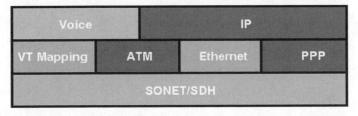

Figure 8.24   The protocol stack for various services.

IP can be carried over SONET/SDH. We show three of the more common ones here. In the next portion of this lesson, we will focus on IP over PPP-over-SONET (Packet over SONET or POS), and IP-over-Ethernet-over-SONET (Ethernet over SONET or EOS).

Questions

1. What does SONET mean?
   a. Synchronous Opportunity Networks
   b. Synchronous Optical Networks
   c. Standards-Based Optical Networks
   d. Standard Optional Networking

2. The SONET link architecture is broken into ____ pieces.
   a. 1
   b. 2
   c. 3
   d. 4

3. The point between two different repeaters is called the line.   T/F

4. The end-to-end communications is called the path.   T/F

5. The basic SONET rate called the OC-1 operates at ____.
   a. 34 Mbps
   b. 49.76 Mbps
   c. 51.22 Mbps
   d. 51.84 Mbps

6. The STM-1 is the equivalent to an OC-4.   T/F

7. PDH stands for:
   a. Plesiochronous Data Header
   b. Plesiochronous Data Hierarchy
   c. Plesiochronous Digital Hierarchy
   d. Plesiochronous Data Header

8. SONET can use ADMs to drop off certain portions of the bandwidth without demultiplexing the entire payload.   T/F

9. Wave-division multiplexing combines the _____ and _____ multiplexing schemes.
   a. Time and space
   b. Frequency and statistical
   c. Frequency and space
   d. Frequency and time

10. WDM can multiplex multiple data streams on the same piece of fiber.   T/F

11. The ability to multiplex as much as 128 or more wavelengths on a piece of fiber is called:

    a. Wave-division multiplexing

    b. SONET

    c. Add/drop multiplexing

    d. Dense wave-division multiplexing

12. SONET and SDH use a ring topology when _____ is required.

    a. A loop

    b. Add/drop multiplexing

    c. Survivability

    d. Duplex operation

13. What lambda spacing does the ITU recommend?

    a. 1 nm spacing

    b. 7 nm spacing

    c. 3 nm spacing

    d. 1552.52 nm center, vendors may step in 50, 100, 200, and so on increments

14. What is the popular wavelength for SONET?

    a. 850 nm

    b. 1310 nm

    c. 1555.52 nm

    d. 1610 nm

15. Which optical signals can be carried by DWDM technology?

    a. ESCON and fiber channel

    b. Gigabit Ethernet

    c. SONET/SDH

    d. All the above

Data Communications

After reading this chapter and completing the questions, you will be able to:

- Describe the steps needed to transmit or receive data
- Understand the need for compression
- Discuss the various alphabets used in data communications
- Describe the various standards used in modems
- Discuss what a modem does

No matter where we travel these days, we run across several people who chastise us as authors. These folks believe that we spend far too much time describing the methods and the meaning of data communications. All too often, we have to defend our position with the reality of the data communications needs. Let's take an example of what we are talking about.

Recently, while in a very large mid-western city, I was asked to speak to a group of academics and business people about the industry and trends. After talking about the status of the industry, the floor was opened to Q&A. Much to my chagrin, many in the audience challenged the fact that I spoke regarding broadband communications only being deployed to approximately 20 percent of users and that the bulk of the access to our networks was through dial-up data communications. Admittedly, if you are in a very large city, the deployment of broadband communications has exceeded these numbers. However, if you are in the suburbs of these cities, the numbers are dramatically different.

After defending my position (and I am not sure I completely convinced these disbelievers) I left for my next stop. I traveled to a small community of about 20 thousand, where I was staying in one of the two local hotels/motels in town. Upon checking in, I decided to check on e-mail. I immediately noticed the absence of a high-speed cable in my room. Moreover, I fired up my wireless LAN card (discussed in Chapter 14) and attempted to find connectivity. Having no luck, I called down to the front desk and inquired about access to the Internet. The front desk ambassador informed me that I could connect to the dial-up line in the room and was very proud to let me know that a connection was available at the base of my lamp, so I did not have to crawl on the floor to plug in my modem. So, here I was in rural America and using a dial-up connection, which I had only recently discussed.

A short-time later, I was on the East Coast in the Baltimore area. Here with a group of telecommunications professionals, the conversation led to the use of broadband communications. (This time, I had high-speed access from my local hotel.) However, many of the people in the group stated that they lived out in the "boonies" and that CATV was not available, and that they were too far from the local CO to get DSL service from the local supplier (both of these are discussed in Chapter 15). The point is and continues to be, the need for dial-up data communications has not gone away and will not do so for some time to come. Thus, you should have an understanding of how it works and why it works the way it does.

Many people think: "If I learn the buzzwords, everyone will think I know what I'm talking about." Nothing could be further from the truth; just knowing the words will not suffice. However, there is really no mystique associated with the use of data communications. Although some complexities do exist in this technology, the basics are fairly straightforward. If you can surmount the initial hurdle of setting up a data transmission, the rest can be fairly well assimilated.

It is important to understand that the data world grew out of the voice world. Voice traditionally paid for the data transmissions on the network. Data is now growing much faster than voice; voice is growing at only 3–4 percent per year, data is growing at 30+ percent per year. The use of the analog dial-up telephone network is where it all started. In order to communicate from a terminal, computer, or other piece of equipment, you merely have to put the pieces together in the proper order:

1. Select and deal with the transmission media
2. Use communicating devices that will present the proper signal to the line (the communicating device is called the DCE)
3. Add a device called the data terminal equipment (DTE)
4. Set up or abide by accepted rules (protocols)
5. Use a preestablished alphabet that the devices understand
6. Ensure the integrity of information before, during, and after transmission
7. Deliver the information to the receiving device

This chapter demystifies the elements involved in all data communications processes. Later chapters focus on specific technologies, using the concepts and terminology introduced here. However, before we traverse down the data communications path, we should point out two definitions:

- *Bit*: A bit is a contraction of two words, which describes a binary digit. In data, all information is represented in either a one (1) or a zero (0). This is the smallest possible representation of data that we can have. Thus the binary digit is contracted into a bit.

- *Byte*: A byte is a group of bits (1s and 0s) that are put together to create a character in an alphabet. Normally, we use the description that a byte is 8 bits. That became the norm, so everyone uses that definition. In reality, however, a byte can be of 5, 6, 7, or more bits depending on the alphabet being used. More will be seen on this below.

Now we can move on to our descriptions of data communications.

Concepts

Like learning computer programming, learning data communications technology is a nonlinear process. That is, whatever starting point one chooses, one almost has to use terms that will be defined elsewhere. The usual solution to this problem is *iterative teaching*: teach a basic set of concepts, and then go back and both use and expand on those concepts, refining them along the way. (I prefer to think it works like this: I am going to tell you what I am going to tell you. I am going to tell you. Then, I am going to tell you what I told you!) Our basic set begins with a discussion of some important concepts that permeate the world of data communications. Those concepts include:

- Standards
- Architectures
- Protocols
- Error detection
- Plexes
- Multiplexing
- Compression
- Standards

A *standard* is a definition or description of a technology. The purpose of developing standards is to help vendors build components that will function together or that will facilitate use by providing consistency with other products. This section discusses what standards are, why they exist, and some of the ways they could affect you. Specific standards are mentioned in other sections where applicable.

There are two kinds of standards: *de facto* and *de jure*. *De facto* means *in fact*. If more than one vendor "builds to" or complies with a particular technology, one can reasonably refer to that technology as a standard. An excellent example of such a standard in data communications is IBM's systems network architecture (SNA). No independent standards organization has ever "blessed" SNA as an "official," or de jure standard. But dozens, if not hundreds, of other vendors have built products that successfully interact with SNA devices and networks.

Note that de facto standards rarely become standards overnight. SNA was available for some time before vendors other than IBM could or would provide products that supported it. Moreover, some technologies become standards because the creating vendors intend them to become standards (e.g., Ethernet), while others become standards despite the creating vendors.

De jure means *in law,* although standards do not generally have the force of law. In some parts of the world, when a standard is set, it in fact becomes law. If a user or vendor violates the rules, the penalties can be quite severe. A user who installs a nonstandard piece of equipment on the links could be subject to steep fines and up to 1 year in prison. These countries take their standards seriously. In the United States, no such penalties exist; we are more relaxed in this area. But a standard is a de jure standard if an independent standards body (i.e., one not solely sponsored by vendors) successfully carries it through a more or less public standards-making procedure and announces that it is now a standard.

You might well ask, "What's the difference? And who cares, anyway?" But understanding which technologies fall into which category, if either, can be a factor in deciding what to buy. Generally, de facto standards are controlled by the vendors that introduced them. For example, Microsoft Windows is a de facto standard; many vendors provide programs that comply with and operate in this environment. But if it decides to change the way a new version of Windows works, Microsoft in theory can obsolete all of those programs. (In practice, Microsoft is most unlikely to do this, at least intentionally, because much of its market power stems from the fact that all those other products are built to its standard. Were Microsoft to make such a change, it is likely that those other software providers would look elsewhere for a target operating system. Microsoft's stock would drop precipitously, to say the least! Or as we saw, the Department of Justice would alter the way Microsoft does business.)

One reason that vendors often build to de facto standards is that the standards-making process tends to be somewhat lengthy. A minimum of a 4- to 12-year period to come out with a new or revised standard is not at all uncommon in the industry. With product cycles under 1 year in some areas of the communications industry, waiting for finalization of a standard before introducing a product could result in corporate suicide. Ethernet is a good example of a standard that started as a de facto standard. Intel, Xerox, and Digital Equipment Corporation (DEC) introduced Ethernet with the intent of making it a de jure standard. But that process took years and the final result was slightly different than the technology originally created by the three vendors. Nonetheless, many networks were created based on Ethernet before the 802.3 de jure standard was finalized, bringing profit to its creators and operating environments to their customers.

In the real world, the standards-making bodies rely in large part on vendors to develop the details of new and revised standards. In fact, most standards bodies have vendor representatives as full participants. It is a fascinating political process with much pushing and pulling to gain advantage in the market. The vendors participate for several reasons, not the least of which is to get the jump on competitors that are not as close to the process. Other reasons include the ability to state in marketing materials that they contributed to or were involved in testing of a new standard, as well as the opportunity to influence the actual details of a standard to favor technology that the vendors are most familiar with.

To be fair, it should be stated that the primary goal of most of those involved in the standards process is to define a good and useful standard. But when the process produces a dual standard, as in the case of the Ethernet and token ring local area network standards, one can presume that the "best" was compromised somewhat in favor of what could be agreed on.

Even de jure standards change in ways that significantly affect the market—and you. One set of standards that affects thousands of users is the set of modem standards, discussed later. But beware a vendor that trumpets compliance with a "new standard!" The vendor's claim might be legitimate, but if no other vendors have products available in the same space, the company might simply be hyping its own product in hopes that it eventually will become a standard. Or there might be a standard under development but not yet approved. In the latter case, if that standard changes before final approval, the vendor's current products will instantly become nonstandard without changing in any way!

Architectures

As with constructing a building, an overall design is needed when planning a communications environment. For a building, that design is described by architectural drawings. A communications architecture is a coordinated set of design guidelines that together constitute a complete description of one approach to building a communications environment.

Several communications architectures have been developed. Some of the best-known include IBM's SNA and DEC's DNA. But for those already familiar with the open systems interconnect (OSI) model described in Chapter 2, most of this chapter (excluding codes, which reside at the presentation layer) addresses the physical and link layers. The newest architecture to run away with the industry and the fancy of all developers is the Internet architecture using TCP and IP protocols described in Chapter 10. Everyday new applications and protocols are being developed to run on the Internet architecture. This includes voice (VoIP), data, streaming audio and video, and multimedia applications (IMS).

The data communications architectures were modeled after the voice architectures. This is understandable, because data is merely a logical extension of the dial-up voice network. Devices are therefore constructed to fit into the overall voice network operation. Data equipment is designed and built to mimic the characteristics of a human speech pattern. Now, however, we see that voice is data and data is voice, too! This paradigm shift marks the true convergence of voice and data onto a single architecture. The world appears ready to embrace the technologies that will fall out from this convergence.

Protocols

Protocols are key components of communications architectures. Architectures are guidelines on how environments connecting two or more devices can be constructed, so most components of a given architecture in a network will be found on each communicating computer in that network. Protocols provide the rules for communications between counterpart components on different devices.

More detail, with examples, is provided in the discussion of the OSI model in Chapter 2. However, there is one aspect of protocols that also applies to hardware: whether they are synchronous or asynchronous. These key characteristics are covered in the following section.

Transmission Protocols (Synchronous vs. Asynchronous)

All lower-level data communications protocols fall into one of the two following categories: synchronous or asynchronous. The words themselves are based on Greek roots indicating that they either are "in" or "with" time (synchronous) or "out of" or "separated from" time (asynchronous). The underlying meanings are quite accurate, so long as one understands to what they must be applied.

All data communications depend on precise timing or clocking. The discussion of analog versus digital transmission covered how voltage levels are sampled in the middle of a bit time in order to maximize the odds that the sample value will be clearly distinguishable as a 1 or a 0. But how does the equipment determine precisely when the middle of a bit time occurs? The answer is clocking; equipment at both ends of a circuit must be synchronized during transmission so that the receiver and the sender agree regarding beginnings, middles, and ends of bits during transmissions. There are two fundamentally different ways to do this clocking: asynchronously and synchronously.

Simply put, asynchronous transmissions are clocked (or synchronized) 1 byte at a time. Synchronous transmissions are clocked in groups of bytes. But the differences in how these two approaches work go beyond the differences between individual bytes and groups of bytes.

Asynchronous communications is also called start/stop communications and has the following characteristics.

Every byte has added to it 1 bit signaling the beginning of the byte (the *start bit*) and at least 1 bit (possibly2) added at the end of the byte (the *stop bits*). Bytes with 7 data bits typically also include a parity bit (which is an error-checking bit), whereas 8-data-bit bytes usually do not. Thus, generally speaking, 10 or 11 total bits are actually transmitted for every asynchronous byte. To get 7 usable data bits, we must transmit approximately 10–11; strictly speaking, we use a 30–35 percent overhead. Figure 9.1 shows the layout of a data byte in an asynchronous form. This was a special concern when data communications was initially used in the late 1950s and early 1960s. Back then, the cost per minute of a dial-up line was $0.60–0.65. Using that value, 30 cents of every dollar were spent just to provide the timing for the line. This amount of waste concerned everyone.

This also makes nominal speed calculations for such connections easy: dividing the rated speed of the circuit (e.g., 9600 bits per second) by 10 bits per byte gives a transmission speed in characters per second (e.g., 960 cps). As a rule, we divide bits per second by 10 to get the nominal speed of an asynchronous circuit. (*Nominal* here means best-case; in the real world, circuits rarely deliver 100 percent of their nominal capacity. But it's a starting point for capacity calculations.)

Bytes are sent out without regard to the timing of previous and succeeding bytes. That means that none of the components in a circuit ever assume that just because one byte just went by, another will follow in any particular period of time. Think of a person banging away on a keyboard. The speed and number of characters sent in a given period doesn't indicate in any way how many or how quickly characters can be sent in the succeeding similar period.

Clocking is controlled by data terminal equipment (DTE). For example, when a personal computer is used to dial into CompuServe, clocking on bytes going toward the service is generated by the sending PC as shown in Fig. 9.2. That first start bit reaching

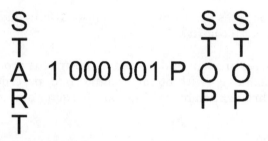

Figure 9.1   To send 7 usable bits of data, we must use 1 start, 1 parity, and 1 or 2 stop bits.

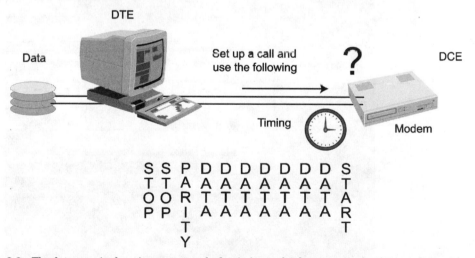

Figure 9.2   The data terminal equipment controls the timing to the data communications equipment (modem), as the bits are sent in an asynchronous protocol—a start bit, and 1 or 2 stop bits help to set the timing.

the modem begins the sequence, with all succeeding bits in the same byte arriving in lockstep at the agreed-on rate until the stop bit is received. Then clocking stops until the beginning of the next byte arrives. Any intervening devices (especially modems) between the communicating DTEs take the clocking from the data sent by the originating DTE for any given byte.

Most PC and minicomputer terminal communications employ asynchronous techniques. The default communications ports on PCs (the "serial" or COM ports) only support asynchronous communications. Interestingly, the serial ports of a PC are now starting to disappear in favor of USB ports. However, the communications port is being internally added in the form of a modem card. Note the RJ-11 jack on the side or back of a PC or laptop, as shown in Fig. 9.3. This is where the special card is used to deliver the serial (COM) port for data communications. To use synchronous communications on a PC, a special circuit board is required.

Synchronous communications have the following characteristics:

- Blocks of data rather than individual bytes (characters) are transmitted.

- Individual bytes don't have any additional bits added to them on a byte-by-byte basis, except for parity.

However, bytes are sent and clocked in contiguous groups of one or more bytes. Each group is immediately (with no intervening time) preceded by a minimum of two consecutive synchronization bytes (a special character defined by the specific synchronous

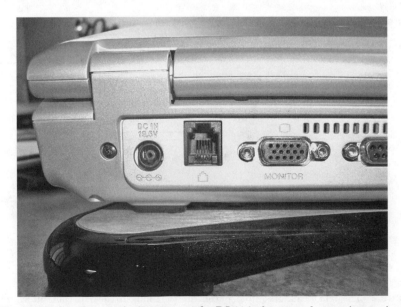

Figure 9.3   The internal modem on the laptop uses the RJ-11 jack, note only two pins are in use.

protocol, of which there are many) that begin the clocking. All succeeding bits in the group are sent in lockstep until the last bit of the last byte is sent, followed (still in lockstep) by an end-of-block byte. This layout of the synchronous characters (SYN) is shown in Fig. 9.4.

Clocking is controlled by data communications equipment (DCE). Specifically, on any given circuit one specific DCE component is optioned (i.e., configured) at installation time as the master device. When the circuit is otherwise idle, the master generates the same synchronization character mentioned above on a periodic basis to all other DCE devices so that all DCE clocks on the circuit are maintained in continuous synchronization.

Except in cases where smaller numbers of bytes (fewer than about 20) are sent at a time, synchronous communications makes more efficient use of a circuit, as can be seen from Table 9.1.

Generally speaking, all circuits running at greater than 2400 bits per second actually operate in synchronous mode over the wire. This is simply because building modems to reliably operate asynchronously at higher speeds over analog circuits is much more difficult than taking this approach. Asynchronous modems that run faster than 2400 bits per second actually incorporate asynchronous-to-synchronous converters; they communicate asynchronously to their respective DTEs, but synchronously between the modems as shown in Fig. 9.5. This doesn't normally impact performance: when smaller groups of characters are sent, there is time to include the additional overhead for synchronous transmission. When larger groups are sent, the reduced overhead of synchronous transmission comes into play. In practice, these higher-speed modems actually communicate with other modems at even higher than their rated speeds; the extra bandwidth is used for overhead functions between the modems.

TABLE 9.1   Comparison of the Utilization of the Circuit

Data Bytes	Asynchronous Bits	Synchronous Bits	Synchronous Savings
1	10	32	−220%
5	50	64	−28%
10	100	104	−4%
20	200	184	8%
30	300	264	12%
100	1,000	824	18%
1,000	10,000	8,024	20%
10,000	100,000	80,024	20%

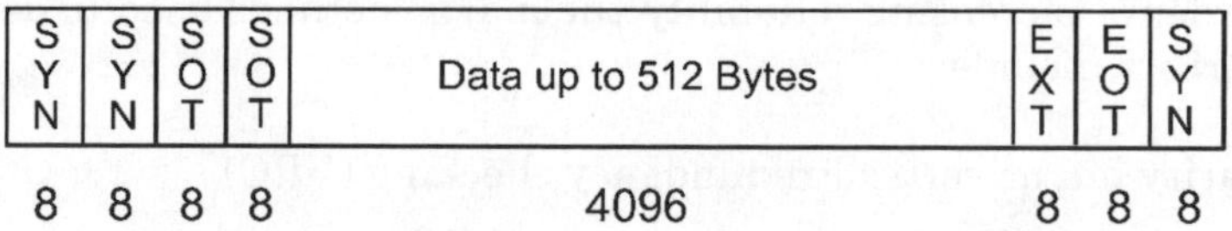

Figure 9.4   The layout of data transmitted synchronously. In this case, the block size is 512 bytes.

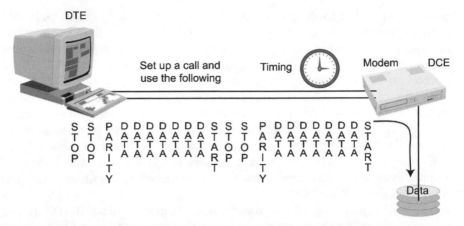

Figure 9.5 The data communications equipment (modem) will set up the communications synchronously. Blocks are used to create the synchronous transfer.

Error Detection

We mentioned at the beginning of the chapter that ensuring the integrity of the information was one of the key responsibilities of a data communications environment. This doesn't mean that the data must be kept honest. Rather, it means that we must somehow guarantee with an extremely high degree of probability that the information is received in exactly the same form as it was sent.

More precisely, there are two tasks required: detecting when transmission errors occur and triggering retransmissions in the event that an error is detected. It is the responsibility of protocols to trigger and manage retransmissions. Here we discuss some of the various approaches that have been developed to detect errors in the first place.

All of the code sets used in data communications (see the following) are designed to use all of their bits to represent characters (letters, numbers, other special characters). A not-so-obvious implication of this fact is that every byte received in such a code set is by definition a valid code. How can we detect whether the received code is the code that was sent?

The solution is to somehow send some additional information, some data about data (sometimes described as *metadata*) along with the primary data. All error-checking approaches depend on sending some additional data besides the original application-related data. The additional data is created during the communications process, used to check the underlying data when it is received, and then discarded before the information is passed to its final destination.

In order of increasing reliability, the major methods used to detect data communications errors include:

- Parity bit, or vertical redundancy checking (VRC)
- Longitudinal redundancy checking (LRC)
- Cyclic redundancy checking (CRC)

Suppose you are my rich aunt and that I am living in Paris (to further my cultural education, of course) and have run out of money. I've called you (collect, of course) to request that you electronically transfer some money into my account at the Banque de Paris. In a fit of generosity, you have decided to send me $1000.00. If the network used is not perfectly reliable and appropriate error detection methods are not applied by the transmitting financial service, a change in a single character—for example, changing the period after the first three 0s to another 0—could result in your sending me considerably more money than you intended: a total of $1000000.

What are the chances of my getting my inheritance early in this way? Not very high, given the odds that only the decimal point would change, and only to a 0 (out of either 126 or 254 other possibilities). But consider the probability of detecting the error, assuming that it has occurred. Using parity bits, the likelihood of detecting this kind of error (which requires several bits to be wrong at one time to change an entire character) is about 65 percent. A somewhat better method, longitudinal redundancy checking, would up the odds of detection to about 85 percent. But the cyclic redundancy checking method improves the odds of detecting and correcting such a multibit error to 99.99995 percent.

Because the networks used to send monetary amounts generally use CRC techniques, it doesn't look as though I'm going to get rich because of their errors. But let's examine these methods in a bit more detail anyway.

Parity Bit/Vertical Redundancy Checking (VRC)

The parity bit approach to error detection simply adds a single "parity" bit to every character (or byte) sent. Whether the parity bit is set to 0 or 1 (the only two possibilities, of course) is calculated by the sending digital device and recalculated by the receiving device. If the calculations match, the associated character is considered good. Otherwise, an error is detected.

This is much simpler than it sounds. Two approaches are typically used: even and odd parity. Other forms of parity exist, such as mark or space parity. It makes no difference which is used; the only requirement is that the sending and receiving devices use the same approach. To illustrate even parity, consider the ASCII bit sequence representing a lowercase letter a: 1100001. Because we are using even parity, we require that the total number of 1 bits transmitted to the receiver to send this a, including the 8 parity bit, be equal to an even number. Their position in the underlying byte is irrelevant. If we count the 1s in the 7-bit pattern, we get 3, an odd number. Therefore, we set the parity bit to 1, resulting in 11100001, an 8-bit pattern with an even number of (i.e., four) 1s. (The parity bit is sent last. In our illustrations the bits farthest to the right are sent first, so we show the parity bit being added at the left.) Figure 9.6 shows an ASCII illustration of the word *hello*, complete with even parity bits. As you can see from the illustration, bytes are represented as vertical sets of numbers, thus vertical redundancy checking: if we orient digits vertically, we add a vertical bit that is redundant to help check the correctness of the underlying byte. The vertical orientation is arbitrary, of course. However, when we illustrate longitudinal redundancy checking, you will see that there is a reason for this display approach.

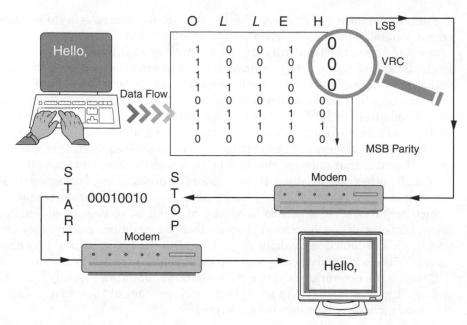

Figure 9.6 The vertical redundancy check shows the flow of data. The parity bit is added after each character is generated.

Having gone to the trouble of describing parity bits, we must confess that they are of limited use in data communications. Parity checking will catch 100 percent of errors where the number of bits in error is odd (1, 3, 5, and so on) and none of the errors where the number of bits in error is even. Put another way, if an error occurs (and communications errors rarely affect only a single bit), there is only about a 65 percent chance that parity checking will detect it. (The probability is better than 50 percent because there are somewhat more 1-bit errors than any one type of multibit error, whether the numbers of the latter are odd or even.)

Parity checking is used extensively inside computers. There it makes sense because it is entirely plausible that errors would occur one at a time (if they occur at all). Parity checking does well in this environment. Also, some networks [e.g., AOL (America on line), CompuServe] still have users set their communications software to use parity checking. But even CompuServe uses a more sophisticated protocol for file transfers. Some more sophisticated error detection protocols are described in the following paragraphs.

Longitudinal Redundancy Checking (LRC)

The concept of LRC follows directly from VRC, taking VRC a step further. This example uses 8-bit rather than 7-bit bytes. But LRC checking needs to operate on a group of bytes, rather than on 1 byte at a time. For this example, it doesn't really matter what the bits represent, so let's create a set of eight 8-bit bytes. As you will see, although the bit patterns don't matter for the example, the number of bytes used does as you can see in Table 9.2.

If we only use VRC (odd parity), as described above, we produce the pattern shown in Table 9.3. But of course, we said that VRC only catches about 65 percent of errors, hardly acceptable. But what if we apply odd parity checking across the bytes in addition to vertically? In that case, the completely filled-in Table 9.4 would be generated.

Adding both the horizontal and vertical checking, together referred to as longitudinal redundancy checking, improves the odds of detecting errors to about 85 percent. Not bad, although we wouldn't want to trust our money to such a transmission. But there is another disadvantage to LRC. Using 8-bit bytes for every 8 data byte, an additional 2 LRC bytes must be transmitted. That works out to 20 percent added overhead for error checking (2 LRC bytes divided by the 10 total bytes transmitted in the set), not counting any degradation due to time required to compute the check bytes. This is not an efficient error-checking mechanism. In fact, considering that error checking is only one of several sources of transmission overhead, it is abysmal.

TABLE 9.2 Setting Up for Vertical Parity Checking

1	0	1	0	1	0	1	0
0	0	1	0	0	0	1	0
1	1	1	0	1	1	1	0
1	0	1	0	0	0	1	0
0	1	1	0	0	1	1	0
1	1	1	0	1	1	1	0
0	1	1	0	0	1	1	0

TABLE 9.3 The Parity Bit Is Inserted in VRC

1	0	1	0	1	0	1	0
0	0	1	0	0	0	1	0
1	1	1	0	1	1	1	0
1	0	1	0	0	0	1	0
0	1	1	0	0	1	1	0
1	1	1	0	1	1	1	0
0	1	1	0	0	1	1	0
1	*1*	*0*	*1*	*0*	*1*	*0*	*1*

TABLE 9.4 The Vertical and Longitudinal Redundancy Checks Are Inserted Here

1	0	1	0	1	0	1	0	1
0	0	1	0	0	0	1	0	1
1	1	1	0	1	1	1	0	1
1	0	1	0	0	0	1	0	0
0	1	1	0	0	1	1	0	1
1	1	1	0	1	1	1	0	1
0	1	1	0	0	1	1	0	1
1	*1*	*0*	*1*	*0*	*1*	*0*	*1*	*0*

LRC does have one advantage over cyclic redundancy checking (CRC), the approach discussed next: far fewer computational resources are required for calculating the LRC bytes than for calculating a CRC (unless the CRC is implemented with hardware). In fact, until recent generations of PCs became available, with their vastly more powerful CPUs, CRC checking for asynchronous data communications in the PC environment was not practical because of its computationally intensive nature. Now, however, it is routinely used. Read on to see why.

Cyclic Redundancy Checking (CRC)

Although no practical error-checking algorithm can guarantee detection of every possible error pattern, CRC comes close. A complete explanation with examples of how CRC works would (and does, in several data communications textbooks) requires several pages of somewhat hairy binary algebra. Rather than put you through that, we'll describe some of the method's key characteristics and indicate how this method is used.

Like the previously described approaches to error detection, CRC relies on on-the-fly calculation of an additional bit pattern (referred to as a *frame check sequence*, or FCS) that is sent immediately after the original block of data bits. The length of the FCS is chosen in advance by a software or hardware designer on the basis of how high a confidence level is required in the error-detection capability of the given transmission. All *burst errors*, or groups of bits randomized by transmission problems, with a length less than that of the FCS will be detected. Frequently used FCS lengths include 12, 16, and 32 bits. Obviously, the longer the FCS, the more errors will be detected.

The FCS is computed by first taking the original data block bit pattern (treated as a single huge binary number) and adding to its end (after the low-order bits) some additional binary 0s. The exact number of added 0s will be the same as the number of bits in the desired FCS. (The FCS, once calculated, will overlay those 0s.) Then, the resulting binary number, including the trailing 0s, is divided by a special previously selected divisor (often referred to in descriptions of the algorithm as P).

P has certain required characteristics:

- It is always 1 bit longer than the desired FCS.
- Its first and last bits are always 1.
- It is chosen to be "relatively prime" to the FCS; that is, P divided by the FCS would always give a nonzero remainder. In practice, that means P is normally a prime number.
- The division uses binary division, a much quicker and simpler process than decimal division. The remainder of the division becomes the FCS.

Specific implementations of CRC use specific divisors; thus the CRC-32 error-checking protocol on one system should be able to cooperate with the CRC-32 protocol on another system; the CRC-CCITT protocol (which uses a 17-bit pattern, generating a 16-bit FCS) likewise should talk to other implementations of CRC-CCITT. Selection of a specific P

can be tuned to the types of errors most likely to occur in a specific environment. But, unless you are planning on engineering a new protocol, you needn't worry about the selection process; it already has been done for you by the designers of your hardware or your communications software.

CRC is typically used on blocks or frames of data rather than on individual bytes. Depending on the protocol being used, the size of the blocks can be as high as several thousand bytes. Thus, in terms of bits of error-checking information required for a given number of bytes of data, CRC requires far less transmission overhead (e.g., CRC-32 sends four 8-bit bytes' worth of error-checking bits to check thousands of data bytes) than any of the parity-based approaches.

Although binary division is very efficient, having to perform such a calculation on every block transmitted does have the potential to add significantly to transmission times. Fortunately, CPUs developed in the last few years are up to the challenge. Also, unlike with most other check-digit types of error correction, the receiving device or software does not have to recalculate the FCS in order to check for an error. Instead, the original data plus the FCS are concatenated together to form a longer pattern, then divided by the same P used as a divisor during the FCS creation process. If there is no remainder from this last division, then the CRC algorithm assumes that there are no errors. And, 99.99995 percent of the time, there aren't.

Plexes—Communications Channel Directions

The next area of discussion is the directional nature of your communications channel. Three basic forms of communications channels exist.

One-Way (Simplex)

This is a service that is one way and only one way. You can use it to either transmit or to receive. This is not a common channel for telephony (voice), because there are very few occasions where one person speaks and everyone else listens. Feedback, one of the capabilities that we prize in our communications, would be eliminated in a one-way conversation. Broadcast television is an example of simplex communications.

Designing an efficient data communications application using a simplex channel can require quite a bit of ingenuity. A good example is stock ticker tape radio signals. Bear in mind that in a true simplex system (such as this one) there is absolutely no feedback possible from the receiver to the transmitter. How then does someone using such a signal get useful, timely information? After all, unless one is simply gawking at the symbols as they go by, it is not practical to wait for on average half of the symbols to go by in order to find out that the particular stock in which you are interested just went up or down a bit.

The answer is a combination of communications and computer technology. The applications that implement this technique memorize locally (on a PC) the entire repeating communications stream once, then accept each new symbol/price combination received as an update to the local "database." The user inquires against that local database, getting what appears to be instant information, even though it might have been received several minutes ago. Naturally, the computer must be set to continually receive; otherwise, the user will have no assurance that the data is even remotely current.

Another approach requires the user to specify in advance to the software a set of symbols to collect. As that stock information goes by, the program snags only the specified information for retention and local query. This is not any faster than the previous approach, but it does require less local storage capability.

Two-Way Alternating (Half Duplex)

This is the normal channel that is used in conversations. We speak to a listener, then we listen while someone else speaks. The telephone conversations we engage in are normally half duplex. Although the line or medium (air, in this case) is capable of handling a transmission in each direction, most human brains can't deal well with simultaneous transmission and reception.

Many computer and communications configurations use half duplex technology. Until a few years ago, most leased-line multidrop modems were half duplex. One of the key differentiators among such modems was their turnaround time, that is, how quickly a pair of such modems could reverse the channel direction. This was measured in milliseconds—the fewer, the better. Entire communications protocols were built around this technology (e.g., IBM's bisynchronous communications or BSC). All-block mode (e.g., IBM 3270s) terminals still operate in half duplex mode only, even if full duplex facilities are available. This simply means that at any given time, the terminal is either sending to its associated computer or receiving from it, not both at once. This does not cause a problem because the entire system is designed around this behavior, and it works quite well. Of course, almost half of any given circuit's raw capacity (if the capacities of the two directions are added together) is wasted. (IBM's more recent SDLC-protocol-based front-end processors can talk to one terminal and receive from another at the same time, minimizing this waste, but the individual terminals are still functioning as half duplex devices.)

With some technologies, half duplex can be used so effectively that the one-way-at-a-time characteristic of the circuit is invisible; it appears to be full duplex (see below). An excellent example of such an approach is local area network communications. Most actual LAN technologies, including both Ethernet and token ring, are actually half duplex on the wire. But the information moves so quickly, and the responses are so fast, that the path appears to an observer to be full duplex.

Two-Way Simultaneous (Duplex) or Full Duplex

True full duplex communications make maximum use of a circuit's capacity—if the nature of the communications on that circuit takes advantage of it. In data communications, a circuit is implemented and used in full duplex mode if a device can send to a computer and receive from the computer at the same time. Although we mentioned that human conversation is typically half duplex, there is an exception to this: conversation among teenagers, who seem to be able to speak and listen (somewhat) at exactly the same time.

TABLE 9.5   Comparing the Capability and Directionality of the Circuit

This Capability Level	Requires All Lower Levels to Have at Least the Following Capability	But Can Also Function without Impairment on top of Levels with the Following Capabilities
Simplex	Simplex	Half or full duplex
Half duplex	Half duplex	Full duplex
Full duplex	Full duplex	(no additional levels)

A common example of full duplex communications is that seen when one dials into an online information system such as CompuServe or others. Most such systems allow users to continue typing at a keyboard even while the service is sending information to the user for display on the screen. Were the connection not a full duplex one, this simultaneous bidirectional communication would not be possible.

One point that confuses some people is that the terms *simplex*, *half duplex*, and *full duplex* can refer to varying levels of a communications architecture. If the three levels are considered to be three points on an increasing scale of capability, one can say that a given level of communications architecture must rely on lower levels with at least the capability of that given level, as presented in Table 9.5.

What does this table mean? It means that a wide-area analog data circuit built to handle full duplex communications (requiring the telephone company to support simultaneous communications in both directions, and use of full duplex modems) can fully support half duplex or simplex communications. But if a similar circuit is implemented with half duplex modems, then full duplex communications on that circuit will not work, although simplex will. A citizens band radio provides a half duplex channel—two directions, but only one way at a time. Simplex would work—one sender could lock down a key and just keep sending—but full duplex would be impossible.

Air is a full duplex channel. But a simplex signal such as the output from a stereo speaker system has no trouble traveling this full duplex channel.

Compression

Although compression is not exactly a modulation technique, it does (usually) produce faster transmissions. To understand how compression works, consider first how human beings communicate. Most human communication is inherently redundant. This does not imply waste; rather, human beings use that redundancy as a continual cross-check on what information is really being sent and meant. For example, in face-to-face conversation much more information is being sent than just the words. Facial expressions, tones of voice, limb positions and movement, overall carriage of the body, and other less obvious cues all contribute to the information stream flowing between two people having a conversation. But much of the information is duplicated. For example, anger can be communicated by the words themselves; but it can also be conveyed by tone of voice, facial expression, involuntary changes in the color of one's complexion, the stress in the voice, arm movement, and other cues. If some of these items were removed, the message received might be just as clear but the total amount of raw information might be reduced.

In data communications, compression is a technique applied either in advance to information to be transmitted or dynamically to an information stream being transmitted. The underlying technology is essentially the same in both cases: removal of redundant information, or expression of the information in a more compact form, is used to reduce the total number of bytes that must pass over the communications medium in order to reduce the time the medium is occupied by a given transmission to a minimum.

A detailed discussion of compression techniques is beyond the scope of this book. But in this section we describe two very basic approaches in order to elucidate the fundamentals of the technology. Later, during the discussion of modems, we will briefly identify and describe the power of some compression techniques that are often built into such devices.

The simplest form of compression is the identification and encoding of repeating characters into fewer characters. For example, consider the transmission of printed output across a network to a printer. A typical report contains a very high number of blank characters, often occurring consecutively. Suppose every such string of four or more consecutive blanks (which are of course themselves ASCII characters) is detected and replaced with a 3-byte special character sequence encoded as follows:

- The first character is a special character (one of the nonprint characters in the ASCII code set, for example) indicating that this is a special sequence.

- The second character is one occurrence of the character that is to be repeated, in this case a blank.

- The third character is a 1-byte binary number indicating how many times the character is to be repeated. With 1 byte (using binary format), we can count up to 255, high enough to get some real savings!

How much can we save? Look at Table 9.6. We'll assume that on average, blanks occur in 10-byte consecutive streams, a very pessimistic assumption.

TABLE 9.6   Quick Analysis of Compression Benefits

Total Characters in Print Stream Before Compression	Blanks in Print Before Compression	Total Characters in Streamprint Stream After Compression	Percentage Savings
1000	10	993	1
1000	100	930	7
1,000	500	650	35
50,000	2,000	48,600	3
50,000	5,000	46,500	7
50,000	20,000	36,000	28

As can be seen from the table, the savings depend on the number of occurrences of the character to be repeated. In practice, this is a reasonably powerful technique. In the example, we addressed only blanks. In practice, any character except the special character would be fair game.

But what if we actually want to send that special character? After all, unlike print jobs, many transmissions must be able to handle every possible code; there are none left over that are "special." No problem—we add the following rules:

- We'll never try to compress multiple occurrences of the special character.

- Every time we encounter the special character as input during the encoding process, we'll simply send it twice. If the receiving hardware sees this character twice, it drops one of the occurrences.

With this approach, we only have to select a special character that is unlikely to occur frequently. If it then does occur frequently in a particular transmission, our compression algorithm doesn't break; it will just be very inefficient for that one transmission.

Note how the overall redundancy is squeezed out of a transmission using this approach. But, just as in human communications, eliminating redundancy increases the risk that some information will be misinterpreted. In human communication, if the reddening of an angry person's face and other visual cues were not visible (e.g., if the conversation were on the telephone) and the speaker was otherwise very self-controlled, the listener might misinterpret angry words as being a joke; after all, many American subcultures routinely use affectionate insults without anger. Unrecognized anger is a very serious loss of information. In data communications without compression, omission of a single space in a series of spaces might cause a slight misalignment on a report, but will most likely not seriously distort its meaning. If compression is used and the binary count field is damaged—i.e., changed to another binary digit—dozens or even hundreds of spaces or other repetitive characters might be either deleted or added to the report, seriously compromising its appearance and perhaps distorting its meaning. Consider the havoc that could be wrought on a horizontal bar chart! The error-checking techniques discussed earlier become much more important in a system that uses compression!

Another more sophisticated method of compression requires pattern recognition analysis of the raw data rather than just detection of repeating characters. Again, some special character must be designated, but now it precedes a special short code that represents some repetitive pattern detected during the analysis. For example, in graphics displays capable of showing 64 K (65,536) colors, every screen pixel has associated with it two 8-bit bytes (which together can represent 65 K different values) indicating the color assigned to that pixel. If someone sets the screen to display white on a blue background, the 2-byte code for blue is going to appear thousands of times in the data stream associated with that display. The repeating 1-byte compression algorithm described earlier will not detect anything to compress. But if analysis shows that a 2-byte pattern occurs many times in succession, a more sophisticated approach might assign a specific character (preceded by the special character) to represent precisely 20 (or some other specific number of) consecutive occurrences of that 2-byte sequence.

The savings can be considerable, but they again depend on the characteristics of the data being transmitted.

A third, very computationally intensive approach to compression has been designed especially for live transmission of digitized video signals. Unlike most other compression methods, this approach does not involve movement of representations of the entire digitized data stream from one point to another. Video signals consist of a number of still frames composed each second (visualize 30 photographs per second, in the highest-quality case). Although the first picture must, of course, be sent in its entirety, special equipment and algorithms must then continuously examine succeeding video frames to be transmitted, identifying which pixels have changed since the last "picture" was taken. Then, information addressing just the changed pixels is sent to the receiver, rather than the entire new frame. The receiving equipment uses this change information combined with its "memory" of the previous frame to continuously, locally build new versions of the picture for display. This approach is particularly fruitful for pictures that in large part remain static; for example, video conferencing. In video conferencing, usually the only moving features of the picture are the human beings. The table(s), walls, and other room fixtures stay still, therefore requiring transmission only once. Frequently, only the lips move for long periods of time.

One other compression-related concept is worth mentioning: lossy vs. lossless compression. "What?" I hear you ask. Does lossy mean what it sounds like? Would we ever tolerate transmission that loses information? The answer, for some applications, is "yes." Moreover, you have probably settled for information loss when working daily with computers, and it caused you no hardship at all. If you use a personal computer with a video graphics adapter (VGA) screen, but display any type of graphic that inherently has Super VGA (SVGA) level resolution, your VGA screen loses the additional definition in the image that is visible only when an SVGA controller card and monitor are used. And in fact, this example, while not involving compression as such, demonstrates precisely the type of situation where lossy compression would be tolerated: transmission of video images. Some compression algorithms used for transmission of video images lose some of the resolution of those images. However, if the received image is acceptably precise, the maintenance of the speed of the moving image might be more important.

Codes

The concept of a *bit*—an electronic expression of a 1 or 0—should now be clear. However, how do you get from 1s and 0s to transmitting your resume over wires?

The alphabet must be built up from sets of 1s and 0s. Specifically, we employ one or more sets of *codes* or *alphabets*, standard definitions of patterns of 1s and 0s that we will agree to use to represent letters, numbers, and other symbols that we wish to transmit and receive.

The alphabets most frequently used are either American Standard Code for Information Interchange (ASCII), which is fairly universal, or Extended Binary Coded Decimal Interchange Code (EBCDIC), which is an IBM alphabet. These two code sets, or alphabets, are used to convert a series of 1s and 0s into an alphabetic or numeric character.

ASCII

One character (also known as a byte or octet) must be represented as a consistent bit pattern by both sender and receiver. As we use a keyboard (standard typewriter keyboards are known as QWERTY *keyboards* because of the sequence of the first row of alphabetic keys), we create a stream of combination of letters, numbers, and symbols.

When ASCII (usually pronounced *ass-key* with a mild accent on the first syllable) was originally defined for use by the U.S. government, the bit pattern was defined to be seven data bits long. With 7 bits, it is possible to differentiate 128 different patterns. So, to re-create these typed characters with 1s and 0s, we can use a combination of up to 128 possible ASCII characters shown in Fig. 9.7. Here the discussion of a byte being, however, many bits it takes to make a character comes true.

Using the combinations in this figure, we should be able to transmit just about everything we presently understand in our vocabulary. And, in fact, for many years, the 7-bit ASCII was used for most non-IBM mainframe communications. But there were two factors that caused this form of ASCII to become less popular.

First, most computers handle data in 8-bit chunks (rather than 7) to represent characters. The terms *byte* and *octet* almost always refer to 8-bit, not 7-bit, patterns. Second, while 7-bit ASCII can indeed represent all the English letters and numbers, with some symbols left over for special characters and control information, there are many other characters used in written communication that cannot easily be expressed in a 128-character code set. Accented characters in the Romance languages, character graphic drawing symbols, and typographical indications in word processors (bolding, underlining, and so forth) are just a few examples of symbols difficult to handle with standard ASCII.

				Bit 7	0	0	0	0	1	1	1	1
				Bit 6	0	0	1	1	0	0	1	1
				Bit 5	0	1	0	1	0	1	0	1
Bit 4	Bit 3	Bit 2	Bit 1	Col	0	1	2	3	4	5	6	7
				Row								
0	0	0	0	0	NUL	DLE	SP	0	@	P		p
0	0	0	1	1	SOH	DC1	!	1	A	Q	a	q
0	0	1	0	2	STX	DC2	"	2	B	R	b	r
0	0	1	1	3	ETX	DC3	#	3	C	S	c	s
0	1	0	0	4	EOT	DC4	$	4	D	T	d	t
0	1	0	1	5	ENQ	NAK	%	5	E	U	e	u
0	1	1	0	6	ACK	SYN	&	6	F	V	f	v
0	1	1	1	7	BEL	ETB	'	7	G	W	g	w
1	0	0	0	8	BS	CAN	(	8	H	X	h	x
1	0	0	1	9	HT	EM	)	9	I	Y	i	y
1	0	1	0	A	LF	SUB	*	:	J	Z	j	z
1	0	1	1	B	VT	ESC	+	;	K	[	k	{
1	1	0	0	C	FF	FS	,	<	L	\	l		
1	1	0	1	D	CR	GS	-	=	M	]	m	}
1	1	1	0	E	SO	RS	.	>	N	^	n	-
1	1	1	1	F	SI	US	/	?	O	_	o	DEL

Figure 9.7 The ASCII 7-bit code set.

Extended ASCII

Extended ASCII is a superset of ASCII. Extended ASCII is the code used inside virtually all non-IBM computers, including personal computers. It is an 8-bit code set, doubling the possible distinguishable characters to 256. The 7-bit ASCII codes are present in extended ASCII in their original form with a 0 prefixed to the base 7 bits. Another 128 characters are also available with the same base 7 bits as the original ASCII, but with a 1 prefixed instead.

But whereas ASCII is a standard, extended ASCII is_._._._well, not quite standard. While the original 128 characters communicate well from vendor to vendor, even in extended ASCII, every application defines its own use of the additional 128 characters. For example, you can easily write out ASCII text from most word processing programs, with the result being readable by most other word processors. But if you attempt to read a document created by a word processor in its native form with another, different word processor, you will only be successful if the latter specifically contains a translation module for material created by the first.

Nonetheless, the lion's share of non-IBM communications is now conducted using extended ASCII. Virtually all personal computers use it, including IBM's. If you set your communications protocol to *N,8,1* (no parity, 8 data bits, 1 parity bit), those 8 data bits are encoded in using extended ASCII.

EBCDIC

IBM, not a company to follow the herd, realized early on that 128-code ASCII did not contain enough patterns for its requirements. So, IBM created an entirely different code set, one twice as large as the original ASCII code set. IBM's 8-bit, 256-character code set, used on all of its computers except personal computers, is called Extended Binary Coded Decimal Interchange Code or EBCDIC. (Most people pronounce it *eb-suh-dick* with a mild accent on the first syllable.)*

As with ASCII, certain of the characters are consistent wherever EBCDIC is used. But other characters vary depending on the specific communicating devices. In Fig. 9.8, the white space can be used differently depending on the EBCDIC dialect in use.

Unicode

Two hundred fifty-six codes might seem to be all anyone would need. But consider the requirements of Chinese, which has thousands of characters. Or the Cyrillic alphabet, which, although it does not have a terribly large number of characters, does not overlap any of those defined in ASCII or EBCDIC. Another code set, called unicode, is now being implemented in some products. Unlike the 8-bit extended ASCII and EBCDIC code sets, unicode uses 16 bits or 2 bytes per character. While only 1s and 0s are used, this allows up to 65,536 (2 to the 16th power) separate character definitions. Of course, each

---

*Actually, IBM had already created the EBCDIC code set before ASCII was created. ASCII was created to have a nonproprietary alphabet.

Bits 8765 \ 4321	0000	0001	0010	0011	0100	0101	0110	0111	1000	1001	1010	1011	1100	1101	1110	1111
0000	NUL	SOH	STX	ETX	PF	HT	LC	DEL			SMM	VT	FF	CR	SO	SI
0001	DLE	DC_1	DC_2	DC_3	RES	N;	BS	IL	CAN	EM	CC		IFS	IGS	IRS	IUS
0010	DS	SOS	FS		BYP	LF	EOB	PRE			SM			ENQ	ACK	BEL
0011			SYN		PN	RS	UC	EOT					DC_4	NAK		SUB
0100	SP										¢	.	<	(	+	|
0101	&										!	$	*	)	;	¬
0110	-	/										,	%	_	>	?
0111											:	#	@	'	=	"
1000		a	b	c	d	e	f	g	h	i						
1001		j	k	l	m	n	o	p	q	r						
1010			s	t	u	v	w	x	y	z						
1011																
1100		A	B	C	D	E	F	G	H	I						
1101		J	K	L	M	N	O	P	Q	R						
1110			S	T	U	V	W	X	Y	Z						
1111	0	1	2	3	4	5	6	7	8	9						

Figure 9.8 The EBCDIC code.

character takes up as much storage and transmission time as two 8-bit characters. But unicode is a truly international code set, allowing all peoples to use their own alphabets if they wish.

Modulation

How does the transmission process work? How does the data get onto the voice dial-up telephone line? We use a device to change the data. This device, known as a modem, changes the data from something a computer understands (numeric bits of information) into something the telephone network understands (analog sine waves, or sound). A modem generates a continuous tone, or carrier, and then modifies or modulates it in ways that will be recognized by its partner modem at the other end of the telephone circuit. The modems available to do this come in variations, each one creating a change in a different way. Remember that the word *modem* is a contraction for *modulation / demodulation*. In order for the communications process to work, we need the same types of modems at each end of the line operating at the same speeds. These modems can use the following types of modulation schemes (or change methods):

Amplitude Modulation (AM)

Amplitude modulation represents the bits of information (the 1s and 0s) by changing a continuous carrier tone. Figure 9.9 illustrates amplitude modulation. Because there are

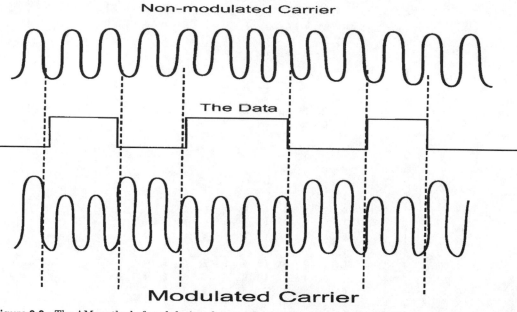

Figure 9.9 The AM method of modulation changes the amplitude of the signal while keeping the frequency constant.

only two stages of the data, 1 or 0, you can let the continuous carrier tone represent the 0 and the modulated tone represent the 1. This type of modem changes the amplitude (think of amplitude as the height or loudness of the signal). Each change represents a 1 or a 0. Because this is a 3-kHz analog dial-up telephone line, the maximum amount of changes that can be represented and still be discrete enough to be recognizable to the line and the equipment is about 2400 per second. This cycle of 2400 changes per second is called the baud rate. Therefore, the maximum amount of data bits that can be transmitted across the telephone line with AM modulation is 2400 bits per second. Most amplitude modulation modems were designed to transmit 300–1200 bits per second, although others have been made to go faster.

As we look at the different ways to change the 1s and 0s generated by the computer into their analog equivalents, we have another choice in the process. Voice communications (or human speech itself) is the continuous variation of amplitude and frequencies, so we could choose to use a modem that modulates the frequency instead of the amplitude. An explanation of this type of modem follows.

Frequency Modulation (FM)

Frequency modulation is provided by an FM modem. This modem represents the 1s and 0s as changes in the frequency of a continuous carrier tone. Because there are only two states to deal with, we can represent the normal frequency as being a 0 and slow down

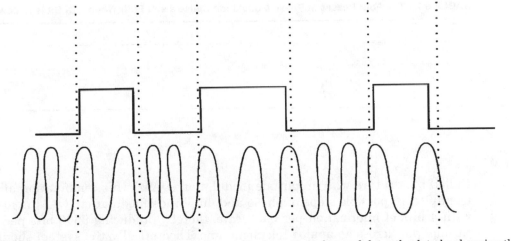

Figure 9.10 Frequency modulation keeps the amplitude constant, but modulates the data by changing the frequency of the carrier.

the continuous carrier frequency when we want to represent a 1 to the telephone line shown in Fig. 9.10. The modem uses the same baud rate on the telephone line as the amplitude modulation technique, that being 2400 baud or discrete changes per second. These modems modulate 1 bit of information per cycle change per second, or a maximum of 2400 bits per second. Note that the baud rate and the bits per second rate are somewhat symmetrical. Although both AM and FM modems are designed around what was once considered pretty fast transmission rates, we have continually been unsatisfied with any rate of speed developed. We want more and more, faster and faster.

Because we (as humans) and our creations (the computers) are never satisfied with the speed of transmission over the telephone line, we demanded faster. Throughput was expensive under the old dial-up telephone network. Therefore, we asked for additional speed to get more throughput and less cost. The engineers came up with a new process that modulates on the basis of phases.

Phase Modulation

If we can change the phase of the sine wave as it is introduced to the line, at positions of 0, 90, 180, and 270 degrees, we can encode the data with more than 1 bit of information at a time. A phase modulation technique allows us to transmit a di-bit of information per signaling-state change. This gives us 4800 bits per second of throughput. The di-bit represents the information, as shown in Table 9.7.

As you can see, two bits of information at 2400 baud gives us the 4800 bits per second. This was a step in the right direction. But we wanted more, so a combination of phase modulation and amplitude modulation was developed.

TABLE 9.7   The Four Phases in Phase Modulation Cause a 90°. Shift When a Di-Bit Is Received

Bits	Phase
00	0
01	90
10	180
11	270

QAM

Called quadrature with amplitude modulation (QAM), this combination allows us to use up to 16 possible steps of phase and amplitude modulation. QAM is mostly used with 4 bits of information per baud rate, thereby producing 9600 bits per second of throughput across an analog telephone line. Theoretically, the system should be able to produce 38,400 bits per second of information (four phases at 4 bits per phase at 2400 baud = 38,400 bits per second).

However, in practice, line rates can rarely support sustained throughput across the telephone network at this speed. Also, the telephone company limits the bandwidth to 3 kHz, and we use 2400 baud. If we try to send more data at a higher baud rate, the band limitation (bandpass filters) will strip the frequencies that go beyond the filters. This is a function of the telephone company equipment on the line at the CO. Thus we usually have to settle for analog data transmission at slower speeds.

The driving force behind improving modulation techniques has always been to increase the speed possible over an analog circuit. Why? In addition to the obvious reason (i.e., accomplishing the task more quickly improves productivity), the cost of communications over dial circuits is directly proportional to the amount of time those circuits are in use; going faster saves money. But, when the absolute best available modulation technology is in use, one has not yet necessarily squeezed the absolute best transmission volumes out of a circuit. One can push it even further by using compression.

Devices

DTE versus DCE

A basic of data communications is that every communicating device is either a terminal-type device (data terminal equipment, or DTE; also sometimes referred to as data circuit terminating equipment, or DCTE) or a communications-type device (data communications equipment, or DCE). DTEs use communications facilities; their primary functions lie elsewhere. DCEs provide access or even implement communications facilities. Their only role is moving information.

You might presume that some cosmic requirement is satisfied by this overall categorization. But in fact the nitty-gritty reality of cabled communications is the primary cause of this division. Although we will get into cabling standards later, consider the following situation:

Two devices, A and B, must be connected. The connection will be via two wires, numbered 1 and 2. Let us assign wire number 1 to transmit the data, and number 2 to receive. But wait! If A transmits on number 1, and B also transmits on number 1, and if they both receive on number 2, neither will listen to what the other is sending. It would be as though two people each spoke into opposite ends of the same tube at the same time, with neither putting the end to his or her ear.

The solution seems simple: have A transmit on wire 1, B listen on wire 1, A listen on wire 2, B transmit on wire 2. But now let us introduce device C. How should C be built? If it is configured as is A, it cannot communicate with A; if it is configured as is B, it cannot communicate with B.

But devices are not configured at random. For example, terminals do not usually connect directly to terminals; printers are never connected directly to printers; and so on. Perhaps if one broad category of devices usually connects not to another in that category but rather to a device in another category, we could standardize on only two default configurations. This is what was done with DTEs and DCEs.

Categories and Examples of DTEs

The grouping is not perfect. Some devices routinely connect to both DTEs and DCEs (e.g., multiplexers). Such devices do not clearly fall into either category, and must be configured depending on the specific installation requirements. But for the most part, any data processing device that can communicate falls cleanly into one of these two categories. Most of the devices covered in this book are DCE devices. Here are some examples of the DTE devices to which we provide data communications services:

- Computers (mainframe, mini, midi)
- Terminals (CRTs, VDT, teletype)
- Printers (laser, line, dot matrix)
- Specialized (bar code readers, optical character recognition)
- Transactional (point of sale equipment, automated tellers)
- Intelligent (personal computers)

The remainder of this section will focus on DCEs and ways of connecting components.

Modems

As mentioned earlier, *modem* is a contraction of two words (*modulator* and *demodulator*). The role of the modem is to change information arriving in digital form into an analog format suitable for transmission over the normal telephone network. Naturally, modems work in pairs (or sets of at least two), and a second modem at the other end of the communications path must return the analog signal to a digital format useful to terminals and computers.

Dozens of manufacturers make modems, and hundreds of models exist. The market can be divided in many ways:

- Speed
- Supported standards
- Leased line versus dial-up
- Two-wire versus four-wire
- Point-to-point versus multipoint (multidrop)
- With or without compression capability
- With or without error correction capability
- Manageable or nonmanageable

Entire texts could be (and no doubt have been) written just on this topic.

V.90 Modems

Practically, all new PCs and laptop computers sold today have a new modem integral to them. The use of modem technology has become commonplace. However, as modems have dropped in price, the ability to go faster has increased. Today, the new modem technology is asymmetrical in that it transmits at one speed and receives data back at a different rate. The world was looking for better ways of moving data, but had to deal with the limits of the wires in the local loop. Over the decades, the cost of modems has dropped while the ability to move the data was going in an upward fashion. Something had to be done because the amount of data we were moving was escalating exponentially. Enter the 56 Kbps modem (V.90 standard), which operates at a 33.6-Kbps transmit rate and a 56-Kbps receive rate.

The rated speeds can be misnomers because in North America, the FCC and the Canadian CRTC limit the speed that a telephone company can offer to a customer to no greater than 53 Kbps. The rate was selected years ago when we were still trying to drive modem communications at 9.6 Kbps. So the arbitrary decision was something that no one ever thought would occur. Alas, here we are with a modem that can achieve 56 Kbps and the regulators have capped it. Moreover, the asymmetrical rate of speed facilitates access to one of the most commonly used networks today—the Internet. The 56-Kbps modem works well because the user has little data to send (typing <www.tcic.com>, for example, requires very little data) but lots to receive (a Web page can be millions of bytes large). So the different speeds allow for dial-up communications on a telephone company circuit (a voice channel) in one direction and a digital-access method for the return path at a much higher rate of speed.

Typically, however, when a user accesses the network with these modems, they will transmit at between 28.8 and 33.6 Kbps upline and receive approximately between 38 and 45 Kbps downstream. One can get a slightly better response from the 56-Kbps modem, but there are still limitations that must be dealt with.

A note that puts this all in perspective though—in the early 1980s we were transmitting data at between 4800 and 7200 Bps, and the modems were expensive (hundreds to thousands of dollars at the time). Here, in a mere decade, we have achieved quantum leaps in technological advancements, and we have seen the cost drop exponentially to a few dollars. What we can expect is faster and better, but cheaper!

V.92 Technology Overview

The newest data standard in modem technology is called V.92, which helps to narrow the gap between dial-up and broadband services by delivering an improved Internet experience to analog modem users. Organizations such as ISPs and long-distance carriers are now offering V.92 to customers. Moreover, the newer PCs come equipped with the V.92 standard as a norm. People who use and support V.92 technology benefit by:

- Becoming more competitive by enabling their network to offer the latest technology to their subscribers and exceeding the service offerings of other ISPs
- Generating more revenue and decreasing customer churn by offering subscribers tiers of services or by charging more for V.92 features like modem-on-hold
- Utilizing quick connect and V.44 compression to decrease usage costs and improve subscriber experience

V.92 presents key enhancements to the V.90 56 K technology, including modem-on-hold, V.44, quick connect, and PCM upstream. Each of these enhancements represents a push forward to a more user friendly dial-up experience.

Modem-On-Hold

Modem-on-hold allows end users to suspend their data connection to either initiate or receive a voice call. If the phone conversation is completed within the allotted time-frame, the user may resume the data connection without redialing.

Under previous standards, analog modems were not compatible with the call waiting service offered by the telephone companies. When the phone line was engaged in a data session, call waiting was either disabled (caller gets a busy signal) or the modem disconnected when interrupted by the call waiting tone. However, V.92 modems use the call waiting beep to trigger the on-hold feature. To receive calls while online, users must subscribe to a call waiting service, and for initiating calls, the three-way calling service.

When a call comes through a phone line tied up by a data connection, the call waiting beep prompts the client modem to alert the user to an incoming call. With software added to the client's PC, the alert message is displayed in a pop-up dialog box. For users who subscribe to a caller ID service, the incoming call's number is also displayed.

Upon dialing in, the network access server (NAS) queries the remote access dial-in server (RADIUS) for modem-on-hold information. That information is stored by the NAS until the end user opts to use modem-on-hold.

If the user decides to suspend surfing and take the call, the client modem requests the server modem to go on hold. The two modems then negotiate and determine the maximum time allowed before the server modem terminates the connection. The client modem flashes the line and connects the user to the voice call.

If the user exceeds the allotted modem-on-hold time set by the server, the NAS disconnects from the client modem and sends a disconnect reason type to the RADIUS server. Although V.92 technology allows a maximum on-hold time of 16 minutes, due to preset timeouts in higher protocol stacks, the client might not be able to take full advantage of the on-hold time without causing interruption of the data application. However, modem-on-hold allows enough time for the user to decide either to drop the data connection or communicate to the calling party about terminating the call. It also may include software to warn the user when the predetermined timeout approaches.

For users who use their primary telephone line for Internet access, modem-on-hold eliminates their risk of missing important phone calls while online. For some households, it saves the cost of buying a second phone line for Internet connections. The ability to seamlessly switch between voice and data services eliminates the time and cost of reconnecting, which also allows fuller line utilization.

V.44

V.44 may improve data compression up to 6:1 compared to the 4:1 maximum with the existing V.42 compression standard. Note that software modems will be able to take advantage of this, but most serial ports limit maximum transfer rate to 115.2 K. With a 48-K connection and 6:1 compression, a data rate of 288 Kbps could be achieved. (Data compression depends upon the nature of the data transfer.) Compressed data files such as .gif, .jpeg, and .zip will not experience additional compression or speed improvement.

Quick Connect

The quick connect feature of V.92 shortens the modem connection time up to 50 percent, where the connection is recognized by the modem. This reduction in modem start-up time is accomplished by storing the calling line parameters in the user's modem, which enables a faster handshake between the modem and the server. On these recognized connections, V.92 may shorten the connection time from the typical 25–30 seconds to about 15 seconds.

Initial implementations have improved connect times by more than 10 percent, and future modem implementations should produce further reductions. With V.90, modems assume that each call is made on a different line to a different destination. The following sequence takes place:

1. The client modem calls the server modem.

2. The two modems perform a "handshake." A handshake is a swapping of information between the two devices, whereby they can agree to communicate at the same rate of speed and use the same alphabet, compression, and so on. As a handshake is conducted between two humans when they introduce themselves, the modem emulates this process.

3. The link layer connection, including error control and data compression, is established. Remember the data link layer in the OSI model describes that error detection and correction is performed.

4. PPP negotiation and authentication take place. Point-to-point protocol (PPP) is a protocol for passing packet data across a circuit switched connection.

With V.92, the client modem learns and remembers the line characteristics of the previous call. During call setup, the client modem probes the line to compare its characteristics with those stored in memory. If there is a match, the handshake starts at the previously negotiated rate and bypasses the full training probe. If it does not recognize the line characteristics, a normal V.90 (slower speed) handshake begins.

Pulse Coded Modulation (PCM) Upstream

PCM upstream increases the upstream data rate from the current V.34 speed (33.6 Kbps) to as high as 48 Kbps. PCM upstream redesigns the upstream modulation process to minimize signal loss during the analog-to-digital conversion. Higher upstream data rate is accomplished by manipulating the client modem settings so that the analog signal it transmits can be reconstructed to a more precise digital signal on the central office PCM Codec. A filter is inserted into the client analog modem transmitter. The server modem determines the channel characteristics and designs coefficients for the client filter to use so that line impairments are mitigated. Said another way, there can be only one digital-to-analog conversion in the circuit to achieve rates higher than 33.6 Kbps. Increasing upstream rate decreases the downstream rate to a maximum 48 Kbps. By increasing the upstream bandwidth, PCM upstream introduces more symmetry to the dial-up connection. This improves the quality of applications that require symmetric data flow, such as Voice over IP calls and multiplayer online gaming. For users who pay local or long-distance toll charges, faster upload speeds up their session, which saves them money.

The most obvious benefit to PCM upstream is faster uploading of files, including ftp uploads or e-mails with large image file attachments. As an example, digital camera users who frequently upload photos for printing or sharing with family and friends can accomplish this task much quicker.

Putting the Pieces Together

Looking at all the pieces discussed in this chapter, we started with a seven step sequence to get the data communication to work. They were as follows:

1. Deal with the medium—in Fig. 9.3 early in the chapter was an RJ-11 jack on the internal modem card. So to deal with the medium, we use the standard two-wire connector and plug that into the wall as seen in Fig. 9.11. We will plug the connector into the wall outlet and into the laptop or desktop modem port. Note that only two wires are needed, one for transmit, the other for receive. This plug and jack combination acts as the interface to the telephone network at layer 1 of the OSI model.

2. Use communicating devices that will present the proper signal to the line (the communicating device is called the DCE). This is the modem which was also represented in Fig. 9.3. Alternately, we may not have an internal modem built into our desktop or laptop device, so we need to add something. A PCI card inside a desktop PC works fine, whereas a PCMCIA card can be used for the laptop device. In Fig. 9.12 is all older V.34 modem that works at 33.6 Kbps for a laptop. Plugging this modem into the laptop when needed gives you a connection capability.

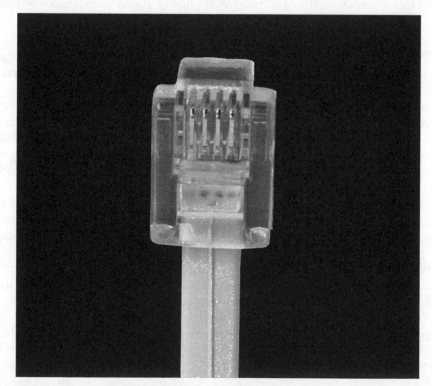

Figure 9.11   The two-wire connection is all we need to plug into the telephone line.

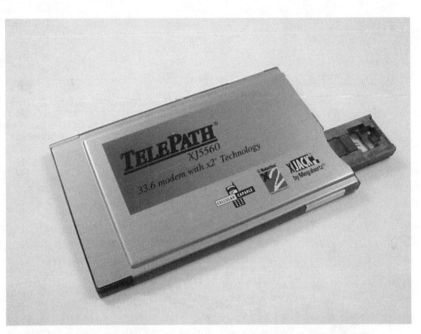

Figure 9.12 A modem used for a laptop. This one is an older version, but still works.

The RJ-11 is located at the right end of this card, which protrudes outside the laptop and the RJ-11 plug is then inserted to provide the connection.

3. Add a device called the data terminal equipment (DTE)—the DTE in this case is the laptop or the desktop PC.

Set up or abide by accepted rules (protocols)—the dial up communications protocols will use the protocols as agreed upon by the two parties.

In Fig. 9.13 we start a session in Windows by clicking on the "start", then "control panel" and "phone and modem options." This brings up the modems screen shown in Fig. 9.14. Finally we selected modems properties and using the drop down menu, we can select the speed at which we want to communicate as shown in Fig. 9.15. In this case we set it at 115 Kbps (note 115 Kbps will be 28.8 at 4:1 compression yielding an effective 115 Kbps rate).

Next we select the "start", "control panel" and "network connections" tabs in windows. We now select "create a new connection at the top left-hand side of this screen as shown in Fig. 9.16. This brings up a new connection wizard as shown in Fig. 9.17. Click "next."

Select the connect to the Internet radial button, seen in Fig. 9.18 and click "next" then select "set my connection manually" as seen in Fig. 9.19. Click "next."

Now select "connect using a dial-up modem," seen in Fig. 9.20. Click "next.

The next screen asks you to type in the ISP name. I am using QWEST, see Fig. 9.21. Click "next." You will now be presented a screen that asks for the phone number as seen in Fig. 9.22. Type in your ISP's phone number and click "next."

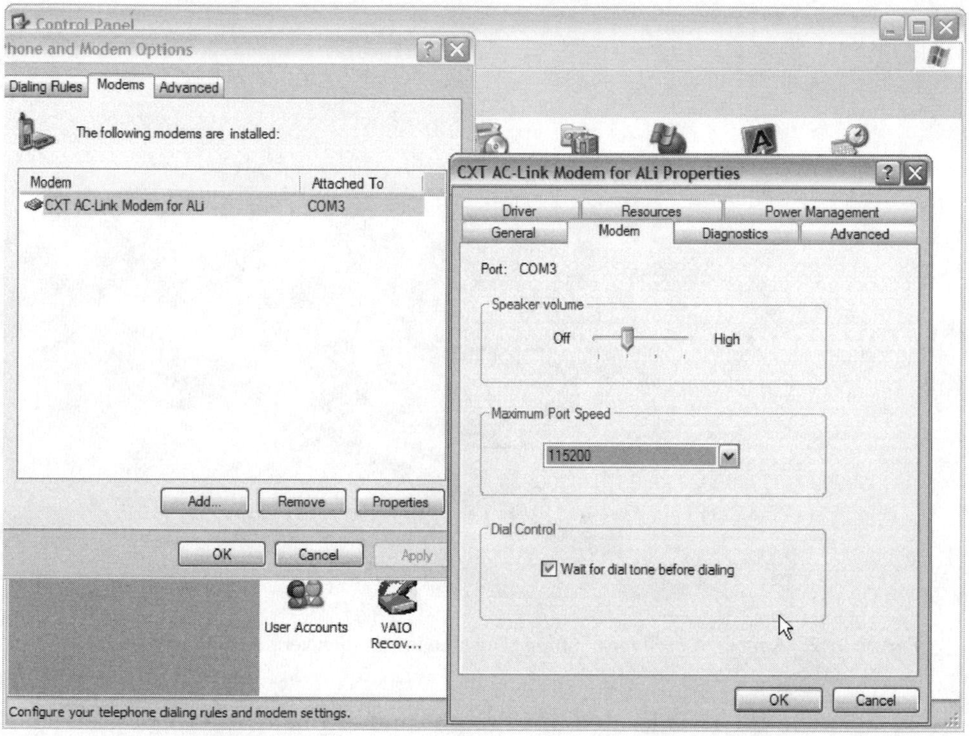

Figure 9.13 Opening the control panel.

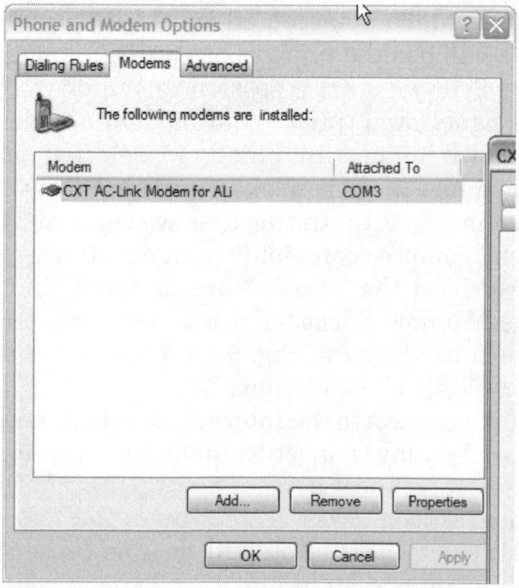

Figure 9.14 The modem options.

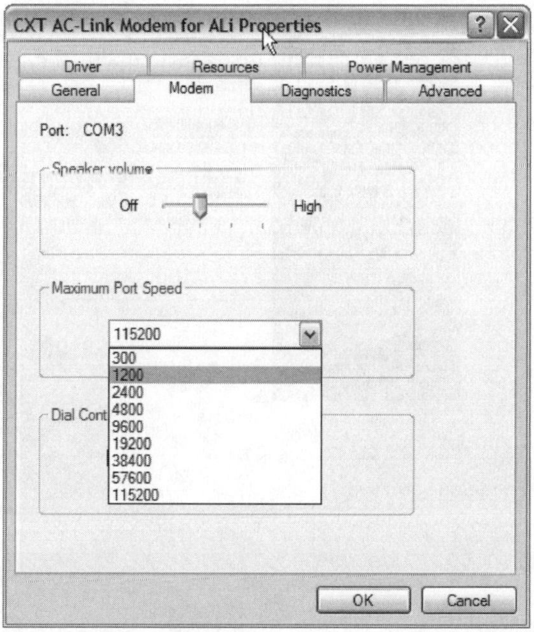

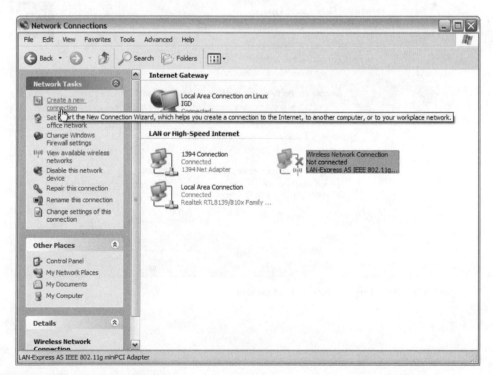

Figure 9.15   Setting the speed from the pull down menu.

Figure 9.16   Creating a new connection.

Figure 9.17   The connection wizard.

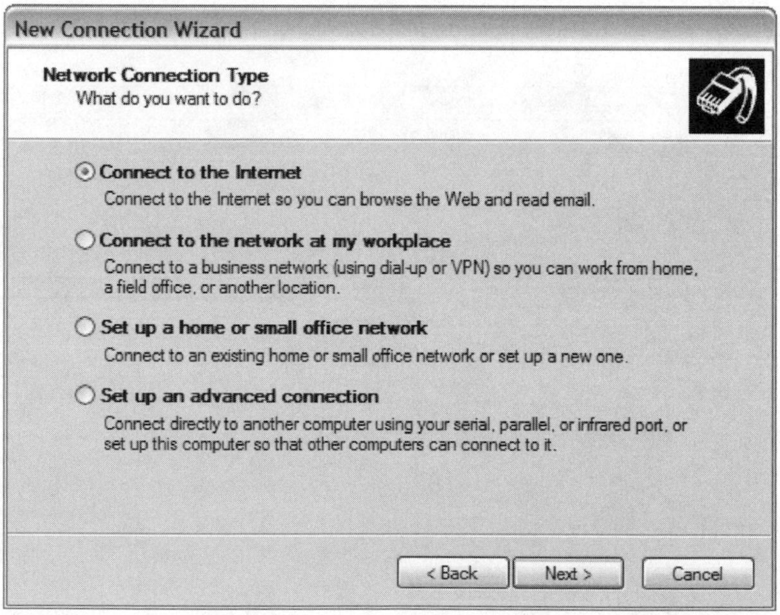

Figure 9.18   Selecting the Internet connection.

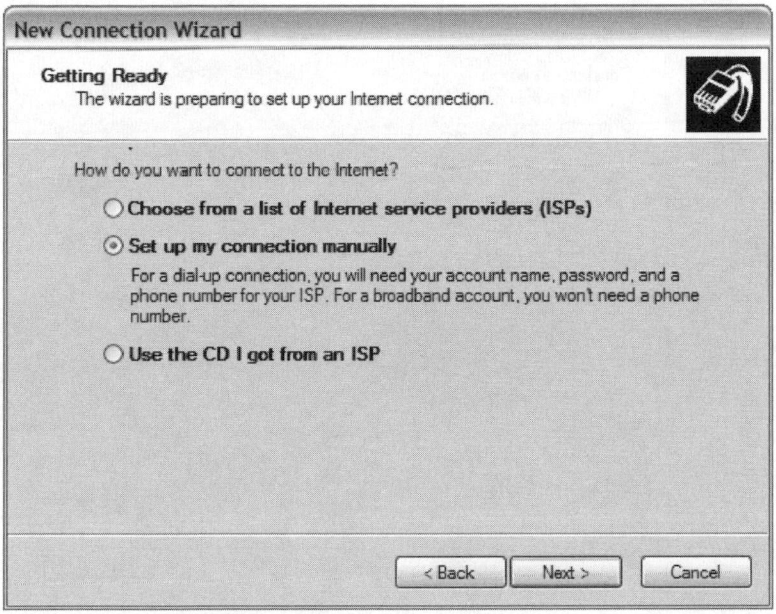

Figure 9.19   Choose to set the connection manually.

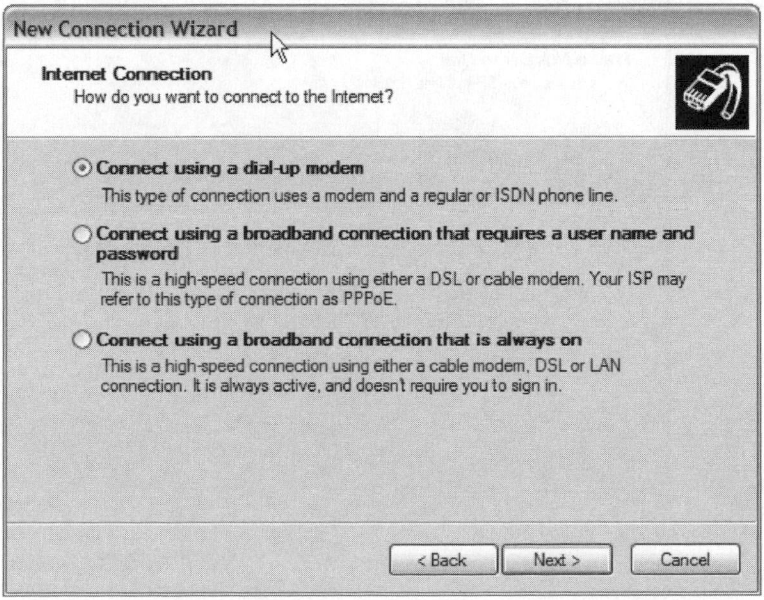

Figure 9.20   Select the dial-up modem choice.

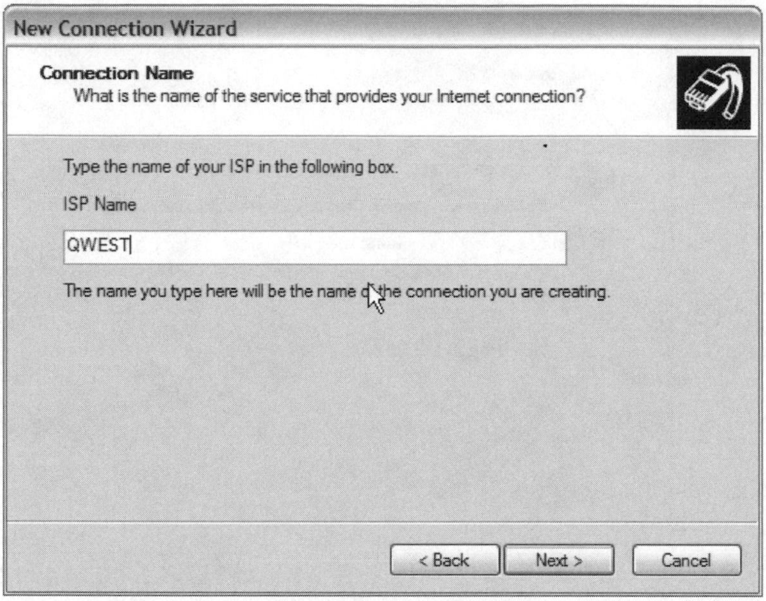

Figure 9.21 Adding the ISP name.

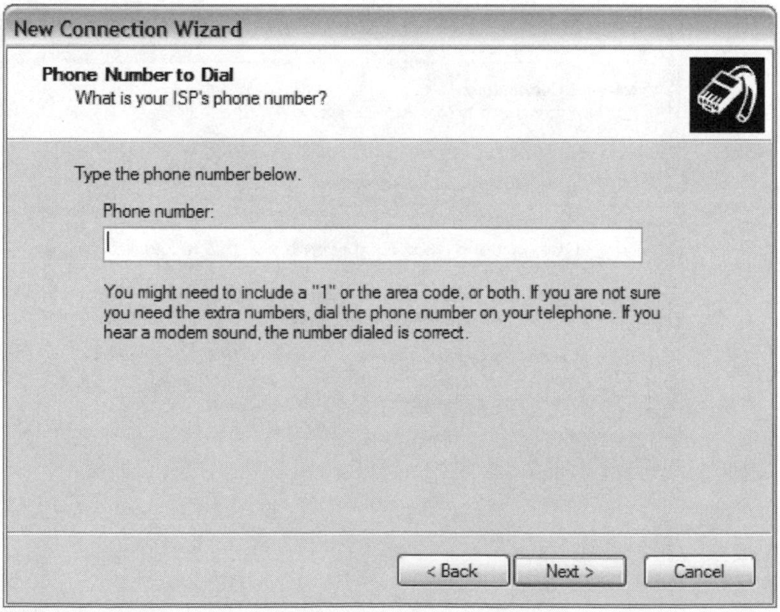

Figure 9.22 Add the ISP telephone number.

The next screen asks you to type in your user name and password. Note that in Fig. 9.23 the password is asked for twice, a confirmation that you typed it in correctly. You can also select or clear the two radial buttons below the password entry as you choose. Click "next."

The final screen asks that you confirm all the information as shown in the middle of the screen, shown in Fig. 9.24; and if satisfied, click "finish".

Now you get the connection screen, shown in Fig. 9.25. Your connection is now ready to go. Click on the connection shown in network connections (QWEST) and the system will dial out to the ISP.

5. Use a preestablished alphabet that the devices understand—the Windows standard for most services today based on the MS Office products, and so on, uses extended ASCII code set.

6. Ensure the integrity of information before, during, and after transmission— done by the protocols and checks errors using a CRC.

7. Deliver the information to the receiving device—display the data in the application you are using.

You are now communicating via a dial-up modem and using a telephone line to do so. Congratulations.

Figure 9.23   Enter user name and password.

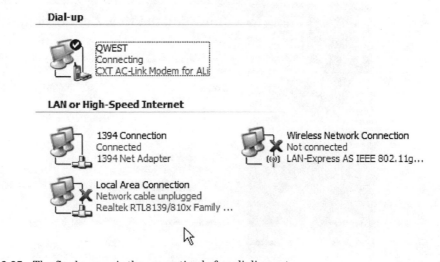

Figure 9.24   Confirm everything and choose finish.

Figure 9.25   The final screen is the connection before dialing out.

Questions

1. The use of data communications is growing at 3–4 percent per year.   T/F
2. The voice networks are actually paying the fare for the data networks.   T/F
3. When we transmit we can send the data either in time or out of time, this is called:
   a. Transmit and receive
   b. Synchronous and asynchronous
   c. STDM
   d. Timing the data sequence
4. The main reason we check the data for errors is because we want to get $1000000.   T/F
5. Data transmission can be classified as either _____ or lossless.
6. The two most common alphabets we use today are _____ and _____.
7. Using the ASCII code set we can get 256 combinations of 1s and 0s.   T/F
8. How many combinations will we get with the IBM code set? _____
9. The modem is called the DTE.   T/F
10. How many bits does it take to create a byte?
    a. 7
    b. 8
    c. 5
    d. Alphabet (code set) dependent
11. What is the baud rate of a 33,600 bps modem?
    a. 33,600
    b. 56,000
    c. 24,000
    d. 2,400
12. When we use a FM modem we typically transmit data at _____ bps.
13. The two ways to get more data on the circuit is to use:
    a. Compression and code sets
    b. Multiplexing and demultiplexing
    c. Compression and rarefaction
    d. Compression and multiplexing

14. Two different forms of standards are used today, they are:

    a. IBM and DEC

    b. De jure and de facto

    c. Telephone company and computer manufacturers

    d. National and international

15. When transmitting at greater than 2400 bps all data transmissions are sent asynchronously.   T/F

16. The standard typewriter keyboard is called _____ because of the position of the keys on the keyboard.

17. Computers, printers, or cash registers are examples of types of:

    a. DCE

    b. Mux

    c. DTE

    d. Code sets

10

TCP/IP

After reading this chapter and completing the questions, you will be able to:

- Describe the importance of using TCP/IP in everyday networks
- Evaluate the various protocols in the TCP/IP suite
- Discuss how IP came about
- Describe what a DHCP and DNS server is
- Explain the process of using IP addresses and subnetworking

Architecture, History, Standards, and Trends

Today, the Internet and World Wide Web (WWW) are familiar terms to just about everyone around the world. It is amazing how many people depend on applications enabled by the Internet, such as electronic mail and Web access. The transmission control protocol/Internet protocol (TCP/IP) suite is the middleware that drives the Internet and networks worldwide. Its simplicity and power has led to its becoming the single network protocol of choice in the world today.

TCP/IP Architectural Model

The TCP/IP suite is so named for two of its most important protocols: transmission control protocol (TCP) and Internet protocol (IP). A less used name for it is the Internet protocol suite, which is the phrase used in official Internet standards documents. Regardless of the names used to define it, TCP/IP is what makes the Internet and most local area networks (LANs) work today.

Internetworking

The primary purpose of TCP/IP was to create a network of networks, or Internet, that provides ubiquitous communication services over heterogeneous physical networks. The obvious benefit of such an interconnected network is the ability to enable communication between myriad hosts on different networks, whether local or spread across the country.

Another point surrounding the use of TCP/IP internetworking is the standard mechanism that facilitates communication between and among various differing networks. Each physical network has its own services provided by a network interface card (NIC), a programming interface that provides basic communication functions and varied application program interfaces (APIs). TCP/IP provides communication services that run between the programming interface of a physical network and user applications. It is the common interface for these applications, regardless of the selection of a physical network. The architecture of the physical network is transparent to the user.

As shown in Fig. 10.1, to be able to interconnect two networks, we need a computer that is attached to both networks and can forward data packets from one network to the other; such a machine is called a router. The term IP router is also used because the routing function is part of the Internet protocol portion of the TCP/IP protocol suite. A router can be a computer with two NIC cards installed in it, or it can be a very specific vendor device that forwards the packets from one side of the network to the other.

An IP network has two very important resources, its IP addresses and the corresponding naming structure within the network. To provide effective communication between hosts or stations in a network, each station must maintain a unique identity. In an IP network this is achieved by the IP address. To identify a host on the network, each computer is assigned a unique address, called the IP address that operates at the equivalent of layer 3 on the OSI model. When a computer has multiple network interface cards, such as with a router, each interface has a unique IP address.

The TCP/IP Protocol Layers

Like most networking software, TCP/IP is built in layers. This layered approach, or protocol stack, refers to the stack of layers in the protocol suite. It can be used for positioning (but not for functionally comparing) the TCP/IP protocol suite against others, such as systems network architecture (SNA) and the open system interconnection model (OSI). Functional comparisons cannot easily be extracted from this, as there are basic differences in the layered models used by the different protocol suites.

Layers communicate with those above and below via concise interfaces. A layer provides a service for the layer directly above it $(N + 1)$ and makes use of services provided by the layer directly below it $(N - 1)$. For example, IP provides the transfer of data from one host to another without any guarantee to reliable delivery or sequencing. Transport protocols such as TCP make use of this service to provide applications with highly reliable, sequenced data stream delivery.

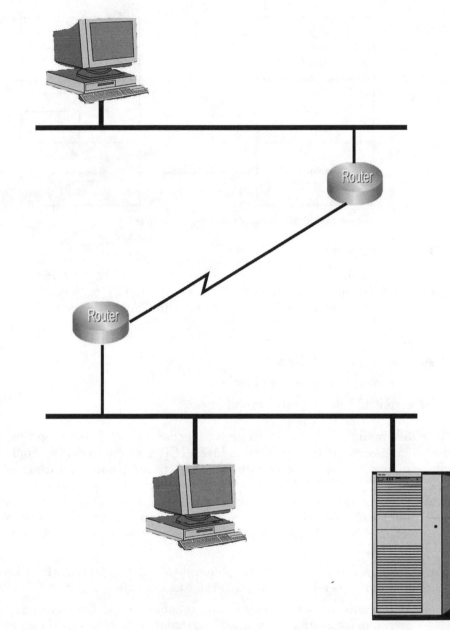

Figure 10.1   Two networks can be interconnected.

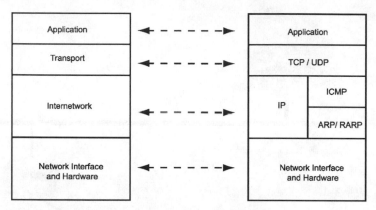

Figure 10.2 Shows how the TCP/IP protocols are modeled in four layers.

Using the four layers of the protocol suite, shown in Fig. 10.2, the TCP layer is responsible for the end-to-end reliable data transport. TCP only exists in the end user equipment, not on the network. TCP is responsible for the following:

- Sequencing of the segments
- Acknowledgment of the data
- Retransmission requests and responses
- Flow control between the two end devices

TCP also maintains the connection (connection-oriented) between the two applications at both ends. At the application layer, TCP uses either native application interfaces or an application program interface (API) to service the end-user needs.

Application layer: It is provided by the program that uses TCP/IP for communication. Examples of applications include Telnet and the file transfer protocol (FTP). The interface between the application and transport layers is defined by port numbers and sockets.

Transport layer: It provides the reliable end-to-end data transfer from an application to its remote peer. Multiple applications can be multiplexed at this layer.

- TCP provides connection-oriented reliable data delivery, duplicate data suppression, congestion control, and flow control.
- User datagram protocol (UDP) is a peer to TCP offering connectionless, unreliable, best-effort service. Applications running on UDP must provide their own end-to-end integrity, flow control, and congestion control. Usually, UDP is used by applications that need a fast transport mechanism and can tolerate the loss of some data such as VoIP and streaming media.

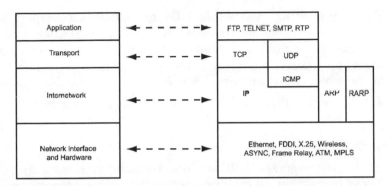

Figure 10.3   The TCP/IP model expanded to support any subnet.

Internetwork layer: IP is the most important protocol in this layer. It is a connection-less protocol that doesn't provide reliability, flow control, or error recovery. These functions are provided by a higher level protocol.

Other internetwork layer protocols are ICMP, IGMP, ARP, and RARP.

Network interface layer: The link layer, or the data-link layer, is the interface to the actual network hardware. A more detailed layering model is included in Fig. 10.3. This interface may or may not provide reliable delivery, and may be packet or stream oriented. TCP/IP does not specify any subnet protocol. Examples of subnets include IEEE 802.2, X.25, ATM, FDDI, frame relay, and MPLS.

TCP/IP Applications

The highest-level protocols within the TCP/IP protocol stack are application protocols. They communicate with applications on other Internet hosts and are the user-visible interface to the TCP/IP protocol suite. All application protocols have some characteristics in common:

- They can be user-written applications or applications standardized and shipped with the TCP/IP product. Indeed, the TCP/IP protocol suite includes application protocols such as:

  - Telnet for interactive terminal access to remote Internet hosts

  - FTP for high-speed file transfers

  - Simple mail transfer protocol (SMTP) e-mail program

  - Real time protocol (RTP) to carry VoIP

  - Simple network management protocol (SNMP) a network management tool

  These are some of the most widely implemented application protocols, but many others exist. Each particular TCP/IP implementation will include a lesser or greater set of application protocols.

- These applications use either UDP or TCP as a transport mechanism. It is often easier to build applications on top of TCP because it is a reliable stream, connection-oriented, congestion-friendly, flow control enabled protocol. As a result, most application protocols will use TCP, but there are applications built on UDP to achieve better performance through reduced protocol overhead.

- TCP/IP is based on the client/server model of interaction.

Multimedia Applications

Bandwidth requirements will continue to increase at massive rates; not only is the number of users growing rapidly; but the applications being used are becoming more advanced and therefore consume more bandwidth such as video, IPTV, and multimedia experience. Technologies such as dense wave-division multiplexing (DWDM) are used to meet these high bandwidth demands being placed on the Internet.

Much of this increasing demand is attributable to the increased use of multimedia applications. An example is VoIP technology. As this technology continues to grow and mature, we are sharing bandwidth between voice and data across the Internet. My old saying that "voice will become data and data will be data" finally rings true.

This raises some interesting opportunities for phone companies. As the VoIP industry continues to erode the minutes away from the voice network, how will the Bell Telephone Companies compete? By 2005 almost 10 percent of the telephone companies' minutes have eroded to VoIP and CATV suppliers. Unless the telephone companies develop a quick plan, they will be sitting on the sidelines watching the industry go by. Inevitably, voice conversations will become video conversations as phone calls become video conferences.

Today, it is possible to hear radio stations from almost any part of the globe via the Internet with FM quality. We can watch television channels from all around the world leading to the clear potential of using the Internet as the vehicle for delivering movies and all sorts of video signals to consumers everywhere. It all comes at a price; however, as the infrastructure of the Internet must adapt to such high bandwidth demands. Thus the telephone companies as an industry might play catch-up and become a part of this market.

Internetworking Protocols

It is appropriate to provide an overview of the most important and common protocols associated with the TCP/IP internetwork layer. These include:

- Internet protocol (IP)
- Internet control message protocol (ICMP)
- Address resolution protocol (ARP)
- Reverse address resolution protocol (RARP)

- Bootstrap protocol (BOOTP)
- Dynamic host configuration protocol (DHCP)
- Domain name service (DNS)

These protocols perform datagram addressing, routing and delivery, dynamic address configuration, and resolve between the internetwork layer addresses and the network interface layer addresses.

Internet Protocol

IP is an Internet Engineering Task Force (IETF) standard protocol. The standard also includes ICMP and IGMP. The current IP specification can be found in Request for Comments (RFC) 791, 950, 919, and 922, with updates in RFC 2474.

IP transparently runs on the underlying physical network. This includes the physical and the data link layers of the OSI model. IP is responsible only for the routing of the datagrams or packets from end to end. IP works with some specifics in handling the transmission of the datagrams across the Internet. IP for example does the following:

- Makes its best attempt to deliver the data
- Guarantees nothing, does not guarantee delivery
- Only determines the route to take with the data
- Ignores the integrity of the data, performs no checks on the data

IP is connectionless, so it doesn't maintain or establish the connection between the two end devices. It doesn't even know whether the device on the other end receives the data. The primary reason for using a connectionless network protocol was to minimize the dependency on specific computing centers that used hierarchical connection-oriented networks.

This was the legacy systems design back then, and the U.S. Department of Defense wanted a network that would still be operational if parts of the country were destroyed after a nuclear holocaust. In the event portions of the network were destroyed, the packets may be sent along a different path. So, conceptually, all IP packets could take a different route to the destination. Realistically today, that rarely happens because the networks are now created in robust fiber rings and are self-healing. The likelihood is that all packets follow pretty much the same route today.

IP Addressing

IP addresses are represented by a 32-bit unsigned binary value. It is usually expressed in a dotted decimal format. For example, 63.1.7.9 is a valid IP address. The numeric form is used by IP software. The mapping between the IP address and an easier-to-read symbolic name, for example mywebsite.com, is done by the DNS discussed later.

The IP Address

IP addressing standards are described in RFC 1166—Internet Numbers. To identify a host on the Internet, each host is assigned an address, the IP address, or in some cases, the Internet address. When the host is attached to more than one network, it is called multi-homed and has one IP address for each network interface. The IP address consists of a pair of numbers:

$$IP\ address = network\ number + host\ number$$

IP addresses are inherently not easy to remember. People find it much easier to remember names and have these names related to individual machines connected to a network. The network number part of the IP address identifies the network within the Internet and is assigned by a central authority and is unique throughout the Internet. The assigning authority is IANA. Currently there are two types of IP addresses in active use: IP version 4 (IPv4) and IP version 6 (IPv6).

IPv4 was initially deployed on 1 January 1983 and is still the most commonly used version. IPv4 addresses are 32-bit numbers often expressed as four octets in "dotted decimal" notation (for example, 192.168.0.12), as shown in Fig. 10.4. Deployment of the IPv6 protocol began in 1999.

IPv6 addresses are 128-bit numbers and are conventionally expressed using hexadecimal strings (for example, 1080:0:0:0:8:800:200C:417A). Users are assigned IP addresses by Internet service providers (ISPs). ISPs obtain allocations of IP addresses from a variety of registries (local, national, and so forth).

The IANA's role is to allocate IP addresses from the pools of unallocated addresses to the registries according to their established needs. When a registry group requires more IP addresses for allocation or assignment within its region, the IANA makes an

Figure 10.4 The IP address is decimal dot delimited.

additional allocation to the appropriate agency. The network number portion of the IP address is administered by one of the three Regional Internet Registries (RIR):

- American Registry for Internet Numbers (ARIN)—is responsible for the administration and registration of IP numbers for North America, South America, the Caribbean, and sub-Saharan Africa.

- Reseaux IP Europeens (RIPE)—is responsible for the administration and registration of IP numbers for Europe, Middle East, and parts of Africa.

- Asia Pacific Network Information Centre (APNIC)—is responsible for the administration and registration of IP numbers within the Asia Pacific region.

Assigning the host number part of the IP address is done within the organization that controls the network identified by the network number. In other words, the individual IS or IT person in an organization is responsible for assigning the host numbers for each of the computing devices in the organization.

IP addresses are 32-bit numbers represented in a dotted decimal form (as the decimal representation of four 8-bit values concatenated with dots). As shown in Fig. 10.5, the IP address is viewed by typing the "cmd" prompt in Windows and then typing "ipconfig /all." Strictly speaking, an IP address identifies an interface that is capable of sending and receiving IP datagrams.

One system can have multiple such interfaces. However, both hosts and routers must have at least one IP address, so this simplified definition is acceptable. IP datagrams (the basic data packets exchanged between hosts) are transmitted by a physical network attached to the host. Each IP datagram contains a source IP address and a destination IP address. To send a datagram to a certain IP destination, the target IP address

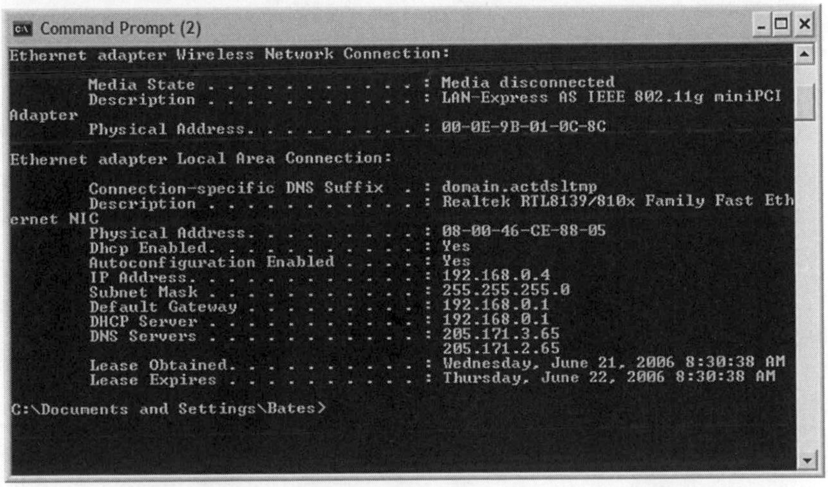

Figure 10.5 The IP address shown on an interface.

must be translated or mapped to a physical address. This may require transmissions on the network to find out the destination's physical network address.

Class-Based IP Addresses

The first bits of the IP address specify how the rest of the address should be separated into its network and host part. The term network address is sometimes used instead of network number, but the formal term, used in RFC 1166, is network number. Similarly, the term host address is sometimes used instead of host number.

There are five classes of IP addresses. They are shown in Fig. 10.6 as the five classes labeled A through E.

IP Subnets

Because of the explosive growth of the Internet, the idea of assigned IP addresses in a class (A through E) became much too inflexible to allow easy changes to local network configurations. Changes typically occur when:

- A new type of physical network is installed at a location, i.e., from an SNA to an Ethernet.

- The cumulative number of hosts requires splitting the LAN into two or more smaller networks.

- Distance expanses require splitting a network into smaller networks, with gateways or routers between them.

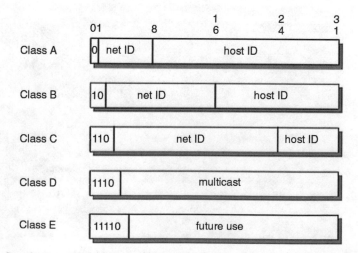

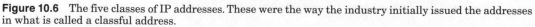

Figure 10.6 The five classes of IP addresses. These were the way the industry initially issued the addresses in what is called a classful address.

To avoid having to request additional IP network addresses, the concept of IP sub-netting was introduced. The assignment of subnets is done locally. The entire network still appears as one IP network to the outside world. The host number part of the IP address is subdivided into a second network number and a host number. This second network is termed a subnetwork or subnet. The main network now consists of a number of subnets. The IP address is interpreted as:

IP address = network number + subnet number + host number

Subnetting is designed to be transparent to remote networks. A host within a network is subnet aware. Yet, a host on a different network is not. The local administrator decides on the ways to subnet and how to deliver appropriate address numbers within the organization. Any bits in the local portion can be used to form the subnet. The division is done using a 32-bit subnet mask. A subnet with a class B network is shown in Fig. 10.7. The 16-bit host field is now divided into 8 bits for the subnet address and 8 bits for the host field.

Bits with a value of 0 in the subnet mask indicate positions allotted to the host number. Bits with a value of 1 indicate positions allotted to the subnet number. Like IP addresses, subnet masks are usually written in dotted decimal form, as shown in Fig. 10.8.

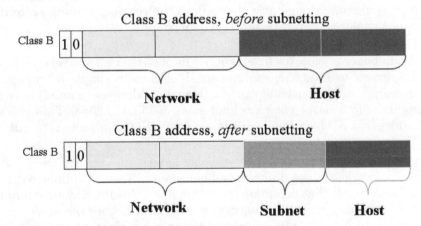

Figure 10.7 A class B address before and after subnetting.

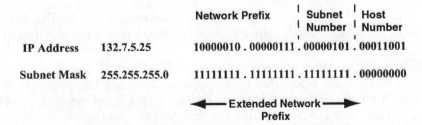

Figure 10.8 The subnet and mask shown in binary and dotted decimal notation.

To create subnets on a class B network, we could use one of the following schemes:

- The first octet is the subnet number; the second octet is the host number. This gives $2^8 - 2$ (254) possible subnets, each having up to $2^8 - 2$ (254) hosts. The subnet mask is 255.255.255.0.

- The first 12 bits are used for the subnet number and the last four for the host number. This gives $2^{12} - 2$ (4094) possible subnets but only $2^4 - 2$ (14) hosts per subnet. The subnet mask is 255.255.255.240.

Before deciding on a subnet structure, the number of subnets and hosts and any future growth must be considered. In the example, the class B network has 16 bits to be divided between the subnet number and the host number fields. Either a larger number of subnets each with a small number of hosts, or a smaller number of subnets each with many hosts can be chosen. However, we never want to go back and renumber our networks if we can help it! So planning is important in this regard.

Types of Subnets

There are two choices of subnets: static and variable length. Variable length subnets are more flexible than static. Sometimes the routing protocols require only static, so this is a choice that may be protocol dependent.

Static Subnets   Static (or fixed) subnet implies that all subnets derived from the original network use the same subnet mask. Although simple to implement and easy to maintain, static subnetting can waste some addresses in small networks. Consider a network of four hosts using a subnet mask of 255.255.255.0. This allocation wastes 250 IP addresses. All hosts and routers are required to support static subnetting.

Variable Length Subnets   When variable length subnets are used, subnets within the same network can use different subnet masks. A small subnet with only a few hosts can use a mask that accommodates this need. A subnet with many hosts requires a different subnet mask. The ability to assign subnet masks according to the needs of the individual subnets helps conserve network addresses. Variable length subnetting divides the network so that each subnet contains sufficient addresses to support the required number of hosts.

An existing subnet can be split into two parts by adding another bit to the subnet portion of the subnet mask. Other subnets in the network are unaffected by the change.

Mixing Static and Variable Length Subnets   Not every IP device supports variable length subnets. Initially, a host that only supports static subnets prevents the use of variable length subnets, or so it would seem. However, this is not the case. Routers interconnecting the subnets are used to hide the different masks from hosts. Hosts continue to use basic IP routing. This offloads subnet complexities to dedicated routers.

Determining the Subnet Mask   Usually, hosts will store the subnet mask in a configuration file. However, sometimes this cannot be done, for example, as in the case of a diskless workstation. The ICMP protocol includes two messages: address mask request and address mask reply. These allow hosts to obtain the correct subnet mask from a server.

Addressing Routers and Multi-Homed Hosts   Whenever a host has a physical connection to multiple networks or subnets, it is described as being multi-homed. By default, all routers are multi-homed since their purpose is to join networks or subnets. A multi-homed host has different IP addresses associated with each network adapter. Each adapter connects to a different subnet or network.

IP Routing

An important function of the IP layer is IP *routing*. This provides the basic mechanism for routers to interconnect different physical networks. A device can simultaneously function as both a normal host and a router.

After IP datagrams are produced and passed to the router for transmission across the link, a sequence of steps is taken to determine where and how to send the datagram. Assume a datagram is produced and delivered to IP for addressing and routing across the Internet. The datagram is being sent to bud@tcic.com

1. The first step for the near-end router to launch the datagram across the network is to determine the destination network. This is from the address (destination addresses are contained in the IP header).

2. The router looks up a table to determine what the next hop IP address is.

3. Determining the outgoing interface from the router to the Internet (the output port and the physical interface).

4. The router determines what encapsulation and header requirements are used for the particular network service being activated (e.g., frame relay).

5. The router appends the frame relay service overhead and addressing information like the data link connection identifier (DLCI).

6. The router stores the destination address and header information in cache.

Additional protocols are needed to implement a full-function router. These types of routers are essential in most networks, because they can exchange information with other routers in the environment. There are two types of IP routing: direct and indirect.

Direct Routing

If the destination host is attached to the same physical network as the source host, IP datagrams can be directly exchanged. This is done by encapsulating the IP datagram in the physical network frame.

Indirect Routing

Indirect routing occurs when the destination host is not connected to the same network as the source host. The only way to reach the destination is through one or more IP routers. The first hop is called an indirect route in the IP routing algorithm. The address of the first router is the only information needed by the source host to send a packet to the destination host. A router is also needed to forward traffic between subnets. Figure 10.9 shows an example of direct and indirect routes.

IP Routing Table

The determination of direct routes is derived from the list of local interfaces. It is automatically composed by the IP routing process at initialization. In addition, a list of networks

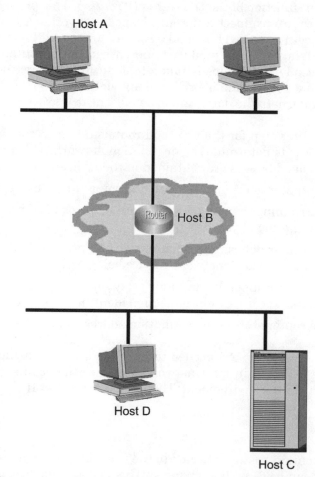

Figure 10.9   C has direct routes to B and D, however, must route through host B to get to A.

and associated gateways (indirect routes) may be configured. This information is stored in a table called the IP routing table. This list is used to facilitate IP routing. Each host keeps the set of mappings between the following:

- Destination IP network addresses
- Routes to next gateway

Methods of Delivery

Four different methods are available for the delivery of a message in an IP world. These include unicast, broadcast, multicast, and anycast.

Unicast

The majority of IP addresses refer to a single recipient; this is called a unicast address. Unicast connections specify a one-to-one relationship between a single source and a single destination. This is shown in Fig. 10.10 with a single host communicating with another host.

Broadcast

Broadcast addresses are never valid as a source address. They must specify the destination address. The different types of broadcast addresses include:

- *Limited broadcast address*: This uses the address 255.255.255.255. It refers to all hosts on the local subnet. Routers do not forward this packet.
- *Network-directed broadcast address*: This is used in a non-subnet environment. Routers will normally forward these broadcast messages.
- *Subnet-directed broadcast address*: If the network number is a valid network number, the subnet number is a valid subnet number and the host number is all 1s, then the address refers to all hosts on the specified subnet. This is shown in Fig. 10.11.

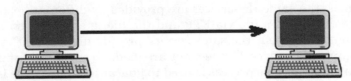

Figure 10.10 A unicast message is between two devices.

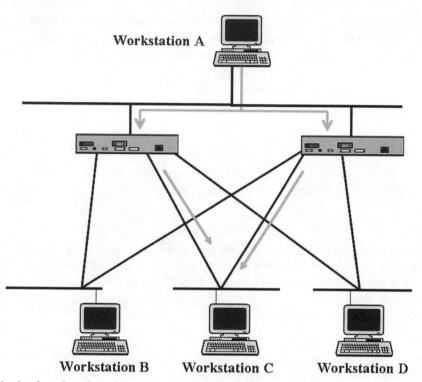

Figure 10.11   A subnet broadcast forwards all packets to all devices on the subnets.

Multicasting

If an IP datagram is broadcast to a subnet, it is received by every host on the subnet. Each host processes the packet to determine if the target protocol is active. If it is not active, the IP datagram is discarded. Multicasting avoids this overhead by selecting destination groups. Each group is represented by a class D IP address. In order to receive a multicast, the device will normally subscribe to the multicast (i.e., a video broadcast, and so forth) The multicast is shown in Fig. 10.12.

Anycast

Sometimes, the same IP services are provided by different hosts. For example, a user wants to download a file via FTP and the file is available on multiple FTP servers. Hosts that implement the same service provide an "anycast" address to other hosts that require the service. Connections are made to the first host in the anycast address group to respond. This process is used to guarantee the service is provided by the host with the best connection to the receiver. The anycast service is included in IPv6 and shown in Fig. 10.13.

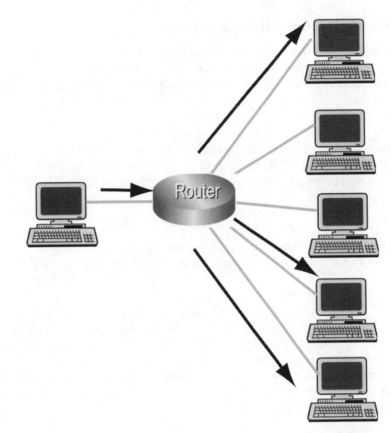

Figure 10.12 Multicast is to those devices that are subscribed to receive the packets.

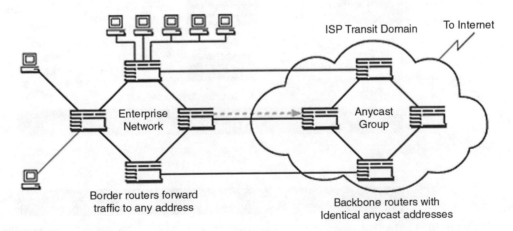

Figure 10.13 Anycast in action.

Classless Inter-Domain Routing (CIDR)

Standard IP routing understands only class A, B, and C network addresses.

Within each of these classful networks, subnets can be used to provide more granularities, however there is no way to specify that multiple class C networks are related. The result of this is the exponential number of entries that are in a routing table. The solution to this problem is called *classless inter-domain routing* (CIDR). CIDR is described in RFCs 1518–1520. CIDR does not route according to the class of the network number. It is based solely on the high order bits of the IP address. These bits are termed the IP prefix. Each CIDR routing table entry contains a 32-bit IP address and a 32-bit network mask, which together give the length and value of the IP prefix.

IP datagram

The unit in an IP network is called a datagram. It consists of an IP header and data relevant to higher level protocols, such as TCP or UDP. IP can provide fragmentation and reassembly of datagrams. The maximum length of an IP datagram is 65,535 octets, this is the same maximum limit of a TCP segment.

All IP hosts must support 576 octet datagrams without fragmentation. Fragments of a datagram each have a header. The header is copied from the original datagram. A fragment is treated as a normal IP datagram while being transported to their destination. However, if one of the fragments gets lost, the complete datagram is considered lost. Because IP does not provide any acknowledgment mechanism, the remaining fragments are discarded by the destination host. The IP datagram header has a minimum length of 20 octets, as seen in Fig. 10.14.

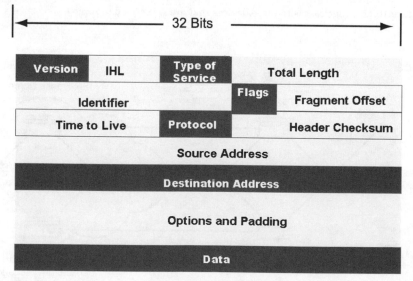

Figure 10.14   The IP datagram has a minimum of 20 octets. The graphic is 4 bytes across and minimum of 5 rows.

Fragmentation

When an IP datagram travels from one host to another, it may pass through different physical networks. Each physical network has a maximum frame size. This is called the maximum transmission unit (MTU). It limits the length of a datagram that can be placed in one physical frame.

IP implements a process to fragment datagrams exceeding the MTU. The process creates a set of datagrams within the maximum size. The receiving host reassembles the original datagram.

IP requires that each link support a minimum MTU of 68 octets. This is the sum of the maximum IP header length (60 octets) and the minimum possible length of data (8 octets). IP implementations are not required to handle unfragmented datagrams larger than 576 bytes. In practice, most implementations will accommodate larger values.

In order to reassemble the fragments, the receiving host allocates a storage buffer when the first fragment arrives. The host also starts a timer. When subsequent fragments of the datagram arrive, the data is copied into the buffer storage at the location indicated by the fragment offset field. When all fragments have arrived, the complete original unfragmented datagram is restored. Processing continues as for unfragmented datagrams.

Internet Control Message Protocol (ICMP)

ICMP is a standard protocol that also includes IP and IGMP. Its status is required. It is described in RFC 792 with updates in RFC 950. Path MTU Discovery is a draft standard protocol with a status of elective. It is described in RFC 1191. ICMP router discovery is a proposed standard protocol with a status of elective. It is described in RFC 1256.

When a router or a destination host must inform the source host about errors in datagram processing, it uses the ICMP. ICMP can be characterized as follows:

- ICMP acts as a higher level protocol. ICMP is an integral part of IP and must be implemented by every IP module.

- ICMP is used to report errors, not to make IP reliable. Datagrams may still be undelivered without any report on their loss.

- ICMP cannot be used to report errors within ICMP messages.

- For fragmented datagrams, ICMP messages are only sent about errors with the first fragment.

- ICMP messages are never sent in response to datagrams with a broadcast or a multicast destination address.

ICMP Messages

ICMP messages are described in RFC 792 and RFC 950, and are mandatory. ICMP messages are sent in IP datagrams. The IP header has a protocol number of 1 (ICMP) and a type of service of 0 (routine). The IP data field contains the ICMP message, shown in Fig. 10.15. The message contains the following components:

- *Type*: Specifies the type of the message:
  - 0: Echo reply
  - 3: Destination unreachable
  - 4: Source quench
  - 5: Redirect
  - 8: Echo
  - 9: Router advertisement
  - 10: Router solicitation
  - 11: Time exceeded
  - 12: Parameter problem
  - 13: Timestamp request
  - 14: Timestamp reply
  - 15: Information request (obsolete)
  - 16: Information reply (obsolete)
  - 17: Address mask request
  - 18: Address mask reply
  - 30: Traceroute
  - 31: Datagram conversion error
  - 32: Mobile host redirect
  - 33: IPv6 Where-Are-You
  - 34: IPv6 I-Am-Here
  - 35: Mobile registration request
  - 36: Mobile registration reply
  - 37: Domain name request
  - 38: Domain name reply
  - 39: SKIP
  - 40: Photuris
- *Code*: Contains the error code for the datagram reported by this ICMP message.
- *Checksum*: Contains the checksum for the ICMP message starting with the ICMP type field. If the checksum does not match the contents, the datagram is discarded.
- *Data*: Contains information for this ICMP message. Typically it will contain the portion of the original IP message for which this ICMP message was generated.

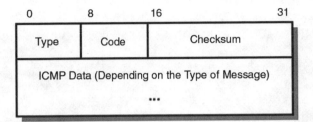

Figure 10.15   The ICMP message with its appropriate data delivers the error messages.

ICMP Applications

There are two simple and widely used applications based on ICMP: ping and traceroute. Ping uses the ICMP echo and echo reply messages to determine whether a host is reachable. Traceroute sends IP datagrams with low time to live (TTL)[1] values so that they expire en route to a destination. It uses the resulting ICMP time exceeded messages to determine where in the Internet the datagrams expired and pieces together a view of the route to a host. These applications are discussed in the following sections.

Ping   Ping is the simplest of all TCP/IP applications. It sends IP datagrams to a specified destination host and measures the round trip time to receive a response. The word *ping*, which is used as a noun and a verb, is taken from the sonar operation to locate an underwater object. It is also an abbreviation for Packet InterNet Groper. Traditionally, if you could successfully ping a host, other applications such as Telnet or FTP could reach that host. Nonetheless, the first test of reachability for a host is still to attempt to ping it. Most of us are familiar with the ping command. Type "Start" "Run" and "cmd" When the command prompt comes up, type the ping command. The results will be the echo response in time to reach the end node. See Fig. 10.16 for the screen capture of the ping. Ping is useful for verifying an IP installation. The syntax that is used in different implementations of ping varies from platform to platform.

ping [-switches] host [size [packets]]

Traceroute   The traceroute program is used to determine the route IP datagrams follow through the network. Traceroute is based upon ICMP and UDP. It sends an IP datagram with a TTL of 1 to the destination host. The first router decrements the TTL to 0, discards the datagram and returns an ICMP time exceeded message to the source. In this way, the first router in the path is identified. In Fig. 10.17 the first router is firewalled and therefore does not return a response. In the screenshot, the first hop is returned with an asterisk (*) as seen in the figure.

---

[1]Time to live is a hop count. As the IP datagram moves through the network, at each hop the counter is decremented. When the counter reaches zero, if the packet is not at the destination, it is discarded.

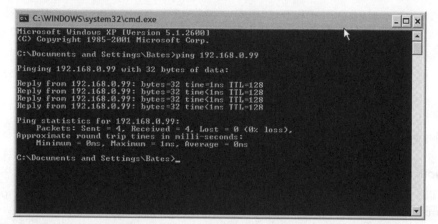

Figure 10.16 A screenshot of a ping.

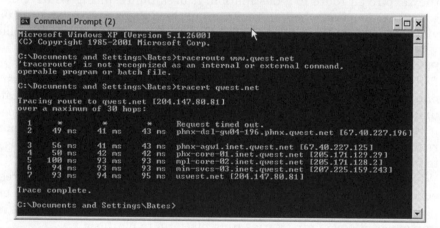

Figure 10.17 A screenshot of a traceroute. (Note the asterisks on line 1 of the screenshot, indicating a firewalled node.)

This process is repeated with successively larger TTL values to identify the exact series of routers in the path to the destination host. Traceroute sends UDP datagrams to the destination host. These datagrams reference a port number outside the standard range. When an ICMP port unreachable message is received, the source determines the destination host has been reached.

Internet Group Management Protocol (IGMP)

IGMP is a standard protocol with STD number 5. That standard also includes IP and ICMP. Its status is recommended. It is described in RFC 1112 with updates in RFC 2236. Similar to ICMP, IGMP is also an integral part of IP. It allows hosts to participate in IP multicasts. IGMP further provides routers with the capability to check if any hosts on a local subnet are interested in a particular multicast.

Address Resolution Protocol (ARP) Overview

On a single physical network, individual hosts are known on the network by their physical hardware address or what is called the MAC address. Higher level protocols address destination hosts in the form of a symbolic address (IP address in this case). When such a protocol wants to send a datagram to destination IP address a.b.c.d, the device driver does not understand this address. Therefore, a module (ARP) is provided that will translate the IP address to the physical address of the destination host. It uses a lookup table (sometimes referred to as the ARP cache) to perform this translation.

When the address is not found in the ARP cache, a broadcast is sent out on the network, with a special format called the ARP request. If one of the machines on the network recognizes its own IP address in the request, it will send an ARP reply back to the requesting host. The reply will contain the physical hardware address of the host. This address is stored in the ARP cache of the requesting host. All subsequent datagrams to this destination IP address can now be translated to a physical address, which is used by the device driver to send out the datagram on the network.

ARP Packet Generation

If an application wishes to send data to an IP destination address, the routing mechanism first determines the IP address of the next hop of the packet (it can be the destination host, or a router) and the hardware device on which to send it. If it is LAN (Ethernet or token ring network), the ARP module is consulted to map the <protocol type, target protocol address> to a physical address.

The ARP module tries to find the address in this ARP cache. If it finds the matching pair, it gives the corresponding 48-bit physical address back to the device driver, which then transmits the packet. If it doesn't find the pair in its table, it discards the packet and generates a network broadcast of an ARP request. The ARP process is shown in Fig. 10.18 and Fig. 10.19.

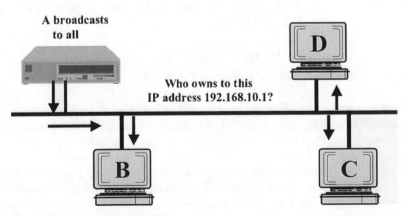

Figure 10.18   The ARP query sent on the LAN.

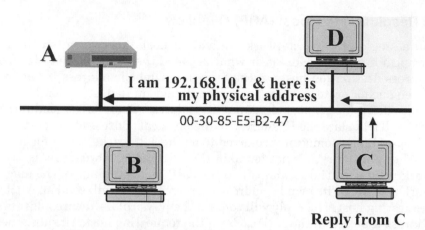

Figure 10.19   The ARP response on the LAN.

Reverse Address Resolution Protocol (RARP)

The RARP protocol is a network-specific standard protocol. It is described in RFC 903. Some network hosts, such as diskless workstations, do not know their own IP address when they are booted. To determine their own IP address, they use a mechanism similar to ARP, but now the hardware address of the host is the known parameter, and the IP address the queried parameter. It differs more fundamentally from ARP in the fact that a RARP server must exist on the network that maintains that a database of mappings from hardware address to protocol address must be pre-configured.

RARP Concept

The reverse address resolution is performed the same way as the ARP address resolution. The same packet format is used as for ARP. An exception is the operation code field that now takes the following values:

- 3: For the RARP request shown in Fig. 10.20
- 4: For the RARP reply shown in Fig. 10.21

And of course, the physical header of the frame will now indicate RARP as the higher level protocol (8035 hex) instead of ARP (0806 hex) or IP (0800 hex) in the EtherType field. Some differences arise from the concept of RARP itself:

- ARP only assumes that every host knows the mapping between its own hardware address and protocol address. RARP requires one or more server hosts on the network to maintain a database of mappings between hardware addresses and protocol addresses so that they will be able to reply to requests from client hosts.

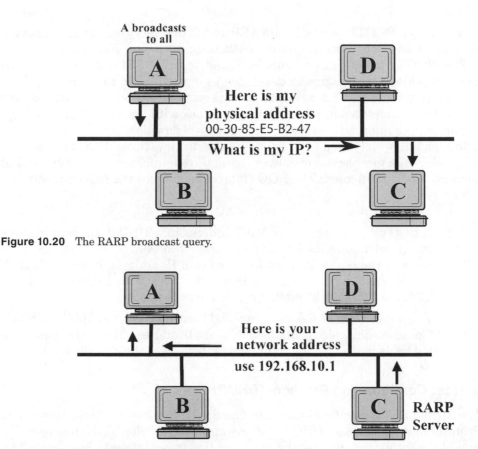

Figure 10.20   The RARP broadcast query.

Figure 10.21   The RARP response message.

- Due to the size this database can take, part of the server function is usually implemented outside the adapter's microcode, with optionally a small cache in the microcode. The microcode part is then only responsible for reception and transmission of the RARP frames, the RARP mapping itself being taken care of by server software running as a normal process in the host machine.

- The nature of this database also requires some software to create and update the database manually.

- In case there are multiple RARP servers on the network, the RARP requester only uses the first RARP reply received on its broadcast RARP request, and discards the others.

Bootstrap Protocol

The bootstrap protocol (BOOTP) enables a client workstation to initialize with a minimal IP stack and request its IP address, a gateway address, and the address of a name server from a BOOTP server. In the ARP and RARP services, the client device had the IP address and needed to resolve it to a MAC address and vice versa.

The BOOTP specifications can be found in RFC 951—Bootstrap Protocol. The BOOTP protocol was originally developed as a mechanism to enable diskless hosts to be remotely booted over a network as workstations, routers, terminal concentrators, and so on. It allows a minimum IP protocol stack with no configuration information to obtain enough information to begin the process of downloading the necessary boot code. Although still widely used for this purpose by diskless hosts, BOOTP is also commonly used solely as a mechanism to deliver configuration information to a client that has not been manually configured. The BOOTP process involves the following steps:

1. The client determines its own MAC address.

2. A BOOTP client sends its MAC address in a UDP datagram to the server. If the client knows its IP address and/or the address of the server, it can use them. If the client does not know its own IP address, it uses 0.0.0.0. If the client does not know the server's IP address, it uses the limited broadcast address (255.255.255.255). The UDP port number is 67.

3. The server receives the datagram and looks up the client MAC address in its configuration file, which contains the client's IP address. The server fills in the remaining fields in the UDP datagram and returns it to the client using UDP port 68.

Dynamic Host Configuration Protocol (DHCP)

The current DHCP specifications can be found in RFC 2131—Dynamic Host Configuration Protocol and RFC 2132—DHCP Options and BOOTP Vendor Extensions. The DHCP provides a framework for passing configuration information to hosts on a TCP/IP network. DHCP is based on the BOOTP protocol, adding the capability to automatically assign reusable network (IP) addresses and additional configuration options. DHCP messages use UDP port 67, the BOOTP server's well-known port and UDP port 68, the BOOTP client's well-known port.

DHCP consists of two components:

1. A protocol that delivers host-specific configuration parameters from a DHCP server to a host/client.

2. A mechanism for the assignment of temporary or permanent network addresses to those hosts.

IP requires the setting of many parameters within the protocol implementation software. Because IP can be used on many dissimilar kinds of network hardware, values for those parameters cannot be guessed at or assumed to have correct defaults. The use of a distributed address allocation scheme based on a polling/defense mechanism, for discovery of network addresses already in use, cannot guarantee unique network addresses because hosts may not always be able to defend their network addresses.

DHCP supports three mechanisms for IP address allocation:

1. *Automatic allocation*: DHCP assigns a permanent IP address to the host from a pool of addresses. The host always gets the same address assigned to it.
2. *Dynamic allocation*: DHCP assigns an IP address for a limited period of time. This network address assignment is called a lease.
3. *Manual allocation*: The host's address is assigned by a network administrator.

In Fig. 10.22 the laptop has two network interface cards installed: a wired and a wireless interface. To get to this screenshot, select "Start" then "Run" and type "cmd" then select "OK." When the DOS command prompt screen appears type in "ipconfig /all" then press "Enter". The result is shown in this figure. Note a few of the pieces include the IP address and subnet mask; also the address of the DHCP server and the lease obtained/expiration time. The leases are for 24 hours on this machine, but they can be modified depending on the system. I have seen leases that last only 1 hour, others 2 weeks.

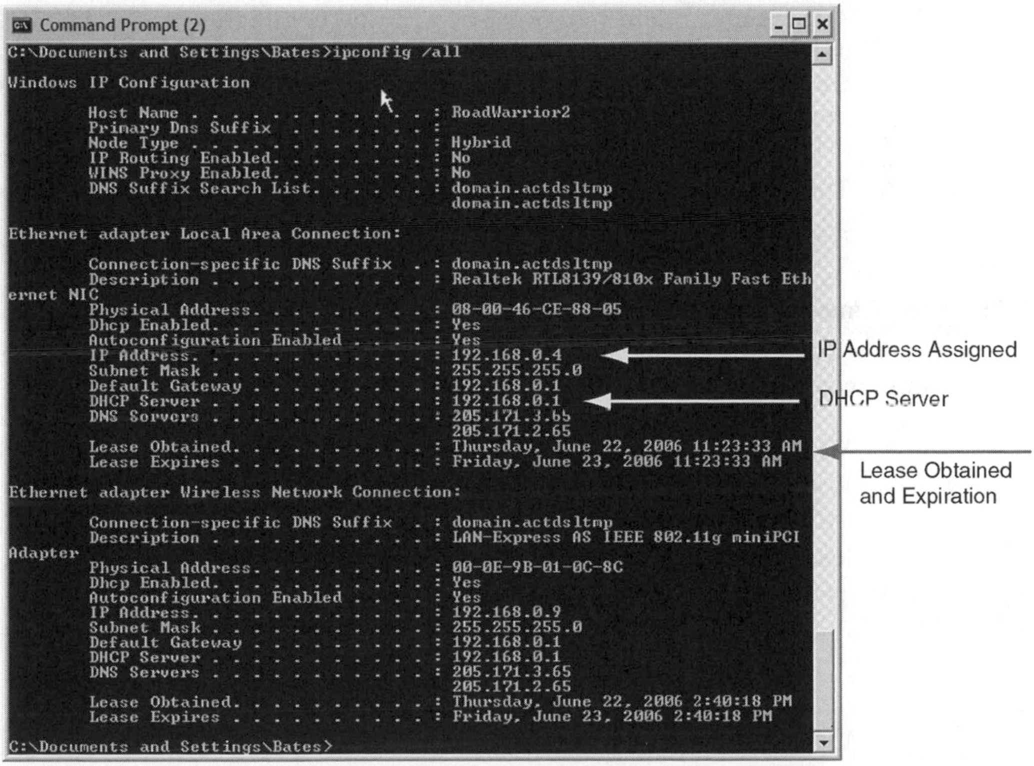

Figure 10.22   This screenshot shows that the host has two interface cards and the assignment of the IP address on the wired card (local network connection) with its associated DHCP server address and the lease time.

The following is a description of the DHCP client/server interaction steps:

1. The client broadcasts a DHCPDISCOVER message on its local physical subnet.

2. Each server may respond with a DHCPOFFER message that includes an available network address (your IP address) and other configuration options.

3. The client receives one or more DHCPOFFER messages from one or more servers. The client chooses one based on the configuration parameters offered and broadcasts a DHCPREQUEST message that includes the server identifier option to indicate which message it has selected and the requested IP address option, taken from your IP address in the selected offer.

4. The server selected in the DHCPREQUEST message commits the binding for the client to persistent storage and responds with a DHCPACK message containing the configuration parameters for the requesting client. The IP address field in the DHCPACK messages is filled in with the selected network address.

5. The client receives the DHCPACK message with configuration parameters. The client performs a final check on the parameters and notes the duration of the lease. At this point, the client is configured.

    If the client detects a problem with the parameters in the DHCPACK message, the client sends a DHCPDECLINE message to the server and starts over. On receipt of a DHCPDECLINE, the server must mark the offered address as unavailable.

    If the client receives a DHCPNAK message, the client starts over.

6. The client may choose to relinquish its lease on a network address by sending a DHCPRELEASE message to the server.

DHCP Lease Renewal Process

Suppose the client already has a DHCP address that has already been configured and wants to start the process that ensures lease expiration and renewal.

1. When a server sends the DHCPACK to a client with IP address and configuration parameters, it also registers the start of the lease time for that address.

2. The client is rightfully entitled to use the given address for the duration of the lease time. At this time, the client is in the BOUND state.

3. Times are options configurable by the server.

4. When one of the timers expires, the client will send a DHCPREQUEST (unicast) to the server that gave it the address asking to extend (RENEWING) the lease. The server usually responds with a new lease time. Timers are reset at the client and server accordingly.

5. If no DHCPACK is received until a timer expires, the client now broadcasts a DHCPREQUEST message (REBINDING) to extend its lease.

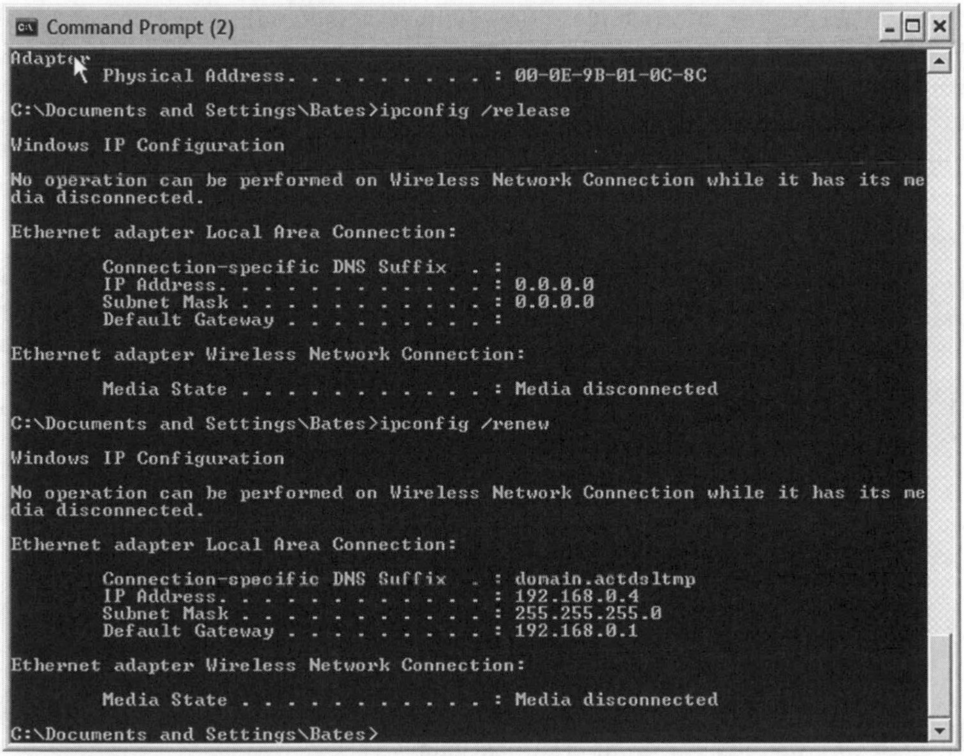

Figure 10.23   The release and renewal of a DHCP address.

6. If the client does not receive a DHCPACK message after its lease has expired, it must stop using its current TCP/IP address. The client issues a DHCPDISCOVER broadcast to obtain a new valid address.

As an alternative, a user can also issue a release and renew message to get a new lease or new IP, on a busy network. The screenshot in Fig. 10.23 is a sample of this being done. The upper portion of the screenshot shows the command "ipconfig /release" with the resultant address returned 0.0.0.0. The lower portion shows the command "ipconfig /renew" with the resultant renewal of 192.168.0.4.

Domain Name Services (DNS)

The domain name server is responsible for maintaining the addresses of all networks and nodes and the IP address translations for them. This server is a distributed name/address mechanism used on the Internet and IP networks. A domain is part of the Internet naming hierarchy. Syntactically, an Internet domain name consists of a sequence of names (labels) separated by periods: for example, mail.smtp.idsweb1.com.us.

When a user enters a plain text address, the domain name server is called upon to translate the text-based address into an IP addressing scheme. The DNS then returns the numerical IP address using the address.subnet.node using the dot delimiter defining the actual users' IP address. The DNS servers reside around the country and use a fully distributed computing architecture to maintain addressing information of all registered domains. The databases can be updated on a 30-minute timer, or other time as set by the ISP. Normal operation requires at least two DNS connections for redundancy purposes.

Regional ISPs provide local DNS servers updated from the master database maintained by Network Solutions, Inc. of Virginia. The InterNIC (short for Internet Network Information Center, a registered service mark of the U.S. Department of Commerce and now a defunct entity. InterNIC began as a collaborative project between AT&T and Network Solutions, Inc. (NSI) supported by the National Science Foundation. InterNIC assigned names and addresses then promulgated the changes on a regular basis, keeping all the databases as current as possible. Separate DNS systems are used for the extensions of the addresses. There are six major extensions:

- .com for commercial organizations
- .gov for government bodies
- .edu for educational institutions
- .mil for military organizations
- .org usually nonprofit organizations
- .net for systems performing network services

There is also a domain assigned for each country such as Canada (.ca). An organization may fit into more than one category and can choose whichever naming domain it prefers.

DNS servers handle the translation of IP addresses to alpha-numeric host names to make it easy to understand an IP topology. There is nothing wrong with using only addresses to communicate on a network and to keep track of where everything is within a network, but it is much easier to remember where Mickey is in relation to Minnie than it is to remember where 192.168.0.23 is in relation to 192.168.17.55. In this scenario Mickey is the host name and 192.168.0.23 is the IP address.

Furthermore, DNS servers are directly responsible for translating URLs (uniform resource locators) like http://www.tcic.com into their IP addresses like 209.35.87.216. As you can see, www.tcic.com is much easier to remember and is the *fully qualified domain name,* and 209.35.87.216 is the IP address. Most systems can accept up to three name server addresses, a primary and up to two backups, contacting each in turn in order to look up the IP address that corresponds to a particular name. To handle the lookups of names and addresses most efficiently, one DNS server can forward a lookup request to another DNS server.

Traditionally this is set up as a static DNS, which requires the network administrator to manually edit and update the lookup table whenever an IP address gets assigned or reassigned to a particular name, or when a name is no longer used because the system is out of service. Needless to say, this can be a burden administratively. This process can be handled dynamically and therefore with much less administrative intervention with a dynamic DNS (DDNS).

Domain Names

Names assigned to subnets, networks, or any arbitrary collection of IP addresses are called domain names. Therefore, a system's fully qualified name might be bud.tcic .com. Domains are designed to save typing and to provide some structure to the naming of systems. The system that has the job of keeping track of which names correspond to which IP addresses is called a domain name services (DNS) server. A DNS server simply contains a table of addresses with their corresponding names. Lookups can be performed in either direction but usually a DNS server translates names into numeric addresses on behalf of clients. For any client to take advantage of domain names, it must know the IP address of at least one name server.

Dynamic Domain Name Services (DDNS)

Dynamic domain name services allow the dynamic updating of the lookup table in order to resolve a dynamic or static host name to a dynamic IP address. DDNS is a service that maps Internet domain names to IP addresses. DDNS serves a similar purpose to DNS: DDNS allows anyone hosting a Web or FTP server to advertise a public name to prospective users.

Unlike DNS that only works with static IP addresses, DDNS works with dynamic IP addresses, such as those assigned by an ISP or other DHCP server. DDNS is popular with home networkers, who typically receive dynamic, frequently-changing IP addresses from their service provider. To use DDNS, one simply signs up with a provider and installs network software on their host to monitor its IP address.

Dynamic update is the basic DDNS operation, letting software such as DHCP clients or servers send special messages to name servers to update zone data. A DHCP server, for example, can send an update message to the primary name server for a particular zone to request that a record be added to that zone to map a DHCP client's name to its new, DHCP-issued IP address. The DHCP server might send a subsequent update message to the primary name server for a reverse-mapping zone to add a pointer (PTR) record for the DHCP client.

Compared to ordinary DNS, the disadvantage of DDNS is that additional host software, a new potential failure point on the network, must be maintained.

With all these complex protocols and pieces one can now see why TCP/IP is so popular with just about every network vendor in the industry. With a single protocol suite, every networking need can be handled. In a later chapter, we will see how all the pieces come together and make TCP/IP the glue that binds all the computing systems around the world.

Questions

1. The predominant protocol that runs on an Internet is:

    a. Novell

    b. IBM SNA

    c. UNIX

    d. TCP/IP

2. To move away from proprietary architecture and systems, what organization was responsible for creating the TCP/IP protocol suite?

    a. SNA

    b. OSI

    c. IETF

    d. DOD

3. What device will maintain a translation table with an entry for each internal host needing Internet access?

    a. DNS server

    b. LDAP server

    c. Microsoft SMS server

    d. Firewall

4. What server will handle the assignment of an address to the client?

    a. DNS

    b. ACP

    c. DHCP

    d. ARP

5. What protocol on the LAN will support the resolution of a MAC address to an IP address?

    a. ARP

    b. RARP

    c. ACP

    d. DHCP

11

Frame Relay, ATM, and MPLS

After reading this chapter and completing the questions, you will be able to:

- Describe frame relay
- Describe the addressing techniques of frame relay
- Understand where frame relay fits in the overall OSI model
- Discuss the concept of cell relay
- Understand why the cells are so important
- Describe the broadband concept with ATM
- Discuss the benefits of using cell relay
- Understand what MPLS is all about
- Understand how MPLS can work with Frame Relay and ATM

One of the data transport systems developed in 1992 is a frame switching technique called *frame relay*. Frames of information are generated by most of the data communications processes today. Although we call them by different names, such as *packets, frames,* or *cells,* they all are just a means of transmitting a specific amount of information across a network. When first introduced, frame relay was met with mild enthusiasm. This is not to say that it is not an efficient means of transferring the data, merely that the industry was confused about what the intended goals would be.

What Is Frame Relay?

Frame relay is a high-performance, cost-efficient means of connecting an organization's multiple local area networks (LANs). Like older packet switching services, frame relay uses the transmission links only when they are needed. Essentially, a virtual circuit is used for network services.

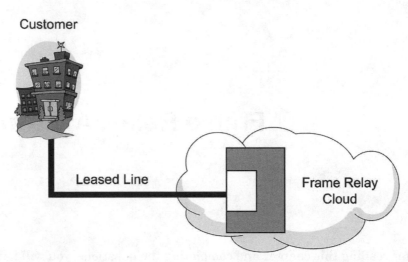

Figure 11.1   The customer leases/ rents a dedicated circuit into the cloud and terminates it on a port.

The customer rents or leases a physical circuit into the network cloud, as shown in Fig. 11.1. This circuit is terminated onto a port in a computer system. The computer system (switch) recognizes the connecting ends of the wires and uses these wires when the customer has traffic to pass into the network. Thus, a virtual circuit connection is established into the cloud for future use as the customer's needs dictate. Because the connection is not always "nailed up," other customers connected to the same network supplier can also transmit traffic across the same physical pairs of wires inside the cloud. Additionally, like private line connections, frame relay transports data very quickly, with only a limited amount of delay for network processing to take place.

Reduced processing allows the transport of data much more quickly. By eliminating the overhead in each of the processors, the network merely looks at an address in the frame and passes the frame along to the next node in the network.

Why Was Frame Relay Developed?

Major trends in the industry led to the development of frame relay services. These can be categorized into four major trends as follows:

1. *The increased need for speed across the network platforms within the end-user and the carrier networks*: The proliferation of high-speed LANs being deployed has shifted the paradigm of computing platforms. The demands of these services will exceed by hundreds to thousands of times the data transport needs of the older text-based services. Users demand connectivity and speed to ensure quick and reliable communications between systems. To accommodate this connectivity, some changes had to be made to the overhead intensity. One way to accommodate the reduced overhead is to eliminate some of the processing, mainly in the error detection and correction schemes.

2. *Increasing intelligence of the devices attached to the network*: The transfer of data between and among devices on the network has moved many of the processing functions to the desktop. The capacity to move the information around the network must meet the demands of each attached device. Increased functionality must be met with increases in the bandwidth allocation for these devices.

3. *Improved transmission facilities*: The days of "dirty" or poor-quality transmission lines required the use of overcorrecting protocols. Because the network now performs better, a newer transmission capability is needed.

4. *The need to connect LANs to WANs and the internetworking capabilities*: Today's users want to connect LANs across the boundaries of the wide area. Users demand and expect the same speed and accuracy across the WAN that they get on the local networks. Therefore, a newer transport system to support the higher-speed connections across a wider area was needed.

The Significance of Frame Relay

As an analog transmission system, the old network was extremely noisy, producing many network errors and corrupting data. When data errors were introduced, a retransmission was required. The more retransmissions were necessary, the less effective was throughput on the network. To solve this problem, the industry introduced the X.25 services, also called *packet switching*. The X.25 was originally designed to handle the customer's asynchronous traffic. Frame relay was designed to take advantage of the low-error, high-performance digital network and to meet the needs of the intelligent, synchronous use of the newer and more sophisticated user applications.

Compared to private leased lines, frame relay makes network design much simpler. The private line network shown in Fig. 11.2 requires a detailed analysis to set all the right connections in place; this further accentuates the traffic-sensitive needs of the user network. The meshed network allows for speed of connectivity, but the network costs are much higher. Depending on the nature of the data traffic, the bursty data needs of a LAN-to-LAN or LAN-to-WAN connection are not required full time. We, therefore, spend significantly more money to support the meshed leased-line network. In Fig. 11.3, a single frame relay access from each site is provided into the network cloud, instead of multiple links shown in the earlier network. Multiple sessions can run on the same link concurrently. Communications from a single site to any other site can be handled using the predefined network connections of the virtual circuits. In frame relay, these connections use *permanent logical links* (PLLs), more commonly referred to as *permanent virtual circuits* (PVCs). Each of the PVCs connects two sites just as a private line would, but in this case the bandwidth is shared among multiple users rather than being dedicated to the one site for access to a single site. Using this multiple-site connectivity on a single link reduces the costs.

Because the PVCs are predefined for each pair of end-to-end connections, a network path is always available for the customer's application to transport data. This eliminates the call setup time associated with the dial-up lines and the X.25 packet arrangements.

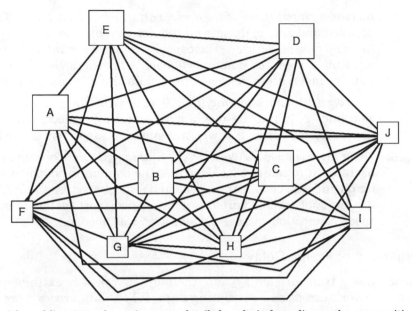

Figure 11.2   A leased-line network requires more detailed analysis depending on the communities of interest.

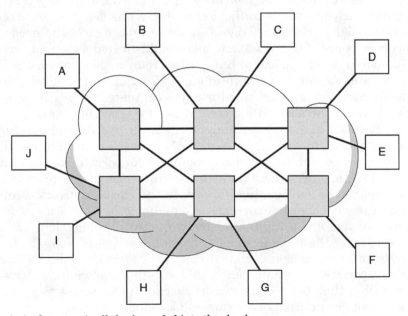

Figure 11.3   A single access is all that's needed into the cloud.

Comparing Frame Relay to Other Services

When the network suppliers and the standards bodies were attempting to define the benefits of frame relay services, they looked at a comparison of the time-division multiplexed (TDM) switched circuit and the packet switched network services.

TDM Circuit Switching

TDM circuit switching creates a full-time connection or a dedicated circuit between any two attached devices for the duration of the connection. TDM divides the bandwidth down into fixed time slots in which there can be multiple time slots, each with its own fixed capacity, available. This is shown in Fig. 11.4, where each attached device on the network is assigned a fixed portion of the bandwidth using one or more time slots. When the device is in transmit mode, the data is merely placed in this time slot without any extra overhead such as processing or translations. Therefore, TDM is protocol transparent to the traffic being carried. Unfortunately, when this attached device is not sending data, the time slots remain empty; wasting the bandwidth. TDM is not well suited for the bursty data that are becoming the norm in today's organization.

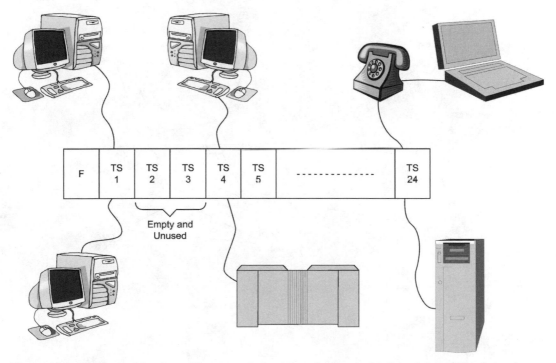

Figure 11.4 TDM switching forces the transmission into a fixed-capacity time slot, and the channels are virtually wasted.

X.25 Packet Switching

Because TDM had its limitations, a service was created that allowed the bandwidth to be allocated "on the fly." Instead of simply putting the data into a fixed time slot, smaller pieces of data called packets, containing the source and destination address information as well as other control functional information, are used. When data bursts are sent, multiple packets are generated and routed across the network based on the address. The network creates a virtual circuit from each source to each destination. This is shown in Fig. 11.5, where multiple virtual circuits can be active on a line at the same time. The major drawback to this scheme is the penalty paid in speed of delivery. Guaranteed data delivery and integrity was a prerequisite for the development of the X.25.

The standards bodies attempted to use the best features of the switched network and the packet services. They arrived at frame relay to meet the needs of the user. This comparison took into account the following service connections:

Speed: The digital networks support high-speed connections of up to 2.048 Mbps. X.25 networks only support speeds of up to 64 Kbps.

Network setup delay: Call setup time on a switched network and packet network is relatively low. The PVC allows this because the call setup time is eliminated.

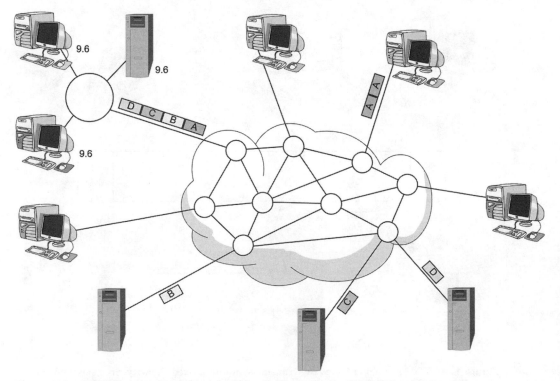

Figure 11.5   Multiple connections on virtual circuits are active on the line simultaneously.

Routing: When one sets up a circuit switched call, the routing is used only once to establish the link. In case of a network delay or a failed link, the user must reestablish the call. The X.25 network is robust in that if a problem occurs on the link, the packet nodes in the network immediately reestablish the connection with the next packet. Therefore, the suppliers and standards bodies opted for the robust and dynamic call setup with very low delay.

Signaling: In the switched network design, the signaling is used only in the initial setup or teardown of the call. In the packet switched networks, the signaling is dynamic—it is contained in every packet and thus is easily reestablished. The standards bodies opted for the dynamic signaling arrangements of the packet switched networks.

Bandwidth: In the circuit switched networks the bandwidth is fixed. The variable length of a packet allows for use of much less bandwidth. Therefore, the standards bodies opted to arrive at a dynamically allocated bandwidth-on-demand concept.

Costs: Circuit switched services are relatively inexpensive. In the packet switched services, the expense is also very low.

Frame Relay Speeds

Frame relay was designed initially to start from 64 Kbps up to 1.544 Mbps in North America. Speeds of 2.048 Mbps were approved in the rest of the world. This speed is based on using T1 or E1 access links.

When designing a frame relay service; the access speed is important both prior to and after installation. The customer must select a specified delivery rate. For small locations, such as branch offices with little predictable traffic, the customer might consider the lowest possible access speed. Carriers offer this as burstable frame relay.

The customer selects a committed information rate (CIR). The committed information rate is a guaranteed rate of throughput when using frame relay. The CIR is assigned to each PVC. Each PVC is assigned a CIR consistent with the average expected volume of traffic to the destination port. Because frame relay is a duplex service, a different CIR can be assigned in each direction making the service asymmetrical. This allows added flexibility to meet the customer's needs. However, because the nature of LANs is that of bursty traffic, the CIR can be burst over and above the fixed rate for 2 seconds at a time in some carriers' networks. This committed burst rate (Bc) can be up to the link rate, depending on the carrier offering. When the network is not very busy, the customer could still burst data onto the network at an even higher rate. The burst excess rate (Be) can be an additional speed of up to the channel capacity, or in some carrier's networks it can be 50 percent above the committed burst rate, but only for 1-second increments. Combining these rates, an example can be drawn as follows:

$$CIR + Bc + Be = \text{Total throughput}$$
$$128 \text{ Kbps} + 128 \text{ Kbps} + 64 \text{ Kbps} = 320 \text{ Kbps total}$$

Guaranteed Delivery

When a committed information rate is used, the guarantee is that the network will make best effort to deliver traffic (frames) at the CIR, but bursts are another situation. As data frames enter the network they will follow the same logical connection in sequence. There should be no out-of-sequence arrival of data, and there should be no loss of frames. Unfortunately, there is no real guarantee! Frames can be lost, discarded, or delayed while en route.

When using the burst rate or the burst excess rate, the network will make its best effort to deliver the frames; but no guarantees are made. As each frame bursts out through the network, it is marked within its overhead with a *discard eligibility bit*. This means that as the network nodes attempt to serve higher rates of throughput, the frames are given a designator by the end-user equipment. This designator lets the other hops on the network know that if the network suddenly begins to get congested, the frames riding the network beyond the CIR can be discarded and other customer frames within the CIR will have priority. In essence, the network provides some breathing room for users by expanding and contracting based on how busy it is. The less busy the network, the higher a customer can burst without risk.

Because the network will only make its best attempt to deliver the data, the end-user equipment must be intelligent enough to recognize that frames have been discarded. In Fig. 11.6, the frame format is shown with the setup of the bytes in the header information, creating the discard eligibility setting. In this framed overhead, other pieces of information are also contained. Designators in each frame that are set by the network nodes along the path alert the nodes and customer equipment when congestion is occurring. The forward explicit congestion notification (FECN) and a backward explicit congestion notification (BECN) are used for this purpose. These are shown in the framing overhead.

Another piece of the frame layout is the data link connection identifier (DLCI) that marks the PVC addressing scheme. The FECN and BECN, along with the DLCI, are parts of the 2-byte sequence. Encapsulated in the frame after the header is the user data, a variable-length frame of user information that can carry up to 1610 bytes. The initial 1610-byte payload can carry a full Ethernet frame with some overhead.

The bytes are not important at this point, but the variable length is. Because this is a variable, there are some inherent delays in the processing of the data across the network.

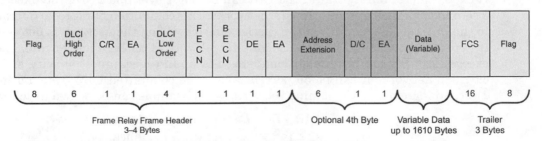

Figure 11.6 The frame format used in frame relay.

For this reason, the packet switching networks have received a negative image. The X.25 and the frame relay networks have timers and delimiters that the nodes must use to process the data across the network. These are set to certain parameters to allow frames or packets to be transmitted at differing sizes. Along with the variable-length data frames, the trailer in Fig. 11.6 represents the overhead associated with the error checking (frame check sequence). However, when transmitting data across the network, buffers must be allocated to receive the frames. Because the data are variable, the full size buffer must be allocated to receive a frame. This happens even if the frame is only half full. The switch cannot process the data until the beginning flag and the ending flag are received and the CRC calculated on what is in between. Therefore, added buffering is required for this system to work. Variable works in some cases, but in others it introduces extra overhead and latency.

The frame relay nodes only perform error checking of the address header; they don't check the user data contained inside. Each node on the network only checks the address and passes the frame along the predefined path (the PVC) to the next node. Nowhere is the data verified. Data integrity is the responsibility of the end devices to perform error checking and retransmission requests. We would expect that the transmission control protocol (TCP) at the receiving node would ask for a retransmission if corruption or data loss occur.

Advantages of Frame Relay Services

Frame relay served the network well, albeit for a short time. Most of the benefits are enjoyed by customers who put networks in place worldwide and have not moved away from them. Newer technologies arrived that pushed frame relay into the background. However, the benefits and advantages of frame relay services were many. These include the following:

Increased Utilization and Efficiency

The network uses frame relay services to allow the user network to "breathe" when necessary and dynamically allocates the bandwidth in real time. The support of multiple connections simultaneously allows multiple sessions to be online concurrently. The nature of the bursty data transmissions on our applications does not require the full-time allocation of bandwidth. This allows shared resources on corporate LANs in remote sites.

Savings Through Network Consolidations

Data from various sources can be applied to the network in various ways, such as LAN bursty traffic from the desktop devices, and traffic from other application-specific devices. The use of a single connection to support all of these connections at various speeds and at variable times allows the end user to consolidate services and therefore save money. Frame relay enables the user to save on transmission and switching costs.

Improved Network Up Time

Network down time is a phrase that will make even the most staunch data processing person shudder. The use of a frame relay service into the virtual cloud allows the reestablishment of the network connections within the cloud automatically. The only single point of failure that really remains is in the local loop or last mile. Up time can achieve 99.9 percent availability on a network of this sort.

Improvements in Response Time

With direct logical connectivity to the multiple locations on the network, a single interface improves the response times. Limiting the number of hops that the frames will traverse through, along with eliminating call setup time, vastly improves response times. Allocation of bandwidth to support the bursty data needs also improves the response times, especially when a burst rate can be accommodated. Frame relay is a reliable transport protocol for high-performance and fast-response interconnection of intelligent end-user devices, providing the highest ubiquitous speed, lowest-overhead protocol standard available for the WAN.

Easily Modifiable and Fast Growth

The logically connected PVCs can be adjusted easily through the network administration group of the carrier. New PVCs can be assigned on a single link quickly, or existing PVCs can be increased in capacity up to the access channel capacity needed to support the dynamics of the organization's transport needs. With the PVC concept, a virtual connection is created quickly and without major modifications to the network.

Standards Based

Frame relay falls into the ITU-TSS and the ANSI standards infrastructure. The interoperability between various switching platforms has been proven, and it is a logical progression toward the future switching services for broader bandwidth services, such as ATM, allowing a smooth transition to these newer, emerging services.

Services Available

Usually, the following services and protocols are readily available from the carriers, allowing the transparent flow of data across the network. Those that are not will be added as the network services proliferate and the interfaces are developed to support the various service offerings.

TCP/IP and Novell IPX/SPX

Using the packet-level routing capabilities of the frame relay network through a certified or type-accepted router (the word internationally is *homologated*), any type of data can be transported. In the event a customer does not have a router capable of internetworking with the suggested network or other pieces, the carriers can rent, lease, or sell the specific routers that work on their networks.

CCITT X.25 Protocol

Convenient interfaces to the X.25 networks are being introduced to allow a customer to connect to and transport data to sites that might not have the frame relay services available. The X.25 interface can connect the host-computing environment to the network interface across a public packet switching service, then into an X.25 gateway on the public network, as shown in Fig. 11.7. Or packets of data can be rerouted across the frame relay network through the router at the customer location seen in Fig. 11.8.

Facsimile (CCITT Group III or IV) Traffic

X.400 protocol electronic messaging service for domestic and international messaging services can be accommodated by the carrier or through the interfaces at the customer location. Facsimile traffic is extremely time-sensitive, and the packetized fax has not been truly developed.

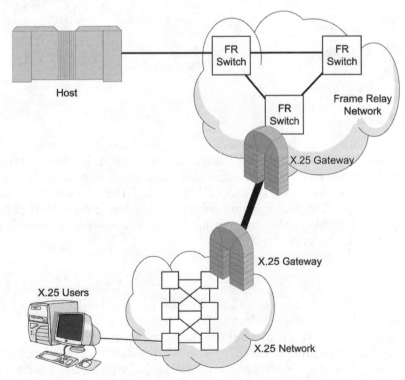

Figure 11.7 Access to frame relay can be through the public packet switching service to an X.25 gateway.

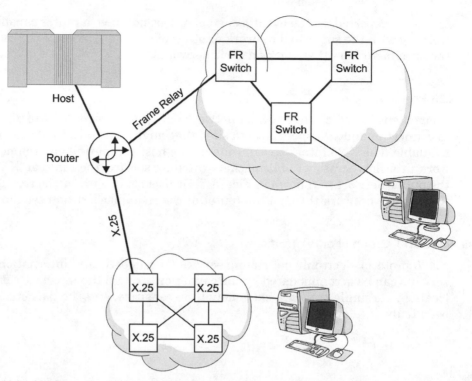

Figure 11.8 An alternative is to use X.25 to a customer's router that redirects the packet onto frame relay.

The Major Players

The two major standards players in the specification and support of frame relay services are the CCITT and ANSI. Together, they have defined a standard data (packet mode) interface for ISDN networks and frame relay services. The basics of frame relay were actually developed in CCITT blue book I.122 (*Packet Mode Bearer Services*) in 1988. The speed at which frame relay was developed from that point on has been directly attributable to the demand for a simple, easy-to-use, high-performance service for LAN-to-LAN connectivity.

Others

In 1989, StrataCom (now a Cisco Company), Digital Equipment Corporation (now Compaq/HP), Northern Telecom, Inc. (Nortel), and Cisco Systems began a joint development effort to specify added frame relay services, under the auspices of the Frame Relay Forum. Their efforts were specifically geared toward addressing the needs of LAN-to-LAN communications, including the need for a local management interface (LMI). The collaboration of these groups led to the publication of a joint specification for the first implementations of frame relay by numerous vendors in 1990. Portions of that specification were adopted by CCITT and ANSI for inclusion in the standards.

In 1988, ITU approved Recommendation I.122, *Framework for Additional Packet Mode Bearer Services,* which is part of a series of ISDN-related specifications. ISDN developers had been using a protocol called link access protocol with D channel (LAP-D) to carry signaling information on the D channel of ISDN (LAPD) as defined by CCITT Recommendation Q.921. LAPD has characteristics that could be useful in other applications, such as provision for multiplexing of virtual circuits at level 2 in the frame level (as opposed to level 3 in the X.25 networks). Therefore, I.122 was written to provide a framework outlining how such a protocol might be used in applications other than ISDN signaling.

In 2003, the Frame Relay Forum merged with the Multiprotocol Label Switching (MPLS) Forum as a means of proliferating frame relay interworking with MPLS. Frame relay is the layer 2 protocol that carries the data, whereas MPLS (discussed later in this chapter) is the management and signaling plane for the protocols.

The Basic Data Flow

In most popular synchronous protocols, data is carried across a communications line based on very similar structures. The standard HDLC (high-level data link control) frame format is used in a myriad of these protocols and services. Frame relay makes a very slight change to the basic frame structure, redefining the header at the beginning of the frame (2 bytes long). The basic frame structure for other synchronous protocols is shown in Fig. 11.9. In this case, the HDLC frame header consists of an address and control information. For frame relay, the header is changed as shown in Fig. 11.10, which uses 2 bytes (octets) to define the following pieces:

- The data link connection identifier (DLCI). This identifier uses up to 1024 LCNs.

- The command/response bit (C/R). This is not used in frame relay.

- The extended address bit (EA). When set to zero, it extends the DLCI address.

- Forward explicit congestion notification (FECN). This is set in the frames going out into the network toward the destination address.

- Backward explicit congestion notification (BECN). This is set in frames returning from the network to the source address.

- Discard eligibility bit (DE). This bit is used by the source equipment to denote whether the frame is eligible to be discarded by the network if the network gets congested. When set to 1, it indicates that the frame is eligible to be discarded during congestion period.

- Extended address bit (EA). When set to 1, it is used to end the DLCI.

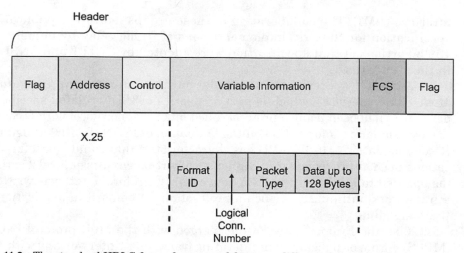

Figure 11.9 The standard HDLC frame format used for many different data protocols.

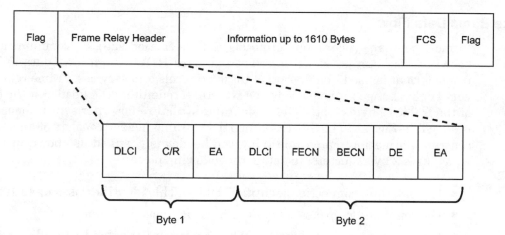

Figure 11.10 The change is in the HDLC frame for frame relay.

Advantages

The chief advantage of this application revolves around the way it is priced. Comparatively inexpensive, frame is priced by bandwidth and by permanent virtual circuit (PVC) access point. It is not distance or usage based as a norm. This is of critical significance when evaluating the potential for the usage-based voice that would be carried.

It is also estimated that approximately 80 percent of Internet servers run on frame relay. This is partly because of its low cost, particularly among Internet access suppliers, who provide service on a monthly access fee with unlimited usage. This has been incorporated in the general strategies of the frame relay deployment.

A second key advantage is that the communications network suppliers carry the frame relay services over existing infrastructure. Much of the upgrade, maintenance, restoration, and repair and other concerns about managing a network are the responsibility of the frame relay carrier as opposed to the end user. This removes most of the networking burden from the end user. Just about everything between the sites is domed, operated, managed, and maintained by the communications provider, removing all of that responsibility from the end-user organization.

Disadvantages

The prime limitation to frame relay has been the ability to transmit time-sensitive applications (such as voice, fax, and video) due to the burst transmission characteristics of the system. The original design was for a data communications network, where these time sensitivities were not as critical. Furthermore, outside the United States, the acceptance and availability of frame relay has been somewhat sporadic. A number of countries still do not offer frame relay access or service capabilities, limiting where frame relay can be used.

ATM

Asynchronous transfer mode (ATM) is another class of packet switching technologies that relays traffic via an address contained within the packet. When packet switching was first developed, the packets used variable lengths of information. This variable nature of each packet caused some latency within a network. As a next step toward creating a faster packet switching service, the industry introduced the concept of *frame relay*. Both of the packet switching concepts used variable-length packets. To overcome this overhead and latency, a fixed cell size was introduced. In early 1992, the industry adopted a fast packet or "cell relay" concept that uses a short (53-byte) fixed-length cell to transmit information across both private and public networks. This cell relay technique was introduced as ATM.

ATM is defined as a transport and switching method in which information does not occur periodically with some reference, such as a frame pattern. All other techniques used a fixed timing reference; ATM does not, hence the name *asynchronous*. With ATM, data arrives and is processed across the network randomly. There is no specific timing associated with ATM traffic, so the cells are generated as data needs to be transmitted. When no traffic exists, idle cells may be present on the network, or cells carrying other payloads will be present including voice, data, and video communication on any user-to-network interface (UNI).

As shown in Fig. 11.11, the ATM concept aggregates a myriad of services onto a single access arrangement. All of these services can be combined at aggregate rates of 622 Mbps to 2.4 Gbps. In the future the carriers will step up to the 10 Gbps and higher rates.

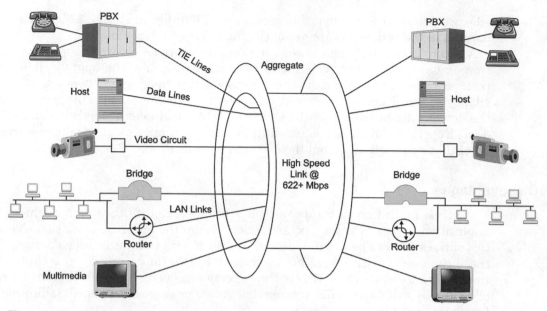

Figure 11.11   Multiple inputs are aggregated onto a single UNI.

Broadband Communications

ATM is an outgrowth of B-ISDN standards that are intended to run on SONET. Therefore, asynchronous transfer mode is designed to run on synchronous facilities. *Broadband* is defined as a higher throughput rate of bursty traffic than is traditionally available on the telephone companies' channel capacities. Instead of a 64-Kbps (DS0) channel, the broadband communications handle multimegabit transport starting at the very low end at 1.544 Mbps, progressing upward in "chunks" or increments up to 155 Mbps, 622 Mbps, and 1+ Gbps.

The Cell Concept

Network suppliers were looking to improve upon the inefficient use of their capacity. They found that they were consistently overbuilding their infrastructure. However, this overbuilding is expensive.

Looking at user demands, a new concept emerged: rather than forcing the user to adapt to the constraints of the network, why not let the network adapt to the needs of the user? Thus ATM was born. ATM gets around the inefficiency of the fixed time slot, rates, and formats of the TDM world by allocating whatever is necessary to the user whenever the user wants it.

Instead of using the processor-intensive slow-speed services of X.25 packet switching, or the speedier frame relay, a mix of packet/frame technology evolved using a fixed-size cell that offers higher throughput.

The Importance of Cells

Cells can get around the waste of frame relay or other frame concepts. In frame relay, the frames are larger, but variable in length. Therefore, if the frame size is set to accommodate LAN traffic, such as an Ethernet frame of 1500 bytes, the network deals with a frame of the same size. Consequently, the 1500-byte frame is used, even if only 150 bytes are to be transmitted. In many implementations, a pad function (filler) is used to fill the frame for transmission. The use of this frame was only 10 percent efficient.

Moreover, when a variable frame size is used, the buffers across the network have to work accordingly. In many cases the buffers in the frame relay switches are set to expect a full frame of 1610 bytes (plus the associated overhead). If a switch has a nearly full buffer, and a frame arrives, the switch must allocate the full-size buffer for the receipt of the frame. If a full frame buffer cannot be allocated, the switch throws the frame away. Although the frame may have been partially filled, the maximum buffer cannot be allocated. Therefore, the network is inefficiently used because the data is discarded when it did not have to be.

On the other hand, a much smaller cell allows the transmitter to break down large blocks of information into more manageable pieces. If the frame used (in this example) is only partially filled, the network need not be concerned. It will only be required to send the 150 bytes of information plus any associated overhead in a couple of cells. Thus, the network performs more efficiently. The processor speed can be used to maximize the throughput and minimize delays across the network.

Deriving Bandwidth

When these fixed cells are used, another benefit is achieved. Using a cell concept, the user would transparently send cells interleaved across the network regardless of the amount of bandwidth needed.

Cell Sizes and Formats

The standard fixed cell size for ATM is 53 bytes (octets). This comprises 5 bytes of overhead for activities such as addressing, and 48 bytes of payload. The cell is shown in Fig. 11.12. The 48-byte payload will be a variable, depending on the information and control necessary. There are several types of cells used that could take 4 bytes of the 48 away for control, leaving the user 44 bytes of effective data; another option gives the user all 48 bytes of payload for data. It depends on the implementation and the service run on ATM. Either way, the cell is still fixed at 53 bytes long. The cell is broken down as follows. Five bytes of overhead are shown in Fig. 11.13.

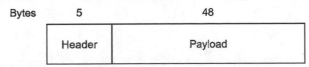

Figure 11.12 The ATM cell consists of 5 bytes of header and 48 bytes of payload.

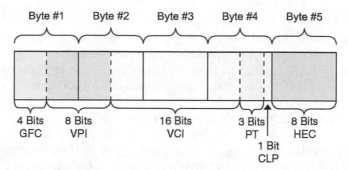

Figure 11.13 The overhead uses 5 bytes to keep addressing in order.

General Flow Control Identifier

The first 4 bits of byte number 1 contain what is known as a *general flow control identifier* (GFC). This is used to control the flow of traffic across the user-to-network interface (UNI) out to the network. This is only used at the user interface, because once the cell goes onto the network-to-network interface (NNI) that is between network nodes, these extra 4 bits will be reassigned for network addressing. The GFC is only used at the entry to the ATM backbone network between the user device and the rest of the network.

Virtual Path Identifier

The next 8 bits of the header are called the *virtual path identifier* (VPI). A VPI is part of the network address. A virtual path is a grouping of channels between network nodes.

Virtual Channel Identifier

The virtual channel identifier (VCI) is a pointer on which channel (virtual) the system is using on the path. The combination of the virtual path and virtual channel make up the data link running between two network nodes. The VCI is 16 bits long, using the second 4 bits of byte 2, all 8 bits of byte 3, and first 4 bits of byte 4.

Payload Type

Three bits in byte 4 are allocated to define the payload type (PT), which indicates the type of information contained in the cell. Because these cells will be used for transporting different types of information, the network equipment might have to handle it differently.

Cell-Loss Priority

Bit number 8 of byte number 4 is a cell-loss priority (CLP) bit. The user can define whether or not to discard the cell if congestion occurs on the network. If congestion occurs and the bit is set to 1 by the user, the network can discard the cell. If the bit is set to 0, then the cell may not be discarded.

Header Error Control

The 5th byte of the overhead is used as a header error control (HEC). This is an error-correcting byte that is conducted on the first 4 bytes of the header. It is used to correct single-bit errors and detect multiple errors in the header information. If a single-bit error occurs, the HEC will correct it. However, if multiple errors occur in the header, it will discard the cell so that cells will not be routed to the wrong address because of errors occurring on the network. The HEC only looks at the header information; it does not concern itself with the user data contained in the next 48 bytes.

The Cell Format for User Data

Once the header is completed, the user information is then inserted, as seen in Fig. 11.14. The user field is either 44 or 48 bytes of information, depending on the process used. Here's how this works.

The Adaptation Layer

Called the ATM adaptation layer (AAL), this is probably the most significant part of ATM. The adaptation layer provides the flexibility of a single communications process to carry multiple types of traffic such as data, voice, video, and multimedia.

Each type of traffic has varying needs. Voice needs constant data traffic; LAN is bursty in nature; video is time sensitive; data transfers from host to host can be delayed without a problem. It is in this adaptation process that the network can deal freely with varying types of information and only route cells on the basis of the routing information in the header.

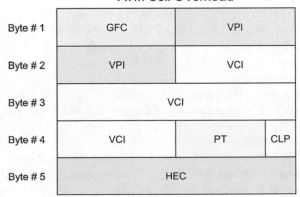

Figure 11.14   The ATM header is shown here.

TABLE 11.1   Summary of the Five Different Adaptation Types

Type	Name	Description
1.	Constant-bit-rate services	Allows ATM to handle voice services at DS0, DS1, and DS3 levels. Recovers timing and clocking for voice services.
2.	Variable-bit-rate (VBR) time-sensitive services	Not finalized but reserved for data transmissions that are synchronized. Also will address packet mode video in a compressed mode using bursty data transmission.
3.	Connection-oriented VBR data transfer	Bursty data generated across the network between two users on a prearranged connection. Large file transfers fall into this category.
4.	Connectionless VBR transfer	Transmission of data without a prearranged connection. Suitable for LAN traffic that is bursty and short. Same reasoning as X.25 where dial-up connection and setup take longer than data transfer.
5.	Simple and efficient adaptation layer	Improved type 3 for data transfer where higher-level protocols can handle data and error recovery. Uses all 48 bytes as data transmission and handles message transfer as sequenced packets.

Just about any type of transmission will require more than a single cell of information (48 bytes), so the ATM adaptation layer divides the information into smaller segments that are capable of being inserted into cells for transport between two end nodes. Depending on the type of traffic, the adaptation layer functions in one of five ways. These are shown in Table 11.1, with various types of information and adaptation layers involved.

The Adaptation Layer Process

The AAL is broken down into two sublayers; first is the convergence sublayer, the second is the segmentation and reassembly sublayer (SAR). The purpose of the process is to break the data down into the 48-byte payloads, yet maintain data integrity and pointers for ID purposes. This process of two sublayers produces a protocol data unit (PDU). The convergence sublayer PDU is of a variable length that is determined by the AAL type and the length of the higher-layer data passed to it. The SAR-PDU is always kept at 48 bytes to fill an ATM cell data stream. This is shown in Fig. 11.15 as it goes through the process.

As the user data, which can be multimegabyte files, is passed down to the convergence sublayer (CS) process, the data is broken down into variable block lengths. A maximum of 64 Kbytes is used in this process. The large user file is broken down into the 64-Kbyte segments. A header and trailer describing the type and size of the CS-PDU are added. This is then passed on to the next sublayer process.

The SAR then receives the CS-PDU and breaks it down into 44-byte cells (if less than 44 bytes, the rest is padded). Additional overhead (2 bytes of header and 2 bytes of trailer)

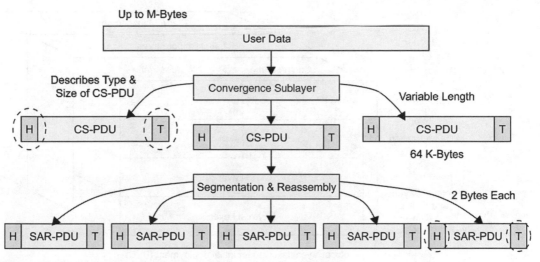

Figure 11.15   Once the header is computed, the payload is attached.

is added to the SAR-PDU. The simple and efficient adaptation layer instead uses all 48 bytes for user information, and therefore uses the bandwidth more efficiently.

Finally, the PDU is then inserted into an ATM cell with the 5-byte header. Following this, the cell is handed down to the physical cable system.

ATM Standards Protocols

ITU recommended that ATM be used in worldwide broadband networks. The first standards were produced in the mid-1980s and provided a basic outline of the service. These recommendations specify ATM among the protocol suites at the lower layers of the OSI reference mode. Most ATM standards were already specified by the international ITU committee.

The B-ISDN protocol reference model shown in Fig. 11.16 is defined in CCITT Recommendation I.121 into multiple planes:

- *The U plane*: The *user plane* provides for the transfer of user application information. It contains the physical layer, the ATM layer, and multiple ATM adaptation layers required for different service users (e.g., continues bit rate and variable bit rate service).

- *The C plane*: The *control plane* protocols deal with call establishment and release and other connection control functions necessary to provide switched service. The C plane shares the physical and ATM layers with the U plane. It also includes the ATM adaptation layer procedures and higher-layer signaling protocols.

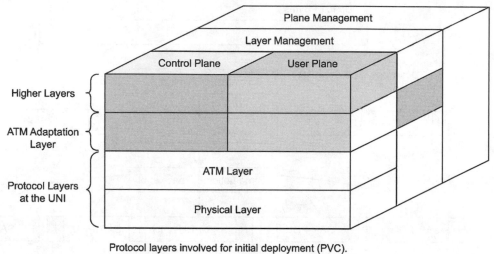

Figure 11.16   The adaptation process goes through two steps to produce the ATM payload.

- *The M plane*: The *management plane* provides management functions and the capability of exchanging information between the U and C planes. The M plane contains two sections: layer management, which performs layer specific management functions, and plane management, which performs management and coordination functions related to the complete system.

ANSI

The ANSI subcommittees active in broadband network standards are T1X1 and T1M1. T1X1 plays a role in SONET rates and format specification, and T1M1 guides the effort to define the standard for operations, administration and maintenance, and provisioning (OAM&P).

The physical-media-dependent (PMD) sublayer deals with aspects that are dependent on the transmission medium selected. The PMD sublayer specifies physical medium and transmission (e.g., timing, line coding) characteristics and does not include framing and overhead information. Physical characteristics of the UNI at the user, subscriber, and terminal interface for broadband services (U_B, T_B, and S_B, respectively) reference points are defined in ANSI T1E1 2/92-020 and shown in Fig. 11.17. The transmission convergence (TC) sublayer specification deals with physical layer aspects that are independent of the transmission medium specifications. B-ISDN-independent TC sublayer functions and procedures involved at the UNI are defined in ANSI T1.105-1991 and T1E1-2/92-020.

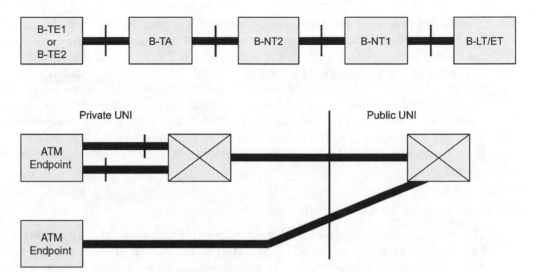

Figure 11.17   The physical access reference points of the UNI developed by ANSI and CCITT (ANSI).

ATM Forum

The ATM Forum is an international consortium of members that is chartered to accelerate the acceptance of ATM products and services in local, metropolitan, and wide-area networks. Although it is not an official standards body, the Forum works with the official ATM standards groups to ensure interoperability among ATM systems. The consortium accelerates ATM adoption through the development of common implementation specifications. The Forum's first specification on the ATM user-network interface (UNI) provided an important platform on which vendors can design and build equipment. The UNI defines the interface between a router or a workstation and a private ATM switch, or between the private ATM switch and a public ATM switch.

In 2004, the ATM Forum merged with the combination of the Frame Relay Forum and the Multiprotocol Label Switching (MPLS) Forum. The new name of this organization is now the MFA Alliance. Through this joint relationship, the MFA Alliance fosters and promotes the acceptance and use of frame relay and ATM interworking with MPLS/IP converged networks.

Public Switches

The public network ATM switch is a larger, more intelligent version of the customer premises switch. A public switch is capable of handling hundreds of thousands of cells per second and has thousands of switch ports, each operating at rates of 622 Mbps and beyond. All cell processing functions are performed by the input controllers, the switch fabric, and the output controllers. In an ATM switch, cell arrivals are not scheduled.

The control processor resolves contention when it occurs, as well as call setup and tear-down, bandwidth reservation, maintenance, and management. The input controllers are synchronized so that cells arrive at the switch fabric with their headers aligned.

The resulting traffic is said to be *slotted,* and the time to transmit a cell across the switch fabric is called a *time slot.* All VCIs are translated in the input controllers. Each incoming VCI is funneled into the proper output port as defined in a routing table. At the output controllers, the cells are formatted in the proper transmission format. For example, a broadband ISDN output controller provides an interface that consists of a line terminator to handle the physical transmission and an exchange terminator for cell processing.

ATM and Frame Relay Compared

The network interworking function provides the transport of frame relay user traffic transparently across the ATM link. It also handles the PVC signaling traffic over ATM. As already discussed, this is sometimes called *tunneling through the network.* Other times it is called *encapsulating the traffic.* Regardless of the name it is given, the function provides for the transparent movement of end-user frame relay information across the ATM network. The benefit is that with the tunneling or encapsulation formatting, the service is as good as though the end-user had a leased line service between the two end points. The benefit of this tunneling approach is connecting two frame relay networks across an ATM backbone. This is shown through the use of the network interworking unit in Fig. 11.18. The interworking function is shown as a sepa-

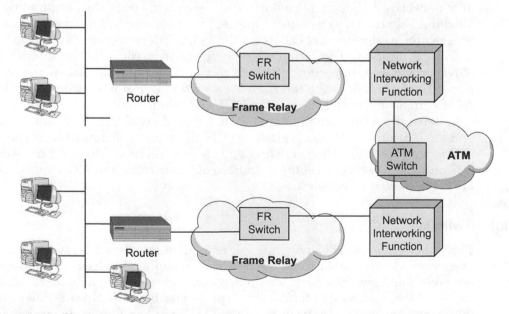

Figure 11.18   The network interworking function.

rate piece of equipment between the frame relay and ATM networks, and in some cases it is just that. However, newer implementations place this function inside an ATM switch. Regardless of where it resides, it is the functionality that is really important, not the location of the box. The interworking function will allow for each frame relay PVC connection to be mapped on a one-to-one basis over an ATM PVC. In other cases, frame relay PVCs can be bundled together across a single higher-speed ATM PVC. The one-to-one or one-to-many services allow more flexibility.

Service Interworking Functions

The use of a service interworking function (IWF) takes away some of the flexibility and transparency across the network. It actually acts more like a gateway (protocol converter) to facilitate the connection and communications between different disparate pieces of equipment. Figure 11.19 is a representation of the interconnection of the service interworking devices across the network. The end user actually sends traffic out across a frame relay network on its own PVC; then it gets passed through the frame relay network to the service interworking function, where the data is then mapped to an ATM PVC. The IWF functionality provides the mapping of the data link control identifier (DLCI) to the VPI/VCI, as well as other optional features. The IWF is shown as a separate box, whereas newer implementations will have the dual mode functionality inside an ATM switch.

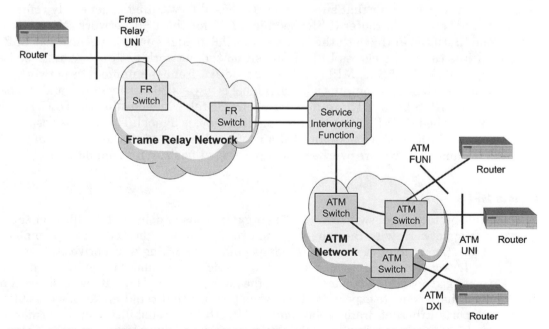

Figure 11.19   Frame/ATM service interworking function.

Frame relay and ATM can interwork and interoperate through several different techniques. This allows the carrier a sense of comfort, knowing that the legacy systems of the past can still be accommodated. The frame relay investments made in the early 1990s are still viable, and the ATM investments will be around for some time to come. Through the ATM protocols such as FUNI, end users have the comfort of knowing their networks are not obsolete. One can now see why the networking and service interworking functions are so important.

MPLS

If one were to listen to every trade magazine and every prophet in telecommunications, the logical conclusion drawn by these people is that ATM and frame relay are dead! Wow, we missed the funeral. But wait; if frame and ATM are dead, what has replaced them? The answer is MPLS, just ask the press.

MPLS is an offshoot of much of the work done on the ATM and Frame Relay Forums. Frame relay and ATM are both layer 2 technologies based on permanent virtual circuits. Network organizations typically terminate these PVCs in an IP router. This approach is complex, because it requires mapping between two architectures designed for fundamentally different functions.

MPLS reduces network complexity in part because MPLS integrates both layer 2 switching and layer 3 routing in a single, uniform, standards-based protocol hierarchy. It deals with a label switching concept of packet forwarding. Using routers and switches across the network, we can now deal more effectively with our layer 3 protocols (IP). A router that supports MPLS-based forwarding is generally referred to as a label-switching router (LSR).See Fig. 11.20 for the LSR network. Normally we call the first LSR in the path the ingress LER (label edge router), and the last LSR in the path is called the egress LER. LSRs sit on the network path between these two and are called core LSRs. MPLS as one can derive from the name is a network protocol where each packet contains a label. A label is always 20 bits in length and is a part of a 32-bit MPLS header. This differs from a frame relay label (called the DLCI) or an ATM label (called the VPI/VCI), but then again a label is a label. The label is assigned at the ingress LSR. Just what we needed a new label on top of all the ones we already have. This amounts to more overhead on a per packet basis. Why then do we need it?

What is MPLS

Multiprotocol label switching enables organizations to deliver IP traffic over the shared, public network with the reliability and security of a dedicated point-to-point network connection making it an increasingly popular networking alternative. As organizations are trying to manage the demands of their voice, video, and data networks into a single converged network, while maintaining the high quality and low latency delivery that their users have come to expect, MPLS is one approach that could make this possible. MPLS supports Ethernet, frame relay, and ATM with high reliability and performance while simultaneously offering the scalability necessary to deliver layer 3 services such as IP.

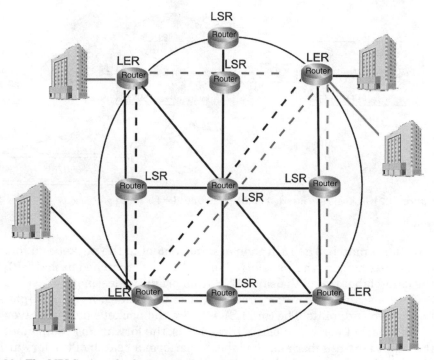

Figure 11.20   The MPLS network of routers includes LER and LSR.

MPLS is a fast-path routing technology (not to be confused with fast packet), where the router makes a forwarding decision on a packet based on a label included in the packet. A forward equivalence class (FEC) is assigned to each packet defining the priority and routing with which it will be handled. The first router to apply an MPLS label to a packet is known as the label edge router (LER). The packet traverses a label switch path (LSP) hopping between label switch routers (LSR) with the forwarding decisions based on the labels they see. The MPLS label is a 32-bit number inserted between the link layer and network layer sections of a packet. An example of a label being added to the network is seen in Fig. 11.21. This is a representation of an envelope being moved across a network, the label is what creates the fast packet routing.

The forwarding function of a WAN is responsible for transporting a packet across the network, based on the information found in a routing table. The WAN control function is responsible for the construction and maintenance of the routing table, as well as for communicating routing information to other nodes. One of the key attributes of MPLS is that it separates the forwarding and control functions. The separation of these two functions allows each function to be independent of the other.

The MPLS control function uses a standard routing protocol such as OSPF to create and maintain a forwarding table. When a packet arrives at an LER, the forwarding function uses information contained in the packet's header to search the forwarding

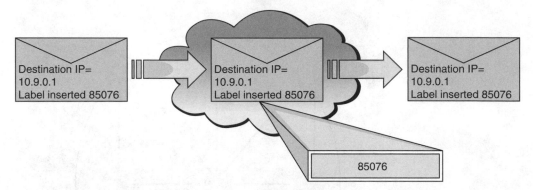

Figure 11.21 Labels are inserted in the packet header for routing decisions.

table for a match. The LER then assigns a label to the packet and forwards the packet to the next hop, in what is referred to as the label-switched path (LSP). All packets with the same label travel the same LSP from origin to destination.

Unlike standard routing protocols, it is possible to have multiple active paths between two endpoints. The core LSRs ignore the packet's network layer header. Instead, when a packet arrives at one of these LSRs, the forwarding component in the LSR uses the input port number and the label to perform a search of the forwarding table. When a match is determined, the forwarding component replaces the label and directs the packet to the outbound interface for transmission to the next hop in the LSP.

Frame Relay and ATM Networks

Frame relay and ATM encapsulations are typically found in WAN-MPLS networks and are often deployed over T3/E3 or OC-3/OC-12 circuits in central sites and in T1/E1 or T3/E3 physical connections at remote offices. When frame relay and ATM are running over MPLS, the packet labeling and/or security services, such as encryption and VPNs (virtual private networks), characteristic of MPLS networks, may mask the application layer details of the traffic over the segments. The challenge now is how to consolidate these multiple networks into a common infrastructure in order to reduce complexity and cost, but also to increase flexibility. Infrastructure technologies like ATM, frame relay, IP, and MPLS co-exist in the service provider infrastructure and are expected to continue to do so for some time yet, which makes the question of how best to internetwork these technologies extremely important. Of course, by some definitions we have convergence today with networks typically sharing the long haul transit at the optical layer. But above the "bit shifting" layer it is typical to have multiple service (or technology-specific) overlays. So, convergence is not just about convergence at a bit transport layer (layer 1)—it is about convergence at layer 2, layer 3, and even above.

This means that service providers will want to sell/market an IP service rather than the underlying ATM or FR service that the IP service may depend on. What the customer gets may be FR- or ATM-based service but packaged as part of an IP service offering.

But the carriers have to go where the money is, and one should know that future networks will be ROI based. The chart in Fig. 11.22 shows the 2005 revenue in the United States based on carrier revenues for the various services they offer.

The money includes that shown in Table 11.2. One can still see that despite all the efforts of the carriers to implement newer packet technologies and/or now the use of IP enabled services with MPLS, the real money still lies in private lines, followed closely by the use of frame relay. One can expect these numbers to change over time, but the MPLS technologies and uses are still in their infancy of evolution. Trying to come up with various new technologies always puts the carriers at risk that they will invest heavily and possibly make a wrong decision. Change happens slowly in the telecommunications industry. The table below is a classic view of that reluctance to make a change until the technology has been tested and proven by years of innovations.

TABLE 11.2   Summary of Revenue for Carriers in 2005

Item	Revenue
Private lines	$11.9 B
Frame relay	$8.9 B
ATM	$3.5 B
Dedicated IP VPN	$2.5 B
Ethernet services	$0.8 B
Other	$3.4
Total	$31

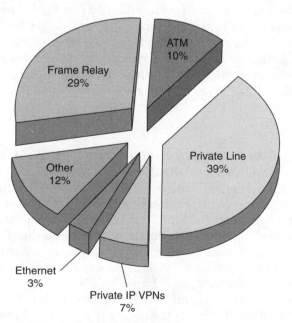

Figure 11.22 The revenue still lies in the older technologies.

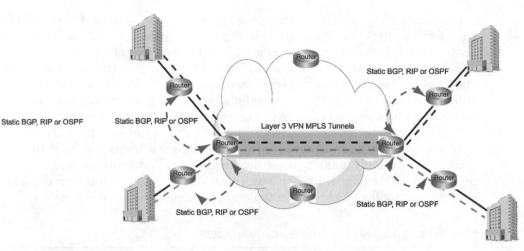

Figure 11.23   Layer 3 VPNs and MPLS.

Layer 3 VPNs

The implementation of L3 MPLS-based VPNs is typically based on IETF RFC 2547 bis. This class of VPN transports traffic across the network through the use of MPLS tunnels and multiprotocol border gateway protocol (MP-BGP) signaling. BB refers to a backbone router that is running MPLS, while BO refers to a branch office router that is not running MPLS. This is the most common way that MPLS-based VPNs are currently deployed. However, an enterprise could also run MPLS in their branch office routers to extend its benefits to the network endpoints. Also note that each BB has a routing instance per VPN, known as a VRF. Two of the advantages of MPLS-based L3 VPNs are that they are standards-based and easy to provision. This type of VPN also supports a wide range of access types and a variety of topologies, including full mesh, partial mesh, and hub and spoke. A layer 3 VPN is shown in Fig. 11.23.

Layer 2 VPNs

L2 VPNs, such as ones based on frame relay and ATM, are extremely common and are inherently multiprotocol. Realizing the importance of L2 VPNs, the IETF L2VPN working group has defined both encapsulation and label-distribution mechanisms that enable transporting non-IP protocols across an MPLS core network. Due to the multi-protocol nature of L2 VPNs, an L2 MPLS-based VPN presents an easy transition step for organizations that currently run legacy protocols, but intend to migrate to an all-IP network over time. For example, a network organization can set up an L2 VPN to transport legacy protocols such as IPX or SNA over the core MPLS network, without having to encapsulate them inside of IP. Layer 2 VPN is shown in Fig. 11.24.

One of the key features of an L2 MPLS-based VPN is the ability to create a tunnel as an LSP. Another key feature is the ability to use control protocols such as MPLS's label distribution protocol (LDP) or BGP to set up emulated virtual circuits.

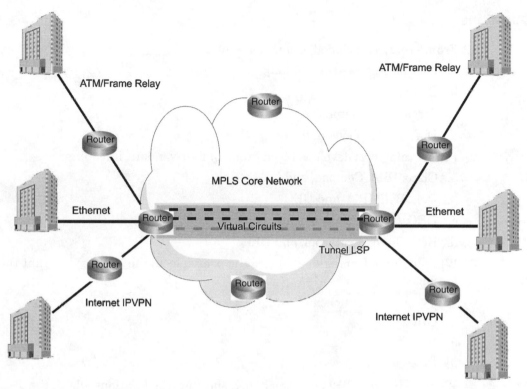

Figure 11.24   Layer 2 VPN and MPLS.

MPLS Traffic Engineering

MPLS traffic engineering (MPLS-TE) sets up label-switched paths (LSPs) along links with available resources, thus ensuring that bandwidth is always available for a particular flow and avoiding congestion both in the steady state and in failure scenarios. Because LSPs are established only where resources are available, overprovisioning is not necessary.

Further optimization of transmission resources is achieved by allowing LSPs not to follow the shortest path, if the available resources along the shortest path are not sufficient. An added benefit of MPLS is that built-in mechanisms such as link protection and fast reroute provide resilience in the face of failure. The catch is that MPLS-TE is oblivious of the class of service (CoS) classification, operating on the available bandwidth at an aggregate level across all classes.

One can see that there is a lot of potential with MPLS in the future, and with time it will displace many of the leased lines and frame relay networks. We believe that ATM and MPLS will be the core network for the near future in what is called the *next generation network.*

Questions

1. Frame relay is included as a member of the _____.
   a. Fast packet switching family
   b. Cell relay family
   c. Circuit relay family
   d. Dial-up telephone network

2. Frame relay was developed by a group of four vendors, inlcuding:
   a. Cisco, IBM, Compaq, and NT
   b. Dell, Bell, IBM, and DEC
   c. DEC, Cisco, Stratacom, and NT
   d. Bell, Cisco, Stratacom, and DEC

3. When using a frame relay service the user selects the_____that they need for speed.
   a. Bc
   b. CIR
   c. Br
   d. Be

4. When using the CIR a customer then specifies the locations where the_____ is logically connected.
   a. SVC
   b. PVC
   c. SNA
   d. TCP

5. The address is called the_____.
   a. IP address
   b. SNA address
   c. Data link connection identifier
   d. Logical channel number

6. The traffic congestion notifications are called the_____.
   a. FECE and BECE
   b. FEBC and REBC
   c. FEA and BEA
   d. FECN and BECN

7. When designing a network between 10 sites, how many links are needed into the cloud?

   a. 9

   b. 10

   c. 90

   d. 100

8. When the variable payload was initially introduced it contained up to_____ bytes.

   a. 2096

   b. 1610

   c. 1518

   d. 4048

9. Frame relay was designed to operate in the_____.

   a. LAN

   b. MAN

   c. WAN

   d. CAN

10. What does ATM stand for?

    a. Automated Teller Machine

    b. Adode Type Manager

    c. Asynchronous Transfer Mode

    d. Asymmetrical Transfer Mode

11. ATM operates at the layer 3 of the OSI model.   T/F

12. The layer sitting on top of ATM provides for convergence of the data is called:

    a. IP

    b. ATMCS

    c. ACP

    d. AAL

13. One of the ATM speeds supported is:

    a. 175 Mbps

    b. 622 Mbps

    c. 1.9 Gbps

    d. 2.048 Gbps

14. ATM uses a cell payload that is_____.
   a. 53 bytes
   b. 44 bytes
   c. 46 bytes
   d. 48 bytes

15. The cell header is_____bytes long.
   a. 48
   b. 5
   c. 53
   d. 44

16. The complete address of a cell is called the_____.
   a. VPP/VCI
   b. VPI/VCC
   c. VPI/VCI
   d. VPP/VCI

17. ATM is a connection-oriented service.   T/F

18. There are_____different forms of AAL.
   a. 3
   b. 4
   c. 5
   d. 6

19. MPLS is a fast packet routing system.   T/F

20. The label is an address.   T/F

21. If one were to want security with MPLS, the the use of a_____
   is recommended.
   a. DLCI tunnel
   b. ATM tunnel
   c. VPI/VCI
   d. VPN

22. MPLS has literally run away with all the revenue.   T/F

12

The Internet

After reading this chapter and completing the questions, you will be able to:

- Discuss the history of the Internet, describing factors that influenced its formulation and progression
- Explain the technologies that lead to the development of Mosaic
- Define the HTTP protocol and World Wide Web
- Describe the function of an ISP (point of presence)
- Explain what applications are shaping the Internet traffic of tomorrow

In the twentieth century the communications world changed forever through the birth of a revolutionary new network. Advances in computers and communications allowed a pairing of the technologies, providing a means of sharing the vast amounts of information compiled all over the world by providing it to almost anyone, with a simple click of the mouse. This invention we all know as the Internet. The Internet is an invention that began worldwide acceptance in the late 1980s and commercialized in 1995 already has over a billion users.

The Internet is a social as well as a technological phenomenon. A huge number of people otherwise unfamiliar with data processing have nonetheless gone out and bought computers, modems, cable modems, or xDSL technologies, and other required paraphernalia. Then, they proceeded to hook up to and actually use a resource based on technologies that, if asked about, they could describe in only the most general terms, if at all.

With some qualifications, the Internet ultimately may be one of the few innovations that actually justifies the hype associated with it. Often described as a "network of networks" or the "information superhighway," it provides a path to incredible amounts of information, much of it free for the taking (free if you don't count the basic network access costs).

A Little History

In U.S. history the 1950s and 1960s invoke images of the Cold War. Today many young people can't totally appreciate the battle between the axis of good and evil. The truth of the situation is that the U.S. government and the former Soviet Union were engaged in a strategic battle over the world. The threat of war was real and life evolved around this struggle.

In 1957 an organization of the U.S. government called the Defense Advanced Research Projects Agency (DARPA) was created in response to advances in the Soviet Union's launch of a space satellite. DARPA's specific goals were to "direct and perform advance projects in the field of research, designated by individual project or category."

DARPA realized, in order to gain superiority in the technology arena, that information from key government research laboratories, and a few universities under contract to the government for various research projects, needed to be shared from these geographically diverse locations. In addition to information, advances in computers allowed raw computing power to be shared as well. The idea of creating a network to accomplish this goal was conceived, and the idea of the DARPAnet was born. The Department of Defense funded this idea with a $20,000 grant.

The DARPA agency is the central research and development agency within the Department of Defense. DARPA has had a change of its name four times in the last century. Originally named ARPA, and then changed to DARPA in 1972, redesignated to ARPA in 1993 and changed to DARPA yet again in 1996. For continuity and research purposes, we will call it DARPA through this book as it reflects the current name of this organization.

DARPA is still very active in the pursuit of technological innovation on advanced research and technologies. You can view some of these initiatives by visiting the DARPA web site located at www.darpa.mil.

At approximately the same time, the U.S. Air Force was contracting researchers to make the nation's telecommunications infrastructure capable of surviving a nuclear attack. One researcher in particular, from the RAND Corporation, Paul Baran, theorized a distributed telecommunications network, where information could flow to the proper destination even if some links in the network were incapacitated or removed. This idea, created what is now known as packet switching. In simplest form packet switching involves breaking up information into smaller more manageable pieces and then routing them to a destination. In Chapter 10, we discussed the TCP/IP protocols that make the Internet work.

In 1965, this technology debuted its first test when MIT's Lincoln Lab connected with DARPA's facilities on a 1200 bps connection. Within four years sites in Stanford Research Institute, University of California Santa Barbara, University of California Los Angeles, and University of Utah were connected forming the DARPAnet. The predecessor of the Internet as we know it today was on line.

Universities

With universities receiving government grants for research, it was only logical that they were added to the DARPAnet. The researchers could now share their results with other research groups working on similar advances in technology. Over time, additional universities, companies dealing with the government, shown in Fig. 12.1, and even some overseas institutions were added, making this an international network.

The bandwidths connecting all these institutions were continuously increased to support all kinds of communications. In reality, the Internet (as we now know it) started out as a 56-Kbps data communications network used to connect these sites together. Although this was an enabling speed, bandwidth was utilized quickly, so multiple 56-Kbps lines were used. Over the years, telecommunication technology advanced, and costs came down which made it feasible to lease T1 lines to connect locations. Not only did this provide more bandwidth to the sites, the quality of transmission over these dedicated facilities made the communication more reliable.

With the increased speeds, demand rose from the private sector to connect to this network. In 1991, the Internet was opened to commercial use and the National Science Foundation began transitioning the DARPAnet into the Internet. With more users on the network, further demand began putting stress on these T1 connections, so the NSF began converting the backbone of the network to T3 lines running at 45 Mbps. This was fine for the government network, but as the private sector gained access it would be too slow and become unusable—therefore the backbone network was upgraded again to a newer faster technology called ATM.

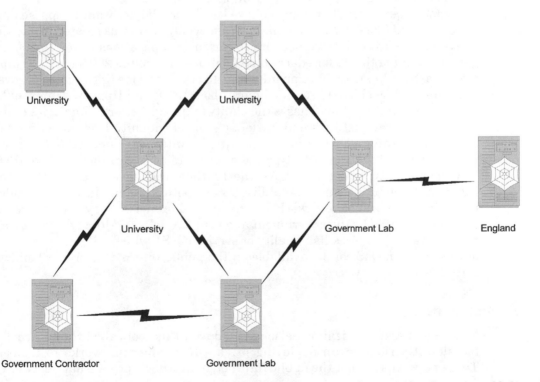

Figure 12.1 The Internet began growing as universities, contractors, and overseas locations were added.

Growth exploded on the Internet during the 1990s with most users connecting to the backbone with dial-up 56K connections. The dot.com businesses began springing up and the Internet quickly became crowded. This was to the lament of the universities and research facilities that have always been connected to a network that was designed for *them*. The academia groups began complaining to the government that their network was too slow to support their applications and wanted something done about it. Since the 1996 Telecom Act, the Internet was to be an unregulated environment, therefore the government had no authority—administration was already in the private sector. This didn't make the universities happy so they pressured the government to do more.

Internet 2

The government had a solution to get by the congestion on the Internet, and in typical government form suggested a separate network for universities and research institutions which would be called I2 (Internet 2) or the Abilene network. This is amazing because the universities never invested and paid for the original Internet; it was a government sponsored project that provided them access. Why should the universities get a private network for free, when they benefit most from research that turns into commercial projects? After all most of the software and hardware that made the Internet work more efficient, came from private businesses (who usually provide their technology at a reduced price to education institutions).

No one is quite sure, but many believe legislators did not want to oppose any legislation that would "benefit" education. In either event, the I2 was created to allow universities to have a less congested network to run their applications faster. In 2000, work began on planning this I2 for educational facilities. As of June 2004, over 240 universities and a partnership with 70 companies and 40 organizations (including the government) are connected. Feel free to research more about the I2 at http://www.internet2.edu.

The one advantage the I2 has is the ability to try out newer technologies and beta test them on a private network and work out some of the initial issues; without crippling the Internet. After all, who could work with the Internet crippled due to a new product rollout? The I2 is currently testing the newer version of Internet protocol IPv6.

Although universities now have the I2, they still have free access to the public Internet. Their users have the ability to use both systems. In reality academia has been given the best of both worlds by having a dual network system to use. Again, all of this is financed by the government and your tax dollars. Although the I2 claims they have newer capabilities like quality of service (QoS), which will be covered at the end of this chapter, QoS can be available on the public Internet (if proper bandwidth and software are employed).

Private Internets

Many business organizations also realized that this tool called the Internet also was too slow. Carriers began deploying private IP enabled networks to transmit data. These networks are not the public Internet, but rather a private data network running

IP protocols. Examples of these networks are IP enabled frame relay networks. Many of these networks provide interface to the public Internet, but filter packets inbound making them inaccessible to the average Internet user. Private networks have been deployed worldwide by the large carriers and can offer guaranteed response time on their networks (<60 ms is common). Private Internets will continue to grow in popularity as Voice over the Internet Protocol (VoIP) becomes more accepted.

Internet is a term that refers to the public Internet; there are also private versions of Internets called *Intranets*. An Intranet is a private company's Web pages and databases that provide access to their channel partners and sometimes customers. Intranets are vital in the business-to-business (B2B) supply model. Intranets often are virtual private networks, meaning they provide the selected users with various pieces of information depending on accessibility levels, e.g., an employee working from home would have access to database files, but a customer might only have limited access to product support pages.

Early Internet Services

We're going to get a little technical here for a moment. TCP/IP was defined in Chapter 10. Recall that TCP/IP is a collection of protocols. The base protocols described by the letters TCP/IP refer to the lower three or four layers of the OSI model. Some layer 7 protocols ride on top of TCP/IP. Among these are Telnet, file transfer protocol (FTP), simple mail transfer protocol (SMTP), and simple network management protocol (SNMP). Newer protocols like the real time protocols (RTP) and network time stamp protocols (NTP) ride at layer 7.

When you use a browser to access a list of files or updates to programs on a Web site, when you actually click on an icon or link to retrieve a file, there's a better-than-even chance that the file is being retrieved using FTP. FTP is not the protocol used for routine browser operations, but the major browsers do incorporate the capability of moving files around using FTP. FTP existed long before the World Wide Web. Most operating systems come with software that enables you to use FTP directly without using a browser. However, FTP typically has a command-line interface in such an environment. If you are comfortable with the C: prompt, then you might want to use FTP in cases where you have problems getting the browser to work properly. A few graphical user interface (GUI)-based FTP implementations are also stand-alones rather than integrated into a browser. This could be very useful in cases where you're going to spend some time doing nothing but retrieving files, for example, from a vendor's support site. We like to use an FTP client, like the one shown in Fig. 12.2 from Mozilla (freeware open source code). This screen shot shows the FTP client logging onto an FTP server.

SMTP

The service that was, and still is used most on the Internet is electronic mail (e-mail). Originally, it was much less sophisticated than the capabilities used today. In fact, most implementations of the time sent only the text of a message, the address of the

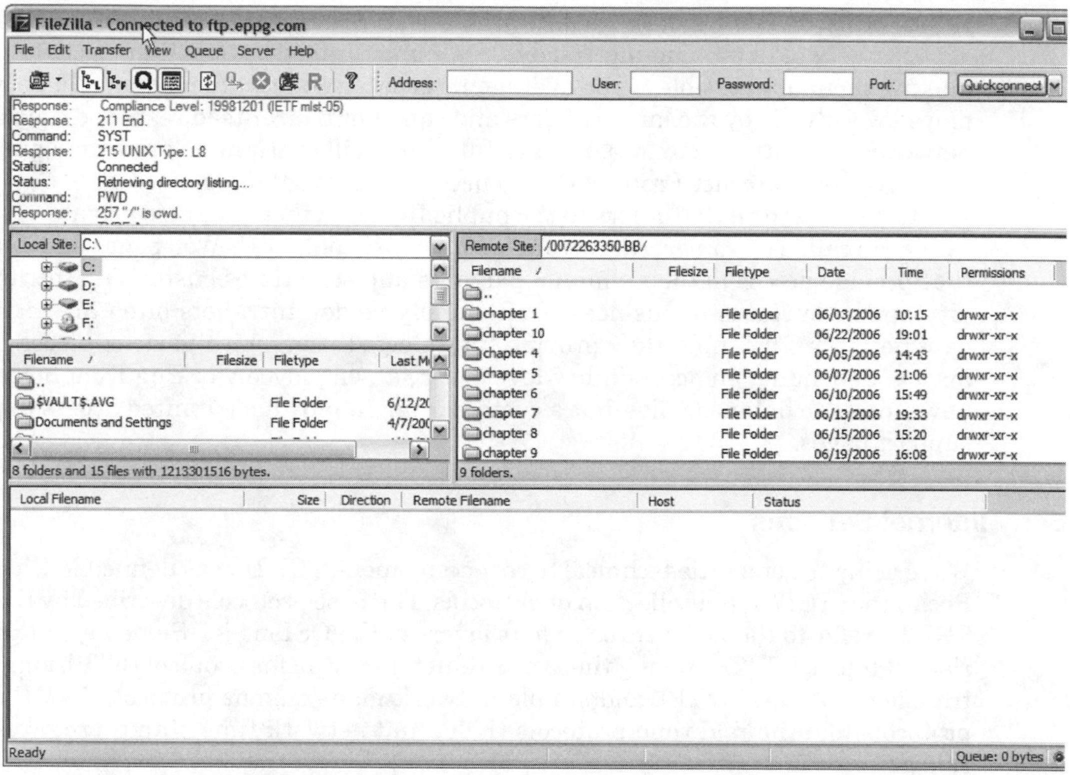

Figure 12.2 An FTP client using Mozilla's FileZilla.

recipient, and a text subject string with no attachments of any kind, no separate names of the addressees (versus just their addresses), and no copy-to's. This rudimentary form of e-mail enabled strictly the exchange of ASCII text to one person at a time.

Nevertheless, this mail capability was based on the same underlying protocol used for most mail on the Internet today: the SMTP. If one were to describe SMTP in terms of the OSI model, it is a layer 7 protocol. It rides on top of TCP/IP, as do other protocols mentioned later in this chapter, see Fig. 12.3.

The SMTP mail protocol was developed around an ASCII text transmission system. This poses an interesting situation when a user wants to transmit information to a colleague.

Has the following ever happened to you? You spend the whole day preparing a report. Great pains are taken to build a table with four columns of text. Background shading is applied in your word processor to highlight certain fields in the file. The headers on each of the columns are bolded and italicized in the word processing formatting service. Lastly, you lay this all out with reverse text for emphasis (white text on a black background for important fields, black text on white background for normal text). Eureka!

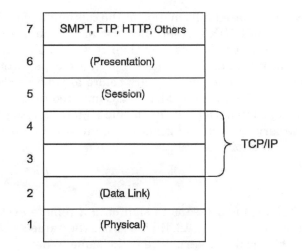

7	SMPT, FTP, HTTP, Others
6	(Presentation)
5	(Session)
4	
3	
2	(Data Link)
1	(Physical)

TCP/IP

Figure 12.3 The protocols used for the application sit on top of TCP.

You have finally finished the document. Now you want to e-mail it to your colleague for review and discussion. A few compliments are also expected for the fruits of your labor. So, you type up an e-mail message announcing your accomplishment, paste the document to the mail message, and let it fly through the Net. Soon you call your colleague and ask what he/she thinks about it. Alas, you are told it is garbage! No, the text is not garbage, but the format of the document that arrives is garbage. The formatting has all disappeared.

No longer is the table and column format intact. The bolding and shading have also disappeared. Moreover, the text is all over the place, indented where it shouldn't be, and so forth. You are crushed! What happened? After all that work, the other end thinks the document is trash. Well, let's analyze what happened.

Today, word processing systems use an extended ASCII code set. That means that an 8-bit code set is used to format the document in current packages. The Net, on the other hand, was built on a true ASCII code set (7-bit ASCII). As a result, when you transmit the document, the receiving device is looking at the 7 bits (not 8) and interpreting the information using a different language. The result is what shows up. To solve this problem, other protocols like file attachments (MIME and binary) are used in the mail programs on the market today. Relief at last!

Gopher and Finger

Several additional layer 7 applications were commonly used until the World Wide Web became popular, and are still probably used by those not enamored of the Web. Among these are the picturesquely named Gopher and Finger. Gopher is a text-based ancestor of the Web; a Gopher client, like a Web browser, jumps from Gopher site (server) to site retrieving text-based information at the command of its user. Finger is a method of identifying users of UNIX systems. Because most Web users don't have or need UNIX accounts, its usefulness is less now than it was in the past. Other search capabilities include Ph, WAIS, and Veronica. All of these capabilities and services were used by thousands of people for many years before anyone used the expression "the Web." Nevertheless, you should not feel left out. Compared to the Web, none of these capabilities were packaged in a user-friendly fashion. Moreover, the types of information available via these services were not generally of interest to typical users. After all, the *R* in ARPAnet did stand for research.

Telnet

Telnet (not Telenet) is a means to sign onto a remote system network directly as a user of that system, see Fig. 12.4. This is not the same as using the World Wide Web, although the physical infrastructure is the same. When you use a browser to access a Web page, every time you click on a link, you send a request for a specific set of information to a specific Web site. That Web site, if it can, sends back just the information you requested. Generally speaking, it then completely forgets it had anything to do with you. No "conversation" takes place: each exchange is a stand-alone transaction.

In the case of Telnet, however, you sign onto a remote machine. To do this, you have to have an account on that machine, although some machines, notably in university environments, may allow you to sign on anonymously or even create your own account. Usually, if you are trying to sign onto a system anonymously, you use the user ID "anonymous" and a password consisting of your complete e-mail address. The software normally does not check the latter; rather, it's just a courtesy and a convention that you comply with in order to get the free service that you're about to use. With the popularity of the Web, Telnet is not a facility you are likely to need on a regular basis. However, if a vendor gives you access to a system for some reason, you may need to access it using this approach. To use it, go to the prompt on your operating system and type Telnet

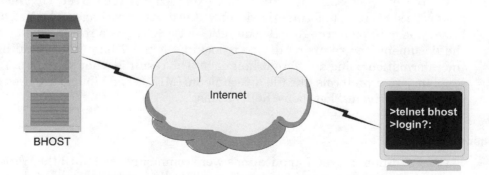

Figure 12.4   Telnet allows remote users to sign on to a system as if they were present locally.

[space] and the name of the system you wish to access. You can also tell Telnet a specific IP address of the form nnn.nnn.nnn.nnn. FTP can also be used to access a remote system in the same way, with the same address and convention.

Telnet enables signing onto a remote computer. SMTP stands for simple mail transfer protocol. You will probably not use this protocol explicitly; however, if you use Internet mail (for example, the mail that is provided as part of Netscape), then you are using the SMTP protocol. As mail protocols go, SMTP is pretty simple. This has caused some problems because it does not in and of itself incorporate ways to send attachments, particularly not binary or program-type attachments. However, a number of vendors have come together, built software, and established conventions that allow these capabilities.

Although among the least sophisticated mail environments in the world, SMTP mail is sort of taking over the world. Why? Because SMTP is built into pretty much all systems that use the Internet. It is the kind of mail that you get when you sign up with an Internet service provier (ISP).

The form of an SMTP or Internet mail address is *name@node.extension*. For example, the Internet mail address of one of the authors of this book is *bud@tcic.com*. Until recently, the list of extensions was very short: only about eight or so. Agreements have since been made that will probably significantly increase the number of suffixes. A whole structure of these is beyond the scope of this book.

One of the major successes in the area of intervendor cooperation was the creation of a couple of standards for including attachments with e-mail. The preferred one of these is called *multipurpose Internet mail extensions* (MIME). A MIME attachment can include just about anything that can be represented in digital form. Moreover, most of the more sophisticated e-mail software packages can automatically create MIME inclusions without users having to go through several steps. MIME extends the format of the Internet mail to allow non-U.S.-ASCII textual messages, nontextual messages, multipart message bodies, and non-U.S.-ASCII information in message headers.

Although SNMP protocol is integral to the management of the Internet, most users will never be involved with it because it is used by people operating the Internet rather than by end users. We will not go further into this topic in this book.

The World Wide Web (or is that world wide wait??) is just a virtual structure running on top of the basic Internet itself. All of the things that were there before the World Wide Web are still there; however, the vast majority of Internet users is not aware of them because the Web itself is so much easier to use. Browsers (and therefore the Web, which really just consists of browsers and Web sites talking back and forth) use a protocol called hypertext transfer protocol (HTTP). One of its key characteristics was mentioned earlier, but bears repeating: exchanges (or transactions) based on HTTP are "stateless." This means that unless special measures are taken, Web sites do not maintain true "conversations" with users of those Web sites.

Every time you access a Web site—that is, every time you get a page from a Web site—the Web site recognizes the request from you, responds to it, and forgets about it. You may be thinking, "But many Web sites that I interact with do seem to keep track of what's going on from one screen to the next."

You are correct; they have figured out ways to do this, but those ways don't use the basic HTTP capability; they use some additional capabilities that are built into browsers. The developers of the major browsers realized that this was a problem that had to be solved. What happens is that when a Web site wants to retain some contacts to an exchange, it causes the browser to create something called a *cookie* on the user's local disk drive, somewhere on a directory below the browser. Cookies can either be line entries in a file of cookies, or they can be one per file; Netscape maintains a file of cookies.

A cookie is just a sequence of information that the Web site places on the local disk to retain some information. It may have the user's name and ID, and possibly some information that the user filled in on a form on the Web site. One very common use of a cookie is to retain an ID and password that is granted to the user as part of the exchange with the Web site in order to allow the user to get into the Web site in the future without having to go through an elaborate sign-on procedure. Thus, cookies can be very beneficial to efficiency and user satisfaction. However, there has been a fair amount of concern that cookies can also be used to compromise the privacy of individuals. Some people do not want a Web site to retain information about them, especially without telling them about it. Discussions are under way to address this concern. By the time you read this, enhancements may be made to browsers that enable them to tell the user when information from a cookie is about to be used. In practice, we don't believe that users will make heavy use of this capability because it will really slow down accessing Web site services.

Archie

The next step in improving utility of the information on the Internet was the development of Archie, which was designed at McGill University in Canada. Archie essentially indexed FTP sites. The target machine had to run the Archie server, while your machine ran the Archie client. The good part was that the Archie server was accessible via an Archie client, e-mail, or Telnet. Archie was a great catalog on the Internet. Archie returned a list in UNIX language that gave you host and file names to use when you set up the FTP session. Archie was a step in the right direction of making the Internet easier to use, but you still needed to know how to use Telnet and FTP.

Gopher

Gopher was also a client-server system. It provided a menu of choices, and it allowed you to set up bookmarks of locations you liked. Like previous Internet accesses, it was designed around the user having a dumb ASCII terminal. Thus, it provided menus and minimalist keystrokes to make a selection. That was the good part. Unfortunately, the single keystrokes were not always intuitive. The intent was that you would launch the Gopher client from your own host and communicate with the Gopher server on the remote host. It was possible to Telnet to a remote host and then to launch Gopher, but this was painfully slow and created excessive network traffic. Remember that the interconnection of hosts was often with 56-Kbps lines.

Veronica

There was some speculation as to the source of this name, but most people think it was named after Archie's girlfriend. Others insist it stood for a very easy, rodent-oriented net-wide index to computer archives, but this is unlikely. Veronica is an extension to Gopher that facilitated searches and returned a list of hits (hits in this case were file names that matched the name in the original search request). Veronica was also a client-server arrangement, where the Veronica server keeps the database being searched.

By selecting one of the returned hits, you could get more information about it or transfer it back to your computer. Veronica, therefore, automated the FTP process, but was still dumb terminal and menu oriented.

WAIS

Wide area information service (WAIS) was another database search engine that allowed you to enter keywords and search a database for entries. Although the number of databases was large, finding this was still not easy because you were using Gopher to search WAIS.

Introduction to Mosaic and the WWW

Early Internet services required a certain user familiarity with the protocols previously mentioned. This turned off many prospective users who found the commands clumsy and difficult to execute. A "friendlier" interface was really needed to gain widespread acceptance and greater participation on the Internet. With the evolution in personal computing from DOS to Windows and the Mac platform, some inventors realized if a graphical user interface (GUI) could be applied to the Internet, it would overcome these frustrations. These developments lead to the development of Mosaic and the World Wide Web.

WWW

The World Wide Web (WWW) has essentially replaced all of these older search engine capabilities. The early WWW often resorted to Gopher or WAIS to actually do the transfer.

The two developments that made the WWW useful were browsers, hypertext, and hyperlinks. Hypertext was a way of encoding formatting information, including fonts, in a document while using plain ASCII characters. Hyperlinks were essentially addresses imbedded in the hypertext Web page. By selecting the hyperlink, you were taken directly to a new page.

Browsers

Browsers basically automated the searching on keyword function that we had done via menus using Gopher. Browsers today are very large and complex programs. Look on your hard drive, and you will find that the Netscape 7.2 application is about 26 megabytes. With each revision, it gets larger and more complex as new features are added.

Microsoft's browser was previously buried in the operating system, but now available as a stand-alone product, is around 12 megabytes in size.

Marc Andresen was instrumental in creating one of the first browsers called *Mosaic*. Mosaic became the foundation of Netscape's Navigator. Netscape's success can be attributed to the fact that it followed the AOL model of giving away the browser software for free. Netscape even gave away their source code to its browser on the theory that thousands of heads are better than a few, and eventually it will result in a better product. This same philosophy made Linux such a strong operating system for PC platforms. AOL later acquired Netscape, so what goes around comes around.

Browsers are also part of the client-server world. The money lies in getting the service providers to buy your suite of server software that provides the data to the browsers. This suite of software may provide many other features and capabilities such as calendar, proxy, LDAP, and mail servers as well.

Hypertext

In the UNIX world (where this entire Internet started), there were only two kinds of files:

1. ASCII text-based files that were all the documentation, source code, and configuration files.
2. Binary files that were the executable program files.

Unfortunately, no one considered fancy formatting, multiple fonts, graphics, and tables. ASCII text was boring in the modern world of animated color. The question became, how can we add this capability?

Individual vendors' products, such as Word (registered trademark of Microsoft), utilize proprietary code sets in which the font and size (for example) are imbedded. Other products, such as WordPerfect (registered trademark of Corel), chose to imbed special tag characters, indicating the beginning and end of special font and size groups of characters. Unfortunately, with special (non-ASCII) characters imbedded in the text, these were no longer text documents, but binary documents that could only be operated on by proprietary vendor-specific programs that were not universally available or free.

How then could we keep the documents on the Internet open, free, standardized, and comprised strictly of ASCII characters so that anyone could read them? How could we extend the capability without making the previous version obsolete? A major problem with a specific vendor's product was that when the new one came out, the older versions couldn't read the newer versions' formats. This was a major inconvenience, designed to force the users to upgrade to the latest version.

The solution was to go with the tag approach. Rather than using special characters as tags, we simply used a sequence of ASCII characters, which meant something specific to the browser and did not impair the ability of a dumb ASCII terminal to read them. For example, the tag <title>Important Subject</title> will cause the browser to display that line as a title. For the curious, you may view the source of a Web page and see all these tags. All you have to do is go to the *View* menu and select *Source*. You are then presented with all the original ASCII information. Although a little difficult to read because of all the tags, all the text is there as are all the references to other Web pages (HREF) and all the font and formatting information. While we are on the subject, you might try converting one of your text documents to Rich Text format. Here the formatting stuff is all in the beginning of the document—just another (standardized) way of sending formatting information in plain ASCII text format.

If you are using an older browser, it simply can't properly display the text within the new tag, but the text is still there, and you can read it. Fortunately, new versions of the browser are readily available and free for the downloading. Hypertext then allows the standard ASCII text characters to define special formatting which the browser can display.

Hyperlink

A hyperlink was simply a pointer to another Web page. It was the complete address to find the specified Web page. The link visible on the browser presented Web page might say something innocuous like "more info." If you viewed the source and searched for the HREF or the "more info," following the href will be the actual path to that page. Selecting the hyperlink caused a lot of background processing. The browser took the uniform resource locator (URL) and fabricated a query to that location just as though you had filled in that value manually in your browser Window. It then set up a connection, downloaded the desired page, and terminated the connection. A hyperlink would like the following:

<u>http://www.tcic.com</u>

The underline is an example of how the hyperlink might work. By holding the Control (CTL) key and clicking you mouse on the link, it will automatically launch your browser and go to the TCIC Web site (assuming of course that you do not have features turned off and/or that the firewall at your site is not blocking the access).

URL

URL was simply the Internet address of the Web page. URLs were displayed in this form *www.tcic.com*. This URL took you to TCIC's main Web page as seen in Fig. 12.5. Selecting a hyperlink from that page took you to a universal resource identifier (URI), which pointed to the files in the directory tree of the host server. Each slash (/) in the name identified a directory level on the server. In some cases where a document management system was employed to build and provide Web pages, these slashes were actually logical divisions within the resource and had nothing to do with actual directories. Today, the trend is to use dynamically built Web pages. They can be better customized (see the discussion on cookies) to the user's needs, you don't have to store thousands of different Web pages, and the processors are fast enough to create them quickly.

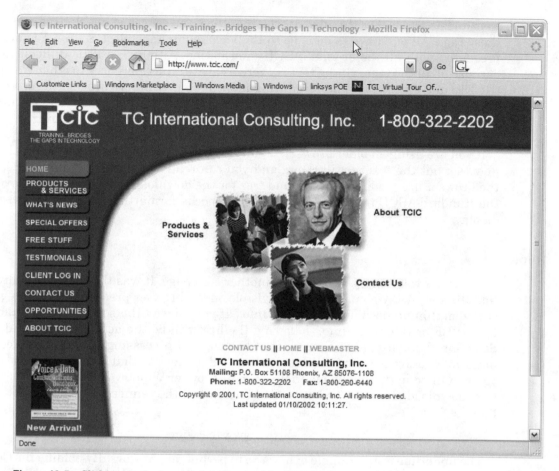

Figure 12.5 Clicking on the hyperlink took me to the URL for TCIC's Web page.

DNS

One of the most interesting and important parts of the Internet is the directory name service or the domain name service (DNS). In short, the DNS system permits human readable names to be quickly translated into IP addresses that are needed to route the packets across the network.

As is described in Chapter 10, the IP address is structured by network and then by host. It is read from left to right by the router in trying to find the proper destination network.

The human readable addresses are hierarchical from right to left. For example, take the address *Bud@TCIC.com*. First, we know that it is somewhere in the .com domain. If I am *George@biguniversity.edu*, I need to find Bud's address. It is very likely that the university has no idea of what the address might be. The local e-mail system, therefore, makes a query of the unnamed "." domain. There are several of these servers around the Internet, which are updated daily by the InterNIC as names are registered.

There is some controversy over the InterNIC's absolute control over domain names. (Someone has to be in charge to prevent chaos, but change is underway with the introduction of competition in this area.) To register a domain name, one (or one's ISP) must contact the InterNIC (or a suitable competitor), and pay an annual fee. (Prior to the commercialization of the Internet, Stanford Research Institute (SRI) performed this function.) There are proposals to open other domains (for example, .biz .store, and so forth) and let other entities administer the names within that domain.

Each country has a domain and administers these domain names themselves. All public entities such as cities, counties, and states are under the .us domain. Some of the country domains are .uk for United Kingdom, .cz for Czech, .de for Germany, .au for Australia, and so forth.

Each domain then has its own DNS server, so when George is trying to send e-mail to Bud, his e-mail server asks the "." domain for Bud's address. The "." domain replies that it can only provide the address of the .com DNS. We then ask the .com DNS that replies with the DNS address of TCIC. Since TCIC is really under an ISP, what we really get is the address of the DNS server at that ISP. Finally, we get Bud's real address. Now, this address is put into the e-mail packets, and they are sent on their way. In addition, we, the users, never knew about all the fooling around that went into finding the address in the first place.

JAVA

The early Internet was strictly ASCII text-based. Then came the inclusion of graphical interchange format (GIF) files. As indicated previously, these were simply references in the hypertext document to a location that contained the graphic file that was displayed. Next, came the desire to automate or animate Web pages.

Sun Microsystems invented a clever (and, to some, controversial) language called *Java*, which is a registered trademark of Sun Microsystems.

The basic problem was that to animate a page the local machine had to execute some software. This opened the door to viruses. Sun's clever idea was to have the browser execute the program, rather than the host hardware. The good part was that you were somewhat protected from malicious programs. The bad part was that the browser was interpreting the Java language on the fly, and this interpretation was slow. (Faster machines help a lot here.) The original idea was that the browser could prevent the Java script from doing any damage (like wiping out the hard drive). Unfortunately, the more powerful we needed the Java to become, the more capability it needed on our host machine. Microsoft, naturally, has its own approach to page automation called Active-X. The good part is that it runs as machine code. The bad part is that it runs as machine code and can therefore contain viruses. The user is given the opportunity to download or not download the Active-X code. If you trust the source, go ahead and run it. If you are not sure, cancel the download and do without the animations.

Surfing the Web

When you select a hyperlink, the browser creates a packet requesting a Web page and sends it to the specified URL. Your browser actually sets up a connection to the server. The server replies with the requested file (Web page) and the browser displays the page. Your browser now stores this page in its cache memory so that after you have followed several other links, you can easily get back by selecting the back button. The button retrieves the page out of cache rather than having to fetch it from the source (which as you have experienced, could take a while). You should periodically empty your cache. First, depending on the settings of your browser it may never use the cache again. Second, if the browser does always check cache first, regardless of age, when you sign onto the site the next time a month later, the page you see is the old one from cache. Actually, this is an exaggeration because the browser has a setting for how old a page can get before a fresh copy is fetched. You can just throw away the cache folder (it is safer to discard the contents); your browser will build a new one when you launch it. If you do a lot of surfing, this cache can take up a lot of disk space.

You can always force the browser to get a fresh copy of the page by selecting the *Reload* (or *Refresh*) button. This causes the browser to ignore whatever was cached. The fact that each page can contain multiple references to other pages anywhere in the world is the reason it is called the World Wide Web (also referred to the World Wide Wait). Links can take you anywhere including back, where you started. There is no hierarchical structure to the Web.

Tracking Visitors

From a commercial point of view, we would like to know how many visitors or hits we have on our Web page. (Here hit is defined as someone accessing our page, for example, setting up a connection to us.) We can tally each connection and present that to potential advertisers as an indication of the popularity of our page. First, the number of connections or hits to our page is only approximately related to the number of viewers. Here is why: If you happen to set the home page to *www.tcic.com*, every time you launch your browser, you go there. It looks like a hit! The fact that you immediately go to some other book-marked page doesn't register. Second, depending on your browser settings, you could revisit a page multiple times, but your browser has that page cached. The Web page owner then has no way of knowing that you are frequently referring to his page during your online session. Third, if the client or user is surfing from behind a proxy, his local proxy server will provide your page whenever requested, saving network bandwidth, but the Web site owner again doesn't know that he has been hit once again.

Cookies

One of the more controversial aspects of the Web is the existence of cookies. Cookies are nothing but an encoded set of information that the Web server asks your browser to keep for it. The cookies simply contain information about you and the sites you visit.

They may contain information, such as your credit card number, that you have entered while visiting a site. They may also contain links you selected from that Web site. If you visit a major *outfitter.com* and you look at hiking boots, the next time you log into that site, the first page may have backpacks and tents prominently displayed. The site read the cookies it left on your machine the last time you visited. It determined that you are an outdoor type (and decided it would be a high probability of sale for you on related outdoor equipment. However, you still have the ability to view all the other parts of the site because the index page always contains an index to other pages on the main page.

Cookies, then, are a convenient way for the vendor to keep information about site visitors without having to keep a huge database of all visitors whether they are casual or frequent visitors.

You can throw away the cookie file anytime you want. The browser will rebuild it when it needs it. You can also read your cookie file by opening it in a text reader. Depending on the browser, the cookie file normally contains ASCII text. The information is normally encoded as a set of numbers that are not meaningful to anyone, but the originator of the cookie. Some Web pages won't work correctly unless you have the cookies enabled. You may leave "accept cookies" turned on and discard the file at the end of your session if you are paranoid about the information that might be stored therein.

Search Engines

Even if we have links to follow, there is no good way to find a specific set of information. We still need a database catalog that we can search that lists sites that might contain the information we want. The search engines (such as Yahoo! and Google) provide a database to search very similar to the way Gopher and Veronica tools did in the past.

Enterprising individuals also developed "Web crawlers" that would follow hyperlinks based on a key word and fetch all the associated pages. You could start these crawlers, go to bed, and wake up with a full disk. Today's databases are a combination of crawling and advertising. The business plan of the search engine provider is to offer advertising along with the database information. Companies that pay more get a better position on each page. In a few cases, the ordering of the hits on the page is a function of how much the information source paid to gets its listing put first. The goal of the game is to entice the Web surfers to your site. Once there, you can either sell them something or present them with advertising for which you have been paid. The more visitors to your site, the more you can charge for the so-called "banner advertisements." For folks looking for information, these banner ads are just background noise. Being enticed to look at one will often lead you on an interesting, but irrelevant, wild goose chase.

Standards

Within the Internet, standards are created and managed on a voluntary basis. The IETF makes recommendations to the IAB for inclusion as standards. Remember that the whole Internet started as a volunteer-based network, each building on what was done before. Anyone who determines a new feature is needed or a problem needs fixing creates a solution. That solution is implemented on one's own network, and when ready, it can be submitted to the IETF as a request for comment (RFC). It is then published on the relevant newsgroups for others to try it and comment on it. After it has survived this torture test, it is ready for formal adoption. Because the whole Internet is voluntary, it is up to the network administrator to decide whether to use that RFC or not. Failure to implement it, however, may mean compatibility problems with other networks.

This process is very practical and very different from that used by the formal international standards organizations, such as the International Standards Organization (ISO) and the International Telecommunications Union (ITU). These have a formal membership and a proposal submission and review procedure that is designed to form a consensus.

Commercial Opportunity

Where do you shop? Chances are that most of your shopping is done at physical storefronts or malls within a few miles of your home. Perhaps you also shop from catalogs that reach you by snail mail (i.e., the post office).

What chance does a small vendor located thousands of miles away from you have of marketing products to you? Until the Internet became available, the vendor had very little chance. That vendor could publish nice color catalogs and mail them out. Many small companies have done just that, and have become large companies by doing so. A good example of this is L.L. Bean.

However, this is an expensive route to take; the production of a good catalog is a costly effort, and postage is very expensive if a large number of pieces are to be distributed. The point here is that the cost of even trying is high.

Enter the Internet. Literally tens of millions of people either have or will have access soon, and, with minimal investment (a few thousand dollars), a vendor can in theory reach all of them. A nice potential market, wouldn't you say? Many think the answer to this question is a resounding yes! However, there are a few flies in the ointment, depending on your point of view.

Currently, one can attempt to reach potential customers via the Internet in several ways:

- Send out a large number of electronic messages (the electronic equivalent of junk mail, referred to as *spam* by those who would prefer not to receive such transmissions).

- Place advertising for products and services on others' Web sites.

- Utilize software to track viewers habits (adware) and send them targeted e-mail based upon their Web browsing statistics.

- Create a Web site (see the following) to describe products and services, and perhaps to actually take orders for those same products and services.

Web Advertising

One of the distinguishing characteristics of computers is that, if programmed correctly, they can aid in focusing transmission of commercial messages (i.e., advertising) to only those people most likely to be receptive to those messages. The Internet embodies a number of ways to advertise to its users. One, mentioned above, is spam. But spam is a sledgehammer approach; by definition, it is not focused. Other, much more subtle approaches, are available. One approach is using "banner ads"—colorful, sometimes animated rectangles on Web pages, similar to magazine ads, but with a significant difference: When clicked on, they normally change the user's current Web page to one on the advertiser's Web site. This is referred to as a *link*. Banner ads are usually placed (for a fee, of course) on sites with a lot of traffic; thus, they are the Net equivalent of putting up a poster for some kind of product or service in the window of a supermarket.

Spam

What is your definition of junk mail? Do you like to receive it? Do you often purchase products as a result of receiving it? We didn't think so. Although people who receive small amounts of postal mail might like receiving anything at all in their mailbox, most would prefer it to be a bit more specific to the person than typical junk mail. Spam is the name of unsolicited e-mail on the Internet. Although new users of the Internet *(newbies)* may initially be excited by messages in their electronic inboxes with titles like ****!!!!***Make big money stuffing envelopes!!!!*****, after the fifth, tenth, or hundredth such message, things become tedious very quickly. The risk that something worthwhile is buried among the garbage is always present. Although the delete button is always there, it takes some time to filter out the spam, and time is usually in short supply.

The good news is that with a small expenditure of money and a little applied intelligence, one can greatly reduce the amount of spam that one actually sees. Products, both for regular e-mail and for newsgroups, are available that are capable of filtering out unwanted messages, see Fig. 12.6. For example, Qualcomm's Eudora Pro e-mail program can select e-mail and delete it before reading it on the basis of an unlimited set of user specified character sequences, whether those sequences appear in a message's subject, in the main body of text, or as part of the sender's name.

If you never want to see a message containing the word "toner" in the subject (many scam artists try to sell copier and printer toner via the Net—we have no idea why), you don't have to. Anawave's Gravity, a sophisticated newsgroup reader program, has similar filtering capabilities. On the other hand, as P. T. Barnum said, "There's a sucker born every minute," and the law of large numbers says that if you send out thousands of such messages, at least a few suckers are going to read them and respond. Because the cost of sending out spam is so much smaller than the costs associated with paper mail, it is likely that people will continue to send it out.

That isn't to say efforts haven't been tried to curb spam; in 2003 the CAN-SPAM Act was passed in the United States. In reality the CAN-SPAM Act didn't cure SPAM because it suggests the bill simply legalizes spam, making it OK for 23 million U.S.

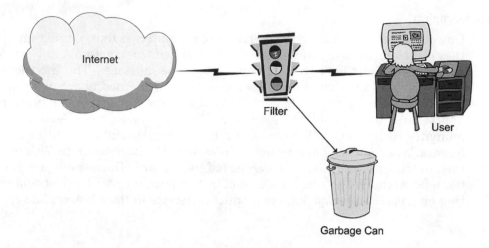

Figure 12.6   Today's e-mail products offer filters for sorting out your regular mail from unsolicited messages. In addition, many of these products provide filters to sort mail by sender, subject matter, so it is easy to retrieve specific messages.

businesses to bombard you with marketing provided they offer you some way to opt out from further mailings, and don't hide behind anonymous headers and misleading subject lines. In 2003, 35 percent of the e-mail sent could be classified as SPAM, and since the bill, the statistic has jumped to 85 percent. In 2004, the cost of SPAM to businesses and consulers alike was estimated at $25 billion.

The alarming growth of spam is mind boggling; some expect e-mail to melt down unless spam is controlled. With over 10 billion messages everyday being sent, in a year that number is expected to triple. Something needs to be done to protect inboxes out there everywhere and free up the valuable bandwidth on the Net today.

The UN has gotten involved and is trying to pass legislation from 60 countries to curb worldwide spam (7/2004). If one regards Internet mail as a faster alternative to the post office, then spam can be considered unavoidable. At least in the case of the electronic version, methods are available to automatically handle a portion of it, no recycling required.

Adware and Spyware

In 2002, few people understood the difference between a Banner Ad, and adware*.

In a sense they are two different approaches toward the same thing; getting an advertising link in front of consumers. Adware differs from Banner ads in the means by which it is presented to the user. Instead of being part of a web site, adware causes a new browser to open with an ad on it.

---

*AdWare is also a registered trademark that belongs to AdWare Systems, Inc. AdWare Systems builds accounting and media buying systems for the advertising industry and has no connection to pop-up advertising, spyware, or other invasive forms of online advertising.

As an Internet user you have definitely experienced this annoying feature. Adware has been criticized because it sometimes includes other software that tracks a user's personal information and passes it on to third parties, without user's knowledge or permission. This practice has been dubbed spyware and has prompted an outcry from computer security and privacy advocate groups.

There are several commercially available products, and many free software packages that remove these threats. However, with the abundance of programs, some are not detected by every package. Both adware and spyware are extremely difficult to eliminate without these tools. In many cases you can delete a program, only to find it restored the next time you power up your system. You certainly want to make sure that if you are running Windows, you must turn off your "System Restore" feature until after deleting the adware and rebooting the machine. This is done in your system properties as shown in Fig. 12.7.

How pervasive is spyware? In one study, Earthlink the ISP revealed that half a million spyware monitors and Trojan horses were discovered in a million and a half scans this year. Each infected computer had an average of 27 spyware programs on it.

This widespread threat of information theft, and privacy implications has lead congress to pursue the Cyber Trespass Act (2004). It implicitly states that "anyone who is not the owner or authorized user of a computer to provide an opt-in screen prior to transmitting or enabling any information collection program, which can collect personally identifiable information or information about Web sites visited." Consumers also must be informed of the type of information the software collects or sends, or the purpose for which the

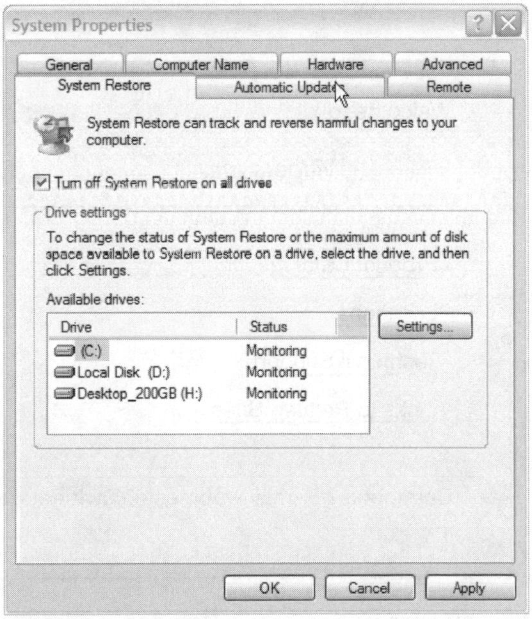

Figure 12.7 Turning off system restore in Windows XP.

information is collected or sent. The bill also requires that spyware that the consumer consents to download must be easily uninstalled "without undue effort or knowledge" on the part of the computer user.

The legislation is pending approval from the Senate and confirmation by the President before it becomes law, but congressional forces have stepped in to prevent widespread theft, and fraud from these malicious programs.

Web Site

Another way one can advertise one's wares on the network is to create a Web site. Creating a Web site is more than just a way to advertise, seen in Fig. 12.8. A Web site puts your corporate or personal image up close and personal in front of any Web user who wants to access it. Unlike spam, however, the creation of a Web site ranges from outright cheap to very expensive depending on features involved. On a per-user basis, it may not be expensive compared to print advertising; however, the skills as well as the resources involved in creating a Web site are completely different.

What does it take to create a Web site? Here are just some of the requirements. For one thing, you need a computer; an ISP may provide one for you if that's the way you'd like to go. An ISP can provide either a dedicated computer—one that is just going to be your own Web site—or a shared (sometimes referred to as a virtual Web site) computer, in which case your Web pages share the computer, the disk space, and so on of a number of other Web sites. Two categories of computers, or rather operating systems, tend to be used for Web sites: UNIX computers and Windows NT computers.

Welcome to

Widgets Inc.

- Product Catalog

- Locations

- Technical Support

- Links to Related Sites

Comments? E-mail webmaster@widgetsinc.com

Figure 12.8 A Web site provides more than advertising, it allows for online sales, product support, and a place where customers can find out further product information.

In practice, any computer that runs UNIX, such as a Sun, an IBM RS 6000, or any other computer capable of running some variant of UNIX can be used. Windows NT and now Windows 2003 Server computers are increasingly popular because they are somewhat easier to manage; however, the size of the Web site you can create tends to be larger with a UNIX computer. Now the implementation of Linux-based systems is becoming the norm because of the simplicity and cost of the software.

You need much more than just a computer, however. To create a Web site, you need connections to the Internet that require an ISP (discussed elsewhere in this book) and a way to create the pages. Initially, when the Web first came into being, one created Web pages by using a text editor where pages were defined in hypertext markup language (HTML). Markup languages have been around for quite some time. They are distinguished from what-you-see-is-what-you-get (WYSIWYG) systems because they are text. Markup languages use what are called *tags*. A tag is a word surrounded by angle brackets (<tag-goes-here>) that tells the system processing the markup language what to do with text that immediately precedes or follows the tag. Markup languages are particularly useful for manipulating truly large amounts of text in a consistent way. If you are going to use a WYSIWYG system, then everybody working on a project must have an entire series of standards defined in excruciating detail. For example, normal paragraphs have to be a certain point size, headers have to be a certain point size, and so on, and every individual must know how those work and set their WYSIWYG editors accordingly. With a markup language, instead of saying exact point size for heading, you would say "heading 1." That will be a tag. Of course, although the WYSIWYG editor requires a great deal of specification of detail, a markup language requires the user to know all of the tags. Because HTML was a relatively new language, not many people initially knew those tags. This is one of the main reasons why so-called Web masters commanded such high salaries. The creation of a Web page is not inherently difficult; however, it requires a skill set that is completely new and therefore rare—at least so far. A fair number of businesses have had Web pages created, then examined what was created and realized that maintenance is not all that difficult, at least at a conceptual level. In any case, now a large number of tools enable Web maintainers to take at least one large step away from the HTML coding that was required until recently. In addition, a number of editors focus on the HTML coding, but have point-and-shoot selections for the various tags so that you don't necessarily have to memorize all of them.

There is a major additional element here. For example, it is very easy to create a basic newsletter document; however, a really good newsletter requires skills far beyond just the use of a word processor, no matter how sophisticated that word processor is. Page layout skills, an understanding of design elements, and of course an understanding of subject matter are all required. In the case of a Web page or site, a significantly larger number of factors must be taken into account. For example, there is always a temptation with modern tools to create strikingly beautiful Web pages with all kinds of wonderful graphics. However, graphics of any size require a considerable amount of bandwidth or network capacity to be moved out to the people who are going to view them. Many people still access the network via dial-up lines. For the most part, those lines at the moment max out at 33.6 Kbps (upload). Faster speeds are available, but it is a mistake to design a Web page for popular use and then not take into account the vast majority of people who do not have fast connections to the Web. The 56 Kbps modems discussed earlier do not produce fast enough connections for very busy Web sites or dense graphic images. Large files only frustrate visitors of a Web site and chase them away forever. This problem is sometimes aggravated by the fact that companies typically have dedicated, higher-speed connections to the Internet and the Web. By higher speed, in this case, we mean as fast as a T1 circuit or 1.544 million bits per second (Mbps). Very large companies have T3s or 45 Mbps. A diagram of these connections is seen in Fig. 12.9. Connect these to a local area network in a developer's area and the people who are doing the testing on the Web site will see all those lovely pictures positively snap onto their screens. Those same graphics, however, will take a long time to reach a typical dial-in user's screen. The Web is not referred to as "World Wide Wait" for nothing. Of course, now that cable modems and DSL services are

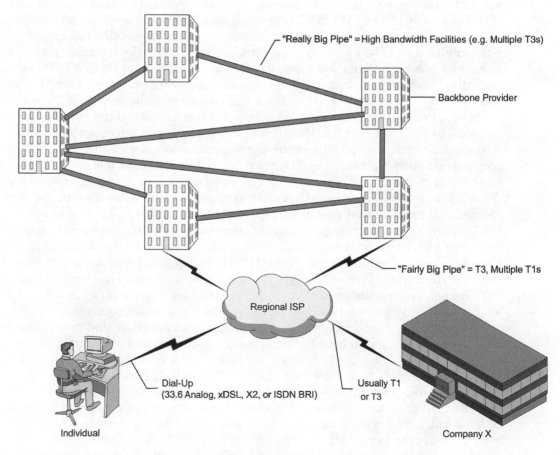

Figure 12.9 A high-speed access line is used in larger companies.

reasonably priced, users will see a ramp-up in the ability to download files and Web sites much faster. Remember, however, that only 15 percent of the population is on these higher speed connections.

The cost of a Web site varies radically. At the low end, it is possible to get an account on America Online and create a Web site for no extra cost. We are talking about $20 per month or so. But for this price, the amount of storage you get is minimal—two or three megabytes—and you do all the work yourself. All you have is a facility. Moreover, anyone who is serious about providing a Web site for access by many other people probably does not want to put it on America Online or Earthlink. The focus of these providers is serving individual users; they're not really set up to provide excellent Web site support. They are changing, but are not yet there. These companies (AOL, Earthlink, and NetZero) are charted as online service providers, not ISPs. Many other companies have gone into business to do just that—notably many ISPs. The real cost of setting up a Web site is not the network; it's the computers themselves, which for high-capacity machines could easily cost in tens of thousands of dollars, possibly even the low hundreds of thousands for a single high-capability server. Some of the more frequently accessed sites are *hit* (accessed) literally millions of times per day. One doesn't want to use a low-end PC to handle something like that. The other major cost is people time. We mentioned previously that the skills aren't all that rarified, but they are still rare. Because of that, people who really know how to do a good job on a Web site still command premium rates. A typical high-end Web site will not come into being for less than $50,000 to $100,000 up front; it can easily cost several times that. Also, there are continuing maintenance costs. One of the most common phenomena seen on the Web today is that a company, possibly very well funded, spends the bucks to create a Web site, puts it online, and gets buried by the number of accesses coming in initially. Those accesses will taper off unless at least two things happen:

1. The Web site is kept up-to-date. That doesn't mean just current information; it means that the Web site undergoes a perceptible change, whether it's in content or layout, on a continuing basis. People won't come back frequently if, when they come back, they don't see anything new.

2. Enough bandwidth is ensured for the site to handle the actual number of users accessing it. Bandwidth in this context is not just the network access; it's also the capability of the server. As with many other environments, everyone typically blames the network itself when access is slow. More often than not, it turns out that the slowness of the access is due to the undersizing of the server's capabilities.

Advertising, of course, is not the only reason to create a Web site. Many companies, like Amazon.com, for example, have created a Web site that is an entire enterprise. Of course, the site has advertising, but it also has a great deal of content regarding products or services for sale. In the most complete cases, products and services are actually for sale directly via the Web.

Sounds like a major opportunity, right? It could be. Billions of people now routinely access the Web on a daily basis. That's a large pool of potential customers. However, people are in some cases still reluctant to put the necessary information on the network to make real purchases. Both of the major vendors of Web browsers, Netscape and Microsoft, have addressed this concern by incorporating something called a *secure sockets layer* (SSL) into their browsers, as have the people who created Web sites that actually sell products and services, see Fig. 12.10. SSL is pretty good, but because very few people understand that the encryption is present, we believe that it will still take some time for Web sales to become the preferred method. It doesn't help that the Web is really slow at times. Often, it's quicker to pick up the telephone and call a vendor than it is to try to go through all the text entry to purchase products and services on the Web.

One should be aware that the Web is almost a science fiction kind of environment. One of the characteristics is that things change rapidly. Web pages come and go, companies appear and disappear, and the features of individual Web pages, as mentioned above, change rapidly. There are some ways to try to keep on top of this. One is to use searchers. A few services or Web sites specialize in helping other users find Web sites. Paradoxically, these services or searchers are free. How do they do it? They accept a great deal of advertising, and this advertising is focused in a way that occurs in no other medium. The Web sites that provide searchers pay attention to what individuals search for, and, based on what those individuals request, different advertising appears along with the responses to the searches.

Major Web services that provide searching are AltaVista (*http://www.altavista.com*), Yahoo (*http://www.yahoo.com*), Google (*http://www.google.com*), and Excite (*http://www.excite.com*). The technology used by these companies is amazing.

They have enormous databases that are kept up-to-date on a continuing basis via automated searchers that go out themselves and collect information from everywhere on the Net. Those databases are then indexed and used for searches for users. The searches are amazingly fast. Of course, to an individual who does not realize what's going on behind the scenes, the searches may not be so amazing. A typical search may return 100,000 results. That would be daunting, but at least in Excite's case, the results are sorted in a descending order according to the likelihood of satisfying the request.

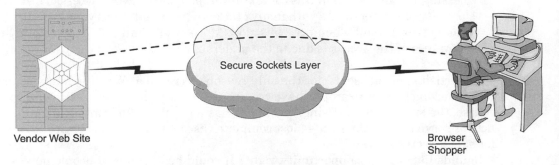

Vendor Web Site

Secure Sockets Layer

Browser
Shopper

Figure 12.10 Secure sockets layer provides encryption for online sales to protect personal information during transmission.

Why the Hype?

It is reasonable to describe the Internet as a peer-to-peer network. This means that, as long as things are set up properly, any computer on the Net can communicate directly with any other computer. What do we mean by *any computer*? Any computer in the world with a connection to the Internet and a properly configured suite of TCP/IP software can participate fully in any service for which it and its users have authorized access. Of course, in practice, performance considerations may limit what one can actually do with any particular computer. Essentially, by buying computer equipment costing under $500, ordering a dial-up telephone line (the extra line can cost as much as $30 a month), and signing up with a local Internet service provider for about $12–22 per month, an individual or an organization can gain full access to the Internet. xdsl and CATV access to the Internet costs just about the same as the dial-up line.

Using the ISP

Obviously, the Internet backbone is critical, but it's just a start. The vast majority of Internet users (both companies and individuals) are not a part of the backbone. Moreover, the backbone providers are generally not in the business of providing end-user (or end-business) connections, other than to their own personnel and customers. Instead, a group of intermediary companies called Internet service providers (ISPs) has sprung into being. The commercialization of the Internet by the Clinton and Gore administration in the United States created this new ISP business. In 1992, the decision was made to commercialize the Internet as the information superhighway. Soon thereafter (1994–1995), the emergence of the ISPs exploded. It is your friendly local ISP that you go to get a connection to the Internet. ISPs themselves connect to the backbone directly, usually for a fee (which is recouped, month by month, from customers like you).

Note that underlying all this is the assumption that actual physical interlocation circuits are still provided by either local telephone companies or interexchange carriers. When a backbone provider, or ISP, is an interexchange carrier, it acts in a dual role. Otherwise, such providers and ISPs construct rooms full of routers, modems, DSUs, and so forth, and use their local Telco to connect up, both among their own locations and to the Internet backbone itself, or to other backbone providers in the case of the central organizations.

To gain access to the Internet, you need an ISP. ISPs come in two flavors, regional and national; also, one might consider an international category. National and international carriers tend to be very well-known companies. Such organizations as AT&T, CompuServe, and IBM fall into this category. They have access points, or points of presence (POPs), all over the world. Interestingly, AOL is probably the most pervasive dial-up service, but the others are also up there. It would be worth your while, if you travel, to check into the dial-in services for these services before choosing an ISP. It is a major factor. All have an 800 number access, but it tends not to work terribly well over long distances because you are going through the dial-up network and, as has been mentioned elsewhere, the dial-up network was not really designed for data.

Regional ISPs tend to have slightly lower access charges than the international ones. This is probably because of the additional cost of those international circuits. Another possible advantage of a regional ISP is that, in the region it focuses on, it probably has more dial-in points than the national carriers. So if one of the dial-in points (or numbers) has a problem, you can use an alternative one in your area. The national and international ISPs are really gunning for your business. They have in most cases brought their prices down to very close to those of the regional carriers. Moreover, they do have the advantage of providing dial-in points across the country and even around the world.

Another factor in selecting an ISP is less obvious than the number of dial-in points. This factor is the ISP's connection to the backbone of the Internet itself. The number of simultaneous users an ISP can effectively handle is directly related to the speed of its connection into the Internet. We discuss high-speed circuits elsewhere in this book. An ISP that has only a T1 connection to the Internet really does not have enough capacity to handle significant numbers of people. This is not normally a problem with the national and international ISPs; however, it is a real consideration when selecting among regional carriers, of which often several are available in any given region. Normally, you probably want to use an ISP that has at least a T3 (a big pipe) connection and perhaps several T3 connections to the Internet. This ISP connection to the Internet factor is particularly important if you are selecting an ISP on behalf of a medium to large company, as opposed to just an individual. A company with hundreds or thousands of individuals connecting to the Internet simultaneously can put a really big load on an ISP. It may increase the ISP's total traffic by a double-digit percentage if it's just a regional ISP. The moral of the story: do your homework. Another consideration in selecting an ISP is the variety of connection alternatives for the user to the ISP. Obviously, dial-up will be supported, but straight dial-up, at the writing of this book, only reaches speeds of 33.6 Kbps upline to the Net, and as much as 53 Kbps downline from the Net.

That's a lot faster than speeds in the past, but it isn't nearly as fast as some available alternatives. Another alternative available now is xDSL. xDSL, sometimes referred to as just DSL (this stands for digital subscriber line), represents a variety of technologies that, as a class, deliver megabit-per second speeds to homeowners (this will be covered in Chapter 15 thoroughly). However, an ISP has to have a special connection to your local telephone company in order for you to access the ISP using xDSL. As a practical matter, xDSL will only be available in limited locations for the next few years. It may not dominate the landscape if other services become generally available (like broadband or fixed wireless), but xDSL has the potential to take off because it provides higher bandwidth than just about any other service to individual homes at a tiny fraction of the cost of equivalent services. Other means of connecting to ISPs involve dedicated circuits, cable, switched 56, or even frame relay. You have to decide what you need and what you are willing to pay for, but you also have to check with the ISP to find out what it is willing to accept. If you are selecting an ISP for a business, two ISPs may be better than one, see Fig. 12.11.

Several ISPs over the past few years have had total network failures for hours at a time (although you don't hear about them). If you are going to purchase a service like this for your business users, then, as with any other service, you need to consider what happens if the provider fails. One way to handle this is to purchase service from two different ISPs. Another way is to use an ISP that can provide redundant dedicated connections into your business. Don't forget to arrange for diverse routing from your

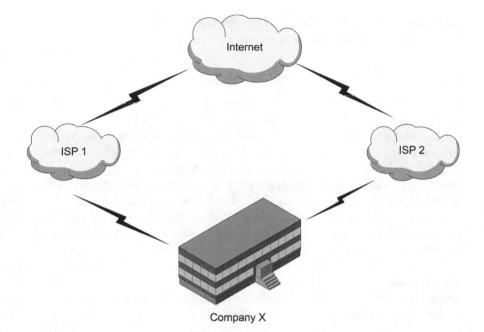

Figure 12.11   By having two ISP's redundancy is achieved. If a problem happens in the local loop on one circuit, the other is still functional.

location to the ISPs as well. This may involve, for example, getting circuits to two different central offices, something that the telephone companies tend to resist, but it is still a good idea if you can swing it.

Some of the other miscellaneous things to consider when selecting an ISP include factors that you might consider when selecting any vendor. Among these are optional services, prices for those services, what support and coaching is available for setting up the use of the ISP, and a hidden gotcha that you really should consider. The key question is, will the ISP still be in business a few months from now? It doesn't take very much equipment to set up an Internet ISP, and many individuals have taken advantage of this fact. We are not recommending that you automatically discriminate against a small ISP; in fact, some of the best ones out there are small organizations. Nonetheless, you may not be comfortable dealing with a very small company, if only because you may have concerns about its ability to handle growth. Again, do your homework.

The Function of the ISP Point of Presence

As previously mentioned, the POP is an ISP's physical location with a connection to the backbone of the Internet. The backbone of the Internet spans the country and passes through three main concentration points where it is broken down into further networks by the various carriers. These points called network access points (NAPs) are located in New York, Chicago, and San Francisco. The Internet backbone has continually been upgraded since its inception. Originally, the backbone was T3 service, but has now been upgraded to multiple paths of OC-192 capacity.

Collocation

Computers are sensitive to environmental conditions and need certain requirements to operate optimally. When a company is running a Web server or business applications, having the system up translates directly into dollars and cents. Therefore, the goal is to ensure up time of their systems. Since over 90 percent of problems in communication happen within the local loop, having a direct connection to the Internet backbone minimizes local loop problems. Since a POP is connecting directly on the Internet backbone, locating equipment within the POP just about eliminates local loop problems.

POPs are located in many major cities across the United States, but not all POPs provide collocation services. Where collocation is available is usually termed a data center, if no space is available it is a generic POP.

Within ISP's POPs there is space for customers to place their Web hosting servers, or an alternate place for data back up. When an ISP allows you to physically locate your equipment in their POP it is called collocation service. There are several benefits for utilizing collocation services, these include the following:

- Physical security—locking cabinets and a secure data center
- Fully redundant power (AC and DC systems)
- Back up generators
- HVAC system to ensure proper air quality
- Controlled environment (temperature, humidity)
- Fire threat detection and suppression systems
- Flexible Bandwidth options that are easily scalable from megabit service up to Gigabit services, and optical networking
- 24×7×365 on site support and remote hands available

If a company decides to host a Web server on their own physical premises, they need to meet the requirements mentioned above. This proves to be quite costly, and in most cases it is financially beneficial to collocate servers at a POP or data center. By sharing the redundant systems within the center with other users, it costs them less than employing their own individual systems. Within a data center, there are cages separating customers so physical security still exists.

Access

Access from the POP to the customer is provided in various forms depending on technology utilized. Access to the backbone within the data center is provided in increments from megabit speeds right up to the hundreds of megabits depending on user requirements. A further advantage of being directly connected to a POP comes when a user needs more bandwidth.

In the outside world ordering a circuit, or more bandwidth, often requires provisioning a new line. This provisioning process takes an average of 30 days (when it's readily available), to months (when new high capacity circuits are needed). By being directly connected to the backbone, more bandwidth can be provisioned within days, as it only requires pulling a line within the POP.

Connections from the customer site to the pop vary, and these access methods are technologies covered in other chapters in this book. Examples for access methods to the POP are T1, T3, frame relay, ATM, MPLS, gigabit Ethernet (called *Metro*), SONET, and fiber optics in various increments (OC3, OC12, OC48).

Internet Futures

Many people are concerned that the Internet will experience spontaneous self-destruction due to its speed of growth. We mentioned earlier that change happens rapidly on the Internet. In fact, a concept called *Internet time* is in common usage. It is difficult to quantify Internet time, but it means that things that one would expect in other environments to take years, take only months or even days on the Internet. A good example of this is the speed at which, for a while, Internet browsers were being revised by their producers. Even now, Netscape releases new beta versions of its Netscape browser on a very frequent basis, sometimes as frequently as once every couple of months. It says something that a high percentage of the people who use browsers on the Internet are actually using beta versions of those browsers just to get the latest features that are being taken advantage of by the sites that they access.

However, we were talking about the growth of the Internet. The two major concerns regarding the growth of the Internet are:

1. The traffic levels will grow to the point where things will bog down completely.
2. The number of nodes or computers on the network will exceed the number that can be handled by the addressing scheme.

Actually, in many respects, portions of the Internet have already run out of gas as far as performance is concerned. For good reason, the Web is described as the "World Wide Wait." All the major backbone providers are adding capacity at a very rapid clip. It remains to be seen whether they can keep up with demand. After all, the growth eventually has to taper off a little bit because it is unlikely that more than one computer can be used by every man, woman, and child. Once everybody has a computer, we're limited to the growth of the population. Moreover, the population has not been growing nearly as quickly as the Internet has. Of course, that point may not be reached for a while, so in the meantime, we may experience a fair amount of pain. We can't predict whether the Net will self-destruct. We suspect that it will go through phases of slowing and speeding as new capacity comes online and new facilities become available on the network, bringing in new users and increasing the use by existing users. Many of the manufacturers are now hyping the optical Internet, meaning that the capacity of fiber optics will enhance the Internet for the foreseeable future. That is of course, if some of the ISPs buy it!

As far as the network address availability is concerned, we're happy to report that the powers that be on the Internet have defined a new standard—IPv6. Going into the details of the IPv6 protocol is really beyond the scope of this book. Suffice it to say that IPv6 will not have any problems with the number of nodes that it can address any time in the near future. Not only that, but the designers have also done a good job of stripping out unnecessary overhead in order to make this protocol inherently slightly faster than the existing IPv4 protocol now in use on the network (version 5 was a specialty protocol that never received general usage). The main question is not whether IPv6 can handle the number of addresses that it will have to handle, but rather how quickly can it be brought online. Naturally, migration issues arise because millions of people are still running software that does not support IPv6 at this time. A certain amount of backward compatibility is built into the new protocol; but we suspect that the people operating the network will have to dance very quickly to get from where they are now to where they want to be in a smooth fashion.

Questions

1. What is the Internet?
   a. A government network
   b. A network of networks
   c. The geeks network
   d. A U.S.-based network

2. Who really invented the Internet?
   a. Al Gore
   b. The U.S. government
   c. DARPA
   d. Bill Clinton

3. When we use the Internet, the core protocols are TCP and IP.   T/F

4. The Internet was developed initially for the transfer of what types of information?
   a. Video and multimedia
   b. Voice and streaming audio
   c. E-mail and small file transfers
   d. Virtual terminal and Telnet

5. When we talk about IP today, what version are we referring to?

   a. 4

   b. 5

   c. 6

   d. 8

6. What does DNS stand for?

   a. Domain Network Service

   b. Domain Name Convention

   c. Domain Name Servers

   d. Digital Naming Systems

7. When we refer to the Web, what are we talking about?

   a. A spider web

   b. The World Wide Web of computers

   c. Web-based mail services

   d. Web naming

8. IP stands for:

   a. Internetwork Packets

   b. Internet Payloads

   c. Internet Protocol

   d. Interworking Protocols

9. By the year 2004, it is expected that the Internet will be carrying _____ percent of the voice.

   a. 3

   b. 10

   c. 20

   d. 50

10. The best way to handle a large file transfer is to use which protocol?

   a. MIME

   b. SMTP

   c. SIP

   d. FTP

11. How can people get access to the Internet?

   a. Through the local computer hardware stores

   b. Through the local banks

    c. From an ISO provider

    d. Through the local or regional ISP

12. If a user wants to get access at high-speed, what inexpensive Telco option is available today?

    a. DSL

    b. Dial-up modems

    c. B-ISDN

    d. T3

13. Normally, the user will use _____ ISP.

    a. Three

    b. Two

    c. One

    d. Four

14. What companies are now competing with the local Telco for access to the ISP?

    a. Long-distance dial-up

    b. Cable TV

    c. Gas and electric companies

    d. All of the above

Chapter 13

Local Area Networks (LANs)

After reading this chapter and completing the questions, you will be able to:

- Explain what a LAN is
- Understand the concept of using a LAN
- Discuss the various means of creating a LAN
- Explain the difference between the LAN and the WAN
- Discuss the various speeds associated with Ethernet
- Understand how an Ethernet frame is created
- Discuss the use of carrier sense multiple access with collision detection (CSMA/CD)
- Describe the throughput constraints

D igital data communications technologies can function over essentially arbitrary distances. Whether at 1 mile or 10,000, they will work about the same. Nevertheless, certain data communications functions would be much more useful (e.g., file sharing and transmission) if higher speeds could be used than are generally available on a wide area network. What if some slick optimization and engineering techniques were used to improve communications performance radically, at least for short distances? The productized answer to this question is local area networks (LANs).

What is a LAN? Originally, the industry defined LANs as data communications facilities with the following key elements:

- High communications speed
- Very low error rate
- Geographic boundaries

- A single cable system or medium for multiple attached devices
- A sharing of resources, such as printers, modems, files, disks, and applications

Let's take these one at a time.

High Communications Speed

At the time (the 1970s), use of communications speeds above 1 Mbps on either a wide or local area basis was exceedingly rare, other than on terminals locally connected to a mainframe. Therefore, "high-speed communications" meant transfer rates in the millions of bits (or megabits) per second. Even then, it was obvious that submegabit speeds would become a significant speed limit unless they could be vastly increased.

Nevertheless, why not simply use the existing wide area network (WAN) protocols for LANs? They certainly can be so used. The reason, in a word, is overhead. One major source of overhead in WAN protocols is their routing capabilities. LAN protocols eliminate routing overhead by functioning as though all nodes are physically adjacent. Another source of overhead is error checking, which is covered in the following paragraphs.

Very Low Error Rate

An error rate is the typical percentage of bits that can be corrupted on a regular basis during routine transmissions. Error checking ensures that such damaged bits are retransmitted so that applications never see the errors. But the data link protocols in use for wide area networks must contend with much higher error rates than would normally be experienced using LAN technologies.

Wide area analog communications typically experience one error in somewhere between 10^5 and 10^6 bits transmitted. A very low error rate is at least two orders of magnitude better than this or one error in 10^8 transmitted bits. Several technologies meet this challenge.

In a typical WAN protocol stack, error checking takes place at multiple stack levels. At each level, that error checking requires both additional bits in the transmitted frames and additional processing time at both ends (at the sending end, to create the error-checking bits; at the receiving end, to determine whether any errors occurred). If some of that error-checking overhead can be eliminated because of fewer errors to catch, higher speeds can more easily be achieved—which, not coincidentally, is another of the prime characteristics of a LAN.

The physical elements of a LAN do not depend on the vagaries of the telephone companies' facilities. Those elements are digital and are designed specifically to deliver high-speed communications with very low error rates. Thus the higher levels of the protocols can be relied on to handle the few errors that do creep in. Most LAN protocols do little or no error checking, and this is one design element that permits the higher speeds.

Geographic Boundaries

A LAN is bounded by some geographic limitation. Engineering considerations and physics impose this limitation; vendors did not impose it by fiat. The technologies employed to meet the other requirements (especially the requirement for high speed at a low error rate) tend to preclude more wide area transmission capabilities.

The geographic limitations of the various LAN technologies are expressed in different ways. There is usually a maximum distance from one node (or connected, network-addressable computer) to the next, expressed in tens or perhaps hundreds of meters. There is usually a maximum distance from one node to any other network node, typically hundreds or a few thousands of meters.

Network technologies that only reach up to the bounds of a single campus, or group of colocated buildings, satisfy these specific limitations. However, as we will see, a number of new technologies and connectivity options have worked together to mitigate the distance limitations significantly, which apply to LANs as they were originally defined and designed.

Single Cable System or Medium for Multiple Attached Devices

One of the less obvious but nonetheless essential characteristics of a LAN is that all devices on it are viewed and, to all intents and purposes, function as being adjacent. This implies that no special routing capabilities are required for communications traffic from one device to another; just put the information on the LAN and it will reach its destination. To put this into the ISO context, no routing functions should be required for a LAN to operate.

To accomplish this feat, all the devices must reside or appear to reside on a single cable system. Thus, each end-node-to-end-node link is also functionally a point-to-point link. No routing choices need be made if every machine you can talk to is right next door. All signals from all devices propagate throughout that cable system. In reality, the LAN is a broadcast multipoint circuit on which all devices have equal access.

What Do Users of LANs See When They Use the Network?

Configurations vary widely. However, when a user turns on his or her workstation, it normally runs a number of programs automatically until the user is prompted to enter identification (i.e., "user ID") and a password. This is called *logging in*. If you ask the user, "Into what are you logging?" he or she will answer, "I'm logging in to the network, of course!"

Logging in to a bunch of wires? Well, not exactly. Because security and access to services is typically (although certainly not always) provided for a given user from a single file server, users often perceive and refer to that server as "the network" or "the LAN." Managers of those servers often go along with this usage in order to avoid confusion—or because they believe it to be the only definition anyway.

However, referring to a server as a LAN can cause quite a bit of confusion in certain cases. The LAN manager will most likely refer to the wiring plant as the LAN. In this usage, LANs provide connectivity among devices, including servers. This book generally refers to the wiring plant together with the active devices providing connectivity as the LAN. File servers are just one category of servers, albeit a very important one.

Why Are LANs Used?

For many, the answer to "Why use LANs?" is "How could we work without them?" Nevertheless, business operated for centuries without LANs, and automated data processing functioned successfully for more than a decade without them. What changed?

Performance

One major change was the increasing popularity of minicomputers. Mainframe communications architectures had been optimized for use of large numbers of terminals. In fact, a special category of communications hardware (front-end processors) was developed in order to off-load the additional work necessary to manage such terminals.

In the minicomputer environment, however, front-end processors could not be used; the minicomputers were not built to handle the high input/output speeds necessary to service such processors.

Minicomputers are designed to respond immediately to certain requests for services called *interrupts*. Every keystroke on terminals connected in this way generates an interrupt on the associated minicomputer. And "interrupt" is exactly what happens; all processing ceases for an instant while the single keystroke is processed. You can easily see that, as additional terminals are added to a minicomputer, the amount of substantive processing accomplished (versus that required merely to receive characters from attached terminals) decreases rapidly!

If the communicated information from the terminals could be presented to the minicomputers more efficiently (i.e., in groups without generating one interrupt per keystroke), the minicomputers could serve far more terminal users. A new input/output method was needed.

Wiring

Another issue, again in the minicomputer environment, was the snarl of wiring that communications was generating in computer rooms throughout the world as well as in buildings containing those same terminal users. Before local area networks, almost every logical (non-wide area) connection from a terminal to a computer required a separate set of physical wires from the terminal all the way back to the computer. Even if not every terminal needed access to every computer, wiring such as this was common. Figure 13.1 shows the spider web of wires that would be required to link the various devices together. This is expensive to install, difficult to manage, and inefficient in the use of ports and facilities.

Data switches, or data PBXs, were alternatives, but they could only support lower speeds—and to configure them economically, they still had to be large and centrally

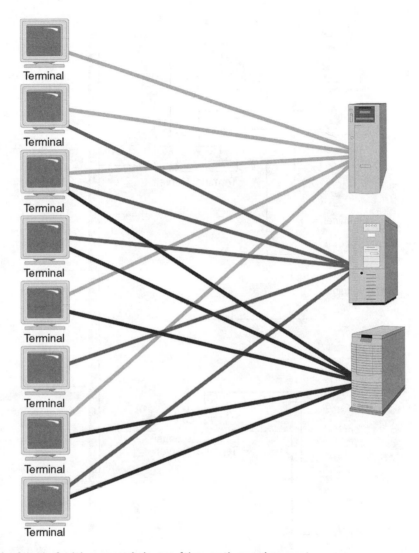

Figure 13.1 A typical wiring scenario in a multicomputing environment.

located, much like the computers! Such devices helped, but they were not an optimal solution. But what if a network device could be used to consolidate the terminal wiring? Terminal servers are LAN devices that can perform such a function as seen in Fig. 13.2.

This might not look all that much better than the previous figure. Nevertheless, terminal servers can be located near the terminals, with one long cable back to the main computer system instead of one per terminal. In a real business setting, this greatly simplifies terminal wiring. A terminal server can allow any given terminal to have

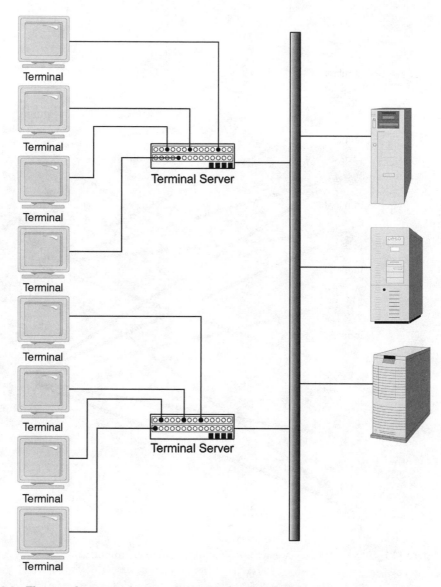

Figure 13.2   The use of a terminal server eliminates the wiring mesh.

more than one session active simultaneously, either with one or several destination computers. If a new computer is added to the environment, only the authorizations change; no wiring other than the new computer's connection to the LAN is required. Best of all, the way LANs are implemented on minicomputers eliminates the inter-rupt-per-keystroke problem. Naturally, the sessions need to be responded to; however,

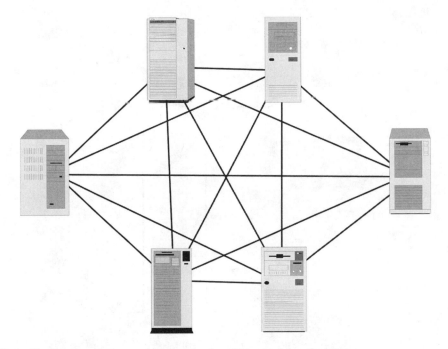

Figure 13.3   The minicomputer connectivity requires the same form of wiring mess.

a much smaller percentage of the minicomputer's resources is devoted strictly to communications functions.

Not only did these terminals generate wiring snarls, but also sites with multiple minicomputers were common. Suppose you had six computers, each with a need to reach all of the others on occasion. You could easily end up with a network wiring diagram like the one shown in Fig. 13.3. The wiring nightmares were so bad that many organizations joked that if the wiring was pulled out, the building would probably fall to the ground.

Imagine what a mess this would be if there were 8, 10, or 20 computers to connect! But if you used a common cable system instead, you might get something as the setup, depicted in Fig. 13.4. Clearly, this is an improvement, but the real question is: Is it easier to manage? You bet! In addition, the number of components required, and therefore the cost, decreases geometrically.

Shared Resources

Much of this progress occurred before personal computers were generally available. With the advent of personal computers, additional requirements surfaced. A general need appeared for resource sharing, where the resources were not connected to a central computer, especially high quality printers.

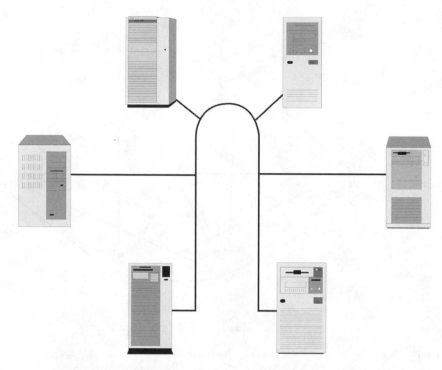

Figure 13.4   A single cabling structure might be a better approach.

The other major resource first shared was file services. File services provide a PC user the ability to reference files on another machine (the server) as though those files were actually located on the user's PC.

As network offerings matured, additional shared resources became common:

- Database servers
- Application servers
- Communications servers
- Backup servers

One of the particularly useful capabilities of a LAN is to allow companies to provide individual processor configurations optimized for specific functions. The ability to provide such servers goes a long way to justify the extra management effort involved in managing LANs.

LANs are not limited to these categories of servers; these are just the most frequently implemented. Other possibilities include scanner servers and facsimile servers. Additional functions will most likely evolve over time.

Distributed Systems

The term distributed processing predates LANs. However, LANs make it much easier to implement. What is distributed processing? It is not simply spreading functions out among multiple computers, although many people believe that is all there is to it. Distributed processing has a few basic premises:

- Do the work close to where the results are required.
- Dedicate processor(s) configured appropriately to their specific functions.

For robustness—the ability to continue key functions in the presence of failures—provide a certain degree of redundancy. Do not have just one processor in any given function category.

Of course, distributed processing is also designed into WANs, but allowing computers to communicate at high speeds among themselves is much easier to accomplish in a LAN environment.

Client/Server Architecture

Client/server design is, depending on one's viewpoint, either an extension or a subset of distributed processing design. Although distributed processing typically begins with the premise that all computers are created equal—at least insofar as their communications patterns—client/server design uses a more asymmetric model. The basic premise of client/server design is similar to that of distributed processing: dedicate processor(s) configured appropriately to their specific functions.

Scalability

A key benefit often provided by both distributed systems and client/server architectures is scalability. Roughly speaking, scalability is the ability to increase the power and/or number of users in an environment smoothly without major redesigns or swapping out of equipment and software. The key difference is that, with smaller machines, each upgrade is less expensive, and the added capacity is readily available.

Scalability is more an argument in favor of many small processors rather than specifically for LANs. However, the easiest way to connect those processors is with a LAN.

How They Work

A LAN environment includes, at a minimum, nodes and wiring. We first cover what makes up a node.

Node Configuration Elements

A LAN node is a computer that has a unique network address. That address consists of a sequence of letters and numbers (or possibly just numbers) that, just like your postal

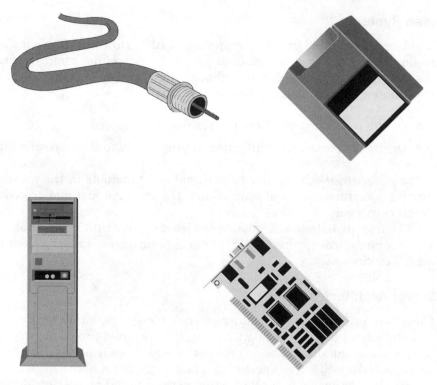

Figure 13.5   The basic components of a LAN.

address, identifies the node so that messages sent to it can be delivered to the correct device. LAN nodes comprise certain basic elements as depicted in Fig. 13.5. The key components of the LAN include:

- Processor (computer, possibly but not necessarily including keyboard and monitor, and so forth)
- Software
- LAN network interface card (NIC)

The processor can be just about any computer currently available. The software and NIC, however, deserve more discussion.

LAN Software for LAN Nodes

Every LAN node requires a complete, functional implementation of the International Standards Organization's (ISO's) Open Systems Interconnect (OSI) model. This simply means that all the functions described in the OSI model must be addressed, one way or another. With the exception of part of layer 1 (the physical layer), all of the OSI functions are accomplished in software, so it should be no surprise that most LAN software involves not one but rather several software modules that collectively allow a node to communicate.

At the bottom layer of the protocol stack (of these software modules) is certain software that is built into the NIC (in read-only memory, or ROM) as part of the physical layer. This is generally invisible to the user—or even to the installer—but it is critical. When installed, the onboard NIC software executes in the same "address space" used by other software on the node; thus certain address space might have to be set aside by the node in order for the software not to get stepped on by other programs. This might be handled directly by the node's operating system, or it might have to be addressed directly by the installer.

The next layer of software is the network driver. This software is the go-between or interface between the rest of the software on the node and the NIC. In the world of PCs, there are two prevalent standards for this software: network distributed interface standard (NDIS, from Microsoft) and open data interface (ODI, from Novell). These standards define not how the software drivers operate, but rather the standard approach for the other software on the computer to interact with the NDIS or ODI drivers.

It is the responsibility of the NIC manufacturers to provide such drivers with their interface cards. Providing such standard software is much more difficult than you might assume. As with all of the other software on a node, the NIC interface software runs under the operating system supporting that node. Computers, especially personal computers, can run many different operating systems. A different driver implementing a given interface standard is required for each operating system. If a vendor supports both ODI and NDIS (and most do), that doubles the number of modules to be provided. Nowadays, the PC-based systems include all the necessary protocols to support either network card driver. An example is Windows 9X, which has all the necessary drivers for both NDIS and ODI.

Above the level of the driver software is the province of network operating systems (NOS), such as Novell's NetWare and Microsoft's Windows operating systems (XP, Server, etc.).

The NOS software on a node provides two major functions:

- It provides all of the communications functions specified in the OSI model above level 2.
- It intercepts and satisfies resource requests on the node for resources that would normally appear on the node, but instead are to be provided via the LAN (e.g., file access, communications access).

LAN Network Interface Cards

Network interface cards shown in Fig. 13.6, typically fit into an expansion slot on a computer. In some cases, however, the network interface is built into the computer in

Figure 13.6   A network interface card, shown in two angles.

the factory. The latter approach usually results in a lower overall cost, but can reduce or eliminate the opportunity to change or upgrade the network interface later.

Functions performed by an NIC include the following:

- Providing a unique LAN address for the node that is built in by the manufacturer.
- Performing the link level functions with other nodes appropriate to the physical connection (e.g., twisted pairs of wire) and protocol (e.g., Ethernet) used on the particular LAN.
- Accepting protocol frames of information at full LAN speed, buffering (storing) them on the card until the computer is ready to process them.
- Recognizing, examining the address information and ignoring received protocol frames that are not addressed to the node in which the NIC is installed.

Responding to certain management signals on the network. These might be inquiries as to the status of the card or recent communications loads imposed on it, or commands to stop communication on the network.

All NOS node software functions in parallel with other software on a node. For example, the computer does not stop doing word processing when LAN communications occur. Thus, the node can on occasion get quite busy, perhaps so busy that frames arriving across the network might not always be dealt with promptly. However, those frames continue to arrive at the NIC at the rated speed of the LAN. What happens if the bits pile up in the NIC? If the buffer on the NIC fills and more bits continue to arrive, some bits will be lost ("dropped on the floor" in the vernacular).

The speed of the NIC is also a factor. However, the speed with which it communicates to its node (the local speed) is independent of the LAN speed. The part of the NIC doing local communications might or might not be as fast as the node receiving the information. If it is not that fast, then the NIC is a communications bottleneck. If overall performance is not satisfactory, this is one possible cause.

Topologies

The word topology is used in at least two different ways when discussing LANs. Unfortunately, speakers rarely identify which of the two meanings they are using. Even worse, they often muddle the two meanings together. We try to distinguish the two meanings by qualifying the term into physical topology and logical topology.

Physical topology constitutes the way one lays out the wires in a building. The major physical topologies include:

- Bus
- Ring
- Star

Logical topology describes the way signals travel on the wires. Unfortunately, logical topologies share much the same terminology as physical topologies. Signals can travel in the following fashions:

- Bus
- Ring
- Star (or switched)

So, is there any difference between physical and logical topologies? Emphatically, yes! Most of the logical topologies can be used on most of the physical topologies. Thus you can use bus communications techniques on a bus or star; ring communications techniques on a bus, ring, or tree; and star communications techniques on a bus or star. Confused? Read on—we sort the main variations out one at a time.

Physical Topologies

The bus physical topology has the following key characteristics:

- All locations on the communications medium are directly electronically accessible to all other points.
- Any signal placed on a bus becomes immediately available to all other nodes on the bus without requiring any form of retransmission.

Physical bus topologies are usually drawn as a line with nodes attached, as shown in Fig. 13.7. Note that the bus is a single high-speed cable with all devices connected to it.

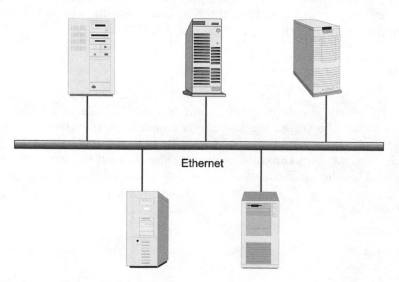

Figure 13.7 The layout of a bus topology.

The ring physical topology has the following key characteristics:

- Each node is connected to only two other nodes.
- Transmissions from one node to another pass via all intervening nodes in the ring.

Rings are typically drawn, as shown in Fig. 13.8. Some types of rings (e.g., fiber distributed data interface [FDDI]) have additional active devices to construct the ring itself, Fig. 13.9. This architecture is not a perfect circle as we think of it, but it is still a ring.

The star physical topology has the following key characteristics:

- Each node connects to a central device with its own wire or set of wires.
- The central device is responsible for ensuring that traffic for a given node reaches it.

Data might or might not pass through multiple nodes on the way to its destination, depending on the specific capabilities of the central device. Star topologies often are drawn something like the one shown in Fig. 13.10.

Note that, although there is always some type of device at the center, star diagrams often do not show it. It depends on whether the focus of the diagram is the nodes or the way the network is built. In the latter case, the diagram would look like this variation, shown in Fig. 13.11.

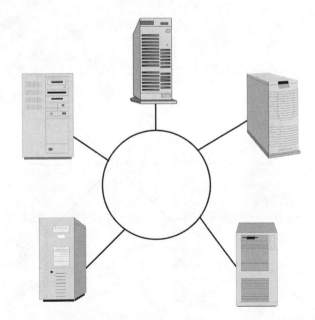

Figure 13.8 The typical physical ring as it evolved.

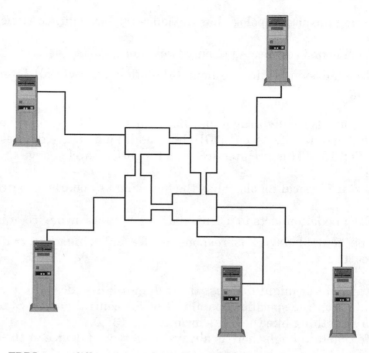

Figure 13.9 The FDDI uses a different type of ring. Not all rings are laid out in perfect circles.

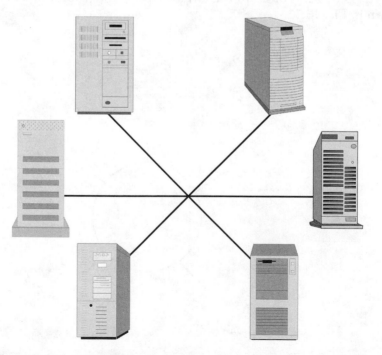

Figure 13.10 The typical star network layout.

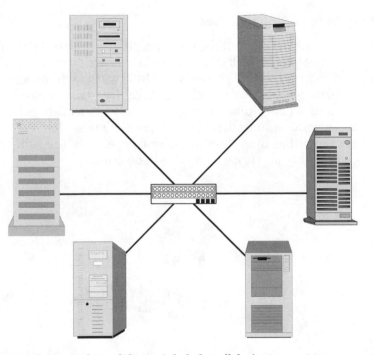

Figure 13.11   The star has some form of electronic hub that all devices connect to.

Logical Topologies

As mentioned earlier, logical topologies include bus, ring, and star (or switched). A logical bus operates with each transmission visible to every other node on the LAN. The easiest way to do this, of course, is with a physical bus; all devices connect to the same wire.

But consider the user of a star physical topology. If the central device instantly retransmits every frame it receives from one wire out to every other wire, how can the individual devices detect whether they are on a physical bus or physical star? Do they care? The answer to both questions is a qualified "no." A certain amount of engineering goes into building such devices. However some LANs were originally designed to function on a physical bus.

Bus topologies require a method of handling collisions—times when two or more nodes attempt to transmit at the same or overlapping times. Different methods are used with different protocols.

A logical ring consists of a network where any given transmission passes from one device to another in a fixed sequence until it reaches its destination. It is naturally most obvious on a physical ring. However, it also can be implemented on a physical bus or a physical star. An advantage of this tightly disciplined line protocol is that there can never be a "collision"; all devices know their turn and follow it. On the other hand, there can be quite a wait until one's turn arrives.

LAN Switching versus Nonswitched

When discussing driving habits, some people say, "Speed kills." That may be true, but in the case of networks, lack of speed can kill. There are many ways to design networks, but one of the most popular and straightforward is to design a backbone, whereby there is a high-speed path for high-speed requirements at a central point (topologically speaking) and all subsidiary networks connect to that backbone, seen in Fig. 13.12. There are several assumptions in this model. One is that there is a need for connections between either the subnetworks or from each of the subnetworks to that central backbone, possibly for server or application access.

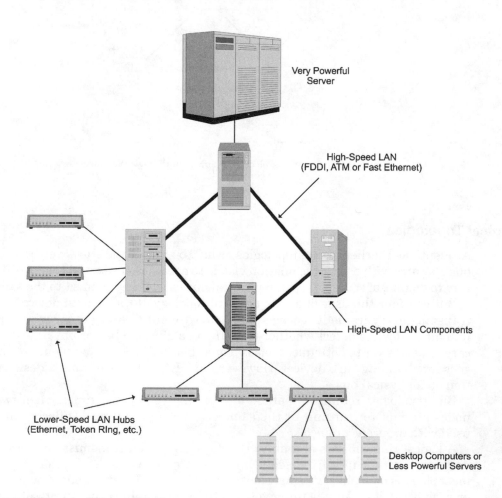

Figure 13.12   A backbone architecture.

There are many cases where backbones are required, so speed is important. Here we are talking about a way to deliver somewhat higher speed to desktops or for small backbones.

The internal bus speeds of even medium-speed desktop computers far exceed the capabilities of cost-effective local area networks. Loading applications takes a long time, relatively speaking. When you have a lot of people doing this at the same time, it can bury a network. You can pay the money to upgrade in the way we're going to describe here, but an easier approach is simply to distribute the applications to the desktop.

The key fact to remember here is that most local area networks employ shared media. Generally, when we refer to shared media, we mean Ethernet hub-based LANs. In modern networks wired with radial or star-type wiring, the equipment at the center causes every node in an Ethernet segment to see all of the traffic generated by all the other nodes. They are designed this way, and it is a good way to design a network for many reasons.

The job of a switch is twofold:

- It has to make the traffic on the wires to the devices to which the switch is connected look exactly the way it was before, from the point of view of the connected devices, because we are not planning on changing the electronics in those devices.

- It examines every packet coming in on every wire and on a packet-by-packet basis, directs those packets outbound to only the port or circuit where the packet has to go.

Switching is done on the basis of the hardware addresses of the connected network devices. Therefore, it's very fast. But the speed alone is not what creates the major benefit here. The major benefit is that the only traffic that is put on a wire going to a device is traffic destined for that device (plus broadcast traffic, unfortunately), see Fig. 13.13. So, that wire only sees traffic to and from that device; what this means is that, in effect, the wire now has the full rated bandwidth of the network dedicated to just that device and the connections it's talking to; that bandwidth is no longer shared. This is a major performance upgrade.

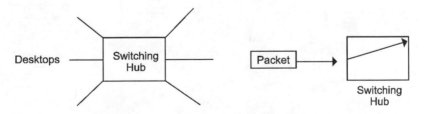

Figure 13.13 Switched LAN—packets go only to correct destination.

There are some limitations, however. Traffic on wires going to workstations without a switch would have lots of traffic that really wasn't designated for those workstations. But in a typical small network, all of the traffic is either going to or from the server if there is only one. So, giving it a switched connection doesn't really help very much because all of the traffic is still going to have to appear on that circuit. A better way to go is to have a switched hub that has a higher backbone speed connection shown in Fig. 13.14.

The beauty of this approach (switching to improve connectivity capacity to workstations) is that you only have to change the central hub. The electronics in the workstations remain the same, as does the wiring.

In addition to a simple lowering of the traffic levels, collisions are usually avoided in this approach, since there aren't other devices on any particular segment that are trying to get in at the same time. Put another way, the segment becomes a single wire connecting, or virtually connecting, two devices talking back and forth through the hub without any interfering traffic to get in the way.

The next variation is more of a topological variant than a technological one. Switching technology described in the preceding paragraphs in the context of delivering full bandwidth to individual desktops. But in many cases, workgroups need greater connection speed to a backbone. Moreover, many companies cascade Ethernet hubs in order to gain connectivity benefits while minimizing wiring costs; see Fig. 13.15. The problem, of course, is that the connections become much more heavily loaded as one moves up the upside-down tree hierarchy that Ethernet uses for its physical configuration.

As mentioned above, switching technologies are sometimes used in order to provide a moderate upgrade in speed in an environment that is running out of gas. They are an alternative to changing technologies. Because of the elimination of collisions in a switched LAN environment vis-à-vis a shared environment, switched LANs provide a significant improvement in to-the-desktop bandwidth.

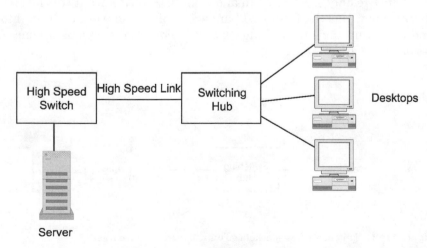

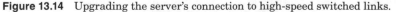

Figure 13.14   Upgrading the server's connection to high-speed switched links.

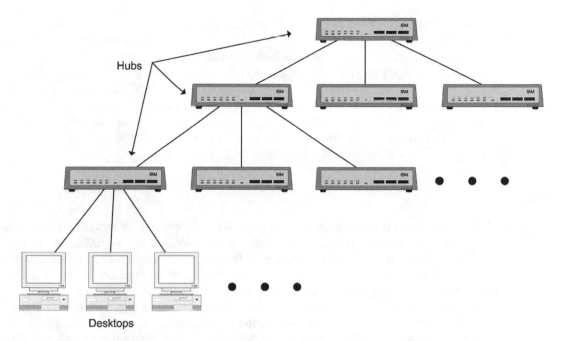

Figure 13.15 Cascaded, shared hubs.

Ethernet

Ethernet was the first commercial approach to using a LAN on a bus topology. Ethernet is the most commonly used LAN technology today. Ethernet still enjoys continued popularity and growth for a number of reasons:

- For its speed, it is by far the least expensive networking approach.
- Its various standards supporting a wide variety of media are sufficiently well defined that products from multiple vendors can be mixed and matched with a reasonable expectation that they will work well together.
- Ethernet equipment exists to allow virtually any intelligent device to connect to an Ethernet.
- It is fast enough for the vast majority of applications in use today.
- The Ethernet standards continue to evolve to keep pace with other LAN techniques.

The Ethernet standards define an approach to building a contention-based LAN on a bus topology. As originally defined and implemented by Xerox, Intel, and Digital Equipment Corporation (the DIX design), the bus appears to be a single straight cable system to all connected devices. The cable is available to multiple users at the same time, even though only one user at a time can send data if a shared bus is installed.

The Institute for Electrical and Electronic Engineers (IEEE) is responsible for the standards setting and administration for LANs. The committees associated with setting these standards are called the *802 committees*. Technically, the LAN protocol implemented most widely and still referred to as Ethernet is actually defined in the 802.3 standard, and is not precisely the same as either of the two "Ethernet" standards (I or II) defined by the Xerox-Intel-DEC triumvirate. However, most equipment available today can support both standards; also, in most cases the devices can interoperate on the same media. In any case, most people, when not attempting to be particularly precise, refer to 802.3 as Ethernet. We do also.

Concepts

The human ear is much better at picking out a single voice from among multiple simultaneous speakers than is any electronic receiver at selecting one signal from among many. Thus every local area network using a bus design must incorporate a contention management or arbitration mechanism that results in only one signal being present at a time. No matter how many devices share the medium, they have to wait their turn. Otherwise, signals on the cable would conflict like voices on the floor of a commodities exchange—but with less profit. Ethernet uses a contention management approach called carrier sense, multiple access with collision detection (CSMA/CD) to ensure that devices "speak" politely, one at a time. CSMA/CD is designed to provide equal use of the network for all attached devices. CSMA/CD actually breaks down into three meaningful two-word terms:

Carrier sense: All stations listen to the cable continuously. Ethernet nodes do not send out any signal at all unless they have something to say. Therefore, when stations monitor the cable, they are listening for the presence of a carrier signal. If a device that wants to transmit detects a carrier on the cable, then it knows that another device either is preparing to send, is sending, or has just finished sending information onto the cable. In any case, the waiting device will hold back until the carrier signal vanishes.

Multiple access: If no one is using the cable, any of the network devices attached to the Ethernet can transmit data onto the network at will; there is no central control, nor is there a need for any. This is a more powerful design element than might be apparent at first blush. Networks degrade (or experience reduced performance) in different ways, depending on their design. One factor that does not in and of itself degrade an Ethernet is the attachment of literally hundreds of devices. Because the wire is truly idle, unless a device is transmitting, only active devices impose any load on the network. Thus a myriad of devices can be connected, so long as most of them are not transmitting at any one time.

Of course, there is a potential fly in this ointment: If all those attached devices need to transmit lots of data, great congestion will ensue. Some networks are built to support primarily word processing, an occasional file transfer, and perhaps some electronic mail. With such networks, the light load per machine allows many devices to be present without degrading the network. Networks that will experience much traffic at all per device need to be engineered more carefully, perhaps by being divided up into multiple bridged segments.

Collision detection: In the event that two devices attempt to transmit at the same time, or even during overlapping time intervals, a collision will occur.

Think of two people simultaneously beginning to speak at a cocktail party. If they both continue to speak, neither will be understood. This might be fine for a New Yorker, who can talk and listen at the same time, but for the type of network under discussion, it can be devastating. On an Ethernet, if a collision occurs, the data is lost and each system must retransmit. However, to retransmit immediately will only cause the exact same result—a new collision.

At the cocktail party (if the attendees are reasonably well behaved), both speakers will stop as soon as they become aware of the problem. On an Ethernet, the first device that detects the problem will stop the regular transmission and send out a special jamming signal, which tells all attached devices that a collision has occurred. The jam signal will be heard by every device because all devices continue to listen to the network even if they are transmitting.

At the cocktail party, each speaker hesitates a moment, then tries again. The one that hesitates the shortest time gets the word in edgewise, while the other will wait for the next opportunity. On an Ethernet, any device that was attempting to transmit at the time the jam signal arrives will assume that a collision occurred. It will therefore calculate and wait a semirandom amount of time. What is semirandom? Each device uses a preprogrammed back off algorithm to wait a certain period of time before retransmitting. The individual devices will therefore wait different amounts of time. The calculation (algorithm) is an attempt to generate a random number, but the (guaranteed unique) address of each device is a part of the calculation. Thus, the amount of time waited in such circumstances will always be different for each involved device, ensuring that the next attempt by the device that waits the shortest time will succeed. Well, almost.

The problem is that the only devices that apply the waiting algorithm are those that experienced the collision. Anyother device that has occasion to transmit will only follow the standard Ethernet approach (listen, then transmit). If a new participant "decides" that it is time to transmit, it could do so just as the "fastest waiter" in the previous group finishes its wait and goes ahead with its second try. If this happens, another collision will occur.

You might well ask, "How does anything ever make it through an Ethernet?" We must emphasize that all of the shilly-shallying described in the previous paragraphs happens in a small number of microseconds. And remember, unless devices attempt to transmit at almost exactly the same time, collisions will not happen; the second device waits its turn, then transmits.

Nonetheless, if you understand how the collision detection and avoidance mechanism works, it should be no surprise that as the number of communicating devices attached to an Ethernet increases, the number of collisions also increases. In practice, close management is indicated when steady traffic on an Ethernet exceeds about 30–40 percent of the

10-Mbps capacity of the network. This really means that a true Ethernet with an average number of users on it will yield an effective throughput of approximately 3.3–4 Mbps.

Half Duplex

If you have ever seen a fast typist using a terminal connected to a minicomputer via Ethernet, you might have concluded that Ethernet is a full-duplex protocol. However, Ethernet is actually a half-duplex protocol. It is so fast, though, that it is functionally full duplex. Although no more than one frame can occupy the wire at a time—and in the case of a typist, it is possible that each 64-byte frame might literally include only 1 byte of data in each direction—the frames are moved back and forth so quickly that it looks to a human being as if the typing and the receiving of characters are simultaneous.

If two files were copied, one from node A to node B and the other from node B to node A, at exactly the same time, the flow of frames in both directions would so intermingle that again it would appear that the transmission was going in both ways simultaneously. Nevertheless, because at any one instant only one frame can occupy the wire at a time, the medium is actually only half duplex.

Bandwidth

Ethernet was created in the beginning to operate at 10 Mbps. There is an advantage to making all implementations run at the same speed: no significant speed matching is required when connecting multiple Ethernet segments, even those built using different media.

However, although all Ethernets run at 10 Mbps, not all devices on an Ethernet actually communicate at 10 Mbps. This concept is difficult to grasp, but it is important. Every node connected to an Ethernet incorporates an interface capable of receiving from and transmitting onto the Ethernet at 10 Mbps—exactly. Otherwise, it does not comply with the Ethernet standard.

As with all protocols, not all of the bandwidth on Ethernet is actually available for carrying application-related data. Some bits are required for overhead functions. Ethernet supports a variable-length "frame"; the minimum frame length is 64 bytes, the maximum frame size is 1518 bytes. The variation results from changing the amount of data transmitted. In the Ethernet (actually, 802.3) protocol, 18 bytes in each frame are dedicated to overhead, as shown in Table 13.1. A graphical layout of the frame is shown in Fig.13.16.

Destination Address

Both the destination and source addresses are 6-byte fields, usually represented in hexadecimal format; for example, BB-BB-BB-BB-BB-BB. Every Ethernet interface on a LAN segment receives and processes all frames transmitted on the LAN. The main job of the receiving interface is to compare the destination address in each received packet with its own address. If the addresses match, the frame is delivered to higher protocol

TABLE 13.1   Composition of an 802.3 Frame

Function	Bytes	Description
Destination address	6	Ethernet address of the node to which the frame is addressed
Source address	6	Ethernet address of the sending node
Length	2	Indicates the number of bytes of data in the next (data) field
Data	46–1500	The "payload"—the actual data being transmitted
CRC	4	Cyclic redundancy error detection bytes

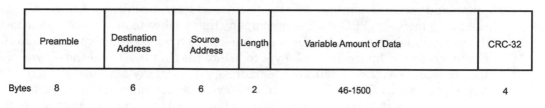

| Bytes | 8 | 6 | 6 | 2 | 46-1500 | 4 |

Figure 13.16   The Ethernet frame.

layers at the node for further processing and eventual handoff to an application. If the addresses do not match, the frame is "dropped on the floor"; that is, it is discarded.

NOTE   In our normal numbering system, decimal or base 10, the digits 0 through 9 are used to count. Note that even though we call it base 10, and there are 10 digits, there is no single digit that represents the quantity 10. Each position (ones, tens, hundreds, etc.) in a number contains a decimal digit (that is, 0 through 9) indicating how many of a power of 10 ($10^0 = 1$, $10^1 = 10$, $10^2 = 100$, and so on) goes into that number. Thus the number 264 is four 1s plus six 10s plus two 100s.

In the hexadecimal or base 16 numbering system, we also use the digits 0 through 9 to count. But we need six additional symbols to represent the values 10 through 15 (there is no need for a single symbol for 16). Hexadecimal uses the capital letters A through F to represent the values 10 through 15, respectively. Each position in a hexadecimal number contains a hexadecimal digit (0 through F) indicating how many of a power of sixteen ($16^0 = 1$, $16^1 = 16$, $16^2 = 256$, and so on) goes into that number. Thus the hexadecimal number 264 is four 1s plus six 16s plus two 256s or, in total as represented in the decimal numbering system, 612. The hexadecimal number BB is eleven 1s plus eleven 16s, or a total of 187 decimal.

The "natural" internal numbering system used in most data processing and communications equipment is binary, or base 2, using only 1s and 0s. Network addresses (and many other items in data communications and data processing) are usually represented in hexadecimal notation because of the ease with which it can represent or be converted into 4-bit binary (base 2) numbers, as follows:

Hex digit	0	1	2	3	4	5	6	7	8	9	A	B	C	D	E	F
Binary value	0000	0001	0010	0011	0100	0101	0110	0111	1000	1001	1010	1011	1100	1101	1110	1111
Decimal value	0	1	2	3	4	5	6	7	8	9	10	11	12	13	14	15

Because it only takes one hexadecimal digit to represent any possible single 4-bit binary value (as illustrated here), and 1 byte equals 8 bits, it takes exactly 2 hexadecimal digits to represent the contents of 1 byte.

Source Address

Every Ethernet node contains an interface device, today mostly these are built-in or installed at the factory, other times provided as part of an add-on printed circuit board that implements the interface. Every single one of those devices worldwide contains (or should contain) a unique 48-bit Ethernet address, usually stored in programmable read-only memory (PROM). Every company that wishes to manufacture such Ethernet devices applies to the IEEE for a unique 3-byte code. As the company manufactures the interfaces, it "burns in" its 3-byte code into the first 3 bytes of the 6-byte address of that device. The other 3 bytes of the address are normally assigned sequentially, 1 per device, but can in fact be assigned in whatever way the manufacturer wishes. The only requirement is that every device has a different 6-byte address. If properly followed, this system guarantees that every manufactured Ethernet device will have its own unique 6-byte physical address.

Length

Valid lengths for Ethernet frames are from 64 to 1518 bytes inclusive. The length field in the frame indicates only the number of payload bytes, and that value can range from 46 to 1500 bytes inclusive. Notice that a frame cannot contain fewer than 46 bytes of data. What happens if the sending device provides fewer bytes to be transmitted? The controller will add "pad" bytes to bring the overall frame size up to the minimum length of 64 bytes. The undersized frames are called *runts*. If a runt gets onto the cable, the interface cards will accept the frame and determine that it is too short, thus discarding it immediately.

Why is there a minimum length? There is an interaction between minimum frame length and the ability to detect collisions. Each medium supported by the Ethernet standard has a defined maximum length for any one segment. One factor that goes into determining that length is the need to ensure that a device transmitting a frame onto the segment will still be listening if a collision occurs—and will recognize that the collision happened to its own transmitted frame. Devices stop listening for their own collisions a very short time after they finish transmitting. Therefore, once a device begins transmitting, it must continue to do so long enough for the most distant device to receive at least the beginning of the frame, plus the time required to receive a jam signal from that distant device if such an event occurs.

If the minimum frame size were smaller, then the defined maximum segment sizes would also have to be shorter. To allow longer-than-specified segment lengths, the minimum frame size would have to be increased, requiring additional pad characters and reducing the efficiency of the Ethernet protocol. The 64-byte minimum cannot be claimed to be "ideal;" rather, it is an engineering judgment call by the original designers of the Ethernet protocol. If installers adhere to the rules regarding segment lengths, no undetected collisions can occur.

Data

This is the frame's payload, the reason the frame is being transmitted in the first place. The data can be up to 1500 bytes. In most cases, the actual number of application-related bytes carried will be smaller than this, because some of the 1500 bytes will be used by higher-level protocols for their overhead bytes, sometimes many more per frame than are required by Ethernet itself. Sometimes people will include 14-byte Ethernet headers, 4-byte 802.1q VLAN tags, and 4-byte CRCs in their counts, for 1514, 1518, 1522. However, 1518 is the most common number. The average size Ethernet frame is judged to be between 350 and 500 bytes. If a frame exceeds the maximum length of 1518 bytes (1500 payload and 18 overhead), the frame is considered a giant. Giants will also be discarded by the receiving interfaces except where there are cards that support "jumbo frames." Jumbo frames are used with Ethernets that operate at gigabit per second speeds. Jumbo frames often mean 9000 bytes for Gigabit Ethernet, but can refer to anything over 1500 bytes.

CRC

The cyclic redundancy check (CRC) digits allow the receiving node's Ethernet interface to determine whether a frame was received intact or not. If not, the frame is discarded. If the interface is one of the more expensive available, it might also keep track of the number of frames discarded in order to facilitate management and detection of network faults. Error checking was covered earlier in this book.

Components

Speaking very generally, the components used to implement a LAN tend to be similar across implementations; there must be an interface built into (or added to) each node. Each node must have driver software installed that communicates between the nodes (network) operating system software and the interface, and the interface must be connected to the network medium. However, when one delves a little deeper, there are significant differences both among LAN architectures and even among variations in the same LAN architecture, such as Ethernet.

For example, Ethernet is probably supported over more different types of media (with truly standard implementations) than any other LAN protocol. And the detailed piece parts, as well as design considerations, vary greatly depending on the specific medium.

The rest of this chapter covers the various components that can be used to build an Ethernet. We also mix in some design information and rules. Before getting down into the details, though, we would like to indicate what happens to people who violate the rules. Actually, at most organizations there aren't network police. However, many network installers and users wish there were. Generally speaking, there are two kinds of consequences that can result when LAN design rules are violated. The network doesn't work. Obvious, right? What could be worse? What could be worse is the alternative: the network that does work...sort of.

The designers of the various LAN standards (not just Ethernet, of course) attempted to specify standards that would result in robust networks—networks that could continue to operate in the presence of certain kinds of problems. But, TANSTAAFL ("there ain't no such thing as a free lunch"). If a network does have some kind of problem and continues to operate anyway, that operation is usually somewhat degraded. In Ethernet's case, for example, intermittent short circuits appear to users as collisions. No data is lost, but overall performance can be slow. Out-and-out failures are often much easier to diagnose and repair.

10BASE5

This is a good time to explain the naming standard used for the various Ethernet substandards. Bearing in mind that these were defined by committees, here goes. Each term is made up of three parts. The first part (here, 10) indicates that the network runs at 10 Mbps. The second part (BASE) indicates that the network is a baseband network. The last part (in this case, 5) indicates some physical component of the cabling system. In the case of 10BASE5, it indicates that one segment can reach up to 500 meters (1640 feet) in length. We explain the variations in these terms as we cover each of Ethernet's supported media.

Ethernet was originally defined to operate over a particularly heavy type of coaxial cable, one thicker than most individuals' thumbs. People in the industry often referred to it as orange hose—a particularly apt name because of its usual color. A more conventional term for the 10BASE5 medium is thick wire Ethernet.

10BASE5 Piece Parts

As with any LAN, every attached device must have a network interface card (NIC). In the case of thick wire, that NIC has a port called an attachment unit interface (AUI), a 15-pin interface designed to connect to a transceiver cable (sometimes also referred to as a drop cable).

The transceiver cable can extend up to 50 meters (164 feet), but usually is much shorter, somewhere between 2 and 10 meters. This cable is not Ethernet cable; it is not coaxial, but rather multipin, similar to RS232, but with fewer wires. The transceiver cable plugs into a transceiver, naturally. The transceivers are shown in Fig. 13.17, whereas the pin-outs are shown in Fig. 13.18.

Transceivers include the componentry for a combined transmitter and receiver. Minimum spacing between transceivers on the cable is 2.5 meters (8.2 feet). When using the orange Ethernet cable, there are black marks spaced on the cable to indicate the appropriate spacing between the taps. If you do not adhere to the distance limits, other problems can occur. Ethernet transceivers are also sometimes referred to as taps or sometimes vampire taps.

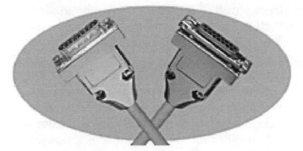

Figure 13.17 Transceivers are used for the AUI connection.

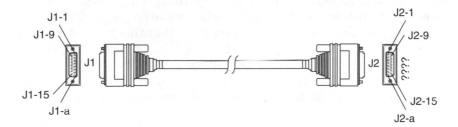

Figure 13.18 The pin-out for the AUI 15-pin connector.

Vampire tap is most descriptive. Thick-wire Ethernet taps can be attached to the orange hose without interrupting the network. Inserting two sharp points into the cable, one deep enough to reach the core, the other stopping at the braid, does this. (A special tool is usually used to predrill the holes.) The tap clamps onto the cable with the two points sunken into the cable. The design might seem somewhat baroque, but the ability to add or remove devices from an active network was a significant advance in network technology at the time Ethernet was first designed.

Not all networks—not even most other Ethernets—require separate transceivers, so it would be worthwhile to indicate their function here. Ethernet transceivers perform several important functions:

- Physical access to the main LAN cable, as described above
- Media conversion from coaxial to multistrand cable
- Electrical protection and isolation in both directions (LAN to NIC and vice versa)

But transceivers are essentially passive devices; the protocol smarts reside in the NICs. Thick wire is the only Ethernet medium that must be configured as a physical bus. As mentioned above, thick wire can be configured in segments up to 500 meters long. Up to three segments can be connected in series using two Ethernet repeaters. If more segments are so connected, the (very small) delays unavoidably introduced by the repeaters might foul up the collision detection part of the protocol.

Up to 100 direct physical attachments can be made to one segment, although there are ways to attach far more network devices than that. Up to 1024 network addresses can reside on a segment or set of segments connected by repeaters. As with the other rules, violators of this configuration rule might be punished by undetected collisions.

Barrel connectors, as shown in Fig. 13.19 (barrel), are small passive devices used to connect two pieces of coaxial cable to make a longer one. Barrel connectors are not defined parts of the Ethernet standard. They can be used, but the rules for segment lengths simply apply to the aggregate length built up of smaller wire pieces; that is, a 500-meter length can include one or more barrel connectors, but it still is limited to 500 meters.

Terminators, as shown in Fig. 13.20, are also small passive devices. But, unlike barrel connectors, terminators are defined Ethernet components and are essential to proper operation of a 10BASE5 Ethernet. Every 10BASE5 segment must have precisely two terminators installed, one on either end. One and only one of those terminators must be properly grounded. We used to tell students that this was required to ensure that the bits do not "fall out of the wire." But actually, in a matter of speaking, terminators are intended to ensure that the bits do "fall out of the wire"; improperly terminated coaxial cable ends can reflect transmissions back onto the wire, interfering with themselves and/or later transmissions and generating unnecessary collisions.

Figure 13.19   A barrel connector.

Figure 13.20   A terminator used on an Ethernet coaxial cable.

Configuration of 10BASE5 Parts

SETUP—Designing 10BASE5 networks is relatively simple. But installing them is less so. If only one segment is needed, typical configurations include those shown in Fig. 13.21. Note a few characteristics of the 10BASE5 cable layouts:

- No loop is created; the cable forms a line, however bendy.
- The cable is strung in such a way that all parts of the building are within reasonable transceiver cable reach.
- The cable is continuous and is most likely not configured to take advantage of any existing cable troughs. In fact, it is probably placed in the ceiling.
- The 500-meter segment length limitation applies to the length of the cable on the reel; how it is laid out does not affect the length limitation at all.

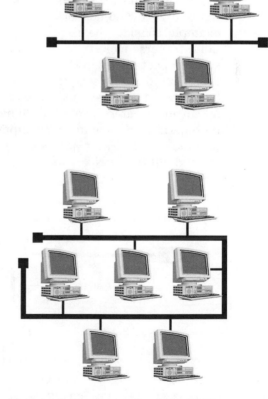

Figure 13.21 Typical 10BASE5 cable layouts.

- Everything that attaches to a 10BASE5 cable connects via a transceiver that is clamped to the cable or via something else that is attached via a transceiver. The cable ends never plug into anything but the appropriate terminator.

- If more than one segment is required, the segments connect as shown in Fig. 13.22.

Because of the complexity of the layout, the differences in building designs, and the difficulty in using this thick-wire coax, this has become a throwback in the installation business. No new 10BASE5 networks are being installed these days, so we will not go into great detail on their possible layouts. But it is a good idea to expand on the two-repeater rule here, because it applies (sometimes in modified form) to other Ethernet topologies as well. The rule says, in effect, that "Thou shall not configure an Ethernet such that traffic must flow via more than two repeaters to get from any node to any other node." Seems straightforward, but there is at least one nonobvious subtlety. If two repeaters are configured so that the cable between them has no other drops (not even one), then for purposes of the two-repeater rule those two repeaters each count as one half of one repeater. Thus, the two add up to one. An Ethernet can thus have up to four repeaters in series without violating the two-repeater rule. Figure 13.23 illustrates a configuration with three repeaters.

The two-repeater rule is not as onerous as might be the case. It is possible to configure a 10BASE5 network with an almost arbitrarily large number of segments. For example, consider the "comb" configuration shown in Fig. 13.24. Here, no single packet must traverse more than two repeaters to reach anywhere on the network, although seven repeaters are in the configuration. Each segment can still be 500 meters; there is opportunity with such layout to connect a great many nodes, if necessary. Nodes can be placed on any segment, although in practice the top segment, which is connected to all seven repeaters, is often designated as a backbone and reserved for repeaters and perhaps network monitoring equipment. The drawback is that whenever a single frame is sent, it will be sent across every link on the network, causing possible congestion throughout the LAN.

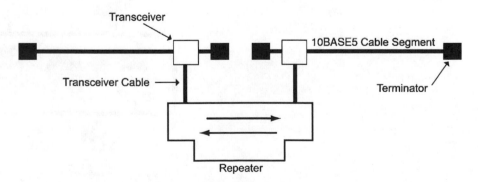

Figure 13.22 Connecting 10BASE5 segments.

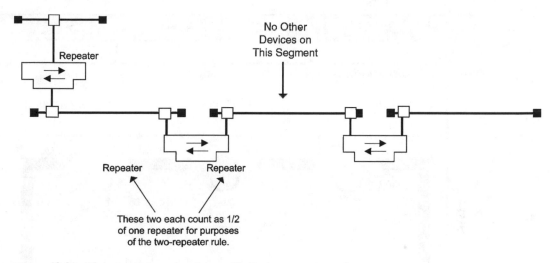

Figure 13.23 Three repeaters complying with the two-repeater rule.

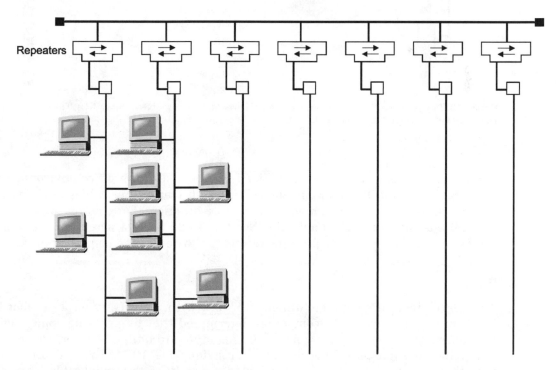

Figure 13.24 Comb 10BASE5 layout.

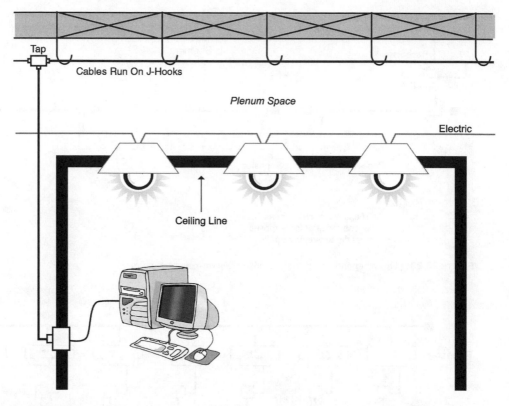

Figure 13.25 To move a station is very complex. It requires going above the ceiling. The drop behind the wall may not lend itself to removal.

Physical access to the main cable itself is required. In an office environment, the main cable is typically strung in the ceiling, with transceiver cables leading to individual offices. Moves and changes can be quite an effort. For this reason and others, 10BASE5 is rarely installed anymore. See Fig. 13.25 for how accessing the cable and the need to add a drop cable from the ceiling to the device can be problematic.

10BASE2

10BASE5 wiring is extremely difficult to work with, and costly on a per-foot basis. With improving technology, companies determined that by applying some engineering smarts, they could design a new Ethernet standard (still 802.3) for use on a much lighter, flexible, and less expensive type of coaxial cable. 10BASE2, also often referred to as thin wire, or cheaper net, is specified to run on RG-58A coaxial cable. This cable is almost identical to the cable that you probably have running into your home for cable television. However, there are quite a number of differences between the configuration of 10BASE5 and that of 10BASE2.

Figure 13.26   The 10BASE2 T connector.

10BASE2 Piece Parts

As with the other 802.3 media, 10BASE2 requires an NIC in each node. However, the NIC is much smarter and the tap much simpler (and less expensive) than in a 10BASE5 configuration. Also, there is no transceiver cable required or even allowed; instead, the tap called a T connector—plugs right into the back of the NIC. The T connector splits the signal on the cable, allowing it to continue on and also sending a copy directly into the connector on the NIC—a coax connector of the same type as on the other two sides of the T. A T connector looks something like the one shown in Fig. 13.26.

T connectors have advantages and disadvantages compared to transceivers. They are far less expensive, about one-tenth the cost. They can be added or removed from a 10BASE2 daisy chain in seconds, much more quickly than a 10BASE5 transceiver. However, unlike with 10BASE5, T connectors are inserted in line in the coaxial cable; if a T connector is to be added or removed, the entire cable will be down for those few seconds during which the change is being made. This is true even if the T connector is being added to the end of the cable. Once a T connector is added to the cable, unplugging it from or plugging it into its attached node does not disrupt the cable—so long as the T connector itself remains in the cable. For this reason, many installations preconfigure many T connectors in each daisy chain to avoid later disruption.

The minimum distance between T connectors is 0.5 meters (1.6 feet). One 10BASE2 segment can be up to 185 meters (607 feet) long, much shorter than a 10BASE5 segment. As with 10BASE5, every segment must end with a terminator, in this case one designed for 10BASE2. As you can see in the next section, there are differences in how the coax is terminated and in how it is laid out when compared with 10BASE5.

Configuration of 10BASE2 Parts

SETUP—10BASE2 is supported in two different kinds of configurations and is also often used in a third not originally envisioned in the specification. The three configurations can briefly be summarized as follows:

- Star with daisy chains
- Pure star configuration
- Daisy chain bus

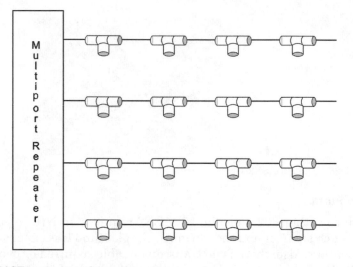

Figure 13.27   10BASE2 using a multiport repeater.

The original specification for 10BASE2 was a star configuration, with each radiating spoke a daisy chain bus. Such a configuration might look like Fig. 13.27.

A multiport repeater (MPR) takes every signal it receives on one daisy chain and sends it out over all of the other daisy chains to which it is connected. Up to 27 T connectors (some vendors support up to 30) can be installed on each daisy chain; the number of daisy chains is limited by the number of ports on the MPR. The last T connector on each daisy chain must have a terminator on one side. The MPR is an active device; it plugs into ac power. As such, it is grounded through its power cord and therefore provides an electrical ground for each attached segment. Thus no separate ground is required (or indeed allowed) for the individual segments. Note that each daisy chain is plugged directly into a port on the MPR; the cable end at the MPR does not require a T connector.

This MPR configuration of daisy chains is very cost effective compared to 10BASE5. However, wiring and maintaining it is rather onerous. Until the last few years, using this approach for wall-plate installations (vs. just running the cable along the floor) was very difficult and often subject to frequent outages as individuals interrupted connections, disrupting the entire daisy chain. More recently, special wall plates have come onto the market that simplify such wiring; however, they are quite expensive. 10BASE2 installations can also use a pure star configuration, as shown in Fig. 13.28.

With only one T connector (and therefore only one Ethernet node) per cable, the per-port cost of a 10BASE2 pure star is much higher than the daisy chain approach; the cost of the MPR itself is spread across far fewer devices than with the previous

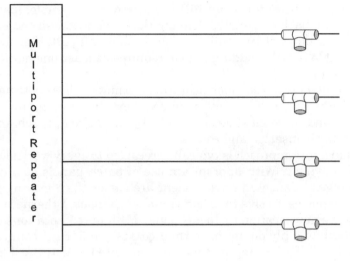

Figure 13.28 10BASE2 pure star.

Figure 13.29 10BASE2 daisy chain bus without repeater.

configuration. Nonetheless, the star has two major advantages over both the daisy chain and 10BASE5:

- Because it is no longer a physical bus (although it is still a logical bus), it can use the physical communications paths installed in buildings for the purposes of telephone wiring because telephone wiring too is star configured.

- Because each node is on its own cable, cable faults generally do not affect other nodes through the MPR.

Both of the two previous 10BASE2 configurations are officially supported by vendors. The following one is not. The pure daisy chain bus Fig. 13.29, without use of any repeater, was not contemplated by the specifiers of the 10BASE2 standard (perhaps because the opportunity to sell equipment to implement it is minimal). The biggest problem with it is that, although every Ethernet segment is supposed to be grounded, daisy chains without repeaters usually are not in practice grounded.

Because such networks are by definition very small (not to exceed 30 T connectors), the problems brought on by not grounding them properly usually do not cause major interruptions. Certainly this is probably the least expensive type of Ethernet configuration on a per-port basis that supports more than two nodes.

Removing a node from any 10BASE2 network is simple; just unplug the T connector from the back of the NIC, leaving the T connector in the cable. Adding a node to either of the daisy chain configurations is more difficult. If dealing with preterminated coaxial cable lengths, adding a node requires at least one additional cable length and a T connector.

The problem is not so much acquiring the materials as getting at the portion of cable to which the new cable length is to be added. In addition, unless the new connectors are used (and these must be preinstalled), the entire daisy chain is down until the new T connector is inserted and connected.

The pure star approach is typically precabled to every work location, just as is normal telephone wiring. With appropriate use of patch panels at a central location, moves and changes in such an environment are easier than moving telephones. (Normally, telephone moves involve telephone number changes; Ethernet moves require only connecting the new location up to any active MPR port.) Locations not requiring Ethernet connectivity simply do not have their coaxial cable runs connected to an active MPR port. If 10BASE-T wiring had not been invented, the 10BASE2 approach might have become much more popular.

10BASE-T

10BASE-T defines a standard for running Ethernet over unshielded twisted pair (UTP) wiring. The much lower wiring cost of 10BASE-T, as well as the availability of people who know how to work with UTP wiring, has made this cabling approach extremely popular. The vast majority of new installations today use 10BASE-T for horizontal wiring.

The possibility of running Ethernet over UTP excited many companies before the actual standard was developed. Several vendors developed an Ethernet-over-UTP variant before the 10BASE-T standard was finalized. These variants worked, but naturally, it was impossible to intermix components from these vendors to build an Ethernet-over-UTP configuration. Most of the vendors did, however, have the integrity to guarantee free conversion, or at least plausible migration paths, from their proprietary hardware to hardware compliant with the 10BASE-T standard when the latter became available.

That promise does not mean, of course, that all customers bothered to take advantage of such upgrades when they became available. You might find yourself dealing with an existing UTP-based Ethernet installation with which you have had no previous involvement. If so, we suggest you verify that the hardware is indeed 10BASE-T compliant rather than an older proprietary variant before blithely assuming that added 10BASE-T hardware will integrate properly.

10BASE-T Piece Parts

10BASE-T NICs are functionally similar to 10BASE2 NICs. That is, there is no separate transceiver as is required with 10BASE5 architecture. The connections are quite different, however. Ethernet UTP wire is terminated at each end with an eight-pin

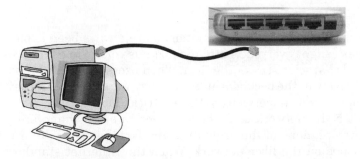

Figure 13.30   The 10BASE-T connection.

modular RJ-45 jack (only four pins are used). The modular jack plugs directly into the NIC; no T connector is required. Each cable supports only one Ethernet node, as with the pure star thin net approach. See Fig. 13.30 for a representation of the 10BASE-T environment. Its length must not exceed 100 meters (328 feet). The minimum category of wire based on standards is CAT 3.

A 10BASE-T hub (sometimes also called a concentrator) is usually required. This is another version of the LAN in a box. The box or hub is the backbone network, whereas the horizontal run to the desktop is the drop. The only exception is if only two devices are to be connected; two 10BASE-T devices can be linked via a crossover 10BASE-T cable. 10BASE-T hubs are functionally identical to multiport repeaters, although some vendors provide sufficiently fast central hubs that the two-repeater rule can be slightly relaxed.

10BASE-T hubs (and, to a large extent, other hubs as well) come in two broad categories:

- Work group hubs, sometimes referred to as stackable hubs
- Backplane chassis, sometimes referred to as concentrators

Work group hubs are relatively inexpensive devices that typically support 12 or 16 connections. If they incorporate SNMP management agents, the cost increases by several hundred dollars. Work group hubs, by definition, have very few options in their configurations. Nevertheless, their low cost and simple environmental requirements (they can be mounted in a rack or simply placed on a table or on the floor) make them extremely popular.

Chassis-based concentrators offer great modular flexibility. Such devices consist of a power supply, some control logic, and several slots into which interface boards can be inserted. Each interface board can support several 10BASE-T cables, often 12. Depending on the manufacturer, other boards might be available to support different types of networks out of the same chassis. Those other network types (for example, token ring) might be interconnected to the Ethernet board either via an additional interface board just for that purpose or via an external device not inserted into the chassis.

10BASE-F (Fiber)

Newer uses of various cabling systems have always been explored. The fiber-optic medium has caught everyone's attention because of the declining costs of the glass and the electrical characteristics of the fiber. When users discovered that the fiber could be used inexpensively in the backbone network, they were thrilled. If they could use a high-speed medium that was impervious to the electrical, mechanical, and radio frequency interference, then the network could be stretched to areas that were previously unavailable. Furthermore, none of the grounding and bonding issues that come with copper cable were issues on the fiber network. When the Ethernet standard ramped up to higher speeds (100-Mbps Ethernet, for example), the fiber would support these higher speeds with ease. Thus, the backbone saw more implementations with the 10BASE-F installed.

The 10-Mbps standard was still used in the backbone network, but UTP wiring was still the least expensive proposition for wiring to the desktop. Therefore, a medium changer is required. In the closets where the LAN will run from floor to floor, or from closet to closet, fiber is used. At the hub, ports exist for the connection from hub to hub via the fiber backbone. Inside the hub, the electronics are present to convert the fiber backbone to a copper station drop, or, in more precise terms, from the light to the electrical pulses needed for the copper. A typical configuration of the 10BASE-F environment is shown in Fig. 13.31. This could be extended to the desktop, but, as already stated, the

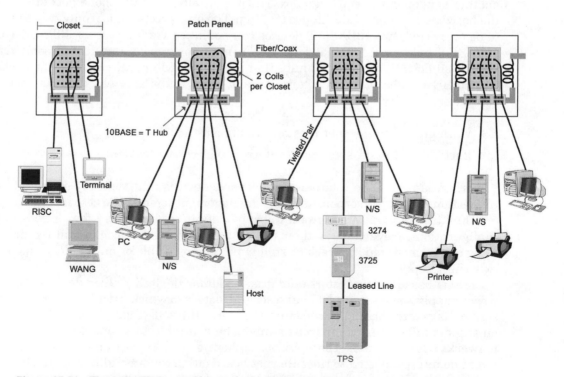

Figure 13.31 The 10BASE-F uses fiber in the backbone but converts to copper to the desk.

cost of putting fiber cards acting as transceivers in a PC or workstation is too steep for the average user. Therefore, this is done in a mixed environment.

10Broad36

Some networks have been built based on a broadband coaxial cable in the backbone. This might be more prevalent in a campus area (such as a college, corporate park, or hospital), where multiple buildings are interlinked. The use of the broadband cable was an expedient to support the needs of the organization's voice, data, and video needs because all of these components were analog transmissions that were connected between buildings. Therefore, the broadband backbone cable was used when the Ethernet was introduced. Customers who needed to link multiple buildings together were constrained by the 500-meter distance limitations of the Ethernet baseband coax. Even with the two-repeater rule, the most that the cable could be extended was 1500 meters, just under a mile. Although this might sound like a lot of cable, which should reach just about anywhere, that one mile of cable gets used very quickly when it needs to be snaked through ceilings, up and down from the ceiling heights, and so on.

Thus, the existing broadband cable offered a significant distance increase to Ethernet users who had to exceed the distance allowances. Using a 10-Mbps transmission speed on a broadband cable, the distance limitations were increased to 3600 meters. This is a sevenfold increase in the distances over which the cable could be run. So the vendors came up with a solution to the distance and the medium needs for the end user. Broadband cable inherently is an analog transmission system. Special devices called frequency agile modems (FAMs) were attached to the cable to modulate the electrical signal onto the carrier. The cable is normally broken down into various channels of 6 MHz each. Using a bridging arrangement, two channels could be connected together as a 12-MHz channel and used to transmit 10-Mbps Ethernet on this coax. This allowed more flexibility in overall networking ability because the Ethernet, as stated in the beginning of this chapter, has been implemented in a variety of media.

Digital Equipment Corporation (DEC) was a supporter of this form of connectivity in their DECNet on Ethernet from the onset. Others also came up with the necessary piece parts to use the broadband cable systems for the 10-Mbps Ethernet standards. This has also been accepted as a connection under the IEEE standards committee. See Fig. 13.32 for a cable using the broadband Ethernet connection.

Fast Ethernet

As described elsewhere, the uses of local area networks have changed over the years. While in the past the primary use was for movement of files and access to data by applications, a frequent use of local area networks now is to load applications from servers. Also, the character of those applications has changed. The executables themselves have moved into the multiple megabyte range, and in some cases graphic files are also now in the millions of bits. What all this means is that faster networks are needed. Another factor driving the need for speed is larger, higher-resolution monitors. A modern

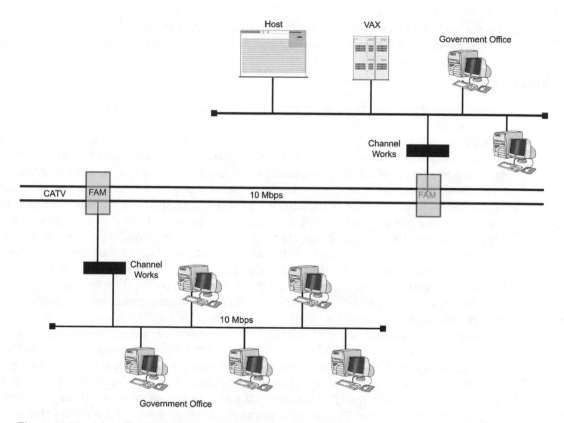

Figure 13.32   A broadband (CATV) application using 10 megabits on coax.

1024×768 monitor displays slightly over 1 million bits for one screen's worth of information. That would require, ideally, slightly more than 1/10 of a second to traverse an Ethernet. In practice, it would take considerably longer. One-tenth of a second may not sound like a great deal, but on a small network of 10 users, a whole second might be eaten up just by the one screen to each user. In practice, it would probably be worse since contention would slow things down.

Some applications are considerably worse than this. Large, high-resolution graphics files make some environments entirely unsupportable by a standard Ethernet. For example, the size of a single-digitized magazine cover can approach 70 megabytes. Bottom line: we need more speed.

The culture of the workforce has also changed considerably. The days of just typing ASCII text characters on a screen have gone. With Internet and Intranet access, the user now does more information processing. Moreover, that information is represented through a GUI, in which the graphics interfaces are much denser. The amount of data traveling across our networks is rapidly becoming exponential. The 10-Mbps Ethernet was pushed aside in favor of the 100-Mbps Ethernet. Some organizations moved to a 10-Mbps switched Ethernet as a means of forestalling the change of all the NIC cards in the PCs. This made sense, but only begs for the actual upgrade later. Now newer switches and hubs are auto detecting where a mix of 10- and 100-Mbps Ethernet NIC cards can be used on the same network.

All computer manufacturers are now installing 100-Mbps Ethernet cards directly in the PCs when they are manufactured. This saves the LAN administrator from having to buy the cards separately. There is a minor issue associated with the manufacturers installing these cards. Not all NIC cards are created equal. Many are made with special features and functions not available to others. Therefore, there could be some conflict on the LAN when these mixed variations are all on the same network. The other problem is that the computer manufacturers who install the NICs usually require special drivers for their machine. Thus a user must be aware that differences will arise and the price we pay for free LAN cards is the added burden of keeping on top of the myriad protocols and drivers required.

As the convergence of voice and data caught on in the industry during the late 1990s, the move is to incorporate voice, data, and streaming video at the desktop on the LAN. Given the limits of the 10-Mbps Ethernet with the specifications discussed before, the movement to 100 Mbps was escalated.

The term *Fast Ethernet* is primarily used today to refer to a technology technically described as 100BASE-T. In 1996, when the technology was introduced, Fast Ethernet actually referred to any of several technologies. There is some confusion here. One of the technologies was switched Ethernet. Likewise, full duplex Ethernet, at least the full duplex variation of 10BASE-T, is no longer referred to as Fast Ethernet. Just as with 1200-bps modems, which once were described as "high-speed;" the advent of better technologies has resulted in changing the terminology used to describe the older technologies.

Two technologies really deserve the name Fast Ethernet. Of the two, the vast majority of analysts have declared 100BASE-T the winner. The other is 100VGAnyLAN.

100BASE-T

When developers were trying to determine what the successor to Ethernet should be, they had two basic choices: try to stick to the basic technology as closely as possible, just increasing its speed, or try to make fundamental improvements to solve flaws that had become more obvious over time. Two camps developed, one taking each approach. The winning camp is the one that took the first approach. Their product: 100BASE-T. The good news about 100BASE-T is that the frame size and characteristics are identical to those in standard Ethernet. It uses CSMA/CD and in general can be understood and managed by network administrators and software in the same way that 10BASE-T could be managed. The bad news is that there are still collisions, and the product still taps out at considerably less than the nominal 100 Mbps that it is supposed to be able to handle. One might describe it as *Ethernet on steroids*. The actual throughput on a 100BASE-T is about 33–40 Mbps if using a hub and about 60 Mbps if using an Ethernet switch.

It is, however, the most popular replacement for standard Ethernet by far. In large part this is due to good marketing, but there is definitely something to be said for not having to do major retraining of your network administrators and technicians.

Like the original Ethernet, 100BASE-T supports several media. Notably absent from this list is coaxial cable. Both standard copper wiring and fiber are supported. As with all high-speed technologies, the copper implementation has severe distance limitations. Most of the high-speed technologies do not support end devices more than 100 meters away from their central electronics locations; Fast Ethernet is no exception.

If one is going to have to put in new wiring, there is no reason to put in anything less capable than category 5. Operating on two pairs, Fast Ethernet is referred to as 100BASE-TX. This is by far the most popular implementation of Fast Ethernet.

The option copper for Fast Ethernet is shielded twisted pair (STP). Generally speaking, STP should only be installed in special cases where the potential interference either to or from the network is an issue. STP is much more difficult to install, with more demanding grounding requirements than UTP. It doesn't increase speed, nor does it improve usage of the pairs in the cable. As far as network performance is concerned, it works the same as on UTP.

In addition to copper wiring, 100BASE-T is supported on fiber. As with category 5; fiber supports both half and full duplex operations. Why might you use fiber? It doesn't improve the speed. The reason is fiber's general superiority over copper. In the case of Fast Ethernet, the main reason to use fiber would be to extend the available distances. Fast Ethernet over copper, as mentioned above, only reaches 100 meters to the desktop. A more severe limitation is that distances between copper-connected Fast Ethernet hubs must not exceed 5 meters, see Fig. 13.33. The use of fiber considerably relaxes these limitations.

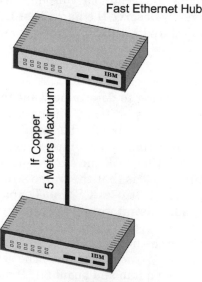

Figure 13.33 Copper-connected Fast Ethernet hubs have to be close!

As with standard Ethernet, there are variations on the way the wiring (either copper or fiber) can be used. Buyers must select among shared, switched, and/or full duplex use of the media and obtain the right electronics to install at both ends of the cable. The default is shared half duplex. One should be aware that just as in standard Ethernet, the contention experienced with a shared half-duplex configuration means that in no case except a two-user network you will be able to count on actually getting anywhere near the 100-Mbps nominal performance of a Fast Ethernet. However, that should not usually be a major problem. Just as with standard Ethernet, medium or even large work groups can be set up that still get a significant performance improvement over standard Ethernet by using shared half duplex Fast Ethernet.

If what you're doing is building a backbone, you probably want to use switched full duplex Fast Ethernet. This will deliver close to the rated 100-Mbit performance to each node, and it costs considerably less than the available alternatives.

Because all Fast Ethernet implementations are based on either copper or fiber, the cabling is done in a star or radial configuration; no physical bus topologies need apply. This means that in theory and in practice, each node can be upgraded individually. The manufacturers build the central electronics (hubs, switches, and so forth) with the capability, in most cases, to handle either 10- or 100-Mbps Ethernet on a port-by-port basis. This means that better electronics can be swapped at the central location, the network can be brought back up, and one-by-one individual users' machines can be upgraded as seen in Fig. 13.34.

Better than this, however, is the advent of dual-speed NICs. Manufacturers make NICs that operate at both 10 and 100 Mbps. These are described as 10/100 cards. But any given computer can run at only one speed at a time—why do we need the dual speed? Most environments upgrade individual computers in groups; certainly it is rare to replace all of the computers in an environment at one time. Often, they are replaced one at a time, as users' needs change. With 10/100 cards, a company can make a long-term decision to move toward 100BASE-T without having to upgrade all the central hubs. The company can upgrade the desktops and then upgrade the hubs as it makes sense to do so. In most cases, the 10/100 cards automatically sense the speed of the connected wire (that is, of the central electronics port) at the time the PC is booted.

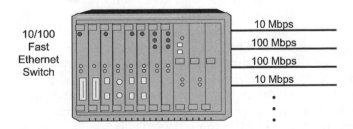

10/100
Fast
Ethernet
Switch

10 Mbps
100 Mbps
100 Mbps
10 Mbps

Figure 13.34 Implementing Fast Ethernet—a 10/100 hub.

100BASE-T Performance Expectations

In an environment with small workgroups (fewer than 20), shared 100BASE-T will probably deliver much better performance to the desktop than shared Ethernet could. Why? With 100BASE-T, each user will average at most 5 Mbits of capacity on the hub if all are active simultaneously. But in most real-world scenarios, not all users are truly simultaneously active. In the typical case, fewer than 10 percent of the users are doing anything on the network at any given instant. Ten percent of 20 people is 2 people. These two active users, in most cases, would share 100 Mbps of capacity, or 50 Mbps each—obviously better than switched Ethernet's delivery of 10 Mbps at best to each user. However, let's cook the numbers a little differently. If there are 100 users on a switched Ethernet segment, each will still get 10 Mbps delivered to the desktop all the time. Fast Ethernet at 100 Mbps, in the worst case, will deliver only 1 Mbps to the desktop. If 10 percent of users are active at a time, then each will get about 10 Mbps. In practice, contention on the 100-Mbps hub will reduce that by 20–30 percent. In this case, switched Ethernet might be a better choice than the Fast Ethernet.

Gigabit Ethernet

While we do not know of anyone who alleges that full duplex switched 100BASE-T is insufficient to handle any likely desktop requirement, if one puts together enough high-speed desktop LANs, the backbone to serve them needs to be a better technology than that desktop LAN technology, whatever it is. Moreover, as the use of voice, data, video, and multimedia finally becomes a reality on a single architecture, the need for more than 100 Mbps to the desk may become a reality. Gigabit Ethernet was developed with the goal of providing these applications to the individual user in the future. In 1998, products were introduced before the standards had been adopted. As with many new technologies, some vendors came out with products early and promised to change or upgrade those products, at no cost to the initial implementers, to whatever the standard becomes. This allowed the vendors to get a leap on the market and assure their market share before others could get there. So the question is, when would you use Gigabit Ethernet and when would you not?

Like 100Base-T, Gigabit Ethernet comes in half and full duplex variations. In its half duplex implementation, it has some very severe limitations regarding delivery of actual capacity. There is an interaction in all Ethernets between minimum packet size and size in terms of radius of the actual maximum network configuration. The smaller the minimum frame size, the smaller the maximum radius of the network. This relationship is compounded in a bad way by increasing the speed of the network transmission. Since the goal in upgrading to a faster variety of Ethernet is to keep the same frame size limitations, the radius of the Gigabit Ethernet without using a special technique is limited to about 20 meters—obviously impractical. What the designers have done is implement a special technique that involves transmission of a special signal in any case, where a frame smaller than 512 bytes is transmitted on a Gigabit Ethernet. This means that for large frames (e.g., those associated with large file transfers), Gigabit

Ethernet might actually deliver close to its full speed. However, many networks being used by human beings as opposed to machines generate large numbers of small frames averaging only 300–350 bytes. In the worst case, such a network, even if implemented on Gigabit Ethernet, would experience performance little better than that delivered by 100BASE-T in its full duplex incarnation. The technique allows for a 200-meter network diameter. This limitation means that any network implementer needs to seriously analyze what kind of traffic is going to be carried by that network, and evaluate the likely bandwidth to actually be delivered by Gigabit Ethernet.

Gigabit Ethernet also provided no quality of service (QoS) guarantees, although the proponents of Gigabit Ethernet are working to provide QoS-like services. This means that even though its nominal speed is very high, it still is not an ideal technology for satisfying isochronous type traffic (for example, video). The new standards, the 802.1Q, are designed to handle quality of service features for Gigabit Ethernet.

If one implements full duplex Gigabit Ethernet, the issue regarding distance pretty much disappears. Gigabit Ethernet requires the use of fiber. There are two kinds of fiber: multimode and single mode. Multimode should be able to reach up to about 550 meters, whereas single mode should be able to reach distances approaching 3 kilometers.

One other caution: Most of the Intel-based servers in service are generally incapable of accepting or transmitting information at speeds significantly greater than those that can be provided by 100BASE-T. Thus hooking a server directly to a gigabit "pipe" would not necessarily deliver improved performance over Fast Ethernet. Higher-end UNIX servers can deliver performance two to four times the above; but even they cannot yet receive or transmit information at true gigabit speeds. Backbone components (routers and the like) also are just now coming on the market that can handle speeds in this range. Therefore, simply buying gigabit devices and dropping them into the network is not likely to be a successful strategy.

Gigabit Ethernet does promise to be a less expensive technology than ATM. In cases where backbones can be successfully implemented with Gigabit Ethernet, it may be more cost effective. However, ATM is available at speed ranges that are at least competitive with Gigabit Ethernet. With the additional capabilities of ATM and its large (carrier-based) installed-base, ATM is probably the preferred technology for high-capacity backbones at least for the next couple of years.

Just when we thought it was safe to come out of the LAN closets and use the technologies, with the knowledge that Gigabit Ethernet is coming along to deal with bandwidth issues, the next in a series of evolutionary steps emerged. Now the talk is focused on 10-Gigabit Ethernet. Nortel Networks announced their strategy in 1999 with the use of 10-Gbps Ethernet over SONET OC-192 based networks. The 10-Gigabit Ethernet standards are still emerging, so many vendors are coming out with their own proprietary solutions to satisfy this demand.

This 10-gigabit strategy also points out that the end user may not need this speed yet, but the carriers (Telcos and ISPs and new providers) will be looking for this throughput. If a carrier chooses to offer 1 Gbps to a consumer (large organization), then the 10 Gbps is necessary for the provider to guarantee the QoS and the effective data rates.

This is particularly true when serving the ISPs and ITSPs (Internet telephony service providers). Through the use of metro area networks running on synchronous optical network (SONET) standards and using dense wave-division multiplexing (DWDM) on the fiber systems, the carriers will be delivering 1–2–54 or 10 Gbps Ethernet.

Virtual LANs

In a traditional shared media network, traffic generated by a station is propagated to all other stations on the local segment. For a given station on shared Ethernet, the local segment is the "collision domain" because traffic on the segment has the potential to cause an Ethernet collision. The local segment is also the "broadcast domain" because any broadcast is sent to all stations on the local segment.

Ethernet bridges and switches divide a network into smaller "collision domains," but they do not affect the broadcast domain. In simple terms, a virtual local area network (VLAN) can be thought of as a mechanism to fine-tune broadcast domains.

The IEEE's 802.1Q standard was developed to address the problem of how to break large networks into smaller parts, so broadcast and multicast traffic wouldn't grab more bandwidth than necessary. The standard also helps provide a higher level of security between segments of internal networks. The 802.1Q specification establishes a standard method for inserting virtual LAN (VLAN) membership information into Ethernet frames.

In a LAN, the data link-layer broadcast and multicast traffic is delivered to all nodes, but this traffic cannot go beyond the LAN boundary. In the past, shared cabling or hubs were the boundaries for LANs. Because network protocols typically rely on broadcast queries to let end stations discover one another, devices on two LANs cannot see each other without the help of a network-layer device with ports in both LANs, such as a router or a layer 3 switch acting as a router. A typical example of a layer 3 switch is a Cisco 3550 or 3750. These are powerful switches that route between domains within a corporate backbone.

Because broadcast messages are sent to all devices on a LAN means the LANs cannot become very large. If they do become large networks, devices become overburdened with the broadcast traffic. The ability of devices on a LAN to discover each other also means that secure devices, like servers housing confidential information, should be placed on a separate LAN from the average user, with router filters controlling access to these servers.

A VLAN is an administratively configured LAN or broadcast domain. Instead of going to the wiring closet to move a cable to a different LAN, network administrators can accomplish this task remotely by configuring a port on an 802.1Q-compliant switch to belong to a different VLAN. The ability to move nodes from one broadcast domain to another by establishing membership profiles for each port on centrally managed switches is one of the main advantages of an 802.1Q VLAN. A VLAN is a collection of switch ports that make up a single broadcast domain. A VLAN can be defined for a single switch, or it can span multiple switches. VLANs are logical entities created in the software configuration to control traffic flow. Membership in workgroup segments can be determined logically instead of by user location, and moves, adds, and changes can be easily configured as the network evolves.

The 1Q enabled switch acts as an intelligent traffic cop and a simple network security device. Ethernet frames are sent only to the ports where the destination device is attached. Broadcast and multicast frames are constrained by VLAN boundaries so only stations whose ports are members of the same VLAN see those frames.

Sharing VLANs between switches is achieved by inserting a tag with a VLAN identifier (VID) of 1–4094 into each frame. Most networks use a few VLANs, however, there are switches out there that support 512. Of course if a company needs more than 512 VLANs, then a serious network design review is needed. A VID must be assigned for each VLAN. By assigning the same VID to VLANs on many switches, one or more VLAN (broadcast domain) can be extended across a large network.

The secret to performing this magic is in the tags. 802.1Q-compliant switch ports can be configured to transmit tagged or untagged frames. A tag field containing VLAN information can be inserted into an Ethernet frame. The use of an 802.1p tag for QoS as needed. If a port has an 802.1Q-compliant device attached, these tagged frames can carry VLAN membership information between switches.

When configuring the switch for VLANs the network administrator must ensure ports with non-802.1Q-compliant devices attached are configured to transmit untagged frames. Many PC and printer NICs are not 802.1Q-compliant. If they receive a tagged frame, they won't know what to do with the frame, so into the bit bucket it goes. Also, the maximum legal Ethernet frame size for tagged frames was increased in 802.1Q (and its companion, 802.3ac) from 1518 to 1522 bytes. This could cause network interface cards and older switches to drop tagged frames as giants.

Quality of Service (QoS)

We mentioned an 802.1p tag above. The IEEE 802.1p standard has a really good prioritization mechanism. Low priority packets are not sent, if there are packets in a higher queue. The IEEE 802.1p standard describes no admission control protocols. It would be possible to give network control priority to all packets, but the network would be easily congested. We can assume that network interface card manufacturers make drivers that support multiple level queues.

IEEE 802.1p standard itself does not limit the amount of resources one application uses, but many implementations do. A mechanism to negotiate a guaranteed end-to-end QoS for each application would be an improvement overall in the delivery of different application traffic. The 802.1p tags are supported on both layer 2 and layer 3 switches.

The way we set the priorities is to use an added tag for the network switches to route the traffic in the priority. We believe that the IEEE committees modeled their QoS parameters after the Olympic Games. Some of the queues are labeled as bronze, silver, gold, and platinum (now there is a new one). The switch manufacturers all created a numeric value for their switches, as follows in Table 13.2.

TABLE 13.2   Summary of 802.1p Tags

Tag	Description	Service
1	BK	Background
2	—	Spare
0 (Default)	BE	Best effort
3	EE	Excellent effort
4	CL	Controlled load
5	VI	Video < 100 ms latency and jitter
6	VO	Voice < 10 ms latency and jitter
7	NC	Network control

Questions

1. What is the reason for installing a LAN?
   a. Making a network
   b. Sharing resources
   c. Because everyone else is doing it
   d. It is cheap

2. When the first LANs were used they were both_____and_____laid out.
   a. Physically and topology
   b. Physiological and topological
   c. Physically and logically
   d. Physically and mentally

3. The three basic forms of a LAN are:
   a. Ring, bus, and star
   b. Ring, star, and hub
   c. Star, spoke, and wheel
   d. Physical, logical, and topological

4. One of the less obvious characteristics of a LAN is that all devices on it are viewed and function as being:
   a. Equals
   b. Subservient
   c. Adjacent
   d. Tangent

5. Every keystroke on terminals connected to a main computer generates a:
   a. Letter
   b. Interrupt
   c. Symbol
   d. Flag

6. The user can always be counted on to backup his/her data.   T/F

7. The card placed inside the PC is called:
   a. The LAN card
   b. The network interface card (NIC)
   c. The server card
   d. A credit card

8. Server-based networks can be and typically are tuned so as to support anywhere from_____to_____users on a single server.
   a. 1–50
   b. 10–100
   c. 20–300
   d. 50–60

9. The NIC card provides a unique LAN address called the :
   a. Big Mac
   b. Apple Interface
   c. LAN address
   d. MAC address

10. LAN switches operate at layer_____of the OSI model.
    a. 1
    b. 2
    c. 4
    d. 6

11. What three companies originally formed the Ethernet standard?
    a. IBM, DEC, and Xerox
    b. Intel, DEC, and IBM
    c. Intel, Xerox, and DEC
    d. Intel, DEC, and IEEE

12. The use of a_____was the first cabling system used.
    a. Thick wire fiber
    b. Thin wire coax
    c. Thick wire coax
    d. Thin fiber

13. The Ethernet operates at_____Mbps.
    a. 10, 50, 100
    b. 10, 100, 1000
    c. 100, 1000, 100000
    d. 1, 10, 100

14. The Ethernet specification that used thin coax is called_____.
    a. 10BASE5
    b. 10BASE2
    c. 100BASE10
    d. 10BASE-F

15. When using a 10/100 card, the hub will_____sense the speed of the card.

16. Regular 10 Mbps Ethernet will deliver approximately what throughput?
    a. 10 Mbps
    b. 6–8 Mbps
    c. 3.3–4 Mbps
    d. 5–6 Mbps

17. The contention standard is called:
    a. CSMA/CA
    b. CSMA/DC
    c. CSMA/CDR
    d. CSMA/CD

18. The Ethernet standard is called:
    a. 802.1
    b. 802.5
    c. 802.11
    d. 802.3

19. The minimum size frame in an Ethernet network is_____bytes.
    a. 46
    b. 64
    c. 128
    d. 1500

20. The frame carries a payload of between_____and_____bytes.
    a. 64–1518
    b. 46–1500
    c. 64–1500
    d. 46–1518

21. 100-Mbps Ethernet is also called_____.
    a. 100BASE-T
    b. VGAnyLAN
    c. 100BASE4
    d. Fast Ethernet

14

Wireless LANs

After reading this chapter and completing the questions, you will be able to:

- Discuss what a wireless LAN is
- Understand what all the hype is about throughout the industry
- Discuss the components of a wireless LAN
- Converse about the protocols used and the services available
- Understand why security is so important in a WLAN

Whenever we discuss LANs as covered in the previous chapter, we are really talking about a wired LAN; more specifically an 802.3 (Ethernet). Why then should we be concerned with the use of a wireless connection? Surely wireless doesn't run as fast as a wired LAN, it probably has more issues than a wired LAN, and it is not as secure as a pair of wires! So why bother at all? The answer is not about wireless, but it is all about mobility. Today's workforce is constantly on the move. In this chapter we cover the major components of 802.11 wireless LANs (WLANs). Fundamental concepts such as medium access mechanisms, frame formats, security, and the physical interfaces build the foundation for understanding more advanced and practical concepts. Many people think of WLANs as wireless Ethernet. Although WLANs are close, they are not Ethernet. They do, however; connect to Ethernets as the means of carrying data onto the wired network. The IEEE created a separate set of standards for WLANs known as the 802.11 standards. This differs from 802.3 wired LANs as we shall see below. Suffice it to say; when we want wireless connectivity the tools are in place; when we want wired connectivity the tools are also in place. Finally, when we need to interconnect between the wired and wireless networks, the pieces and tools are also in place. Recall from Chapter 1 that we discussed the various means of transmitting our information. We had choices of using copper, radio, and infrared. These choices were also made available when the IEEE committees created the standards for WLANs. The use of wireless LANs was not confined to the late 1990s, however. In the late 1980s and early 1990s, the authors dealt with WLANs from various vendors. Examples were a product produced and marketed by Motorola called *Altair,* which was an RF-based network, using a licensed 18 GHz radio channel. Another was the use of a direct sequence spread spectrum service from a company called Telesystems of Canada.* In the infrared WLAN arena companies like BICC had their InfraLAN product. It wasn't until 1996 that the IEEE created a set of standards in the 802.11 committees. That is when WLANs began to skyrocket in popularity.

WLAN Opportunities

The market for wireless communications has enjoyed tremendous growth. Wireless technology now reaches or is capable of reaching virtually every location on the face of the earth. Billions of people exchange information every day using pagers, cellular telephones, and other wireless communication products. With tremendous success of wireless telephony and messaging services, it is hardly surprising that wireless personal and business computing was the next evolution. No longer bound by the harnesses of wired networks, people will be able to access and share information on a global scale nearly anywhere they venture.

WLANs

Looking at all of the possible combinations of a wireless architecture includes the opportunities to ramp up the speeds on the local area network. Mobile communications and now, the mobile data networking has been one of the areas where transmission is contingent upon the following:

1. Distances from the radio equipment
2. Interference from other devices in the environment
3. Power output capabilities of the mobile set
4. Overall distance/speed ratio for the mobile device

Each of the factors above will have a direct impact upon the speed and reliability of the data throughput in a mobile communicating service. However, the use of high-speed communications in the mobile environment was on an overall transmission of up to 2 Mbps with UMTS. When the device is not as mobile, higher speeds can now be achieved. In a LAN a wireless approach can be just what the data doctor ordered!

---

*Approximately 1986–87 Telesystems originally created the ARLAN, which later after a merger of Telexon became Aironet in 1994. Later Aironet was acquired by Cisco.

In LANs, we have seen wired speeds move up the overall curve from an Ethernet speed, originally at 10 Mbps to today's current speed on Ethernet being 1 Gbps. We know that 10 Gbps is available, but typically not widespread in the LAN.

However, in the wireless environment we have seen a different approach. Instead of having unlimited bandwidth, we had been using WLAN technologies that deliver much less than the wired networks. Reality shows that 2–11 Mbps speeds were the norms of the past. However, newer techniques are allowing us to run at speeds of up to 54 Mbps today and 100+ in the near future. We do not actually achieve near the full 54 Mbps, but then again we saw that wired Ethernet only delivered between 33 and 40 percent of its rated speeds.

The speeds are not as important as the overall throughput, yet the way we measure things is where everyone gets excited. Note that the speeds of the wired and the wireless networks are impacted by more than just the medium—the protocols add a significant amount of overhead to the transmission and therefore reduce the overall throughput. One must always be aware of the raw data rate and what can actually be achieved when considering the use of a network topology and medium.

Where wireline networks can achieve higher data throughput, the wireless networks allow the mobility and flexibility unavailable on a wired network. This trade-off is one of the benefits of reviewing the procedures and capabilities without the hype. Remember that there is the sizzle and then there is the steak!

Defining the WLAN

A WLAN is a flexible data communication system implemented as an extension to or as an alternative for, a wired LAN within a building or campus. One should consider these as complimentary products rather than competitive products.

Early WLANs used electromagnetic waves to transmit and receive the data, such as:

- Radio
- Light
- Infrared

WLANs transmit and receive data over the air, minimizing the need for wired connections, although they typically connect to our wired networks at some point. Usually the connections use an access point connected to a backbone Ethernet, as shown in Fig. 14.1.

WLANs combine data connectivity with user mobility. Through simplified configuration possibilities, they enable movable LANs. Most network users are much more mobile within the office than ever before. However, there are combinations of LANs that play into the everyday installation and operation.

Not all LANs are wired, in some cases the network is installed as a WLAN based on each terminal device using a wireless interface (NIC card). Remember the NIC card discussion from the previous chapter. It provides layers 1 and 2 connections for our LANs. Most laptop computers come equipped with a wireless NIC today.

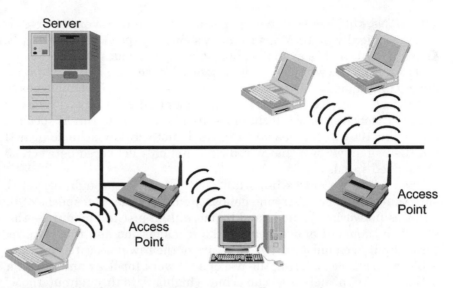

Figure 14.1   Wired and wireless connectivity is how we usually connect the user.

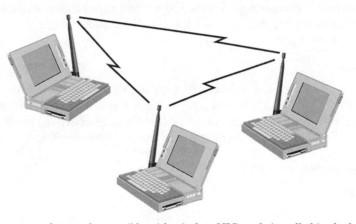

Figure 14.2   Ad hoc networks are also possible with wireless NIC cards installed in the laptop.

The "ad hoc" nature of the connection is what is achieved, as shown in Fig. 14.2. This form of a WLAN has always been considered the most limited because of the distances and the coverage areas in a large office building where the environment is surrounded by concrete and steel—all of which limit throughput and distances.

Over the last decade, WLANs have gained popularity in a number of vertical markets, including the health-care, retail, manufacturing, warehousing, and academic arenas. These industries have profited from the productivity gains of using handheld terminals and notebook computers to transmit real-time information to centralized hosts for processing. Today WLANs are becoming more widely recognized as a general-purpose connectivity alternative for a broad range of business customers.

Applications for WLANs

Wireless LANs augment rather than replace wired LAN networks—providing the final few meters of connectivity between a backbone network and the in-building or on-campus mobile user. The following list describes some of the many applications made possible through the power and flexibility of WLANs:

1. Medical staffs in hospitals use handheld PDAs or notebook computers with WLAN capability. This delivers patient information instantly.

2. Consulting or accounting audit teams or small workgroups improve communications with quick or ad hoc network setup.

3. Network managers in dynamic environments minimize the overhead of moves and changes.

4. Corporate training sites and students at universities use wireless connectivity to facilitate access to learning information.

5. Portable classrooms are available in the event of a shortage of space, as seen in Fig. 14.3.

6. Retail store IS managers use wireless networks to simplify frequent network reconfiguration and allow sidewalk and parking lot sales to occur without the heavy cost of wiring these locations.

7. Trade shows where workers minimize setup requirements by installing preconfigured WLANs reducing local MIS support.

8. Warehouse workers use WLANs to exchange information with central databases within the shop as well as wireless bar code readers to check inventory, as seen in Fig. 14.4.

Figure 14.3 Mobility can be added to classroom environments.

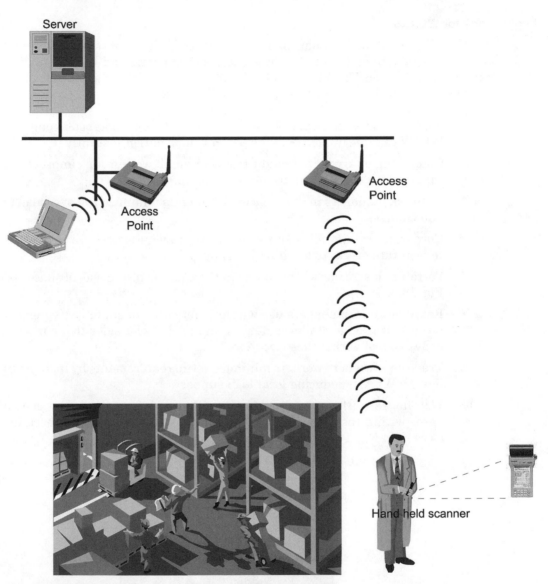

Figure 14.4   Warehousing and shipping areas benefit from WLAN.

9. Restaurant staff and car rental service representatives provide faster service with real-time customer information input and retrieval. The use of a handheld input RF device prevents people from standing in long lines, and speeds their service delivery.

10. Historical building owners use WLANs because of limits on what can be done to the structure of the building (e.g., no coring floors).

WLANs provide all the functionality of wired LANs, but without physical constraints of the wire. WLAN configurations include independent networks (offering peer-to-peer connectivity) and infrastructure networks (supporting fully distributed data communications).

How WLANs Work

Wireless LANs use electromagnetic airwaves to communicate information from one point to another. Radio waves are often referred to as radio carriers because they simply perform the function of carrying the energy to a remote receiver. The data being transmitted is superimposed on the radio carrier so that it can be accurately extracted at the receiving end. This is generally referred to as modulation of the carrier by the information being transmitted, which we discussed earlier in this book. Once data is superimposed (modulated) onto the radio carrier, the radio signal occupies more than a single frequency, because the frequency or bit rate of the modulating information adds to the carrier.

Multiple radio carriers can exist in the same space at the same time without interfering with each other if the radio waves are transmitted on different radio frequencies. To extract data, a radio receiver tunes in (or selects) one radio frequency while rejecting all other radio signals on different frequencies.

In a typical WLAN configuration, a transmitter/receiver (transceiver) device, called the *access point*, connects to the wired network from a fixed location using standard Ethernet cable, as shown in Fig. 14.5. At a minimum, the access point receives, buffers, and transmits data between the WLAN and the wired network infrastructure. A single access point can support a small group of users and can function within a range of less than one hundred to several hundred feet. The access point (or the antenna attached to the access point) is usually mounted high, but may be mounted essentially anywhere practical as long as the desired radio coverage is obtained.

End users access the WLAN through WLAN adapters, which come in the form of:

- PC cards in notebook computers, as shown in Fig.14.6.
- ISA or PCI adapters in desktop computers shown in Fig.14.7.
- Fully integrated devices within handheld computers.

Figure 14.5 The access point connects the user to the Ethernet cable.

Figure 14.6 This wireless NIC card for a laptop is dual radio capable.

Figure 14.7 A PCI card with external antenna is installed in a desktop PC.

WLAN adapters provide an interface between the client network operating system (NOS) and the airwaves (via an antenna). The nature of the wireless connection is transparent to the NOS.

IEEE Standards

In 1996, the IEEE created and ratified a set of standards for wireless connectivity known as the 802.11 standards. Back then the data rates for wireless connectivity was at a roaring 1 or 2 Mbps. As we saw in the previous chapter on Ethernet, at that same time users were accustomed to using a 10 Mbps Ethernet connection. The actual throughput on the 10 Mbps Ethernet was about 3.3–4 Mbps. Therefore, when considering a WLAN implementation, 1–2 Mbps was not all that bad.

TABLE 14.1   Summary of IEEE Standards and Working Committees

Committee Designation	Purpose
802.11	Wireless LANs at 1–2 Mbps using radio at 2.4GHz or infrared
802.11b	Wireless LANs at 1–2–5.5 and 11 Mbps using 2.4 GHz
802.11a	Wireless LANs at 6 9–12–18–24–36–48 and 54 Mbps in 5 GHz radio
802.11g	Wireless LANs that are backward compatible with the 2.4 GHz radios operating at 1–2–5.5–11–6–9–12–18–24–36–48 and 54 Mbps
802.11 d	A modification to the channel use for international countries
802.11e	Quality of services introduced and wireless multimedia (WMM) and wireless multimedia extensions (WME) for the client device
802.11f	A recommendation for interoperability between vendor products using inter-access point protocol (IAPP)
802.11h	Automatic selection of frequency (channel) and power control
802.11i	Security (WPA2) for robust secure networks
802.11j	A standard accepted by Japan to use certain 4.9 GHz channels
802.11s	Mesh networks defined
802.11r	Defines seamless and fast roaming for primarily VoIP applications over WLAN
802.11k	Under consideration for radio resource management
802.11n	Under consideration for faster data at 100–400 Mbps and uses MIMO technology
802.11p	Under study WLAN in a vehicular environment
802.11u	Under study to link WiFi to external networks (like WiMAX and Cellular)
802.11v	Under study for network management systems
802.11w	Under study for protecting management frames in WiFi
802.1y	Under study to use 3.6–3.7 GHz radio channels

Later evolution became a potpourri of standards including the following as shown in Table 14.1, which lists the standards for 802.11 committees and the purpose.

IEEE 802.11 Wireless LANs

The IEEE 802.11 standard defines the physical layer and media access control (MAC) layer for a WLAN. The standard defines three different physical layers for the 802.11 wireless LAN, each operating in a different frequency range and at rates of 1 Mbps and 2 Mbps. In this section we focus on the architecture of 802.11 LANs and their media access protocols. We'll see that although it belongs to the same standard family as Ethernet, it has a significantly different architecture and media access protocol. The IEEE 802.11 represents the first standard for WLAN products from an internationally recognized, independent organization. The IEEE manages most of the standards for wired LANs. We saw the standards at work when we reviewed the Ethernet (802.3) and the token ring (802.5). The WLAN standard (802.11) represents an important milestone in WLAN systems because customers can now have multiple sources for the components of their WLAN systems. There are still applications where the existing proprietary data communications are a good fit because they may optimize some aspect of the network performance. However, 802.11 compliant products expand the users' options.

802.11 LAN Architecture

The principal components of the 802.11 wireless LAN architecture are shown in any architectural drawing. The fundamental building block of the 802.11 architecture is the cell, known as the basic service set (BSS) in 802.11 parlance. A BSS typically contains one or more wireless stations and a central base station, known as an access point (AP) in 802.11 terminology, as shown in Fig. 14.8. The stations, either fixed or mobile, and the central base station communicate amongst themselves using the IEEE 802.11 wireless MAC protocol. Multiple access points may be connected together (e.g., using a wired Ethernet or another wireless channel) to form a so-called distribution system (DS). The DS appears to upper level protocols (e.g., IP) as a single 802 network, in much the same way that a bridged, wired 802.3 Ethernet network appears as a single 802 network to the upper layer protocols.

How It Will Be Used in End Applications

The IEEE 802.11 standard defines the protocol for two types of networks: ad hoc and client/server networks.

- An ad hoc network is a simple network where communications are established between multiple stations in a given coverage area without the use of an access point or server. The standard specifies the etiquette that each station must observe so that they all have fair access to the wireless media. It provides methods for arbitrating requests to use the media to ensure that throughput is maximized for all of the users in the base service set. IEEE 802.11 stations can also group themselves together to form an ad hoc network—a network with no central control and with no connections to the "outside world." Here, the network is formed "on the fly," simply because there happen to be mobile devices that have found themselves in proximity to each other, that have a need to communication, and that find no preexisting network infrastructure (e.g., a preexisting 802.11 BSS with an AP) in the location. An ad hoc network is also called an *independent basic service set* (IBSS) because it

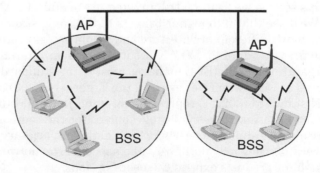

Figure 14.8   A basic service set is shown using an AP and multiple end points connected.

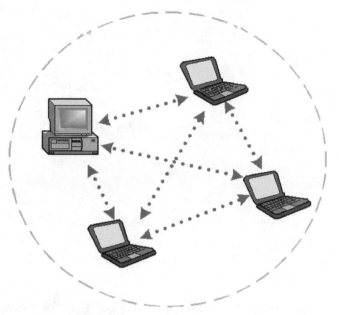

Figure 14.9 The ad hoc network is an IBSS.

is independent of an access point. An ad hoc network might be formed, for example, when people with laptops meet together (e.g., in a conference room, a train, or a car) and want to exchange data in the absence of a centralized access point. There has been a tremendous recent increase in interest in ad hoc networking, as communicating portable devices continue to proliferate. This is shown in Fig. 14.9.

■ The client/server network uses an access point that controls the allocation of transmit time for all stations and allows mobile stations to roam from cell to cell. The access point is used to handle traffic from the mobile radio to the wired or wireless backbone of the client/server network. This arrangement allows for point coordination of all of the stations in the basic service area and ensures proper handling of the data traffic. The access point routes data between the stations and other wireless stations or to and from the network. Typically, WLANs controlled by a central access point will provide better throughput performance.

Physical Layer Implementation Choices

The physical layer in any network defines the modulation and signaling characteristics for the transmission of data. At the physical layer, two RF transmission methods and one infrared are defined. Operation of the WLAN in unlicensed RF bands requires the offspread-spectrum modulation to meet the requirements for operation in most countries. The RF transmission standards in the standard are frequency hopping spread spectrum (FHSS) and direct sequence spread spectrum (DSSS). Both architectures are

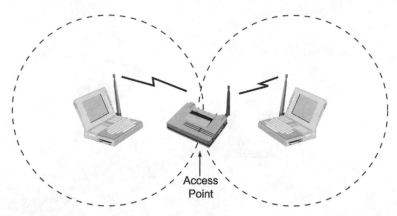

Figure 4.10   The client/server approach to wireless LANs.

defined for operation in the 2.4 GHz frequency band, typically occupying the 83 MHz of bandwidth from 2.400 to 2.483 GHz.

1. Differential BPSK (DBPSK) and DQPSK is the modulation for the direct sequence.

2. Frequency hopping uses 2–4 levels Gaussian FSK as the modulation signaling method.

Different frequencies were approved for use in Japan, United States, and Europe, and any WLAN product must meet the requirements for the country where it is sold. The physical layer data rate for FHSS system is 1 Mbps. For DSSS both 1 Mbps and 2 Mbps data rates are supported. The choice between FHSS and DSSS, will depend on a number of factors related to the users, application and the environment that the system will be operating.

Infrared Physical Layer   One infrared standard is supported, which operates in the 850—950 nm band with peak power of 2 W. The modulation for infrared is accomplished using either 4- or 16-level pulse-positioning modulation. The physical layer supports two data rates: 1 and 2 Mbps.

Direct Sequencing Spread Spectrum (DSSS) Physical Layer   The DSSS physical layer uses an 11-bit Barker sequence to spread the data before it is transmitted. Each bit transmitted is modulated by the 11-bit sequence. This process spreads the RF energy across a wider bandwidth than would be required to transmit the raw data. The receiver reverses the RF input to recover the original data. The advantage is reduced effects of narrowband sources of interference.

The IEEE 802.11 protocol can also use a short request to send (RTS) control frame and a short clear to send (CTS) frame to reserve access to the channel. When a sender wants to send a frame, it can first send an RTS frame to the receiver, indicating the

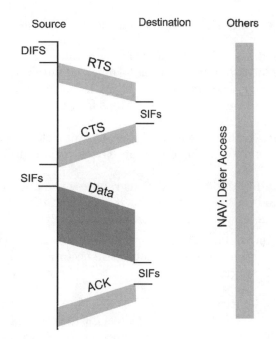

Figure 14.11   The RTS/CTS sequence.

duration of the data packet and the ACK packet. A receiver that receives an RTS frame responds with a CTS frame, giving the sender explicit permission to send. All other stations hearing the RTS or CTS then know about the pending data transmission and can avoid interfering with those transmissions. An IEEE 802.11 sender can operate either using the RTS/CTS control frames, or can simply send its data without first using the RTS control frame. The RTS sequence is shown in Fig. 14.11.

The use of the RTS and CTS frames helps avoid collisions in three important ways:

1. Because the receiver's transmitted CTS frame will be heard by all stations within the receiver's vicinity, the CTS frame helps avoid both the hidden station problem and the fading problem.

2. Because the RTS and CTS frames are short, a collision involving an RTS or CTS frame will only last for the duration of the whole RTS or CTS frame.

3. When the RTS and CTS frames are correctly transmitted, there should be no collisions involving the subsequent DATA and ACK frames.

Frequency Hopping Spread Spectrum (FHSS) Physical Layer   The FHSS physical layer has 22 hop patterns to choose from. The frequency hop physical layer is required to hop across the 2.4 GHz ISM band covering 79 channels. Each channel occupies 1 MHz of bandwidth and must hop at the minimum rate specified by the regulatory bodies of the intended country. A minimum hop rate of 2.5 hops per second is specified for the United States.

Each of the physical layers uses their own unique header to synchronize the receiver and to determine signal modulation format and data packet length. The physical layer headers are always transmitted at 1 Mbps. Predefined fields in the headers provide the option to increase the data rate to 2 Mbps for the actual data packet.

The MAC Layer   Unlike the 802.3 Ethernet protocol, the wireless 802.11 MAC protocol does not implement collision detection. There are a couple of reasons for this:

1. The ability to detect collisions requires the ability to both send (one's own signal) and receive (to determine if another station's transmissions are interfering with one's own transmission) at the same time. This can be costly.

2. More importantly, even if one had collision detection and sensed no collision when sending, a collision could still occur at the receiver. This situation results from the particular characteristics of the wireless channel.

Given the difficulties with detecting collisions at a wireless receiver, the designers of IEEE 802.11 developed an access protocol, which aimed to avoid collisions (hence the name CSMA/CA), rather than detect and recover from collisions (CSMA/CD).

First, the IEEE 802.11 frame contains a duration field, in which the sending station explicitly indicates the length of time that its frame will be transmitting on the channel. This value allows other stations to determine the minimum amount of time (the so-called network allocation vector, NAV) for which they should defer their access. The MAC layer specification for 802.11, as shown in Fig. 14.12, has similarities to the 802.3 Ethernet wired line standard. The protocols for 802.11 use a protocol scheme known as carrier-sense, multiple access, collision avoidance (CSMA/CA). This protocol avoids collisions instead of detecting a collision like the algorithm used in 802.3. It is difficult to detect collisions in an RF transmission network and it is for this reason that collision avoidance is used. The MAC layer operates together with the physical layer by sampling the energy over the medium transmitting data. The physical layer

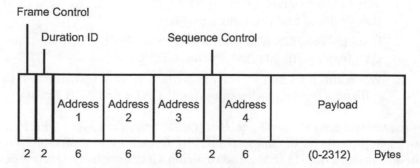

Figure 14.12   The MAC layer frame for 802.11 is similar to an Ethernet frame.

uses a clear channel assessment (CCA) algorithm to determine if the channel is clear. This is accomplished by measuring the RF energy at the antenna and determining the strength of the received signal. The best method to use depends upon the levels of interference in the operating environment. The CSMA/CA protocol allows for options that can minimize collisions by using request to send (RTS), clear-to-send (CTS), data and acknowledge (ACK) transmission frames, in a sequential fashion.

Communication is established when one of the wireless nodes sends a short message RTS frame. The RTS frame includes the destination and the length of message. The message duration is known as the *network allocation vector* (NAV). The NAV alerts all others in the medium, to back off for the duration of the transmission. The receiving station issues a CTS frame, which echoes the sender's address and the NAV. If the CTS frame is not received, it is assumed that a collision occurred and the RTS process starts over. After the data frame is received, an ACK frame is sent back verifying a successful data transmission. A common limitation with WLAN systems is the "hidden node" problem. This can disrupt 40 percent or more of the communications in a highly loaded LAN environment. It occurs when there is a station in a service set that cannot detect the transmission of another station to detect that the media is busy. The hidden node is shown in Fig. 14.13.

With the emphasis now on Voice over IP (VoIP) telephone applications, the 802.11 standard allows the interconnection of the traditional PBX and LANs, as shown in Fig. 14.14. Most of the Voice over WiFi solutions use the 802.11b or 802.11g standards. The 802.11b

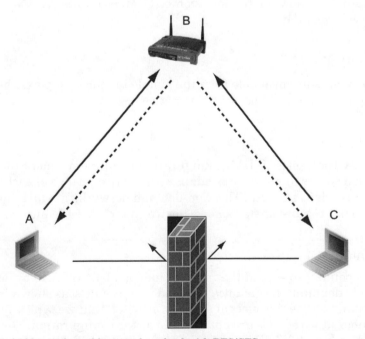

Figure 14.13 The hidden node problem can be solved with RTS/CTS.

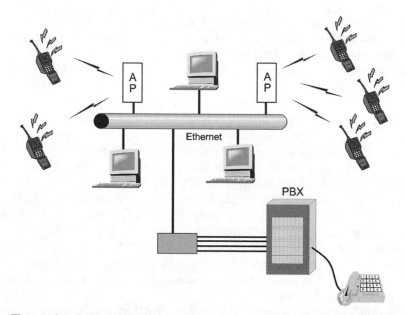

Figure 14.14   The wireless LAN and PBX integration.

standard will allow the transmission of 11 Mbps on the WLANs with new speeds being promised every day.

WLAN Configurations

Many choices are available from the simple to more complex. The benefit is that these configurations can change on short notice.

Independent WLANs

Probably the easiest WLAN configuration is an independent (or peer-to-peer) WLAN. Anytime two or more wireless adapters are within range of each other, they can set up an independent network. These on-demand networks are fast and easy to use, because they do not require any expensive devices nor do they require any configuration.

Extended WLANs

Access points can extend the range of independent WLANs by acting as a repeater effectively doubling the distance between wireless PCs, as shown in Fig. 14.15. These access points create the effect of a hub or a switch that we typically see in a closet, where a number of wired PCs are homed in to a star configuration. The hub was popularized in 1984 when 10BASE-T networks were introduced. By using this access point as a

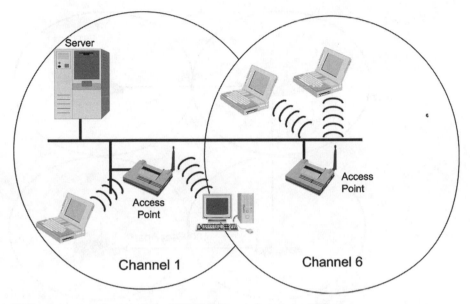

Figure 14.15   Access points extend the WLAN distances for wireless PCs.

substitute to the hub, the WLAN can be extended beyond two independent devices. Normally, the short distances between the two independent devices can be doubled with the use of the access point.

Infrastructure WLANs

In infrastructure WLANs, multiple access points link the WLAN to the wired network and allow users to efficiently share network resources. The access points not only provide communication with the wired network but also mediate wireless network traffic in the immediate neighborhood. Multiple access points can provide wireless coverage for an entire building or campus. Many of the WLAN companies recommend that the access points (APs) are placed at 100 feet on center. If one calculates the math on this, using a radius of 50 feet (look at Fig. 14.16 for this). Looking at this, we calculate the area of coverage to be as follows:

$$\text{Area} = \Pi\, r^2$$
$$\text{Area} = 3.1416 \times 50^2 \text{ feet}$$
$$\text{Area} = 3.1416 \times 2{,}500 \text{ square feet}$$
$$\text{Area} = 7854 \text{ square feet}$$

Now if a single access point is designed to cover 7800+ square feet, one can assume that the amount of people in this area will be significant. The IEEE suggested that the number of users supported by an AP is 75 users. Most WLAN manufacturers suggest

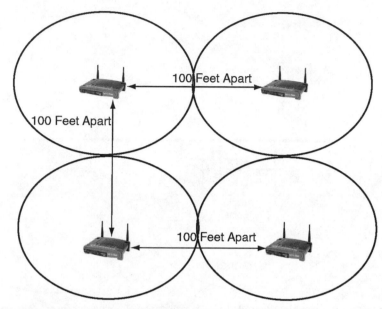

Figure 14.16   The placement of APs at 100 feet on center.

that 12–20 simultaneous users as a realistic number. (If using VoIP then the number drops quickly to 5–7 simultaneous users). Think of 12–20 users on line in an area this size and wonder what might happen with congestion. The WLAN is a half-duplex service so the user must send, wait for an acknowledgement, then listen again before sending more. A lot of time is wasted in the overall performance of the network, but it still works pretty well!

WLAN Technology Options

Manufacturers of WLANs have a range of technologies to choose from when designing a WLAN solution. Each technology comes with its own set of advantages and limitations.

Spread Spectrum

Most WLAN systems use spread-spectrum technology, which trades off bandwidth efficiency for reliability, integrity, and security. The WLAN consumes more bandwidth than in a narrowband transmission, but the trade-off produces a signal that is stronger and easier to detect. This assumes that the receiver knows the parameters of the spread-spectrum signal being broadcast. If a receiver is not tuned to the right frequency, a spread-spectrum signal looks like background noise. A look at a spread spectrum is shown in Fig. 14.17, using the 22-MHz channel for the spread spectrum. Not that the channels only are 1–6 and 11 that are nonoverlapping.

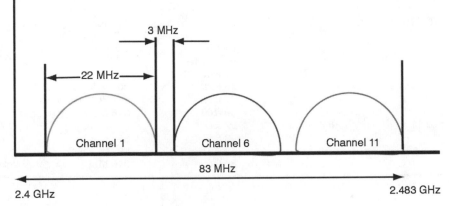

Figure 14.17 Spread spectrum across a 22-MHz channel.

WLAN Customer Considerations

Compared with wired LANs, WLANs provide installation and configuration flexibility as well as the freedom that is inherent in network mobility. When considering the use of a WLAN, the network manager must take into account that the WLAN requires consideration of some or all of the following issues.

Range/Coverage

The distance over which RF waves can communicate is a function of product design (including transmitted power and receiver design) and the propagation path, especially in indoor environments. Interactions with objects, including walls, steel beams, file cabinets, people, doors, etc., can affect how energy propagates, as can be seen in Fig. 14.18. The result is that these objects will affect the range and coverage of a particular system. Most WLAN systems are RF based because radio waves can penetrate many indoor walls and surfaces. The range for typical WLAN systems varies from approximately 50 to 300 feet depending on manufacturer, power output, area to be covered, and interference/noise in the area. Note in this figure that the coverage areas are not perfectly symmetrical due to obstructions from the walls.

We try to use a concept of range, throughput and reading of received signal strength indicators (RSSI). The ranges that we like to use are as given in Table 14.2:

Throughput

The actual throughput in a WLAN is product and setup dependent, but can be seen in Table 14.2. Factors that affect throughput include airwave congestion (number of us-

TABLE 14.2 Distances and Speeds Used in WLAN

Technology	Frequency	Distance	Bandwidth	RSSI
802.11b	2.4 GHz	22 feet	11 Mbps	−83 dBm
		45 feet	5.5 Mbps	−85 dBm
		67 feet	2 Mbps	−89 dBm
		90–100 feet	1 Mbps	−90 dBm
802.11g	2.4 GHz	22 feet	54–48 Mbps	−83 dBm
		45 feet	36–24 Mbps	−85 dBm
		67 feet	18–12 Mbps	−89 dBm
		90–100 feet	9–6 Mbps	−90 dBm
802.11 a	5.3 GHz	22 feet	54–48 Mbps	−84 dBm
		43 feet	36–24 Mbps	−87 dBm
		62–63 feet	18–12 Mbps	−90 dBm
		80 feet	9–6 Mbps	−93 dBm

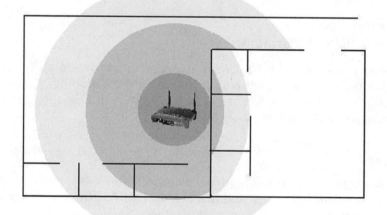

Figure 14.18 The coverage areas.

ers), propagation factors such as range and multipath, the type of WLAN system used, as well as the latency and bottlenecks on the wired portions of the WLAN. Typical data rates range from 1 to 54 Mbps today with more that 100+ Mbps for the future. WLANs provide sufficient throughput for the most common LAN-based office applications. Heavy graphic orientation or streaming video/voice may have a significant degrading factor on the WLAN. The consideration of using a WLAN for these applications is application dependent. On average when using an 802.11b approximately 5–6 Mbps is the expected throughput under ideal conditions. When using an 802.11g device we can expect to get approximately 9–12 Mbps of throughput under normal conditions.

Finally, when using an 802.11a system, we can expect to get 12–18 Mbps of throughput. Remember, this is the actual throughput due to overhead, retransmissions, timing, and the like. The signaling rate is probably going to be 11 Mbps with the 802.11b, and 54 Mbps with an 802.11g/a device. This is a big difference that most people feel shocked when they hear the results.

Integrity and Reliability

Wireless data technologies have been used for more than 50 years. Wireless applications in both commercial and military systems are proven technologies. While radio interference can cause degradation in throughput, it is limited in the workplace. Vigorous designs and the limited distances result in connections that are far more robust than cellular phone connections and provide data integrity performance equal to or better than wired networking.

IEEE 802.11 Specifications

Progress and development in silicon technology coupled with lower prices and product interoperability have led to the 802.11x (where x is b, g, or a) WLANs specification. IEEE 802.11b and g use direct-sequence spread-spectrum (DSSS) technology (the g standard also can support the use of OFDM described later). DSSS modulates the data string of ones and zeros with a coded chip sequence. In 802.11, that coded chip sequence is called the Barker code, this is an 11-bit pattern (10110111000). The coded chip has certain mathematical properties that lend it toward modulating radio waves. The original data is coded with this Barker code. This creates a series of "chips." Each bit is "encoded" by the 11-bit Barker code, and each group of 11 chips encodes one bit of data.

Wireless radios generate a 2.4-GHz carrier wave (2.4–2.483 GHz), and modulate that wave using a variety of techniques. With 802.11x devices, as you move away from the radio, the radio adapts and uses a less complex (and slower) encoding mechanism to send data.

IEEE 802.11 Architectures

IEEE's standard for WLANs (IEEE 802.11), there are two different ways to configure a network: ad hoc and infrastructure. In the ad hoc network, computers are brought together to form a network "on the fly." There is no structure to the network; there are no fixed points; and usually every node is able to communicate with every other node. A good example of this is the aforementioned meeting where employees bring laptop computers together to communicate and share design or financial information. Although it seems that order would be difficult to maintain in this type of network, algorithms such as the spokesman election algorithm (SEA) have been designed to "elect" one machine as the base station (master) of the network with the others being slaves. Another algorithm in ad hoc network architectures uses a broadcast and flooding method to all other nodes to establish who's who.

The second type of network structure used in WLANs is the infrastructure. This architecture uses fixed network access points with which mobile nodes can communicate. These network access points are sometimes connected to landlines to widen the LAN's capability by bridging wireless nodes to other wired nodes. If service areas overlap, handoffs can occur. This structure is very similar to the present day cellular networks around the world.

IEEE 802.11 Layers

The IEEE 802.11 standard places specifications on the parameters of both the physical (PHY) and medium access control (MAC) layers of the network. The PHY layer, which actually handles the transmission of data between nodes, can use either direct sequence spread spectrum, frequency-hopping spread spectrum, or infrared (IR) pulse position modulation. IEEE 802.11 makes provisions for data rates of either 1 Mbps or 2 Mbps, and calls for operation in the 2.4–2.4835 GHz frequency band (in the case of spread-spectrum transmission), which is an unlicensed band for industrial, scientific, and medical (ISM) applications, although we will concentrate on the use of RF in this chapter.

The MAC layer is a set of protocols which is responsible for maintaining order in the use of a shared medium. The 802.11 standard specifies a carrier sense multiple access with collision avoidance (CSMA/CA) protocol. In this protocol, when a node receives a packet to be transmitted, it first listens to ensure no other node is transmitting. If the channel is clear, it then transmits the packet. Otherwise, it chooses a random "backoff factor" which determines the amount of time the node must wait until it is allowed to transmit its packet. During periods in which the channel is clear, the transmitting node decrements its backoff counter. (When the channel is busy it does not decrement its backoff counter.) When the backoff counter reaches zero, the node transmits the packet. Because the probability that two nodes will choose the same backoff factor is small, collisions between packets are minimized. Collision detection, as is employed in Ethernet, cannot be used for the radio frequency transmissions of IEEE 802.11. The reason for this is that when a node is transmitting it cannot hear any other node in the system which may be transmitting, because its own signal will drown out any others arriving at the node.

Physical Signals

The wireless physical layer is split into two parts, called the PLCP (physical layer convergence protocol) and the PMD (physical medium dependent) sublayer.

- The PMD takes care of the wireless encoding.
- The PLCP presents a common interface for higher-level drivers to write to and provides carrier sense and CCA (clear channel assessment), which is the signal that the MAC layer needs to determine whether the medium is currently in use. The PLCP is shown in Fig. 14.19. Note the size of the frame is much larger than an Ethernet frame (so WLANs are not Ethernet) and the addressing introduces two added fields over the addresses used in an 802.3 frame.

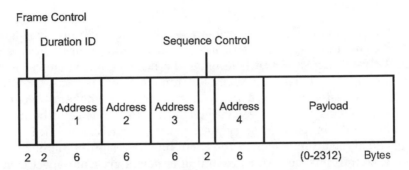

Figure 14.19   PLCP frame for 802.11.

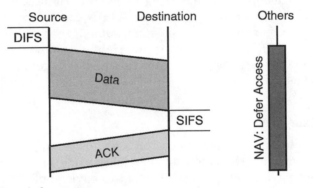

Figure 14.20   The timing window.

Timing Is Everything

The most basic portion of the MAC layer is the ability to sense a quiet time on the network and then choose to transmit. Once the host has determined that the medium has been idle for a minimum time period, known as DIFS (DCF [distributed coordination function] inter-frame spacing), it may transmit a packet. If the medium is busy, the node must wait for a time equal to DIFS, plus a random number of slot times. The time between the end of the DIFS period and the beginning of the next frame is known as the contention window. Figure 14.20 is a representation of this timing window.

Each station listens to the network, and the first station to finish its allocated number of slot times begins transmitting. If any other station hears the first station talk, it stops counting down its backoff timer. When the network is idle again, it resumes the countdown. In addition to the basic backoff algorithm, 802.11 adds a backoff timer that ensures fairness. Each node starts a random backoff timer when waiting for the contention window. This timer ticks down to zero while waiting in the contention window. Each node gets a new random timer when it wants to transmit. This timer isn't reset until the node has transmitted.

Roaming

In a typical environment, two or more access points will provide signals to a single client. The client is responsible for choosing the most appropriate access point based on the signal strength, network utilization, and other factors. Whenever a station determines the existing signal is poor, it begins scanning for another access point. This can be done by passively listening or by actively probing each channel and waiting for a response.

When information has been received, the station selects the most appropriate signal and sends an association request to the new access point. If the new access point sends an association response, the client has successfully roamed to a new access point (make, then break behavior). Roaming is now a critical aspect of a WLAN. Roaming means that the user can pass between and among access points without having to log out and back in. In effect the user stays connected the whole time. Looking at Fig. 14.21, we see a client device moving from left to right and passing between two different access points served by the same WLAN controller, whereas a second controller and third access point are in the same subnet, then seamless roaming occurs as the client device continues to move to the right. Conversely, if we do not have seamless mobility, as shown in Fig. 14.22, then the client will get dropped and have to reauthenticate and associate anew.

MAC Layer and Data Payload

In addition to collision avoidance, timing, and roaming, the MAC layer is also responsible for identifying the source and destination address of the packet being sent, as well as the data payload and a CRC. The entire payload of the packet, including the MAC header, is transmitted at the rate specified in the PLCP.

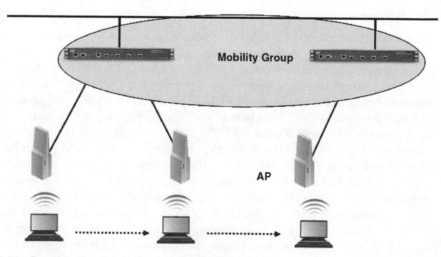

Figure 14.21 Seamless roaming is the goal of most organizations.

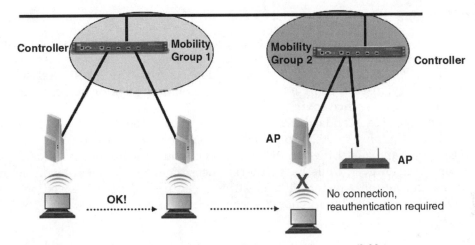

Figure 14.22   Dropped connections occur when seamless roaming is not available.

Wireless Access Point

Wireless access points make part of the LAN wireless. The wireless access point connects to the LAN like any other device and then lets any computer connected to it wirelessly act as if it were on the same LAN. Combined wireless access points and routers are available to extend the reach of the LAN and limit the amount of boxes in use.

Units are configured by either connecting a computer to it with a USB or a serial connector. You need to set the name of your ESSID (your logical WLAN). The access points allow encryption using the wire equivalent privacy (WEP) in its setup.

Wireless Adapter

To connect wirelessly, the PC or laptop needs a wireless adapter. The wireless adapters use a normal PCMCIA Type-II card that goes into the slot of a laptop just like a LAN card. The antenna sticks out. There are adapters for desktop PCs that let you use the wireless PC cards. You plug the adapter boards into a PCI slot and then plug the same type of card you use on a laptop into that board.

Realities of Wireless

Line-of-sight outdoors can work across a great distance. However indoors, with walls and electrical devices, more interference is prevalent. This reduces coverage patterns. Other 2.4-GHz devices such as cordless phones, microwave ovens, baby monitors, and bluetooth devices can cause temporary gaps in operation. When mounting the access point—higher is better. The higher the device is mounted typically the fewer obstacles in the transmission path.

Faster Wireless Standards—802.11a

The 802.11a standard, on the other hand, was designed to operate in the more recently allocated 5-GHz UNII (unlicensed national information infrastructure) band. Unlike 802.11b, the 802.11a standard departs from the traditional spread-spectrum technology; instead using a frequency-division multiplexing scheme that's intended to be friendlier to office environments.

The 802.11a standard, which supports data rates of up to 54 Mbps, is the Fast Ethernet analog to 802.11b, which only supports data rates of up to 11 Mbps. Like Ethernet and Fast Ethernet, 802.11b and 802.11a use an identical MAC (media access control). However, while Fast Ethernet uses the same physical-layer encoding scheme as Ethernet (only faster), 802.11a uses an entirely different encoding scheme, called OFDM (orthogonal frequency-division multiplexing).

Frequencies for All

The 802.11a standard is designed to operate in the 5-GHz frequency range in a band set aside by the FCC called the unlicensed national information infrastructure (UNII). The FCC allocated 300 MHz of spectrum for unlicensed operation in the 5-GHz block.

The total bandwidth allotted for IEEE 802.11a applications is almost four times that of the ISM band; the ISM band offers only 83 MHz of spectrum in the 2.4 GHz range, while the newly allocated UNII band offers 300 MHz. The 802.11b spectrum is plagued by saturation from several wireless technologies. The 802.11a spectrum is currently relatively free of interference due to the lack of devices operating in that spectrum.

The 802.11a standard gains some of its performance from the higher frequencies at which it operates. Moving up to the 5-GHz spectrum from 2.4 GHz, however, will lead to shorter distances, although we have tested the ranges and found them to be very close (90 percent). In addition, the encoding mechanism used to modulate the RF can encode one or more bits per radio cycle. Power is increased to compensate for loss in the frequencies over the distances. Power by itself is not enough to maintain the same distances in an 802.11b environment. A summary of the channels in the 2.4-GHz and the 5-GHz range is shown in Fig. 14.23. What we especially like about the 802.11a channels is the fact that there are many more of them and they are not overlapping. In this figure we also took the liberty of adding some newer channels shown as additional UNII channels. The FCC has recently opened up additional channels in the UNII band, although no vendors have products yet, expect them soon.

A new physical-layer encoding technology that departs from the traditional direct-sequence technology is being used. This technology is called COFDM (coded OFDM). COFDM was developed specifically for indoor wireless use and offers performance much superior to that of spread-spectrum solutions. COFDM works by breaking one high-speed data carrier into several lower-speed subcarriers, which are then transmitted in parallel. Each high-speed carrier is 20 MHz wide as shown in Fig. 14.24 and is broken up into 52 subchannels, each approximately 300 kHz wide, as shown in Fig. 8.19. COFDM uses 48 of these subchannels for data, while the remaining four are used for error correction.

WiFi Standard	Frequencies	Channels	Spacing	Modulation	Power Max
802.11 b/g	2.400-2.4835 GHz	1,2,3,4,5,6,7, 8,9,10,11,12, 13 & 14	25 MHz	DSSS and CCK ERP-OFDM	1W for N America 100 mW for Europe
802.11 a	Name/Range	24 total channels			
	U-NII lower 5.150-5.250	36,40,44,48	20 MHz	OFDM	40 mW N 200 mW E
	U-NII middle 5.250-5.350	52,56,60,64	20 MHz	OFDM	200 mW N 200 mW E
	Additional U-NII bands 5.470-5.725	100,104,108 112,116,120 124,128,132 136, 140	20 MHz	OFDM	1000 mW N 1000 mW E
	U-NII upper 5.725-5.825	149,153,157 161	20 MHz	OFDM	800 mW N N/A
	ISM 5.825-5.850	165	20 MHz	OFDM	800 mW N N/A

Figure 14.23   Channel comparisons by numbers, bands, and output power limitations.

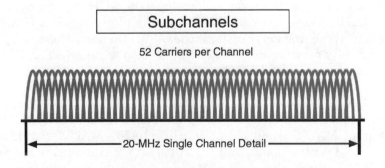

Subchannels

52 Carriers per Channel

────── 20-MHz Single Channel Detail ──────

Each channel is subdivided into 52 subchannels, each about 300 KHz wide.

Figure 14.24   The 52 subchannels per carrier.

COFDM delivers higher data rates and a high degree of multipath reflection recovery, thanks to its encoding scheme and error correction.

802.11a will support data rates of 6, 9, 12, 18, 24, 36, 48, and 54 Mbps, as per the standard. The de facto standard for 802.11a networking appears to be 54 Mbps. Data rates of 54 Mbps are achieved by using 64-QAM with throughput being somewhere in

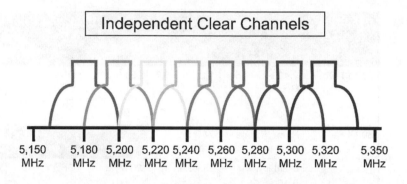

Figure 14.25   Independent clear channels.

the 18–26 Mbps range. Vendors are now stating that they will offer an additional proprietary mode that combines two carriers for a maximum theoretical data rate of 108 Mbps and conservatively estimates that data throughput of 72 Mbps will be possible when using its proprietary dual-channel mode.

Bran Anyone?

In Europe, the HiperLAN/2 standard led by the ETSI called BRAN group (broadband radio access networks) has wide acceptance as the 5-GHz technology of choice. HiperLAN/2 and 802.11a share some similarities at the physical layer. However, HiperLAN/2 is more like asynchronous transfer mode (ATM) than to Ethernet. The HiperLAN/2 standard actually grew out of the effort to develop wireless ATM. HiperLAN/2 shares the 20-MHz channels in the 5-GHz spectrum in time, using TDMA (time division multiple access) to provide QoS (quality of service) through ATM-like mechanisms.

802.11a on the other hand shares the 20-MHz channel in time using CSMA/ CA (carrier sense multiple access with collision avoidance). Logically, HiperLAN/2 uses a different MAC than 802.11a. The HiperLAN/2 MAC design has proven to be problematic and controversial, and the HiperLAN/2 standard is not yet complete. In contrast, 802.11a uses the same MAC as 802.11b, which gives developers only one task to complete: a 5-GHz IEEE 802.11a-compliant radio. No simple task, but easier than redesigning the radio and the MAC controller.

Taming the Standards Beast

Manufacturers are concerned over the competing 802.11a and HiperLAN/2 standards. Building and supporting two separate products is a nightmare in both development and marketing. The increased development costs will be handed down to the end user, which will detract from the acceptance of the standards and products. This becomes a lose-lose situation for the vendors. The IEEE 802.11 committees are working on the interoperability standards.

Backward Compatibility Problems

Because 802.11a and 802.11b operate in different frequencies, there's no chance they'll be interoperable. Thus, any vendor or end user that has made large investments in 802.11b technology faces the "forklift technology" dilemma. The only way to change the architecture is to bring in the forklifts and take away the 802.11b, and then bring in the 802.11a boxes. A migration path exists for the future when more bandwidth is required, however, extensive retooling is required. The 802.11a and 802.11b technologies can coexist, however, because there is no signal overlap.

Installing a WLAN

Setting up a WLAN is fairly simple, using a D-link wireless AP, we use the following steps for the basic setup.

Hardware needed:

One CAT5 cable

One wireless router

One laptop with a wireless card

Start

1. Plug the D-link wireless access point in and with a pen or something small press and hold the reset button for about a couple of seconds. This is located on the back of the device next to the Internet Port.

2. Connect the CAT5 cable into the wired port and the other end into the switch.

3. Plug a CAT5 cable into your computer and the other end into the switch. You will have to set the wired NIC to 192.168.0.x to be on the same subnet as the access point. We used 192.168.0.100 as shown in Fig. 14.26.

4. Open Internet Explorer on your PC and type in 192.168.0.50 in the address bar and press enter.

5. A username and password dialog box will appear, type "admin" as the username and leave the password blank. This is shown in Fig. 14.27, not the address typed into Explorer is the 192.168.0.50.

6. Once you are logged in, the home screen will appear.

7. The first thing you want to do is to set up the system, so click on the **Run Wizard** button.

8. The wizard will show you a list of options you can configure as seen in Fig. 14.28. Click *next*.

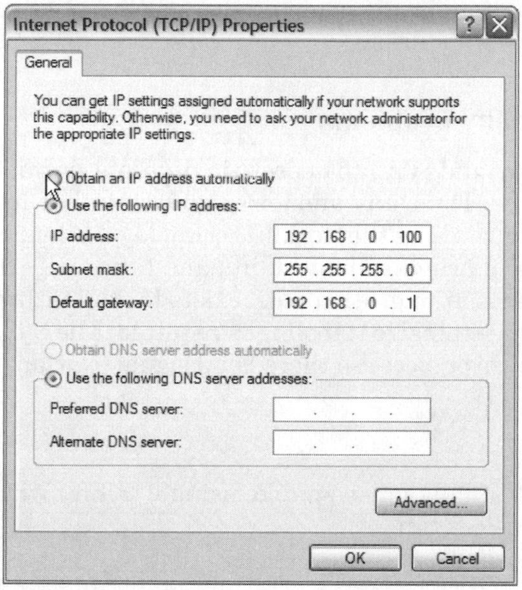

Figure 14.26 Set up your wired NIC on the same subnet as the AP.

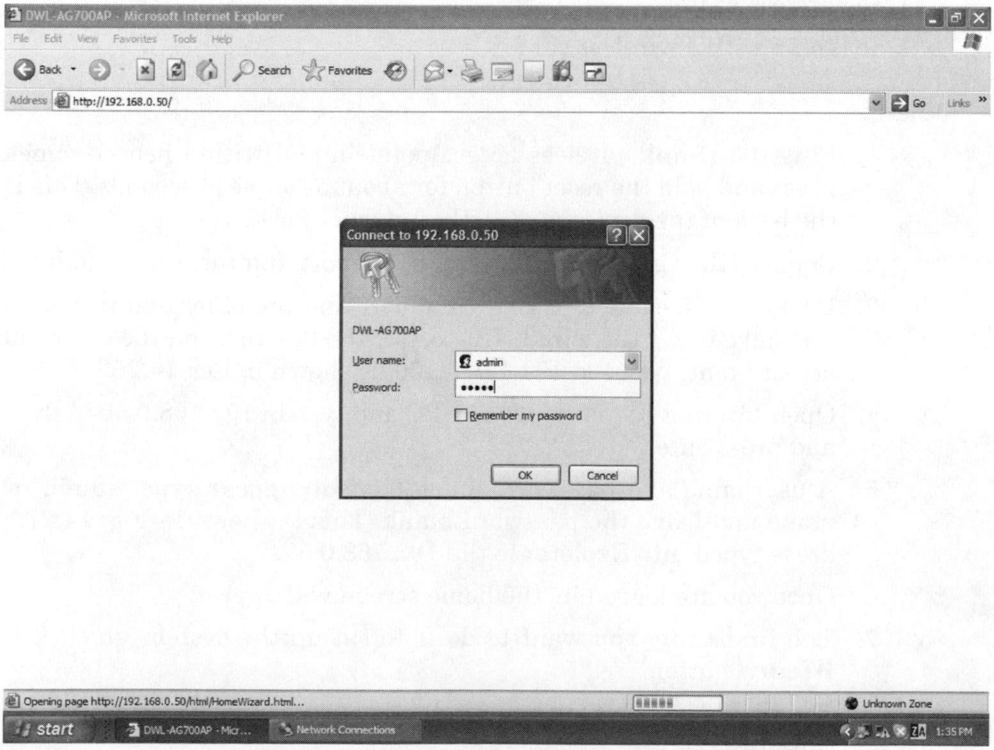

Figure 14.27 Connect to the AP at the address shown and type admin as password.

9. Set up your password, use "Iamnotsure" and type it again in the verify space. Click *next*.

10. Now set up the 802.11a WLAN network. The default SSID is set to default and channel 52. Change the SSID to **AMEN** and leave the channel at **52.**

11. The access point is capable of three levels of wireless encryption: 64, 128, or 152 bit using either a HEX or ASCII key. By default encryption is disabled. Leave it disabled, as seen in Fig. 14.30. Click *next*.

12. Next, the 802.11g screen will appear. The default SSID is set to default and channel 6. Change the SSID to **GWHIZ** and the channel to **11**. Click *next*.

13. The access point is capable of three levels of wireless encryption: 64, 128, or 152 bit using either a HEX or ASCII key. By default encryption is disabled. Leave it disabled. Click *next*.

14. Setup is now complete. Click *restart* to save and reboot the access point. This will take a few seconds.

15. Restart your browser and connect to 192.168.0.50 and log in.

16. You will be asked for a username and password again, "admin" for username and "Iamnotsure" for the password.

Going Wireless

1. Unplug the CAT5 cable from the back of your computer.

2. Look in the taskbar on your computer in the lower right hand corner of the screen—next to the clock. You should see two network icons, one with a red X which looks like two monitors and another with a red X with 3 green curved lines next to a single monitor. Right click on the network icon with the green lines and select view available wireless network.

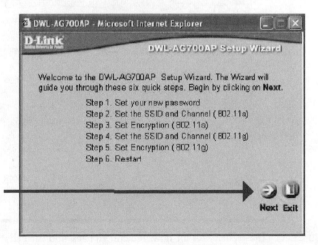

Figure 14.28   Next runs the wizard.

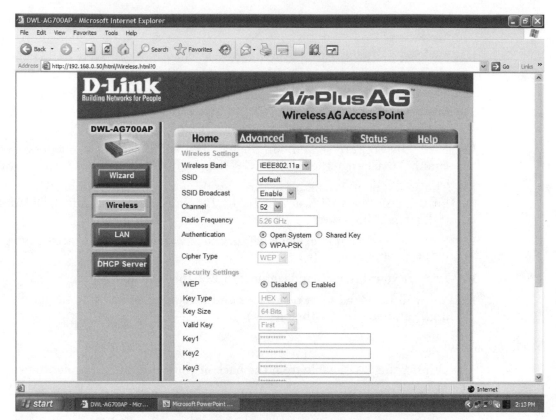

Figure 14.29 Set the radio to 802.11a and use AMEN for the SSID and channel 52 for the radio.

Figure 14.30 Leave the security off for now, you can go back and turn that on later.

3. A list will appear with all wireless network connections available to you. If you have connected to anyone of these networks, click *disconnect* from each one that it connects.

4. Next, you want to locate the name of your access point, the SSID that you entered before (use AMEN). Click on this name and then click *connect*. A window will pop up warning you that the connection is not secure, click *connect* anyway.

5. Windows will then connect you to your wireless access point using the 802.11a network.

6. Open your browser and click *home* to go to the home page, you should see MSN's Web site if we have an external connection. (You may have to plug in the DNS address to get the system to connect you to the outside world).

7. If outside access is available and you do not see this, take the power cable out of the back of the access point and wait 10 seconds.

8. Plug the AP back in and try to go to your home page again. If this does not work, check your settings.

These settings should get you where you need to go. Regardless of the access point you are using, the steps are pretty much the same throughout the industry. We also had to assume that by now you had a wireless NIC in your laptop or a USB connection on your PC. If you need to get a wireless card on your desktop, we prefer to use a USB connector, because it is awkward for many people to install a PCI card, and the like. Here are the basic steps for this to work.

Installing the USB Wireless Network Card

1. Put the CD for the wireless NIC into the CD ROM tray and install the drivers. The program should take you through an installer, and add the drivers to the computer. Do not plug the USB device in yet.

2. After the drivers are installed restart your computer.

3. After the computer reboots, plug the small end of the USB cable into the network card, then plug the other end into the USB port on the computer.

4. Look at the wireless network card. Is the power light on? If not, go to step#5. If it is, go to step #9.

5. Click on *control panel* in the *start menu*.

6. Then click on *administrative tools.*

7. Then click on *services*.

8. When the service menu loads, scroll down to *wireless zero configuration*. Make sure the service is started. If not, right click it and go to *properties*. Under the *start up type* make sure automatic is selected from the drop down

menu, then click on *start* under the *service status*. (A popup should load informing you the service has been started). Then click *apply* (at the bottom) of the tab, then *OK.* Go back to step #4 and make sure the power light is on.

9. The wireless network card should be active. If it isn't, click on *My Computer*. Click on *my network places* (in the left side column), Then click on *view network connections* (again on the left side column). Make sure the wireless connection is enabled. (You can do this by right clicking on the *wireless network connection.*) If it isn't enabled, select *enable* from the list.

You are now ready to use your WLAN!

Questions

1. How many different types of WLAN are available?
   a. 802.11
   b. 802.11a
   c. 802.11b
   d. 802.11d
   e. 802.11e
   f. 802.11g
   g. 802.11i
   h. 802.11n

2. What standards body has been setting the rules for WLANs?
   a. IETF
   b. ITU
   c. IEEE
   d. ISO
   e. OSI

3. What is the recommended distance from the manufacturers to place the access points (APs) apart?
   a. 100 feet
   b. 50 feet
   c. 90 feet
   d. 300 feet

4. When did WLANs become popular?

   a. 1992

   b. 1994

   c. 1996

   d. 1998

   e. 2000

5. What speeds are achievable in an 802.11 WLAN?

   a. 1 Mbps

   b. 2 Mbps

   c. 5.5 Mbps

   d. 11 Mbps

   e. All of the above

6. 802.11 has the same framing format as 802.3 standard framing.   T/F

7. When the 802.11a standard is used what is the frequency band used?

   a. 900 MHz ISM band

   b. 2.4 GHz ISM band

   c. 5 GHz UNII band

   d. 5.3 GHz ISM band

7. How much throughput can a user get on a 802.11g network typically?

   a. 5–6 Mbps

   b. 9 Mbps

   c. 18 Mbps

   d. 54 Mbps

8. If we install a wireless LAN AP on channel 6, what channel should the adjacent AP be on?

   a. 1 or 6

   b. 6 or 11

   c. 1 or 11

   d. 1 and 11

9. How far can the distance be from the AP for a client using a signaling rate of 36–24 Mbps?

   a. 22 feet

   b. 45 feet

   c. 67 feet

   d. 90 feet

15

Digital Subscriber Line (DSL) and CATV

After reading this chapter and completing the questions, you will be able to:

- Describe the benefits of using *x*DSL
- Understand the capabilities of the various types of *x*DSL
- Discuss the limitations of the local loop
- Describe the modulation techniques used
- Discuss why the CATV vendors jumped into the data business
- Describe the cable systems they use for data
- Understand the speeds that they offer
- Describe the technique they use to link users on their network

While the industry had been scurrying around looking for new ways of transmitting data from the consumer's door, the local telephone companies (called the LECs) found new life in their copper cable plant. Clearly, these telephone companies had a personal stake in finding something that would allow them to continue to use the copper cable plant connected to every home and business. The movement to a data communications era gave them the impetus they needed.

What Is xDSL?

One of the major problems facing the incumbent local exchange carriers (ILECs) was the ability to maintain and preserve their installed base. After the Telecommunications Act of 1996 was passed there was mounting pressure on the ILECs to provide faster and more accurate Internet access. Therefore, they needed a new form of communications to work over the existing copper cable plant. One of the technologies selected was the use of *x*DSL. The *x*DSL family includes several variations of what is known as digital subscriber line. The lowercase *x* in front of the DSL stands for the many variations. These will include:

- Asymmetric digital subscriber line (ADSL and ADSL+)
- ISDN-like digital subscriber line (IDSL)
- High-bit-rate digital subscriber line (HDSL)
- Consumer digital subscriber line (CDSL)
- Rate-adaptive digital subscriber line (RADSL)
- Very high speed digital subscriber line (VDSL)
- Symmetric or single digital subscriber line (SDSL)
- Single pair high speed digital subscriber line (SHDSL)

One can see that the variations are many. Each DSL capability carries with it differences in speed, throughput, and facilities used. The most popular of this family under today's technology is ADSL, yet very high data rate DSL (VDSL) is also making headway because the ILECs are now providing fiber to the home (FTTH).

ADSL is a technology provided primarily by the ILECs because the existing cable plant can support the speeds, which can vary depending on the quality of the copper and the distances involved from the central office (CO) to the customer premises. The most important and critical factor in dealing with ADSL technology is the ability to support speeds from 1.5 up to 8.192 Mbps. The ILECs can also support plain old telephone service (POTS) for voice or fax communications on the same physical pair of wires. What this means is that the ILECs do not have to install new cabling to support high-speed access to the Internet.

Asymmetric Digital Subscriber Line (ADSL)

Asymmetric digital subscriber line is the modem technology that converges the existing twisted-pair telephone lines into the high-speed communications access capability for various services. Most people consider ADSL as a transmission system instead of a modification to the existing transmission facilities. In reality, ADSL is a modem technology used to transmit speeds of 1.5–6 Mbps under current technology. ADSL is expected to support downloadable speeds up to 8 Mbps and up speeds of approximately 1 Mbps. This definition of the higher range of ADSL speeds is truly yet to be proven; however, with changes in today's technology one can only imagine that the speeds can be achievable.

ADSL Capabilities   Many of the capabilities introduced with the DSL family are the services for converging voice, data, multimedia, video, and Internet streaming protocol services. The carriers see their future in the rollout of products and services to the general consuming public so they can access the Internet. Table 15.1 lists the speeds and standards covering the various ADSL technologies.

TABLE 15.1   Speeds and Standards Based xDSL

Family	ITU	Name	Ratified	Maximum Speed Capabilities
ADSL	G.992.1	G.dmt	1999	7 Mbps down, 800 Kbps up
ADSL2	G.992.3	G.dmt.bis	2002	8 Mbps down, 1 Mbps up
ADSL2plus	G.992.5	ADSL2plus	2003	24 Mbps down, 1 Mbps up
ADSL2-RE	G.992.3	Reach extended	2003	8 Mbps down 1 Mbps up
SHDSL	G.991.2	G.SHDSL	2001	5.6 Mbps up/down
VDSL	G.993.1	Very-high-data-rate DSL	2004	55 Mbps down, 15 Mbps up
VDSL2	G.993.2	Very-high-data-rate DSL 2	2005	100 Mbps up/down

TABLE 15.2   Summary of Distances and Speeds for DSL

Data Rates for ADSL			
Current Data Rate, Mbps	Wire Gauge	Distance, ft	Distance, km
1.5–2.048	24	18,000	5.5
1.5–2.048	26	15,000	4.6
6.3	24	12,000	3.7
6.3	26	9,000	2.7

Remember that the speeds shown here are theoretical. If the copper has been damaged or impaired in any way, the speed and distances will change accordingly (downward), and we all know what condition the wiring is in from years of abuse and dealing with the elements. Reality and the actual distances and speeds very likely will be less than shown here in Table 15.2, the typical distances are shown with the requisite speeds. What is most important is the assumption that these speeds can be established and maintained on the installed base of unshielded twisted pair (UTP) wire. As long as the ILECs can approximate these speeds today, the consumer will most likely not complain.

Modem Technologies   Before proceeding too far in this discussion, a quick review of modem technology is probably in line. Modems, or modulator/demodulators, were designed to move data across the voice communications network. Users still struggle to transmit data across the voice networks at speeds up to 33,600 bps. Even with the newer modems called the V.92, which are supposed to operate at 56 Kbps, we still see significant reductions in speed. Although this may seem like high-speed communication, our demands and needs for faster communications have quickly outstripped the capabilities of our current modem services, making the demand for newer services more evident. Higher-speed modems could be produced, but the economics and variations on the wiring system prove this somewhat impractical. Instead, the providers looked for a better way to provide data communications that mimic the digital transmission speeds we readily accept.

Using the telephone company's voice services, the end user installs a modem on the local loop. This modem is the data circuit–terminating equipment (DCE) for the link. A modem is used to communicate across the wide area networks, as shown in Fig. 15.1. The ILEC installs a voice-grade line on the copper cable plant and allows the end user

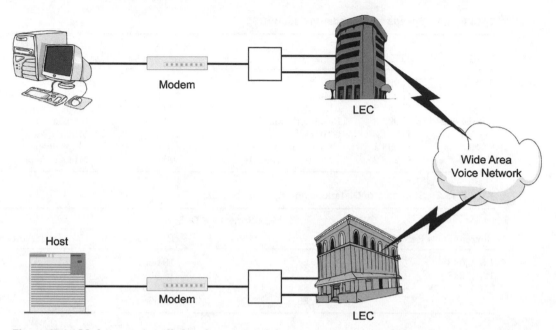

Figure 15.1   Modems are installed at the customer's location and use the existing telephone wires to transmit data across the voice network.

to connect the modem. The modem then converts the data into an analog signal. There is no real magic in modem communications today, but in the early days of data communications, this was considered voodoo science. The miracle of data compression and other multibit modulation techniques quickly expanded the data rates from 300 bps to today's 33.6 Kbps. Newer modems are touted to handle data at speeds of up to 56 Kbps, but few come close to these rates. So, the reality of all the pieces combined still has the consumer operating at approximately 33.6 Kbps.

ISDN-Like Digital Subscriber Line (IDSL)

DSL refers to a pair of modems installed on the last mile of line, facilitating higher data speeds. Network providers use the existing wires and add the DSL modems to increase the throughput. DSL modems offer duplex operations. The speed of a DSL modem may be 128 Kbps on copper at distances up to 18,000 feet using the twisted-pair wires. The bandwidth used is from 0 to 80 kHz. IDSL uses the 128-Kbps full-duplex basic rate interface (BRI). As shown in Fig. 15.2, the IDSL technique is all digital, operating at two channels of 64 Kbps for voice or nonvoice operation and a 16-Kbps data channel for signaling, control, and data packets. ISDN was very slow to catch on, but the movement to the Internet created a whole new set of demands. Now more ILECs and the CLECs(Competitive Local Exchange Carrier) offer ISDN services. As the deployment of IDSL was speeding up on the local loop, the providers developed a new twist, called

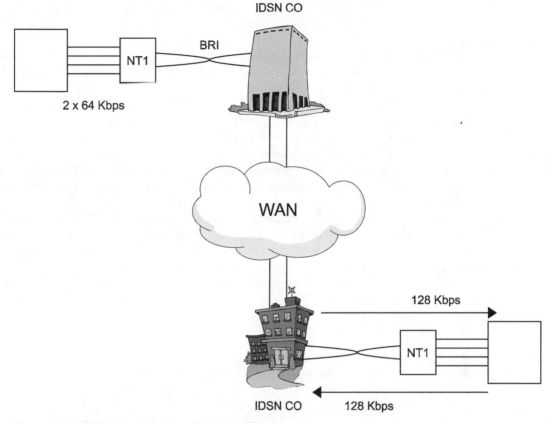

Figure 15.2 IDSL line connection allows 128 Kbps.

always on ISDN, mimicking a leased set of channels that are always connected. Bonding the channels together, users can surf the Net at speeds of 128 Kbps. Note that this is a *symmetrical* digital subscriber line.

High-Bit-Rate Digital Subscriber Line (HDSL)

In 1958, Bell developed a voice multiplexing system that uses the 64-Kbps pulse code modulation (PCM). Using the PCM techniques, voice calls were sampled 8000 times per second and coded using an 8-bit encoding. These samples were then organized into a framed format, using 24 time slots to bundle and multiplex 24 simultaneous conversations onto a single four-wire circuit. Each frame carries 24 samples of 8 bits and 1 framing bit, 8000 times a second. This produces a data rate of 1.544 Mbps. We now refer to this as a *digital signal level 1* (DS-1) at the framed data rate. This rate of data transfer is used in the United States, Canada, and Japan.

Throughout the rest of the world, standards were set to operate using an E1 with a signaling rate of 2.048 Mbps. The differences between the two services (T1 and E1) are significant enough to prevent their seamless integration.

However, in the digital arena, T1 required that the provider install the circuits to the customer's premises. The local provider installs a four-wire circuit. Repeaters are spaced at every 5000–6000 feet. When installing the T1 on the local loop, limitations of the delivery mechanism get in the way. Alternate mark inversion (AMI) consumes all the bandwidth and corrupts the surrounding cable spectrum quickly. Consequently, the providers can only use a single T1 in a 50-pair cable. Figure 15.3 is a representation of this cable layout. This inefficient use of the wiring makes it impractical to install T1s to small office and residential locations. Further limitations require the providers to remove bridge taps, clean up splices, and remove load coils from the wires to get the T1 to work.

To circumvent these cabling problems, HDSL was developed. HDSL does not require the repeaters on a local loop of up to 12,000 feet. Bridge taps will not bother the service, and the splices are left in place. This means that the provider can offer HDSL more efficiently for 1.544 Mbps. The modulation rate on the HDSL service is more advanced. Sending 768 Kbps on one pair and another 768 Kbps on the second pair of wires splits the T1. This is shown in Fig. 15.4.

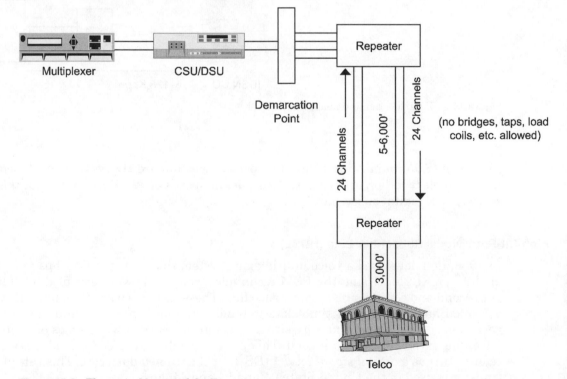

Figure 15.3   The typical layout of the T1.

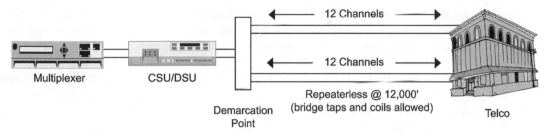

Figure 15.4 HDSL is impervious to the bridge and splices. The T1 is split onto two pairs.

Originally, HDSL used two pairs at distances of up to 15,000 feet. HDSL at 2.048 Mbps uses three pairs of wire for the same distances. The most recent version, HDSL-2, uses only one pair of wire and is more acceptable to the providers. Nearly all providers today deliver T1 capabilities on some form of HDSL.

Symmetric or Single Digital Subscriber Line (SDSL)

The goal of the DSL family was to continue to support and use the local cable plant. Therefore, providing high-speed communications on a single cable pair became paramount. Most local loops already employ single cable pair today; thus, it is only natural to assume that providers would want this capability. SDSL was developed to provide high-speed communications on that single cable pair but at distances no greater than 10,000 feet. Despite this distance limitation, SDSL was designed to deliver 1.544 Mbps on the single cable pair. Typically, however, the providers provision SDSL at 768 Kbps. This creates a dilemma for the carriers because HDSL can do the same things as SDSL.

Asymmetric Digital Subscriber Line (ADSL)

SDSL uses only one pair of wires to provide duplex high-speed communications but is limited in distance. Not all users require symmetrical speeds at the same time. ADSL was, therefore, designed to support different speeds in each direction at distances of up to 18,000 feet. Because the speeds requested are typically to access to the Internet, most users look for higher download speeds and lower upload speeds. Therefore, the asymmetrical nature of this service meets those needs.

Rate-Adaptive Digital Subscriber Line (RADSL)

Typically, when equipment is installed, assumptions are made based on minimum performance characteristics and speeds. In some cases, special equipment is used to condition the circuit to achieve those speeds. However, if the line conditions vary, the speed will be dependent on the sensitivity of the equipment. In order to achieve variations in throughput and be sensitive to the line conditions, rate-adaptive DSL was developed. This allows the flexibility to adapt to changing conditions and adjust the speeds in each direction to potentially maximize the throughput on each line. In addition, as line conditions change, one could see the speeds changing in each direction during the transmission. Many of the ILECs have installed RADSL as their choice given the local loop conditions. Speeds of up to 768 Kbps are the preferred rates offered by the incumbent providers.

Consumer Digital Subscriber Line (CDSL)

Not all consumers need symmetrical high-speed communication to access the Internet. Furthermore, ADSL speeds are more than the average consumer may be looking for. Lower-speed communications capability was developed using CDSL. With other forms of DSL, splitters are used on the line. CDSL was designed to eliminate the splitter on the line. Moreover, speeds of up to 1 Mbps in the download direction and 160–384 Kbps in the upward direction are provided. It is expected that the speeds and CDSL will meet needs of the average consumer for some time to come. A universal ADSL working group developed what is called ADSL-*lite*, also called *G.lite*. This specification was ratified in late 1998, using the working group's specifications for service delivery to the average consumer.

Very High Speed Digital Subscriber Line (VDSL)

It was only matter of time until some users demanded higher-speed communications than was offered by the current DSL technologies. VDSL was introduced to achieve the higher speeds. In fact, speeds ranging from 13 to 52 Mbps are available, but the distance limitations of the local cable will be a big factor. In order to achieve the speeds, one can expect that a fiber feed will be used to deliver VDSL. This technique will most likely carry ATM (cells) as its primary payload. We can expect some hybrid arrangements to deliver this speed to the door for high-speed data at up to 52 Mbps downward and 1.5–6 Mbps upward.

Table 15.3 summarizes the current speeds and characteristics of the DSL technologies discussed here. These are the typical installation and operational characteristics; others will certainly exist in variations of installation and implementation.

Single Pair High Speed Digital Subscriber Line (SHDSL)

SHDSL is the newest member of the DSL family being currently standardized at ITU (G.SHDSL) and ETSI (TM6) in 2001. G.SHDSL targets the small business market. Multiple telephone and data channels, videoconferencing, remote LAN access, and leased lines with customer-specific data rates are among its many exciting characteristics. Spectrally friendly with other xDSLs, it supports symmetric data rates at 5.6 Mbps (both up and down speeds) across greater distances than other technologies. SHDSL uses a Trellis coded pulse amplitude modulation (TC PAM)-based modulation scheme,

TABLE 15.3   Summary of DSL Speeds and Operations Using Current Methods

Service	Explanation	Download	Upload	Mode of Operation
ADSL	Asymmetric DSL	7 Mbps	800 Kbps	Different up and down speeds, one pair of wire.
ADSL 2	Asymmetric DSL	8 Mbps	1 Mbps	Different up and down speeds, one pair of wire.
ADSL 2 plus	Asymmetric DSL	24 Mbps	1 Mbps	May start involving fiber.
ADSL 2 RE	Extended reach	8 Mbps	1 Mbps	Different up and down speeds, one pair of wire.
RADSL	Rate-adaptive DSL	64 Kbps–8.192 Mbps	16–768 Kbps	Different up and down speeds. Many common operations on 768 Kbps. One pair of wire.
CDSL	Consumer DSL	1 Mbps	16–128 Kbps	Now ratified as DSL-lite. No splitters. One pair of wire.
HDSL	High data rate DSL	1.544 Mbps in North America; 2.048 Mbps in rest of world	1.544 Mbps 2.048 Mbps	Symmetrical services. Two pairs of wire.
IDSL	ISDN DSL	144 Kbps (64 + 64 + 16) as BRI	144 Kbps (64 + 64 + 16) as BRI	Symmetrical operation. One pair of wire. ISDN BRI.
SDSL	Single DSL	1.544 Mbps 2.048 Mbps	1.544 Mbps 2.048 Mbps	Uses only one pair, but typically provisioned at 768 Kbps. One pair of wire.
SHDSL	Single pair high-bit rate DSL	5.6 Mbps	5.6 Mbps	Uses one pair, aimed at small residential customers.
VDSL	Very high speed DSL	55 Mbps	15 Mbps	Fiber needed and ATM probably used.
VDSL 2-12 MHz	Very high speed DSL	55 Mbps	30 Mbps	Fiber needed and ATM probably used.
VDSL 2-30 MHz	Very high speed DSL	100 Mbps	100 Mbps	Fiber needed and ATM probably used.

which is different from the other forms of xDSL. It will operate over a single-pair of wires at ranges from 6000 feet to 20,000 feet (2.3 Mbps to 192 Kbps rates, respectively) on 26 AWG copper. This will produce a 35–50 percent improvement in rate at a given range over traditional symmetric DSL and a 15–20 percent improvement in distance at a given rate over traditional symmetric DSL. G.SHDSL is also known as G.991.2 standard.

The Hype of DSL Technologies

The local providers are extremely excited at the possibility of installing higher-speed communications and preserving their local cable plants. No one wants to abandon the local copper loop, but getting more data reliably across the local loop is imperative. Therefore, the ability to breathe new life into the cable plant is an extension of the facilities in place. This also means that they can create a new form of revenue streams from the old copper. Consumers are looking for higher-speed access (primarily to access the Internet) for whatever the application. Yet, at the same time, consumers are looking for a bargain. They do not want to spend a lot of money on their communications services.

The providers are trying to bump up their revenues, without major new investments. They would like to launch as many new service offerings on their existing cable plant and increase the costs to the end user. This is a business decision, not a means of trying to rake the consumer over the coals. Yet, there has to be a happy medium of providing services and generating revenues with limits on expenses. To do this, the *x*DSL family offers the opportunity to meet the demands while holding down investment costs. The key ingredient for success is to minimize costs and satisfy the consumer. Make no mistake, if the local provider does not offer high-speed services, someone else will.

xDSL Coding Techniques

Many approaches were developed as a means of encoding data onto *x*DSL circuits. The more common are carrierless amplitude phase (CAP) modulation and discreet multi-tone (DMT) modulation. Quadrature with phase modulation (QAM) has also been used, but the important part is the standardization. The industry as a rule selected DMT, but several developers and providers have used CAP. It is, therefore, appropriate to summarize both of these techniques.

Discreet Multitone (DMT) Modulation

DMT uses multiple narrowband carriers, all transmitting simultaneously in a parallel transmission mode. Each of these carriers carries a portion of the information being transmitted. These multiple discrete bands—or, in the world of frequency-division multiplexing, subchannels—are modulated independently of each other, using a carrier frequency located in the center of the frequency being used. These carriers are then processed in parallel form.

In order to process the multicarrier frequencies at the same time, a lot of digital processing is required. In the past this was not economically feasible, but integrated circuitry has made this more feasible.

The American National Standards Institute (ANSI) selected DMT with the use of 256 subcarriers, each with the standard 4.3125-kHz bandwidth. These subcarriers can be independently modulated with a maximum 15 bps/Hz. This allows up to 60 Kbps per tone used. Figure 15.5 shows the use of the frequency spectrum for the combination of voice and two-way data transmission. In this representation, voice is used in the normal 0–4 kHz band on the lower end of the spectrum (although the lower 20 kHz is provided). Separation is allowed between the voice channel and the upstream data communications, which operates between 20 and 130 kHz. Then a separation is allowed between the upstream and the downstream channels. The downstream flow uses between 140 kHz and 1 MHz. As shown in this figure, the separation allows for the simultaneous

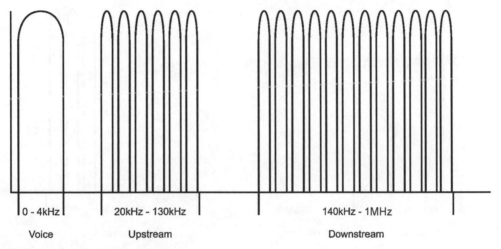

| 0 - 4kHz | 20kHz - 130kHz | 140kHz - 1MHz |
| Voice | Upstream | Downstream |

Figure 15.5   The ANSI DMT specification.

up and down streams and the concurrent voice channel. It is on this spectrum that the data rates are sustained. Each of the subchannels operates at approximately 4.3125 kHz, and a separation of 4.3125 kHz between channels is allocated.

Using DMT for the Universal ADSL Service (G.Lite)

Provisions for the high-speed data rates of full ADSL are good, but not every consumer is looking for the high data rates afforded on ADSL. Therefore, the universal ADSL working group decided to reevaluate the need for the end user. What they determined is that many consumers need downloads of 1–1.5 Mbps and uploads of 160– 640 Kbps. Consequently, ADSL-lite specification was designed with these speeds for the future. Initially introduced in early 1998, the specification was ratified in late 1998 to facilitate the lower throughput needs of the average consumer. DMT is the preferred method of delivering G.lite service. There is no way to know if the network providers can support hundreds of multimegabit ADSL upload and download speeds on their existing infrastructure. However, using the G.lite specification can support lower-demand users more efficiently. Similar to the DMT used in the ANSI specification, the carriers are divided as shown in Fig. 15.6. Note that in this case the high end of the frequency spectrum tops out at approximately 550 kHz instead of the 1 MHz range with ADSL.

Carrierless Amplitude Phase (CAP) Modulation

CAP is closely aligned to quadrature amplitude modulation (QAM). QAM as a technique is widely understood in the industry and well deployed in older modems. Both CAP and QAM are single carrier signal techniques. The data rate is divided in two and modulated onto two different orthogonal carriers before being combined and transmitted. The main difference between CAP and QAM is in the way they are implemented.

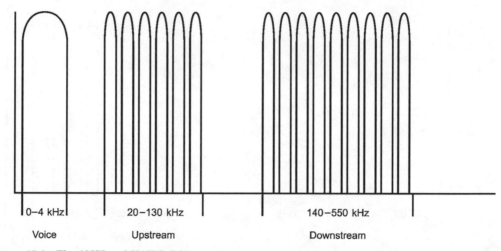

| 0–4 kHz | 20–130 kHz | 140–550 kHz |
| Voice | Upstream | Downstream |

Figure 15.6   The ANSI and UAWG G.lite spectrum.

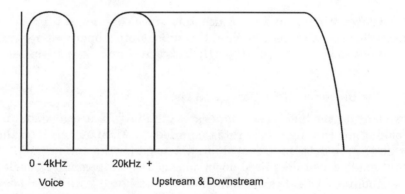

0 - 4kHz   20kHz +

Voice   Upstream & Downstream

Figure 15.7   The spectral use of CAP.

QAM generates two signals with a sine/cosine mixer and combines them onto the analog domain.

CAP was one of the original proposals for use with ADSL technology. Unfortunately, this was a proprietary solution offered by a single vendor, which turned heads away from acceptance. CAP's use of the frequency spectrum of the line is shown in Fig.15.7. Most industry vendors agree that CAP has some benefits over DMT, but also that DMT has more benefits over CAP. The point here is that two differing technologies were initially rolled out for ADSL (and the other family members), which contradict each other in their implementation.

CAP uses the entire loop bandwidth (excluding the 4-kHz baseband analog voice channel) to send the bits all at once. There are no subchannels as found in the DMT technique. The lack of subchannels removes the concern about and problems with individual channel transmission.

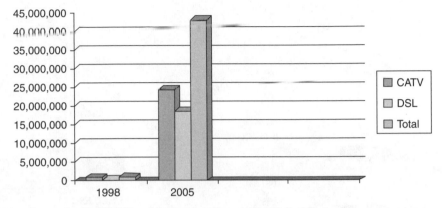

Figure 15.8   Comparison of CATV and DSL subscribers in the United States.

Comments on Deployment

ADSL service finally caught on. However, the ILECs were dragging their feet. As of late 1998, there were only about 150,000 ADSL modem pairs installed in the United States. In contrast, there were over 800,000 cable modems installed in residences and businesses across the country. The local owners of the copper loop needed to take a more aggressive approach to delivering high-speed services, or consumers go somewhere else. As the market continues to mature and standards continue to develop, the local providers must preserve their infrastructure. At the end of 2005 the numbers changed significantly with cable TV data users approximating 24.5 million and DSL users at approximately 18.5 million and look like the chart shown in Fig. 15.8. At one time U.S.-based CATV users outnumbered DSL users by 2:1; that margin is now approximately 1.5:1, which shows great strides by the ILECs.

Although consumers are reluctant to proceed with ADSL, the HDSL and SDSL services are still very attractive alternatives, offering 1.544- to 2.048-Mbps symmetrical speeds or some variation, as already discussed.

In the future, when high-speed media are installed to the door or to the curb, the logical stepping stone will become the VDSL service, perhaps sometime in 2002–2003. Although trials are already under way, too much time passes until the results are complied and analyzed. Therefore, the reality of VDSL for the masses is still a long way off.

Voice over DSL

In general, a Voice over DSL (VoDSL) system functions as an overlay solution to a DSL broadband access network, enabling a CLEC to extend multiline local telephone service off of a centralized voice switch. For example, Jetstream's VoDSL solution allows up to 16 telephone lines and high-speed continuous data service to be provided over

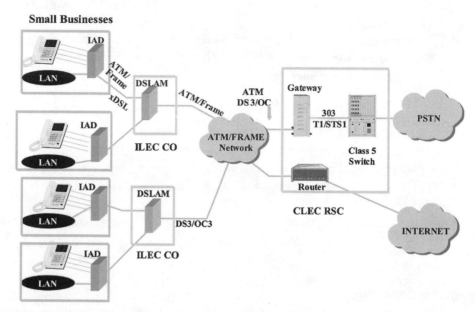

Figure 15.9 Integrating Voice over DSL onto ATM or frame relay.

a single DSL connection as shown in Fig. 15.9. A VoDSL solution typically consists of three components.

- First, a carrier-class voice gateway that resides in the regional switching center (RSC) and serves as a bridge between the circuit-based voice switch and the packet-based DSL access network.

- Second, an integrated access device (IAD) resides at each subscriber premises and connects to a DSL circuit. It also serves as a circuit/packet gateway and provides the subscriber with standard telephone service via up to 16 analog POTS (Plain Old Telephone Service or basic dial tone) ports and Internet service via an Ethernet connection.

- Third is the management system.

With VoDSL solutions, DSL broadband access networks now have the coverage, capacity and cost attributes to enable CLECs to deliver local telephone services as well as data services to the small and mid-size business markets. It has already been established that DSL access networks have the right bandwidth to serve the data needs of small and mid-size businesses. With VoDSL access solutions, this is true for serving the local telephone service needs of those subscribers as well.

Some VoDSL solutions are capable of delivering 16 telephone lines over a DSL circuit along with standard data traffic. Because 95 percent of small businesses use 12 or fewer telephone lines, a single DSL circuit provides sufficient bandwidth to serve the voice needs of the vast majority of the market. In addition, if more than 16 lines are required, most VoDSL solutions allow a provider to scale service by provisioning additional DSL connections. In addition to providing the right capacity for providing local telephone service, DSL broadband access networks are very efficient in the way they deliver service. TDM-based transport services, such as a T1 line, require the bandwidth of the line to be channelized and portions dedicated to certain services, such as a telephone line. Even if a call is not active on that line, the bandwidth allocated to that line cannot be used for other purposes. DSL access networks are packet based, allowing VoDSL solutions to use the bandwidth of a DSL connection dynamically. VoDSL solutions only consume bandwidth on a DSL connection when a call is active on a line. If a call is not active, then that bandwidth is available for other services, such as Internet access. This dynamic bandwidth usage allows providers to maximize the potential of each DSL connection, delivering to subscribers the greatest number of telephone lines and highest possible data speeds.

Because telephony traffic is more sensitive to latency than data traffic, VoDSL solutions guarantee the quality of telephone service by giving telephony packets priority over data packets onto a DSL connection. In other words, telephony traffic always receives the bandwidth it requires and data traffic uses the remaining bandwidth. Fortunately, telephony traffic tends to be very bursty over the course of a typical business day, so the average amount of bandwidth consumed is minimal. For example, over a single 768-Kbps symmetric DSL connection, a CLEC could provide eight telephone lines (serving a PBX/KTS with 32 extensions) and still deliver data service with an average speed of 550 Kbps.

VoATM over DSL

Voice over ATM (VoATM) unites ATM and DSL technologies to deliver on the promise of fully integrated voice and data services. VoATM meets all requirements in terms of QoS, flexibility, and reliability because the underlying technology is ATM, a highly effective network architecture developed specifically to carry simultaneous voice and data traffic.

ATM Suitability for Voice Traffic   Sometimes mistakenly associated with VoIP, VoATM is a completely separate technology that predates VoIP. In contrast to IP and frame relay, ATM uses small, fixed-length data packets of 53 bytes each that fill more quickly, are sent immediately, and are much less susceptible to network delays. (Delays experienced by voice in a frame relay or IP packet network can typically be 10 times higher than for ATM and increase on slower links.) ATM's packet characteristics make it by far the best-suited packet technology for guaranteeing the same QoS found in "toll-quality" voice connections.

The part of ATM responsible for converting voice and data into ATM cells, the ATM adaptation layer (AAL), allows various traffic types to have data converted to and from the ATM cell and translates higher layer services (e.g., TCP/IP) into the size and format of the ATM protocol layer. A number of AAL definitions exist to accommodate the various types of network traffic. Those AAL types most commonly used for voice traffic are AAL1, AAL2, and AAL5.

VoATM with AAL1 is the traditional approach for constant bit rate (CBR), time-dependent traffic such as voice and video and provides circuit emulation for trunking applications. ATM with AAL1 is still suitable for voice traffic, but is not the ideal solution for voice services in the local loop because its design for fixed bandwidth allocation means network resources are consumed even when no voice traffic is present. AAL5 is used by some equipment manufacturers to provide VoATM, provides support for variable bit rate (VBR) applications, and is a better choice over AAL1 in terms of bandwidth used. However, the means for carrying voice traffic over AAL5 is not yet fully standardized or widely deployed, and implementations are usually proprietary.

ATM with AAL2 is the newest approach to VoATM. Figure 15.10 shows how AAL2 provides a number of important improvements over AAL1 and AAL5, including support for CBR and VBR applications, dynamic bandwidth allocation, and support for multiple voice calls over a single ATM permanent virtual circuit (PVC). An additional and significant advantage of AAL2 is that cells carry content information. This feature allows traffic prioritization for packets (cells) and is the key to dynamic bandwidth allocation and efficient network use.

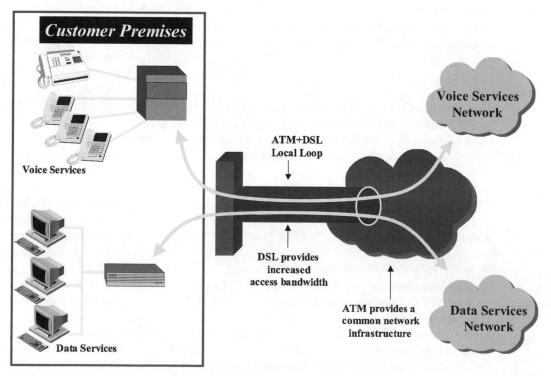

Figure 15.10   Voice over ATM with AAL2.

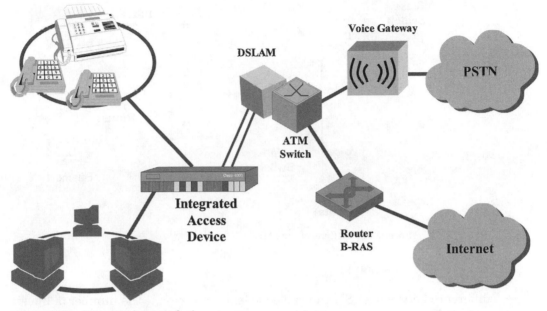

Figure 15.11   Integrated access devices.

VoATM and DSL   Since DSL links are readymade for voice and data, and ATM excels at carrying varied traffic, using VoATM over DSL over the local loop to the customer is a natural extension of these services. To enable the combination, equipment that supports VoATM is needed at each end of the local loop: a next generation integrated access device (NG-IAD) at the customer premises, and a voice gateway at the central office (CO). The integrated access device concept is shown in Fig. 15.11. The integrated devices can use many applications, as shown in Fig. 15.12.

The real benefit here is that the telephone line that once carried a single phone call for voice, data, or fax traffic can now be expanded to carry data and voice simultaneously on the same pair of wires. Because we use the data protocols (IP), we can multiplex several (16) conversations and Internet access on the higher bandwidth, and still have the lower end (0–4 kHz) available as a full time fax line. The use of the bandwidth that was once arbitrarily curtailed is now a reality.

How Does ADSL Compare to Cable Modems?

ADSL provides a dedicated service over a single telephone line; cable modems offer a dedicated service over a shared media. While cable modems have greater downstream bandwidth capabilities today (up to 30 Mbps), that bandwidth is shared among all users on a line, and will therefore vary, perhaps dramatically, as more users in a neighborhood get online at the same time. Cable modem upstream traffic will in many cases be slower than ADSL, either because the particular cable modem is inherently slower, or because of rate reductions caused by contention for upstream bandwidth slots. The big

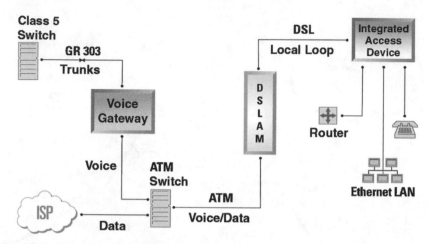

Figure 15.12   Multiple applications of the IAD.

difference between ADSL and cable modems, however, is the number of lines available to each. There are far fewer cable connected homes in the world, and many of the older cable networks are not capable of offering a return channel; consequently, such networks will need significant upgrading before they can offer high bandwidth services.

Cable Modem Systems and Technology

In the late 1970s, a major battle arose in the communications and the computer industries. Convergence of the two industries was happening as a result of the implementation of the local area networks (LANs). In the local networking arena, users began to implement solutions to their data connectivity needs within a localized environment. Two major choices were available for their installation of wiring: baseband coaxial (coax) cable and broadband coaxial cable.

The Ethernet Cable

The baseband cable was based on Ethernet development, using a 20-MHz, 50-Ω coax. Designed as a half-duplex operation, Ethernet allowed the end user to transmit digital data on the cable at speeds of up to 10 Mbps. Clearly, the 10 Mbps was maximum throughput, but it was attractive in comparison to the technology of twisted pair at the time (telephone wires were capable of less than 1 Mbps bursty data). Moreover, the use of the baseband technology allowed the data to be digitally applied directly onto the cable system. No analog modulation was necessary to apply the data. It was DC input placed directly onto the cable. The signal propagates to both ends of the cable before another device can transmit. This is shown as a quick review in Fig. 15.13. To control the cable access, the attached devices used carrier-sense multiple access with collision

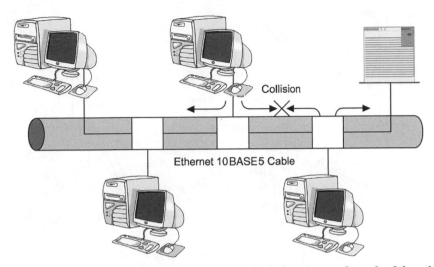

Collision

Ethernet 10BASE5 Cable

Figure 15.13 The Ethernet device propagates the signal in both directions to the ends of the cable.

detection (CSMA/CD) as the access control. CSMA/CD allowed for the possibility that two devices may attempt to transmit on the cable at the same time, causing a collision and corruption of the actual data. Consequently, use of the cable had to be controlled.

A second alternative at the time was to use the broadband coaxial cable, operating with a bandwidth of approximately 350 MHz on a 75-Ω cable. Broadband systems were well known because this is the same as CATV, which had surfaced in the early 1960s. Therefore, the technology was well deployed and commodity priced. Moreover, the 350-MHz capacity was attractive to the computer industry and the communications industry partisans. The issues began to surface quickly regarding the benefits and losses of using each technique. This is shown in Fig. 15.14.

The issue boiled down to one of analog versus digital and the baseband versus broadband implementations to achieve this goal. This was a hot issue throughout both industries. The issue included using a broadband cable under the turf of the voice communications departments, whereas the baseband cables were under the primary control of the data-processing departments. If one technology were chosen over another, the lines in the sand would be washed away, and the convergence of voice and data would force the convergence of the two groups.

The issue was, therefore, not whether to use a cable, but what type of cable to use, so the LAN would fall under the correct jurisdictional authority within the organization. Unfortunately, control is not the goal of organizations, but access and profitability are. As an industry, too much time was wasted over semantics. What ultimately rolled out of the bandwidth argument, though, was the baseband cable systems were better for the LAN. This was the decision of the 1980s, when all traffic on the LAN was geared to data only at speeds of 10 Mbps and less.

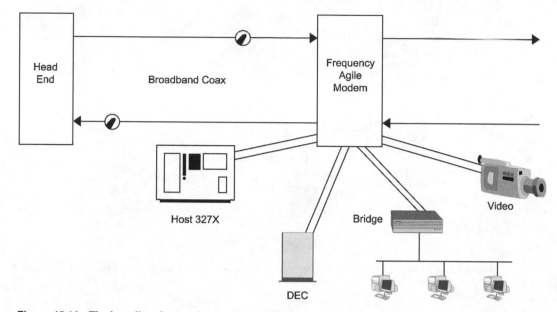

Figure 15.14   The broadband coaxial cable is an alternative to the Ethernet cable.

Cable TV Technology

Cable television (CATV) has been around since the early 1960s and is a proven technology. In the early days of Ethernet, Digital Equipment Corporation (DEC) rolled out many systems using baseband (Ethernet) cable. However, some organizations needed more than just data on a large localized network. They worked with two major providers at the time to develop the interfaces for the broadband cable systems to attach an Ethernet to the CATV cable.

DEC developed several working arrangements with various suppliers to provide a frequency agile modem (FAM) to work on the CATV systems. A FAM is a modem that has the capability to tune to any of the various analog frequencies traversing the coaxial cable. The CATV companies did not necessarily own the broadband cable. Instead, this cable was locally owned in a high-rise office or a campus complex by the end user. The cable system provided a high bandwidth, but it was very complex for the data and LAN departments to understand. The reason is obvious: the broadband coax operated using frequency-division multiplexing (FDM) (analog techniques), which was beyond the scope of the LAN administrators and the data-processing departments. The voice people knew of analog transmission, but they had a hard time with digital transmission in those days. A silent department was in the crux of all the arguments—the video departments within many organizations stayed out of the fight.

As DEC began to roll out various choices, the average user had to justify the connection of the analog technologies (used as a carrier) with the digital-data demands of the LAN. What many organizations did on a campus was to consolidate voice, data, LAN, and video on a single cable infrastructure. What the industry came up with was a specification for 10Broad36 to satisfy the LAN needs over a coax cable. 10Broad36 stands for 10 Mbps, on a broadband cable up to 3600 meters long. A classic representation of the combined services on 10Broad36 is shown in Fig. 15.15.

The data industry was distraught because this encouraged the use of an analog carrier system to move digital data. Over the years, however, this has been revisited several times.

Later in the evolution of this service, the term "broadband LAN" became popularized. Ethernet grew to 100 Mbps, and then onto the gigabit range. A broadband LAN is any LAN connected with a multichannel network or a network that can support high-speed modulated data. Recall that modulation is the process of applying the data through some change, such as AM or FM. Therefore, the inherent nature of coaxial cable popularized this term and provided it with data rates in excess than those of Ethernet. Ethernet uses a baseband cable in which the transmitter (a network card) sends a pulse, using the entire bandwidth of the cable (digital), instead of modulating any data on a carrier signal on the cable. Justifying this high-speed communication met with resistance until the use of the various fiber and coaxial systems emerged. By taking a

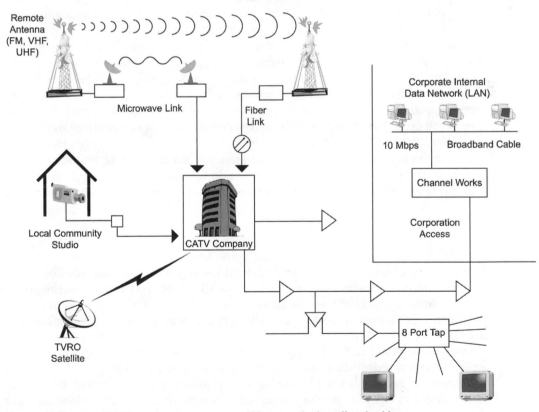

Figure 15.15 The CATV services are represented here on the broadband cable.

quantum leap in the industry, the data and voice departments saw both the benefit and the need to converge services to the desktop by offering voice and video over the LAN. The 10-Mbps Ethernet and coaxial cables could not handle this offering. Moreover, access to the Internet continued with demands to add speed and capacity (voice and video on the Internet). The industry began to seek a new method of bypassing the telephone companies' local loops. A technology already at the door, of course, was CATV. So, a new idea emerged: use CATV to support high-speed Internet access and bypass the local loop from telephone companies. Hence, cable-modem technology changed the way we will do business in the future.

The New Market

The cable television companies are still in the midst of a transition from their traditional core business of one-way entertainment video programming to a position as a full-service provider of video, voice, and data-telecommunications services. Among the elements that have made this transition possible are technologies such as the cable data modem. These companies have historically carried a number of data services. These have ranged from news and weather feeds—presented in alphanumeric form on single channels or as scrolling captions—to one-way transmission of data over classic cable systems. Often, the cable companies were carrying data feeds in the non-image portions of the video signal in an out-of-band channel. Today, these carriers bring closed captioning and secondary audio signals to augment conventional video images.

Information providers are targeting the upgraded cable network architecture as the delivery mechanism of choice for advanced high-speed data services. These changes stem from the commercial and residential data communications markets. More people now work from home and depend on connectivity from commercial online services to the global Internet.

Increased awareness has led to increasing demand for data service, and for higher speeds and enhanced levels of service. Cable is in a unique position to meet these demands. There appear to be no serious barriers to cable deployment of high-speed data transmission.

System Upgrades

The cable platform is steadily evolving into a hybrid digital and analog transmission system. Cable television systems were originally designed to optimize the one-way, analog transmission of television programming to the home. The underlying coaxial cable, however, has enough bandwidth to support two-way transport of signals. The hybrid network is shown in Fig. 15.16.

Growth in demand for Internet access and other two-way services has dovetailed with the trend within the industry to enhance existing cable systems with fiber-optic technology. The resultant product of this pairing is called *hybrid fiber coax* (HFC). Many cable companies are in the midst of upgrading the HFC plant to improve the existing cable services, and support data and other new services. Companies are

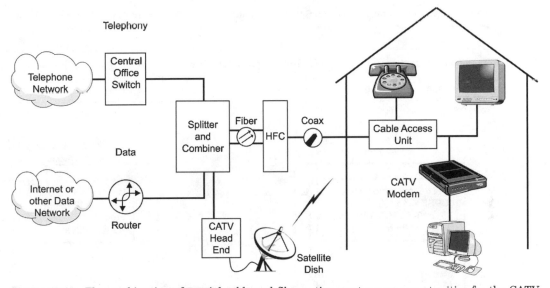

Figure 15.16 The combination of coaxial cable and fiber optics creates new opportunities for the CATV companies to offer high-speed data access and telephony services.

taking different approaches to online service access. For some applications, customers may be accessing information stored locally at or near the cable headend or regional hub. This may be temporary until wide-area cable interconnections and expanded Internet backbone networks are in place to allow information access from any remote site. Regardless, the CATV companies are striving for what the industry terms the "triple play." The triple play means that the CATV company offers voice, data, and video services bundled on a single interface via the cable infrastructure already connected to homes and businesses.

Cable Modems

Digital data signals are carried over radio frequency (RF) carrier signals on a cable system. Digital data utilizes cable modems, devices that convert digital information into a modulated RF signal and convert RF signals back to digital information. The conversion is performed by a modem at the subscriber's premises, and again by head-end equipment handling multiple subscribers. See Fig. 15.17 for a block diagram of the cable modem.

A single CATV channel can support multiple data streams or multiple users using shared LAN protocols, such as Ethernet, commonly in use in business-office LANs today. This is where Ethernet networks can be applied to the broadband coaxial networks. Different modulation techniques are being tried to maximize the data speed that can be transmitted through a 6-MHz channel. Comparing the data traffic rates for different types of modems shows why the cable modem is so popular under today's

TABLE 15.4   A Comparison of the Speeds Available and the Download Times for a 500-KB File

Method	Rate	Time
Telephone modem	28.8 Kbps	6–8 min
ISDN	128 Kbps	1–1.5 min
Cable modem	10 Mbps	Approximately 1 sec

(Source: CABLELABS)

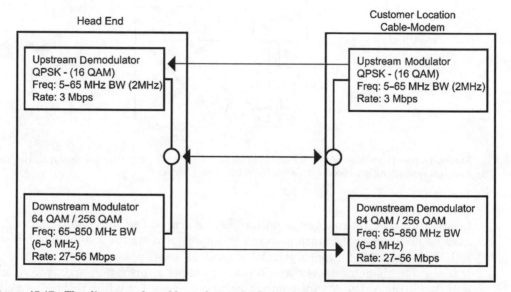

Figure 15.17 The diagram of a cable modem is fairly straightforward, but note that the upstream and downstream speeds are different.

environment. Table 15.4 shows a comparison of a file download of 500 KB using different techniques.

Careful traffic engineering is being performed on cable systems, so data speeds are maximized as customers are added. Just as office LANs are routinely subdivided to provide faster service for each individual user, cable data networks can also be custom tailored within each fiber node to meet customer demand. Multiple 6-MHz channels can be allocated to expand capacity as well.

Some manufacturers have designed modems providing asymmetrical capabilities, using less bandwidth for outgoing signals from the subscriber. CATV companies in some locations may not have completed system upgrades. Therefore, manufacturers have built migration strategies into such modems to allow for eventual transmission of broadband return signals when the systems are ready to provide such service and customers demand it. A representative sample of the way data speeds are provided on cable modems is shown in Table 15.5.

TABLE 15.5   Comparative Capabilities of a Few Vendors Show Differences

Manufacturer	Upstream	Downstream
General instrument	1.5 Mbps	30 Mbps
Hybrid/Intel	96 Kbps	30 Mbps
LANcity	10 Mbps	10 Mbps
Motorola	768 Kbps	30 Mbps

What Does a Cable Modem Do?

The cable modem performs the following functions:

- Transports subscriber IP traffic across the HFC system. The cable modem receives traffic on its Ethernet port from the subscriber's equipment and forwards the appropriate IP packets on upstream RF channels to the cable router, as shown in Fig. 15.18. The subscriber's equipment is any device that supports the TCP/IP protocol. It receives IP packets destined for its attached subscriber's equipment on downstream channels and transmits them across the Ethernet interface.

- Provides monitoring information to the cable router. The cable modem monitors the performance of the downstream channel and its internal operations, and it forwards the downstream channel statistics to the cable router when queried.

- Indicates connectivity status. The front panel LEDs indicate connectivity status and act as a diagnostic aid. See Fig. 15.19 for a connectivity scheme using a cable modem. Figure 15.20 is a drawing of the rear of the cable modem with the various connections in place.

- Participates in encryption sessions with the cable router when passing upstream and downstream data.

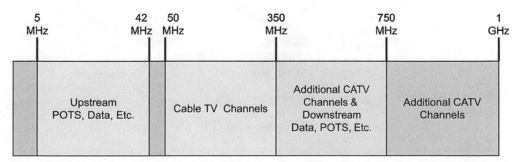

Figure 15.18   The cable modem handles all the RF management and the assignment of the channels on the cable for upstream and downstream services.

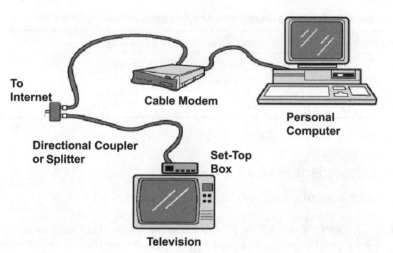

Figure 15.19 The cable modem is attached to the incoming cable splitter on one side and the PC on the other.

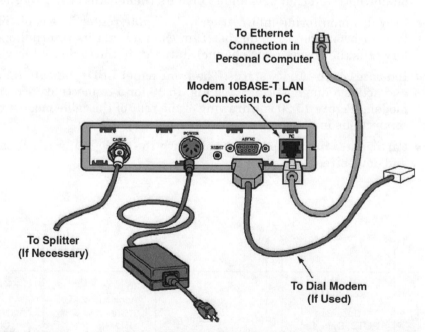

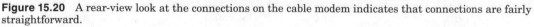

Figure 15.20 A rear-view look at the connections on the cable modem indicates that connections are fairly straightforward.

What Does the Cable Router Do?

The cable router interfaces the HFC system to local and remote IP networks. The cable router is located at the headend and performs functions in the following areas:

- Routing
- Spectrum management
- Variable length subnet mask (VLSM)
- Dial upstream
- Service levels
- $\pi/4$ DQPSK modulation
- 16 QAM modulation
- Network management
- Trap management
- Security

Table 15.6 gives more detail on the functions of the router.

Network Ports

The network ports on the cable router connect to standard Internet routers and remote devices for the purpose of transporting IP traffic. Each network port contains a processor for distributed IP routing, and handles both input and output. Traffic received on each of these ports is routed by its local processor to the appropriate port of the cable router for transmission. No routing is done between network ports.

Network Port Types

The maximum number of network ports on the cable router is two, excluding the controller Ethernet port; unless you are using an ATM network port card, and then you can have only one network port.

The types of network ports are:

- 100BASE-T Ethernet
- Asynchronous transfer mode (ATM)
- Fiber distributed data interface (FDDI)

The HFC ports on the cable router transmit data to and receive data from the subscriber. These ports handle the upstream and downstream channels on the receivers and transmitters. Modems are assigned to the upstream and downstream channels by the cable router.

Table 15.6 A Summary of the Cable Modem Activities and Features

Feature	Function
Routing	■ Performs IP routing. It uses the standard routing information protocol (RIP) to advertise its routes to other routers in the IP network. ■ Routes traffic from cable subscribers to the Internet, cable subscribers, and service provider applications. ■ Filters upstream packets according to the rules you configure. ■ Controls group access for IP multicast. ■ Routes traffic to subscriber premise routers connected to cable modems located on the HFC subnet.
Spectrum management	■ Maximizes data-passing efficiency with its management of upstream and downstream channels. ■ Performs load balancing on upstream and downstream channels by managing the bandwidth allocation to the cable modems. ■ Performs forward error correction (FEC) to overcome transient ingress (impulse) noise. ■ Provides automatic congestion control for the upstream channels. ■ Performs upstream frequency agility to avoid ingress noise.
Variable length subnet mask (VLSM)	■ Allows configuration of different subnets other than the class C subnets supported in the past.
Dial upstream	■ Provides an alternate return path for passing data. ■ Provides secure communication.
Service levels	■ Enables each modem in an HFC subnet to have a configured level of service. ■ Prevents users from experiencing extreme performance variations across different loading conditions. ■ Protects bandwidth by preventing any one user from monopolizing all the bandwidth.
/4 DQPSK modulation	■ Provides 768 Kbps data signaling rate in the upstream data path. ■ Encodes two bits as one-of-four possible phase shifts.
16 QAM modulation	■ Doubles the data rate by encoding four bits per symbol as 1-of-16 possible amplitude and phase combinations. ■ Provides 1.5 Mbps data-signaling rate in the upstream path.
Network management	■ Configures and controls all cable modems. ■ Acts as software download server for the cable modem. ■ Stores usage statistics for cable modems, including information on following: 　■ Upstream and downstream HFC channels 　■ Receivers and transmitters 　■ IP traffic 　■ Automatically discovers modems
Trap management	■ Filters and forwards traps, based on configuration.
Security	■ Provides secure communications between each registered modem and the cable router using special data-encryption techniques. ■ Provides management security by filtering unauthorized SNMP, Telnet, or FTP packets. The cable router accepts management traffic from trusted IP hosts only. ■ Provides firewall protection of the headend server complex from the HFC side of the network.

Each downstream channel occupies 6 MHz of bandwidth and supports 30 Mbps. Encryption and FEC are also included on all downstream data channels. Subscriber modems receive downstream data at a 30-Mbps burst rate. However, the maximum sustainable downstream throughput is 10 Mbps. In reality, the CATV companies use Ethernet switches and offer between 3 and 6 Mbps. This is a limitation of the Ethernet port on the cable modem. A downstream channel is assigned to the transmitter during configuration and the range of downstream channels is 3 through 116. The list of possibilities of up and down speeds is as extensive as the number of manufacturers of cable modems and CATV companies.

Standards

Modems are available today from a variety of vendors, each with its own unique technical approach. These modems are now making it possible for cable companies to enter the data communications market. In the longer term, modem costs must drop and greater interoperability is desirable. Customers who buy modems that work in their current cable system need assurance that the modem will work if they move to a different geographic location served by a different cable company. Further, agreement on a standard set of specifications allows the market to enjoy economies of scale, and drives down the price of each individual modem. Ultimately, these modems will be available as standard peripheral devices offered as an option to customers buying new personal computers at retail stores. The cable companies and manufacturers came together formally in December 1995 to begin working toward an open standard.

Leading U.S. and Canadian cable companies were involved in this development toward an open-cable modem standard. Specifications were to be developed in three phases, and then be presented to standards-setting bodies for approval as standards. Individual vendors were free to offer their own implementations with a variety of additional competitive features and future improvements. A data interoperability specification will comprise a number of interfaces. The resultant specification is called the *data over cable service interface specification* (DOCSIS).

Some interfaces reside within the cable network. Several of these system-level interfaces also will be specified to ensure interoperability.

Return Path

The portion of bandwidth reserved for return signals (from the customer to the cable network) is usually in the 5- to 40-MHz portion of the spectrum. This portion of the spectrum can be subject to ingress and other types of interference, so cable systems offering two-way data services have been designed to operate in this environment.

Industry engineers have assembled a set of alternative strategies for return-path operation. Dynamic frequency agility (shifting data from one channel to another when needed) may be designed into modems, so data signals may avoid unwanted interference as it arises. Other approaches utilize a "gate" that keeps the return path from an individual subscriber closed, except for those times when the subscriber sends a return signal. Demarcation filters, different return laser types, and reduced node size are among the other approaches, each involving tradeoffs between capital cost and maintenance effort and cost.

Return-path transmission issues have already been the subjects of 2 years of lab-and-field testing and product development. The full, two-way capability of the coaxial cable already passes most U.S. homes is now being utilized in many areas and will soon be available in most cable systems. Full activation of the return path in any given location will depend on individual cable company circumstances, ranging from market analysis to capital availability.

Applications

Cable modems open the door for customers to enjoy a range of high-speed data services, all at speeds, hundreds of times faster than telephone modem calls. Subscribers can be fully connected, 24 hours a day, to services without interfering with cable television service or phone service. Among these services are:

- Information services—access to shopping, weather maps, household bill paying, and so forth.
- Internet access—electronic mail, discussion groups, and the World Wide Web.
- Business applications—interconnecting LANs or supporting collaborative work.
- Cable commuting—enabling the already popular notion of working from home.
- Education—allowing students to continue to access educational resources from home.

The promises of advanced telecommunications networks, once more hype than fact, are now within reach. Cable modems and other technology are being deployed to make this happen. Regardless of the technology selected, the main goal is to get the high-speed data communications on the cable adjacent to the TV and entertainment. This gives the CATV companies the leverage to act in an arbitrage situation, competing with the local telephone companies who have dragged their feet in moving high-speed services to the consumer's door.

Questions

1. What does DSL stand for?
   a. Direct Subscriber Link
   b. Digital Subscriber Loop
   c. Digital Speed Lines
   d. Digital Subscriber Line

2. The x in xDSL stands for the speed of the DSL line.   T/F
3. ADSL can support download speeds up to:
    a. 6 Mbps
    b. 8 Mbps
    c. 52 Mbps
    d. 26 Mbps
4. What distance can ADSL run on a 26-AWG cable?
    a. 8–12 kft
    b. 10–12 kft
    c. 15–24 kft
    d. 15–18 kft
5. The newest family member of the DSL family is_____.
    a. SDSL
    b. SHDSL
    c. CDSL
    d. VDSL
6. VDSL2 will bring us download speed of up to 100 Mbps Ethernet.   T/F
7. The ANSI specification uses bandwidth from:
    a. 18–350 kHz
    b. 18–550 kHz
    c. 4–550 kHz
    d. 18 kHz–1 MHz
8. The three types of modulation used today are _____.
    a. CAP, MDT, and QAM
    b. CAP, MDT, and TCM
    c. CAP, DMT, and TCAM
    d. CAP, DMT, and QAM
9. The use of repeaters is required to run xDSL on the copper cable pairs.   T/F
10. The main types of xDSL use two pairs of wires.   T/F
11. The VDSL service will be symmetrical at 52 Mbps, which is the same as ATM.   T/F
12. In the late 1970s a major battle arose in the _____and the computer industries.
    a. Cable TV
    b. Data

   c. Internet

   d. Communications

13. To control the cable access, the attached devices used _____ as the access control.

   a. CSMA/CA

   b. CSMA/CD

   c. RTS/CTS

   d. QAM 64

14. Traditional Ethernet ran on a _____ cable.

   a. Broadband coax

   b. Thin broadband cable

   c. Baseband coax

   d. Thick broadband cable

15. The CATV companies used a _____ as their primary means of carrying their traffic.

   a. Baseband coax

   b. Unshielded twisted pair

   c. Broadband coax

   d. Twinax coax

16. A new idea emerged to use _____ for Internet access and bypass the local loop.

   a. UTP

   b. Coax

   c. STP

   d. CATV

17. Digital data signals are carried over _____ signals on a cable system.

   a. CSMA/CD

   b. RF

   c. DOCSIS

   d. CSMA/CA

18. The CATV channel _____ bandwidth used to transmit Ethernet.

   a. 10 MHz

   b. 24 MHz

   c. 350 MHz

   d. 6 MHz

19. The typical upload speed offered by the CATV companies is:
    a. 128 Kbps
    b. 100 Mbps
    c. 10 Mbps
    d. 1 Mbps

20. Download speeds on the Internet using CATV will yield somewhere around:
    a. 10 Mbps
    b. 5 Mbps
    c. 2 Mbps
    d. 1 Mbps

21. The portion of bandwidth reserved for _____ is usually in the 5- to 40-MHz portion of the spectrum.
    a. Ethernet
    b. Return path
    c. Forward path
    d. Multiuser path

22. The CATV service is very secure.   T/F

23. As many as 2500 users can be on a single cable leg running in a neighborhood.   T/F

16

Routers and Switches in the Networking Role

After reading this chapter and completing the questions, you will be able to:

- Discuss the role of a router
- Understand a layer 2 versus layer 3 switches
- Discuss the components of a LAN to WAN connection
- Converse about putting all the pieces together
- Understand the need for interconnection devices

We covered a lot of ground up to now in the first 15 chapters. Now we can apply many of the concepts discussed into a single application; the transmission of data across a network. The network may be a local area network (LAN), campus area network (CAN), a metropolitan area network (MAN), or the wide area network (WAN). Each of these pieces has already been discussed in great detail in their respective chapter. To transfer the data across a network element, we can either use a switching or routing process. We start with a discussion of the routing concepts compared to switching concepts. Next we look at layer 2 and 3 switching, finally at routing protocols. Keep in mind the areas we discussed earlier, such as the layer 2 and 3 switching, remember the use of Ethernet. As for routing protocols remember the use of frame relay, asynchronous transfer mode (ATM), and multiprotocol label switching (MPLS). A sidebar to this is the use of a dial-up (telephony with modem) connection or a leased line (for example T1) as a means of connecting locations together for the purpose of transferring data. IP datagrams are now the norm for moving data through many of the architectures within business and corporations.

Routing Concepts

The concept of routing involves two basic activities:

1. Determination of routing paths
2. Transport of information groups (packets) through an internetwork

The latter of these will be referred to as "switching." Switching is relatively straight-forward. Path determination, on the other hand, can be very complex.

Path determination may be based on a variety of metrics (values resulting from algorithmic computations on a particular variable, for example, network delay) or metric combinations. Software implementations of routing algorithms calculate route metrics to determine optimal routes to a destination. To aid the process of path determination, routing algorithms initialize and maintain routing tables, which contain route information. A simplified routing table is shown in Fig. 16.1. Route information varies depending on the routing algorithm used.

Some routing algorithms fill routing tables with destination/next hop associations. These associations tell a router that a particular "destination" can be gained optimally by sending the packet to the node identified in the "next hop."

Other algorithms provide destination/metric associations. These associations tell a router that a particular "destination" is some "metric" (sometimes referred to as "distance") away. The router compares metrics to determine optimal routes. The metric differs depending on the design of the routing algorithm that is being used.

Still other routing algorithms provide destination/path associations. These associations relate destinations to the path to be taken to reach that destination. Routers simply forward packets along this path until the destination is achieved.

Routers communicate with one another (and maintain their routing tables) through the transmission of a variety of messages. The routing update message is one such message. Routing updates generally consist of all or a portion of a routing table. They are the means by which routers communicate path information with one another. Armed with path information from other routers, routers can determine optimal routes. Routing updates may be sent on a regular basis, or when a network topology change affects route paths, or both.

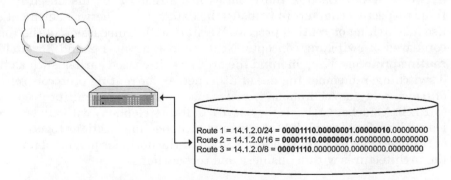

Figure 16.1   A sample of a routing table in a router.

The Switching Process

Switching algorithms are relatively simple, and the same for many routing protocols. In most cases, they operate as follows: A host (often called an end system) determines that it must send a packet to another host. Having acquired a router's address by some means, the source host sends a packet addressed specifically to a router's physical (MAC-layer) address, but with the protocol (network-layer) address of the destination host.

Upon examining the packet's destination protocol address, the router determines that it either knows or does not know how to forward the packet to the "next hop." In the latter case (where the router does not know how to forward the packet), the packet is typically dropped. In the former case, the router sends the packet to the next hop by changing the destination physical address to that of the next hop and transmitting the packet.

The next hop may or may not be the ultimate destination host. If not, the next hop is usually another router, which executes the same switching decision process. As the packet moves through the internetwork, its physical address changes, but its protocol address remains constant.

Layer 2 switching takes place near the front of the frame. As a result you expect to have the switches operate quickly. Many organizations implement a network backbone throughout entire buildings or campuses as shown in Fig. 16.2. This allows data connectivity throughout the information system's environment. Isolating localized network

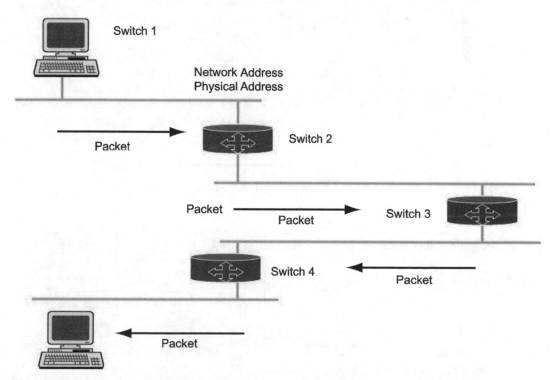

Figure 16.2   A campus switching and routing plan.

traffic is a critical step toward supporting future growth and maintaining optimal performance. When switches segment departmental LANs, network traffic typically remains local to the department.

Backbone networks are best used for transporting interdepartmental or core traffic or for providing connectivity to shared resources and other host systems similar to what is seen in Fig. 16.3. Departmental LANs can interconnect with the backbone via a switch. Many networks include switches housed in the wiring closets for interconnectivity to the backbone systems.

Usually, LAN technologies are half-duplex operations. With a half-duplex operation, a network adapter can transmit or receive data at any given time, but it cannot perform

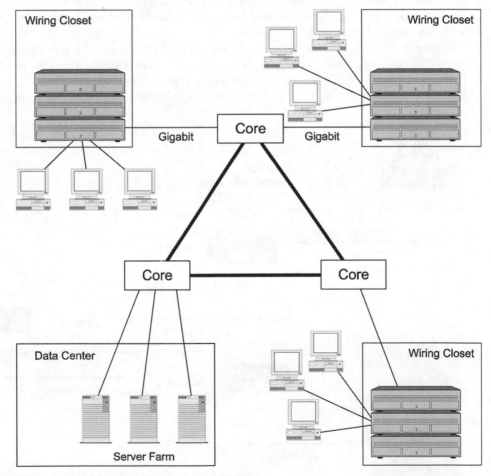

Figure 16.3 A core switch links departmental LANs.

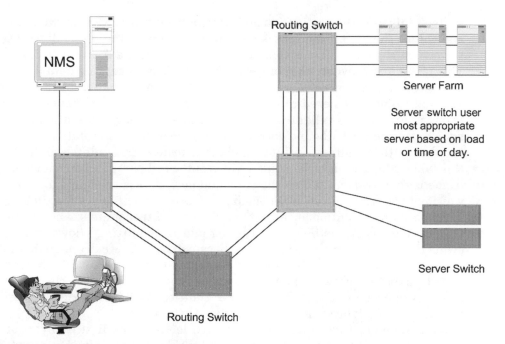

Figure 16.4 A high-speed switch allows direct connections and low latency.

both operations simultaneously. Some switch vendors have implemented full-duplex adapters, allowing stations directly connected to the switch to transmit and receive data from the switch simultaneously. This allows for higher throughput between the adapter and the switch, as might be seen in Fig. 16.4, where users and servers might be connected directly to a high-speed switch (layer 2 or 3).

The cut-through Ethernet switch achieves very low latency times. It does this by making a connection between inbound and outbound ports as soon as the frame header information has arrived on the inbound port and is processed by the switch. To process the header information, the switch checks the destination address against a table of learned MAC (media access control) addresses. The switch uses this table information to determine which outbound port should receive the frame. The frame is then transmitted on the outbound port, usually while it is still being received on the inbound port. Exceptions to this process occur if the outbound port has buffered frames waiting to be transmitted or if the media is in use by another station. In these cases, the switch buffers the frame and transmits it, when possible.

Error Checking

Cut-through switches typically do not perform error checking on the inbound frame when the destination address in the header information matches an address in the switch's tables. If the destination address is unrecognized, the switch buffers the frame and checks the FCS (frame check sequence) to validate the frame. If the frame is good, the switch copies the frame to all outbound ports. If the frame is bad, it is discarded. This technique prevents header errors from causing false transmits.

A store-and-forward Ethernet switch operates much like a multiport bridge. Each inbound frame is buffered completely, and the FCS shown at the end of the Ethernet frame in Fig. 16.5, is validated before the frame's header information is processed and transmitted on the outbound port. To process the header information, the switch checks the destination address against a table of learned MAC addresses. The switch uses this table information to determine which outbound port should receive the frame. The frame is then transmitted on the outbound port, unless the outbound port has frames waiting to be transmitted or the media is in use by another station. In these cases, the switch buffers the frame at the outbound port and transmits it when possible.

Buffering the frame before processing and transmitting allows store-and-forward switches to provide extended features. Because the FCS is calculated for all frames, the switch can eliminate transmission of corrupted frames. Some switch vendors provide added, virtual subnet and extended broadcast domain services by checking the network layer information in the buffered frame. Additional frame filtering capabilities (again based on network layer information) may also be available.

With fragment-free switching, the switch looks at the first 64 bytes of a frame. If these are valid, it forwards the frame out of the designated port. Fragment-free switching forwards after 64 bytes have been received and analyzed. This eliminates runts and it enables filtering.

Some switches offer adaptive cut-through. The switch to 64 bytes is made after 8–16 bytes, if there are excessive runts. The switch has a fall-back mode. It automatically falls back to store-and-forward mode if excessive CRC (cyclic redundancy check) errors exist. The threshold is set by the installer.

Switches are used like bridges to isolate traffic and separate collision domains. The goal is to increase throughput to each user by decreasing the number of stations that must contend for the shared bandwidth. The switch separates collision domains. It also maintains a matrix of destination addresses and physical ports associated with the address so that it can switch frames. An incoming frame is transmitted only on the port associated with the frame's destination address. The number of destination addresses supported by each port depends on the vendor and model of a switch, but it can range from one to over one thousand.

Layer 2 switching can be implemented for Ethernet or other layer 2 LANs. Layer 2 switching:

- Is used for local LAN-to-LAN connections
- Does not logically separate networks
- Does not interconnect different data link architectures
- Uses the MAC-layer learning process, forwarding process, and filtering process
- Does not alter the frame

- Is upper-layer protocol independent
- Forwards to multicasts and broadcast traffic

The learning process involves examination of each frame's source address; it then records that address in the filtering database. Each source address is updated to the filtering database only if the following conditions occur:

- The port on which the frame was received is in a state that allows learning.
- The source address field of the frame denotes a unique end node and is not a group address.
- A static entry for the associated MAC address does not already exist.
- The resulting number of entries does not exceed the capacity of the filtering database. Some filtering databases allow new entries to overwrite older entries, such as FIFO (first in, first out). Other vendors may not update their databases at all and instead flood all new entries.

When a switch receives the destination MAC address found within a frame, the switch compares that address with what it has in its switching tables. If that destination address does not match any addresses in its table, the switch floods that frame out of all ports except the port that it came in on.

A switch makes a forwarding decision from the destination address found within the frame. When the switch receives the destination address, it compares the address to what it has in its switching tables. If the switch finds a match, it forwards the packet out of a specific port only.

Once a switch has learned the address on a specific LAN, it does not forward local traffic. When both devices reside on the same LAN, the switch filters the traffic.

Why Are Switches So Fast?

Hardware-based switches are used with:

- ASICs (application-specific integrated circuits)
  - Contain specific applications
  - Make the forwarding decision for both layer 2 and layer 3
- RISC (reduced instruction set computing) processors
  - Very fast processors
  - Used within the CPUs (central processing units)

Traditional bridges and routers are software-based devices. A software-based device makes its decision by reading instructions from local memory. The forwarding time average is 800 microseconds for traditional bridges and 1000 microseconds for routers.

With early lower speed networks, the latency times were acceptable. As network speeds increased to 100/1000 megabits, the slower latency times became unacceptable. With ASICs the instructions are in the hardware and carried out there. When a switch makes its forwarding decision at both layer 2 and layer 3, its latency times average 7–50 microseconds. The ASIC chips use the RISC processors for processing internally.

Layer 3 Switching

Traditionally, layer 3 switching acts like a router, where the switch still uses the routable layer 3 address to make a forwarding decision. The main difference between layer 3 switches and routers is that layer 3 switches make forwarding decisions within hardware, and routers make forwarding decisions within software. Today, switches have latency times averaging 7–50 microseconds, and routers average 700–1000 microseconds. A typical layer 3 switch is shown in Fig. 16.5 with a figure of a Cisco 3550 switch. Layer 3 switches process data based on the IP addresses rather than on a MAC address. They perform the function of routing between virtual LANs (VLANs) in a layer 3 architecture.

Routing Algorithm Types

Routing algorithms may be classified by type. For example, algorithms may be:

- Static or dynamic
- Distributed or centralized
- Single-path or multipath
- Flat or hierarchical
- Host-intelligent or router-intelligent
- Intra-domain or inter-domain
- Link state or distance vector

Static routing algorithms are hardly algorithms at all. The network administrator establishes static routing table mappings prior to the beginning of routing.

Dynamic routing algorithms adjust, in real time, to changing network circumstances. They do this by analyzing incoming routing update messages. If the message indicates

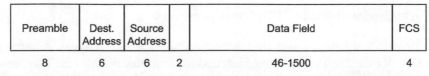

Preamble	Dest. Address	Source Address		Data Field	FCS
8	6	6	2	46-1500	4

Figure 16.5   A Cisco 3550 is a layer 3 switch.

that a network change has occurred, the routing software recalculates routes and sends out new routing update messages.

Routing algorithms may be centralized or distributed. Centralized algorithms calculate all routing paths at one central device. Unfortunately, centralized routing also suffers from several serious flaws that have severely restricted its use. Distributed algorithms calculate routing paths at each individual router. Each router periodically exchanges route information with (at a minimum) each of its neighbors. Distributed algorithms are more fault-tolerant than centralized algorithms. They also distribute update traffic over the entire internetwork, so traffic bottlenecks are not such a serious problem. Like centralized routing, they may still generate routing loops. Overall distributed routing algorithms are much more common than centralized routing algorithms.

Some sophisticated routing protocols support multiple paths to the same destination. These multipath algorithms permit traffic multiplexing over multiple lines; single-path algorithms do not. The advantages of multipath algorithms are obvious; they can provide substantially better throughput and redundancy.

Some routing algorithms operate in a flat space, while others utilize routing hierarchies. In a flat routing system, all routers are peers of all others. In a hierarchical routing system, some routers form what amounts to a routing backbone.

Routing systems often designate logical groups of nodes called domains, autonomous systems, or areas. In hierarchical systems, some routers in a domain can communicate with routers in other domains, while others can only communicate with routers within their domain. In very large networks, additional hierarchical levels may exist. Routers at the highest hierarchical level form the routing backbone.

The primary advantage of hierarchical routing is its ability to limit the pervasiveness of routing exchanges. Hierarchical routing limits routing exchanges because it mimics the organization of most companies and therefore supports their traffic patterns very well.

Most network communication occurs within small company groups (domains). Intra-domain routers only need to know about other routers within their domain, so their routing algorithms may be simplified. Depending on the routing algorithm being used, routing update traffic may be reduced accordingly.

Some routing algorithms assume that the source end node will determine the entire route. This is usually referred to as source routing. In source routing systems, routers merely act as store-and-forward devices, mindlessly sending the packet to the next stop.

Other algorithms assume that the hosts know nothing about routes. In these algorithms, routers determine the path through the internetwork based on their own calculations. In the first system, the hosts have the routing intelligence. In the latter system, routers have the routing intelligence.

Algorithm Metrics

As eluded to previously, routing tables contain information used (by switching software) to select the best route. Nevertheless, how, specifically, are routing tables built? What is the specific nature of the information they contain?

Many different metrics have been used in routing algorithms. Sophisticated routing algorithms can base route selection on multiple metrics, combining them in a manner resulting in a single (hybrid) metric. All of the following metrics are used:

- Reliability
- Delay
- Bandwidth
- Load
- MTU
- Communication cost

These characteristics can be set in the Type of Service field in the IP header. Reliability, in the context of routing algorithms, refers to the reliability of each network link. Some network links may go down more often than others.

Common Routing Protocols

Routing algorithms are implemented by routing protocols. Routing protocols not only define the metric(s) and metric weightings to be used for optimal route calculations, they also define the size, contents, exchange frequency, and exchange pattern of routing updates and other messages. A summary table is shown as Table 16.1 compares the routing protocols.

Routing protocols should not be confused with routed protocols. A routing protocol implements a particular routing algorithm. Physically, software calculates routing paths through an internetwork. Routed protocols, on the other hand, are network protocols that can be routed by a routing protocol. Routing protocols include:

- IGRP (interior gateway routing protocol)
- OSPF (open shortest path first)
- RIP (routing information protocol)

TABLE 16.1   Comparison of Routing Protocols

Factor	RIP	IGRP	OSPF	EIGRP
Algorithm	Distance vector	Distance vector	Link state	Hybrid
Metric	Hops	Aggregate	Cost	Aggregate
Convergence	Slow	Slow	Fast	Fast
Scales well	No	Yes	Yes	Yes
Bandwidth consumption	High	High	Low	Low
Router resource consumption	Low	Low	High	Low
Address flexibility	No	No	Yes (variable length subnet mask)	Yes (variable length subnet mask)
Routed protocol	IPX	IP	IP	IPX/IP
Proprietary	No	Yes (Cisco)	No	Yes (Cisco)
Configuration complexity	Low	Low	High	Low

Routed protocols include:

- IP (Internet protocol)
- IPX (Internet packet exchange)

Based on the two most common routing algorithm types (distance vector and link state), the routing protocols correspond to several of the most common routed protocols. Based on the routed protocol environment they are most commonly found in, routing protocols are often divided into three categories. The three categories are:

- TCP/IP
- OSI
- Proprietary

TCP/IP Routing Protocols

RIP is a distance vector, intra-domain routing protocol originally designed for PUP (Xerox PARC Universal Protocol, 1980) and used in XNS (Xerox Network Systems, 1981). RIP became associated with both UNIX and TCP/IP in 1982 when the Berkeley Standard Distribution (BSD) implementation of UNIX began shipping with a RIP implementation referred to as routed. RIP is formally defined in RFC (request for comments) 1058, written in 1988.

RIP was widely adopted by computer network vendors. For example, AppleTalk's routing protocol (RTMP) is a modified version of RIP. RIP was also the basis for the older routing protocols of Novell, 3Com, Ungermann-Bass, and Banyan.

RIP was designed for reasonably homogeneous small or moderate-sized networks. In this capacity, RIP is quite useful. However, in larger, more complicated internetworks, RIP has several drawbacks. First, RIP's hop count limit is 16, so destinations may not be more than 16 hops distant. Second, the protocol cannot choose routes based on real-time parameters such as delay or load. Due to these and other inadequacies, RIP has been replaced in many installations with more modern routing protocols.

Level 1 and Level 2 Areas

Levels of routers can be assigned in an internetwork, as seen in Fig. 16.6. These routers handle the data transfer within their own network groups (called areas) and between network groups. Area 1 routers handle the intranetwork group, whereas area 2 routers handle the interconnectivity.

IGRP is an intra-domain distance vector routing protocol developed in the mid-1980s by Cisco Systems, Inc. It is designed for use in large, complex IP and OSI networks.

Unlike RIP, IGRP uses a combination (vector) of metrics. Internetwork delay, bandwidth, reliability, MTU, and load are all factored into the routing decision. Network administrators can set the weighting factors for the metrics. IGRP uses either the administrator-set or the default weightings to automatically calculate optimal routes.

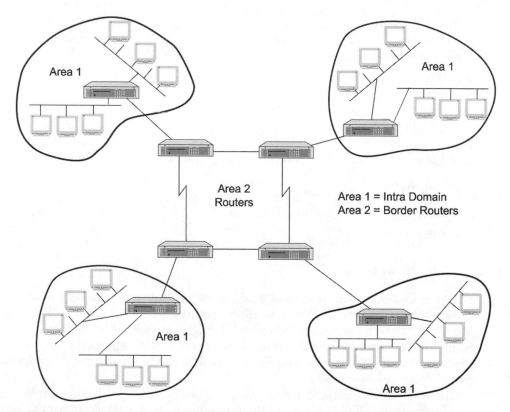

Figure 16.6 Area 1 and area 2 routers provide the necessary routing infrastructure.

To provide additional flexibility, IGRP permits multipath routing. Multiple equal-bandwidth paths may run a single stream of traffic in round-robin fashion, with automatic switchover to the second line if one line goes down.

IGRP contains a number of features designed to enhance its own stability. These include:

- Hold-downs
- Split horizon updates
- Poison reverse updates

Hold-downs are used to prevent regular update messages from inappropriately re-instating a route that has gone bad. When a route goes down, neighboring routers will detect this via the lack of regularly scheduled update messages. These routers then calculate new routes and send out routing update messages to inform their neighbors of the route change. This activity begins a wave of routing updates that filter through the network.

These triggered updates do not instantly arrive at every network device. It is therefore possible that a device that has yet to be informed of a network failure may send a regular update message (indicating that a route that has just gone down is still good) to a device that has just been notified of the network failure. In this case, the latter device will now contain (and potentially advertise) incorrect routing information.

Hold-downs are a way of telling routers to "hold down" any changes that might affect recently removed routes for some period. The hold-down period is usually calculated to be just greater than the period necessary to update the entire network with a routing change.

Split Horizon

Split horizon updates derive from the fact that it is never useful to send information about a route back in the direction from which it came. Router R1 initially advertises that it has a route to Network A. There is no reason for R2 to include this route in its update back to R1, as R1 is closer to Network A. The split horizon rule says that R2 should strike this route from any updates it sends to R1.

The split horizon rule helps prevent routing loops. For example, consider the case where R1's interface to Network A goes down. Without split horizons, R2 continues to inform R1 that it can get to Network A (through R1). If R1 does not have sufficient intelligence, it may actually pick up R2's route as an alternative to its failed direct connection, causing a routing loop. Although hold-downs should prevent this, split horizons are implemented in IGRP because they provide extra algorithm stability. This is shown in Fig. 16.7.

Whereas split horizons should prevent routing loops between adjacent routers, reverse poison updates are intended to defeat larger routing loops. The idea is that increases in routing metrics generally indicate routing loops. Reverse poison updates are then sent to remove the route and place it in hold-down. In Cisco's implementation of IGRP, reverse poison updates are sent if a route metric has increased by a factor of 1.1 or greater.

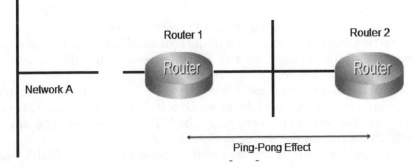

Figure 16.7 Split horizon prevents the "ping-pong" effect of a routing loop.

OSPF

OSPF (open shortest path first) is a relatively recent intra-domain, link state, hierarchical routing protocol developed for IP networks by the Internet engineering task force (IETF).

Information on attached interfaces, metrics used and other variables are included in OSPF routing updates. This information is flooded throughout the routing area. As OSPF routers accumulate link state information, they are able to calculate the shortest path to each node. Updates are only required when a link state changes. "Hello" messages act as keep-alive messages to let routers know that other routers are still functional.

Additional OSPF features include equal cost multipath routing and routing based on upper-layer type of service (TOS) requests. TOS-based routing supports those upper-layer protocols that can specify particular types of service. For example, an application might specify that certain data is urgent. If OSPF has high-priority links at its disposal, these may be used to transport the urgent datagram.

OSPF supports one or more metrics. If only one metric is used, it is considered arbitrary, and TOS is not supported. If more than one metric is used, TOS is optionally supported with a separate metric (and, therefore, a separate routing table) for each of the eight combinations created by the three IP TOS bits (the "delay," "throughput," and "reliability" bits). For example, if the IP TOS bits specify low delay, low throughput, and high reliability, OSPF calculates routes to all destinations based on this TOS designation. Obviously, this calculation can be extremely resource intensive.

EGP

Exterior gateway protocol (EGP) is the primary inter-domain routing protocol used in the Internet. Originally documented in RFC 904 in April 1984, EGP is used for communication between the "core" Internet routers. These core Internet routers form the Internet's routing backbone. Information is passed from individual source networks up to the core routers, which pass the information through the backbone until it may again be passed down to the destination network. In some cases, the links between lower-level domains and the core routers remain static. In other cases, EGP is used for these links.

Although EGP is a dynamic routing protocol, it uses a very simple design. It does not use metrics and therefore cannot make true intelligent routing decisions. EGP routing updates contain network reachability information. In other words, they specify that certain networks are reachable through certain routers.

EGP updates are sent to neighboring routers at regular intervals. In the updates, each router indicates those networks to which it is directly attached. This network reachability information eventually permeates the EGP environment. The information is used to construct and maintain routing tables.

Although it served the Internet well for close to 10 years, EGP's weaknesses became more apparent with the phenomenal growth of the Internet. For example, EGP had no

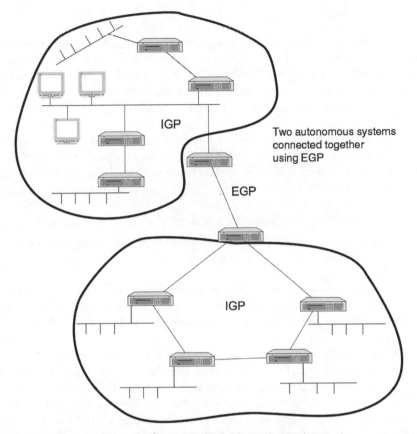

Figure 16.8 An exterior gateway protocol connects two autonomous systems.

way of dealing with the routing loops that can occur in multipath networks. In addition, EGP routing updates are often very large and cumbersome. Finally, EGP could not make intelligent routing decisions because it did not support link metrics. For these reasons, EGP was phased out of the Internet. An example of an EGP connection is shown in Fig. 16.8.

EIGRP

Cisco's enhanced interior gateway routing protocol (EIGRP) is a proprietary routing protocol that uses a hybrid of distance vector and link state and uses bandwidth and delay as its primary calculations. As a proprietary routing protocol, the EIGRP was designed to create a fast convergence process and extend the addressing capabilities of routers beyond the older RIP. Where the EIGRP can benefit a customer is in the replacement for RIP in a Novell environment. Novell's proprietary SPX/IPX protocol can be handled nicely in EIGRP, but so too can IP. Because EIGRP can support both IPX and IP, it is attractive to suppliers and carriers alike.

BGP

Border gateway protocol (BGP) represents an attempt to address the most serious of EGP's problems. Like EGP, BGP is an inter-domain routing protocol created for use in the Internet core routers. Unlike EGP, BGP was designed to detect routing loops and to use a metric so that intelligent routing decisions may be made. BGP may be thought of as next-generation EGP. Indeed, BGP replaced EGP in the Internet. BGP is specified in RFC 1163.

Although designed as an inter-domain protocol, BGP may be used both within and between domains. Two BGP neighbors communicating between domains must reside on the same physical network. BGP routers within the same domain communicate with one another for two reasons:

- To ensure that they have a consistent view of the domain
- To determine which BGP router within that domain will serve as the connection point to/from certain external domains

Some domains are merely pass-through channels for network traffic. In other words, some domains carry network traffic that did not originate within and is not destined for them. BGP must interact with whatever intra-domain routing protocols exist within these pass-through domains.

BGP update messages consist of network number/domain path pairs. The domain path contains the string of domains through which the specified network may be reached. These update messages are sent over the TCP reliable transport mechanism.

The initial data exchange between two routers is the entire BGP routing table. Incremental updates are sent out as routing tables change. Unlike some other routing protocols, BGP does not require periodic refresh of the entire routing table. Instead, routers running BGP retain the latest version of each peer routing table. Although BGP maintains a routing table with all feasible paths to a particular network, it only advertises the primary (optimal) path in its update messages.

The BGP metric is an arbitrary unit number specifying the "degree of preference" of a particular path. The metrics are typically assigned by the network administrator through configuration files. Degree of preference may be based on any number of criteria, including domain count (paths with a smaller domain count are generally better), type of link (is the link stable? fast? reliable?), and other factors.

Dial On-Demand

In some cases, routers can use a dial on-demand feature, also possible with a bridge. By using this dial on-demand feature, expensive WAN bandwidth can be used only when needed. The cost of a circuit switch dial-up connection using either ISDN or some other circuit switching technique can become prohibitive. One would only use this when excessive demand exists, or a link state failure occurs. It is better to have a connection, albeit a slow connection, instead of no connection at all.

The use of the dial on-demand capabilities, therefore, requires some form of a switched connection. This may be based on a destination IP address typically to more than one address or destination. The dial on-demand may well be used to a single circuit switch connection to various locations, but only one at a time. This dial on-demand capability may be based on any LAN traffic (a MAC address) to a single address.

Point-to-Point Protocol

If a switched on-demand service or other fast relay service is used for dial on-demand capabilities, a different protocol may well suit the needs. In this particular case, the point-to-point protocol (PPP) was designed to establish a communication over a point-to-point link. The originating entity would first use a link control procedure (LCP) to configure and test the data circuit. The link is established and optional facilities are negotiated on an as-needed basis by this link control procedure. The originating PPP will send its network control protocol packets to choose and configure one or more of the network layer protocols. These network layer protocols may include X.25 circuit switch, dial-up communications, ISDN or other. Once this is completed, datagram traffic from each of the network layer protocols can now be sent. The link will remain configured for communications between the two entities until some external event occurs, or an explicit packet is issued to close down the link. This external event could be user intervention (human error) or some activity timer timing-out in an expiration period.

Using the PPP, any form of a DCE/DTE interface can be used. PPP is designed around a duplex circuit only for; dedicated or circuit switched; asynchronous or synchronous communications without great restrictions; and greater control and performance. The physical layer is transparent to the data link layer of the PPP. Many organizations now use Internet and Intranet capabilities that involve the circuit switched dial-up communications across the public switch network, circuit switch capabilities, or ISDN. In this environment, network is operating with TCP/IP protocols. The PPP protocol is used to establish the connection between the calling and the called location. Upon establishment of this PPP link, the network control protocols will establish the ability to begin routing IP packets.

Gateways

Gateways are devices that work at the higher levels of the OSI model. Actually, it works at the layers one through six, stopping at the presentation layer. The gateway is responsible for the protocol conversions if two disparate networks need to communicate, and use different language and formats.

Traditionally, when using a LAN and an IBM mainframe environment, the gateway has been in high demand. Converting SNA traffic into TCP/IP traffic, or SNA into SPX/IPX on a Novell LAN is the role of the gateway.

These devices may be hardware or software, or both. The gateway is also used when an X.25 access is used from a LAN to a UNIX host or a DECnet host. It will convert X.25 to LAN traffic, then pass the data into a 3270 gateway allowing an IBM host to use the data.

Switching

Routers can become bottlenecks in networks. They continually attempt to keep up with the increased traffic capacity of high-speed switches. Added intelligence in routers further slows down packet forwarding. Conventional routers compute data paths (and scheduling information, if the router supports differentiated service) on a packet-per-packet basis. Internetworking vendors have announced several new routing solutions that combine network layer routing with link layer switching, as shown in Fig. 16.9.

Layer 2 switching can be used to make decisions on a per-flow basis not per packet, and most network layer processing can be eliminated. Approaches included Cisco Systems' tag switching as well as Ipsilon Networks' IP switching.

The growth of the Internet presented challenges to Internet service providers and equipment suppliers to keep up with the traffic demands and the number of users. Cisco introduced the idea of tag switching technology as a key component in their plans to meet the challenge. Tag switching is a proprietary technology proposed by Cisco Systems and a precursor to MPLS discussed earlier in Chapter 11. Tag switching combines the performance and traffic management capabilities of layer 2 (data link layer) switching with the proven scalability of layer 3 (network layer) routing. Tag switching integrates routing and switching for an Internet-scale environment. It is one of several multilayer switching technologies being pioneered by Cisco. A conceptual view of tag switching is shown in Fig. 16.9. Routes will be selected by L3 routing protocols instead of a specified traffic engineering route.

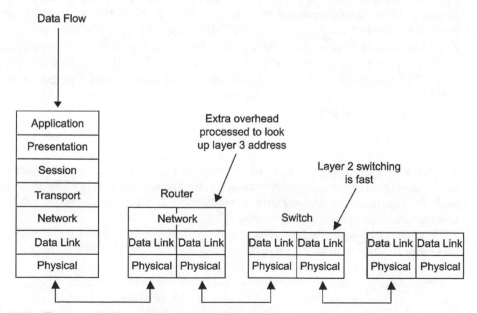

Figure 16.9 The protocols that work between layer 2 and layer 3.

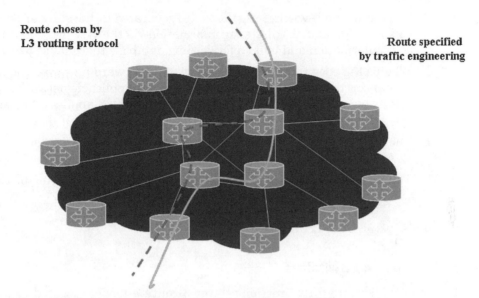

Figure 16.10   Conceptual view of tag switching as a precursor to MPLS.

Tag switching is a technique for high-performance packet forwarding that assigns "tags" to multiprotocol frames for transport across packet or cell-based networks. It is based on the concept of "label swapping," in which units of data (e.g., a packet or a cell) carry a short, fixed length label that tells switching nodes how to process the data. A tag-switching internetwork consists of the following elements:

1. *Tag edge routers*: Located at the boundaries of an Internet, perform value-added network layer services and apply tags to packets.

2. *Tag switches*: Switch-tagged packets or cells based on the tags. Tag switches may also support full layer 3 routing or layer 2 switching, in addition to tag switching.

3. *Tag distribution protocol (TDP)*: In conjunction with standard network layer routing protocols, TDP is used to distribute tag information between devices in a tag switched Internet.

The basic processing within a tag-switching internetwork works as follows:

1. Tag edge routers and tag switches use standard routing protocols (e.g., EIGRP, BGP, OSPF) to identify routes through the network. These edge routers fully interoperate with non-tag switching routers.

2. Tag routers and switches use the tables generated by the standard routing proto-
    cols to assign and distribute tag information via the TDP. Tag routers receive the
    TDP information and build a forwarding database that makes use of the tags.

3. When a tag edge router receives a packet for forwarding across the tag network,
    it analyzes the network layer header, performs applicable network layer services,
    selects a route for the packet from its routing tables, applies a tag, and forwards
    the packet to the next hop tag switch.

4. The tag switch receives the tagged packet and switches the packet based solely
    on the tag, without reanalyzing the network layer header.

5. The packet reaches the tag edge router at the egress point of the network,
    where the tag is stripped off and the packet delivered.

Sounds just like MPLS, doesn't it?

Tag Edge Routers and Switches

Tag edge-routers are fully functional layer 3 routing devices located at the edge of a
tag-switching network (now called an MPLS network). The routers apply tags to incoming packets and remove tags from outgoing packets. As full-function routers, tag edge
routers also apply value-added layer 3 services, such as security, accounting, and QoS
classification.

One of the functions of an edge router is to examine incoming packets and apply the
proper tag before forwarding the packet. Tag switching provides flexibility in the algorithms and techniques it supports for mapping tags to packets. Examples include:

- *Destination prefix*: The tag edge-router uses normal router procedures to match the
  packet destination IP address against the destination prefix entries in the router's
  forwarding tables.

- *Traffic tuning*: Packets can be tagged so that they flow across specific routes, allowing network managers to load balance.

- *Application flows*: This method looks at both the source and destination address, as well as other layer 3 information. This can be used to provide finer
  granularity in processing the tagged packets and maintain a given quality of
  service through the network for a specific source/destination flow of packets,
  such as for RSVP.

Tag Switches

Tags, as we saw in the Chapter 11 discussion of MPLS, are short fixed-length labels,
enabling tag switches to do simple and fast table lookups. These enable tag switches
to implement the lookup and forwarding capabilities using fast hardware techniques,
including ATM cell switching.

Because tag switching decouples the tag distribution mechanisms from the data flows, a wide variety of methods of associating a tag with a packet can be used and will interoperate in a tag network, including:

- In the layer 2 header [e.g., in the VCI(Virtual connection identifier) field for ATM cells]
- In the layer 3 header (e.g., in the flow label field in IPv6)
- In between the layer 2 and layer 3 headers

These techniques allow tag switching to be used over a wide variety of media, including ATM links, Packet-over-SONET (POS) links, and Ethernet. Tag switching is also not specific to IP. With tag switching software installed, standard routers can act as tag switches. By supporting the tag distribution protocol, and adding the ability to switch tagged packets based on the tag values, Internet core routers can participate in a tag network backbone.

ATM switches can also participate as tag switches. To act as a tag switch, an ATM switch will implement the appropriate, standard layer 3 routing protocols, as well as the tag distribution protocol.

Tags will be placed in the VCI fields of cells by the tag edge routers, and the ATM switch will switch cells based on the VCI values, as it normally does for all cells. A fundamental difference between tag switching and ATM is that standard ATM uses a connection setup procedure to allocate VCIs and program the ATM switching hardware, while tag switching uses standard routing protocols and the tag distribution protocol. The result is that ATM switches performing tag switching do not need to handle high call setup rates.

Tag switching and ATM forum-compliant ATM can coexist on the same ATM switch, so do both Internet service and ATM services on the same platform. Tag switching avoids the use of switched virtual circuits (SVCs) for highly dynamic IP packet flows and frees CPU processing power for P-NNI (private network to network interface) and the needs of longer-lived ATM virtual circuits, such as real-time voice or video flows.

Application in Router-Only Internets

Layer 3 switching can be used on standard routers. An Internet built exclusively from routers can deploy software to gain the advantages of traffic tuning provided by tag switching. For high performance in this environment, tag switching can support POS OC-3 interfaces on core routers. Tag switching can work on higher performance router platforms and can enable multigigabit speeds to OC-12, OC-48, and OC-192.

Application in Multiservice Networks

In networks that provide both Internet and ATM/frame relay services on a common core ATM infrastructure, tag switching provides a way to integrate the ATM platforms into

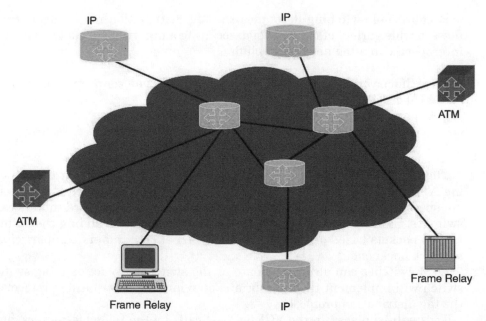

IP   IP

ATM

ATM

Frame Relay   IP

Frame Relay

Figure 16.11 Multiservice networks are possible with label switching such as ATM, frame relay, and tag switching.

a high-performance Internet service offering as represented in Fig. 16.11. It enables an ATM platform to simultaneously support Internet core switching via tag switching, and standard ATM switching using ATM forum and other industry standard protocols. Tag switching enables a closer coupling of the ATM switch into the Internet service, providing a stronger reason for using a common ATM core for all service offerings.

IP Switching

IP switching is a related technology for combining ATM layer 2 switching with layer 3 routing (IP switching is also a type of multilayer switching). IP switching typically allocates a label per source/destination packet flow. An IP switch processes the initial packets of a flow by passing them to a standard router module that is part of the IP switch. When an IP switch sees enough packets to consider a flow long-lived, the IP switch sets up labels for the flow with its neighboring IP switches or edge routers. Subsequent packets for the flow can be label-switched at high speed (e.g., in an ATM switching fabric), bypassing the slower router module. Special IP switching gateways are responsible for converting packets from non-labeled to labeled format, and from packet media to ATM.

Tag switching enhances the label-swapping concept, resulting in a highly scalable and flexible technology. The tag switching destination prefix algorithm, coupled with standard routing protocols, supports more efficient use of labels than per-flow schemes, avoiding flow-by-flow setup procedures. This may produce the scalability required for public Internet service networks, where the number of flows is enormous and the rate of change is very high. By preestablishing tag mappings at the same time as routing tables are populated, tag switching can tag switch both short-lived flows and the initial packets of long-lived flows, avoiding bottlenecks in high-performance applications.

IP switching is an open and proprietary, published technology developed by Ipsilon Networks. It is designed for ATM-based IP networks. Support for frame relay is planned for the future. IP switching aims to optimize IP throughput by switching most traffic across the ATM network, bypassing the routing infrastructure.

IP switching works as follows. Each IP node sets up a default virtual channel (VC) on each of its ATM physical links. This virtual channel is used to forward packets in the normal, nonoptimized manner. An IP switch controller decides which of the packets arriving on the default VC belong to a long-lived flow, like ftp, Telnet, WWW, or real-time data.

IP Switch Operation

Long-lived flows are worth optimizing by giving them their own virtual channel and switching them on the ATM level. Short-lived traffic (e.g., DNS queries, SNMP queries, and SMTP data) continues to be forwarded on the default VC. A flow is characterized by a source—destination pair and other header fields as configured. Once the IP switch controller has identified a flow, it asks the upstream IP node to send that traffic on a new ATM virtual channel.

Independently, the downstream IP switch controller will have identified the flow in the same way and requests that the traffic is sent on a new virtual channel. At this point, the flow does not use the default VC anymore. It is isolated to a particular input channel and a particular output channel. The flow can then be optimized by "cut-through" switching in the ATM hardware, bypassing the routing software and the associated processing overhead. When a flow is switched on the ATM level, packets do not need to be reassembled from cells. This process decreases transmission delays. The general concept is that long-lived flows are switched on the ATM level while short-lived traffic is routed as usual. The efficiency of IP switching depends on the traffic pattern. IP switching works best when a high percentage of traffic can be classified as long-lived flows. The longer the duration of the flows, the less overhead there is for setting up and tearing down virtual channels.

IP Switching Protocols

Ipsilon uses a newer set of protocols to facilitate the IP switching in their systems. These include the general switch management protocol (GSMP) and the Ipsilon flow management protocol (IFMP). Both are covered under the RFCs shown on the drawing. The goal of these protocols is to simplify the IP switching process in the Ipsilon switches and any others employing the IP switching open standard.

Address Mapping Simplified

Ipsilon also stresses that the IP switching is more efficient than normal routing in an ATM environment. Where the ATM and ATM-forum standard switching involves many protocol lookup tables for converting IP packets onto an ATM world, the IP switching skips many of the steps involved.

Multicast Advantage

Using these products and protocols in a multicast environment to handle the LAN bottlenecks and switching architectures, the strategy is to reduce the bottlenecks caused by routers. High-end routers/switches can simplify the process by using the legacy router equipment and newer equipment.

   These switching and routing choices allow for a very robust set of choices to handle the movement of the data as we have been building upon the choices. One merely has to understand and use the technologies that best serves the need.

Questions

1. At what layer of the OSI model does the router work?
   a. Data link layer
   b. Application layer
   c. Transport layer
   d. Session layer
   e. Network layer

2. A switch is much faster than a router.   T/F

3. Today, when considering a network, the administrator will likely use the following in the enterprise network:
   a. Layer 2 switches
   b. Layer 3 switches
   c. Layer 3 routers
   d. Layer 2 routers

4. Considering the networks can work well together, what device will not bother examining the FCS of the packets as they are processed:
   a. Half duplex switches
   b. Full duplex switches
   c. Cut-through switches
   d. High-end routers

5. What protocol can still only be used in a small office network?
   a. OSPF
   b. IGRP
   c. EIGRP
   d. RIP
6. What is the synonym for using a tag on any packet?
   a. Label switching
   b. IP switching
   c. Tag switching
   d. RSVP switching
7. Tag and IP switching can equally work on IP, ATM, and frame relay networks.   T/F
8. The primary inventor of IP switching products was:
   a. Cisco
   b. IBM
   c. IETF
   d. Ipsilon
9. The following protocol can help to prevent routing loops:
   a. OSPF
   b. Split horizon
   c. Poison reverse
   d. RIP
10. The TOS field of an IP packet can carry the following types of information, except:
    a. Time of day
    b. MTU
    c. Cost
    d. Load
    e. Delay

Voice over Internet Protocols (VoIP)

After reading this chapter and completing the questions, you will be able to:

- Discuss the desire to place Voice over IP
- Understand the protocols used
- Discuss the H.323 and SIP protocols for end users
- Converse about putting all the pieces together
- Understand carriers' desire for a different set of protocols called Megaco (H.248)

We now enter the world of convergence, where all the providers, carriers, and end users alike want to run voice over data networks. As we always say to people when we discuss this; voice will be data and data will be too! To transfer voice across a data network we can gain efficiencies and cost savings that have heretofore eluded us. We start with a discussion of the protocols compared to methods and concepts of converting voice into data packets. Next we look at some of the many choices.

It seems everybody's talking about VoIP these days. One of the reasons is that talk is cheap when it comes to VoIP—or at least cheaper. The technology is one that cost-conscious businesses and consumers are following because it can lower the cost of communication services. However, VoIP means a whole lot more than cheaper long-distance calls—VoIP technology is at the forefront of a dynamic evolution in the world of business communications, a move to networks that do it all.

In the simplest of terms, VoIP converts voice and fax calls into a digital stream of data packets. These packets are transmitted over the Internet or other IP-based networks as a stream of data, circumventing the much more expensive circuit-switched voice networks that major telephone carriers have used for over 100 years.

An entire communications industry has sprung up around VoIP, with services available from Primus, Sprint, MCI, Vonage, Skype, and nexVortex, among others.

All major carriers are also betting on IP technology, spending hundreds of millions of dollars on the IP communications infrastructure needed to support both voice and data transmission on their networks. In fact, estimates are that now more than 1100 service providers worldwide offering VoIP, either through online software or as a monthly package.

But cheap voice service is the tip of the iceberg. VoIP points the way to powerful communication networks that do much more than carry mere conversations. Voice and data sharing the same network is part of a grander scheme described as "network convergence"—complicated-sounding jargon for a single network that transports not just voice and data, but also high-quality, real-time video cheaply and efficiently.

If you send an e-mail or file, any small delays as it travels across the Internet or a company's local area network are not a big deal. On the other hand, if the packets for a voice call are delayed, the conversation can get choppy, the sound quality falls, and in the worst-case scenario a call will simply fail. The delay problem was licked by creating prioritizing schemes like multiprotocol label switching (MPLS) that distinguishes voice packets from general data. It works like a traffic cop, ensuring voice always moves ahead of data in an expeditious manner.

Now that traffic prioritization has been worked out, the stage is set for even more demanding things like video to come to the fore, bringing true network convergence. The main issue that's holding us back from even more compelling voice, video and data integration on a single network is a lack of business applications that can take full advantage of a converged network. The programs aren't exactly flooding the market en masse yet, but there are a few good ones that show what's possible.

Voice over the Internet

Over the past 10 years, the hype in the industry has been the convergence of the voice and data transmission systems. This is nothing new; we have been trying to integrate voice and data for decades. However, a subtle difference exists with today's convergence scenarios:

- In the beginning, the convergence operation mandated that data be made to look like voice; then it could be transmitted on the same circuitry. Circuit-switched voice and data used the age-old techniques of a network founded in voice techniques.

- Now, the convergence states that voice will look like data and the two can reside in packetized form on the same networks and circuitry. Circuit-switching technologies are making way for the packet-switching technologies.

These changes take advantage of the idle space in voice conversations, where it has been determined that during a conversation, only about 10–25 percent of the circuit time is actually utilized to carry the voice. The rest of the time, we are in idle condition by either:

1. Listening to the other end
2. Thinking of a response to a question
3. Breathing between our words

In this idle capacity, the compression of voice can facilitate less circuit usage, and encourage the use of a packetized form of voice. Data networking is more efficient because we have been using data packetization for years through packets, frames, or cells.

The use of a packet-switching transmission system allows us to interleave voice and data packets (video too) where there is idle space. As long as a mechanism exists to capture the information and reassemble it on the receiving end, it can be a more efficient use of bandwidth. It is just this bandwidth utilization and effective saving expectations that has driven the world into frenzy over packetizing voice and interleaving it on a data network, especially the Internet. Carriers have been told that by packetizing voice they can get an 11-fold increase of traffic (and subsequent revenues) on the existing wires they have today. Can you imagine any carrier turning this down? However, they need a carrier class operation that supports lifeline services similar to the circuit-switched network that we have evolved over the years to a network that produces 99.9999 percent uptime and reliability.

Currently, the drive is to get free voice on a data network. In the early years of data communications, data always was given a free ride on the voice networks. Telecommunications managers diligently fine-tuned their voice networks and allowed the data to run over the voice networks during the off-hours (after hours). This use of the circuitry was paid for through the dial-up voice communications.

This method of providing data over the voice networks crept into some of the business hours when real-time communications were needed. However, many times, the voice tie-lines and leased lines (point-to-point circuits) usually had some reserve capacity. Therefore, the data was placed on the point-to-point circuits that were justified by voice. As the competition in the telecommunications market heated up in the late 1990s, we saw the costs for a minute of long-distance drop from $0.50–0.60 per minute in North America down to an average cost today of about $0.05–0.07 per minute.* This significant drop in cost has been the result of competition and technological enhancements. At the same time, the data convergence took advantage of this falling cost factor. Meanwhile, data was migrating from a point-to-point technique on a dial-up connection to a more robust packet form of transmission using X.25 or IP packet-switching techniques. The cost per bit of data transmission was dropping even more rapidly. When the introduction of the Internet came to the commercial world in 1995, the floodgates started to pour open. The cost of data transmission has been touted as being free on the Internet, the only cost being the access fees. However, the cost of data networking has been rapidly declining on private line (Intranets), drawing the attention from both a public and a private networking focus.

This convergence has everyone looking for free voice by interleaving voice on the data networks. We agree with the scenario and would not attempt to detract from that goal. However, the other side of the equation is the circuit-switched networks that are

---

*It still amazes the authors that, in 2006, many small business and residential customers are still paying as much as $0.20–0.25 per minute for long-distance calling. This means that the consuming public is not looking for the deals and the carriers are not offering them as much as they say. Every carrier has a plan to offer flat rate long distance or free calls, so long as you sign up for about $20–25 monthly for the plan. Calculate the amount of time you are on the outbound dialed calls and divide that number of minutes into the cost of the plan. You may be surprised what your average cost per minute is!

continually driving the cost per minute for voice down. Closely aligned to this paradigm is the fact that the North American long-distance companies are now offering specials in every aspect of their service to compete with the Internet providers.

The convergence of voice and data networks onto a single IP network, as shown in Fig. 17.1, also provides some inherent flexibility, in terms of being able to easily add,

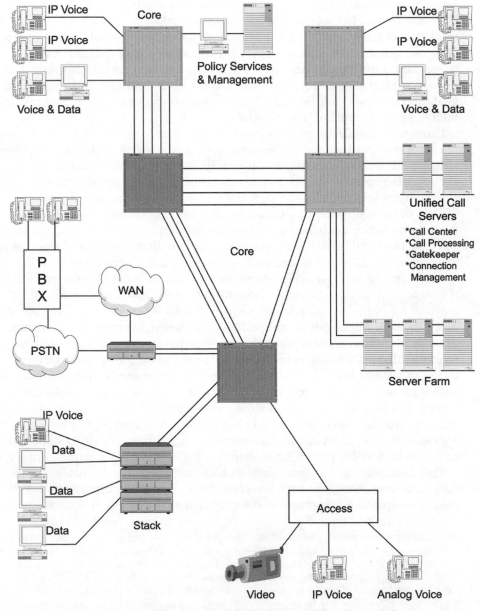

Figure 17.1 A converged network includes voice, data, and video over an IP network.

change or remove nodes (e.g., phones) on the network. As a result, organizations can easily deploy and then redeploy equipment to maximize their investments, without having to do a "truck roll" or require special expertise on hand. In fact, when an office moves or closes, it will be a simple matter to move the phones to another location rather than having to sell off old equipment or try to salvage what you can.

VoIP delivers many nice new features, such as advanced call routing, computer integration, unified messaging, integrated information services, long-distance toll bypass, and encryption. Because of the common network infrastructure, it is also possible to integrate other media services, like video or even electronic white boards, to name a few. An example of such features would be the "follow-me" feature where a person is always reachable at the same extension, whether telecommuting from his Lake Michigan cabin, staying in a hotel abroad, or sitting at his desk in the office. Another feature would be the integration of VoIP with customer relationship management (CRM) software. Caller ID or dialed numbers could be linked to a customer's record, which automatically opens on the desktop when the sales person receives or places a call. Because of the cost-effectiveness, flexibility, and promise that leveraging a single IP network offers, VoIP technology certainly merits study.

As you begin this project, the first challenge is to determine if there would be enough justification for a VoIP implementation. Clearly what we found was that the possibility exists between and among offices, as well as to other locations. In reality what we found was that the amount of traffic originating/terminating between offices is limited. This means that although an organization could develop a VoIP strategy, the bulk of the traffic will be to and from customers.

Voice over Internet Protocol

The public telephone network and the circuit-switching systems are usually taken for granted. Over the past few decades, they have grown to be accepted as almost 100 percent reliable. Manufacturers built in all the necessary stopgaps to prevent downtime and increase lifeline availability of telephony. It was even assumed that when the commercial power failed, the telephony business continued to operate. This did not happen accidentally, but through a very concerted development cycle jointly by the carriers and the manufacturers alike.

Access to a low-cost, high-quality worldwide network is considered essential in today's world. Anything that would jeopardize this access is treated with suspicion. A new paradigm is destined to replace (or at least complement) our basic communications. As data and voice is transported via IP packet networks the cost of telephony is plummeting. Packet data networking has matured over time that the voice technologies were maturing. The old basic voice and basic data networks have been replaced with highly reliable networks that carry voice, data, video, and multimedia transmissions.

Proprietary solutions manufactured by various providers have fallen to the side, opening the industry to a more open and standards-based environment. Admittedly, industry pundits are still saying that 70 percent of the revenue in this industry is generated by voice applications. This may be so, because on average, 57 percent of all international calls originating in North America going to Europe and Asia are actually carrying fax, not voice. They are considered dial-up voice communications transmissions because of the methodology used. Because data traffic is growing much faster than telephony traffic, there has been considerable interest in transporting voice over data networks (as opposed to the more traditional data over voice networks).

Support for voice communications using the Internet protocol (IP), which is usually just called *Voice over IP* or *VoIP,* has become especially attractive given the low-cost, flat-rate pricing of the public Internet and the IP networks that were built by the CLECs during the heyday of the competition.

In fact, toll-quality telephony over IP has now become the most important step leading to the convergence of the voice, video, and data communications industries. The feasibility of carrying voice and call-signaling messages over the Internet has already been demonstrated over the past 5 years. Delivering high-quality commercial products, establishing public services, and convincing users to buy into the vision are all still in their infancy, despite what we read in the trade press. The evolution of all networks begins this way, so there is no mystique in it. A recent survey by a prestigious R&D company indicated that more than 57 percent of the Fortune 1000 companies has already migrated to VoIP. Although this is partially true, some semblance of balance is required. Many of these organizations have installed test beds, pilots, and other experiments to determine the feasibility of using VoIP for conducting mission critical business. One large company CEO, whom the authors respect immensely, recently stated that "for internal calls, this is a great solution. But for customer calls and from financial analysts for discussions on the company's performance, the POTS network is still the best solution for now." Although this is not a disparaging remark, it is a fact of life.

VoIP is the packetizing of voice over the Internet protocol using current technologies as shown in Fig. 17.2. IP telephony, which is a different subset, will also have to change, somewhat. We will expect it to deliver interpersonal communications that end users are already accustomed to using in our traditional PBX and central office services. These added capabilities will include (but not be limited to features such as):

- Calling line ID (CLID)
- Three-way calling
- Call transfer
- Voice mail
- Voice-to-text conversions

Users are very comfortable with the services and capabilities delivered by the telephone companies on the standard dial-up telephone set using the touch-tone pad. IP telephony will have to match these services and ease-of-use functions in order to be successful.

Telecom buyers aren't beating the path to VoIP because it's the latest and greatest. Research companies that track VoIP and PBX installations are finding that even though VoIP/IP telephony accounts for an increasing number of PBX lines, those lines that are being deployed as legacy systems are reaching the end of their natural lifespan.

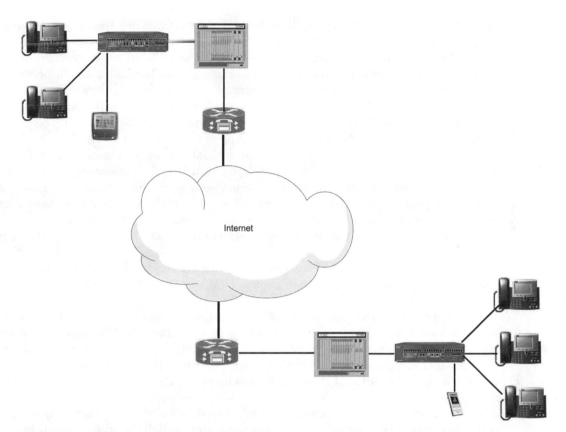

Figure 17.2   VoIP is the use of packetized voice over the Internet.

Telecom managers are not abandoning their natural caution and rushing to VoIP. Rather, it appears that they are buying VoIP as a replacement technology, not as displacement or disruptive. The good news is that VoIP will still beat TDM; it will just take longer than some might expect. IP telephony and VoIP will not replace the circuit-switched telephone networks overnight; coexistence will be here for the next decade. Analysts expect that in 2006 the amount of VoIP will amount to 20–25 percent of all voice traffic domestically, and approximately 30–40 percent of international traffic. One must be prepared for both alternatives to carrying voice in the next decade. Thus, the differences between the two opposing network strategies will settle and the world will shift into a packet-switched voice network over the next decade. We stated this in 2000 with the fourth edition of this book; we further agree that this is inevitable.

Quality of Service

We recently read a report that really threw a monkey wrench into the VoIP mechanics. A research house recently reported in August 2006 that over the past 5 years the quality of VoIP calls has steadily declined. We were flabbergasted on first blush, but then after re-reading the report, could easily believe it. After all, every network company that wants to sell "free voice" offers VoIP to a consumer market without any guarantees. Since March 2004, more than one million VoIP users tested their systems' call quality through the company's portal. Of those one million calls, about 20 percent were considered low quality and therefore unacceptable. The graph shown in Fig. 17.3 is a summary of the conclusions. Around the same time last year, only about 15 percent of VoIP calls were considered to be of unacceptable quality. In 2005, roughly 82 percent of calls tested had acceptable quality; that slipped to 80 percent in the first half of 2006; another decline in the first half of the year. A small drop may not seem significant, but when we consider the innovations in technology, this is devastating!

A Yankee Group vice president said of this that most enterprise users need not worry about call quality degradation because many run VoIP over their own networks, but call quality could plummet for companies using hosted services or services where the hosting company doesn't own the network. He felt that there's a lot of truth to the degradation.

Most users run some sort of instant messaging service (called presence), file sharing software and video, while also using voice. That can destroy call quality and introduce latency and jitter.

The largest argument against VoIP today is the lack of quality of service (QoS). The manufacturers and developers are working to overcome the objections by producing transmission systems that will assure a QoS for lifeline voice communications. Lifeline services include the ability to dial 911 calls (999 in other parts of the world), and be confident that the call will go through much the same as it does on the current voice networks.

When "I have fallen and can't get up," I need to be assured that help is a phone call away (or an IP call). If this assurance cannot be delivered, there will be less acceptance of the service. Mission-critical applications in the corporate world will also demand the ability to have a specified grade of service available. Most of the domestic

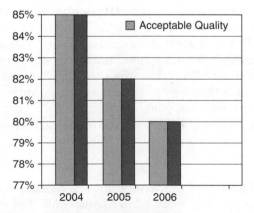

Figure 17.3   Level of acceptable quality calls in a 3-year period.

long-distance carriers offering to carry VoIP are demanding that the enterprise use an MPLS solution to guarantee the QoS standards.

CTI applications with call centers being web-enabled, interactive voice recognition, response, and other speech-activated technologies will demand a quality of service to facilitate the use of these systems. Each will demand the grade and quality of service expected in the telephone industry.

Another critical application for VoIP will be the results of quality of voice transmission. Noisy lines, delays in voice delivery, and clicking and chipping all tend to frustrate users on a voice network. Packet data networks carrying voice services today may produce the same results. Therefore, overcoming these pitfalls is essential to the success and acceptance of Voice over IP telephony applications. Merely installing more capacity (bandwidth) is not a solution to the problem; it is a temporary fix. Instead, developers must concentrate on delivering several solution sets to the industry such as those shown in Table 17.1. The QoS requirements for IP telephony can therefore be summarized as shown in Table 17.2, which considers the layered approach that vendors will be aggressively pursuing.

IP telephony datagrams entering the network will be treated with a priority to deliver the QoS expected by the end user. The routers and switches in the network will assign a high-priority marking on each datagram carrying voice, and treat these datagrams specially. Queues throughout the network will be established with variable treatments to handle the voice datagrams first, followed by the data datagrams.

Given the differences, why should we even consider the use of IP telephony? If the IP telephony world is only going to account for a small percentage of domestic traffic, is it worth all the hassles? The answer is a mixed bag, but overall the efficiencies of VoIP will outweigh the need to develop better control mechanisms to satisfy the telephony industry.

TABLE 17.1   Different Approaches to QoS

Strategy	Description
Integrated services architectures (Int-Serv)	Int-Serv includes the specifications to reserve network resources in support of a specific application. Using the RSVP protocol, the application or user can request and allocate sufficient bandwidth to support the short- or long-term connection. This is a partial solution because Int-Serv does not scale well, because each networking device (routers and switches) must maintain and manage the information for each flow established across their path.
Differentiated services (Diff-Serv)	Easier to use than Int-Serv, Diff-Serv uses a different mechanism to handle the flow across the network. Instead of trying to manage individual flows and per-flow signaling needs, Diff-Serv uses DS bits in the header to recognize the flow and the need for QoS on a particular datagram-by-datagram basis. This is more scalable than Int-Serv and does not rely solely on RSVP to control flows.
802.1p Prioritization	The IEEE standard specifies a prority scheme for the layer 2 switching in a switched-LAN. When a packet leaves a subnetwork or a domain, the 802.1p priority can be mapped to Diff-Serv to satisfy the layer 2 switching demands across the network.

TABLE 17.2   QoS Requirements for IP Telephony

Layer Addressed	Technique	Variable
1	Physical port	Variations of port definitions, or the prioritization of port interfaces based on application
2	IEEE 802.1p bits	Dedicated paths or ports for high bandwidth applications, but very expensive to maintain IP addressing
3	RSVP protocol (Int-Serv)	DS bits in the IP header (Diff-Serv)

LAN Protocols

Using IP to carry voice or fax, the IP datagram will encapsulate a UDP datagram which has the real-time protocol inside that, as seen in Fig. 17.4. As a result, a sequence numbering (counter is arbitrary), a synchronization source, a time stamp, and a payload type (the compression used inside the RTP) are all listed in header information.

This LAN addressing is an encapsulation of the IP datagram that sits inside the frame of information. Looking further down the rows, we encounter the IP addresses for the source and the destination IP device. In this case, the source IP is the originating gateway as the source and the terminating gateway as the destination addresses. The IP header information provided by the gatekeeper uses information such as the type of service field, which describes the variable selection criteria for the route. In this field we will see such fields as the precedence (priority), bandwidth, availability, least delay (latency), quality, cost, and loading. The variable parameters such as quality of service are handled herein.

Next we come to another set of headers, which are used by the gateway, the user datagram protocol (UDP) header. This defines the logical protocol port that the devices are sending the data to. Not only do we have a location to send to, we must also address the protocol port. The computer will have a set of VoIP programs running and will have specific ports assigned to handle the processing of the data inside those programs. The protocol port and the IP address are bound together to create a socket into the program (this is like placing the round peg in the round hole).

Finally, we come to the last piece of header information addressing the real time protocols (voice), which have many variable parameters, invoked in this header. The header carries the time stamp to be sure that the voice arrives within the specified period of time.

1. If voice arrives early, it can be held in memory and played out as needed.

2. However, if voice arrives late, it has no value and must be discarded.

This point is crucial to keeping the VoIP networks functioning. The average tolerable delay for a voice call in the PSTN is approximately 30–50 milliseconds. With VoIP the delay creeps up significantly because of all the devices and the memory buffers that

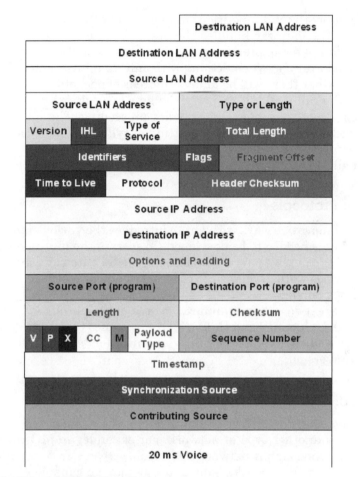

Destination LAN Address						
Destination LAN Address						
Source LAN Address						
Source LAN Address				Type or Length		
Version	IHL	Type of Service		Total Length		
Identifiers				Flags	Fragment Offset	
Time to Live		Protocol		Header Checksum		
Source IP Address						
Destination IP Address						
Options and Padding						
Source Port (program)				Destination Port (program)		
Length				Checksum		
V	P	X	CC	M	Payload Type	Sequence Number
Timestamp						
Synchronization Source						
Contributing Source						
20 ms Voice						

Figure 17.4   The LAN frame with VoIP inside.

must "hold and forward" the information. By hold and forward, the issue is that the gateway (or any router) holds the data for a short time only to analyze the information that it needs to process. The first piece looked at is the time to live (TTL). If the packet has not timed out, the gateway will then take the next step. Then the gateway analyzes the IP packet for the destination address (where do I send this next?). Upon that analysis, the gateway then has to determine the optimal route in a plurality of route choices (at this point the TOS field is analyzed for the variables). The route is selected on the basis of the information being provided. The address may now be stored in another memory (cached) so that a multitude of IP packets can all be processed in rapid succession. The IP data file is then timed to a synchronization source, counted, checked, and then played out. Throughout this entire process the data file is continually analyzed to determine the optimal routing. Information is stored and held in memory so that the information can be validated and checked. Finally, the memory of the duration (length) and repetition (frequency) of calls is used for billing and accounting purposes. The gateway handles the optimal route choice selection upon the analysis of the data file being presented. It should also be noted that a voice call lasts for 3–5 minutes on average. When dealing with only 20 milliseconds of voice per IP datagram, the logic is that there will be many hundreds of packets involved in a single phone call. To keep the call working properly, the network equipment must continually monitor, on a real-time basis, how the calls are proceeding. The latency must continually be monitored or echo and clipping (cutting of syllables) can occur. Each of these parameters requires that the network continually analyze the properties of the data file and continually select the optimal route.

VoIP Signaling Protocols

With the innovative ways we want to introduce the various new media on the Internet, new protocols needed to be developed. To sustain the multimedia, voice over and video over the Internet, we saw the creation of media gateway controllers and gatekeepers. These devices were developed to control the access methods and the sessions between the various parties.

There are two other standards worth mentioning: MCGP and closely related MEGACO. Unlike SIP and H.323, MGCP assumes that edge systems are unintelligent gateways and, therefore, the gateway controller handles all aspects that go beyond media conversion.

Media Gateway Control Protocol (MGCP)

The media gateway (MG) converts media provided in one type of network to the format required in another type of network. For example, an MG could terminate channels from a switched circuit network and media streams from a packet network (e.g., RTP streams in an IP network). This gateway may be capable of processing audio, video, and voice alone or in any combination, and will be capable of full duplex media translations. The MG may also play audio/video messages and perform other interactive voice recognition and response (IVR) functions, or may perform media conferencing. Media gateway control protocols are used by the CATV companies as they offer their VoIP solutions to the end user.

The Media Gateway Control Protocol (MEGACO)

When MGCP was initially introduced for standardization to the IETF, the name was changed to MEGACO and an agreement was reached with the ITU to work on a parallel standards activity: H.248. The key difference between MEGACO and H.248 is that H.248 mandates the support of H.323 (see below). To simplify things and reduce costs, vendors have been implementing systems that use the original MGCP signaling proposal.

MEGACO/H.248 shown in Fig. 17.5 is a current draft standard and represents a cooperative proposal from the IETF and ITU standards bodies. MEGACO has many

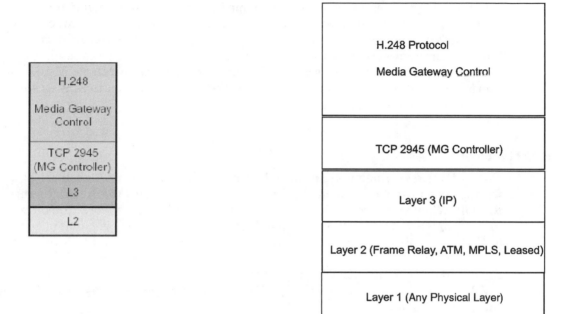

Figure 17.5   The MEGACO protocol stack.

similarities to MGCP and borrows the same naming conventions for the VoIP elements. The MEGACO architecture defines media gateways that provide media conversion and sources of calls, while media gateway controllers provide call control, MEGACO addresses the same requirements as that of MGCP and, as a result, there is some effort to merge the protocols. It defines a series of transactions coordinated by a media gateway controller for the establishment of call sessions. The primary focus of MEGACO is the promotion to standardize IP telephony equipment. Some of the design goals are as follows:

- MEGACO IP phone meets the basic needs of the business user from day one.

- Provides a path for rapid expansion to support sophisticated business telephony features.

- Allows for a wide range of telephones and similar devices to be defined from very simple to very feature rich.

- Implements a simple, minimal design.

- Allows device cost to be appropriate to capabilities provided. Package and termination types have characteristics that enable reliability.

- Meets the appropriate MEGACO/H.248 protocol requirements, as provided in the MEGACO requirements document, and are a straightforward application of the MEGACO/H.248 protocol.

MEGACO provides a means to manage media gateways that convert the user traffic between telephony and packet networks. The MEGACO standard may become more widely accepted across the data (Internet) and telephony worlds and better defined to handle enhanced services. It enables multimedia applications, IVR support, conferencing solutions, wiretap, speech-to-text conversion, and many others. Media gateway controller (MGC) controls the parts of the call state that pertain to connection control for media channels in an MG.

H.323 Protocol

Current voice traffic on circuit-switched networks has a very high level of quality because each connection is guaranteed a certain bandwidth (64 Kbps) for the life of the call. When voice traffic is transmitted over an IP-based network, the data is compressed down to 7.9 or 6.3 Kbps depending on which standard is being used (G.729A or G.723.1). This saving in bandwidth comes at a price in the quality level of the call. On an IP-based network, packets can travel over any number of different routes so the quality of the transmission is tied to the quality of the network. Lost packets in a VoIP network degrade the quality of the system by appearing as gaps of silence in the conversation.

As with any technology that is still in its infancy there are various standards that are being proposed as the best way to achieve industry acceptance. There are several standards in place that deal with IP telephony implementations at the moment. H.323 is the ITU standard. It is a packet-based multimedia communication system that is a set of specifications. These specifications define various signaling functions, as well as media formats related to "packetized" audio and video services.

H.323 from the ITU, which was first approved in 1996, but had its beginnings in the early 1990s. H.323 standards were generally the first to classify and solve multimedia delivery issues over LAN technologies. The H.323 protocol stack is shown in Fig. 17.6. However, as IP networking and the Internet became prevalent, many Internet RFC standard protocols and technologies were developed and based on some of the previous H.323 ideas. Today there is a cooperation between the ITU and IETF in solving existing problems, but it is fair to say that the RFC process of furthering the standards has had greater success than the H.323 counterparts.

H.323 is a comprehensive protocol, which tries to address all aspects of a VoIP system. It is an umbrella system, which includes a number of other specifications such as:

1. H.225—call control signaling, registration, and admission
2. H.235—security issues: authentication, integrity, privacy, and nonrepudiation
3. H.245—channel usage negotiation
4. H.261—Video codecs (coder/decoders)
5. G.723 and G.729—Audio codecs

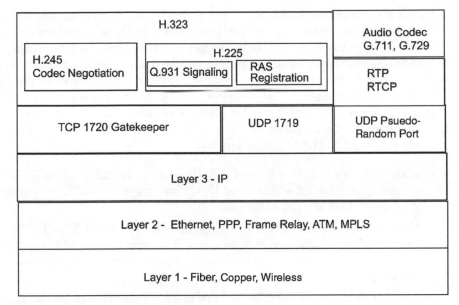

Figure 17.6   The ITU standard-based H.323 protocols.

An H.323 system is composed of four main components:

1. *Terminal*: This is an end-user device, which supports two-way voice, data, and/ or video traffic with another terminal. An end-user terminal would be an IP telephone or a PC with VoIP software and hardware.

2. *Gateway*: Gateways are responsible for communicating with other or different networks. If the connecting device on the other network is not an H.323 device, the gateway will translate between the two protocols. A gateway allows a connection from a PSTN to IP-based LAN.

3. *Multipoint control unit*: An MCU provides support for multiconferencing between several end-user terminals.

4. *Gatekeeper*: Gatekeepers provide authentication services to allow end users to register on the VoIP network. It also manages access policies and address translation.

H.323 networks consist of call processing servers, (media) gateways, and gatekeepers. Call processing servers provide call routing and communication to VoIP gateways and end devices. Gateways serve as both the H.323 termination endpoint and interface with non-H.323 networks, such as the PSTN. Gatekeepers function as a central unit for call admission control, bandwidth management and call signaling. Although the gatekeeper is not a required element in H.323, it can help H.323 networks to scale to a larger size, by separating call control and management functions from the gateways.

H.323 specifications tend to be heavier (due to chattiness, in terms of control signaling) and with an initial focus in LAN networking. These standards have some shortcomings in scalability, especially in large-scale deployments. Primarily, limitations are due to chattiness or the heavy signaling required establishing H.323 sessions. H.323 is dependant on TCP-based (connection-oriented) signaling. There is a challenge in maintaining large numbers of TCP sessions because of the substantial overhead involved. However, most H.323 scalability limitations are based on the prevalent version two of the specification. Subsequent versions of H.323 have a focus on solving some of these problems. The main H.323 process includes:

- With each call that is initiated, a TCP session (H.225.0 protocol) is created, using an encapsulation of a subset of Q.931 messages. This TCP connection is maintained for the duration of the call.

- A second session is established using the H.245 protocol. This TCP-based process is for capabilities exchange, master-slave determination, and the establishment and release of media streams. This group of procedures is in addition to the H.225.0 processes.

- The H.323 quality of service delivery mechanism of choice is the resource reservation protocol (RSVP). This protocol is not considered to have good scaling properties due to its focus and management of individual application traffic flows. Although H.323 many not be well suited in service provider spaces, it is well positioned to deploy enterprise VoIP applications. As a service provider, it might be necessary to bridge, transport, or interface H.323 services and applications to the PSTN.

Voice over IP currently implements the ITU's H.323 specification within Internet telephony gateways (ITGs) to signal voice call setup.

Session Initiation Protocol (SIP)

SIP shown in Fig. 17.7 is a new protocol developed by the Internet engineering task force (IETF) and multiparty multimedia session control (MMUSIC) working group as an alternative to H.323.

A SIP network is composed of five types of logical SIP entities. Each entity has specific functions and participates in SIP communication as a client (initiates requests), as a server (responds to requests), or as both. One "physical device" can have the functionality of more than one logical SIP entity. For example, a network server working as a proxy server can also function as a registrar at the same time. The logical SIP entities are:

- User agent
- Proxy server
- Redirect server
- Registrar server
- Back-to-back user agent (B2BUA)

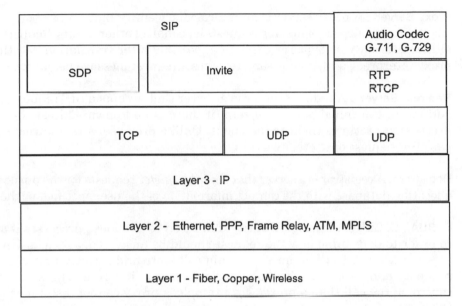

Figure 17.7 The SIP protocol stack is the IETF standard.

User Agent   In SIP, a user agent (UA) is the endpoint entity. User agents initiate and terminate sessions by exchanging requests and responses.

SIP is a less complicated protocol and hence, some would argue, more flexible. It is a challenge-response–based system similar to the HTTP protocol. The main components of a SIP-based system are:

1. *User call agent or user agent client*: The UAC is responsible for initiating a call by sending a URL-addressed INVITE to the intended recipient.

2. *Proxy server*: Proxy servers are responsible for routing and delivering messages.

3. *Redirect server*: A redirect server keeps a user database, which allows it to inform proxy server's of a user's location.

RFC 3261 defines the user agent as an application, which contains both a user agent client and a user agent server, as follows:

- User agent client (UAC)—a client application that initiates SIP requests.
- User agent server (UAS)—a server application that contacts the user when a SIP request is received and that returns a response on behalf of the user. Some of the devices that can have a UA function in a SIP network are workstations, IP phones, telephony gateways, call agents, and automated answering services.

Proxy Server   A proxy server is an intermediary entity that acts as both a server and a client, for the purpose of making requests on behalf of other clients. Requests are serviced either internally or bypassing them on, possibly after translation, to other servers. A proxy interprets, and, if necessary, rewrites a request message before forwarding it.

Redirect Server   A redirect server is a server that accepts a SIP request, maps the SIP address of the called party into zero (if there is no known address) or more new addresses and returns them to the client. Unlike proxy servers, redirect servers do not pass the request onto other servers.

Registrar   A registrar is a server that accepts *register* requests for the purpose of updating a location database with the contact information of the user specified in the request.

B2BUA   A B2BUA is a logical entity that receives a request, processes it as a UAS and, in order to determine how the request should be answered, acts as a UAC and generates requests. A B2BUA must maintain call state and actively participate in sending requests and responses for dialogs in which it is involved. The B2BUA has tighter control of the call than a proxy—for example, a proxy cannot disconnect a call or alter the messages.

The above descriptions lead us to believe that the industry is in a state of flux because so many protocols are developed by differing groups. Actually, we have seen that from an end-user perspective, H.323 or SIP can be used. In the carrier community, they can accept H.323 or SIP signaling into the H.248 MEGACO office and process it across their backbone networks, so interoperability is becoming a reality.

H.323, the call signaling protocol defined by the International Telecommunications Union (ITU-T) in 1996, was the first industry standard defined for IP telephony and multimedia communications over packet networks. Because of the overlap between the scope of SIP and H.323, work is currently underway to define interworking between the two protocols. Both H.323 and SIP are call-signaling protocols that define mechanisms for call routing, call signaling, capabilities exchange, media control, and supplementary services. Next generation networks will have to deliver end-to-end interoperability across multiple protocols.

The industry is settling on SIP as the desired protocol of choice for the future. The SIP is best described as a catalyst for the next phase of open communications over IP. SIP is an interoperable protocol in a multi-vendor environment that creates new possibilities for system flexibility in multiservice networks. Organizations can pick the best of breed from a variety of vendors to create a seamless converged communication network.

The SIP is part of IETF's multimedia data and control protocol framework. SIP is a powerful client-server signaling protocol used in VoIP networks. SIP handles the setup and tears down multimedia sessions between speakers; these sessions can include multimedia conferences, telephone calls, and multimedia distribution.

SIP is a text-based signaling protocol transported over either TCP or UDP, and is designed to be lightweight. It inherited some design philosophy and architecture from the hypertext transfer protocol (HTTP) and simple mail transfer protocol (SMTP) to ensure its simplicity, efficiency, and extensibility.

SIP uses *invitations* to create session description protocol (SDP) messages to carry out capability exchange and to set up call control channel use. These invitations allow participants to agree on a set of compatible media types. SIP supports user mobility by proxying and redirecting requests to the user's current location. Users can inform the server of their current location (IP address or URL) by sending a registration message to a *registrar*. This function is powerful and often needed for a highly mobile voice user base.

The SIP client-server application has two modes of operation; SIP clients can either signal through a *proxy* or *redirect* server. Using proxy mode, SIP clients send requests to the proxy and the proxy either handles requests or forwards them on to other SIP servers. Proxy servers can insulate and hide SIP users by proxying the signaling messages; to the other users on the VoIP network, the signaling invitations look as if they are coming from the proxy SIP server.

A user with multiple devices like a cell phone, desk phone, PC client, and PDA can rely on SIP to seamlessly integrate these entities for increased efficiency and productivity. SIP is differentiated from similar communications protocols by its wide industry support, providing a practical means of multi-vendor integration at the highest level of the protocol stack—the application layer.

Although a growing number of companies are considering an organization-wide migration to converged communications, the majority are testing the waters on an application-by-application basis. Initially, savings associated with business continuity, toll bypass and ease of administration for moves/adds/changes fueled VoIP deployment, but it is the increased flexibility in deploying new capabilities and application integration that will drive the migration to converged communications in enterprise environments.

Converged business communication solutions embrace the principles of:

- Open, standards-compliant software and system architectures

- Solutions that are highly scalable and reliable

- Communication features transparent to the means of access

- Services rendered across multiple forms of access devices

- User productivity optimized to handle operational challenges

- Fork lift solutions are avoided to cut costs and service disruptions

- Enhanced service integration with service providers as opposed to siloed solutions

- Interoperability with multiple vendors creating end-to-end solutions

SIP is a new text-based Internet signaling protocol to be used for establishing real-time calls and conferences over IP networks, as defined by the International Engineering Telecommunications Foundation (IETF).

Real-Time Streaming Protocols (RTSP)

RTSP takes advantage of streaming, which breaks data into many packets sized according to the bandwidth available between client and server. When the client has received enough packets, the user's software can be playing one packet, decompressing another and downloading the third. The user may start listening almost immediately without having to get the entire media file. Both live data feeds and stored clips can be the sources of data. RTSP acts as a "network remote control" for multimedia servers. The delivery mechanisms are based solely on the real-time protocol (RTP). RTSP has been designed to be on top of RTP to both control and deliver real-time content. Real-time streaming protocol can also be used with the RSVP to set up and manage reserved-bandwidth streaming sessions.

One can see that the use of multimedia (voice, data, and video) on the Internet opens the door for a myriad of new protocols. These are but a few.

Call Quality and Integrity

If a data packet is lost while being transmitted over an IP network it can easily be retransmitted. Lost VoIP packets, however, will directly affect the quality of the voice transmission. Denial of service attacks have, unfortunately, become all too common in today's Internet environment. As corporations convert more and more of their voice traffic to traverse their regular data networks, the threat of DOS attacks will take on heightened meaning because now normal telephone service could fall prey to simple hacker tools that anyone can download off the Internet. VoIP servers will need to be placed behind "VoIP aware" firewalls. There are many security-related patches available that pertain to DOS attacks. Network administrators will need to pay particular attention to the VoIP servers on their network to make sure that the servers are always up-to-date with the latest security fixes.

Another threat that must be guarded against is the possibility of a hacker taking over a gateway device. This could be achieved by emulating VoIP signals that the gateway is expecting. This would require that the hacker has access to the gateway's network and has an in-depth understanding of the VoIP protocols. This would not be an easy endeavor, but in today's world of ingenious hacking exploits, if something can occur, it will probably.

Authentication

Just as in the data world, users of VoIP may occasionally have the need to ensure that the person on the other end of a call is really who they say they are. The H.323, SIP, and MGCP standards provide mechanisms for authenticating users.

The H.235 component of H.323 specifies two types of authentication:

1. *Symmetric encryption*: This method of authentication is less processor intensive and requires no previous communication between the two devices.

2. *Subscription based*: This method can be either symmetric or asymmetric. It requires the sharing of a secret key or certificate before the communication can occur. Diffie-Hellman key exchange can be used to generate the shared secret key. Symmetric encryption methods are generally very secure; however, they require large amounts of CPU processing power and time.

H.235 also allows for the use of IPSEC to handle the authentication between the VoIP devices.

The SIP protocol allows for three different types of authentication, all of which are challenge-response based.

1. Basic authentication
2. Digest authentication
3. PGP authentication

MGCP recommends the use of IPSEC for encryption and authentication.

VoIP Security

Voice over IP is not a monolithic technology with a set number of standards. Rather, there are multiple protocols that provide voice over the Internet. The most popular VoIP protocols in use today are H.323 and SIP. MGCP is seen more in large networks such as those used by service providers to coordinate between different VoIP deployments. SCCP, or Skinny, is a Cisco proprietary protocol that is often seen in legacy VoIP deployments.

Even within a given protocol or standard, firewalls must deal with multiple protocols for a single VoIP phone call. A signaling protocol is used to find the two parties involved and set up the call. The actual conversation is carried by RTP and RTCP, the media protocols. For H.323, setting up a call involves standards such as H.225 and H.245. Making it even more confusing is the number of variants for each protocol. For example, versions 2, 3, and 4 of H.323 are commonly seen in VoIP deployments.

Likewise, SIP can come in many formats such as SIP over UDP or SIP over TCP that firewalls must understand and secure. Many organizations have many VoIP variations in use because of mergers and purchasing policies that give divisions or locations control over IT decisions, or simply because multiple applications have been deployed over time.

The complexity of VoIP goes beyond the variety of protocols and extends to how they interact with security. H.323 is a prime example of why VoIP is difficult to secure. A traditional firewall secures the perimeter by defining specific ports through which traffic may enter. For example, Web traffic travels across Port 80 so perimeter firewalls allow traffic to enter on Port 80. However, H.323 uses both static ports, such as Port 1720 for call setup, and random dynamic ports. For a traditional perimeter firewall to allow H.323 to cross the firewall, thousands of dynamic and static ports must be left open for voice traffic—creating large holes for attackers to exploit.

Because H.323 traffic is encoded in a binary format based on ASN.1, even advanced firewalls have a difficult time analyzing and making proper security decisions about VoIP traffic entering the network. Each instance of the VoIP application will place important information—such as delivery address data— in a slightly different location within a packet. As a result, traditional firewalls do not have the intelligence to parse the message and find the proper information to make security decisions. Solving VoIP security complexity involves moving beyond the traditional firewall to a security solution that is highly aware of VoIP protocols and how these protocols work.

Bandwidth Considerations

Network bandwidth requirements are based on the total number of IP trunks or IP stations installed in the system. The multiple algorithms make available the bandwidth needed for a voice call-out to an IP network can range from 10.7 to 96 Kbps. The most common algorithm used for IP trunks is G.729A, which allows the voice to be compressed to 8 Kbps. Once the layer 3 (IP) overhead is added to the voice payload, the approximate bandwidth is 16 Kbps for a single voice stream out of the PBX to an IP network. This bandwidth calculation does not include layer 2 overhead and will vary depending on the type of transport (frame relay, ATM, Ethernet, and the like). Depending on what type of algorithm is in place and how many devices are deployed dictates the amount of bandwidth needed.

The bandwidth for call setup for the SS7 signaling channel over IP is 7.2 Kbps per call and the complete signaling channel is 83.2 Kbps per call. Call teardown requires the same amount of bandwidth. This number varies, and 7.2 and 83.2 Kbps are average values from the start sequence until setup or teardown is accomplished.

This means to make an SS7 call from one PBX to another, the first PBX will transmit 83.2 or 7.2 Kbps (SS7) until the call is established. Once the call is established, the first PBX will stop sending the 83.2 Kbps (7.2 Kbps) setup information and will begin sending the appropriate voice payload per encoding/decoding algorithm selected (G.711, G.729A, G.723.1).

To make multiple calls, the system will send 7.2 or 83.2 Kbps for each call until all the calls are established. During teardown 7.2 or 83.2 Kbps will be transmitted for each call again. If an IP station has been idle for up to 4 seconds, a 7.6 Kbps "Keep Alive" packet will be sent to those respective devices. A Keep Alive packet is not generated to an idle station if it is configured across a WAN. This same process occurs on IP trunk routes. A Keep Alive packet is sent to the trunk route for each system or point code in the network. If traffic is present on either IP station or trunk route, no Keep Alive packet is generated.

Table 17.3 shows the amount of bandwidth for IP overhead per the fill times set in the PBX system. The higher the fill time used, better performance from the PBX and IP network can be realized due to the smaller number, yet larger (in size) packets generated.

TABLE 17.3   Bandwidth Utilization for Various Samples

Codec	Sample Time			
	10 ms	20 ms	30 ms	40 ms
G.711 (64 Kbps)	32 Kbps	16 Kbps	10.67 Kbps	8 Kbps
G.729A (8 Kbps)	32 Kbps	16 Kbps	10.67 Kbps	8 Kbps
G.723.1 (6.3 Kbps)	N/A	N/A	10.67 Kbps	N/A
G.723.1 (5.3 Kbps)	N/A	N/A	10.67 Kbps	N/A

Table 17.4 shows the total amount of bandwidth in layer 3 per voice call during the transmit stream from an IP trunk or IP station. The value shown is based on the fill time from the table above and the bandwidth required by the encoding/decoding algorithm that is used (codec).

Looking at a group of sites and the offered load (call minutes between and among the sites) we see in Table 17.5 a list of the minutes offered, the busiest hour and the number of circuits needed to carry an equivalent number of circuit-switched calls.

Converting the traffic from voice traffic engineered load to an IP bandwidth need, assuming a high-speed connection to the Internet telephony service provider (ITSP), we then calculate the bandwidth based on various rules as follows:

1. Codec protocols used

2. Sample size for VoIP traffic listed above in Tables 17.3 and 17.4

3. Protocol stack (IP, PPP, frame relay, and the like)

4. Transmission network (DSL, ATM, etc.)

5. Voice paths recommended

6. Echo cancellation

7. Equivalent bandwidth

As a general rule of thumb the bandwidth for one call in one direction is between 10 and 110 Kbps.

TABLE 17.4   Bandwidth Utilized at Layer 3 Overhead Combined

	Total Bandwidth per Transmit Stream			
Codec	10 ms	20 ms	30 ms	40 ms
G.711 (64 Kbps)	96 Kbps	80 Kbps	74.67 Kbps	72 Kbps
G.729A (8 Kbps)	40 Kbps	24 Kbps	18.67 Kbps	16 Kbps
G.723.1 (6.3 Kbps)	N/A	N/A	16.97 Kbps	N/A
G.723.1 (5.3 Kbps)	N/A	N/A	15.97 Kbps	N/A

TABLE 17.5   Traffic Statistics and Number of Circuits Needed

Location	Maximum Offered (minutes)	Busiest Hour	Circuits Needed	Equivalent Circuitry in PRI
Site A	3450	10–11	75	< 4
Site B	1836	10–11	53	< 3
Site C	2283	3–4	36	< 2
Site D	1367	11–12	34	< 2
Site E	1224	10–11	31	1 (E1)
Site F	210	10–11	14	< 1

TABLE 17.6   Codec protocols compared

Location	Coding Protocol	Packet Size (ms)	Bandwidth Kbps	Voice Paths	IP Mbps	Trunking
Site A	G.711	20	64	75	6	T2 or Fractional T3
	G.723.1	30	5.3	75	1.2	T1
	G.729A	20	8	75	1.8	T1C or E1
Site B	G.711	20	64	53	4.2	T2
	G.723.1	30	5.3	53	.848	Fractional T
	G.729A	20	8	53	1.3	T1
Site C	G.711	20	64	36	2.88	T1C
	G.723.1	30	5.3	36	.576	Fractional T
	G.729A	20	8	36	.864	Fractional T
Site D	G.711	20	64	34	2.72	T1C
	G.723.1	30	5.3	34	.581	Fractional T
	G.729A	20	8	34	.816	Fractional T
Site E	G.711	20	64	31	2.48	E1 borderline
	G.723.1	30	5.3	31	.496	Fractional E1
	G.729A	20	8	31	.744	Fractional E1
Site F	G.711	20	64	14	1.12	T1
	G.723.1	30	5.3	14	.224	Fractional T
	G.729A	20	8	14	.336	Fractional T

Table 17.6 is a comparison of the various codec protocols that can be used along with the appropriate bandwidth to offer the same load as shown.

Using the figures shown in Table 17.6, we can say that the best possible combination is to use the G.723.1 coding algorithm (codec protocol) and a sample size of 30 milliseconds. Codecs convert analog voice signals into data streams through sampling and quantization. Codecs vary in their quality and delay characteristics and, although there is not yet an agreed standard, G.723.1 and G729A are the most common codecs used for Internet voice transmission.

The frequency at which the voice packets are transmitted has a significant bearing on the bandwidth required. The selection of the packet duration (and therefore the packet frequency) is a compromise between bandwidth and quality. Lower durations require more bandwidth. However, if the duration is increased, the delay of the system increases, and it becomes more susceptible to packet loss; 20 milliseconds is a typical figure.

The use of a codec will produce the results that most people comfortably accept when using compressed voice. A summary of MOS (an ITU mean opinion score) for assessing quality of a channel on a scale of 1–5 (5 being best) is shown in Table 17.7. Actually there is a very lengthy calculation performed to produce the MOS result. Interestingly, the MOS for the G.723.1 codecs is higher than the G.729 A and B, even though the bandwidth used is less. If a greater MOS is required, then the G.711 will be required, but that is the same as PCM voice on the PSTN. No bandwidth gain will be achieved with G.711. Our recommendation is to use the G.723.1 with MP-MLQ where available.

MOS is not the entire story. When selecting to use VoIP there are several issues that must be addressed, such as various forms of delay. The primary goal of the ITU and

TABLE 17.7   Summary of MOS for Various Coding Techniques

Codec	Encoding	Clock Rate	Data Rate kbps	Framing Delay (ms)	Framing Size (Bytes)	Look-Ahead Delay (ms)	DSP Processor Delay	MOS
G.711	PCM	8000	64	10	80	0	13	4.1
G.723.1	MP-MLQ (Multipulse Maximum Likelihood Quantization)	8000	6.3	30	24	7.5	23	3.8
G.723.1	ACELP	8000	5.3	30	20	7.5	23	3.8
G.729A	CS-ACELP with smaller codebook	8000	8	10	10	5	13	3.7
G.729B	CS-ACELP with silence suppression	8000	8	10	10	5	13	3.7

IETF in assessing the acceptability of VoIP falls into a calculated one-way delay budget. For the most part, keeping the one-way delay to a minimum is the goal, but the budget is set to be somewhere around 140–150 milliseconds. Anything greater than 150 milliseconds delay will become uncomfortable for your users.

We have taken some time to discuss some of the various forms and causes of delay so that when you implement a VoIP solution, these characteristics can be considered. The sources of delay are:

- Coder (processing) delay
- Algorithmic delay
- Packetization delay
- Serialization delay
- Queuing and buffering delay
- Network switching delay
- De-jitter delay

When T1s are used for access, many of the delay concerns are avoided. Considering that the cost for 1.536 Mbps (megabits per second) T1 access line typically adds about $900–$1500 per month more than 56 Kbps (kilobits per second) access, adding bandwidth can be expensive. The good news is that the extra capacity may be needed to make bandwidth hungry data communications run much faster, helping to justify the increased costs.

Coder or processing delay is the time that the DSP (digital signal processor) requires to perform the encoding. Because different codec (coder/decoder) algorithms have various degrees of complexity, the delay varies with the codec and the DSP's power. For example, ACELP (algebraic code excited linear production) algorithms work by analyzing a 10-millisecond block of PCM (pulse code modulation) samples, and then compressing them. The compression time for a G.729 ranges from 2.5 to 10 milliseconds, depending on the processor load of the DSP. If the DSP is busy handling four calls, the processing delay will be 10 milliseconds. If the DSP is processing only one call, then the processing delay will be 2.5 milliseconds. Prudent design dictates that the worst case time of 10 milliseconds should be used when calculating overall delays. Decompressing the voice time is much less complex, and requires about 10 percent of the compression time for each block. Since there may be multiple samples in each frame, the decompression time is proportional to the number of samples per frame. If a 20-millisecond frame is used, the worst case decompression time for a frame with two samples is 2×1 milliseconds, or 2 milliseconds. Sometimes three samples are included in a single voice packet, and the processing delay would be 3×1 milliseconds = 3 milliseconds. The case for processor time is shown in Table 17.8.

G.729 and G.723.1 compress voice based on the last sample, the current sample, and the next sample. This obviously implies that the compression algorithm must wait for part of the next sample to compress the current one. The amount of information collected from the next sample is called the look-ahead, and causes additional delay. This look-ahead delay is called the algorithmic delay. The amount of algorithmic delay varies by codec.

Often algorithmic delay, processor delay, and decompression delay are added together into a single number. With the case of G.729, the lumped processor delay for G.729 = 10 milliseconds processor delay + 3 milliseconds decompression delay + 5 milliseconds algorithmic delay = 18 milliseconds.

Packetization delay is the time required to capture the voice so that it can be stored in a packet prior to sending. The smallest packetization delay is dictated by the framing size of the codec, which is shown in Table 17.9. The IETF (Internet engineering task force) recommends a 20-millisecond packetization delay in RFC (request for comments) 1989. The advantage of the larger packetization delay is twofold. First, the longer packetization delay reduces overhead since less voice packets must be sent because each packet is larger. Secondly, the DSP does not have to work as hard because fewer packets are being sent. Some vendors recommend against using payloads smaller than 30 milliseconds because processor delays start to undermine the delay you are saving by using a smaller packetization delay.

TABLE 17.8   Codec Processing for Various Methods

Codec	Rate (Kbps)	Sample Size (ms)	Best Case (ms)	Worst Case (ms)
G.711	64	20	2.5	10
G.723.1	5.3	30	5	20
G.729A	8	20	2.5	10

TABLE 17.9   Packetization Delay

Codec	Kbps	Payload Size (Bytes)	Packetization Delay (ms)	Payload Size (Bytes)	Packetization Delay (ms)
G.711	64	160	20	240	30
G.723.1	5.3	20	30	40	60
G.729A	8.0	20	20	30	30

Serialization delay is determined by the bit rate of the link you are using. Serialization delay is calculated by determining how long it will take to transmit a packet of a given size. Remember that frame size must include all overhead, including the layer 2 headers. For instance, the serialization delay for a common Ethernet frame of 1500 bytes over a 56 circuit is 214.29 milliseconds, shown in Table 17.10. A 64-byte voice frame would experience a 9.14-millisecond serialization delay over the same 56-Kbps link. For this reason we believe that a full T1 using a frame size of 30 milliseconds should give you sufficient throughput and minimize delay.

Once the voice frame is created and sent, often times it cannot pass directly through the network without any further delay. This statement is made even after making the assumption that the voice frame will be given absolute priority over any other non-voice frame. In spite of all this priority, the voice frame will still have to wait in queue along the way toward its destination. If proper queuing systems are in place, the voice frame will have to wait for other voice frames ahead of it, plus it may also have to wait for a lower priority data frame that is partially transmitted and still in the process playing out.

Queuing delay equals the serialization delay of any frames in the output queue that are ahead of it. Since the amount of data in the outbound queue is changed from one moment to the next, queuing delay is a variable. Obviously, if the link speeds are made higher, the queuing delay is reduced.

Queuing problems arise with slow speed links. For instance, consider a 56- Kbps link that just begins the process of forwarding a 1500-byte data packet just 1 microsecond prior to a high-priority voice packet showing up. Even though the voice packet is a higher priority, the router must complete the sending of the 1500-byte data packet. This will require 214 milliseconds, and the voice packet must wait in queue. Increasing priority of the voice frame will not solve this queuing problem.

The jitter buffer functions make sure all packets are restored to temporal order. The jitter buffer function is generally under the control of the RTP (Real-time transport protocol) application. RTP can detect voice packet loss, as well as reassemble the voice packets in proper time. RTP uses a timestamp number to put the packet back into

TABLE 17.10   Serialization Delay in Millisecond Based on Link Speed

Frame	Link Speed										
Size (Bytes)	19.2	56	64	128	256	384	512	768	1024	1544	2048
38	15.83	5.43	4.75	2.38	1.19	0.79	0.59	0.40	0.30	0.20	0.15
48	20.00	6.86	6.00	3.00	1.50	1.00	0.75	0.50	0.38	0.25	0.19
64	26.67	9.14	8.00	4.00	2.00	1.33	1.00	0.67	0.50	0.33	0.25
128	53.33	18.29	16.00	8.00	4.00	2.67	2.00	1.33	1.00	0.66	0.50
256	106.67	36.57	32.00	16.00	8.00	5.33	4.00	2.67	2.00	1.33	1.00
512	213.33	73.14	64.00	32.00	16.00	10.67	8.00	5.33	4.00	2.65	2.00
1024	426.67	146.29	128.00	64.00	32.00	21.33	16.00	10.67	8.00	5.31	4.00
1500	625.00	214.29	187.50	93.75	46.88	31.25	23.44	15.63	11.72	7.77	5.86
2048	853.33	292.57	256.00	128.00	64.00	42.67	32.00	21.33	16.00	10.61	8.00

proper order. The timestamp field is generally based on a free running clock ticking at 8000 ticks per second. Using timestamps, the RIP clocks in each packet and learns that each packet experienced various delays through the network.

Interestingly, the receiving RTP application does not need to know what the latency is from one end to the other. All RTP needs to know is that voice packets should be arriving every 20 milliseconds, and when they don't, it calculates the variation. In this case, there are 35 milliseconds of jitter. The jitter buffer must now make sure that all other packets experience the same amount of delay by removing the jitter. This means that a packet that arrives with a network delay of 50 milliseconds must be held an additional 35 milliseconds so that it will be delayed 85 milliseconds, which matches the slowest packet. The jitter buffer performs this process of making sure all packets experience the same delay. This indeed restores temporal order, but it should be clear to you that there is no advantage to getting most of the voice packets to the other end quickly. They all need to get to the other end quickly. This changes everything about routing. The best effort packet forwarding process of routers is now unacceptable.

It is necessary to prioritize voice packets and get all of them delivered immediately to the other end of the network. It should also be clear that the jitter buffer should be tuned to hold packets long enough to reestablish temporal order, but not too long that the buffer overruns or too short that the buffer underruns.

Business Case for VoIP ROI

VoIP business cases follow the traditional ROI formula:

$$ROI = cumulative\ net\ benefits\ /\ total\ costs \times 100\%$$

As with any IT project, a complete model calculates the total hard and soft costs. Proven metrics and standards are hard to come by due to the infancy of the technology, forcing companies to quantify ROI for their specific organization since comparable case studies likely don't exist. That said companies can generate an ROI figure by accounting for the following hard and soft benefits and costs (including risk):

Hard Benefits   Some of the many hard benefits that can be considered are shown below. We recognize that these are not all inclusive, but know that the starting point must be established.

- Eliminate or reduce intra-office toll charges.
- Avoid service and support contracts on existing telecommunication system hardware and software, or fee-based services (like Centrex).
- Reduce expansion costs via lower costs for adds, moves, and changes; lower user hardware costs.
- Reduce the costs of telecommunications management and support via convergence of resources, which can support the network and telecomm systems with an integrated set of less staff personnel.

Soft Benefits   Some soft benefits, those that are harder to quantify, also play into this model. We tried to at least give you some idea of what you can expect at a minimum.

- Provide productivity benefits for remote and traveling workers who can be empowered with the same integrated capabilities as office workers.
- Reduce user training and learning on phone and messaging systems.
- Cost-effectively implement unified messaging for improved productivity handling voice messages, e-mail, and faxes.
- Reduce systems downtime and improve performance.
- Empower call centers with advanced automation, productivity, and service applications.

Cost Considerations

- VoIP telecommunication hardware and software
- IP phone sets or soft phones
- Network upgrades for possible quality of service and performance upgrades
- Implementation labor and professional services
- Ongoing support and administration labor
- Support and maintenance contracts
- Increased support calls and potential user downtime losses on initial deployment
- IT and user training
- Write-off, write-down, and disposal costs for existing telecommunication assets
- Potential project risks
- Quality of service/performance
- Administration and support skill levels and resources
- Proprietary vs. open systems interoperability

Questions

1. Voice over IP is mainly a movement to get free voice.   T/F
2. VoIP came into existence in the year _____.
   a. 2002
   b. 1990
   c. 1996
   d. 2000

3. The main protocol that the carriers want to use is _____.

    a. PSTN

    b. H.323

    c. SIP

    d. H.248

4. What protocol is fast becoming the accepted standard for end users?

    a. SIP

    b. H.323

    c. H.248

    d. MGC

5. The ITU standard that allows H.323 devices to register and gain admission onto the network is called:

    a. H.323

    b. H.245

    c. H.248

    d. H.225

6. The quality of voice calls is continually rising to the point that it is the same as PSTN calls.   T/F

7. What protocol advertises the sessions that are created?

    a. SDP

    b. SIP

    c. SCP

    d. SAP

8. What device is the equivalent of a traffic cop using H.323 protocols?

    a. Gateway

    b. MCU

    c. Codec

    d. Gatekeeper

9. One can say honestly that there is no ROI in VoIP, instead it is strictly an emotional decision.   T/F

10. The majority of corporations today are at least experimenting with VoIP.   T/F

11. What layer 4 protocol (OSI layer) does RTP depend on?

    a. TCP

    b. IP

    c. UDP

    d. SDP

Session Initiation Protocol (SIP)

After reading this chapter and completing the questions, you will be able to:

- Discuss the hype over SIP
- Understand the protocols used in a SIP network
- Discuss use of a media gateway
- Converse on how to put all the pieces together

In the previous chapter, we covered the generic version of H.323, SIP, and H.248. Because the industry is headed toward acceptance of SIP in the norm, it is appropriate that we cover this topic in greater detail. Moreover, many users and organizations are using some form of SIP through companies like Packet 8 and Vonage. Thus we shall look at the components and see how we might create a connection. This chapter is therefore more of a how to hook it up section rather than what it is.

Throughout this chapter we discuss the use of SIP for the VoIP (Voice over Internet protocol) interconnection. SIP is an application layer control (signaling) protocol for creating, modifying, and terminating sessions with one or more participants. These sessions include Internet multimedia conferences, Internet telephone calls, and multimedia distribution. Members in a session can communicate via multicast or via a mesh of unicast relations, or a combination of these.

SIP itself is not sufficient to set up a phone call. Other IETF (Internet engineering task force) standards are required to support a VoIP phone call. The most important ones are listed here, but this is by no means an exhaustive list. For instance, this list does not include any QoS (quality of service) controls or any of the advanced RTP-oriented standards as well. In order to understand the basics of SIP, a well-rounded understanding of these protocols is sufficient.

- *SIP*: Sets up and tears down calls.
- *SDP*: Describes the media session similar to H.245.

- *RTP*: Carries the voice over a packet switched network.

- *RTSP*: Supports services like voice mail or any service where you want to remotely control a media server that stores recordings of voice only, voice and video, video only, and music.

SIP compares with H.323 in many ways. Some features of SIP are like H.323, and some of the standards are identical, such as RTP. SIP is the signaling protocol that sets up and tears down calls, so it compares with H.225 and RAS (restoration, admission, and status protocol) because H.225 is the protocol that H.323 uses to set up and tear down calls. RAS is the protocol used in H.323 that permits communications with a gatekeeper. The SIP standard includes this capability inside the SIP standard, but the SIP gatekeeper is called a SIP server. The SIP protocol describes communications to and from the SIP servers.

- SDP replaces H.245. The difference is that SDP performs the same task as H.245 in far fewer steps than is required in H.323 slow start.

- SIP uses RTP and RTCP (RTP control protocol), so in this case both H.323 and SIP use the same voice transport standard.

- SIP can use RTSP to provide voice mail services.

SIP uses a text-based protocol that makes it easy to integrate into Java-based systems, especially HTTP (hypertext transfer protocol). H.323, like most protocols from the ITU, uses abstract syntax notation, which is more precise and compact than text-based protocols. Many people think that the benefit of ASN1 (abstract syntax notation one) is outweighed by its complexity and unfriendliness toward an all-text-based Web mentality.

SIP uses all-text and signaling strategies that are very similar to HTTP (Web) and SMTP (e-mail) protocols. This makes SIP the favorite for people that have lots of experience working with e-mail and Web server code. H.323 uses ISDN's Q.931-based mentality that is poorly understood outside of telecom circles.

We will now discuss the very rich portfolio of services that are available through SIP-based communications. This functionality will drive improved productivity by making it easier and more efficient for end-users to communicate no matter where they are in the world. At the same time, SIP-based communications enhance flexibility by providing enterprises a variety of platforms, endpoints, and servers to utilize.

Some of the integrated features of SIP are:

1. Groupware integration with IP messaging

2. Lotus messenger integration

3. Presence server integration with Microsoft Live Communications Server (LCS)

4. Standards adoption such as XML, VXML, and Java

5. Common subscriber database and administration

TABLE 18.1   Comparison of H.323 and SIP

Factor	H.323	SIP
Design	Complex (736-page spec)	Simple (128-page spec)
Number of elements	100s	37
Messages	Based on ASN1	HTTP and RTSP
Call setup	Multiple requests	Single request
Extensibility	Nonstandard	Use session description protocol
Large phone number domains	Designed for LAN	Designed for IP networks
Conferencing	Limited	Open to all sizes
Firewall support	Difficult	Easier
Interoperability among vendors	Poor	Good

The SIP proxy compares to the H.323 gatekeeper. In fact, the SIP proxy has two modes of operation, the SIP proxy arid SIP redirect mode, which compares closely with H.323's gatekeeper routed and direct endpoint signaling, respectively.

Compare SIP with H.323 and other signaling protocols. They all need to perform the same function, which is to set up and tear down calls. The need for so many different protocols that largely do the same thing is based mostly on the type of telephone service being supported, as well as the network that the phone call will traverse. Some protocols, like SS7 (signaling system 7), make very strict assumptions on the bearer channel. SIP, on the other hand, makes no assumptions on the channel that will ultimately carry the voice. In fact, SIP does not assume that a voice call is being set up, and it can just as easily set up a video, voice and video, text session, or any other instant communications session you can imagine. The extreme flexibility of SIP is one of the reasons that SIP is becoming so popular. A comparison of the protocols is shown in Table 18.1.

SIP Servers Should Be Called SIP

Because you are probably expecting a much more complicated explanation, have you noticed that Web servers are called www? Do not think that it is required to call your Web sever www? You may call it something other than www, but it is normally not in your interest to do so. Consider this example. Suppose you work at xyz corporation. If your company was on the ball, many years ago it obtained the subdomain xyz.com. So you name your server www.xyz.com, because people expect you to name your Web server www. Could you name your Web server "my_fantasticlittleweb_server.xyz.com?" Of course, you could. If you do, keep in mind that the only people that will find your Web server are hackers, because no one would ever think that your Web server would have that name. For the same reason, you are to name your SIP server SIP. This means that xyz would name its SIP server: sip.xyz.com.

SIP methods are the commands sent by SIP clients to start, end or modify a call. SIP methods also can support instant messaging (IM)-type services that can tell you when your friends log into the network. The SIP methods originally described in RFC 2543 where telephony oriented, but now they have been expanded to support not only telephony but also IM services like America Online offers. When a SIP method is sent, the receiving end is expected to respond to the method with a number code, called a SIP response that indicates how the method is being processed.

SIP URIs (uniform resource indicators) are used to identify the called party, as well as the server that knows the whereabouts of the calling party. Sometimes, the SIP URI indicates only the peak of a chain of servers that ultimately knows the whereabouts of the called party.

Transport layer security (TLS) creates a private tunnel between communicating applications. When a client and a server exchange information, TLS keeps the communications private so that no third party may eavesdrop or tamper with any message. Secure sockets layer (SSL) is the predecessor to TLS. To accomplish this, TLS is composed of two layers: the TLS record protocol, which can optionally provide encryption, and the SIP handshake protocol, which performs authentication.

The SIP phone consists of a user agent, which in turn consists of two logical elements, called the SIP UAC (user agent client) and SIP UAS (user agent server). The SIP UAC is the client portion of the UA, so it gives the orders by sending SIP methods and receiving response codes. The SIP UAS receives SIP methods and processes them, and in turn sends SIP responses. Usually, the UAS and the UAC are viewed as a single software entity, the SIP user agent.

A SIP server processes SIP calls, providing advanced features as well as call routing. The STP server is expected to be online at all times unlike a SIP phone that may be unplugged at anytime.

The SIP location server is a database of any type you may choose that stores the whereabouts of SIP users. Each caller in a SIP call is uniquely identified by three fields: To, From, and Call-ID. This facilitates modifications to this call, such as adding multiple parties to a call, dropping parties out of a call, reconnecting a dropped party, and forwarding to voice mail. The list of things that can happen during a call is endless. There needs to be a way to keep track of all the callers and which call each belongs to. A dialog does just that. Now SIP servers can keep track of SIP calls in order to process each correctly.

Content-type contains a description of the message body, SDP in this case. Content-length contains an octet (byte) count of the message body. The details of the session, such as the type of media, codec, or sampling rate, are not described using SIP. Rather, the body of a SIP message contains a description of the session, encoded in some other protocol format. One such format is the SDP (RFC 2327). An SDP message is carried by the SIP message in a way that is analogous to a document attachment being carried by an e-mail message, or a Web page being carried in an HTTP message.

Because SIP uses SDP, it is possible that messages could be dropped by the network and never reach the intended destination. SIP uses the response codes as an acknowledgment of the SIP request. The INVITE message uses a three-step handshake because the response to an INVITE must also be reliable. In this case, the 100 and 200 messages are dropped by the network for an unknown reason.

Perhaps it was congestion or bit errors. The reason for the lost packet is not important to SIP. It simply retransmits when an acknowledgment fails to be received.

The final ACK confirms the 200 OK was received, and the called party stops sending responses to the INVITE. In reality, lost packets are rare, and in a scenario like this where five packets out of 12 are dropped is so poor, the connection could not support a VoIP call anyhow.

The Zultys phone, shown in Fig. 18.1, is an IP phone that runs SIP software. It comes with a three-Ethernet jacks, a connection to the network and external power module as shown in Fig. 18.2. You program the phone through a built-in Web interface. It is possible to power the phone over Ethernet (PoE). If you power the phone at the desktop, that is not a problem. The Zultys phone is ideal if you want a solid entry level device. Other phones like Cisco's 7960, shown in Fig. 18.3, are now SIP software driven.

RTSP is like a VCR (video cassette recorder) remote control. The protocol is designed to permit a remote device to control a media server. Just like a VCR remote control,

Figure 18.1   The Zultys phone is a SIP driven phone.

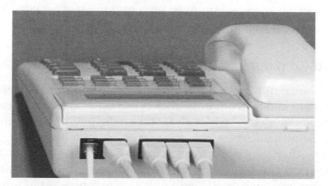

Figure 18.2   The back side of the Zultys phone reveals multiple ports for connections to the uplink and other devices (printer, PC, and the like).

Figure 18.3   The Cisco 7960 is now software driven SIP phone.

RTP provides a protocol that allows an application, like Windows Media Player or RealOne Player, to control the streaming of data to the video screen and audio card. You can fast forward, rewind, halt, erase, and the like, just like a VCR remote control. The application for RTSP in Voice over IP is to provide a voice mail retrieval interface.

RTSP is an application-level protocol with syntax and operations similar to HTTP, but works for audio and video. It uses URLs (uniform resource locators) like those in HTTP. An RTSP server needs to maintain states using SETUP, TEARDOWN, and other methods. Unlike HTTP, in RTSP both servers and clients can issue requests. RTSP is implemented on multiple operating system platforms and allows interoperability between clients and servers from different manufacturers.

The media description is stored on a Web server W, and is accessed via HTTP. The SDP provides the media description of the movie's audio and video streams; including the codecs that are available, dynamic RTP payload types, the protocol stack, and content information such as language or copyright restrictions. The timeline of the movie may also be provided.

Presence-Based Communications and Instant Messaging

Presence shown in Fig. 18.4 is a new and core communication capability not available in circuit-switched telecom networks. A simple example of "presence" is an instant message client's "buddy list," which lists the user's "buddies" and their current state—online or offline. Additional state information, such as whether they are currently active or idle and whether they are currently typing a message response or not, is also provided using presence. This type of primitive presence coupled with an advanced signaling and presence protocol such as SIP will give rise to a new set of advanced services currently unknown to telephony.

Figure 18.4 Presence creates an instant "buddy list" on the phone.

Presence can be used for such services as:

- Make "polite" calls, only when you see a smiley icon.
- Avoid phone tag during busy hours.
- Automatic callback on presence.
- Ad hoc conference calls based on presence.
- Avoid waiting for call center agents—replace ACD (automatic call distributor) with agent presence.
- On-the-air presence for mobile phones.
- Presence coupled with location.

The popularity of multifaceted icons for buddies in IM clients illustrate the potential not only of presence, but also the possibility of replacing the familiar phone pad with an IM-like caller's "dial pad." New interfaces in communication devices may have much more in common with the IM interface than with the telephony dial pad. Presence is also the key for tying endpoints across multiple network boundaries and thus will be a critical tool for fixed-mobile convergence.

Several features distinguish enterprise IM services from consumer presence and IM:

- Security that can adequately support authentication and privacy for sensitive business communications
- Ability to expand presence functionality beyond short text communications; it also can be used to initiate voice calls, start conferences, and generate automatic callback
- Standards-based approach to signaling, message transfer, and XML-based data formats
- Using the same SIP-enabled infrastructure, applications, and data for all communications services in the enterprise—text, voice, video, data, and application sharing
- Choice of clients, servers, and applications from different vendors
- Avoiding duplicate databases for customer and service related data

Unified Messaging (UM): Voice Mail, E-mail, IM, SMS

IP communication supports the seamless integration of voice and video mail with e-mail, IM, and wireless short message service (via mobile network to SIP/IP gateways). An application example is shown in Fig.18.5 for voice mail.

In Fig. 18.5, a mobile user or a user on the PSTN is trying to call a user that has an IP communication service and can be reached at a SIP phone and/or IP devices. The call (1) is first routed by the PSTN gateway to the SIP server for the called party (2) and from

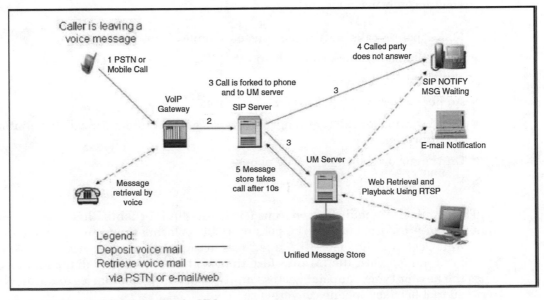

Figure 18.5   A mobile user using the UM.

there to the SIP phone (3). If the called party does not answer (4), the SIP servers will proxy the call to the UM server. The caller can now deposit the voice message (5).

The notification for "message waiting" will appear (a) as a flashing light on the SIP phone—as is usual on PBX and mobile phones, (b) as an e-mail notification and also (c) on a UM Web page. Message waiting notification by e-mail and the Web has the advantage of playback control, using any standard compliant Web media player. An SMS (short messaging system) message can also be sent to a mobile phone. Voice mail can also be retrieved the old fashioned way by calling in from the PSTN or from a mobile phone.

An integrated package with Microsoft Exchange or Outlook can be easily accomplished with many of the SIP packages, such as with AVAYA and INN Corp. A list of messages shows both e-mail and voice mail and can also display fax messages. Upon clicking on a voice mail entry, the media player will play out the voice message.

Multiple Conferencing Modes and Media

SIP-based conferencing can be implemented in many models, and covers scheduled PSTN-like conferences, small ad hoc conferences, the transition from a two-way call to a multiparty conference and multicast group conferences. SIP conferences can be used for text only as in IM, for voice, voice and video, with data, and for games. As mentioned, presence can be used for the setup of ad hoc conferences, and it enables a new spectrum of conference services, from spontaneous to rigorously scheduled controlled conferences.

Call Routing Options and Route Recording

In the PSTN, the commercially most valuable services of the intelligent network are based on call routing, depending on various criteria, such as origination, destination, and time of day. The SIP protocol takes routing to its full potential and also adds routing control by the end user as an additional feature in caller preferences.

ENUM and Directory Services

E.164 telephone NUMber (ENUM) mapping to IP allows finding all communication contact addresses, such as mail, PSTN, mobile phones, fax, and SIP when given a standard E.164 telephone number. ENUM technology has many service routing applications, among them directory services that can return all of an individual's listed phone and fax numbers, e-mail addresses, IM, SMS, and paging address, and so on.

Contact Addresses

The SIP protocol allows you to resolve an *address of record* to multiple *contact addresses* with preferences selected by the user, so that calls can be routed based on who the caller is, based on time/date and on the location of the called party (work, travel, home). The call will then be routed to the preferred communication device.

Secure Communications

The IP communication architecture deploys multiple Internet security mechanisms for secure and confidential signaling and media. The high security possible for IP communications has to be harmonized with the legal intercepts required by law enforcement agencies and is a topic still under discussion.

SIP provides the ability to authenticate callers based on a shared secret, such as username and password. It will also provide, in the future, the ability to send all signaling messages over a secure transport, such as SSL (secure sockets layer), so that the nature of SIP signaling would not be discernable from captured IP packets without breaking the encryption scheme.

Global Mobility

Application level mobility for IP communications has three facets:

Personal Mobility

The user is reachable under the same identifier on several networks, at several terminals, and possibly at the same time.

Service Mobility

Ability to obtain the same services while roaming: services, personalized GUI (graphical user interface), directory, "dial plan" and other "sticky" service features.

Terminal Mobility

The user is reachable by the same SIP address, using dynamically acquired IP addresses. This can support pre-call mobility, mid-call mobility, and recovery from disconnect.

User Preferences

Callers can specify via the SIP user agent the routing and disposition of their calls, while the called party can specify a rich portfolio of preferences for receiving calls. For example, a caller can specify if they wish to avoid speaking to machines and a called party may block all work-related calls during nonwork hours. Many services can be built using these capabilities. The important point to keep in mind is the standard nature of communicating these preferences when routing calls between networks from different service providers—a capability that is impossible between proprietary IP PBXs or proprietary softswitches.

Gateway Services

While the majority of the global public telephone traffic still uses the PSTN, and most of the installed PBXs are also circuit-switched of the TDM (time division multiplexed) type, most phone calls to and from IP devices require gateways, such as:

- Network gateways in carrier networks that support SS7 (signaling system 7) for high call volumes
- Enterprise gateways to connect legacy PBXs to a local area or wide area networks
- Local gateways for 800 calls, 911 emergency calls, and 411 directory calls

Improvements of PSTN Functionality

Leaving aside for now the significant voice traffic migration to mobile telephone networks, the advent of the Internet and its associated technologies are forcing telecommunication companies and their vendors to face the facts that

1. Telecommunication networks have a competitor in the Internet.
2. The deployed technology is obsolete.

What Is a Closed System?

Closed systems, such as the traditional PBX or telephone company switch have the design and change control entirely in the hands of the respective vendor. To enhance this control, switch vendors will also protect the design with as many patents as possible, so that intellectual property claims may keep the competition at bay.

As a result of the intelligent network concept, telephone companies have embraced the need for control of the services to be outside the switch, in server farms that may be procured from other sources. End users still have no control over the service, and innovation by third parties is practically impossible.

The Internet and the World Wide Web by contrast are built entirely on public standards and without intellectual property claims or the notion of end-to-end control. Services are in the hands of users, which provide a wide open field for innovation.

In the context of Voice over IP, a closed system cannot be expanded with components from competing vendors using public standards. Examples of closed systems are "softswitches" and proprietary IP PBXs. In such systems, it is not possible to choose the following from different sources:

- IP phones
- IP-PSTN gateways
- Service controllers
- SIP servers
- IVRs, VoiceXML, and speech recognition systems

- Media and announcement servers
- Conference bridges
- Voice mail and UM

Closed systems may support standard protocols to the outside, such as having ISDN trunks or SIP ports on the IP side, but this does not make them open systems. Besides open protocols between all the mentioned components, standard data formats are also required.

One of the penalties of closed systems is the need to maintain multiple instances of similar user and service data in multiple systems. This is not a trivial task and may lead to increased cost of ownership, besides the occasional errors when duplicating data.

An interesting point is the claim that "open" application programming interfaces (APIs), qualify softswitches and some IP PBXs to be open systems. APIs have usually two intellectual property owners:

1. The owner of the operating system and
2. The owner of the softswitch system.

Java and Jinni occupy an interesting middle ground, since no accredited standards body has intellectual property and change control. The Internet in most cases does not standardize APIs, but rather protocols, for architectural reasons. It does not matter how an IP device is implemented (this is best left to the designer and to the competition in the marketplace), but only how it speaks and behaves over the Net.

Examples of How SIP Improves upon Traditional Telephony

The fast ascent of the Web and e-mail was due in part to the fact that telecom services simply had nothing comparable to offer. But even for such telecom services as telephony, the existing telephone networks are technically obsolete regarding the services potential. Following are several examples of traditional telephony functionality that are enhanced in a SIP environment.

Call Transfer in Voice Mode Only

Many or most telecom engineers are challenged when trying to transfer a voice call due to the difficult and primitive user interfaces (compared to icons and mouse clicks) found in various telephony systems. But even attendants, who understand how to transfer a voice call, may prefer to do the "attended" part of an attended call transfer using IM with the transferred-to party, before making the transfer. Thus when a call from a customer comes in, the attendant may quickly send an IM to ask what to do, while still talking to the caller. Upon receiving an IM reply, the call may be transferred to the requested called party or somewhere else, such as voice mail.

Automatic Callback

Presence can be used for automatic callback. Thus if the called party becomes available, for example, has the cell phone on the air, or the called IP phone is no longer busy, an application can initiate a callback, thus saving unsuccessful call attempts and the resulting phone tag.

Internet communication engineers believe presence to be a key ingredient of the radically new capabilities of IP communications, since there are many other applications enabled by presence, for example, ad hoc conference calls and the replacement of automatic call distributors (ACD) in call centers.

Ad Hoc Conference Call

Scheduling multiparty conference calls to accommodate busy calendars is often hard work. Many e-mails are exchanged to find a suitable date/time for a multiparty conference call. Presence enables applications that automatically invoke a conference call when the intended participants are online and available to users in a convenient fashion.

Call Distributor Queue

Customers calling an 800 number for assistance are often frustrated by long waiting times to get to an agent that can answer specific questions, only to wait again when transferred from one 3 agent to another. Presence enables agents with the desired skills, selected by the calling customer to call back, thereby avoiding waiting by the customer online.

Web-Sharing and Data Collaboration

An agent talking to a customer or employees in a conference cannot exchange documents during the call, except sending files by e-mail or by looking up Web pages so as to share information. The telephone network has no means of pushing Web pages during a voice call using the same signaling mechanisms as used to set up and maintain the conference call. There are no shared whiteboard capabilities, file transfer or data capabilities of any type; no possibility to facilitate understanding between speakers familiar with different languages, so the Internet has to be used anyway.

Mobility

The most sophisticated PBX or PSTN/Centrex services are lost to the user outside the premises of the enterprise. Even such common services as 800 numbers are not valid outside the country or calling area. This is in contrast to the Internet and the Web, where public IP addresses and URLs have global significance, and services like e-mail and Web pages can be accessed in the same way wherever the user may be and, typically, whatever device, operating system and application is employed for access to Internet services. Advanced enterprise IP services can also be securely accessed by roaming users from anywhere.

These are only some examples to illustrate the technical obsolescence of local class 5 and PBX services for consumers and for enterprises alike. There are many applications enabled by integrating voice communications with Internet and Web applications. Such applications are given in various Internet drafts related to the SIP protocol, though we believe some of the most successful may not yet be invented.

Installing a SIP Box

We have a Sipura telephone adapter that allows us to connect an old analog phone to it. From there we add a LAN connection and can program the IP address to our local network addressing. Next we connect the LAN to our backbone router (or DSL modem in this case) and we are ready to make a phone call across the LAN or across the WAN. See the diagram created in Fig. 18.6 for the layout.

We also can use a similar situation with a connection to a hub and SIP gateway as seen in Fig. 18.7. This one uses a Cisco 4200 device and a small hub for connection to the LAN and WAN.

Functionally, we can see a model being laid out as seen in Fig. 18.8 with a key telephone system, a PBX, or any other telephony device connecting through the SIP gateway and then to the WAN.

LAN and Power

2 Analog Phones or Fax Machines. FXS Connections

Figure 18.6   The layout of the Sipura box and the network.

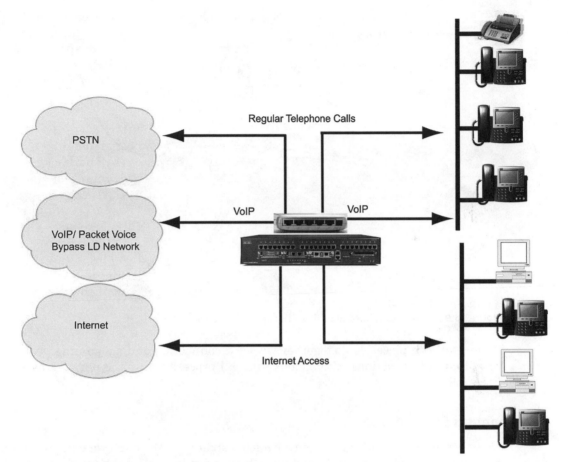

Figure 18.7   The higher end system with a Cisco 4200.

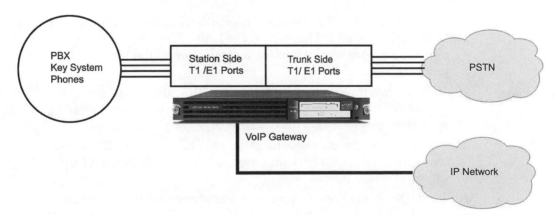

Figure 18.8   The SIP model for any device.

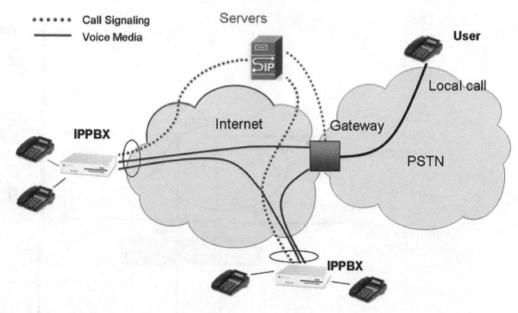

Figure 18.9   The final connection using SIP across the network.

Once all the pieces come together we see a connection and a signaling protocol that coordinate the functions of telephony and call process across the network as shown in Fig. 18.9.

Implementing SIP

How does one go about implementing such a strategy? Although we will not attempt to create a full implementation plan here, because it is beyond the scope of our engagement, there are some basic steps we can suggest to get the process started.

1. Begin by determining the user expectations and requirements. (Will the use of VoIP place any added burden on the LAN? The case we have presented should not be as we are recommending a connection to the legacy PBX connected to a gateway.)
2. Do you have the capacity in the legacy PBX to add one or more PRI interfaces or T1 cards? Are these cards available? Order them early in the game or reuse ones that may free up with the shift in traffic.
3. Conduct a readiness assessment on your LAN and WAN connections (in many cases the circuits that are proposed may just be swung over to a VoIP gateway in lieu of a new installation).
4. Train the IT staff on the protocols and standards interfaces for VoIP.
5. Assess the present utilization on the current links.

6. Determine the QoS requirements. (Should an MPLS solution be considered?)

7. Determine the codec to be used. (We suggested the G.723.1, but you may choose a different codec.)

8. What signaling protocol will you use? (We recommended SIP as a solution because it is fast becoming an industry standard.)

9. Select the one-way latency budget. (We recommend keeping it under 150 milliseconds, but if targets allow, shoot for 120 milliseconds.)

10. What is an acceptable level of packet loss? (1–4% should be average.)

11. What is the jitter buffer sized to do? (We suggest that you keep this around 25 milliseconds or less if possible.)

12. Serialization delay is a consideration, but we recommended a full T1 in all cases, which should minimize the delay on a packet size of <160 bytes.

13. Should you support multiple protocols? (SIP and H.323 are the main choices. H.323 is an ITU standard, so perhaps you may want to consider both.)

14. Does the gateway support these protocols? (The gateways we discussed will support both H.323 and SIP.)

15. What about the routing protocols used in your data network? (Are these in any way impacted by a VoIP solution for your network?)

16. What security such as authentication, NAT, and firewall will be required? (We recommend some form of proxy server from the ITSP to block DoS attacks and a myriad of other issues.)

17. Can you get CDR records? (The ITSP we recommended states that real time CDR records are available online.)

18. Size the circuits appropriately. (We recommended a full T1 in all cases. However, you can choose to select less for some sites.)

19. Order the equipment and the local loops.

20. Order the ITSP services.

21. Install as appropriate.

22. Train the people on the use of hard or soft phones that you may choose to experiment. On legacy phones, there should be transparency in the system. If any reprogramming is needed for the legacy PBX routing, program the changes as appropriate.

23. Select the test group in each site that will assess quality and service fairly. In some cases you may want to experiment with different codecs and packet sizes to see if there are any perceivable differences. Select the MOS (mean opinion score) best befitting the organization.

24. Continually monitor the legal and regulatory scenes for changes in countries that will allow VoIP.

Questions

1. What layer 4 (OSI) does SIP run on?

    a. Layer 3

    b. Layer 4

    c. Layer 7

    d. Layer 2

2. What is the SIP gateway called?

    a. Gatekeeper

    b. Proxy

    c. Registrar

    d. Gateway

3. What is the standards committee settling on SIP?

    a. ITU

    b. ANSI

    c. IETF

    d. IEEE

4. Who stands to benefit from the use of SIP?

    a. Consumers

    b. Carriers

    c. Both a and b

    d. None of the above

5. What services are not part of SIP right now?

    a. TV

    b. Video

    c. Voice mail

    d. Instant messaging

6. In RTSP who issues a request for services?

    a. Servers

    b. Clients

    c. Both a and b

    d. Neither a nor b

7. RTSP maintains both _____ and _____ states.
   a. Setup
   b. Teardown
   c. Invite
   d. Release
   e. Failure

8. The name we give to services of SIP is called_____.
   a. SCP
   b. Presence
   c. Instant messaging
   d. Unified messaging

9. What device connects the analog network user to the SIP network?
   a. The terminal adapter
   b. The router
   c. The IP telephony system
   d. All of the above

IP Telephony

After reading this chapter and completing the questions, you will be able to:

- Discuss the hype over IP telephony (IPT) solutions
- Understand how IPT is replacing traditional TDM systems
- Discuss the range of features available
- Converse on how all the pieces come together

As the convergence of voice and data continues, one of the enablers will be the broadband network. Increasing bandwidth, which translates into greater productivity and the extension of new applications for remote workers, will have a fundamental impact on the corporation.

PBX Equipment and IP Telephony Comparisons

An organization's goal should be to answer the following questions:

1. What vendors can service the organization's needs?
2. What products are available to meet the company's needs?
3. What are the protocols available?
4. Is there a ROI (return on investment) in using IPT and VoIP?
5. Are managed services a possibility?
6. What should an organization do for the new corporate and branch offices?
7. Is there a benefit of using VoIP between sites?
8. Can VoIP deliver a ROI for customer calls?
9. What about international calls?

In this converged world, the corporate enterprise, which includes both voice and data, will be extended to all locations—creating "virtual cubicles" in employees' homes and in satellite offices. With the addition of remote business voice, off-premises employees can have the same level of voice and data services they had in the office, including access to the Internet, the corporate intranet, and the private branch exchange (PBX). Industry still primarily uses separate voice and data networking tools, offering some opportunities for convergence over the longer term. To date, no compelling reason had been found for converging the PBX and the data networking standards in use. That said, we all have an opportunity to sit back and wait for VoIP to mature before being forced to implement. This offers some unique opportunities to experiment (in advance of roll out) with the tools and capabilities. The current PBX technologies installed at most organizations are used for voice only, as a PBX is normally used. The manufacturers continue to support the system and state that they will provide one more upgrade to the current PBX before ceasing to support it in the future. This means that we all could squeeze as much as 5 years of extended life from the current system.

VoIP will offer many new opportunities to converge the technologies, but still requires added tools and services before being used en masse. Thus, we see the migration being handled only when the vendors offering the products can demonstrate the maturity and convergence unequivocally.

One converged network for both voice and data has many benefits:

- For the remote worker, there is one network to manage, one piece of remote access equipment and one service provider for both voice and data.

- From a management standpoint, ease of administration and consolidation of services through fewer providers is attractive.

Business voice is the inclusion of the digital set on the desktop and the PBX with all of its features and applications typically like that, seen in Fig. 19.1. It is the most valuable business tool for many employees, and it's also one of a corporation's largest infrastructure investments. The overall cost of installing a PBX and the associated wiring infrastructure (albeit separate from the data wiring) is significant to most organizations. For many companies this could amount to an investment starting at $1 million or more.

Imagine the impact on employee productivity and customer satisfaction if business phones were not installed in your office. Instead of 3- or 4-digit dialing for internal calls to speak to a coworker, the caller would have to dial ten digits and would not have the ability to transfer a caller to another department. Conferencing of customers and vendors at the touch of a button would not exist. Equally important are the applications running behind the scenes on the corporation's PBX—least cost call routing, automated call distribution (ACD) applications, departmental expense tracking and client billing options. Providing all employees with these business voice capabilities is critical to a company's success.

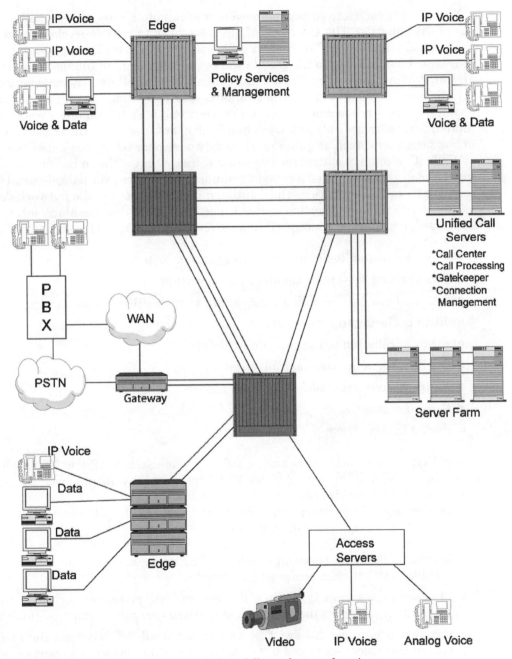

Figure 19.1 An IP telephony solution includes a full complement of services.

Yet, when it comes to remote employees and remote access, the phone has been left out of the equation. The extension of business voice to remote workers is much more than just delivering VoIP or central office (CO) voice. It includes providing the same full-featured digital set to the remote worker, providing all of the features on the PBX and supporting applications, and delivering a reliable, toll-quality call every time.

Delivering voice over packet networks is relatively simple; delivering toll-quality business voice is much more complex. For users to have a high-quality voice experience there needs to be not only sufficient bandwidth, but also all of the features important to business users, such as guaranteed quality of service (QoS) and network security.

While it's simple to extend the corporate voice system within a building or over dedicated circuits between fixed locations, extending PBX voice over packet-based networks requires more sophistication. The solution must be able to handle network delays and packet bursts while supporting a wide range of network devices. Many issues must be addressed, which affect voice performance and call quality, including:

- IP packetization (voice and signaling) and prioritization
- Fixed or user selectable compression algorithms
- PBX and handset signaling (proprietary to each PBX manufacturer)
- Jitter buffering to compensate for network delays
- Echo cancellation to compensate for delays
- Double talk detection and compensation
- Ambient noise creation
- Error detection
- Packet loss recovery

Some typical characteristics and benefits for the use of VoIP and IP telephony that might be considered are seen in Table 19.1. The table lists the potential benefits of the new technologies, which further push toward acceptance.

The most significant perceived benefits and drivers of VoIP and IPT are financial savings and easy implementation of innovative services:

- Internet telephony service providers (ITSP) may use a single infrastructure to provide both Internet access and Internet telephony.
- Cheaper voice service is the tip of the iceberg. VoIP points the way to powerful communication networks that do much more than carry mere conversations.
- Data-oriented layer 2/3 switches can be deployed for switching data as well as packetized voice. Voice and data sharing the same network is part of a grander scheme described as "network convergence"—a single network that transports not just voice and data, but also high-quality, real-time video efficiently.
- Multiplexing data and voice together also results in better bandwidth utilization than in today's over-engineered voice-or-nothing links.

TABLE 19.1   Characteristics and Benefits of IP Telephony

Characteristics	Key IP Solution Aspect	Potential Benefit
Small sites, in cases where there is less investment in existing infrastructure and a low level of functionality	Packaged solutions allow exceptional functionality in a box for relatively low prices	High
Large strategic locations, which see IP as a competitive advantage	May be using IP trunking between sites already. Can offer integrated multimedia solutions to clients and customers	High
Greenfield sites	Lack of existing TDM and circuit switched infrastructure means cost avoidance possible	High
Visionary businesses wishing to become knowledge-led, and to break down the boundaries between customer and the enterprise	IP communication can roll out throughout the enterprise. Applications can be more quickly developed and deployed in an IP environment	High
Virtual site creation with overseas or domestic sites	Reduce call costs by IP trunking (especially overseas)	Medium
Doubled infrastructure management (telephony and IT)	Writing off the telephony network will save money on salaries and maintenance, but it is important to make sure the network staff understands voice as well as data	Low-Medium
Brownfield sites in the right stage of technology refresh cycle (switch end-of-life)	Cost avoidance for TDM-based switch, but still need to consider how applications will reside on an IP PBX, and cost of upgrade to the network	Low-Medium

- Corporations could take advantage of flat Internet pricing vs. hierarchical public switched telephone network (PSTN) pricing and save money while routing long-distance calls over the Internet. This is especially true in Europe and Asia, where the prices of long-distance calls are still much higher than in the United States.

- The use of IPT may also lead to profit from its software-oriented nature: software solutions are more easily extended and integrated with other services and applications, e.g., white-boarding, corporate-wide electronic calendar, instant messaging (presence) or WWW.

- Deployment of new IP telephony services requires significantly lower investment in terms of time and money than in the traditional time-division multiplexing (TDM) telephone environment. Although this is the general industry feeling, it is not as evident when first attempting to price services, because there is no equal TDM product in many cases.

However, widespread business deployment is still somewhat hindered by lower quality of Voice over IP, particularly by higher delay and jitter. The delay problem was improved by creating prioritizing schemes like multiprotocol label switching (MPLS) that distinguishes voice packets from general data. It works like a traffic cop, ensuring that voice always moves ahead of data in an expeditious manner. Moreover, many technical aspects of accounting, billing, charging, and roaming still remain partially unsolved. These issues must be addressed before any major undertaking is considered.

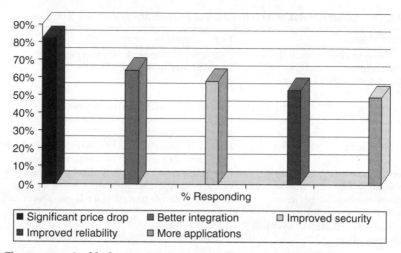

Figure 19.2   Changes required before companies move to IP telephony and VoIP.

Many organizations are still considering the move to IP telephony and VoIP, but feel that changes must occur before they are willing to use it. In January 2005, the Gartner Group surveyed 200 mid-sized and large organizations in the United States and Western Europe. The main changes that need to be addressed before acceptance are shown in Fig. 19.2.

This chart shows the number who expressed a concern about the specific products and services. Security of VoIP became the third ranked issue when the question was posed.

Keeping the traditional telephone usage procedures the same, while changing the core infrastructure, will aid in the transition to a new technology. The telephone as we know it still must be able to set up and complete a telephone call. The difference between VoIP and IP telephony is that VoIP refers to transferring digitized audio data across an IP network; IP telephony implies that this audio data is received by a plain old telephone service (POTS) telephone.

This is not an academic distinction: the usefulness of the telephone lies largely in the huge number of people who can be reached via traditional means. Conversely, VoIP usually reduces "telephony" to a LAN or WAN network service, similar to printing, file sharing or web browsing. VoIP is a nice, neat, technical issue that can be solved with technology alone.

Telephony on the other hand is a complex business, with a mass of technological, legal, regulatory, financial, and business issues that can only be solved with the proper mix of technology and business relationships.

VoIP allows members of an organization to make internal phone calls over their LAN or across their WAN. VoIP implies the same non-POTS phone equipment on either end.

IP telephony allows members of an organization to make phone calls anywhere in the world that is served by the PSTN. IP telephony implies a trusty POTS phone on the called party's end. A comparison of various attributes of VoIP and IP telephony is shown in Table 19.2.

Table 19.2 Summary of Differences between VOIP and IP Telephony

Aspect	Voip	IP Telephony
Functionality	Transfers audio data over an IP network	Transfers audio data to and from the PSTN
Access	Usually LAN or Intranet, now more readily moving to the WAN and Internet	Usually WAN or Internet
Business part	Technology to connect two phone-like devices	Legal, business and regulatory negotiations; billing, accounting system; large enough number of gateways to make economic sense
Uses	Connect members of the same organization for internal phone calls	Connect anyone with the necessary device with anyone on the planet with a phone

Why IP Telephony?

For a private U.S. customer calling within the United States, IP telephony is not a very interesting proposition. After all, domestic U.S. service has excellent quality, and is relatively cheap and extremely reliable. For a private U.S. customer calling abroad, the value proposition is better, but still not very compelling to many places as long-distance fees continue to plummet.

For the commercial U.S. customer there is a base benefit in using the company's network for both telephony and computer communication: if only one network needs to be built and maintained, time and money are saved. If data and your telecom traffic share a common network, then when data traffic is low, more calls can be made and when calls are low, more data can be transferred. In addition, internal phone calls, however far apart workers are, bear no added cost.

For a foreign customer calling within their own country, there are likely to be few savings because of regulation and government regulation. For a foreign customer calling into the United States, IP telephony can be much cheaper than local government-controlled rates offered by the traditional post, telephone, telegraph (PTT) companies. While PTT rates are dropping in many places, those rates are still substantially higher than IP telephony rates.

Voice over IP

IP is "packet-based," which means that the basic unit of exchange in the protocol is a packet. The alternative to packet-based communications is direct or circuit-switched communications. Direct communications are like straws: a one-way, dedicated pipe into which one can pump data at one end and from which one can draw data at the other. Examples of direct communication include serial connections such as those that connect modems to computers, and parallel connections such as those that connect printers to computers. Note that these connections have signaling mechanisms, by which either end can take control of the pipe. This signaling means that the two ends can trade off using the pipe, so the pipe can be two-way, but only in one direction at a time.

If direct connections are like plumbing from a single sink to a single tank with liquid data flowing in only one direction at a time, then packet communications are like a pair of pipes through which packets of data flow like marbles. The marbles are color-coded, so more than one process can send or receive marbles through the same pipe without confusion. The marbles jumble together through the pipe, allowing more than one data stream at a time to flow, as long as the sorter faithfully separates the marbles at the other end.

Of course, sometimes the marbles collide and deflect each other, which delays them, so the marbles do not arrive in any particular sequence or at any fixed interval. Because the packets are marked with a sequence number, this is usually not a problem. TCP/IP guarantees delivery of all packets by requesting retransmission of lost packets in the right order. Collecting packets into a buffer and then passing them along in sequence number order accomplish this.

Using IP means that more data can flow around the network, because the connections aren't direct. If you have a direct connection and you aren't sending or receiving data 100 percent of the time, then some of the connection's capacity (bandwidth) is idle. No one else can use the idle bandwidth; it is just wasted. But if you have an IP connection, then other processes on your computer or other users on the computer, or even other users on other computers, can use whatever bandwidth is idle.

VoIP phone calls are less expensive, because you don't have to pay for a telephone company to build and maintain an expensive, special-purpose network. Instead, you use the Internet or a private converged network whose cost is widely distributed and shared by many groups of people in many different contexts.

For domestic U.S. calls, this argument is not compelling because we have excellent, cheap, and dedicated phone service. However, for many people trying to call long distance in Ireland, Greece, Turkey, Israel, Mexico, and so forth, the cost of a VoIP call can be as little as 10 percent of local PTT rates.

VoIP calls can be made over the same IP infrastructure that IT uses, so businesses would no longer have to maintain separate phone and IT infrastructures. At present, however, VoIP is still not fully formed. It is not widespread or convenient. VoIP has the following restrictions:

- VoIP requires a shared protocol with two aspects: call control and audio data exchange protocol. Universal standards for this protocol are still emerging.

- VoIP suffers from QoS problems. When the network is congested, the quality of a VoIP call is quite bad. Unlike POTS, VoIP bandwidth is not dedicated. Some people may argue with this statement, yet recent studies indicate that the QoS has been steadily declining over the period 2001–2006.

- The IP infrastructure was designed to send data in non-real time. So long as data files and e-mail arrived, the original architects of the Internet were happy. They did not foresee real-time communications over the Internet.

Thus, we see the migration being handled only when the vendors offering the products can demonstrate the maturity and convergence unequivocally. Our recommendation is to use the existing PBX for the next 3–5 years and draw as much benefit from it as possible, while allowing the VoIP products and networking services to mature. When specific applications arise, some organizations may wish to implement VoIP to the desktop to meet that need primarily.

The Switch Is On

Enterprise voice communications are in the midst of a transformation, however. Many pioneering businesses are experimenting and/or migrating from traditional PBX systems, based on TDM, to systems that use IP telephony. The benefit to the enterprise is convergence; IP telephony is just the mechanism.

Converged systems have been available for only a few years, but already account for one-third of all spending on business communications systems. Leading manufacturers have all announced plans to discontinue production of TDM systems. Initially, the introduction of IP telephony systems from large companies like Avaya, Cisco, and Nortel was costly and complex, and the systems lacked even the base functionality of older generation TDM systems. A traditional PBX, for example, may have over 400 features, whereas the IP telephone systems have 200 or less. Start-up companies like Zultys Technologies now offer feature-rich systems that make IP telephony affordable for small- or medium-sized businesses all the way up to large enterprises. Some of the commonly used manufacturers and distributors are:

- Alcatel
- Avaya
- Cisco
- Inter-Tel
- Mitel
- Nortel
- ShoreTel
- Siemens
- Vonexus
- Zultys

What Protocols Are Available?

While a summary of benefits worked out from the perspective of gaining an appreciation of the vendors and the capabilities offered, there was no easy way to compare actual configured systems because of all the variations. Therefore, we chose to compare some of the functionality and protocols used by the various vendors to show what is readily available. This view allowed us to compare the products in different ways and draw some conclusions for any company to follow. Table 19.3 summarizes some of the key factors used by a sampling of the vendors.

While the comparison in the table shows a limited amount of information, the intent was to cover those companies that could support small to large systems and that offered the protocol that is becoming the standard for IP telephony: SIP. This creates a scenario that best fits most organizations that have multiple sites, where many smaller sites may not be able to justify the installation of a new IP PBX, but could benefit from a small unit or a remote server that connects through and to a larger device. The actual implementation would be contingent upon the system at hand when the time comes.

The point now evolves back to the protocol issues, because these are crucial from the perspective of using an IPT solution in conjunction with VoIP. Critical to the consideration is whether to use any forms of encoding and compression protocols when dealing with an IPT and VoIP solution. The most common encoding and compression used are shown in Table 19.4.

So what are the motivations for the switch? According to several of the research houses, two primary driving forces include profits (reduced expenses) and productivity improvements with these new feature sets.

The initial purchase cost of a traditional telephone system is approximately half of the final cost. When we consider the expenses of training, wiring, equipment racks and rooms, air-conditioning, and so on, one can see that a small office system starting at $100,000 can easily pass the $250,000 mark. Operating expenses such as maintenance and replacement costs of a TDM system also add up quickly, where the overall life cycle of a telephone system is 2–2.5 times the initial purchase price. If we use a 10-year straight-line depreciation cycle, then the average cost of such a system is $50,000+ per year. An IP telephony system for roughly the same parameters would be approximately

TABLE 19.3   Key Factors Considered with IP Telephony Systems

	Protocols	Units Networked	Total Users	Encryption	OS
Avaya	SIP, H.323, H.248	250	12,000	Yes	Linux
Cisco	SIP, Skinny (SCCP), H.323	6	100,000+	TLS	Linux
Mitel	H.323, SIP, TAPI, TSAPI JTAPI, CSTA	8 per controller	Unlimited	TLS	VS Works
Siemens	SIP, H.248 MGCP, H.323	Unlimited	Unlimited	TLS, IPSec	Suse Linux
Zultys	SIP, TAPI, VoiceXML	32	10,000	AES	Monta Vista Linux

TABLE 19.4   Common Compression Protocols Used

Usage Scenario	Type Endpoint	Coder	Packet Loss Potential	Latency (One-Way)	Jitter
Traveler	Soft-phone	G.729	1%	100 ms +	± 20 ms
Warehouse	IP wireless	G.729	0	< 5 ms	0
Local office	IP phone	G.711	0	< 5 ms	0
Teleworker	IP phone	G.729	1%	+ 100 ms	± 20 ms

$25,000 per year. (We used a 50 percent value because we have always maintained that a TDM system costs approximately $1000 per user, whereas an IP telephony solution is roughly between $400 and $500, using typical telephone sets. If all high-end telephone sets are used, the cost will obviously escalate dramatically.)

Moves, Adds, and Changes

On average moves, additions, and other changes are expensive depending on the mobility of the organization. A service call to the vendor to relocate a telephone set and modify system software can average $300 or more. One of the best benefits of an IP telephony solution is the savings achieved by moves and changes.

The cost of a move can be as little as $0 when moving a phone in an IP telephone system. Users can plug in the telephone anywhere on the network and still make and receive calls from the new location with little to no intervention from an administrator.

Every IP phone registers with the local call controller that keeps track of location status and personalized configuration details such as speed dials, hunt groups, message routing, and other applications. As the user picks up the handset, the dial tone is delivered to the earpiece and a call request message is initiated between the IP phone and the local call controller via SIP. The local branch call controller detects the number dialed, determines that it is a local call within its known call routing rules, and routes it through integrated analog or digital gateway ports to the PSTN for public network call handling. All the expected call progress messages (line busy or ringing tones) are interpreted and delivered to the display (if so configured) and or earpiece of the handset.

VoIP and IP telephony create new concerns for the IT departments. QoS is a large issue, but others such as "911" calls, power supplies, privacy and security, and Ethernet switches must all be addressed by strategy development.

Growth

Growing a system beyond the initial installation is also fairly simple. In traditional TDM systems, the racks of equipment necessary have been replaced with a PC-based (sized) system. No longer do we need a huge room for the telephone system; now a much smaller area is all that is required.

The cost of the phone itself could be greater, depending on the set. However, wiring, programming, installing, and testing are all reduced to nothing. A single set of wires can support both the data and the voice network needs, replacing about a $350 per port charge on the PBX.

As the business needs change, companies add capacity to the TDM system. In addition to telephones, we need circuit cards to add capacity to the central switching unit. But, what if you grow more than the maximum capacity? Now you will be in a "forklift technology" retrofit that may require a complete system change out. It certainly will cost a lot more than just a few line cards.

Many of the IP telephony solutions from the vendors are merely a software enhancement (albeit you still need to buy the handsets). You can also cluster many systems together such as the way we tied PBX systems together in the old days, but for significantly less money. So the biggest benefit is cost savings? Possibly, but let's continue and see more.

Features

Similarly, the cost of adding major enhancements like voice mail, call center functionality, or integrated voice response (IVR) to a PBX system easily increases the cost to exceed the original cost of the entire system. Also many of the integrated vendor solutions in the PBX world are proprietary architectures. In many cases you are stuck with the same vendor for your whole system, even if there are better choices. If you choose not to use the integrated solution, then the pieces may not work properly together, or the cost of making them work compatibly may far exceed the benefit.

IP-based systems usually include voice mail, instant messaging, IVR, ACD, and (now) presence, along with all of the standard PBX functionality. Future enhancements are just a software upgrade.

One Wire to the Desktop

For businesses opening or moving to new offices, the savings in cabling alone will be significant. Because both voice and data travel over the same LAN, the number of wiring runs (cables pulled) declines by 50 percent. PCs and telephones use the same Ethernet ports. Beyond the fewer cables pulled (we use $350 per cable pull on average) the cost of maintaining the wiring, the number of termination ports and the maintenance costs for this equipment are all cut in half.

Centralized Administration

IP telephony systems do not require a PBX or remote partitions at every remote office. All services, features and functions are controlled and administered from a central location and terminal. A small, inexpensive gateway device at each branch office guarantees interoperability across the entire enterprise, which can span the world. Many times a star-and-spoke solution may be used for robustness and redundancy.

Reduced Toll Costs

Although toll costs have dropped dramatically over the last 20 years, long-distance charges are still a big portion of a company's expenses. With IP-based systems, voice traverses the company private WAN or the Internet. There is no incremental added cost to do this. Businesses already have high-speed private networks, thus adding voice and video means more economical costs. The savings can be substantial—nearly 20–60 percent.

Presence Technologies

Presence is a technology we use to determine when a "buddy" is available. Moreover, the presence technologies allow us to see the "buddy's" status (i.e busy, on a call, etc.) so that we can leave an instant message, a voicemail or an e-mail in lieu of bothering our buddy.

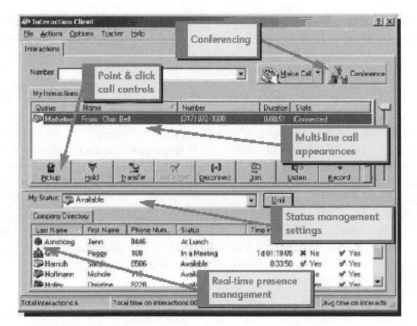

Figure 19.3 A presence screen shows a buddy list.

Calls can be redirected automatically to a forwarded number, if the called party has set the forwarding arrangement. Now we have a truly integrated solution that can handle all the technologies that we have heretofore tried to patch together.

Presence, shown in Fig. 19.3, is defined as knowing that a person is online, and on a connected device with a certain device profile. Each part of that definition is critical to fully understanding presence and how it is changing, and will continue to change, the face of business communications. If we have a dozen people on our "buddy list," we can tell at a glance if any of their computers are logged onto the network and whether they've been active recently. We can tell if Sally in Finance is open to communications, and we can send her a quick IM to ask a question. Her reply by IM or phone can resolve the problem efficiently.

Although AIM started as a consumer-grade technology, it was quickly adopted by many businesses that saw its advantages in enabling quick communications and providing presence information. Identity, presence, and location are three characteristics that lie at the core of some of the most critical emerging technologies in the market today: real-time communications (including VoIP, instant messaging, and mobile communications), collaboration, and identity-based security.

Reliability

Reliability is probably the most important criteria of a business phone system. You pick up the phone and you get a dial tone, no other choice! Some of the vendors deliver IP telephony systems with unmatched reliability, using an approach that is fundamentally different from that of any other IP PBX supplier in the world. Architecture and design not only deliver high reliability, but do so in a very simple and cost-effective manner.

When voice system reliability is discussed, people are typically talking about hardware reliability. Without reliable hardware, you don't have a reliable system. Reliability is measured by determining how often the hardware (components) in a system fails, and how long it takes to fix it after it fails. One can also add in the value of how many people are affected by a single failure.

In telephony, the accepted benchmark is "five-nines" availability, or a system that is available at least 99.999 percent of the time. We have always built our telephone systems as "lifeline services." Although *availability* is usually what is actually computed; it is often mistakenly referred to as reliability, and spoken of as "five-nines of reliability."

Availability is predicted by taking into account the type and number of hardware components in a system and calculating the mean time between failure (MTBF). Currently shipping IP PBX units have a predicted MTBF of approximately 10–15 years, and each failure requires at least 4 hours of mean time to repair (MTTR).

$$\text{Availability} = \frac{\text{MTBF}}{\text{MTBF} + \text{MTTR}}$$

This availability equation represents the standard definition of "reliability," and shows that a typical unit will achieve five-nines of availability. Stated another way, a switch on average is unavailable for 1 hour every 10 years.

IP PBXs can achieve five-nines of availability by using redundancy (two of all critical components) and thus increasing the cost and complexity of the system. All of the major IP PBX vendors use a call control server to set up phone calls and provide telephony features. The most common method is to use a centralized call control server that provides dial tone for all phones and trunks.

Current Status

For VoIP users, the good news is that IP telephony in the enterprise is on track to almost totally replace its TDM counterpart. The bad news is that it's only replacing, not displacing.

According to Infonetics Research, 75 percent of the PBX lines sold in the world in the first quarter of 2006 were of the IP variety. That's up from 63 percent in 2004 and 71 percent in 2005 as shown in Fig. 19.4.

Dell'Oro Group, which uses different measures on the market, found that 14 percent of lines sold in Q1 were in pure IP PBXs, 51 percent in hybrid IP/TDM boxes, and 37 percent in TDM-only PBXs. It also found, however, that the IP portion of the total installed base of enterprise phones was just 27 percent in 2005, up from 21 percent the year before as shown in Fig. 19.5.

These studies indicate that IP PBXs offer enough features and benefits to increase their share of the total PBX market, but are not compelling enough to boost the growth

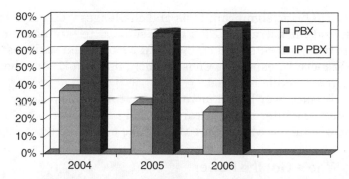

Figure 19.4   Infonetics study shows IP PBX installs are on the grow.

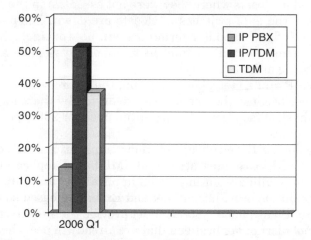

Figure 19.5   Dell'Oro numbers show the split between TDM only and hybrid/IP PBX sales.

of that market itself. The market is still growing very slowly. The shift could happen if IP PBXs were displacing rather than replacing existing TDM PBXs—that is, if enterprises were buying them even when their old boxes had plenty of life cycle left in them.

It all means that organizations are buying IP PBXs, mostly for the same reason they bought their TDM predecessors. Sometimes IP PBXs are the best choice specifically because they are IP-based. In new buildings, for example, the use of IP telephony makes it possible to run both voice and data over Cat 5 Ethernet cable. When using a green field location the opportunity to introduce the IP PBX is there. When nothing is changing and the TDM suppliers are still supporting their legacy systems, then no changes will occur.

Technology enthusiasts won't want to wait for the natural replacement cycle to bring the benefits of VoIP to their organizations. The good news is there are signs that enterprises are becoming increasingly willing to swap out their TDM PBXs for new IP ones, even though the old ones have not been fully depreciated.

IP can still bring significant costs and challenges. You may need to upgrade the data network and infrastructure. You will also have to buy new IP phones to replace the proprietary digital sets used on the TDM system. You will most definitely require significantly more IT expertise. Consequently, using VoIP ups the ante for both network equipment and skills required.

"Hosted" Voice over IP is a more attractive alternative for small businesses than for larger ones. The interexchange carriers and LECs all offer a choice here. Like any new choice, it will take a while before the uptake on this reaches any critical mass.

Power-Power, Who's Got the Power

The need for Power over Ethernet (PoE) surfaces as backup power and generators are now required in closets where they were not essential in the past. If the power is interrupted today, the data switches in closets are down. The data switch is not required because none of the computer terminals will be working. At the same time, a battery backup and generator will sustain the telephone system because telephony carries the burden of being a "lifeline" service.

With a VoIP and IP telephony solution, the data switches in all closets will require backup power because the telephones are driven by these switches. Added to this concern over physical facilities is the potential need for 208 V power in the closets to power the PoE switches.

When deploying IP telephony solutions, applications are equally important. Unified messaging, CRM, voice integration, and XML-based applications running on IP-enabled telephones may all have an impact on applications and future directions. Any unified messaging solution must be Outlook and Exchange based so that new applications are not introduced. The phone systems must provide the same basic look and feel as they do today and not disrupt applications that are already in use. These points are crucial when considering a new direction.

PoE is a revolutionary technology that integrates data, voice, and power over standard LAN infrastructure. It supplies reliable, uninterrupted power to Internet protocol (IP) telephones, wireless LAN access points, network cameras, and other Ethernet devices, using existing cable infrastructure.

PoE technology saves time and the cost of installing additional power cabling and AC outlets and eliminates the need for a dedicated UPS (uninterrupted power source) for individual devices. The power delivered over the LAN automatically activates when a compatible terminal is identified, and is blocked to legacy devices that are not compatible. This feature allows users to freely and safely mix legacy and PoE-compatible devices on their network. The main key drivers for Power over LAN in the IP telephony market are availability and simplicity of installation.

Availability Is a Key Consideration in IP Telephony

Think about running telephony over data networks, where you can benefit from new applications, such as unified messaging together with significant cost-savings in personnel and equipment using a single voice-data network. Before PoE, organizations would not commit their mission-critical voice systems to run on their data networks.

Losing data during a power outage is one thing, but losing data and voice (a lifeline service) during an outage is something else entirely. By supplying power over the same cable as the data network, these systems can now deliver the kind of reliability expected from a business class phone system.

Everyone has high expectations for voice service availability. A common goal is to consistently achieve 99.999 percent as we saw above.

Connecting a UPS to a PoE mid-span in the communication room allows the entire IP telephony network to be more reliable and ensures continuous operation during a power outage. However, one needs only to look at a few of the recent events such as Hurricanes Katrina, Rita, Cindy, and Dennis, all in 2005, plus the 2003 North America power grid outages that severely impaired business' ability to perform their primary missions. Intermittent power outages occur on a daily basis.

Based on the theoretical availability and the power protection strategy, the availability levels of five-nines or higher require the installation of PoE mid-spans backed up by a UPS system with a minimum of 1 hour battery life. Power over LAN technology, when implemented in a VoIP installation, ensures full reliability and availability of the telephony network by eliminating power outages effects.

Simple Installation

PoE offers a simple means for IP handset installation, eliminating the need for a separate Ethernet link and dedicated ac power outlet. A single cable is used to transport voice, data, and power to the desktop. The IP phone is plugged into the Ethernet switch and the mid-span, from which it gets data and power, and the PC is connected to an Ethernet port on the phone.

IP telephones can be powered via one of three options:

1. *PoE mid-span*: Power supplied over the Ethernet cable via an external Power over LAN mid-span, as shown in Fig. 19.6.

2. *PoE end-span*: Power over LAN integrated into an Ethernet switch, shown in Fig. 19.7, which offers standard IEEE 802.3af Power over Ethernet.

3. Power supplied via an ac adapter, as seen in Fig. 19.8.

In the market, different PoE products exist; however, not all are compatible with the PoE standard IEEE 802.3af. Like all global standards, it is important to maintain an open environment to enable interoperability between different terminal vendors.

In environments where an existing Ethernet switch has been previously installed and is providing VoIP QoS capabilities, there is no need to purchase and install a new Ethernet switch to provide PoE functionality. In this case, the simplest means to power the IP phones over the LAN infrastructure is to add a dedicated external Power over LAN mid-span. The advantages include savings in installation costs, preservation of existing infrastructure while supporting pre-standard as well as IEEE 802.3af standard terminals.

Figure 19.6   A mid-span PoE box.

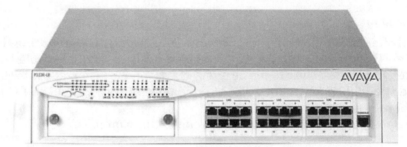

Figure 19.7   A PoE end-span.

Figure 19.8   A stand-alone injector that uses ac power.

There are different types of IP telephony installations, which vary in the following parameters:

1. *Infrastructure type*: VoIP system can be installed in a legacy infrastructure, using the existing Ethernet switches and cabling infrastructure, or in a totally new environment (Greenfield installation).

2. *VoIP PBX*: The PBX can be IP-enabled PBX or pure LAN PBX. IP-enabled PBXs are being offered by the traditional PBX vendors by accommodating a range of IP-oriented components—Voice over IP trunks and gateways, IP line and station cards, IP telephones, and the like—in order to IP-enable existing circuit-switched telephony systems. Pure LAN PBX is based solely on IP packets routing.

3. *Installation size*: Number of IP phones installed.

4. *Variety of end terminals in the installation*: Different types of terminals can be installed in a LAN infrastructure, such as wireless LAN access points, network cameras, and security devices.

Implementation

When we ask "converged enterprises" in our research to identify the main factors that contribute to a successful IPT implementation, four activities come up on nearly every list:

Conduct an Objective Skills Self-Assessment   A successful IPT deployment starts with an enterprise asking itself—do we have all of the necessary in-house expertise and skills to handle this ourselves? Very few businesses can answer this question with a resounding "yes."

Appoint a Competent Project Manager   A successful implementation of IP telephony requires tight planning and the coordination of multiple activities: conducting the up-front assessment, resolving identified issues, optimizing the network design, staging the solution for testing, working with the service providers to augment data network capacity, training the end users, and synchronizing all of the players during the physical cutover—just to name a few. Approaching an IPT implementation with the belief that "things will just fall in place" is a sure path for disaster.

Perform a Rigorous IPT Network Readiness Assessment and Resolve Any Deficiencies   IT managers with converged networks have been emphatic—do not implement IPT without first assessing the underlying data network. The reason for this lies in the fact that voice calls have unique performance requirements that differ fundamentally from most other types of traffic on a packet network.

If deficiencies are detected in the network, they need to be corrected before proceeding with the IPT deployment. It's generally a good idea to repeat the assessment after modifications have been made.

Ensure End-User Awareness and Training Prior to Cutover   In addition to having technical expertise, network assessments, and project management, IPT implementations that were declared "rousing successes" had one additional common element—end-user support.

Reaping the Rewards

"Seeing is believing" as the old saying goes, and the adage is highly apropos in any discussion of convergence. The major business benefits that enterprises expect when adopting IP telephony include:

- Lowering total operating costs
- Enhancing end-user productivity
- Improving IT organization efficiency
- Reinforcing market differentiation and brand image

System Parameters

Below is a list of parameters that should be taken into consideration when dealing with the IP telephony solution. These are not all-inclusive, but more items that have the highest priorities when considering and selecting a system.

Carrier-Class Availability   Availability is the probability that service is available when needed. Carrier-class performance generally means 99.999 percent or better—a maximum of about 5 minutes of downtime per year. Many current phone systems provide carrier class service. *An IP telephony solution must provide equal or better service.*

Availability of telephone stations must also be considered. Their vulnerability to failure or power outages can be mitigated by telephones that support IEEE 802.3af Power over Ethernet (PoE). IP phones with PoE support, for instance, provide a degree of availability over and above server performance and eliminate the need for transformers attached to the IP phone. Additionally, the presence of pass-through Ethernet ports—when connected to laptops with battery-support—strengthens computing and telephony availability in the event of power failure.

IPT Servers and L2 Switches   Moreover, the IP telephone servers and L2 switches should be on an uninterrupted power supply (UPS). These UPS devices can ensure no single point of failure, enable hours of business continuity, and provide for stable turndowns during sustained power outages such as those that might accompany natural disasters.

Demands of Business   The ability to pick up the handset of a telephone, get a dial tone, and place a call is an expectation resulting from over a hundred years of successful telephony and the demands of business obligations. *It has to be there; and it has to be there all the time.*

Infrastructure Changes   Some of the infrastructure changes necessary throughout the organization, that will impact the overall cost of implementation, is the purchase of PoE and managed switches in the telephone closets. These are not there today, so the added cost of providing PoE and managed layer 2/3 switches *amounts to approximately 25 percent* of the cost of the Greenfield system worked up for the corporate headquarters building estimates.

Newer L2 Switches   Currently throughout many sites, newer L2 switches *may be required,* that must be factored into the equation. These switches will be managed, PoE and should support VLAN tagging. The recommendation is to use a different VLAN per rack in a closet, or better yet set up multiple VLAN categories such as tagged, non-tagged and use 802.1p as well as 802.1Q tagging. The 802.1p tags can set the device QoS, whereas the Q tags can be used to define the various VLANs.

Use of 208V Electricity   From a facilities standpoint this may also require the use of 208V electricity in the closets to support the PoE switches, adding to the initial start-up costs. This unfavorably biases the case against the use of IPT. There may be more attractive cost solutions to provide the switches on 110 V and still support PoE on all ports. A company like Power DeZine has been gaining a lot of traction in this arena.

Summary

So what have we learned when it comes to selecting and implementing an IP telephony solution?

1. *Convergence is a safe bet for your enterprise*: IP telephony is the clear going forward standard for voice communication systems.

2. *The business benefits of IP telephony are real*: The potential operating cost, end-user productivity, and IT efficiency impacts that IPT system manufacturers and distribution channels promote are genuine and can be achieved regardless of whether an enterprise is starting from a TDM, Centrex, or Greenfield environment.

3. *All IP telephony providers are not equal*: There are significant differences between vendors when it comes to IPT expertise, experience, and support capabilities, as well as business style. Take the time to compare suppliers. Talk to trusted peers that have already embraced convergence.

4. *Architecture matters*: Your choice of vendor will largely determine whether your converged network will have a centralized or distributed architecture. Don't minimize the importance of this decision—your network design can have a real impact on reliability and ease-of-management.

5. *Involve your end users*: Understanding end-user requirements is critical to ensuring that the IPT features and applications you choose will meet their needs. Ease of use varies highly between vendors and is one of the most important factors when it comes to end-user acceptance of new technology.

6. *Get the help you need*: Convergence brings business benefits as well as the potential for added complexity. If in doubt about the skill levels of your existing IT resources, don't hesitate to consult an expert.

7. *Don't cut corners during implementation*: Bringing advanced IPT technology to your business can be a real career enhancer. Ensure a successful implementation—use a skilled project manager.

8. *A network assessment is a must*: Don't assume that your underlying data network is ready to carry IPT traffic with high quality. Failure to conduct a rigorous IPT readiness assessment early in the implementation phase is almost certain to cause unwanted surprises later.

9. *Go into convergence with your eyes open*: Having a clear up-front understanding of your business communications requirements—especially those involving network performance, total cost of ownership, interoperability, manageability, and growth—is essential to realistically set expectations on the scope and magnitude of IPT benefits.

10. *Do your homework*: If tracking the business benefits of IPT is a desired or required activity, proper preparation is essential. Ensure that you have baseline measurements of your key processes before IPT, and have created the necessary mechanisms to quantify the postdeployment improvements in operating costs, organizational efficiency, and end-user productivity.

Questions

1. What is the single most important benefit of using IP telephone systems?
   a. Improved e-mail and voice mail
   b. Improved profitability
   c. Presence
   d. Gets you away from TDM

2. What is a goal of the organization when choosing an IP telephony solution?
   a. Produce an ROI on the system
   b. Install the latest and greatest technologies
   c. Carry VoIP at any cost
   d. Improve the visibility in the industry

3. If voice and data converged, then the reliability should be at least:
   a. 98.8888%
   b. 99.000%
   c. 99.999%
   d. 100%

4. One of the added benefits of IP telephony includes:
   a. Ease of administration
   b. Expensive new telephones for everyone

c. Network awareness

d. CIT

5. What is the most preferred protocol being accepted as a standard for VoIP and IP telephony?

a. H.323

b. H.248

c. H.225

d. SIP

6. One of the areas where IP telephony can add high benefit is:

a. Greenfield sites

b. Brownfield sites

c. Double infrastructure sites

d. Single use sites

7. To assure high availability we should include the following in the budget:

a. UPS

b. PoE

c. New layer 2 and layer 3 switches

d. All of the above

8. Most organizations want improved security before they implement IP telephony.   T/F

9. Costs of an IP telephone system may exceed ____ of the original TDM system.

a. 50%

b. 100%

c. 200%

d. 10%

10. IP phones are not very expensive.   T/ F

Index

C

M

U

V